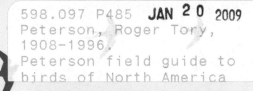

PETERSON FIELD GUIDE

TO

BIRDS

of North America

Specially produced video podcasts, viewable on a computer desktop or on the go, include

- overviews of common and popular species
- comparisons of groups of similar species
- helpful birding tips
- tutorials to help you get the most out of this field guide
- a mini-biography of Roger Tory Peterson
- songs and calls of featured birds

To register for access, go to
www.petersonfieldguides.com

Topography of a bird

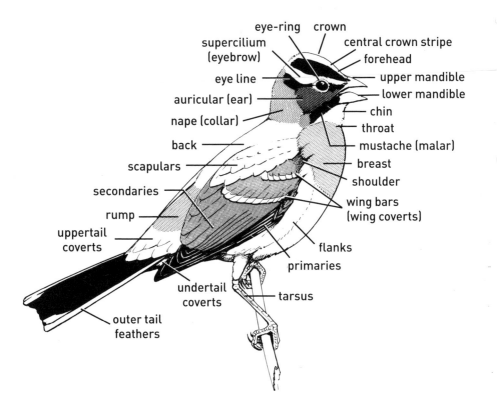

eye-ring · crown
supercilium (eyebrow) · central crown stripe
forehead
eye line · upper mandible
auricular (ear) · lower mandible
nape (collar) · chin
throat
back · mustache (malar)
scapulars · breast
shoulder
secondaries · wing bars (wing coverts)
rump
uppertail coverts
flanks
primaries
undertail coverts · tarsus
outer tail feathers

Undersurface of wing

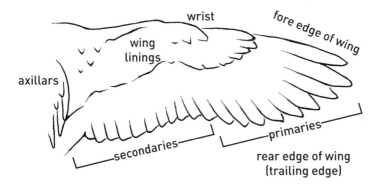

wrist
wing linings · fore edge of wing
axillars
secondaries · primaries
rear edge of wing (trailing edge)

On the upper surface of the secondaries, some waterfowl have a bright-colored patch, called a *speculum.*

Pages listed are first occurrences.

ONE-PAGE INDEX

CONTENTS

PLATES

FOREWORD

Sometime in my early teens, or just before, I became intensely interested in bird watching. This is not to say that I had not previously spent significant time learning about and watching birds—not surprising, given the household in which I was raised. It is just that it then became a very focused pursuit. I spent countless hours wandering the woods and slogging through the salt marshes near our home in Old Lyme, Connecticut, in search of new birds. In the process, I managed to wear out several copies of the Peterson Field Guide—and had a great time. I also acquired a much deeper understanding of my surroundings.

This period did not last more than a year or so, and eventually I shifted emphasis to other interests—first geology and then botany. The fallout, however, has lasted a lifetime. Birds and their identification became my window into the natural world. In this I am not alone. I think most people get their start in natural history this way. In fact, I can remember someone assuring me that at one time virtually 100 percent of the heads of environmental organizations in this country got their start with a Peterson Field Guide in hand.

Being able to recognize and identify the birds we see is a crucial key to understanding the world around us. My father used the comings and goings of birds as both a biological clock of sorts and a litmus test for the condition of the environment. The arrival and departure of migrating birds signaled to him changes in weather or climatic conditions. The increase or decrease in the population of certain species gave him insight into the overall health of the environment—changes for good or ill. As his friend Bob Lewin once noted, "Roger was always interested in numbers." Whether it was counting the number of moths on our screen door or the number of flamingos on a lake in Africa, the results were equally significant.

Dad always likened writing a field guide to serving a prison sentence. The projects are always lengthy and the spatial and visual constraints pronounced. The writing is not stream of consciousness but more akin to writing a telegram—fitting the maximum amount of information into the minimum amount of space. The illustration can never be free and loose but always tightly controlled, showing the essence of the bird in question. In both these endeavors, Dad excelled. Someone once confided to me that Dad's rendition of a robin was not just any old robin, but the perfect robin. Somehow, he was able to convey a bird not at a specific moment in time, awkwardly posed with feathers in disarray, but rather, as the mind saw it, the robin idealized, with feathers neatly patterned and plump. His results were all the more remarkable when one watched how they were achieved. He worked mostly from memory, using only a dry, beat-up specimen of the bird for details of anatomy and occasionally a photograph or two. And he was able to piece together an image of the bird as it should have been. Not just any robin, but all robins.

Dad's innovative approach was the product of a rich variety of influences. He was born in Jamestown, a small town in upstate New York known primarily for farming and light manufacture. His first foray into art was with the encouragement of his seventh-grade schoolteacher, and much of what he learned about birds was self-taught or picked up from the people around him. His family could not afford to send him to college, so he put himself through art school in New York City instead. This was fortuitous, as his time in New York shaped much of what was to come. There he found inspiration from such luminaries in the birding world as Louis Agassiz Fuertes and Ludlow Griscom, and he fell in with a group of avid young birders who called themselves the Bronx County Bird Club, many of whom went on to prominent careers in the biological sciences.

In 1929, Bill Vogt, the editor of *Audubon* magazine's precursor, *Bird-Lore*, suggested that Dad combine his expertise in art and bird identification to create an identification guide. This was at a time when definitive identification was made more often than not with a shotgun and a dissecting knife. The Peterson system of identification, which uses arrows to point out differences in similar-looking species, seems both simple and obvious in hindsight, but at the time, it was an enormous innovation. Suddenly the average person could confidently identify the birds around him with just a pair of binoculars and one small book. Birding went from being the slightly odd pursuit of an eccentric few to being one of the largest spectator sports in America today. The repercussions have been enormous.

Each of Dad's many skills and talents was noteworthy in and of itself, but pieced together, they made him truly unique. His skills as an illustrator were unquestioned. Because of his early training, his first response was to place things in visual rather than technical terms—an especially useful trait when trying to design an identification guide for the uninitiated. At the same time, he was a lifelong student of birds and had a tremendous reservoir of technical information. His writing style was simple, direct, and entertaining. He had a great ability to reduce complex information to the essential bones without losing a certain lyric quality. He also had a talent for pulling together scattered information and synthesizing it into original observation.

Less frequently mentioned, but well known to his peers, was his extraordinary hearing. Yale University School of Medicine tested his hearing late in his life and found it to be exceptional—well into the 99th percentile of human capability—with Dad registering frequencies far above the norm. Bird walks with him were always a source of wonder. He was forever hearing and identifying distant birds that the rest of us could barely discern. I am still amazed by his uncanny ability to render bird calls into written English in such a way as to make them immediately recognizable. Overlaying all this was his incredible focus. For 70 or more years, his single overriding pleasure was the pursuit and identification of birds, to which he brought an energy, skill, and enthusiasm that were inspirational.

In the foreword to the fifth edition of *A Field Guide to the Birds of Eastern and Central North America*, Robert Bateman referred to Dad's lifework as causing ever-expanding "ripples on a pond." This is very apt. More than anything else, Dad thought of himself as a teacher. His whole life was about communication. His greatest wish was to pass along his love of birds and the outdoors, to imbue the rest of us with the same sense of wonder and responsibility that he had derived from bird watching. His childhood interest had morphed into something larger. While birds remained ever the focus, they became only the most visible aspect of a much greater system. For him, they became the markers, the early warning system for the condition of the overall environment. By opening up the world of birds to us through his field guides, he hoped to shift our relationship to our surroundings from one of exploitation to one of stewardship. In this, he has had more than a little success. With each new field guide owner, our world becomes a little richer, a little more full of promise. It may indeed be as Bateman says: "Roger Tory Peterson's life has been one of the most important lives of the last 100 years."

—LEE ALLEN PETERSON
July 2007

EDITOR'S NOTE

In the past 75 years, ever since Roger Tory Peterson's pioneering *Field Guide to the Birds* changed the way we look at birds and jump-started the environmental movement, many birders have grown up using their Peterson Field Guide, and the book holds a special place in their hearts. Today, however, there are more field guides than ever, and more on the way. The Peterson guide is still set apart by its original concept. The Peterson Identification System is a powerful tool, just as useful and easy to understand today as it was when the first Peterson Field Guide was published. We now honor the centennial of Roger Peterson's birth with this new combined edition that is not simply a commemoration but a useful, up-to-date resource.

Peterson was an innovator. If he were a young bird watcher today, there's a good chance he would be at the forefront of new birding technology. In this book, we've included a URL (www.petersonfieldguides.com) where readers can access a set of video podcasts that are easy to use, educational, and fun. These supplements to the book cover key individual species, popular groupings of birds, and such topics as how to use range maps, identification basics, and bird topography.

Additionally, the book's content has been revised. All of the taxonomy has been updated (to include, for example, splits, such as Canada and Cackling geese, and name changes, such as Oldsquaw to Long-tailed Duck). Birds newly recorded in North America, such as Fea's Petrel, Black-tailed and Yellow-legged gulls, and La Sagra's Flycatcher, are included. The text has been revised to accurately reflect our current knowledge of birds. The range maps are all new. The art has been updated where necessary. New paintings were done for birds that didn't previously occur in North America and for figures that Peterson painted over or discarded as he adapted the plates from one book to another. For some birds, the information we have about them is better than what was available when Peterson was painting, so a few of his paintings have been replaced with new ones; others have been digitally enhanced.

When Roger Tory Peterson died, we lost a uniquely talented artist and naturalist. He had a profound influence on a vast number of young naturalists, however, who have devoted their lives to birds and other animals, the environment, education, art, and other vocations and avocations. The team of expert birders who brought a wealth of knowledge to the creation of this new volume worked diligently to enhance Peterson's legacy while ensuring that all of the content was current and highly useful for today's birder. Paul Lehman and Bill Thompson III revised all the text. Michael O'Brien painted the new species, laid out the plates, directed the digital work, and consulted editorially. Paul Lehman supplied the information for the new range maps, graphic artist Larry Rosche created the maps digitally, and Marshall Iliff reviewed them all. Michael DiGiorgio did the digital enhancements of the art and executed the layout of the plates digitally. Kimball Garrett reviewed and revised some of the voice descriptions. Elizabeth Pierson undertook the enormous job of copyediting the revised text. Barbara Jatkola proofread, and Ned Brinkley reviewed the page proof. At Houghton Mifflin, Shelley Berg, Anne Chalmers, Beth Burleigh Fuller, Teresa Elsey, Clare O'Keeffe, Katrina Kruse, Jill Lazer, and Taryn Roeder all played critical roles in producing this book. Jeffrey Gordon and Bill Thompson III created the video podcasts, which we hope will enhance your enjoyment of birds and bird watching.

At a time when environmental concerns are paramount, it's essential that we as readers revisit the sources that inspired and deepened our appreciation of the natural world. Roger Tory Peterson's voice is for the generations, and it's with tremendous pride that we present it to you, revitalized and as relevant as always.

—LISA A. WHITE

PETERSON FIELD GUIDE

TO

BIRDS

of North America

INTRODUCTION

How to Identify Birds

Veteran birders will know how to use this book. Beginners, however, should spend some time becoming familiar in a general way with the illustrations. The plates, for the most part, have been grouped in taxonomic sequence. However, in cases where there is a great similarity of shape and action, similar-appearing birds may be grouped outside their strict taxonomic order. This should aid in field identification and not frustrate the true taxonomist to any great degree.

Birds that could be confused are grouped together when possible and are arranged in identical profile for direct comparison. The arrows point to outstanding field marks, which are explained opposite. The text also gives aids such as voice, actions, and habitat, not visually portrayable, and under a separate heading discusses species that might be confused. The general range is not described for most species in the text. The annotated three-color range maps in the back of the book (pp. 410–496) provide detailed range information. Thumbnail versions of the maps also appear next to the species accounts for quick reference.

In addition to the plates of birds normally found in North America north of Mexico, there are also plates depicting accidentals from Eurasia, the sea, and the Tropics, as well as some of the exotic escapes that are sometimes seen.

What Is the Bird's Size?

Acquire the habit of comparing a new bird with some familiar "yardstick"—a House Sparrow, robin, pigeon, etc.—so that you can say to yourself, "Smaller than a robin, a little larger than a House Sparrow." The measurements in this book represent lengths in inches (with centimeters in parentheses) from bill tip to tail tip of specimens on their backs as in museum trays. For species that show considerable size variation, a range of measurements is given. For less variable species, only one measurement is given.

What Is Its Shape?

Is it plump like a starling (left) or slender like a cuckoo (right)?

What Shape Are Its Wings?

Are they rounded like a bobwhite's (left) or sharply pointed like a Barn Swallow's (right)?

What Shape Is Its Bill?

Is it small and fine like a warbler's (1), stout and short like a seed-cracking sparrow's (2), dagger-shaped like a tern's (3), or hook-tipped like a bird of prey's (4)?

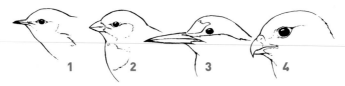

What Shape Is Its Tail?

Is it deeply forked like a Barn Swallow's (1), square-tipped like a Cliff Swallow's (2), notched like a Tree Swallow's (3), rounded like a Blue Jay's (4), or pointed like a Mourning Dove's (5)?

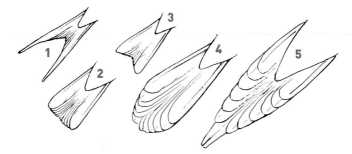

How Does It Behave?

Does it cock its tail like a wren or hold it down like a flycatcher? Does it wag its tail? Does it sit erect on an open perch, dart after an insect, and return as a flycatcher does?

Does It Climb Trees?

If so, does it climb upward in spirals like a creeper (left), in jerks like a woodpecker (center) using its tail as a brace, or go down headfirst like a nuthatch (right)?

How Does It Fly?

Does it undulate (dip up and down) like a flicker (1)? Does it fly straight and fast like a dove (2)? Does it hover like a kingfisher (3)? Does it glide or soar?

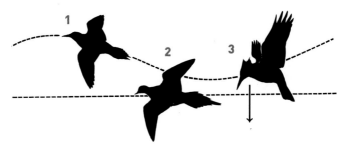

Does It Swim?

Does it sit low in the water like a loon (1) or high like a gallinule (2)? If a duck, does it dive like a scaup or a scoter (3) or dabble and upend like a Mallard (4)?

Does It Wade?

Is it large and long-legged like a heron or small like a sandpiper? If one of the latter, does it probe the mud or pick at things? Does it teeter or bob?

What Are Its Field Marks?

Some birds can be identified by color alone, but most birds are not that easy. The most important aids are what we call field marks, which are, in effect, the "trademarks of nature." Note whether the breast is spotted as in a thrush (1), streaked as in a thrasher (2), or plain as in a cuckoo (3).

Tail Pattern

Does the tail have a "flash pattern"—a white tip as in the Eastern Kingbird (1), white patches in the outer corners as in the Eastern and Spotted towhees (2), or white sides as in the juncos (3)?

Rump Patch

Does it have a light rump like a Cliff Swallow (1) or flicker (2)? Northern Harrier, Yellow-rumped Warbler, and several shorebirds also have distinctive rump patches.

Eye Stripes and Eye-ring

Does the bird have a stripe above, through, or below the eye, or a combination of these stripes? Does it have a striped crown? A ring around the eye, or "spectacles"? A "mustache" stripe? These details are important in many small songbirds.

Wing Bars

Do the wings have light wing bars or not? Their presence or absence is important in recognizing many warblers, vireos, and flycatchers. Wing bars may be single or double, bold or obscure.

Wing Pattern

The basic wing pattern of ducks (shown below), shorebirds, and other water birds is very important. Notice whether the wings have patches (1) or stripes (2), are solidly colored (3), or have contrasting black tips.

Bird Songs and Calls

Using sounds to identify birds can be just as useful as using visual clues. In fact, in many situations, birds are much more readily identified by sound than by sight. The species accounts here include a brief entry on voice, with interpretations of these songs and calls, in an attempt to give birders some handle on the vocalizations they hear. Authors of bird books have attempted, with varying success, to fit songs and calls into syllables, words, and phrases. Musical notations, comparative descriptions, and even ingenious systems of symbols have also been employed. To supplement this verbal interpretation, there are recording collections available for nearly every region of the world and for individual groups of birds. The *Peterson Birding by Ear* CDs provide a step-by-step method for learning how to develop your listening and identification skills. Preparation in advance for particular species or groups greatly enhances your ability to identify them. Some birders do a majority of their birding by ear, and there is no substitute for actual sounds—for getting out into the field and tracking down the songster and committing the song to memory. However, an audio library is a wonderful resource to return home to when attempting to identify a bird heard in the field. Many such collections can now be taken into the field on digital audio devices. *Caution:* When using recordings to attract hard-to-see species, limit the number of playbacks, and do not use them on threatened species or in heavily birded areas.

Bird Nests

The more time you spend in the field becoming familiar with bird behavior, the more skilled you'll become at finding bird nests. It is as exciting to keep a bird nest list as it is to keep a life list. Remember, if you happen to find a nest during the breeding season, leave the site as undisturbed as possible. Back away, and do not touch the nest, eggs, or young birds. Often squirrels, raccoons, and several other mammals, grackles, and cowbirds are more than happy to have you "point out" a nest and will raid it if you disrupt the site or call attention to it. Many people find young birds that have just left the nest and may appear to be alone. Usually they are not lost but are under the watchful eye of a parent bird and are best left in place rather than scooped up and taken to a foreign environment. In the winter, nest hunting can be great fun and has little impact, as most nests will never be used again. They are easy to see once the foliage is gone, and it can be a challenge to attempt to identify the maker. Books such as *A Field Guide to*

Birds' Nests and *A Field Guide to Western Birds' Nests,* both in the Peterson Field Guide series, will expand your ornithological expertise.

Conservation

Birds undeniably contribute to our pleasure and quality of life. But they also are sensitive indicators of the environment, a sort of "ecological litmus paper," and hence more meaningful than just chickadees and cardinals that brighten the suburban garden, grouse and ducks that fill the sportsman's bag, or rare warblers and shorebirds that excite the field birder. The observation and recording of bird populations over time lead inevitably to environmental awareness and can signal impending changes.

To this end, please help the cause of wildlife conservation and education by contributing to or taking part in the work of the following organizations: **The Nature Conservancy** (4245 North Fairfax Drive, Suite 100, Arlington, VA 22203; www.nature.org), **National Audubon Society** (700 Broadway, New York, NY 10003; www.audubon.org), **Defenders of Wildlife** (1130 17th Street NW, Washington, DC 20036; www.defenders.org), **Roger Tory Peterson Institute of Natural History** (311 Curtis Street, Jamestown, NY 14701; www.rtpi.org), **National Wildlife Federation** (11100 Wildlife Center Drive, Reston, VA 20190; www.nwf.org), **World Wildlife Fund** (1250 24th Street NW, PO Box 97180, Washington, DC 20090; www .wwf.org), **Cornell Laboratory of Ornithology** (159 Sapsucker Woods, Ithaca, NY 14850; www.birds.cornell.edu), **Ducks Unlimited** (One Waterfowl Way, Memphis, TN 38120; www.ducks.org), **BirdLife International** (Wellbrook Court, Girton Road, Cambridge CB3 0NA, U.K.; www.birdlife.org), **Partners in Flight** (www.partnersinflight.org), **American Bird Conservancy** (PO Box 249, The Plains, VA 20198; abcbirds.org), as well as your local land trust and natural heritage program and your local Audubon and ornithological societies and bird clubs. These and so many other groups that have come into the forefront of bird conservation in the last 20 years merit your support.

The Maps and Ranges of Birds

The ranges of many species have changed markedly over the past 50 or more years. Some species are expanding because of protection given them, changing habitats, bird feeding, or other factors. Some "increases" may simply be the result of more field-guide-educated birders being in the field, helping to more thoroughly document bird populations and distributions. Other avian species have diminished alarmingly and may have been extirpated from major parts of their range. The primary culprit here has been habitat loss, although other factors such as increased competition or predation from other species may sometimes be involved. Species that are in serious decline in North America run the gamut, from Ivory Gull to Lesser Prairie-Chicken and Loggerhead Shrike to Bewick's Wren, Rusty Blackbird, and Red Knot.

Successful introductions of some species, such as Trumpeter Swan and Eurasian Collared-Dove, have resulted in self-sustaining, growing populations (the latter was introduced to the Bahamas, then arrived in the U.S. on its own). And a good number of additional vagrant species—out-of-range visitors from faraway lands—continue to be found (such as a Red-footed Falcon in Massachusetts). Some species that were formerly thought to occur only exceptionally have, over the past several decades, become much more regular visitors (such as Lesser Black-backed Gull) and sometimes even local breeders (such as Clay-colored Robin). It is not always certain if such changes in status are the result of actual population increases or if they merely reflect better observer coverage and advances in field identification skills.

Range maps need to be of sufficient size to denote adequate detail and to include written information on such topics as population trends and extralimital occurrences. Thus, the range maps in this guide have been purposely placed near the back of the book where they can be reproduced in a large size not possible in the main body of the text. The maps are organized taxonomically, following the order published by the American Ornithologists' Union. In addition, thumbnail versions of the same maps are placed in the main text next to the species accounts to provide a quick overview of a species' range without needing to turn the page. The key to the range maps is located on page 411 and also on the inside of the front cover, for quick reference.

Range maps don't depict how abundant a particular species is within its range. The following list defines terms of abundance used throughout the book. The definitions presume you're in the habitat and season in which a species would occur.

Common: Always or almost always encountered daily, usually in moderate to large numbers.

Fairly common: Usually encountered daily, generally not in large numbers.

Uncommon: Occurs in small numbers and may be missed on a substantial number of days.

Scarce: Present only in small numbers or difficult to find within its normal range.

Rare or very rare: Annual or probably annual in small numbers but still largely within its normal range.

Casual: Beyond its normal range; occurs at somewhat regular intervals but usually less frequently than annually.

Accidental: Beyond its normal range; one record or a very few records.

Vagrant: Beyond its normal range.

Local: Limited geographic range within the U.S. and Canada.

Introduced: Not native; deliberately released.

Exotic: Not native; either released or escaped. A term used especially for species that are present in limited numbers and may or may not be breeding. Other species, such as House Sparrow and European Starling, were also introduced but are so well established that, in the sense used here, they are no longer considered exotic.

Unestablished exotic: Nonnative releasee or escapee that does not have a naturalized breeding population, though some may be breeding in very localized areas.

Habitats

Gaining a familiarity with a wide range of habitats will greatly enhance your overall knowledge of the birds in a specific region, increase your skills, and add to your enjoyment of birding. It is unlikely you will ever see a meadowlark in an oak woodland or a Wood Thrush in a meadow. Birders know this, and if they want to go out to run up a large day list, they do not remain in one habitat but shift from site to site based on time and species diversity for a given type of habitat.

A few birds do invade habitats other than their own at times, especially on migration. A warbler that spends the summer in Maine might be seen, on its journey through Florida, in a palm. In cities, migrating birds often have to make the best of it, like the American Woodcock found one morning on the window ledge of a New York City office. Strong weather patterns can also alter where a bird happens to appear. Hurricanes, for example, can be a disaster for many species. As these violent storms sweep over the ocean, the eye can often "vacuum" up oceanic species that seek shelter in its calmness. Upon reaching land, these normally offshore species are faced with an entirely strange habitat and account for sightings such as a Yellow-nosed Albatross heading up the Hudson River, a White-tailed Tropicbird in downtown Boston, and numbers of storm-petrels on an inland reservoir in the desert Southwest.

Most species, however, are quite predictable for the major portion of their lives, and for the birder who has learned where to look, the rewards are great.

To start, familiarize yourself with individual habitat types. Become familiar with the dominant plant types that are indicators—for example, oak-beech woods, grass-shrub meadows, salt- or freshwater wetlands—and keep accurate records of what species you find in each. In a short time you will have a working knowledge of the predominant species in each habitat, and this will help you with identification by allowing you to anticipate what might be found there.

The seasonal movements of birds at your sites will provide an overview of migrant species that come through at a given time and will be a reference point for future visits during these migration periods. A forest dotted with migrant warblers in spring may revert to relative quiet accented by the repetitive calls of a Red-eyed Vireo or the drawn-out call of a Western Wood-Pewee in midsummer.

Be sure not to overlook cities and towns, where well-adapted species can be found. Peregrine Falcons have shown remarkable adaptability, nesting on strategic ledges in the walled canyons of many cities. The fertile grounds for hunting Rock Pigeons and European Starlings seem to suit this raptor quite well.

Ecotones are edges where two habitat types interface—a forest and a shrub meadow, for example. As this is not a gradual change, ecotones offer habitat for species from both of the adjoining areas and are therefore rich in bird life.

The changes in habitat over the years will also affect your favorite birding areas. Fields turn to shrubby lots and then woodlands. Bobwhite and meadowlarks may move on, but Indigo or Lazuli buntings and Field or Lincoln's sparrows establish themselves. This dynamic is normal in the natural world. However, humankind's alterations to this process have had a great impact. Forest fragmentation is an example. As land development continues, it is affecting numerous species. A sudden disruption has a more drastic effect than a slow change, which allows for adaptation. As we divide up habitat with roadways, we have created a greater edge effect, and this allows Brown-headed Cowbirds to penetrate into forest areas where they would not have ventured in the past. They now parasitize many more species than before, and such parasitization is leading to marked declines in total numbers of many species. This forest fragmentation is also affecting the success rate of nestling fledging by increasing the numbers of some predators and by altering prime habitat requirements for obtaining food to raise the young.

Some species are obligates to a specific habitat type, and searching these areas greatly improves your chances of finding such birds. These include Golden-crowned Kinglet nesting in coniferous woodlands and Kirtland's Warbler in Michigan, which breeds only in jack pine woodlands of a specific height. Even in migration, many species remain faithful to selected habitats, such as waterthrushes along watercourses. Running or dripping water has proven to be an important attractant for migrating land birds, and in areas where fresh water is scarce, a water drip can be a gold mine for migrant warblers and other passerines.

Subspecies and Geographic Variation

Many species of birds inhabit wide geographic areas. The Song Sparrow *(Melospiza melodia)*, for example, breeds throughout North America, from Mexico north into Alaska. In such a wide-ranging species, there are geographic subsets within the population that show distinct local plumage patterns and song variants. When the distinct geographic forms of a species reach a point when the population is dominated by individuals that are recognizably different from typical individuals of the "parent" species, the local group is formally designated a subspecies of the parent species. The subspecies is named by attaching a third, subspecific name to the scientific name of the species. Thus, the pale Song Sparrow of the southwestern deserts of North America is called *Melospiza melodia saltonis,* to distinguish that form from another subspecies. With at least 31 recognizable subspecies, the Song Sparrow ranks among the highest of North American birds in the number of its geographic varieties.

Often a subspecific group is so distinct from the parent species that several members can be easily recognized in the field by bird watchers. A good example of this is the Dark-eyed Junco *(Junco hyemalis)*. With 12 subspecies, at least 5 are easily discerned: the "Oregon," "Pink-sided," "White-winged," "Slate-colored," and "Gray-headed." For the birder, identification of subspecies can add greater challenges to birding and, when documented, valuable information, especially when subspecies are reclassified to full species status. Such has been the case, for example, with the splitting of Western Flycatcher *(Empidonax difficilis)* into Pacific-slope Flycatcher *(E. difficilis)* and Cordilleran Flycatcher *(E. occidentalis)*. Field studies of Sage Grouse *(Centrocercus urophasianus)* leading to the separation of Greater Sage-Grouse *(C. urophasianus)* and Gunnison Sage-Grouse *(C. minimus)* prove how valuable these studies of subspecific populations can be. The differences between Bicknell's Thrush *(Catharus bicknelli)* and Gray-cheeked Thrush *(C. minimus)* illustrate how subtle the field marks can be between species and why they had been relegated to subspecific status. The shifting of this line between subspecies and species is ongoing. Recording data on location and numbers can prove helpful in completing a picture of a species' distribution or even a new species that has been overlooked.

In this edition, species that have distinct subspecies that are easily recognized, such as Yellow-rumped Warbler *(Dendroica coronata)* and Dark-eyed Junco *(J. hyemalis),* have been represented. When in the field, challenge yourself to discern the subspecies. It will increase your visual and listening skills and add a new level of understanding and enjoyment of birds.

PLATES

GEESE, SWANS, AND DUCKS Family Anatidae

Web-footed waterfowl. **RANGE**: Worldwide.

GEESE

Large, gregarious waterfowl; heavier bodied, longer necked than ducks; bills thick at base. Noisy in flight; some fly in lines or V formations. Sexes alike. Geese are more terrestrial than ducks, often grazing. **FOOD**: Grasses, seeds, waste grain, aquatic plants; eelgrass (Brant); shellfish (Emperor Goose).

GREATER WHITE-FRONTED GOOSE   Fairly common **M3**
Anser albifrons (see also p. 24)
28 in. (71 cm). Gray-brown with *pink* bill; adult with *white patch on front of face* and variable *black bars* on belly. The only other N. American goose with yellow or orange feet is Emperor Goose. *Immature:* Dusky with pinkish bill, yellow or orange feet. May be confused with some domestic barnyard geese. **VOICE**: High-pitched tootling, *kah-lah-a-luk,* in chorus. **HABITAT**: Marshes, prairies, agricultural fields, lakes, bays; in summer, tundra.

EMPEROR GOOSE *Chen canagica* (see also p. 24)   Scarce, local **M4**
26 in. (66 cm). Alaskan. *Adult:* A small blue-gray goose, *scaled* with black and white; identified by its *white head and hindneck*. Throat *black* (not white as in dark-morph Snow and Ross's geese). Golden or *orange legs*. *Juvenile:* Has dark head and bill. **HABITAT**: In summer, tundra; in winter, rocky shores, mudflats, seaweed.

SNOW GOOSE *Chen caerulescens* (see also p. 24)   Locally common **M5**
White morph: 25–33 in. (64–84 cm). *White* with *black primaries.* Head often rust-stained from feeding in muddy or iron-rich waters. Bill pink with black "lips." Feet pink. Base of bill curves back slightly toward eye. *Immature:* Pale gray; dark bill and legs. Dark morph ("Blue" Goose): 25–30 in. (64–76 cm): Suggests Emperor Goose, but has *white throat, dark "lips," and lacks scaly pattern.* Intermediates with white morph of Snow are frequent. *Immature:* Similar to young Greater White-fronted Goose, but feet and bill *dark.* **VOICE**: Loud, nasal, double-noted *houck-houck,* in chorus. **SIMILAR SPECIES**: White morph: Ross's Goose. **HABITAT**: Marshes, grain fields, ponds, bays; in summer, tundra.

ROSS'S GOOSE *Chen rossii* (see also p. 24)   Uncommon **M6**
23 in. (58 cm). Like a small Snow Goose, but neck shorter, head rounder (steeper forehead). Bill with *gray-blue or purple-blue base,* stubbier (with *vertical border* between base and facial feathering), *lacking distinctive "grinning black lips"*; warts at bill base difficult to see. *Immature:* Whiter than young Snow Goose. Rare "Blue" morph shows more extensively dark neck, whiter wing patches than "Blue" Snow Goose; hybrids with Snow Goose occur. **VOICE**: Higher than Snow, suggesting Cackling Goose. **SIMILAR SPECIES**: Snow Goose. **HABITAT**: Same as Snow Goose.

GEESE

GREATER WHITE-FRONTED GOOSE

immature

adult

immature

adult

EMPEROR GOOSE

adult

immature

adult

adult

SNOW GOOSE dark morph ("Blue" Goose)

adult

immature

adult

ROSS'S GOOSE

immature

adult

Snow

intergrade between dark and white morphs

SNOW GOOSE white morph

Ross's

Snow

BRANT *Branta bernicla* (see also p. 24)　　　　　　Locally common **M7**
24–26 in. (59–66 cm). A small black-necked goose. Has white stern, conspicuous when it upends, whitish flanks, and band of white on neck (absent in immature). Travels in large irregular flocks. Eastern subspecies, "Pale-bellied" Brant *(B. b. hrota)*, has *light belly, less contrasty flanks, and two separated neck patches.* Pacific Coast subspecies, "Black" Brant *(B. b. nigricans),* has dark belly and complete white band across foreneck. **VOICE:** Throaty *cr-r-r-ruk* or *krr-onk, krrr-onk.* **SIMILAR SPECIES:** Foreparts of Canada and Cackling geese not black to waterline, and those species have large white face patch. Brant is more strictly coastal. **HABITAT:** Salt bays, estuaries; in summer, tundra.

BARNACLE GOOSE *Branta leucopsis*　　　　　　　　Vagrant
26–27 in. (66–69 cm). Similar in size to Brant. Has white sides and black chest to waterline, strongly contrasting with white belly. Note white face encircling eye. Back distinctly barred. Some reports likely represent escapees. **VOICE:** Like Snow Goose, but higher-pitched, doglike barks. **SIMILAR SPECIES:** Canada Goose larger and brown-bodied (not gray), lacks barring, has dark face. Brant has all-dark head. **RANGE:** Casual winter visitor from Greenland and Europe to Atlantic Coast; accidental farther west. Provenance of some birds in question. **HABITAT:** Ponds, lakes; grazes in fields.

CACKLING GOOSE *Branta hutchinsii*　　　　　　　Uncommon **M8**
23–32 in. (58–81 cm). Recently elevated to full-species rank separate from Canada Goose, this species includes the variably sized subspecies *hutchinsii* ("Richardson's"), *taverneri* ("Taverner's"), *minima* ("Ridgway's"), and *leucopareia* ("Aleutian"). Like Canada Goose, shows variable breast color and neck collar. **VOICE:** High, cackling *yel-lik.* **SIMILAR SPECIES:** Told from Canada by smaller size, shorter neck, smaller, rounder head, stubbier bill, and higher-pitched voice. But distinctions between larger Cacklings and smaller Canadas subtle. **HABITAT:** Lakes, marshes, fields; in summer, tundra. Individuals will flock with larger Canadas and are usually noticeably smaller.

CANADA GOOSE *Branta canadensis* (see also p. 24)　　　Common **M9**
30–43 in. (76–109 cm). The most widespread goose in N. America. Note black head and neck, or "stocking," that contrasts with pale breast and *white chin strap.* Flocks travel in strings or in Vs, "honking" loudly. Substantial variation in size and neck length exists among populations. **VOICE:** Deep, musical honking or barking, *ka-ronk* or *ka-lunk.* Small subspecies (and Cackling Goose) have higher-pitched calls. **SIMILAR SPECIES:** Cackling Goose. **HABITAT:** Lakes, ponds, bays, marshes, fields. Resident in many areas, frequenting parks, lawns, golf courses.

GEESE

"Pale-bellied" (Atlantic)

immature

BRANT

"Black" (Pacific)

BARNACLE GOOSE

"Richardson's"

"Aleutian"

CACKLING GOOSE

"Lesser"

"Dusky"

CANADA GOOSE

SWANS

Huge, all-white swimmers; larger and longer necked than geese. Young are pale gray-brown. Sexes alike. Swans migrate in lines or Vs. Feed by immersing head and neck or by "tipping up." **FOOD**: Aquatic plants, seeds.

MUTE SWAN *Cygnus olor* Fairly common, local M10
60 in. (152 cm). Introduced from Europe. This graceful ornamental park swan often swims with an S curve in neck; wings often arched over back. *Black-knobbed orange bill* tilts downward. Wingbeats make a "whooshing" sound. *Immature:* Dingy, with pinkish bill. **VOICE**: It is not mute but makes hissing and wheezing sounds, weak bugling. **SIMILAR SPECIES**: Other swans. **HABITAT**: Ponds, fresh and salt; coastal lagoons, salt bays.

TUNDRA SWAN Uncommon to locally common M12
Cygnus columbianus (see also p. 24)
52–53 in. (132–135 cm); wingspan 6–7 ft. (183–213 cm). Our most wide-spread native swan. Often heard long before a high-flying flock can be spotted. All-white wings and very long neck mark them as swans. Bill *black*, usually with *small yellow basal spot*. Eurasian form ("Bewick's" Swan), casual from AK to CA, has *much yellow on bill* above nostrils. *Immature:* Dingy, with pinkish bill variably dark at base and tip. **VOICE**: Mellow, high-pitched cooing: *woo-ho, woo-woo, woo-ho*. **SIMILAR SPECIES**: Trumpeter and Mute swans. **HABITAT**: Lakes, large rivers, bays, estuaries, grain fields; in summer, tundra.

TRUMPETER SWAN *Cygnus buccinator* Uncommon M11
58–60 in. (147–152 cm). Larger than Tundra Swan, with longer, heavier, *all-black bill*, which has *straight ridge* recalling Canvasback. Black on lores wider, *embracing eyes* and lacking yellow spot (some Tundras also lack this spot). Bill base forms *V shape* (rather than U shape) on forehead. *Immature:* Keeps dusky body color later into first spring and summer than does Tundra. **VOICE**: *Deeper, more nasal calls* than Tundra Swan. **HABITAT**: Lakes, ponds, large rivers; in winter, also bays, grain fields, marshes.

WHISTLING-DUCKS

Formerly called "tree ducks," these rather gooselike ducks with long legs and erect neck are indeed more closely related to geese than they are to other ducks, which taxonomists place in a different subfamily. They are named for their high-pitched calls. Gregarious. **FOOD**: Seeds of aquatic plants and grasses.

BLACK-BELLIED WHISTLING-DUCK Locally common M1
Dendrocygna autumnalis
21 in. (53 cm). A gooselike duck with long pink legs. Rusty with *black belly*, gray face, bright *coral red* bill. Broad *white patch* along forewing, visible in flight. Thrusts head and feet down when landing. Frequently perches in trees. *Immature:* Has gray bill and legs. **VOICE**: High-pitched squealing whistle. **SIMILAR SPECIES**: Fulvous Whistling-Duck. **HABITAT**: Ponds, freshwater marshes.

FULVOUS WHISTLING-DUCK Uncommon M2
Dendrocygna bicolor (see also p. 46)
20 in. (51 cm). Long-legged, gooselike. Note *tawny* body, dark back, *pale side stripes*. Flies with neck slightly drooped and feet trailing, showing *black underwings, white band* on rump. **VOICE**: Squealing slurred whistle, *ka-whee-oo*. **SIMILAR SPECIES**: Black-bellied Whistling-Duck, female Northern Pintail. **HABITAT**: Freshwater marshes, ponds, irrigated land. Seldom perches in trees.

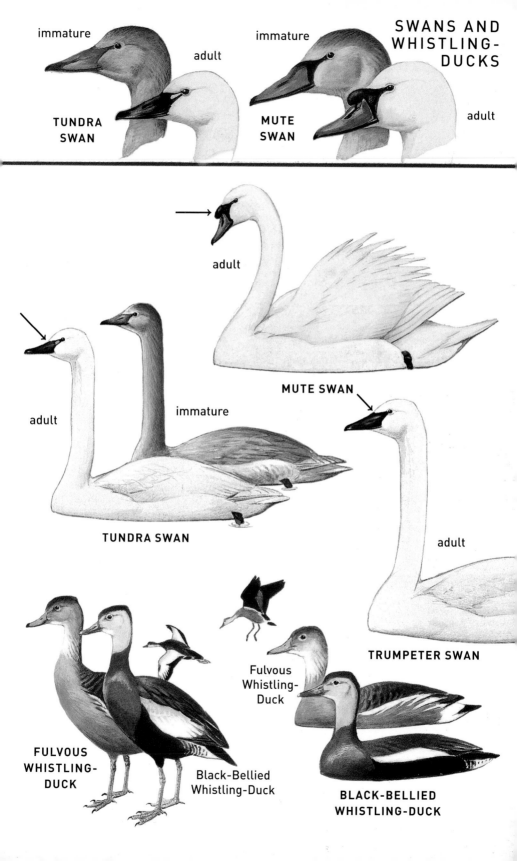

SWANS AND
WHISTLING-
DUCKS

immature

adult

TUNDRA
SWAN

immature

MUTE
SWAN

adult

adult

MUTE SWAN

adult

immature

adult

TUNDRA SWAN

TRUMPETER SWAN

Fulvous
Whistling-
Duck

FULVOUS
WHISTLING-
DUCK

Black-Bellied
Whistling-Duck

BLACK-BELLIED
WHISTLING-DUCK

Geese and Swans in Flight

CANADA GOOSE *Branta canadensis*   p. 20

BRANT *Branta bernicla*   p. 20
Small; black head and neck, white stern.

GREATER WHITE-FRONTED GOOSE *Anser albifrons*   p. 18
Adult: Gray-brown neck, black bars or splotches on belly.
Immature: Dusky, with light bill and feet.

EMPEROR GOOSE *Chen canagica*   p. 18
Gray with white head, black throat, white tail.

TUNDRA SWAN *Cygnus columbianus*   p. 22
Very long neck. *Adult:* Plumage entirely white.

SNOW GOOSE (WHITE MORPH) *Chen caerulescens*   p. 18
Adult: White with black primaries.

SNOW GOOSE (DARK MORPH, "BLUE" GOOSE) *Chen caerulescens*   p. 18
Adult: Dark body, white head.
Immature: Dusky, with dark bill and feet.

ROSS'S GOOSE *Chen rossii*   p. 18
Smaller, slightly shorter necked and shorter billed than Snow Goose.

Many geese and swans fly in line or V formation.

GEESE AND SWANS

CANADA GOOSE

"Pale-bellied"

BRANT

"Black"

GREATER WHITE-
FRONTED GOOSE

adult

immature

immature

EMPEROR
GOOSE

TUNDRA SWAN

adult

SNOW
GOOSE
white
morph

ROSS'S GOOSE

adult

SNOW GOOSE
dark morph
("Blue" Goose)

Dabbling Ducks

Feed by dabbling and upending; sometimes feed on land. Take flight directly into air. Most species have an iridescent speculum on secondaries above. Sexes not alike; in midsummer, males molt into drab "eclipse" plumage, usually resembling females. **FOOD:** Aquatic plants, seeds, grass, waste grain, small aquatic life, insects.

MUSCOVY DUCK *Cairina moschata*   Scarce, local
Male 32 in. (81 cm); female 28 in. (66 cm). Black, gooselike duck with large white wing patch and underwing coverts. *Male:* Bare, knobby, red face. *Female:* Duller, may lack facial knobs. Flight slow, heavy. **VOICE:** Usually silent. Occasionally utters a soft quack or a hiss when threatened. **SIMILAR SPECIES:** Domestic Muscovies show more white on head and belly. Widespread domestic Muscovy Ducks vary in pattern. **RANGE:** Native of tropical America (Mex. to n. Argentina). Recent colonizer of lower Rio Grande Valley, TX. Feral populations established in FL and near Brownsville, TX. **HABITAT:** Freshwater ponds and backwaters; wooded river corridors of Rio Grande in TX.

WOOD DUCK *Aix sponsa* (see also p. 44)   Fairly common M13
18–19 in. (45–49 cm). Highly colored; often perches in trees. In flight, white belly contrasts with dark breast and wings. Note also the long, almost square, dark tail; short neck; and angle at which bill points downward in flight. *Male:* Bizarre face pattern, sweptback crest, and rainbow iridescence unique. In eclipse, more like female but with brighter bill and suggestion of breeding head pattern. *Female:* Dull-colored; note dark crested head and *white eye patch.* **VOICE:** Male, hissing *jeeeeeeb,* with rising inflection. Female, a loud, rising squeal, *oo-eek,* and sharp *crrek, crrek.* **HABITAT:** Wooded swamps, rivers, ponds, marshes.

EURASIAN WIGEON *Anas penelope*   Rare M15
19–20 in. (48–51 cm). *Male:* Note *red-brown* head, *buff* crown. A *gray-sided* wigeon with rufous-pinkish breast. May show weak suggestion of green patch behind eye. *Female:* Very similar to female American Wigeon, but in many Eurasians head is tinged with *rust* or *orange-buff;* in others it is not. Surest point is dusky (not white) axillars, or "wingpits." **VOICE:** Male, a long whistle, *wheeee-oo.* Female, a purr or quack. **HABITAT:** Same as American Wigeon, with which it is usually found.

AMERICAN WIGEON *Anas americana* (see also p. 44)   Fairly common M16
19–20 in. (48–51 cm). In flight, recognized by *large white patch on forewing.* (Similarly placed blue patch of Northern Shoveler and Blue-winged Teal often appears whitish.) When swimming, rides high, picking at water like a coot. Often grazes on land. *Male:* Warm brownish; head pale gray with green eye patch. Note *white crown* (nicknamed "Baldpate"). *Female:* Brown; gray head and neck; whitish belly and forewing. **VOICE:** Male, a two-part whistled *whee whew.* Female, *qua-ack.* **SIMILAR SPECIES:** Told from female Gadwall and Northern Pintail by whitish patch on forewing, small bluish bill. See Eurasian Wigeon. **HABITAT:** Marshes, lakes, bays, fields, grass.

DABBLING DUCKS AND MUSCOVY DUCK

adults

domestic variation

MUSCOVY DUCK

♀

♂

♂ in eclipse (summer)

WOOD DUCK

♀

♂

EURASIAN WIGEON

♀

♂

AMERICAN WIGEON

SILHOUETTES OF DUCKS ON LAND

dabbling ducks (dabblers) | sea and bay ducks (divers) | mergansers (divers) | Ruddy Duck (diver) | whistling-ducks (dabblers)

GADWALL *Anas strepera* (see also p. 44) Fairly common M14
19–20 in. (48–51 cm). *Male: Gray* body with brown head and *black rump, white speculum* on rear edge of wing, and dull ruddy patch on forewing (may be difficult to see). When swimming, wing patches may be concealed. Belly white, feet yellow, bill dark. *Female:* Brown, mottled, with *white speculum,* yellow feet, orange sides on gray bill. **VOICE:** Male, a low, reedy *bek;* a whistling call. Female, a nasal quack. **SIMILAR SPECIES:** Female told from female Mallard by steeper forehead, wing pattern, more nasal call. **HABITAT:** Lakes, ponds, marshes.

AMERICAN BLACK DUCK Fairly common M17
Anas rubripes (see also p. 46)
22–23 in. (55–58 cm). A dusky duck, darker than female Mallard. In flight, shows flashing *white wing linings.* Sooty brown, with paler head and violet wing patch with only thin white trailing edge; feet red or brown. Sexes similar, except for bill (yellow in male, dull green in female). Hybridizes with Mallard. **VOICE:** Male, a low croak. Female quacks like female Mallard. **SIMILAR SPECIES:** Mallard, Mottled Duck. **HABITAT:** Marshes, bays, estuaries, ponds, rivers, lakes.

MOTTLED DUCK *Anas fulvigula* Fairly common M19
22–23 in. (55–58 cm). Like a pale brownish version of American Black Duck. Note tan head, unstreaked buffy throat, and unmarked yellow bill with *dark spot at base of "lips."* Sexes alike. Darker than female Mallard and lacking black on bill and broad white border to speculum. **VOICE:** Very similar to Mallard's. **SIMILAR SPECIES:** American Black Duck, Mallard. **HABITAT:** Marshes, ponds.

"MEXICAN" MALLARD *Anas platyrhynchos diazi* Uncommon, local
20–21 in. (51–54 cm). This subspecies of Mallard was formerly regarded as a distinct species called Mexican Duck. Intergrades with Mallard are frequent. Both sexes very similar to female Mallard but with *grayish brown* instead of whitish tail. Bill of male like bill of male Mallard (unmarked yellowish green). Yellow-orange bill of female has a dark ridge. Not as dark overall as American Black Duck; has white border *on both sides* of wing patch, thinner than in female Mallard. **VOICE:** Same as Mallard's. **SIMILAR SPECIES:** Mallard, American Black Duck, Mottled Duck. **RANGE:** Resident from se. AZ to sw. TX. **HABITAT:** Ponds.

MALLARD *Anas platyrhynchos* (see also p. 46) Common M18
22–23 in. (55–59 cm). *Male:* Note uncrested *glossy green head* and *white neck ring,* grayish body, chestnut chest, white tail, yellowish bill, orange feet, blue speculum. *Female:* Mottled brown with *whitish tail.* Dark bill patched with orange, feet orange. In flight, shows white bar *on both sides* of blue speculum. **VOICE:** Male, *yeeb;* a low *kwek.* Female, boisterous quacking. **SIMILAR SPECIES:** Female Gadwall, American Black Duck. **HABITAT:** Marshes, wooded swamps, grain fields, ponds, rivers, lakes, bays, city parks.

NORTHERN PINTAIL *Anas acuta* (see also p. 44) Fairly common M23
Male 25–26 in. (63–66 cm); female 20–21 in. (51–54 cm). *Male:* Slender, slim-necked, white-breasted, with long, *needle-pointed tail.* A conspicuous *white point* runs onto side of dark head. *Female:* Mottled brown; note rather pointed tail, slender neck, *gray bill.* In flight both sexes show a *single light border* on rear edge of brown speculum. **VOICE:** Male, a double-toned whistle: *prrip, prrip;* wheezy notes. Female, a low *quack.* **SIMILAR SPECIES:** Compare female's overall shape and bill with those of other dabbling ducks. **HABITAT:** Marshes, prairies, ponds, lakes, salt bays.

dabbling ducks
tip up

DABBLING DUCKS

GADWALL

♂ ♀

dabbling ducks
spring directly
from the water

**MOTTLED
DUCK**

♂ ♀

AMERICAN BLACK DUCK

♂ (female similar)

"MEXICAN" MALLARD

MALLARD

♂ ♀

**NORTHERN
PINTAIL**

♀

♂

BLUE-WINGED TEAL *Anas discors* (see also p. 44)   Fairly common M20
15–16 in. (38–41 cm). A half-sized dabbling duck. *Male:* Note *white facial crescent* and large *chalky blue* patch on *forewing.* Molting males hold eclipse plumage late in year, resemble females. *Female:* Brown, mottled; dark eye line; partial eye-ring; pale loral spot; blue on forewing. **VOICE:** Male, quiet whistled peeping notes. Female, a high quack. **SIMILAR SPECIES:** Cinnamon and Green-winged teal. **HABITAT:** Ponds, marshes, mudflats, flooded fields.

CINNAMON TEAL *Anas cyanoptera*   Fairly common M21
16–17 in. (41–43 cm). *Male:* A small, *dark chestnut* duck with large chalky blue patch on forewing. Adult has *red eye,* which it retains in eclipse plumage. In flight suggests Blue-winged Teal. *Female:* Very similar to female Blue-winged but tawnier; bill slightly larger (more shoveler-like), face pattern duller. *Juvenile:* Even more similar to female Blue-winged, with slightly smaller bill, somewhat bolder face pattern than adult female Cinnamon. **VOICE:** Like Blue-winged. **HABITAT:** Marshes, freshwater ponds, flooded fields.

NORTHERN SHOVELER *Anas clypeata* (see also p. 44)   Fairly common M22
18–19 in. (46–49 cm). The long *spoon-shaped bill* gives this duck a front-heavy look. When swimming, it sits low, with bill angled toward or in water, straining water. *Male: Rufous* belly and sides; *white breast;* pale blue patch on forewing; orange feet. *Female:* Brown. Note large spatulate bill, blue-gray forewing patch, white tail, orange feet. Bill color variable. **VOICE:** Male, a soft *thup-thup.* Female, short quacks. **SIMILAR SPECIES:** Cinnamon Teal. **HABITAT:** Marshes, ponds, sloughs; in winter, also salt bays.

GREEN-WINGED TEAL   Common M24
Anas crecca carolinensis (see also p. 44)
14–15 in. (36–39 cm). Teal are small, fly in tight flocks. Green-wingeds lack light wing patches (speculum *deep green*). *Male:* Small, compact, gray with brown head (a green head patch shows in sunlight). On swimming birds, note *vertical white mark* near shoulder, butter-colored streak near tail. *Female:* A small speckled duck with *green* speculum, pale undertail coverts. **VOICE:** Male, a high, froglike *dreep.* Female, a sharp *quack.* **SIMILAR SPECIES:** Female Blue-winged and Cinnamon teal slightly larger and larger-billed, have light blue wing patches; in flight, males show dark belly. Green-winged has white belly, broader dark border to underwing. **HABITAT:** Marshes, rivers, bays, mudflats, flooded fields.

GREEN-WINGED ("COMMON") TEAL (EURASIAN SUBSPECIES)   Rare
Anas crecca crecca
15–15½ in. (38–40 cm). Considered conspecific with "American" Green-winged Teal by most N. American taxonomists but as a separate species by Europeans. *Male: Longitudinal* (not vertical) white stripe above wing, bolder buffy borders to eye patch. *Female:* Largely indistinguishable from N. American race. Intergrades known. **RANGE:** Regular visitor to w. AK; rare but regular along Pacific Coast; very rare along Atlantic Coast; casual inland. **HABITAT:** Same as "American" Green-winged Teal, with which it usually associates.

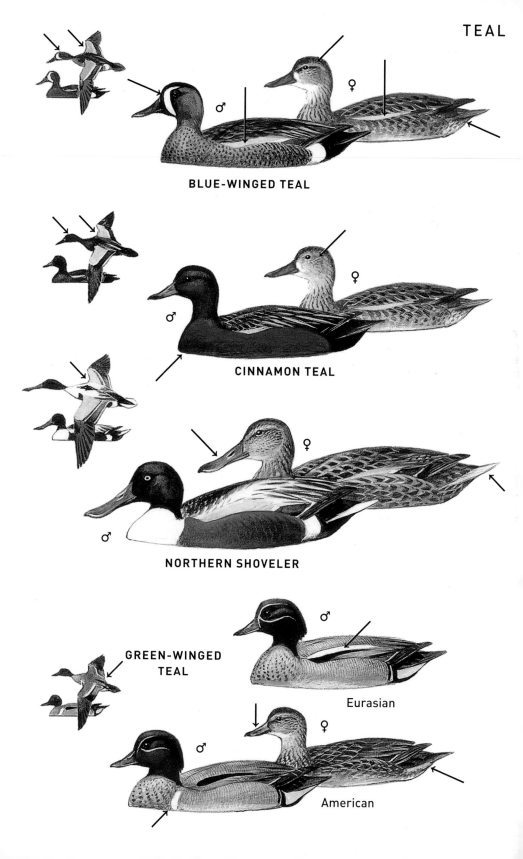

TEAL

BLUE-WINGED TEAL

♂ ♀

CINNAMON TEAL

♂ ♀

NORTHERN SHOVELER

♂ ♀

GREEN-WINGED
TEAL

♂ Eurasian

♂ ♀ American

DIVING DUCKS

Also called "sea ducks" or "bay ducks," but many are found on lakes and rivers and breed in marshes. All dive; dabbling ducks rarely do. Legs close to tail; hind toe with a paddlelike flap (lacking in dabblers). In taking wing, they must patter across surface of water while getting airborne. Sexes not alike. **FOOD:** Small aquatic animals and plants. Seagoing species eat mostly mollusks and crustaceans.

EIDERS

Eiders are seldom seen ashore except in summer when breeding. They usually mass in flocks off shoals and rocky coasts and often fly in line formations. In flight, males show white shoulders. **FOOD:** Mostly mollusks, crustaceans.

SPECTACLED EIDER *Somateria fischeri*   Rare, local **M31**
21–22 in. (53–56 cm). *Male:* Boldly patterned head; black below, white above, suggesting male Common Eider, but head largely pale green, with large *white "goggles"* narrowly trimmed with black. *Female:* Brown and barred like other female eiders, but with pale *ghost image of goggles.* Feathering at base of bill extends far down upper mandible. **VOICE:** Mostly silent. Both sexes give calls similar to Common Eider, but softer. **SIMILAR SPECIES:** Female Common Eider larger and often shows broad pale eyebrow, not goggles. See King Eider. **HABITAT:** In summer, Arctic coasts, tundra ponds; in winter, leads in pack ice.

KING EIDER *Somateria spectabilis* (see also p. 48)   Rare to uncommon **M32**
22 in. (56 cm). *Male:* A stocky sea duck; on water, foreparts appear white, rear parts black. Note protruding *orange bill-shield.* In flight, wings show large white patches. *Female:* Stocky; warm brown, weak pale eye-ring and thin stripe curving behind and down from eye, flanks barred with crescent-shaped marks. Note facial profile. *Immature male:* Dusky, with light breast, dark brown head; may have orangey bill. **VOICE:** Courting male, a low crooning phrase. Female, grunting croaks. **SIMILAR SPECIES:** Common Eider larger, with flatter head profile, longer bill-lobe before eye; male Common Eider has *white* back, female has evenly barred flanks. Immature male King Eider has darker head than immature Common and lacks white shoulder stripe of immature Common. Compare eclipse male in flight with White-winged Scoter. **HABITAT:** Rocky coasts, ocean. Nests on tundra.

COMMON EIDER   Fairly common **M33**
Somateria mollissima (see also p. 48)
24–25 in. (61–64 cm). This bulky, thick-necked duck is oceanic, living in flocks near shoals. Flight sluggish and low; flocks usually in a line. *Male:* This and Spectacled Eider are only ducks in N. America with *black belly and white back.* Forewing and back white; head white with black crown, greenish nape. *Female:* Large, brown, *closely barred, with pale eyebrow;* long, flat profile. *Immature male:* At first brownish; later dusky with white breast and collar; may develop chocolate head or breast; white areas come in irregularly. **VOICE:** Male, a moaning *ow-ooo-urr.* Female, a grating *korr-r.* **SIMILAR SPECIES:** King Eider. Female scoters smaller, lack heavy dark barring of female eiders. Compare eclipse male eider in flight with White-winged Scoter. **HABITAT:** Rocky coasts, shoals; in summer, also islands, tundra.

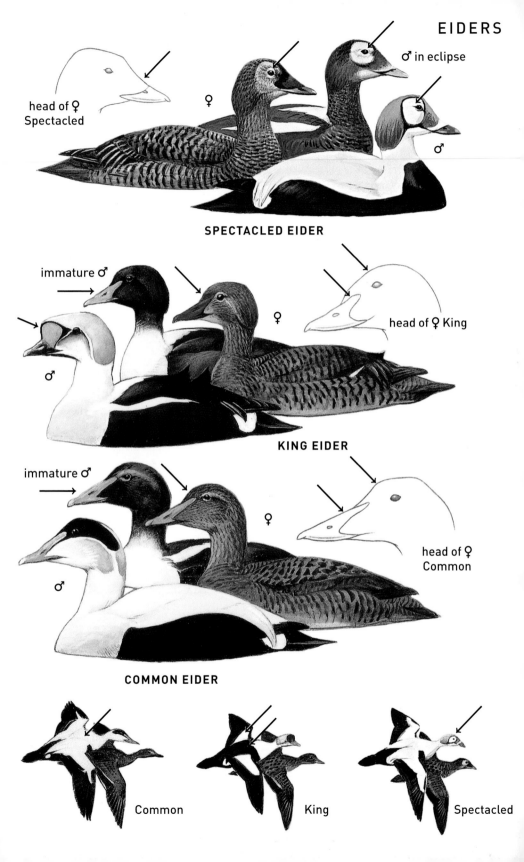

EIDERS

head of ♀ Spectacled

♀

♂ in eclipse

♂

SPECTACLED EIDER

immature ♂

♂

♀

head of ♀ King

KING EIDER

immature ♂

♀

♂

head of ♀ Common

COMMON EIDER

Common

King

Spectacled

STELLER'S EIDER *Polysticta stelleri*   Scarce, local **M30**
17 in. (43 cm). Unlike other eiders in shape, bill. *Male:* Black and white, with *yellow-buff underparts, white head,* black throat, and green bump on back of head. Note *round black spot* on side of breast. As in other eiders, white forewing is conspicuous in flight. *Female:* Dark brown, mottled, with pale eye-ring; distinguished from other eiders by much smaller size and *shape of its small head and blue-gray bill.* Purple speculum bordered in white, visible at short range, suggests a female Mallard. **VOICE:** Usually silent. Male's crooning note resembles Common Eider's but is quieter. Female has a low growl. **SIMILAR SPECIES:** Other eiders, Long-tailed Duck. **HABITAT:** Coasts, ocean.

HARLEQUIN DUCK   Uncommon **M34**
Histrionicus histrionicus (see also p. 48)
16–17 in. (41–44 cm). Dark and spectacularly patterned. *Male:* A small-ish, slaty duck with chestnut sides and odd white patches and spots. In flight, has stubby shape of a goldeneye but appears uniformly dark. *Female:* A small dusky duck with three round white spots on each side of head; no wing patch. **VOICE:** Usually silent. Male, a squeak; also *gwa gwa gwa.* Female, *ek-ek-ek-ek.* **SIMILAR SPECIES:** Female Bufflehead has white wing patch and only one face spot. Female scoters larger, with larger bills. **HABITAT:** Turbulent mountain streams in summer; rocky coastal waters in winter.

LONG-TAILED DUCK (OLDSQUAW) Fairly common in East, rare in West **M38**
Clangula hyemalis (see also p. 48)
Male 21–22 in. (53–56 cm); female 16 in. (41 cm). The only sea duck combining much *white on body and unpatterned dark wings.* It flies in bunched, irregular flocks, rocking side to side as it flies. *Nonbreeding male:* Note needlelike tail, pied pattern, dark cheek. *Breeding male:* Dark with white flanks and belly. Note white eye patch, pink on bill. *Nonbreeding female:* Dark unpatterned wings, white face with dark cheek spot. *Breeding female:* Similar but darker. Lacks pink on bill. *Immature:* Lacks long tail feathers. **VOICE:** Talkative; a musical *ow-owdle-ow* or *owl-omelet.* **SIMILAR SPECIES:** Bufflehead. In flight, sometimes confused with alcids because of dark underwings and rapid wingbeats. **HABITAT:** Ocean, harbors, large lakes; in summer, tundra pools and lakes.

DIVING DUCKS

♂ in eclipse

♀

♂

STELLER'S EIDER

Labrador
Duck
extinct 1878

♂

♀

♂

HARLEQUIN DUCK

nonbreeding
♀

breeding ♀

LONG-TAILED DUCK

nonbreeding
♂

breeding ♂

SCOTERS

Scoters are heavy, blackish ducks seen in large flocks along ocean coasts. They often fly in thin line formation. They are usually in flocks, either single species or mixed, so look them over carefully. Scoters are usually silent but during courtship and mating may utter low whistles, croaks, or grunting noises; wings whistle in flight. **FOOD:** Mainly mollusks, crustaceans.

WHITE-WINGED SCOTER
Uncommon to fairly common M36

Melanitta fusca (see also p. 48)

21 in. (53 cm). White-winged, largest of the three scoters, has a bill feathered to nostril. On water, white wing patch is often barely visible or fully concealed (wait for bird to flap or fly). *Male:* Black, with a "teardrop" of white near eye; bill orange with black basal knob. *Female:* Sooty brown, with white wing patch and two light oval patches on face (sometimes obscure; patches more pronounced on young birds). Asian subspecies *stejnegeri*, very rare in w. AK, has hornlike knob at base of bill. **VOICE:** Usually silent. **SIMILAR SPECIES:** Other scoters. **HABITAT:** Salt bays, ocean; in summer, lakes.

SURF SCOTER *Melanitta perspicillata* (see also p. 48)   Fairly common M35

19–20 in. (48–51 cm). The "skunkhead-duck." *Male:* Black, with one or two *white patches* on crown and nape. Heavy, sloping bill patterned with orange, black, and white. *Female:* Dusky brown; dark crown; two light spots on each side of head (sometimes obscure; more evident on young birds), one mostly vertical, the other more horizontal. **VOICE:** Usually silent. A low croak; grunting sounds. **SIMILAR SPECIES:** Female White-winged Scoter slightly larger overall, has more extensive feathering on bill, more horizontal, oval face patches, and white wing patch (may not show until bird flaps). Black Scoter has rounder head profile (more like Redhead, whereas Surf Scoter more like Canvasback), lacks feathering on bill, and has silvery underside to flight feathers; female and immature have entirely pale cheeks. **HABITAT:** Ocean, salt bays; in summer, lakes.

BLACK SCOTER
Rare to fairly common M37

Melanitta nigra (see also p. 48)

18½–19 in. (47–48 cm). *Male:* An all-black sea duck. Bright *orange-yellow knob* on bill ("butter nose") is diagnostic. In flight, underwing shows two-toned effect (silvery gray and black), more pronounced than in other two scoters. *Female:* Sooty; *entirely light cheeks* contrast with dark cap. **VOICE:** Usually silent. Male, melodious cooing notes. Female, growls. **SIMILAR SPECIES:** Some young male Surf Scoters may lack head patches and appear all black, but they have round black spot at base of higher-sloping bill. Female and immature scoters of other two species have smaller light spots on side of head, not entirely pale cheeks. Female Black Scoter may suggest nonbreeding adult male Ruddy Duck. **HABITAT:** Seacoasts, bays; in summer, tundra and taiga ponds.

SCOTERS

scoters fly in line or V formation

Surf

Black

White-winged

♂ ♀ immature

WHITE-WINGED SCOTER

♂ ♀ immature ♂

SURF SCOTER

immature ♂ ♀

♂

BLACK SCOTER

diving ducks (sea ducks and bay ducks) raft on water, skitter when taking wing

CANVASBACK *Aythya valisineria* (see also p. 50)   Uncommon M25
21–22 in. (53–56 cm). *Male:* Very white looking, with *chestnut red* head sloping into *long blackish* bill. Red eye, rufous neck, black chest. *Female:* Pale grayish brown, with brown chest; pale rust on head and neck. Both sexes have *long, sloping head profile.* Flocks travel in lines or V formations. In winter often form mixed flocks with Redheads, scaup. **VOICE:** Male, in courtship, cooing notes. Female, raspy *krrrr*, etc. **SIMILAR SPECIES:** Redhead not as white on body, lacks long sloping forehead and bill. **HABITAT:** Lakes, salt bays, estuaries; in summer, freshwater marshes and lakes.

REDHEAD *Aythya americana* (see also p. 50)   Uncommon M26
19–20 in. (48–51 cm). *Male:* Gray; black chest and *round rufous head;* bill bluish with black tip. *Female:* Brown overall; *diffuse light patch* near bill. Both sexes have *gray* wing stripe. **VOICE:** Male, in courtship, a harsh catlike *meow;* a deep purr. Female, soft *krrr* notes. **SIMILAR SPECIES:** Male Canvasback much whiter, with sloping forehead and black bill. See female Ring-necked Duck, scaup. **HABITAT:** Lakes, salt bays, estuaries; in summer, freshwater marshes and ponds.

RING-NECKED DUCK *Aythya collaris* (see also p. 50)   Fairly common M27
17–17½ in. (43–46 cm). *Male:* Like a scaup with *black back.* Note *vertical white mark* before wing; bill crossed by a white ring. In flight, a broad *gray* (not white) wing stripe. *Female:* Shaped somewhat like female Lesser Scaup, but with *indistinct* light face patch, darker eye, *white eye-ring,* and *pale ring on bill.* Wing stripe *gray.* **VOICE:** Female a quacking growl: *arrp-arrp-arrp.* Male silent except during courtship, when it gives a low-pitched whistle. **SIMILAR SPECIES:** Told from female Redhead by peaked head, darker crown, grayer face. Male Tufted Duck, rare in e. U.S., has wispy crest, white sides, white wing stripe. Male scaup have pale gray back, female scaup distinct white facial patch. **HABITAT:** Wooded lakes, ponds; in winter, also rivers, bays.

LESSER SCAUP *Aythya affinis* (see also p. 50)   Common M29
16½–17 in. (42–44 cm). Scaup (both species) have a broad white stripe on trailing edge of wing; it is shorter in Lesser. *Male:* On water, black at both ends, whitish or pale gray in middle. Bill *blue;* head has "peaked" shape, glossed with dull purple. Flanks and back very finely barred. *Female:* Dark brown, with clean-cut white patch near bill. May have a pale crescent on ear coverts in breeding season. **VOICE:** Male, in display, a soft whistle. Female, a loud *scaup;* also purring notes. **SIMILAR SPECIES:** Greater Scaup, Ring-necked Duck, Redhead. **HABITAT:** Lakes, bays, estuaries, nearshore ocean waters; in summer, marsh and taiga ponds.

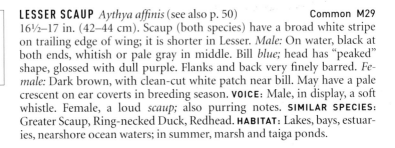

GREATER SCAUP *Aythya marila* (see also p. 50)   Common M28
18–18½ in. (46–48 cm). Very similar to Lesser Scaup, but slightly larger, with more gently rounded—sometimes almost flat-topped—head, bill slightly wider with larger black tip (nail), and *white wing stripe longer,* extending onto primaries. *Male:* Whiter on sides than Lesser; head glossed mainly with dull green rather than dull purple, but use this field mark with caution. *Female* (not shown): Averages slightly paler brown than Lesser, averages a larger white patch at base of bill, and may show pale ear patch in fall and winter, which Lesser typically lacks in these seasons. **VOICE:** Male, in display, soft, wheezy whistles. Female, raspy *scaup-scaup.* **SIMILAR SPECIES:** Lesser Scaup, Ring-necked Duck, Redhead. **HABITAT:** Lakes, rivers, bays, estuaries, nearshore ocean waters; in summer, tundra and taiga ponds.

DIVING DUCKS

CANVASBACK

♂

♀

diving ducks
run and patter

REDHEAD

♂

♀

RING-NECKED DUCK

♂

♀

Lesser

Greater

Greater

Lesser

♂

GREATER SCAUP

♀

LESSER SCAUP

COMMON GOLDENEYE   Fairly common M40
Bucephala clangula (see also p. 50)
18½–19 in. (47–49 cm). *Male:* Note large, *round white spot* before eye.
White looking, with black back and puffy, green-glossed head that appears black at a distance. In flight, short-necked; wings whistle or "sing,"
show large white patches. *Female:* Gray, with white collar and dark brown
head; wings with large square white patches that may show on closed
wing. **VOICE:** Wings "whistle" in flight. Courting male has harsh nasal
double note, suggesting *pee-ik* of Common Nighthawk. Female, a harsh
gaak. **SIMILAR SPECIES:** Barrow's Goldeneye. Male scaup have black chest.
Male Common Merganser long, low, with different bill. **HABITAT:** Forested
lakes, rivers; in winter, also lakes, salt bays, seacoasts.

BARROW'S GOLDENEYE *Bucephala islandica*   Scarce M41
18 in. (46 cm). *Male:* Note *white facial crescent.* Similar to Common Goldeneye, but blacker above; head glossed with *purple* (not green); nape puffier; shows *dark "spur"* on shoulder toward waterline. *Female:* Similar to
female Common; head slightly darker, with steeper forehead and suggestion of puffy nape, bill shorter and more triangular, less white in wing.
Bill may become all *orangey yellow,* often a good field mark but subject to
seasonal change. Female Common Goldeneye often has band of yellow
on bill. **VOICE:** Usually silent. Courting male, a grunting *kuk, kuk.* Female
near nest, a soft *coo-coo-coo.* Wings of both species whistle in flight. **SIMI-
LAR SPECIES:** Common Goldeneye, Bufflehead. **HABITAT:** Wooded lakes,
ponds; in winter, lakes and rivers, protected coastal waters.

BUFFLEHEAD *Bucephala albeola* (see also p. 50)   Common M39
13½–14 in. (34–36 cm). Small. *Male:* Mostly white with black back; puffy
head with *large, bonnetlike white patch.* In flight, shows large white wing
patch. *Female:* Dark and compact, with *white cheek spot,* small bill, smaller
wing patch. **VOICE:** Male, in display, a hoarse rolling note. Female, a harsh
ec-ec-ec. **SIMILAR SPECIES:** Male Hooded Merganser has spikelike bill,
dark sides. See female Black Scoter and nonbreeding adult male Ruddy
Duck. See also Long-tailed Duck. **HABITAT:** Lakes, ponds, rivers; in winter,
also salt bays.

STIFF-TAILED DUCKS

Small, chunky divers, nearly helpless on land. Spiky tail. Sexes not alike. **FOOD:** Aquatic
life, insects, water plants.

RUDDY DUCK *Oxyura jamaicensis* (see also p. 50)   Fairly common M45
15 in. (38 cm). Small, chubby; note *white cheek* and dark cap. Often cocks
tail upward. Flight "buzzy." Can barely walk on land. *Breeding male:* Rusty
red with white cheek, black cap, large, strikingly blue bill. *Nonbreeding
male:* Gray with *white cheek,* dull blue or gray bill. *Female:* Similar to nonbreeding male, but duskier cheek crossed by dark line. **VOICE:** Courting
male, a sputtering *chick-ik-ik-ik-k-k-kurrrr,* accompanied by head bobbing. **SIMILAR SPECIES:** Female Bufflehead, Black Scoter, Masked Duck
(rare). **HABITAT:** Freshwater marshes, ponds, lakes; in winter, also salt bays,
harbors.

DIVING DUCKS

COMMON GOLDENEYE

♂

♀

BARROW'S GOLDENEYE

♂

breeding ♀
(winter/spring)

nonbreeding ♀
(summer/fall)

BUFFLEHEAD

♂

♀

RUDDY DUCK

breeding ♂

nonbreeding ♂

♀

MERGANSERS

Long-lined, slender-bodied diving ducks with spikelike bill, saw-edged mandibles. Most species have a crest. In flight, bill, head, neck, and body are on a horizontal axis. Sexes not alike. **FOOD:** Chiefly fish.

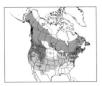

COMMON MERGANSER
Fairly common M43

Mergus merganser (see also p. 46)
24–25 in. (62–64 cm). In flight, lines of these slender ducks follow the winding courses of rivers. Whiteness of adult males and merganser shape (bill, neck, head, and body held horizontally) identify this species. *Male:* Note long whitish body, black back, green-black head. Bill and feet red; breast tinged rosy peach. *Female and immature:* Gray with crested rufous head contrasting with white chin and clean white chest; large square white wing patch. **VOICE:** Male, in display, low staccato croaks. Female, a guttural *karrr.* **SIMILAR SPECIES:** Female Red-breasted Merganser very similar to female Common. Note distinct cut-off of rusty head and neck from breast in Common; this is diffuse in Red-breasted. Female mergansers, which are rusty-headed, suggest male Canvasback or Redhead, but those have black chest, no crest. **HABITAT:** Wooded lakes, ponds, rivers; in winter, open lakes, rivers, rarely coastal bays.

RED-BREASTED MERGANSER
Common M44

Mergus serrator (see also p. 46)
22½–23 in. (56–58 cm). *Male:* Rakish; black head glossed with green and *crested;* breast at waterline dark rusty, separated from head by *wide white collar;* bill and feet red. *Female and immature:* Gray, with crested, dull rusty head that *blends* into color of neck; large white wing patch; red bill and feet. **VOICE:** Usually silent. Male, a hoarse croak. Female, *karrr.* **SIMILAR SPECIES:** Male Common Merganser whiter, without collar and breast-band effect; lacks crest. In female Common, white chin and chest *sharply delineated* from brighter rufous head and pale gray body. Common's bill slightly thicker at base. **HABITAT:** Woodland and coastal lakes, open water; in winter, also bays, tidal channels, nearshore ocean waters.

HOODED MERGANSER
Uncommon to fairly common M42

Lophodytes cucullatus (see also p. 46)
17–18 in. (43–46 cm). *Male:* Note vertical *fan-shaped white crest,* which may be raised or lowered. Breast white, with two black bars on each side. Wing with white patch; *flanks rusty brown. Female:* Recognized as a merganser by silhouette and spikelike bill; known as this species by its small size, dusky look, and *dark head, bill, and chest.* Note loose *tawny crest.* **VOICE:** In display, low grunting or croaking notes. **SIMILAR SPECIES:** Male Bufflehead chubbier, with *white* sides. Other female mergansers larger and *grayer,* with rufous head, reddish bill. In flight, wing patch and silhouette separate female Hooded Merganser from female Wood Duck. **HABITAT:** Wooded lakes, ponds, rivers; in winter, also tidal channels, protected bays.

MERGANSERS

mergansers fly with bill, head, body, and tail on the same horizontal axis

saw-edged mandibles of merganser

♂ ♀

COMMON MERGANSER

♂ ♀

RED-BREASTED MERGANSER

♂ crest down

♂ crest up

♀

♂ in eclipse

HOODED MERGANSER

Common

Red-breasted

Hooded

Flight Patterns of Dabbling Ducks

Note: Only males are diagnosed below. Although females are unlike the males, their wing patterns are quite similar. The names in parentheses are common nicknames used by hunters.

NORTHERN PINTAIL (SPRIG) *Anas acuta*   p. 28
Overhead: Needle tail, white breast, thin neck.
Above: Needle tail, neck stripe, single thin white border on speculum.

WOOD DUCK *Aix sponsa*   p. 26
Overhead: White belly, dusky wings, long square tail.
Above: Stocky; long dark tail, white border on dark wing.

AMERICAN WIGEON ("BALDPATE") *Anas americana*   p. 26
Overhead: White belly, pointed dark tail.
Above: Large white shoulder patch.

NORTHERN SHOVELER (SPOONBILL) *Anas clypeata*   p. 30
Overhead: Dark belly, white breast, white tail, spoon bill.
Above: Large pale bluish shoulder patch, spoon bill.

GADWALL *Anas strepera*   p. 28
Overhead: White belly, white underwing, square white patch on rear edge of wing.
Above: White patch on rear edge of wing.

GREEN-WINGED TEAL *Anas crecca*   p. 30
Overhead: Small; light belly, dark head, broad dark borders to underwing.
Above: Small, dark-winged; green speculum.

BLUE-WINGED TEAL *Anas discors*   p. 30
Overhead: Small; dark belly, narrow dark borders to underwing.
Above: Small; large chalky blue shoulder patch.

upper wing of a dabbling duck showing the iridescent speculum (secondaries)

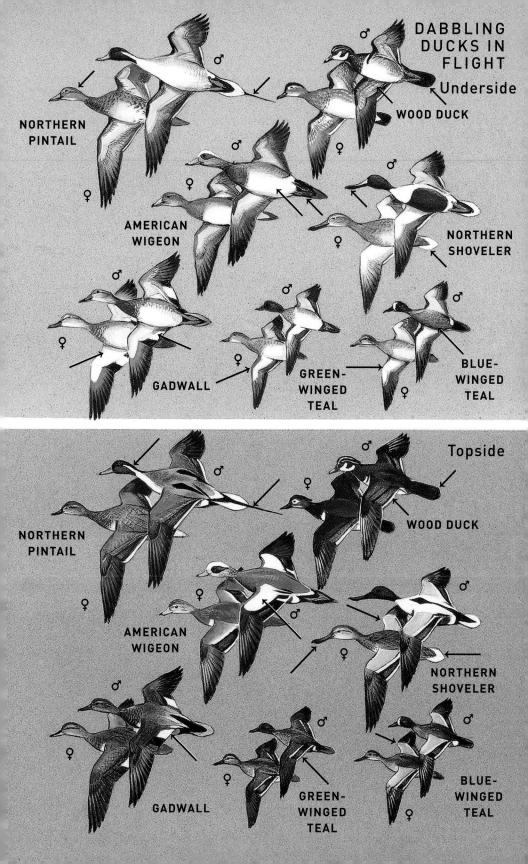

DABBLING
DUCKS IN
FLIGHT

Underside

WOOD DUCK

NORTHERN
PINTAIL

AMERICAN
WIGEON

NORTHERN
SHOVELER

GADWALL

GREEN-
WINGED
TEAL

BLUE-
WINGED
TEAL

Topside

NORTHERN
PINTAIL

WOOD DUCK

AMERICAN
WIGEON

NORTHERN
SHOVELER

GADWALL

GREEN-
WINGED
TEAL

BLUE-
WINGED
TEAL

FLIGHT PATTERNS OF DABBLING DUCKS AND MERGANSERS

Note: Only males are diagnosed below. Although most females are unlike the males, their wing patterns are quite similar. Mergansers have a distinctive flight silhouette. Duck hunters often call mergansers "sheldrakes" or "sawbills."

MALLARD *Anas platyrhynchos* p. 28
Overhead: Dark chest, light belly, white neck ring, white tail.
Above: Dark head, neck ring, two white borders on bluish speculum.

AMERICAN BLACK DUCK *Anas rubripes* p. 28
Overhead: Dark body, white wing linings.
Above: Dark body, paler head, purplish speculum lacks forward border.

FULVOUS WHISTLING-DUCK *Dendrocygna bicolor* p. 22
Overhead: Tawny, with blackish wing linings.
Above: Dark, unpatterned wings; white band on rump.

COMMON MERGANSER *Mergus merganser* p. 42
Overhead: Merganser shape; dark head, white body, white wing linings.
Above: Merganser shape; white chest, large white wing patches.

RED-BREASTED MERGANSER *Mergus serrator* p. 42
Overhead: Merganser shape; dark chest band, white collar.
Above: Merganser shape; dark chest, large white wing patches.

HOODED MERGANSER *Lophodytes cucullatus* p. 42
Overhead: Merganser shape; dusky wing linings.
Above: Merganser shape; small white wing patches.

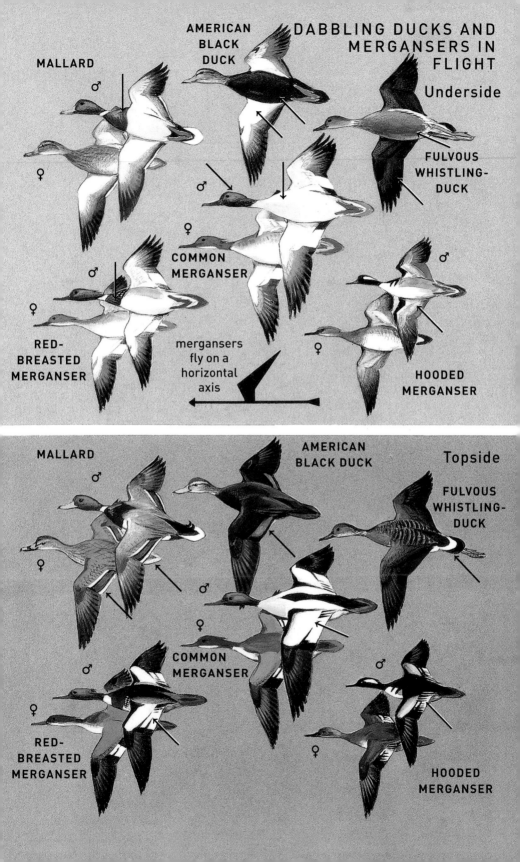

DABBLING DUCKS AND MERGANSERS IN FLIGHT
Underside

MALLARD

♂
♀

AMERICAN BLACK DUCK

FULVOUS WHISTLING-DUCK

♂
♀

COMMON MERGANSER

RED-BREASTED MERGANSER
♂
♀

mergansers fly on a horizontal axis

♂
♀
HOODED MERGANSER

Topside

MALLARD
♂
♀

AMERICAN BLACK DUCK

FULVOUS WHISTLING-DUCK

♂
COMMON MERGANSER
♀

♂
♀
RED-BREASTED MERGANSER

♂
♀
HOODED MERGANSER

FLIGHT PATTERNS OF DIVING DUCKS

Note: Only males are diagnosed below.

LONG-TAILED DUCK (OLDSQUAW) *Clangula hyemalis*　　　p. 34
Overhead: Dark unpatterned wings, white belly.
Above: Dark unpatterned wings, much white on body.

HARLEQUIN DUCK *Histrionicus histrionicus*　　　p. 34
Overhead: Solid dark below, white head spots, small bill.
Above: Dark with white marks, small bill, long tail.

SURF SCOTER *Melanitta perspicillata*　　　p. 36
Overhead: Black body, white head patches (not readily visible from below), sloping forehead.
Above: Black body, white head patches, sloping forehead.

BLACK SCOTER *Melanitta nigra*　　　p. 36
Overhead: Black plumage, paler flight feathers, rounded forehead.
Above: All-dark plumage. Body slightly smaller and pudgier than Surf Scoter's, rounded forehead.

WHITE-WINGED SCOTER *Melanitta fusca*　　　p. 36
Overhead: Black body, white wing patches.
Above: Black body, white wing patches.

COMMON EIDER *Somateria mollissima*　　　p. 32
Above: White back, white forewing, black belly.

KING EIDER *Somateria spectabilis*　　　p. 32
Above: Whitish foreparts, black rear parts.

DIVING
DUCKS
IN
FLIGHT
Underside

HARLEQUIN DUCK ♂

♀

LONG-TAILED
DUCK

♂

♀

SURF SCOTER

♂

♀

BLACK
SCOTER

♂

♀

WHITE-WINGED
SCOTER

Topside

♂

♀

♂

♀

HARLEQUIN DUCK

ONG-TAILED
DUCK

♂

♀

♂

COMMON
EIDER

KING EIDER

♂

♀

♂

♀

♂

BLACK
SCOTER

SURF
SCOTER

WHITE-
WINGED
SCOTER

Flight Patterns of Diving Ducks, etc.

Note: Only males are diagnosed below. The first five all have a black chest. The names in parentheses are common nicknames used by hunters.

CANVASBACK *Aythya valisineria*   p. 38
Overhead: Black chest, long profile.
Above: White back, long profile. Lacks contrasty wing stripe of next four species.

REDHEAD *Aythya americana*   p. 38
Overhead: Black chest, roundish rufous head.
Above: Gray back, broad gray wing stripe.

RING-NECKED DUCK *Aythya collaris*   p. 38
Overhead: Not safe to tell from scaup overhead; gray wing stripe sometimes evident.
Above: Black back, broad gray wing stripe.

GREATER SCAUP (BLUEBILL) *Aythya marila*   p. 38
Overhead: Black chest, white stripe showing through wing.
Above: Broad white wing stripe (extending onto primaries).

LESSER SCAUP (BLUEBILL) *Aythya affinis*   p. 38
Above: Wing stripe shorter than in Greater Scaup.

COMMON GOLDENEYE (WHISTLER) *Bucephala clangula*   p. 40
Overhead: Dark wing linings, white wing patches, rounded dark head.
Above: Large white square wing patch, short neck, dark head.

RUDDY DUCK *Oxyura jamaicensis*   p. 40
Overhead: Stubby; white face, dark chest, long tail.
Above: Small; dark with white cheeks, long tail.

BUFFLEHEAD (BUTTERBALL) *Bucephala albeola*   p. 40
Overhead: Like a small goldeneye; note head patch.
Above: Small; large wing patches, white head patch.

Silhouettes of Ducks on Land

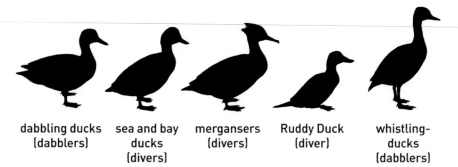

dabbling ducks
(dabblers)

sea and bay
ducks
(divers)

mergansers
(divers)

Ruddy Duck
(diver)

whistling-
ducks
(dabblers)

DIVING DUCKS IN FLIGHT

Underside

CANVASBACK ♂ ♀

REDHEAD ♂ ♀

RING-NECKED DUCK ♂ ♀

GREATER SCAUP ♂ ♀

BUFFLEHEAD ♂ ♀

COMMON GOLDENEYE ♂ ♀

RUDDY DUCK ♂

Topside

CANVASBACK ♂ ♀

REDHEAD ♂ ♀

RING-NECKED DUCK ♂ ♀

GREATER SCAUP ♂ ♀

wing of LESSER SCAUP

BUFFLEHEAD ♂ ♀

COMMON GOLDENEYE ♂ ♀

RUDDY DUCK ♂

GARGANEY *Anas querquedula*   Vagrant
15½ in. (38 cm). *Male:* Broad white eyebrow stripe, silvery shoulder patch (in flight). *Female:* Told from Blue-winged and Cinnamon teal by bolder face pattern (shared by Green-winged Teal), dark legs, paler primaries (in flight), and bold white borders on speculum. **RANGE:** Very rare visitor from Eurasia to w. Aleutians; casual elsewhere in N. America, with widespread records. Many records from West and East coasts, fewer inland.

MASKED DUCK *Nomonyx dominicus*   Vagrant
13–13½ in. (33–34 cm). *Male:* Rusty, dark-striped body with all-black face and blue bill. Stiff tail feathers held upright at times. *Female:* Buffy with black crown and two distinct face stripes. Heavily barred back. **SIMILAR SPECIES:** Ruddy Duck. **RANGE:** Very rare and irregular visitor from Mex. and Caribbean to TX and FL; accidental elsewhere. **HABITAT:** Ponds and marshes with dense vegetation. Often hidden.

TUFTED DUCK *Aythya fuligula*   Regular vagrant
16½–17 in. (41–43 cm). *Male:* Differs from male Ring-necked Duck in having thin wispy crest, entirely *white* sides, and *white* (not gray) wing stripe; from scaup, by black back and wispy crest. *Female:* Resembles female scaup or Ring-necked but may have faint trace of a tuft, broad band at bill tip, and lacks eye-ring and ring on bill of Ring-necked. May or may not have white at base of bill. **VOICE:** Similar to Ring-necked Duck. **RANGE:** Regular visitor from Eurasia to NL, w. AK; very rare elsewhere along Atlantic and Pacific coasts; casual inland. **HABITAT:** Sheltered ponds, bays, reservoirs. Usually with scaup.

SMEW *Mergellus albellus*   Vagrant
16 in. (41 cm). Smaller and shorter-billed than other mergansers. *Male:* Very white, with *black eye patch* and slight drooping black-and-white crest behind eye. In flight, shows conspicuous black-and-white wings. *Female:* Small and gray, with *white cheeks, chestnut cap.* **RANGE:** Rare but regular spring visitor from Asia to w. AK; accidental elsewhere. Some birds might be escapees.

Unestablished Exotic

CHINESE GOOSE *Anser cygnoides*   Exotic

EGYPTIAN GOOSE *Alopochen aegyptiacus*   Exotic

WHITE-CHEEKED PINTAIL *Anas bahamensis*   Provenance in question
(West Indies) 17 in. (43 cm). Numerous reports from FL; scattered records elsewhere. Most birds are likely escapees.

GRAYLAG GOOSE *Anser anser*   Provenance in question

BAR-HEADED GOOSE *Anser indicus*   Exotic

MANDARIN *Aix galericulata*   Exotic

COMMON SHELDUCK *Tadorna tadorna*   Exotic

RUDDY SHELDUCK *Tadorna ferruginea*   Provenance in question

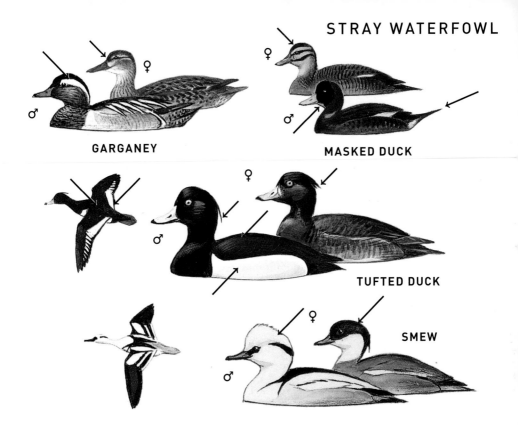

STRAY WATERFOWL

GARGANEY

MASKED DUCK

TUFTED DUCK

SMEW

UNESTABLISHED EXOTICS

CHINESE GOOSE

EGYPTIAN GOOSE

WHITE-CHEEKED PINTAIL

BAR-HEADED GOOSE

GRAYLAG GOOSE

MANDARIN

COMMON SHELDUCK

RUDDY SHELDUCK

Curassows and Guans Family Cracidae

Tropical forest birds with long tails. Only one species reaches extreme s. U.S. **FOOD:** Insects, fruit, leaves, seeds. **RANGE:** New World Tropics.

PLAIN CHACHALACA *Ortalis vetula*   Fairly common, local M46
22 in. (56 cm). A large olive-brown bird shaped somewhat like a half-grown turkey with a small head. Long, rounded, pale-tipped tail, bare red throat. Difficult to observe; best found in morning when calling raucously from treetops. **VOICE:** Alarm a harsh chickenlike cackle. Characteristic call a raucous three-syllabled *cha-ca-lac,* repeated in chorus from treetops, especially in morning and evening. **SIMILAR SPECIES:** Greater Roadrunner. **HABITAT:** Woodlands, tall brush, well-vegetated residential areas.

Gallinaceous, or Chickenlike, Birds
(Turkeys, Pheasants, Grouse, Partridges, and Old World Quail) Family Phasianidae

Often called "upland game birds." Turkeys are very large, with wattles and fanlike tail. Pheasants (introduced) have long pointed tail. Grouse are plump, chickenlike birds, without long tail. Partridges (of Old World origin) are intermediate in size between grouse and quail. Quail are the smallest. **FOOD:** Insects, seeds, buds, berries. **RANGE:** Nearly worldwide.

WILD TURKEY *Meleagris gallopavo*   Fairly common M62
Male 46–47 in. (117–120 cm); female 36–37 in. (91–94 cm). A streamlined version of barnyard turkey, with rusty instead of white tail tips (southwestern birds have buff-white tail tips). *Male:* Head naked; bluish with red wattles, intensified in display. Tail erected like a fan in display. Bronzy iridescent body; barred wings (primaries and secondaries); prominent "beard" on breast. *Female and immature:* Smaller, with smaller and duller head; less iridescent; less likely to have a beard. **VOICE:** "Gobbling" of male like domestic turkey's. Alarm *pit!* or *put-put!* Flock call *keow-keow.* Hen clucks to her chicks. **HABITAT:** Woods, mountain forests, wooded swamps, field edges, clearings. Reintroduced in many areas, and such birds are adapting well to being near people.

GUNNISON SAGE-GROUSE *Centrocercus minimus*   Scarce, very local M52
Male 21–22 in. (53–56 cm); female 18–19 in. (46–49 cm). Recently split taxonomically from Greater Sage-Grouse, this species is found only in a very geographically restricted region of sw. CO and se. UT. Differs from Greater Sage-Grouse by its slightly smaller size, longer "crest," and greater amount of white barring on tail. Identification by range is most reliable.

GREATER SAGE-GROUSE *Centrocercus urophasianus*   Uncommon M51
Male 27–28 in. (69–71 cm); female 22–23 in. (56–58 cm). A large grayish grouse of open sage country, as large as a small turkey; identified by its contrasting *black belly patch* and spikelike tail feathers. Male is considerably larger than female, has black throat, and, in communal dancing display, puffs out its white chest, exposing two yellow air sacs on neck, at same time erecting and spreading its pointed tail feathers in a spiky fan. **VOICE:** Flushing call *kuk kuk kuk.* In courtship display, male makes a popping sound. **SIMILAR SPECIES:** Gunnison Sage-Grouse, but these two resident species do not overlap. See female Ring-necked Pheasant. **HABITAT:** Sagebrush plains; also foothills and mountain slopes where sagebrush grows.

MISCELLANEOUS CHICKENLIKE BIRDS

♂

♂ display

♀

WILD TURKEY

PLAIN CHACHALACA

GREATER
SAGE-GROUSE

♂ display

♀

♂ display

GUNNISON
SAGE-GROUSE

RUFFED GROUSE *Bonasa umbellus*   Uncommon M50

17 in. (43 cm). Note short crest, bold flank bars, and fan-shaped tail with broad black band near tip. A large chickenlike bird of brushy woodlands, usually not seen until it flushes with a startling whir. Two color morphs occur: "rusty" with rufous tail and "gray" with gray tail. Rusty birds more common in southern parts of range (and in Pacific Northwest), gray birds more common northward. **VOICE:** Sound of drumming male suggests a distant motor starting up. Low muffled thumping starts slowly, accelerating into a whir: *Bup . . . bup . . . bup . . . bup . . . bup bup up r-rrrrr.* **SIMILAR SPECIES:** Sharp-tailed, Sooty, Dusky, and Spruce grouse. **HABITAT:** Ground and understory of deciduous and mixed woodlands.

SPRUCE GROUSE *Falcipennis canadensis*   Scarce M53

16–17 in. (41–43 cm). Look for this *tame*, dark grouse in deep coniferous forests of North. *Male:* Sharply defined *black breast,* with some white spots or bars on sides and *chestnut band* on tip of tail. Comb of erectile red skin above eye is visible at close range. Birds of n. Rockies and Cascades, known as "Franklin's" Grouse, lack chestnut tail tip and have large white spots on uppertail coverts. *Female:* Dark rusty or grayish brown, thickly barred, and with black-and-white spotting below; tail short and dark, with rusty tip (except in "Franklin's" race). **VOICE:** Female, call an accelerating, then slowing, series of *wock* notes; also cluck notes. Wing flutter from male's courtship display may sound like distant rumble of thunder. **SIMILAR SPECIES:** Sooty and Dusky grouse slightly larger and grayer, lack bold black-and-white spotting below. **HABITAT:** Coniferous forests, jack pines, muskeg, blueberry patches.

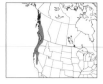

DUSKY GROUSE   Uncommon M57

Dendragapus obscurus [formerly Blue Grouse]

20 in. (51 cm). This is the more interior of the two species formerly lumped as Blue Grouse. *Male:* In courtship display, eye combs may change from yellow to red. Neck sacs *purplish red* with broad border of white feathers. *Female:* See Sooty Grouse. **VOICE:** Courting male gives a series of five to seven low, muffled booming or hooting notes, ventriloquial, usually from ground; lower pitched and substantially softer than calls of male Sooty Grouse. **SIMILAR SPECIES:** Sooty Grouse tends to be darker overall; male has yellowish neck sacs, more obvious gray tail tip; no range overlap. See Spruce Grouse. Female Dusky Grouse may be confused with Ruffed Grouse; see under Sooty Grouse. **HABITAT:** In summer, all forest types, alpine meadow edges; may move to higher-elevation coniferous forests in winter.

SOOTY GROUSE   Uncommon M58

Dendragapus fuliginosus [formerly Blue Grouse]

20 in. (51 cm). This is the more coastal of the two species formerly lumped as Blue Grouse. A large dark grouse with long neck and tail. Distinct gray band on tail tip. *Male:* In courtship display shows yellow eye combs and inflates bright yellow neck sacs with narrow white border. *Female:* Gray-brown, mottled with blackish, belly paler than male's. **VOICE:** Courting male gives a series of five to seven low, muffled booming or hooting notes, ventriloquial, usually from perch in a tree; much louder than calls of Dusky Grouse. **SIMILAR SPECIES:** See Dusky and Spruce Grouse. Females of both Sooty and Dusky grouse may be confused with Ruffed Grouse, but Ruffed has slight crested look, bold flank bars, and lighter tail with *black band* near tip. **HABITAT:** In summer, all forest types, mountain meadow edges; may move to higher-elevation coniferous forests in winter.

GROUSE

RUFFED GROUSE

♂ display

gray morph

rusty morph

SPRUCE GROUSE

♂

♀

♂

♂ display

typical

West ("Franklin's")

♂

♀

♂

♂ display

♂ display

DUSKY GROUSE

SOOTY GROUSE

SHARP-TAILED GROUSE *Tympanuchus phasianellus*   Uncommon M59
17 in. (43 cm). A pale, speckled-brown grouse of prairies and brushy draws. Note *short pointed tail,* which in display or flight shows *white* at sides. Slight crested look. Marked below by dark bars, spots, and chevrons. Displaying male has yellow eye combs and inflates *purplish* neck sacs. **VOICE:** Cackling *cac-cac-cac,* etc. Courting note a single low *coo-oo,* accompanied by quill-rattling, foot-shuffling. **SIMILAR SPECIES:** Prairie-chickens have *rounded, dark* tail and are more barred, rather than spotted, below. Female Ring-necked Pheasant has *long pointed* tail. Ruffed Grouse has banded, *fan-shaped* tail and black neck ruff. **HABITAT:** Prairies, agricultural fields, forest edges, clearings, coulees, open burns and clear-cuts in coniferous and mixed forests.

GREATER PRAIRIE-CHICKEN   Uncommon, local M60
Tympanuchus cupido
17 in. (43 cm). A henlike bird of prairies. Brown, heavily barred. Note *rounded dark tail* (black in male, barred in female). Courting males in communal "dance" inflate orange neck sacs, show off orangey yellow eye combs, and erect black hornlike neck feathers. **VOICE:** "Booming" male in dance makes a hollow *oo-loo-woo,* suggesting sound made by blowing across a bottle mouth. **SIMILAR SPECIES:** Lesser Prairie-Chicken. Sharp-tailed Grouse, often called "Prairie-Chicken," slightly paler overall, has more spots or chevrons on underparts, and has more pointed, white-edged tail. Female Ring-necked Pheasant slightly larger, has long pointed tail. **HABITAT:** Native tallgrass prairie, now very localized; agricultural land.

LESSER PRAIRIE-CHICKEN   Scarce, local M61
Tympanuchus pallidicinctus
16 in. (41 cm). A small, pale brown prairie-chicken; best identified by range. Male's neck sacs are dull *purplish* or *plum colored* (not yellow-orange as in Greater Prairie-Chicken). Breast barring usually paler and thinner than Greater's. **VOICE:** Male's courtship "booming" not as rolling or loud as Greater Prairie-Chicken's. Both sexes give clucking, cackling notes. **SIMILAR SPECIES:** Greater Prairie-Chicken, Sharp-tailed Grouse. **HABITAT:** Sandhill country (sage and bluestem grass, oak shrublands).

GROUSE

SHARP-TAILED GROUSE

♂

♂ display

GREATER PRAIRIE-CHICKEN

♂

♂ display

LESSER PRAIRIE-CHICKEN

♂

♂ display

PTARMIGANS

Hardy Arctic and alpine grouse with feathered feet. They molt three times a year; camouflaging themselves to match the seasons, they change from dark plumage in summer to white in winter. During spring and fall molts they have a patchy look. A red comb above eye may be erected or concealed. **FOOD:** Buds, leaves, seeds.

WILLOW PTARMIGAN *Lagopus lagopus*   Fairly common M54
15 in. (39 cm). Willow and Rock ptarmigans are fairly similar. In breeding season, Willows are variable, but most males are chestnut brown, redder than any Rock; females are warm buffy brown that can overlap brown of Rock. White of wings retained all year and, in flight, contrast with summer body plumage. In winter, white overall with black tail, the latter retained year-round. There is much variation between various molts. **VOICE:** Deep raucous calls. Male, a staccato crow, *kwow, kwow, tobacco, tobacco,* etc., or *go-back, go-back.* **SIMILAR SPECIES:** Rock Ptarmigan always has smaller and more slender bill that lacks strong curve on ridge shown by Willow. In winter, male Rock has *black mark* between eye and bill, lacking in both sexes of Willow. Habitats overlap, but Rock tends to prefer higher, more barren hills. See White-tailed Ptarmigan. **HABITAT:** Tundra, willow scrub, muskeg; in winter, sheltered valleys at slightly lower altitudes.

ROCK PTARMIGAN *Lagopus muta*   Uncommon M55
14 in. (36 cm). Breeding male is usually browner or grayer than breeding Willow Ptarmigan, lacking rich chestnut around head and neck. Some Rocks may be even paler than shown here, or are like dark birds from w. Aleutians (shown in center). Females of the two species are similar, but Rock has smaller bill. In winter, white male Rock has *black mark* between eye and bill. This is absent in most females, which may be told from female Willow by Rock's smaller bill. **VOICE:** Croaks, growls, cackles; usually silent. **SIMILAR SPECIES:** Willow and White-tailed ptarmigans. **HABITAT:** Tundra, above timberline in mountains (to lower levels in winter); also near sea level in bleak tundra of northern coasts.

WHITE-TAILED PTARMIGAN *Lagopus leucura*   Uncommon M56
12½–13 in. (31–33 cm). The only ptarmigan normally found south of Canada. Note *white tail*, particularly in flight. In breeding season, brown with white belly, wings, and tail. In winter, pure white except for black eyes and bill. **VOICE:** Cackling notes, clucks, soft hoots. **SIMILAR SPECIES:** The other two ptarmigans have *black* tail. **HABITAT:** Alpine tundra, including rocky outcrops and stunted willow thickets.

PTARMIGANS

nonbreeding

♀

♂

nonbreeding

♂

breeding

♀

breeding

spring

WILLOW PTARMIGAN

nbreeding

♂

♀

♂ western
Aleutians

♂

nonbreeding ♂

breeding
♀

breeding

ROCK PTARMIGAN

nbreeding

♂

♀

♂

nonbreeding

breeding
♀

molting

breeding

WHITE-TAILED PTARMIGAN

RING-NECKED PHEASANT *Phasianus colchicus*   Fairly common **M49**
Male 31–33 in. (79–84 cm); female 21–23 in. (53–59 cm). A large chicken-like bird introduced from Eurasia. Note long pointed tail. Runs swiftly; flight strong, takeoff noisy. *Male:* Highly colored and *iridescent,* with *scarlet wattles* on face and *white neck ring* (not always present). *Female:* Mottled brown, with *long pointed tail.* **VOICE:** Crowing male gives loud double squawk, *kork-kok,* followed by brief whir of wings. When flushed, harsh croaks. Roosting call a two-syllable *kutuck-kutuck,* etc. **SIMILAR SPECIES:** Female sage-grouse have black belly patch. **HABITAT:** Farms, fields, marsh edges, brush, grassy roadsides. Periodic local releases for hunting.

GRAY PARTRIDGE *Perdix perdix*   Uncommon **M48**
12½–13 in. (32–34 cm). Introduced from Europe. A rotund gray-brown partridge, larger than a quail; note short *rufous* tail, *rusty face,* chestnut bars on sides. Male has dark U-shaped splotch on belly. **VOICE:** Loud, hoarse *kar-wit, kar-wit.* **SIMILAR SPECIES:** Chukar (another introduced species of West, which also has rufous tail) prefers rockier habitat, has red bill and legs, black "necklace." **HABITAT:** Cultivated land, hedgerows, bushy pastures, meadows.

CHUKAR *Alectoris chukar*   Uncommon **M47**
13½–14 in. (34–36 cm). Introduced from Asia. Like a large quail; gray-brown with *bright red legs and bill;* light throat bordered by clean-cut black "necklace." Sides *boldly barred.* Tail *rufous.* **VOICE:** Series of raspy *chucks;* a sharp *wheet-u.* **SIMILAR SPECIES:** Gray Partridge. Mountain Quail smaller and darker, with long head plume, dark bill, dull legs. Red-legged Partridge *(Alectoris rufa),* an occasional escapee, is similar but has streaked breast. **HABITAT:** Rocky, grassy, or brushy slopes; arid mountains, canyons. Birds recently released for hunting may be found well out of range and habitat.

HIMALAYAN SNOWCOCK *Tetraogallus himalayensis*   Very local
28 in. (71 cm). An Asian species, introduced to Ruby Mts. of n. NV. Large, gray-brown body; paler face and neck with rusty brown stripes. Shows white in wing in flight. Flies downslope in the morning to forage and walks upslope during the day. **VOICE:** Calls include cackles and clucks; display call a loud whistle. **SIMILAR SPECIES:** Chukar. **HABITAT:** Rugged alpine slopes.

RING-NECKED PHEASANT

GRAY
PARTRIDGE

CHUKAR

Red-legged Partridge
for comparison

HIMALAYAN SNOWCOCK

NEW WORLD QUAIL Family Odontophoridae

Quail are smaller than grouse. Sexes alike or unlike. **FOOD:** Insects, seeds, buds, berries. **RANGE:** Nearly worldwide.

CALIFORNIA QUAIL *Callipepla californica*   Common M65
10 in. (25 cm). A small, plump, grayish, chickenlike bird, with a *short black plume* curving forward from crown. Male has *black-and-white face* and throat, *scaled belly pattern*. Female duller. **VOICE:** Three-syllable *qua-quergo,* or *Chi-cago.* Also light clucking and sharp *pit* notes. Male on territory, a loud *kurr*. **SIMILAR SPECIES:** Gambel's Quail has rufous brown crown, different belly pattern; ranges barely overlap. **HABITAT:** Broken chaparral, woodland edges, coastal scrub, parks, estates, farms.

GAMBEL'S QUAIL *Callipepla gambelii*   Common M66
10½–11 in. (26–28 cm). Replaces California Quail in most desert habitats. Similar to that species, but male Gambel's has *black patch* on light, *unscaled belly;* flanks and crown more russet (a local name is "Redhead"). Female also *unscaled* on belly. **VOICE:** Loud *kaaaa;* also *ka-KAA-ka-ka* and sharp *ut, ut* notes. **HABITAT:** Variety of shrubby desert environments, including parks, suburbs.

MOUNTAIN QUAIL *Oreortyx pictus*   Uncommon M63
11 in. (28 cm). A gray-and-brown quail of mountains. Distinguished from California Quail by long *straight* head plume and *chestnut* (not *black) throat.* Note chestnut-and-white side pattern. Female similar to male but duller, with shorter plume. **VOICE:** Mellow *wook?* or *to-wook?* repeated at intervals by male; loquacious *wew-wew-wew-wew* series. **HABITAT:** Open pine and mixed forests, brushy ravines, montane chaparral.

SCALED QUAIL *Callipepla squamata*   Fairly common M64
10 in. (25 cm). A pale grayish quail (sometimes called "Blue Quail") of arid country, with scaly markings on breast and back. Note *short bushy white crest,* or "cotton top," a common nickname for this species. Runs; often reluctant to fly. **VOICE:** Guinea hen–like *che-kar* (also interpreted as *pay-cos*). **HABITAT:** Shrub-grasslands, brush, arid country.

NORTHERN BOBWHITE   Uncommon to fairly common, declining M67
Colinus virginianus
9½–10 in. (24–26 cm). A small, rotund fowl, near size of a meadowlark. Ruddy, barred and striped, with short dark tail. Male has conspicuous white throat and white eyebrow stripe; in female these are buff. A dark Mexican subspecies, "Masked" Bobwhite, with *black throat* and *rusty underparts,* was once found in s. AZ, where it has been locally reintroduced. **VOICE:** Clearly whistled *Bob-white!* or *poor, Bob-whoit!* Covey call *ko-loi-kee?* answered by *whoil-kee!* **SIMILAR SPECIES:** Ruffed Grouse larger with fanlike tail. **HABITAT:** Farms, brushy open country, fencerows, roadsides, open woodlands. Recent hunting releases fairly widespread.

MONTEZUMA QUAIL *Cyrtonyx montezumae*   Scarce, local M68
8½–9 in. (21–23 cm). A rotund quail of Mexican mountains and canyons. Note male's oddly striped *clown's face,* bushy crest on nape, and *spotted sides.* Female brown, with less obvious facial striping. Tame (sometimes called "Fool's Quail"). **VOICE:** Male gives a descending whistle; a soft whinnying or quavering cry; ventriloquial. **HABITAT:** Grassy oak canyons, wooded mountain slopes with bunch grass.

QUAIL

♀
CALIFORNIA
QUAIL
♂

♀
GAMBEL'S
QUAIL
♂

♂
MOUNTAIN
QUAIL

♂
SCALED
QUAIL

♂
"Masked"
♀
♂

♂
NORTHERN
BOBWHITE

MONTEZUMA
QUAIL
♀

LOONS Family Gaviidae

Large, long-bodied swimmers with daggerlike bill; dive from surface or sink. Thrash along water on takeoff. Airborne, loons are slower and more hunch-backed than most ducks. Large webbed feet project beyond stubby tail. Seldom on land except at nest. Sexes alike. Immatures more scaly above than nonbreeding adults. **FOOD:** Small fish, crustaceans, other aquatic life. **RANGE:** Northern parts of N. Hemisphere.

RED-THROATED LOON *Gavia stellata*   Common M69

25 in. (64 cm). Note slim snakelike head and neck, thin, slightly *upturned bill, often uptilted head.* Often flies with neck drooped. *Breeding:* Plain brown back, gray head, *rufous throat patch. Nonbreeding:* Slimmer than other loons with paler, spotted upperparts; adult has extensively white neck and face; first winter has smudgy gray neck. **VOICE:** When flying, a repeated *kwuk.* Guttural ptarmigan-like calls on breeding grounds; also falsetto wails. **SIMILAR SPECIES:** Other loons, Western and Clark's grebes. **HABITAT:** Nearshore ocean, bays, estuaries; in summer, tundra lakes.

PACIFIC LOON *Gavia pacifica*   Common M71

25–26 in. (64–66 cm). Smaller than Common Loon, with slightly thinner straight bill, often puffier look to head. Often travels in sizable flocks in offshore waters. *Breeding: Pale gray nape.* Back divided into four checkered patches. *Nonbreeding:* Note sharp, straight separation of dark and white on neck. Dark feathering around eye. Often has trace of chin strap (do not confuse with dusky neck band of young Red-throated). **VOICE:** Deep, barking *kwow;* falsetto wails, rising in pitch. Silent away from breeding grounds. **SIMILAR SPECIES:** Nonbreeding adult Red-throated Loon also has straight separation of dark and white on neck but shows much more white. Other loons, grebes. **HABITAT:** Ocean, bays, large lakes; in summer, tundra lakes and sloughs.

ARCTIC LOON *Gavia arctica*   Rare, local M70

27–28 in. (69–73 cm). A bit larger than Pacific Loon, with more angular head and white rear-flank patches. In breeding plumage lacks pale nape, has bolder black-and-white streaking on neck. **SIMILAR SPECIES:** Red-throated Loon also may show white flanks. **HABITAT:** Same as Pacific Loon.

COMMON LOON *Gavia immer*   Common M72

31–32 in. (78–81 cm). Large, long-bodied, low-swimming; bill *stout,* daggerlike. In flight shows large, trailing feet. *Breeding:* Black head and bill. *Checkered back,* broken white necklace. *Nonbreeding:* Note *irregular or broken (half-collared) neck-pattern. Pale "eyelids."* **VOICE:** In breeding season, falsetto wails, weird yodeling, maniacal quavering laughter; at night, a tremulous *ha-oo-oo.* In flight, a barking *kwuk.* Usually silent in nonbreeding season. **SIMILAR SPECIES:** Other loons and cormorants. **HABITAT:** In summer, lakes, tundra ponds; in winter, larger lakes, bays, ocean.

YELLOW-BILLED LOON *Gavia adamsii*   Rare M73

34–35 in. (86–89 cm). Similar to Common Loon, but bill *pale ivory* (sometimes with darker base) and slightly uptilted: straight above, slightly angled below. In nonbreeding plumage, slightly *paler* head and neck than Common, usually with small *dark ear patch.* **SIMILAR SPECIES:** Bill of nonbreeding Common Loon is somewhat pale, but culmen (upper ridge) is *dark to tip* (outer half of bill is pale in Yellow-billed). **HABITAT:** In summer, tundra lakes; in winter, coastal waters. May appear on inland lakes.

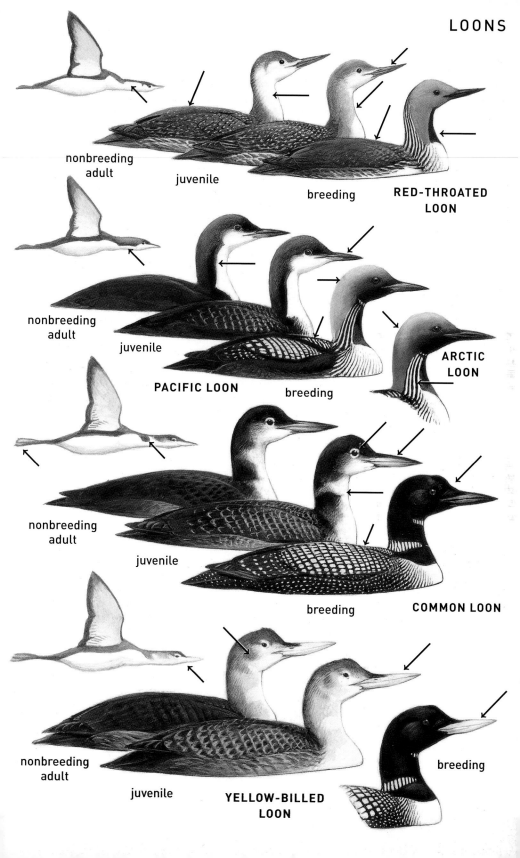

LOONS

nonbreeding
adult

juvenile

breeding

**RED-THROATED
LOON**

nonbreeding
adult

juvenile

PACIFIC LOON

breeding

**ARCTIC
LOON**

nonbreeding
adult

juvenile

breeding

COMMON LOON

nonbreeding
adult

juvenile

**YELLOW-BILLED
LOON**

breeding

GREBES Family Podicipedidae

Ducklike divers with flat, lobed toes; thin neck; tailless look. All but Pied-billed Grebe have white wing patches, pointed bills. Sexes alike. Most young have striped heads. May dive from surface or sink. Flight labored. FOOD: Small fish, other aquatic life. RANGE: Worldwide.

PIED-BILLED GREBE *Podilymbus podiceps* Fairly common M75
13–13½ in. (33–34 cm). A small brown diver. Note "chicken bill," puffy white stern. No wing patch. *Breeding: Black throat patch* and *ring* around pale bill. *Nonbreeding:* Lacks black markings. *Juvenile:* Striped on head. VOICE: Song *kuk-kuk-cow-cow-cow-cowp-cowp-cowp;* also a sizzling whinny and sharp *kwah*. HABITAT: Ponds, lakes, marshes; in winter, also salt bays and estuaries.

HORNED GREBE *Podiceps auritus* Fairly common M76
13½–14 in. (34–36 cm). *Breeding: Golden ear patch* and *chestnut neck*. *Nonbreeding:* Black cap *clean-cut to eye level;* white foreneck, thin straight bill. VOICE: Loud *gamp*, trills on breeding grounds. Usually silent in non-breeding season. SIMILAR SPECIES: Birds in transition plumage have dusky neck and may be confused with Eared Grebe, but note flatter crown, pale lores, straighter, pale-tipped bill. HABITAT: Lakes, ponds, coastal waters.

EARED GREBE *Podiceps nigricollis* Common M78
12½–13 in. (32–33 cm). Note peaked crown, skinny neck, and slightly up-turned, all-dark bill. Often floats high in the water. Gregarious. *Breeding: Wispy golden ear tufts, black neck. Nonbreeding:* Dark cap extends *below eye,* neck usually dusky. VOICE: Musical *poo-ee-chk.* On breeding grounds a froglike *poo-eep* or *krreep.* Usually silent in nonbreeding season. HABI-TAT: Prairie lakes, ponds; in winter, also open lakes, including those with high salt concentration, coastal bays and estuaries.

RED-NECKED GREBE *Podiceps grisegena* Uncommon M77
18–19 in. (46–49 cm). A largish grebe. *Breeding:* Long *rufous neck, light cheek,* black cap. *Nonbreeding:* Grayish (including neck); white crescent on face; variable dull *yellowish* base of bill. In flight, double wing patch. VOICE: Loud braying on breeding grounds. Silent in nonbreeding season. SIMILAR SPECIES: Loons, Red-breasted Merganser. HABITAT: Lakes, ponds; in winter, large lakes, salt water.

LEAST GREBE *Tachybaptus dominicus* Uncommon, local M74
9½ in. (24 cm). Smaller, darker than Pied-billed Grebe, with white wing patches (usually concealed), puffy undertail coverts, slender *black bill, golden eyes.* VOICE: A chattering whinny. HABITAT: Ponds and lake edges.

WESTERN GREBE *Aechmophorus occidentalis* Common M79
25 in. (64 cm). A large slate-and-white grebe with long neck. Bill long, greenish yellow with dark ridge. Black of cap extends *below eye.* VOICE: Loud, reedy *crik-crick.* SIMILAR SPECIES: Clark's Grebe, Red-throated Loon. HABITAT: Rushy lakes, sloughs; in winter, large lakes, bays, coasts.

CLARK'S GREBE *Aechmophorus clarkii* Uncommon M80
25 in. (64 cm). Formerly regarded as a pale morph of Western Grebe. In-termediates are known. Bill *orange-yellow.* Dark eye *surrounded by white* (may be dusky in nonbreeding plumage). Back and flanks slightly paler than Western's, and gray on nape slightly narrower. Downy young are white, not gray. VOICE: Single-noted *creet* or *criik.* HABITAT: Similar to Western, but scarce in ocean waters.

lobed foot of grebe

GREBES

PIED-BILLED GREBE

nonbreeding adult

juvenile

downy young

breeding

nonbreeding variant

HORNED GREBE

breeding

bill of Horned

nonbreeding variant

nonbreeding

non-breeding

nonbreeding

breeding

EARED GREBE

bill of Eared

immature

non-breeding

breeding

RED-NECKED GREBE

nonbreeding

breeding

LEAST GREBE

♂ display

WESTERN GREBE

CLARK'S GREBE

ALBATROSSES Family Diomedeidae

Birds of open ocean, with rigid gliding and banking flight. Much larger than gulls; wings proportionately longer. "Tube-nosed" (nostrils in two tubes); bill large, hooked, covered with horny plates. Sexes alike. Largely silent at sea. **FOOD:** Cuttlefish, fish, squid, other small marine life; some feeding at night. **RANGE:** Mainly cold oceans of S. Hemisphere; three species nest north of equator in Pacific.

BLACK-BROWED ALBATROSS *Thalassarche melanophris*   Vagrant
34–35 in. (86–88 cm); wingspan 7½ ft. (229 cm). Suggests a huge Great Black-backed Gull, but with short blackish tail and very large yellow bill (adult) with hooked tip. Dark eye streak gives it a frowning look. In stiff-winged gliding flight, shows white underwing *broadly outlined* with black. *Immature:* Bill dark. **RANGE:** Accidental off Atlantic Coast.

YELLOW-NOSED ALBATROSS *Thalassarche chlororhynchos*   Vagrant
31–32 in. (79–81 cm); wingspan 7–7½ ft. (213–229 cm). Similar to Black-browed Albatross, but bill *black with yellow ridge* on upper mandible. In flight, underwing whiter, with *narrower* black edging. **RANGE:** Accidental along Atlantic and Gulf coasts.

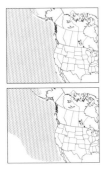

LAYSAN ALBATROSS *Phoebastria immutabilis*   Scarce M81
32 in. (81 cm); wingspan 6½ ft. (198 cm). White body with *dark back and wings*, suggesting a huge, dark-backed gull with extra-long wings. Whitish underwing has some *dark smudges.* Bill and feet pale pinkish gray. Immature similar.

BLACK-FOOTED ALBATROSS *Phoebastria nigripes*   Uncommon M82
32–33 in. (81–84 cm); wingspan 7 ft. (213 cm). Great size, *sooty color,* tremendously long saberlike wings, and rigid shearwater-like gliding identify this species, the albatross found most regularly off our Pacific Coast. Seldom seen from shore. At close range shows whitish face and pale areas toward wingtips. Bill and feet *dark.* Older adults develop more white on head and white patches at base of tail. **SIMILAR SPECIES:** Immature Short-tailed Albatross slightly larger, has *pinkish bill and feet.*

SHORT-TAILED ALBATROSS *Phoebastria albatrus*   Casual
36–37 in. (91–94 cm); wingspan 7½ ft. (229 cm). *Adult: White back, pink bill,* yellowish nape. Underwing white with dark edge. *Immature:* Dark brown, bill and feet *pinkish.* **SIMILAR SPECIES:** Black-footed and Laysan albatrosses. **RANGE:** Breeds on islands off Japan. *Formerly near extinction, slowly recovering.* Ranges from Bering Sea to CA.

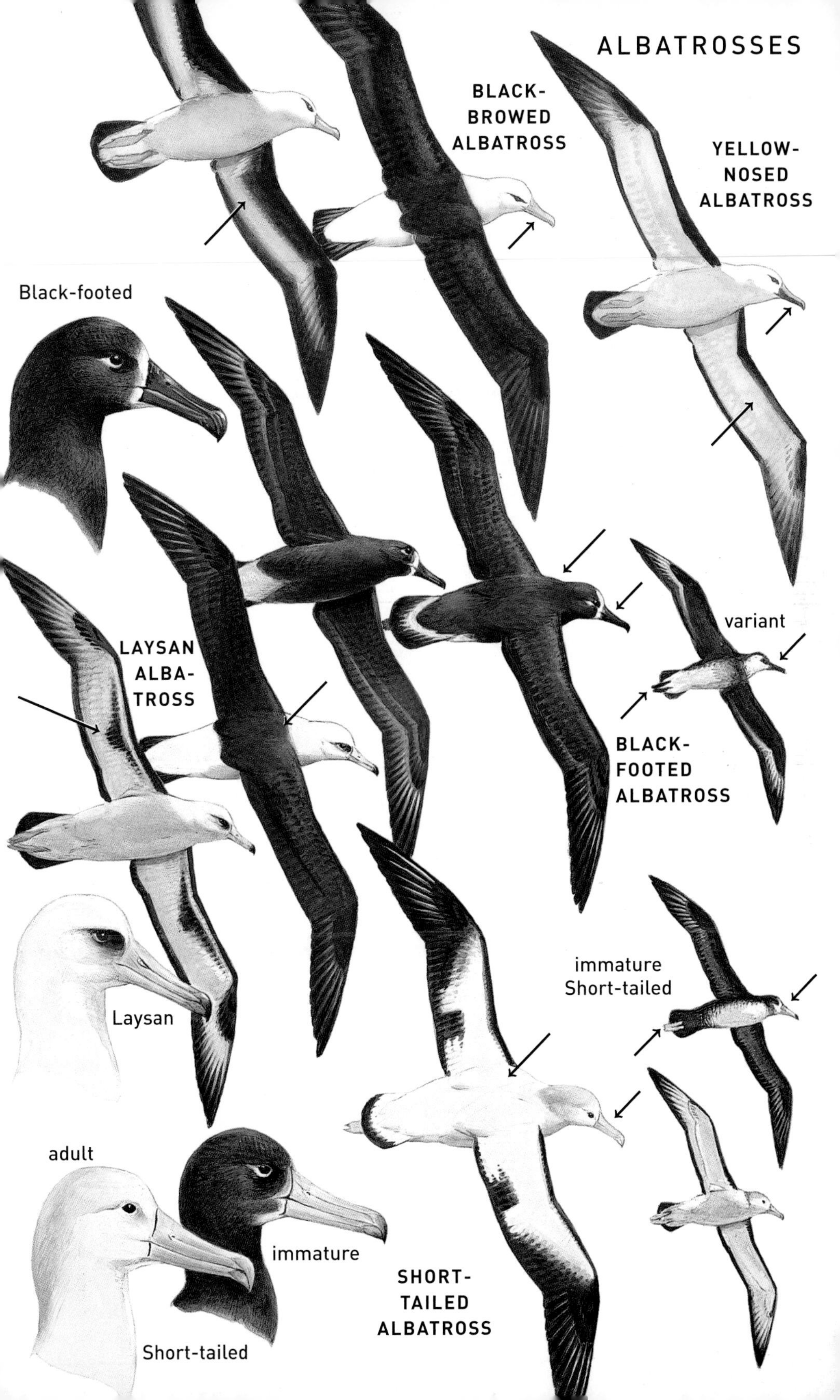
ALBATROSSES
BLACK-BROWED ALBATROSS
YELLOW-NOSED ALBATROSS
Black-footed
LAYSAN ALBA-TROSS
variant
BLACK-FOOTED ALBATROSS
immature Short-tailed
Laysan
adult
immature
Short-tailed
SHORT-TAILED ALBATROSS

SHEARWATERS AND PETRELS Family Procellariidae

Gull-like birds of open sea that glide low over waves (usually with wings more stiffly extended than shown here). They often bank, or arc, up and down like a roller coaster, particularly in strong winds. Typically fly with several flaps and then a glide. Wings narrower than those of gulls. Shearwaters and petrels, along with albatrosses and storm-petrels, have tubelike external nostrils on bill, so are often called "tubenoses." Largely silent at sea; most apt to call at feeding frenzies. **FOOD:** Fish, squid, crustaceans, ship refuse. **RANGE:** Oceans of world. Most species only occasionally or rarely seen from our mainland shores.

NORTHERN FULMAR *Fulmarus glacialis*   Uncommon to fairly common M83
18½–19 in. (47–49 cm). A stiff-winged oceanic seabird; shearwater-like, but stockier with larger head, shorter, rounder wings; flies like shearwater but with quicker wingbeats, less gliding. Note rounded forehead; *stubby, yellowish, tubenose bill;* longish tail. Primaries may show a *pale flash or patch.* Leg color variable. Comes in several color morphs. *Light morph:* Gull-like in plumage. *Intermediate morph:* Variable. *Dark morph* (less common in Atlantic, breeds mostly from Aleutians southward): Smoky gray, wingtips darker. All morphs may be found together in winter. **VOICE:** Hoarse, grunting *ag-ag-ag-arrr* or *ek-ek-ek-ek-ek.* **SIMILAR SPECIES:** At a distance, shape and flight style distinguish light morh from gulls and dark morph from Sooty, Short-tailed, and Flesh-footed shearwaters. **HABITAT:** Open ocean; breeds colonially on sea cliffs.

MURPHY'S PETREL *Pterodroma ultima*   Rare
15½–16 in. (40–41 cm). A dark petrel with wholly *dark underwing linings,* faint dark M across back and wings, somewhat wedge-shaped tail, and *pale face and throat.* **SIMILAR SPECIES:** Sooty Shearwater, dark-morph Northern Fulmar. Accidental Great-winged Petrel (*Pterodroma macroptera;* not illustrated) slightly larger, browner, more white on face. **RANGE:** Breeds in sw. Pacific; rare but regular visitor far offshore from CA to s. BC, mostly in spring.

COOK'S PETREL *Pterodroma cookii*   Rare
10½–11 in. (27–28 cm). *Dark M across gray back and upperwing and gleaming white* underwings suggest much larger Buller's Shearwater, but note Cook's paler head with black ear patch and light sides of tail. **RANGE:** Nests off New Zealand; ranges across Pacific, rarely but perhaps regularly to waters well off West Coast from s. AK to Baja CA.

MOTTLED PETREL *Pterodroma inexpectata*   Rare
14 in. (36 cm). *Dark M across back and upperwing suggests Buller's Shearwater or Cook's Petrel, but note contrasting *dark belly* and *heavy diagonal black bar* across underwing. **RANGE:** Nests in New Zealand; regular summer visitor to deep offshore Alaskan waters, very rare though probably somewhat regular south to well off CA, mostly in late fall and winter.

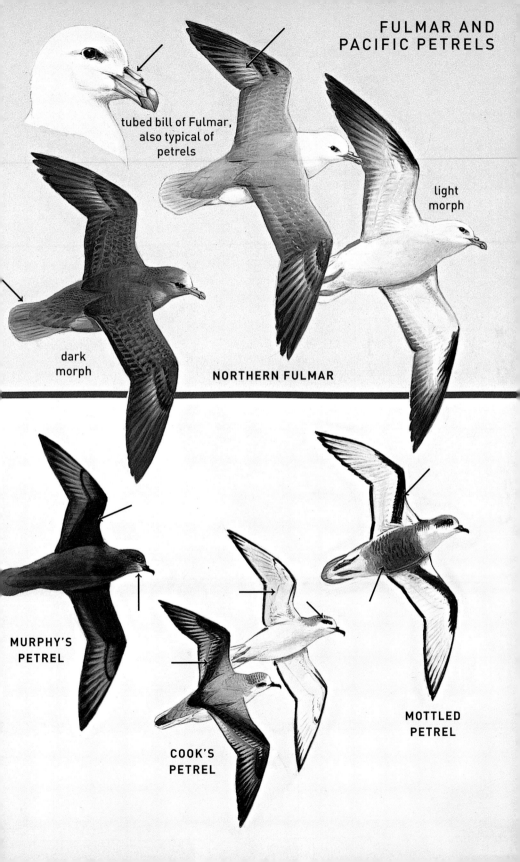

FULMAR AND PACIFIC PETRELS

tubed bill of Fulmar, also typical of petrels

light morph

dark morph

NORTHERN FULMAR

MURPHY'S PETREL

COOK'S PETREL

MOTTLED PETREL

BLACK-CAPPED PETREL *Pterodroma hasitata*   Scarce, local M84
16 in. (41 cm). Larger than Audubon's or Manx shearwater and looks quite similar to Greater Shearwater. Note white forehead, variable white collar, *white rump* patch extending to tail, thick bill. Rarely seen outside Gulf Stream. Nests on Hispanola and Cuba.

BERMUDA PETREL (CAHOW) *Pterodroma cahow*   Casual, endangered
15 in. (38 cm). Breeds only on Bermuda. One of the world's rarest seabirds. Differs from Black-capped Petrel by *smudgy gray* rump, absence of white collar, small bill. **RANGE:** Known only from certain small islets off ne. end of Bermuda, where it comes and goes at night. Sightings becoming more regular in Gulf Stream off NC coast as protection efforts in Bermuda enhance breeding success.

HERALD PETREL *Pterodroma arminjoniana*   Rare, local
15½–16 in. (40–41 cm). Dark, intermediate, and pale morphs. Most N. American records are dark, differing from Sooty Shearwater by *dark* wing linings, longer tail, and slower wingbeat. Light area at primary base suggests a jaeger. Feet and legs black. **RANGE:** Reported annually in Gulf Stream off NC coast from May to September. Nests in tropical Southern Hemisphere.

FEA'S PETREL *Pterodroma feae*   Very rare, local
14–15 in. (36–38 cm). Brownish gray above, with M pattern across wings. Distinguish from Black-capped Petrel by less contrasty pale *gray rump and tail,* pale gray cowl on head, and *dark underwing.* **RANGE:** Breeds on islands off W. Africa. A rare but regular spring and summer visitor to Gulf Stream waters off Cape Hatteras, NC; casual elsewhere. Nests on islands off West Africa.

ATLANTIC PETRELS

BLACK-CAPPED
PETREL

BERMUDA
PETREL

HERALD PETREL
dark morph

FEA'S PETREL

CORY'S SHEARWATER *Calonectris diomedea*   Fairly common **M85**
18–20 in. (46–51 cm). Large, pale seabird; gray brown head *blends* into white of throat; bill dull *yellow*. Belly all white; rump usually dark with indistinct or no white. **SIMILAR SPECIES:** Greater Shearwater has dark cap, black bill, white rump, dark smudges on belly and underwing. Cory's has more pronounced bend to wing than Greater, and wingbeat tends to be slightly slower.

GREATER SHEARWATER *Puffinus gravis*   Fairly common **M88**
19 in. (48 cm). A shearwater dark above and white below, rising above waves on stiff wings, is likely to be this or Cory's Shearwater. Greater has dark cap separated by a light band across nape. Note also white rump patch and dark smudges on belly and underwing. **SIMILAR SPECIES:** Cory's Shearwater.

SOOTY SHEARWATER   Common in Pacific, uncommon in Atlantic **M90**
Puffinus griseus
17–18 in. (43–46 cm). Often seen in massive flocks in summer in Pacific, uncommon in Atlantic. Looks all dark at a distance; rises over and arcs above waves on narrow, rigid wings. In good light, note *whitish linings* on underwings. **SIMILAR SPECIES:** Dark jaegers (white in primaries), Short-tailed and Flesh-footed shearwaters, dark-morph Northern Fulmar.

MANX SHEARWATER *Puffinus puffinus*   Uncommon **M92**
13½ in. (34 cm). A small black-and-white shearwater; half the bulk of Greater Shearwater; no white rump patch. Note dark cap extends below eye; *white undertail*. **SIMILAR SPECIES:** See Audubon's Shearwater. Wingbeat quicker than in Greater or Cory's shearwater. In Pacific, rare but increasing Manx is similar to Black-vented Shearwater but is slightly blacker above, with whitish undertail coverts and paler face.

AUDUBON'S SHEARWATER *Puffinus lherminieri*   Fairly common **M94**
12 in. (30 cm). A very small shearwater, similar to Manx Shearwater but with slightly browner upperparts, *dark undertail*. Wings slightly shorter, *tail longer*. Often has *white markings* around eye. **HABITAT:** Prefers warmer water than Manx Shearwater.

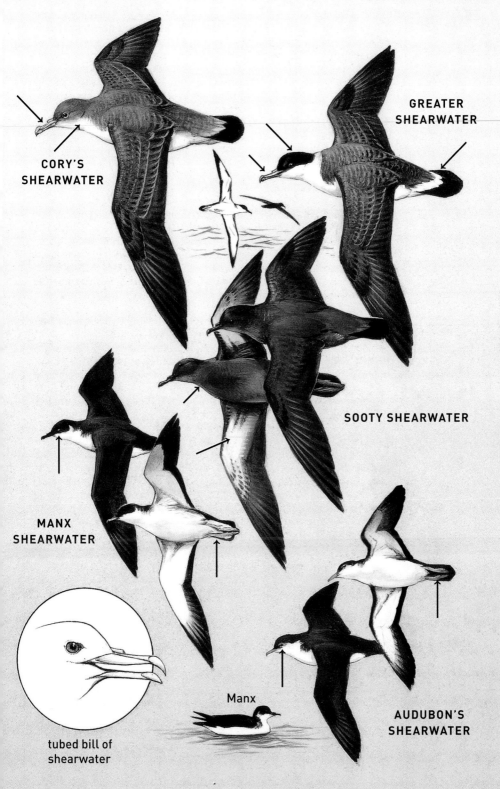

ATLANTIC SHEARWATERS

GREATER
SHEARWATER

CORY'S
SHEARWATER

SOOTY SHEARWATER

MANX
SHEARWATER

Manx

AUDUBON'S
SHEARWATER

tubed bill of
shearwater

SHORT-TAILED SHEARWATER *Puffinus tenuirostris*   Uncommon M91
16–17 in. (40–43 cm). Very similar to Sooty Shearwater; best distinguished by *shorter bill, rounder head,* and *variably smoky gray* wing linings, slightly smaller size and narrower wing, more rapid wingbeats. May have contrasty pale throat. Sooty has whiter wing linings. **RANGE:** South of Alaskan waters (where common in summer and early fall), usually found only in small numbers and mostly between late fall and late winter.

FLESH-FOOTED SHEARWATER *Puffinus carneipes*   Rare M87
17–17½ in. (43–45 cm). This dark-bodied shearwater is a rare but regular visitor. *Larger* than Sooty Shearwater; flight more sluggish. Distinguished by *pale pink bill* (with dark tip), *pinkish feet,* dark wing linings (and slightly paler flight feathers). **SIMILAR SPECIES:** Dark-morph Northern Fulmar, Sooty Shearwater.

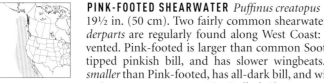

PINK-FOOTED SHEARWATER *Puffinus creatopus*   Fairly common M86
19½ in. (50 cm). Two fairly common shearwaters with *mostly white underparts* are regularly found along West Coast: Pink-footed and Black-vented. Pink-footed is larger than common Sooty Shearwater, has dark-tipped pinkish bill, and has slower wingbeats. Black-vented is much *smaller* than Pink-footed, has all-dark bill, and wingbeats faster with little arcing. **SIMILAR SPECIES:** See Buller's Shearwater.

BLACK-VENTED SHEARWATER   Fairly common, local M93
Puffinus opisthomelas
13½–14 in. (34–36 cm). A small shearwater, dark brown above and whitish below with dusky breast sides, dark undertail coverts, dark cap extending below eye. Smaller size, contrasting *dark-and-white* pattern, and rapid wingbeats with short glides are distinctive. Often seen in flocks from shore, mostly in fall and winter. **SIMILAR SPECIES:** Manx, Pink-footed, Buller's, and Sooty shearwaters.

BULLER'S SHEARWATER *Puffinus bulleri*   Uncommon, irregular M89
16 in. (41 cm). A white-bellied shearwater. Separated from the two other white-bellied species—Pink-footed and Black-vented shearwaters—by broad *dark M* pattern on back and wings. Underparts more *gleaming white.* Cap dark. Tail wedge-shaped. Feet pale, but variable. Occurs in fall (late Aug. through Oct.) in variable numbers from year to year. **SIMILAR SPECIES:** Pink-footed Shearwater is larger with *dingier* underwings, more *uniform* upperparts, more *blended* face pattern.

PACIFIC SHEARWATERS

**SHORT-
TAILED
SHEARWATER**

Sooty
Shearwater
(p. 76) for
comparison

**FLESH-FOOTED
SHEARWATER**

**PINK-FOOTED
SHEARWATER**

**BLACK-VENTED
SHEARWATER**

**BULLER'S
SHEARWATER**

Manx
Shearwater
(p. 76)
for
comparison

STORM-PETRELS Family Hydrobatidae

Dark little birds that flutter or bound over open ocean; they nest colonially on islands, returning to burrows at night. Nostrils in a fused tube over top of bill. Usually silent at sea; most apt to call at feeding frenzies. **FOOD**: Plankton, crustaceans, small fish. **RANGE**: All oceans except Arctic.

WILSON'S STORM-PETREL *Oceanites oceanicus*　　　Common M95
7¼–7½ in. (18–19 cm). A small storm-petrel with somewhat triangular wings and *white rump patch that wraps around sides;* tail slightly rounded or square-cut, *not forked.* Feet yellow-webbed (hard to see), show *beyond tail* in flight. Direct flight, with short glides, pausing to flutter over water. **SIMILAR SPECIES**: Leach's and Band-rumped storm-petrels. **HABITAT**: Open ocean. Often follows ships (Leach's does not). Can be "chummed in" by tossing out ground fish, suet, puffed wheat in fish oil, etc. May be seen from shore.

LEACH'S STORM-PETREL *Oceanodroma leucorhoa*　　　Uncommon M97
8 in. (20 cm). Note obscurely divided *white rump patch* and slightly forked tail. Pale bar on upperwing often reaches leading edge. In flight, bounds about erratically on fairly long angled wings, changing speed and direction — all suggesting a nighthawk. This is the breeding storm-petrel of N. Atlantic (but less often seen than Wilson's Storm-Petrel). *Does not follow ships.* Birds nesting in Mex. and fall visitors off s. CA lack white rump. **VOICE**: At night on breeding grounds, nasal chattering notes and long crooning trills. **SIMILAR SPECIES**: Wilson's Storm-Petrel; Black Storm-Petrel similar to dark-rumped Leach's.

BAND-RUMPED STORM-PETREL *Oceanodroma castro*　　　Scarce M99
8½–9 in. (21–23 cm). A white-rumped storm-petrel, larger than Wilson's, similar to Leach's. Feet do not project beyond *squarish* tail. Pale bar on upperwing much less distinct than in Leach's or Wilson's; rump band more clean-cut than Leach's, less extensive under tail than Wilson's. A stiff-winged flier, with short glides, reminiscent of a shearwater.

WHITE-FACED STORM-PETREL *Pelagodroma marina*　　　Casual
7½ in. (19 cm). A storm-petrel with white head and underparts, two-toned underwing, dark crown and eye patch. Very long legs. When feeding, bounds "kangaroo style" over water on stiff flat wings. **RANGE**: Se. Atlantic, sw. Pacific, Indian Ocean. Casual but almost annual Aug.–Sept. off Atlantic Coast from MA to NC, usually far offshore.

EUROPEAN STORM-PETREL *Hydrobates pelagicus*　　　Vagrant
6 in. (15 cm). Smaller than Wilson's Storm-Petrel; shorter legs, which do not extend beyond square tail. Yellow on feet, not on webs. Shows whitish underwing patch. **RANGE**: Nests in ne. Atlantic and Mediterranean. Casual off NC, NS.

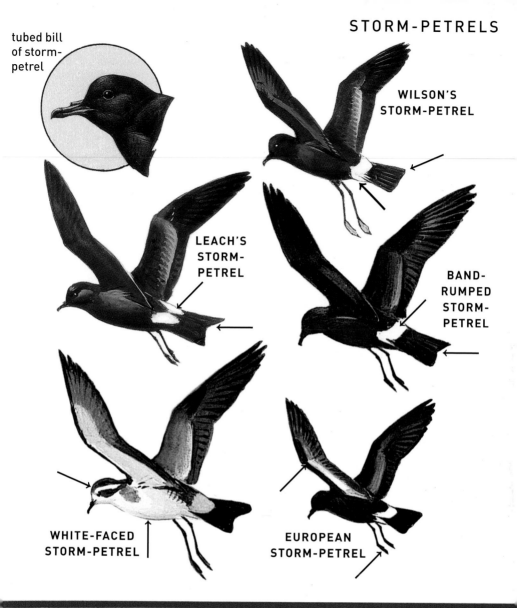

tubed bill
of storm-
petrel

STORM-PETRELS

WILSON'S
STORM-PETREL

LEACH'S
STORM-
PETREL

BAND-
RUMPED
STORM-
PETREL

WHITE-FACED
STORM-PETREL

EUROPEAN
STORM-PETREL

WHITE-RUMPED STORM-PETRELS

Leach's

Wilson's

Band-rumped

European

FORK-TAILED STORM-PETREL *Oceanodroma furcata*   Scarce M96
8½ in. (22 cm). *Pale gray* overall, with contrasting *slaty underwing linings;* our other Pacific storm-petrels are blackish overall. Dark eye patch; faint dark bar across upperwing.

LEAST STORM-PETREL *Oceanodroma microsoma*   Rare M101
5¾ in. (15 cm). A late-summer and fall visitor in variable numbers. Small. Our only regularly occurring storm-petrel with *very short rounded or wedge-shaped* tail. Flight similar to Black Storm-Petrel. **SIMILAR SPECIES:** Ashy Storm-Petrel is larger and paler with forked tail and quicker, shallower wingbeats.

ASHY STORM-PETREL *Oceanodroma homochroa*   Uncommon M98
8 in. (20 cm). Separated from Black and dark-rumped Leach's storm-petrels by slightly smaller size, shorter wings, more fluttery, direct flight (shallower wingbeats). At close range, plumage looks more ashy colored; underwings and rump show *pale cast.*

BLACK STORM-PETREL *Oceanodroma melania*   Fairly common M100
9 in. (23 cm). The largest all-black storm-petrel found off CA, primarily from late spring through early fall. Forked tail. Larger than Ashy Storm-Petrel, with longer wings and *more languid flight.* Separated from dark-rumped Leach's Storm-Petrel by larger overall size, slower wingbeats, and more direct flight; Leach's tends to be farther offshore than Black.

FORK-TAILED STORM-PETREL

LEACH'S STORM-PETREL
dark-rumped form
(see p. 80)

LEAST STORM-PETREL

ASHY STORM-PETREL

BLACK STORM-PETREL

GANNETS AND BOOBIES Family Sulidae

Seabirds with large, pointed bill and pointed tail, making them appear tapered at both ends. Larger and longer necked than most gulls. Sexes alike. Boobies sit on buoys, rocks; fish by plunging from air like Brown Pelicans. Mostly silent at sea, except when at feeding frenzies. **FOOD**: Fish, squid. **RANGE**: Gannets live in cold seas (N. Atlantic, S. Africa, Australia), boobies in tropical seas. All nest colonially on islands.

BLUE-FOOTED BOOBY *Sula nebouxii* Casual M105
32–33 in. (81–83 cm). *Adult:* White body, whitish head, *light patches on upper back and rump,* dark mottled back and wings, *blue feet. Immature:* Has slightly darker head and neck. **SIMILAR SPECIES**: Immature Masked and Brown boobies. Adult male Brown Booby in w. Mex. also has pale head, grayish bill.

BROWN BOOBY *Sula leucogaster* Scarce, local M106
29–30 in. (74–76 cm). *Adult:* Sooty brown with *white belly in clean-cut contrast* to dark breast. White wing linings contrast with dark flight feathers. Bill and feet yellowish. Males of w. Mex. race pale around head, have grayer bill. *Immature:* Underparts mostly dark, with little contrast between breast and belly; bill grayish. **SIMILAR SPECIES**: Immature Northern Gannet lacks clean-cut breast contrast; shows some white patches or mottling above; feet dark (not yellowish). Immature Red-footed Booby (which has dark tail) more buffy overall with dark underwing; has lilac color at base of bill; feet orangey pink. Immature Masked Booby resembles adult Brown Booby, but brown of head not as sharply demarcated from paler underparts. Blue-footed Booby has weaker contrast below, shows whitish patches on upper back and rump.

RED-FOOTED BOOBY *Sula sula* Vagrant
27–28 in. (69–71 cm). The smallest booby. *Adult:* Feet *bright red,* tail *white.* Two color morphs. *White morph:* Gannetlike; white, with black tip and trailing edge of wing (as in Masked Booby), tail white. *Dark morph:* Brown back and wings, paler head; white tail and belly; in flight, *underwing dark,* thin dark trailing edge on upperwing. *Immature:* Tan overall with *dark underwing,* pink and lilac base of bill, dull pink or orangey pink feet. **SIMILAR SPECIES**: Brown Booby. **RANGE**: Nests in tropics. Very rare, mostly young birds, at Dry Tortugas, FL; casual elsewhere in FL and along West Coast.

BOOBIES

adult

juvenile

adult

adult

BLUE-FOOTED
BOOBY

adults

♂

♀

♀

♂

subadult

BROWN BOOBY

white-tailed
brown morph

brown
morph

adults

RED-FOOTED
BOOBY

white
morph

NORTHERN GANNET *Morus bassanus*　　　Common M107

37–38 in. (94–97 cm). A goose-sized seabird that scales over ocean and plunges headlong for fish. Migrates in long lines. Much larger than Herring Gull, with pointed tail, longer neck, larger bill (often pointed toward water). *Adult:* White with extensive black primaries. *Immature:* Dusky, but note "pointed-at-both-ends" shape. Young birds in transition may have a piebald look. **VOICE:** Commonly heard at sea in winter. In colony, a low barking *arrah*. **SIMILAR SPECIES:** Boobies. In windy conditions, gannets in flight may arc up and down, suggesting a large tubenose such as an albatross. **HABITAT:** Ocean, but seen regularly from shore. Breeds colonially on sea cliffs.

MASKED BOOBY *Sula dactylatra*　　　Scarce, local M104

31–32 in. (79–81 cm). *Adult:* White; smaller than Northern Gannet, with *black tail*, black along entire *rear edge* of wing, and black in *face*. Greenish yellow bill. Mostly white underwing. *Immature:* Variably mottled with dark on upperwing and head, but shows white collar. **VOICE:** Usually silent. In nesting colony, a variety of whistles, grunts, bill-rattling. **SIMILAR SPECIES:** Other boobies, immature Northern Gannet.

TROPICBIRDS Family Phaethontidae

These seabirds resemble (but are unrelated to) large terns with two greatly elongated central tail feathers (adults) and stouter, very slightly decurved bill. White-tailed and Red-billed tropicbirds fly with rapid, shallow wingbeats; all three species dive headfirst and swim with tail held clear of water. Sexes alike. Largely silent at sea. **FOOD:** Squid, fish, crustaceans. **RANGE:** Tropical oceans.

WHITE-TAILED TROPICBIRD *Phaethon lepturus*　　　Rare M102

15 in. (38 cm), adults to 30 in. (76 cm) with tail-streamers. *Adult:* Distinguished from other tropicbirds by its *diagonal black bar* across each wing. Note two extremely long central tail feathers. Bill yellow to orange-red. *Immature:* Lacks tail-streamers; has *white*, not black, primary coverts, *coarsely* barred with black above; bill yellow. **VOICE:** Harsh ternlike scream. Also *tik-et, tik-et.* **SIMILAR SPECIES:** Red-billed Tropicbird.

RED-BILLED TROPICBIRD *Phaethon aethereus*　　　Rare M103

18 in. (45 cm), adults to 37 in. (94 cm) with tail-streamers. *Adult:* A slender white seabird with *two extremely long central tail feathers, heavy red bill*, black patch through cheek, black primaries, and *finely barred back. Immature:* Lacks long tail, has orange-yellow bill. **SIMILAR SPECIES:** White-tailed Tropicbird. Red-billed slightly larger and larger-billed; has more *finely barred* back than immature White-tailed, bright red to slight orange (not yellow) bill, more black on wing, including on *primary coverts,* black ear patch *extending to nape.*

RED-TAILED TROPICBIRD *Phaethon rubricauda*　　　Casual

18 in. (46 cm), adults to 37 in. (94 cm) with tail-streamers. Slower wingbeats than other tropicbirds. *Adult:* Whiter above than other two tropicbirds; tail-streamers *red. Immature:* Lacks tail-streamers, thinly barred on back, bill dusky. **RANGE:** Nests in tropical and subtropical Pacific. Casual far off CA coast, perhaps rare but regular.

GANNET, BOOBY, AND TROPICBIRDS

juvenile

adults

NORTHERN GANNET

subadult

adults

diving

MASKED BOOBY

juvenile

immature

adult

WHITE-TAILED TROPICBIRD

ED-BILLED ROPICBIRD

dults

RED-TAILED TROPICBIRD

White-tailed adult

Red-tailed adult

Red-billed adult

PELICANS Family Pelecanidae

Huge waterbirds with long flat bill and great throat pouch (flat when deflated). Neck long, body robust. Sexes alike. Flocks fly in lines or Vs or kettles, alternating several flaps with a glide. In flight, head is hunched back on shoulders, the long bill resting on breast. Pelicans swim buoyantly. **FOOD**: Mainly fish, crustaceans. **RANGE**: N. and S. America, Africa, s. Eurasia, E. Indies, Australia.

AMERICAN WHITE PELICAN *Pelecanus erythrorhynchos*   Common M108
62 in. (157 cm). Huge; wingspan 8–9½ ft. (244–290 cm). White, with black primaries and a great orange-yellow bill. Adults in breeding condition have "centerboard" on ridge of bill; reduced or lacking at other seasons. *Immature:* Dusky wash on head, neck, and wings. This pelican does not plunge from air like Brown Pelican but scoops up fish while swimming, often working in groups. Flocks may fly in lines and broken Vs and circle high in air on thermals. **VOICE**: In colony, a low groan. Young utter whining grunts. **SIMILAR SPECIES**: Swans have no black in wings. Wood Stork and Whooping Crane fly with neck extended, long legs behind. Snow Goose much smaller, with small bill; noisy. **HABITAT**: Lakes, marshes, salt bays, beaches.

BROWN PELICAN *Pelecanus occidentalis*   Common M109
48–50 in. (122–127 cm); wingspan 6½ ft. (198 cm). A ponderous dark waterbird. *Adult:* Much white and buff on head and front of neck. Dark chestnut brown on back of neck when breeding. *Immature:* Duskier brown overall, with dark head, paler underparts. Size, shape, and flight (a few flaps and a glide) indicate a pelican; dark color and habit of *plunging bill-first* proclaim it as this species. Lines of pelicans glide low over water, almost touching it with wingtips. **VOICE**: Adults silent (rarely a low croak). Nestlings squeal. **HABITAT**: Salt bays, beaches, ocean; more rarely inland lakes. Perches on posts, piers, rocks, buoys, beaches.

FRIGATEBIRDS Family Fregatidae

Dark tropical seabirds with extremely long wings (greater span in relation to body weight than that of any other bird). Bill long, hooked; tail deeply forked. Frigatebirds normally do not swim. **FOOD**: Fish, jellyfish, squid, young seabirds. Food snatched from water in flight, scavenged, or pirated from other seabirds. **RANGE**: Pantropical oceans.

MAGNIFICENT FRIGATEBIRD   Fairly common, local M117
Fregata magnificens
39–40 in. (100–102 cm); wingspan 7½ ft. (230–235 cm). A large, mostly black seabird with extremely long angled wings and *scissorlike* tail (often folded in a *point*). Soars with extreme ease. Bill long, hooked. *Male:* All black, with *red throat pouch* (inflated like a balloon in display). *Female:* White breast, dark head. *Immature:* Head and breast white. Most birds seen in w. U.S. are juveniles. **VOICE**: Voiceless at sea. A gargling whinny during display. **SIMILAR SPECIES**: Great Frigatebird (*Fregata minor*) of HI (not illustrated) is accidental off CA and elsewhere. Adult male retains light brown wing coverts, but very difficult to separate from Magnificent; female has whitish or grayish throat, red eye-ring; juvenile has rust-tinged head. Lesser Frigatebird recorded in WY, CA, MI, and ME. Adult male has white spur on axillars. Juvenile has russet head. **HABITAT**: Tropical oceans. May follow ships.

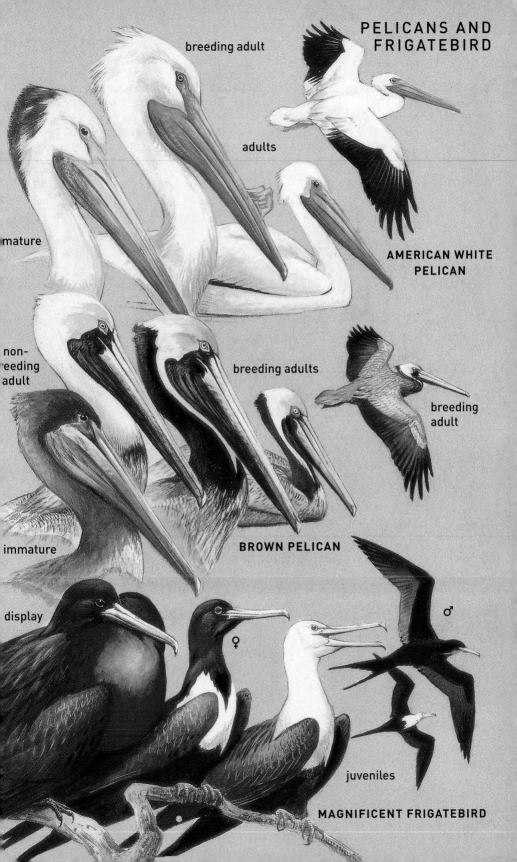

PELICANS AND
FRIGATEBIRD

breeding adult

adults

mature

AMERICAN WHITE
PELICAN

non-
feeding
adult

breeding adults

breeding
adult

immature

BROWN PELICAN

display

♂

♀

juveniles

MAGNIFICENT FRIGATEBIRD

CORMORANTS Family Phalacrocoracidae

Large blackish waterbirds that often stand erect on rocks, posts, or dead limbs with neck in an S; may rest with wings spread out to dry. Adults may have colorful facial skin, throat pouch, and eyes. Bill slender, hook-tipped. Sexes alike. Cormorants swim low like loons, but with bill tilted up at an angle. They often fly in lines or Vs, somewhat in manner of geese. Silent except for occasional low grunts at nesting colonies. **FOOD**: Fish, crustaceans. **RANGE**: Nearly worldwide.

BRANDT'S CORMORANT *Phalacrocorax penicillatus*　　Common M110
34 in. (86–89 cm). *Adult:* Almost size of Double-crested Cormorant, but has dark chin (*blue* when breeding) and flies without marked kink in neck. *Buffy throat patch* behind pouch. *Immature:* If a young cormorant along Pacific Coast has whitish breast, it is Double-crested; if it appears more uniformly dark, it is most likely Brandt's (buffy or pale brown breast) or Pelagic (deep brown breast). **SIMILAR SPECIES**: Other cormorants, loons. **HABITAT**: Ocean, coasts, littoral; nests colonially on sea cliffs.

PELAGIC CORMORANT *Phalacrocorax pelagicus*　　Fairly common M115
26–29 in. (66–73 cm). *Adult:* Noticeably smaller and more iridescent than other Pacific cormorants, with more *slender neck* (with no kinks in flight), longish tail, small head, and *thinner bill*. In breeding condition (late winter through midsummer), has double crest and *white patch* on flanks. Throat pouch and part of face dull red (obvious only at close range). *Immature:* Deep brown all over, darkest on back. Note thin bill. **SIMILAR SPECIES**: Other cormorants, loons. **HABITAT**: Ocean, coasts, bays, sounds. Despite name, seldom seen far from shore.

RED-FACED CORMORANT *Phalacrocorax urile*　　Uncommon, local M114
30–31 in. (76–79 cm). *Adult:* Note *bright red* face (extending to forehead and behind eye). Throat pouch *bluish; bill mostly pale.* Has white flank patches when breeding. Otherwise similar to Pelagic Cormorant, which is slightly smaller, has dull red pouch, restricted dull red on face, and thinner, all-dark bill. *Immature:* Differs from Pelagic in having thicker, mostly pale bill. **SIMILAR SPECIES**: Other cormorants, loons. **HABITAT**: Ocean, coasts; nests on sea cliffs.

CORMORANTS

immature

adult

cormorants
swim with
bill uptilted

breeding
adult

**BRANDT'S
CORMORANT**

PELAGIC CORMORANT

adult

Pelagic
immature

Pelagic adult

adult

immature

**RED-FACED
CORMORANT**

IMMATURE CORMORANTS
IN FLIGHT

Pelagic

Neotropic
(p. 92)

Double-crested
(p. 92)

Brandt's

Great
(p. 92)

DOUBLE-CRESTED CORMORANT *Phalacrocorax auritus*   Common M112
32–33 in. (81–84 cm). Almost any cormorant found inland can be called this species except for a few Great Cormorants and, in s.cen. and sw. states, Neotropic Cormorant. Coastally, it may be told from others by its *orangey* throat pouch and *loral stripe* (adult). In flight, shows *kink* in neck. *Adult:* All black, perches with erect posture. Crest seldom evident. *Immature:* Brownish belly, pale throat and chest. **SIMILAR SPECIES:** Other cormorants, loons. **HABITAT:** Coasts, bays, lakes, rivers; nests colonially on rocky islands, sea cliffs, or in trees at lakes.

GREAT CORMORANT *Phalacrocorax carbo*   Uncommon M113
36–37 in. (91–94 cm). *Adult:* Slightly larger than Double-crested Cormorant; note heavier bill and *yellow* throat pouch, bordered by *white throat* strap. In breeding plumage, has *white patch* on flanks. *Immature:* Dark breast and *pale belly.* Young Double-crested has the reverse: pale breast and dark belly. Young Great often shows suggestion of pale throat patch. **HABITAT:** Coasts and bays, locally inland on rivers, lakes. Nests on rocky islands and headlands.

NEOTROPIC CORMORANT *Phalacrocorax brasilianus*   Uncommon M111
25–26 in. (64–66 cm). *Adult:* Similar to Double-crested Cormorant, but smaller, slimmer, and *longer tailed.* In breeding plumage, white filoplumes on neck. Note smaller and duller throat pouch and, in breeding plumage, *narrow white border* outlining it, forming a point at rear. Lacks orangey loral stripe of Double-crested. *Immature:* Paler below. **SIMILAR SPECIES:** Other cormorants. **HABITAT:** Freshwater wetlands, ponds, lakes; tidal waters, lakes near coasts.

DARTERS Family Anhingidae

This family is represented in N. America by one species. **FOOD:** Fish, small aquatic animals. **RANGE:** N. and S. America, Africa, India, se. Asia, Australia.

ANHINGA *Anhinga anhinga*   Fairly common M116
34–35 in. (86–89 cm). Similar to a cormorant, but neck snakier, bill more pointed, tail much longer. Note large silvery upperwing patch. Male black-bodied; female has buffy neck and breast; immature brownish. In flight, flaps and glides with neck extended, long tail spread. Often soars high, hawklike, with wings held flat (arched in comorants). Perches like a cormorant, often with wings half-spread. May swim submerged, with only head emergent, appearing snakelike. **VOICE:** Occasional grunts and croaks. **SIMILAR SPECIES:** Soaring Double-crested Cormorant, sometimes with tail slightly splayed, regularly misidentified as Anhinga. **HABITAT:** Cypress swamps, rivers, wooded ponds.

CORMORANTS

DOUBLE-CRESTED CORMORANT

immature

adult

breeding adult

GREAT CORMORANT

immature

Double-crested

adult

GREAT CORMORANT
breeding

DOUBLE-CRESTED CORMORANT
breeding

NEOTROPIC CORMORANT
breeding

ANHINGA

♀

♂

♂

♀ swimming

BITTERNS, HERONS, AND ALLIES Family Ardeidae

Medium to large wading birds with long neck, spearlike bill. They stand with neck erect or head back on shoulders. In flight, neck is folded in an S; legs trail. Many herons have plumes when breeding. Sexes similar. **FOOD:** Fish, frogs, crawfish, other aquatic life; mice, gophers, small birds, insects. **RANGE:** Worldwide except colder regions.

GREAT BLUE HERON *Ardea herodias* Common M120
45–47 in. (115–120 cm). A lean gray bird, often miscalled a "crane"; may stand 4 ft. (122 cm) tall. Long legs, long neck, daggerlike bill, and, in flight, folded neck indicate a heron. Great size and blue-gray color mark it as this species. White subspecies, known as "Great White" Heron, is on p. 96. **VOICE:** Deep harsh croaks: *frahnk, frahnk, frahnk.* **SIMILAR SPECIES:** Sandhill Crane, Reddish Egret. **HABITAT:** Marshes, swamps, shores, tidal flats, moist fields.

"WÜRDEMANN'S" HERON *Ardea herodius* (in part) Uncommon, local
45–47 in. (115–120 cm). Resident in FL Keys. Like Great Blue Heron, but white head lacks black plumes. Presumably an intergrade of Great Blue– "Great White" heron complex. See "Great White" Heron, p. 96.

LITTLE BLUE HERON *Egretta caerulea* Fairly common M123
24 in. (61 cm). A small, slender heron. *Adult:* Bluish slate with deep maroon-brown neck; legs dark, bill pale blue with dark tip. *Immature:* All white with *grayish wingtips.* Legs *dull olive;* base of bill pale *blue-gray;* lores dull grayish or gray-green. Birds in transition are boldly pied white and dark. See p. 96. **VOICE:** Loud, nasal *scaaah.* **SIMILAR SPECIES:** Reddish Egret slightly larger overall and longer billed, with paler eye, medium gray color overall, and pinkish-based bill in breeding condition. Immature Little Blue like Snowy Egret except bill slightly thicker and grayer based, lores duller, and wingtips (usually) dusky. **HABITAT:** Marshes, ponds, mudflats, swamps, rice fields.

TRICOLORED HERON *Egretta tricolor* Uncommon M124
26 in. (66 cm). A very slender, dark heron with contrasting *white belly* and white rump. *Long* slender bill. *Adult:* Mostly bluish above and on neck. White crown plumes and pale rump plumes when breeding. *Immature:* Neck rusty brown. **VOICE:** Series of drawn-out nasal quacks. **SIMILAR SPECIES:** Great Blue and Little Blue herons. **HABITAT:** Marshes, swamps, shores.

REDDISH EGRET *Egretta rufescens* Uncommon M125
30–31 in. (76–79 cm). Note pinkish, black-tipped bill of adult in breeding condition. Loose-feathered; neck shaggy (adult). Pale eye. Two color morphs: (1) neutral gray, with rusty head and neck (immature duller, with all-dark bill); (2) white with blue-gray legs (see p. 96). Adults of both morphs have two-toned bill. When feeding, races about with spread wings. **VOICE:** Infrequently vocal; sometimes a harsh *kraaak!* **SIMILAR SPECIES:** Gray morph resembles adult Little Blue Heron, which is darker with bill pale bluish at base. White morph suggests Great or Snowy egret, but legs and feet blue-gray. **HABITAT:** Salt marshes, tidal flats, beaches.

DARK HERONS AND EGRET

herons fly with neck pulled in

juvenile

herons' necks may stretch or be looped in when they are standing

"WÜRDEMANN'S" HERON (intergrade)

adult

adult

GREAT BLUE HERON

adult

LITTLE BLUE HERON

(juvenile on p. 97)

juvenile

adult

TRICOLORED HERON

adult

REDDISH EGRET

dark morph

(white morph on p. 97)

Reddish Egret "dancing" while feeding

GREAT EGRET *Ardea alba*   Common M121

38–39 in. (97–100 cm). A tall, stately, slender white heron with largely *yellow bill*. Legs and feet *black*. When breeding, *straight plumes* on back extend beyond tail; bill may have dark ridge; lores greenish. When feeding, assumes an eager, forward-leaning pose, with neck extended. **VOICE:** Low, hoarse croak. Also *cuk, cuk, cuk*. **SIMILAR SPECIES:** Snowy Egret has all-black bill, yellow feet. Cattle Egret much smaller. **HABITAT:** Marshes, ponds, shores, mudflats, moist fields.

SNOWY EGRET *Egretta thula*   Common M122

24 in. (61 cm). Note the *"golden slippers."* A medium-sized heron, with *slender black bill*, black legs, and *yellow feet*. *Recurved plumes* on back during breeding season. Lores yellow (briefly red in high breeding condition). When feeding, rushes about, shuffling its feet to stir up food. Nonbreeding and young birds may show yellowish or greenish on much of rear side of legs, lores duller. **VOICE:** Low croak; in colony, a bubbling *wulla-wulla-wulla*. **SIMILAR SPECIES:** Great Egret larger, has largely yellow bill. Cattle Egret has yellow bill. White immature Little Blue Heron has blue-gray base to thicker bill, grayer lores, less active feeding style. **HABITAT:** Marshes, swamps, ponds, shores, tidal flats.

LITTLE EGRET *Egretta garzetta* (not shown)   Vagrant

25 in. (64 cm). A vagrant from Eurasia to East Coast, very similar to Snowy Egret, but slightly larger, larger billed, and with duller lores and feet. In breeding plumage, has two long head plumes. Young birds of both species very difficult to distinguish. **VOICE AND HABITAT:** Similar to Snowy Egret.

LITTLE BLUE HERON *Egretta caerulea* (adult on p. 94)

Immature: White with dusky wingtips. Also pied pattern with blue-gray plumage. Base of bill blue-gray, lores greenish gray, legs dull olive. May be confused with immature Snowy Egret. Less active feeding style.

CATTLE EGRET *Bubulcus ibis*   Common M126

19–20 in. (48–51 cm). Slightly smaller, stockier, and thicker necked than Snowy Egret. In breeding plumage shows *buff-orange* on crown, breast, and back (but may appear whitish at a distance); little or no buff at other times. Bill relatively short and yellow (orange-pink when nesting). Legs coral pink (nesting); immature may have yellow, greenish, or dusky legs. **VOICE:** Usually silent. Near breeding colony, a series of nasal grunts. **SIMILAR SPECIES:** Snowy Egret has black bill. Immature Little Blue Heron has blue-gray bill. Great Egret much larger. **HABITAT:** Farms, marshes, highway edges. Often associates with cattle.

REDDISH EGRET *Egretta rufescens* (dark morph on p. 94)

White morph: Note size, structure, feeding behavior, entirely blue-gray legs and feet. Adult has pink bill with black tip.

"GREAT WHITE" HERON *Ardea herodius* (in part)   Uncommon, local

47 in. (120 cm). Our largest white heron, found regularly only in s. FL. All white with yellow bill and dull horn-colored legs, the latter separating it from slightly smaller Great Egret, which has blackish legs. Formerly believed to be (and may be) a distinct species *(A. occidentalis);* currently regarded as a white subspecies of Great Blue Heron, p. 94. **HABITAT:** Mangrove keys, salt bays, marsh banks, open mudflats.

WHITE HERONS
AND EGRETS

SNOWY EGRET

GREAT EGRET

changing

juvenile

CATTLE
EGRET

LITTLE BLUE
HERON
(adult on p. 95)

nonbreeding

breeding

REDDISH
EGRET

white morph

(dark morph
on p. 95)

"GREAT WHITE"
HERON

(see also
Great Blue
Heron on
p. 95)

BLACK-CROWNED NIGHT-HERON

Uncommon M128

Nycticorax nycticorax

25 in. (64 cm). This stocky, thick-billed, short-legged heron is usually hunched and inactive; flies to feed at dusk. *Adult: Black back and cap* contrast with pale gray or whitish underparts. Eyes red; legs yellowish or greenish (pinkish in high breeding condition). Breeding birds have two long white head plumes. *Immature:* Brown, streaked and spotted with buff and white. Bill with greenish base; eyes small, reddish. **VOICE:** Flat *quok!* or *quark!* Most often heard at dusk. **SIMILAR SPECIES:** Immature may be confused with American Bittern and immature Yellow-crowned Night-Heron. **HABITAT:** Marshes, shores; roosts in trees.

YELLOW-CROWNED NIGHT-HERON

Uncommon M129

Nyctanassa violacea

24 in. (61 cm). A chunky heron with longer neck and legs than Black-crowned. *Adult:* Gray overall; head black with buffy-white cheek patch and yellowish crown. *Immature:* Similar to young Black-crowned Night-Heron, but grayer, more finely streaked and spotted; wing coverts have pale edges. Bill thicker and lacks greenish yellow base. In flight, entire foot and some of lower leg extend beyond tail. **VOICE:** *Quark*, higher pitched than call of Black-crowned. **HABITAT:** Swamps, mangroves, bayous, marshes, streams.

GREEN HERON *Butorides virescens*

Fairly common M127

17–18 in. (43–46 cm). A small dark heron that looks crowlike in flight (but flies with bowed wingbeats). When alarmed, stretches neck, elevates shaggy crest, and jerks tail. *Adult:* Comparatively *short* legs are *greenish yellow* or *orange* (when breeding). Back with blue-green gloss; neck deep chestnut. *Immature:* Streaked neck and breast, browner above. **VOICE:** Loud *skyow* or *skewk;* series of *kuck* notes. **HABITAT:** Lakes, ponds, marshes, streams.

LEAST BITTERN *Ixobrychus exilis*

Uncommon, secretive M119

12–13 in. (31–33 cm). Very small, thin, furtive; straddles reeds. Note large *buff wing patch* (lacking in rails). Back black in adult male, rusty brown in female and immature. The dark "Cory's" form has not been recorded since the 1930s. **VOICE:** Song a low, muted *coo-coo-coo;* also gives a raspy, rail-like *khak-khak-khak* series. **SIMILAR SPECIES:** Green Heron. **HABITAT:** Freshwater marshes, reedy ponds.

AMERICAN BITTERN *Botaurus lentiginosus*

Uncommon M118

28 in. (71 cm). A stocky brown heron; size of a young night-heron but warmer brown with longer yellowish bill. In flight, *entire trailing edge of wing is black* and bill held horizontal. Wingbeats much more rapid than night-herons'. At rest or when approached, often stands rigid, bill pointing up. *Black stripe shows on neck.* **VOICE:** "Pumping" sound, a low, deep, resonant *oong-ka´ choonk*, etc. Flushing call *kok-kok-kok.* **SIMILAR SPECIES:** Immature night-herons, Green Heron, and (much smaller) Least Bittern. **HABITAT:** Marshes, reedy lakes. Unlike night-herons, seldom sits in trees.

HERONS AND BITTERNS

adult

**BLACK-CROWNED
NIGHT-HERON**

juvenile

juvenile

adult

**YELLOW-CROWNED
NIGHT-HERON**

"Cory's"

typical

**LEAST
BITTERN**

juvenile

adult

GREEN HERON

**AMERICAN
BITTERN**

LIMPKINS Family Aramidae

A monotypic family, represented by one species. **FOOD**: Mostly large freshwater snails (mainly apple snails); a few insects, frogs. **RANGE**: Se. U.S., W. Indies, s. Mex. to Argentina.

LIMPKIN *Aramus guarauna*   Uncommon, local M177
26 in. (66 cm). A large, spotted swamp wader, a bit larger than an ibis. Long legs and drooping bill give it an ibislike aspect, but no ibis is brown with white spots and streaks. Flight cranelike, with smart upward flaps. **VOICE**: Piercing, repeated wail, *kree-ow, kra-ow*, etc., especially at night and on cloudy days. **SIMILAR SPECIES**: Immature ibises, night-herons, American Bittern. **HABITAT**: Fresh swamps, marshes with large snails.

IBISES AND SPOONBILLS Family Threskiornithidae

Ibises are long-legged, heronlike waders with slender, decurved bill. Spoonbills have spatulate bill. Both fly in Vs or lines and, unlike herons, fly with neck outstretched. **FOOD**: Small crustaceans, small fish, insects, etc. **RANGE**: Tropical and temperate regions.

WHITE-FACED IBIS *Plegadis chihi*   Fairly common M132
23–24 in. (58–62 cm). A long-legged wader with *long decurved bill.* Flies in lines with neck outstretched, alternately flapping and gliding. *Breeding adult:* Dark, with chestnut and bronzy sheen; suggests a blackish curlew. *White border* around face meets behind eye; variably red legs; pinkish to red lores; *red eye. Immature and nonbreeding adult:* Lack most of white on face; body and legs duller; pale streaks on head and neck. **VOICE**: Deep gooselike quacking. **SIMILAR SPECIES**: Glossy Ibis has thin cobalt blue borders on face, which do not meet behind dark eye; dark lores; less or no red on legs. Some immatures may be impossible to identify at least until the iris of young white-faced turns red (as early as midwinter). Hybrids with White-faced are known. **HABITAT**: Freshwater marshes, irrigated land.

GLOSSY IBIS *Plegadis falcinellus*   Fairly common M131
23–24 in. (58–62 cm). A medium-sized marsh wader with long decurved bill, thin pale blue lines edging dark face. At a distance, appears quite black, like a large dark curlew. Flies in lines with neck extended, flapping and gliding with quick wingbeats. *Adult:* Body a deep glossy bronzy chestnut. In nonbreeding season, duller with pale streaks on head and neck. *Immature:* Browner with no gloss. **VOICE**: Guttural *ka-onk*, repeated; low *kruk, kruk.* **SIMILAR SPECIES**: White-faced Ibis. **HABITAT**: Marshes, rice fields, swamps.

WHITE IBIS *Eudocimus albus*   Common M130
24–25 in. (62–64 cm). *Adult:* White. Note *red face*, long *decurved red bill,* and *restricted black in wingtips.* Flies with neck outstretched; flocks fly in "roller-coasting" strings, flapping and gliding; may soar in circles. *Immature:* Dark brownish, with *white belly, white rump,* decurved *orangey pink bill.* **VOICE**: Low and nasal *uuhhnn!* or *quaahh!* **SIMILAR SPECIES**: Wood Stork larger, with much more black in wing. Immature Glossy Ibis differs from immature White Ibis by its uniformly dark appearance. **HABITAT**: Salt, brackish, and fresh marshes, rice fields, mangroves.

LIMPKIN AND IBISES

WHITE-
FACED
IBIS

facial
comparison
in breeding
season

Glossy
Ibis

LIMPKIN

GLOSSY
IBIS

adult

immature

WHITE IBIS

adult

immature

ROSEATE SPOONBILL *Platalea ajaja*   Uncommon M133
32 in. (81 cm). A *bright pink* wading bird with long, flat, spoonlike bill. When feeding, sweeps its bill from side to side. In flight, extends neck and often glides between series of wing strokes. *Adult: Shell pink,* with blood red "drip" on shoulders; tail orange. Head naked, greenish gray. *Immature:* Spatulate bill; whitish plumage tinged pale pink, brightest on underwing. **VOICE:** At nesting colony, a low grunting croak. **SIMILAR SPECIES:** Greater Flamingo. **HABITAT:** Coastal marshes, lagoons, mudflats, mangroves.

STORKS Family Ciconiidae

Large, long-legged, and heronlike, with straight, recurved, or decurved bill. Some have naked head. Sexes alike. Walk is sedate; flight deliberate, with neck and legs extended. **FOOD:** Frogs, crustaceans, lizards, rodents. **RANGE:** S. U.S. to S. America; Africa, Eurasia, E. Indies, Australia.

WOOD STORK *Mycteria americana*   Uncommon M134
39–41 in. (100–105 cm). Very large; wingspan 5½ ft. (168 cm). White, with *dark naked head* and *much black in wing;* black tail. Bill long, thick, slightly decurved. *Immature:* Bill yellowish. When feeding, keeps head down and walks. In flight, alternately flaps and glides. Often soars very high on thermals. **VOICE:** Hoarse croak; usually silent. **SIMILAR SPECIES:** In flight, American White Pelican, Whooping Crane. **HABITAT:** Marshes, ponds, lagoons.

FLAMINGOS Family Phoenicopteridae

Pinkish white to vermilion wading birds with extremely long neck and legs. Thick bill is bent sharply down and lined with numerous lamellae for straining food. **FOOD:** Small mollusks, crustaceans, blue-green algae, diatoms. **RANGE:** W. Indies, Yucatán, Galápagos, S. America, Africa, s. Eurasia, India.

GREATER FLAMINGO *Phoenicopterus ruber*   Rare, local
46–47 in. (115–118 cm). W. Indian subspecies of this widespread flamingo is an extremely slim, rose pink wading bird as tall as a Great Blue Heron but much more slender. Note thick, sharply bent bill. Feeds with bill or head immersed. In flight, shows much black in wings; extremely long neck is extended droopily in front, and long legs trail behind, giving impression the bird might as easily fly backward as forward. Pale, washed-out birds may be escapes from zoos, as color often fades under captive conditions. Immatures also much paler than normal adults. **VOICE:** Gooselike calls, gabbling: *ar-honk,* etc. **SIMILAR SPECIES:** Roseate Spoonbill. Escapees of all five other flamingo species have been recorded in N. America. **RANGE:** Closest colonies in Bahamas, Cuba, and Yucatán. Rare visitor to Florida Bay; accidental elsewhere. **HABITAT:** Salt flats, saline lagoons.

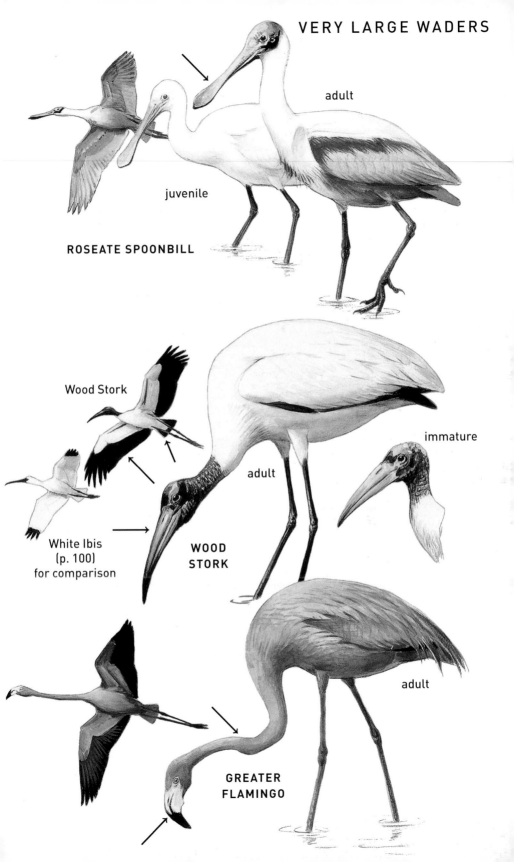

VERY LARGE WADERS

adult

juvenile

ROSEATE SPOONBILL

Wood Stork

immature

White Ibis
(p. 100)
for comparison

adult

WOOD STORK

GREATER FLAMINGO

adult

CRANES Family Gruidae

Stately birds, more robust than herons, often with red facial skin. Note tufted appearance over rump. In flight, neck extended. Migrate in Vs or lines like geese. Large herons are sometimes wrongly referred to as cranes. **FOOD**: Omnivorous. **RANGE**: Nearly worldwide except Cen. and S. America and Oceania.

WHOOPING CRANE *Grus americana*   Rare, very local M179
51–52 in. (130–132 cm); wingspan 7½ ft. (229 cm). The tallest N. American bird and one of the rarest. Large *white* crane with *red face*. Primaries *black*. Young birds washed with rust, especially on head. **VOICE**: Shrill, buglelike trumpeting, *ker-loo! ker-lee-oo!* **SIMILAR SPECIES**: Wood Stork has dark head, more black in wing. Egrets and swans lack black in wings. See also American White Pelican and Snow Goose. **HABITAT**: Prairies, fields and pastures, coastal marshes; in summer, muskeg. *Endangered* but slowly increasing.

COMMON CRANE *Grus grus*   Vagrant
44–50 in. (112–127 cm). Eurasian. Note black neck, white cheek stripe. Feathers arching over rump are blacker than those of Sandhill Crane. Inasmuch as this stray (probably from Asia) has been recorded in AK, AB, NE, IN, and QC to date, it should be looked for among flocks of Sandhill Cranes. Some escapees have also occurred (e.g., in NY, NJ).

SANDHILL CRANE *Grus canadensis*   Uncommon; scarce in East M178
36–48 in. (90–122 cm); wingspan 6–7 ft. (183–213 cm). Note *bald red crown*, bustlelike rear. A long-legged, long-necked, gray bird, often stained with rust. Immature browner. In flight, neck extended and wings flap with an upward flick. **VOICE**: Rolling, bugled *garoo-a-a-a*, repeated. Young birds also give a very different, cricketlike call. **SIMILAR SPECIES**: Great Blue Heron is sometimes wrongly called a crane. **HABITAT**: Prairies, fields, marshes, tundra. Lesser (subspecies) nests in tundra, Greater (subspecies) in grasslands and bogs.

CRANES

storks, ibises, and cranes fly
with neck outstretched

WHOOPING CRANE

adult

juvenile

COMMON CRANE

adult

SANDHILL CRANE

adult

juvenile

NEW WORLD VULTURES Family Cathartidae

Blackish; often seen soaring high in wide circles. Their naked heads are relatively smaller than those of hawks and eagles. Vultures are often locally called "buzzards." Silent away from nest site. **FOOD:** Carrion. **RANGE:** S. Canada to Cape Horn.

TURKEY VULTURE *Cathartes aura* (see also p. 134)   Common M136
26–27 in. (66–69 cm); wingspan 6 ft. (183 cm). Nearly eagle-sized. Overhead, note dark color with *two-toned wings* (flight feathers paler). Soars with wings in dihedral (shallow V); rocks and tilts unsteadily. At close range, small, naked *red head* of adult is evident; immatures have dark head. **SIMILAR SPECIES:** Black Vulture; Zone-tailed Hawk, which "mimics" Turkey Vulture; and eagles, which have larger, feathered head, shorter tail, and soar in a steady flat plane. **HABITAT:** Usually seen soaring in sky or perched on dead trees, posts, or on ground feeding, or sunning with wings outstretched.

BLACK VULTURE *Coragyps atratus* (see also p. 134)   Common M135
25 in. (64 cm); wingspan less than 5 ft. (152 cm). This dark scavenger is readily identified by short, square tail that barely projects beyond rear edge of wings and by *whitish patch* toward wingtip. Legs longer and whiter than Turkey Vulture's. Note *quick flapping*, alternating with short glides. **SIMILAR SPECIES:** Turkey Vulture has longer, rounded tail; flapping is slower, less frequent; soars with noticeable dihedral. *Caution:* Young Turkey Vulture has dark head. **HABITAT:** Similar to Turkey Vulture's but avoids higher mountains, prefers swampy areas.

CALIFORNIA CONDOR *Gymnogyps californianus*   Rare, local M137
46–47 in. (117–120 cm); wingspan 8½–9½ ft. (259–290 cm). Was heading toward extinction; last wild birds captured in 1987. Captive breeding program successful, and some of these birds released to wild in CA, AZ, and Baja CA. Much larger than Turkey Vulture. *Adult:* Extensive *white underwing linings* toward fore edge of wing. Head yellow-orange. *Immature:* Dusky-headed and lacks white wing linings, but almost twice the size of Turkey Vulture and has much broader proportions and shorter tail. Condor has *flatter wing-plane* when soaring; does not rock or tilt. **SIMILAR SPECIES:** Many Golden Eagles show some white under wing, but this color is placed differently; overall shape also different. **HABITAT:** Mountains, grassy foothills, chaparral. Nests on mountain ledges.

VULTURES

adult

immature

TURKEY VULTURE

adult

BLACK VULTURE

adult

CALIFORNIA CONDOR

Birds of Prey

We tend to call all diurnal (day-flying) raptors with a hooked bill and hooked claws "birds of prey." Actually, they fall into two quite separate families:

1. The hawk group (Accipitridae)—kites, harriers, accipiters, buteos, and eagles
2. The falcon group (Falconidae)—falcons and caracaras

The illustrations on the following pages present the most obvious field marks. For a more in-depth treatment of variable plumages, see the various specialty guides that deal with raptors.

The many raptors can be sorted out by their basic shapes and flight styles. When not flapping, they may alternate between soaring, with wings fully extended and tail fanned, and gliding, with wings slightly pulled back and tail folded. These two pages show some basic silhouettes.

glide

full soar

BUTEOS are stocky, with broad wings and a wide, rounded tail. They soar and wheel high in the open sky.

glide

full soar

ACCIPITERS have a small head, short rounded wings, and a longish tail. They typically fly with several rapid beats and a short glide.

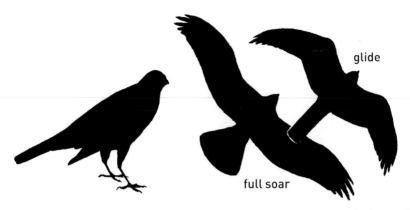

HARRIERS are slim, with long, slim, round-tipped wings and a long tail. They fly in open country and glide low, with a vulturelike dihedral.

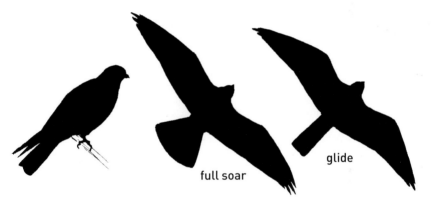

KITES (except for Snail Kite and Hook-billed Kite) are falcon-shaped, but unlike falcons, they are buoyant gliders, not power fliers.

FALCONS have long pointed wings and a long tail. Their wing strokes are strong and rapid.

HAWKS, KITES, EAGLES, AND ALLIES
Family Accipitridae

Diurnal birds of prey, with hooked bill, hooked talons. Though persecuted and misunderstood by many, they are very important in the ecosystem. **RANGE:** Almost worldwide.

EAGLES

Distinguished from buteos, to which they are related, by their greater size and proportionately longer wings. Powerful bill is nearly as long as head. **FOOD:** Golden Eagle eats chiefly rabbits, large rodents, snakes, game birds; Bald Eagle, fish, injured waterfowl, carrion.

BALD EAGLE   Uncommon, locally common M144
Haliaeetus leucocephalus (see also p. 134)
31–37 in. (79–94 cm); wingspan 7–8 ft. (213–244 cm). National bird of U.S. *Adult:* With its *white head* and *white tail,* this bird is "all field mark." Bill yellow, massive. Wings held flat when soaring. *Immature:* Variable, depending on age; first year mostly dark overall with *whitish in wing linings.* Two- and three-year-old birds very mottled with white on belly, flight feathers, tail, and back; some may show pale head with darkish patch through eye, reminiscent of Osprey. **VOICE:** Harsh, high-pitched cackle, *kleek-kik-ik-ik-ik,* or lower *kak-kak-kak.* **SIMILAR SPECIES:** Golden Eagle, Turkey Vulture. **HABITAT:** Coasts, rivers, large lakes; in migration and winter, also mountains, open country.

GOLDEN EAGLE   Uncommon to scarce M161
Aquila chrysaetos (see also p. 134)
30–40 in. (76–102 cm); wingspan 7 ft. (213 cm). This majestic eagle glides and soars flat-winged with occasional shallow wingbeats. *Adult:* Uniformly dark below, or with slight lightening at base of obscurely banded tail. On hindneck, a *wash of buffy gold. Immature:* In flight, shows *white flash in wings* at base of primaries, and *white tail* with *broad dark terminal band.* **VOICE:** Seldom heard, a yelping bark, *kya;* also whistled notes. **SIMILAR SPECIES:** Immature Bald Eagle has larger head, usually has *extensive blotchy white in wing linings* and often on body. Tail may be mottled with white at base but is not cleanly banded. Dark morphs of Rough-legged and Ferruginous hawks are smaller, have whitish flight feathers. **HABITAT:** Open mountains, foothills, plains, deserts, open country.

OSPREYS

Formerly considered a monotypic family comprising a single large bird of prey that hovers above water and plunges feet-first for fish. Sexes alike. **FOOD:** Fish. **RANGE:** All continents except Antarctica.

OSPREY *Pandion haliaetus* (see also p. 134)   Locally common M138
23–24½ in. (58–62 cm); wingspan to 6 ft. (183 cm). Large. Our only raptor that hovers over water and plunges into it feet-first for fish. (Bald Eagle may pick up fish from surface.) *Adult:* Blackish above, *white below;* head largely white, suggesting Bald Eagle, but with *broad black mask through eyes.* Flies with gull-like kink or crook in wings, showing black "wrist" patch below. *Juvenile:* Has scaly pattern on back. **VOICE:** Series of sharp, annoyed whistles: *cheep, cheep* or *yewk, yewk,* etc. Near nest, a frenzied *cheereek!* **SIMILAR SPECIES:** Large gulls. Immature Bald Eagle may show dusky "mask." Rough-legged Hawk also has dark wrist mark and hovers over marshes, but it lacks wing crook and bold mask, and usually shows dark belly patch. **HABITAT:** Rivers, lakes, marshes, coasts.

EAGLES AND OSPREY

overhead flight patterns
on p. 135

BALD
EAGLE

adult

juvenile

GOLDEN
EAGLE

juvenile

Golden Eagle
adult

hovering

OSPREY

adult

KITES

Graceful birds of prey of southern distribution. U.S. species (except Snail Kite and Hook-billed Kite) are falcon-shaped with pointed wings. **FOOD:** Large insects, reptiles, rodents. Snail Kite and Hook-billed Kite specialize in snails.

SWALLOW-TAILED KITE *Elanoides forficatus*　　Uncommon M140
22–23 in. (55–58 cm). A sleek, elegant, black-and-white hawk that flies with incomparable grace. Note blue-black upperparts, clean white head and underparts, and long, mobile, deeply forked tail. **VOICE:** Shrill, keen *ee-ee-ee* or *pee-pee-pee*. **HABITAT:** Wooded river swamps and pine lands, where it feeds mainly on snakes.

MISSISSIPPI KITE　　Fairly common M143
Ictinia mississippiensis (see also p. 128)
14–14½ in. (36–37 cm). Falcon-shaped, graceful, and gray. Gregarious; spends much time soaring. *Adult:* Dark above, lighter below; head *pale gray;* tail and underwing blackish. No other falconlike bird has *black unbarred tail.* Broad *white patch* shows on rear edge of upperwing (not visible from below on birds soaring overhead). *Immature:* Lacks pale patch on wing, has weak white bands on tail. *Juvenile:* Heavily streaked on rusty underparts. **VOICE:** Usually silent; near nest, a two-syllable *phee-phew*. **SIMILAR SPECIES:** Male Northern Harrier. **HABITAT:** Nests in riparian woodlands, residential areas, groves, shelterbelts.

WHITE-TAILED KITE *Elanus leucurus* (see also p. 128)　　Uncommon M141
15½–16 in. (39–41 cm). This whitish kite is falcon-shaped, with long pointed wings and *long white tail* that is slightly notched, not forked. Soars and glides like a small gull; *often hovers. Adult:* Pale gray above, with white head, underparts, and tail. *Large black patch* on fore edge of upperwing is obvious on perched birds. Overhead, shows oval black patch at carpal joint ("wrist") of underwing. *Juvenile:* Like adult, but has *rusty breast,* brown back, and narrow dark band near tip of pale grayish tail. **VOICE:** Whistled *kew kew kew,* abrupt or drawn out. **HABITAT:** Open groves, river valleys, marshes, grasslands, roadsides. May form communal roosts at night in nonbreeding season.

SNAIL KITE *Rostrhamus sociabilis*　　Scarce, local M142
17 in. (43 cm). Suggests Northern Harrier at a distance, but with broader wings and without gliding, tilting flight; flies more floppily on cupped wings, head down, searching for snails. *Male:* All black except for broad white band across base of tail; legs, bill, and face red. *Female:* Heavily streaked on buffy body; white stripe over eye; white band across black tail. **VOICE:** Cackling *kor-ee-ee-a, kor-ee-ee-a*. **HABITAT:** Freshwater marshes and canals with apple snails (*Pomacea* spp.).

HOOK-BILLED KITE *Chondrohierax uncinatus*　　Rare, local M139
16½–17½ in. (42–45 cm). A scarce resident in s. TX. Bill has long, hooked tip. Legs yellow. Plumage varies from blackish or grayish in males to rufous brown in females to much paler below in juveniles. Adults have horizontally barred underparts. Note *paddle-shaped wings.* **HABITAT:** Subtropical woodlands. Spends most of its time in the woods, soaring only briefly as it travels to and from feeding areas.

KITES

additional overhead
flight patterns
on p. 129

**SWALLOW-TAILED
KITE**

adult

juvenile

**MISSISSIPPI
KITE**

adult

juvenile

juvenile

adult

adult

juvenile

WHITE-TAILED KITE

juvenile

♂

♂

black
morph

♀

♀

SNAIL KITE

**HOOK-
BILLED
KITE**

ACCIPITERS (BIRD HAWKS)

Long-tailed woodland raptors with short, rounded wings, adapted for hunting among trees. Typical flight mixes quick beats and a glide. Sexes similar; females larger. Size helps distinguish species but not always reliable in the field. **FOOD:** Chiefly birds, some small mammals. Sharp-shinned and Cooper's often seen hunting birds at backyard feeders.

SHARP-SHINNED HAWK
Fairly common M146

Accipiter striatus (see also p. 126)
10–14 in. (25–36 cm). A small, slim woodland hawk, with slim *square-tipped* tail and *short, rounded wings. Adult:* Dark back, *rusty-barred* breast. Orange eye. *Immature:* Dark brown above, *thickly streaked* with rusty brown on underparts. Yellow eye. **VOICE:** Like Cooper's Hawk, but shriller; a high *kik, kik, kik* given near nest. **SIMILAR SPECIES:** Female Cooper's obviously larger, with *larger head, rounded* tail, with thicker white tip, thicker legs; male Cooper's and female Sharp-shinned closer in size. Adult Cooper's has more defined cap. Immature Cooper's *tawnier* on head and has whiter, more *finely streaked* breast. **HABITAT:** Breeds in extensive forests; in migration and winter, open woodlands, wood edges, residential areas.

COOPER'S HAWK
Fairly common M147

Accipiter cooperii (see also p. 126)
14–20 in. (36–51 cm). Very similar to Sharp-shinned Hawk but larger, particularly female. See Sharp-shinned Hawk. **VOICE:** About nest, a rapid *kek, kek, kek;* suggests a flicker. Also a sapsucker-like mewing. **SIMILAR SPECIES:** Sharp-shinned Hawk, Northern Goshawk. **HABITAT:** Like Sharp-shinned but prefers more open areas.

NORTHERN GOSHAWK *Accipiter gentilis* (see also p. 126)
Scarce M148

21–26 in. (53–66 cm). Larger, broader-winged, broader-tailed, more buteo-like than Cooper's Hawk. *Adult:* Crown and cheek blackish; *broad white stripe over eye.* Underparts *pale gray, finely barred;* back paler than in Cooper's or Sharp-shinned hawk. *Immature:* Buffier overall than immature Cooper's with bolder eyebrow, more extensive streaking below, and wavy, irregular tail banding. **VOICE:** *Kak, kak, kak* or *kuk, kuk, kuk,* heavier than Cooper's, given near nest. **SIMILAR SPECIES:** Cooper's Hawk. A soaring goshawk may be initially misidentified as a buteo. **HABITAT:** Coniferous and mixed forests, especially in mountains; forest edges; winters also in wooded lowlands. Periodic irruptions in fall and winter farther to south.

HARRIERS

Slim raptors with slim wings, long tail. Flight low, languid, gliding, with wings held in shallow V (dihedral). Sexes not alike. They hunt in open country.

NORTHERN HARRIER
Fairly common M145

Circus cyaneus (see also p. 128)
18–21 in. (46–54 cm). A slim, long-winged, long-tailed raptor of open country. Glides and flies buoyantly and unsteadily low over ground, with wings held slightly above horizontal, suggesting Turkey Vulture's dihedral. In all plumages shows *white rump patch. Adult male:* Pale gray, whitish beneath. Overhead, wingtips have "dipped-in-ink" look. *Adult female:* Brown, with heavy streaks below. *Immature:* Russet below without streaks. **VOICE:** Weak, nasal whistle, *pee, pee, pee.* **SIMILAR SPECIES:** Short-eared Owl. **HABITAT:** Marshes, fields, prairies.

ACCIPITERS AND HARRIER

additional overhead flight patterns on pp. 127 and 129

adult

juvenile

accipiters have small head, short rounded wings, long tail

SHARP-SHINNED HAWK

juvenile

adult

COOPER'S HAWK

juvenile

adult

NORTHERN GOSHAWK

juvenile

NORTHERN HARRIER

♂

♀

Buteos and Buteo-like Hawks

Large, thickset hawks, with broad wings and wide, rounded tail. Many buteos habitually soar high in wide circles. Much variation; sexes similar, females slightly larger. Young birds usually streaked below. Dark morphs often occur. **FOOD:** Small mammals, sometimes small birds, reptiles, grasshoppers. **RANGE:** Widespread in New and Old Worlds.

GRAY HAWK *Buteo nitidus* (see also p. 128)   Scarce, local M153
17 in. (43 cm); wingspan 3 ft. (91 cm). A small buteo. *Adult:* Distinguished by its buteo-like proportions, gray back, *thickly barred gray* breast, white rump band, and *banded* tail (similar to Broad-winged Hawk's). *Immature:* Narrowly barred tail, striped buffy breast, bold face pattern, *white U-shaped bar* across rump. **VOICE:** Drawn-out whistles, *ka-lee-oh* or *kleeeeoo*. **SIMILAR SPECIES:** Young Broad-winged Hawk has weaker face pattern, lacks white U on rump, has shorter tail, more pointed wings. **HABITAT:** Streamside and subtropical woodlands.

WHITE-TAILED HAWK   Fairly common, local M156
Buteo albicaudatus (see also p. 128)
21–23 in. (53–58 cm); wingspan 4 ft. (122 cm). Large, with long pointed wings. Flies with marked dihedral. *Adult:* White underparts contrasting with dark flight feathers; white tail with black band, shoulders rusty red. *Immature:* Narrower wings and longer tail than adult. Blackish below with white breast patch. Pale U across upper tail. May show Red-tailed Hawk–like dark belly patch. Tail pale gray with weak barring. **VOICE:** Nasal note followed by high-pitched series of doubled notes: *aaraahh kee-REEK, kee-REEK kee-REEK.* **SIMILAR SPECIES:** Adult Swainson's Hawk smaller, has dark chest. Juvenile White-tailed may be confused with other large buteos, particularly Red-tailed Hawk. **HABITAT:** Coastal prairies, brushlands.

HARRIS'S HAWK   Fairly common M150
Parabuteo unicinctus (see also p. 132)
20–21 in. (50–53 cm); wingspan 3½ ft. (107 cm). A blackish brown hawk of *Buteo* type, with flashing *white rump* and *white band* at tip of tail. Often hunts cooperatively in small groups. *Adult: Chestnut areas* on thighs and shoulders. *Immature:* Light, streaked underparts, *rusty shoulders;* conspicuous *white* at base of tail. **VOICE:** Low-pitched, harsh *raaaah!* **SIMILAR SPECIES:** Dark forms of Ferruginous and Red-tailed hawks lack bold rusty shoulders and white tail base. **HABITAT:** Mesquite, cactus deserts.

ZONE-TAILED HAWK   Uncommon M157
Buteo albonotatus (see also p. 132)
20 in. (51 cm); wingspan 4 ft. (122 cm). Dull *black,* with more *slender* wings than most other buteos. Often mistaken for Turkey Vulture because of proportions, two-toned underwing, and up-tilted wings—but hawk has larger feathered head, square-tipped tail, barred underwing, yellow cere and legs. *Adult: White tail bands* (pale gray on topside). *Immature:* Narrower tail bands, *small white spots* on breast. **VOICE:** Nasal, drawn-out *keeeeah.* **SIMILAR SPECIES:** Turkey Vulture, Common Black-Hawk, other dark-morph buteos. **HABITAT:** Riparian woodlands, mountains, canyons.

COMMON BLACK-HAWK   Scarce, local M149
Buteogallus anthracinus (see also p. 132)
21 in. (53 cm); wingspan 4 ft. (122 cm). A buteo-type hawk with chunky shape, exceptionally wide wings, and *long* yellow legs. *Adult:* All black with broad white *band* crossing middle of short tail. In flight, whitish spot shows at base of primaries. *Immature:* Dark-backed with heavily striped *buffy* head and underparts; tail white with five or six wavy dark bands. **VOICE:** Series of loud whistles. **SIMILAR SPECIES:** Zone-tailed Hawk. **HABITAT:** Wooded river and stream bottoms.

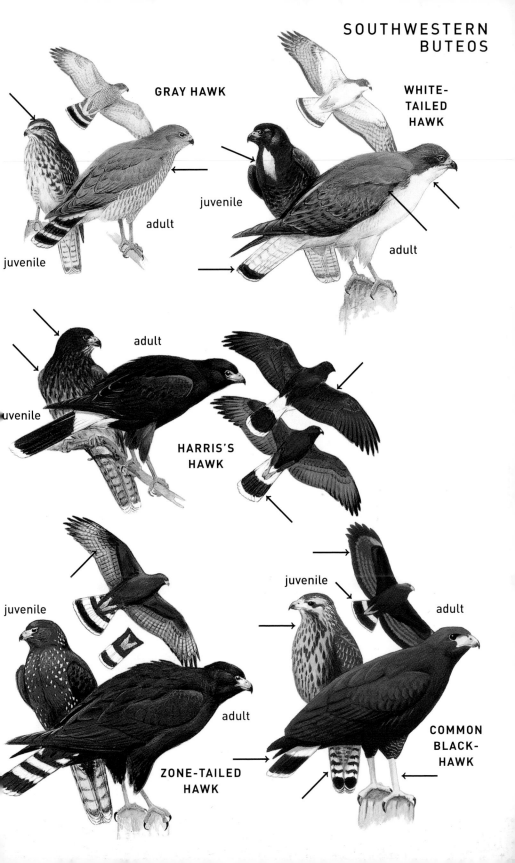

SOUTHWESTERN
BUTEOS

GRAY HAWK

WHITE-
TAILED
HAWK

juvenile

adult

juvenile

adult

adult

juvenile

HARRIS'S
HAWK

juvenile

juvenile

adult

adult

ZONE-TAILED
HAWK

COMMON
BLACK-
HAWK

ROUGH-LEGGED HAWK
Uncommon M160

Buteo lagopus (see also pp. 130 and 132)

21–22 in. (53–55 cm). This hawk of open country often *hovers on beating wings,* more so than other buteos. Somewhat longer, narrower wings and tail than other Buteos except Ferruginous Hawk. Many birds show *solid or blotched dark belly* and *black patch* at "wrist" (carpal joint) of underwing. Some adult males have dark bib but lack blackish belly band. Tail *white,* with *broad black band or bands* toward tip. White flash on upperwing. Legs feathered, feet small. Dark morph may lack extensive white on tail, but broad terminal band and extensive white on underwing are good field marks. **VOICE:** High-pitched squeal, mostly near nest site. **SIMILAR SPECIES:** Red-tailed Hawk, Northern Harrier, dark-morph Ferruginous Hawk. **HABITAT:** Nests on tundra escarpments, Arctic coasts; in winter, open fields, plains, marshes.

RED-SHOULDERED HAWK
Uncommon to fairly common M151

Buteo lineatus (see also p. 130)

16–20 in. (40–50 cm). In flight, note *translucent patch,* or "window," at base of primaries, longish tail. *Adult:* Heavy black-and-white bands on wings and tail, dark *rufous shoulders* (not always easy to see) and wing linings, rufous red underparts. *Immature:* Variably streaked and/or barred below; recognized by proportions, tail bands, and, in flight, wing "windows." Western Red-shouldereds darker with quicker wingbeats; do not commonly soar like eastern birds. Florida birds paler. **VOICE:** Two-syllable scream, *kee-yer* (dropping inflection), repeated in series. **SIMILAR SPECIES:** Other reddish-breasted hawks: Broad-winged Hawk has paler wing linings, more pointed wing, broader bands on tail, lacks wing "windows." See also Cooper's and Red-tailed hawks. **HABITAT:** Woodlands in valleys, canyons, along rivers. Also wooded swamps and residential areas.

BROAD-WINGED HAWK
Common M152

Buteo platypterus (see also pp. 130 and 132)

15–16 in. (38–41 cm). A small, chunky buteo, size of a crow. Often seen migrating in East in fall in spiraling flocks called "kettles." *Adult:* Note tail banding: high overhead shows one obvious thick white band (Red-shouldered shows multiple bands). Wing linings whitish, the edge trimmed with black. *Immature:* Heavily streaked along sides of neck, breast, and belly; chest often unmarked. Tail has several narrow dark bands; terminal dark band twice as wide as the rest. Rare dark morph, which breeds in Prairie Provinces, has dark wing linings but shows usual Broad-winged tail pattern. **VOICE:** High-pitched, shrill, two-part downward *pwe-eeeee.* **SIMILAR SPECIES:** Young Red-shouldered Hawk similar to immature Broad-winged but has streaking heaviest on breast, barred secondaries, blunter wingtips with bold pale "window." Missing flight feathers on worn Broad-wingeds in spring may appear like Red-shouldered's pale wing crescents. See also accipiters. **HABITAT:** Woods, groves.

SHORT-TAILED HAWK
Uncommon, local M154

Buteo brachyurus (see also p. 132)

15–16 in. (38–41 cm). A small black or black-and-white buteo, size of a crow. Two morphs: (1) blackish brown body and black wing linings; (2) blackish above, white below, dark cheeks, *two-toned* underwing pattern, white wing linings. No other FL buteo would be blackish or clear white below. **VOICE:** Descending, high-pitched scream: *kleeear!* **SIMILAR SPECIES:** Broad-winged Hawk in flight shows slimmer wings, whiter flight feathers below. Often perches in open, unlike Short-tailed. See Swainson's Hawk. **HABITAT:** Pines, woodland edges, cypress swamps, mangroves.

BUTEOS

additional overhead
flight patterns on
pp. 131 and 133

dark
morph

light morph

**ROUGH-LEGGED
HAWK**

adult

juvenile

Eastern

pale
FL
form

RED-SHOULDERED HAWK

adult

juvenile

adult

**BROAD-WINGED
HAWK**

juvenile

light-
morph
juvenile

dark-morph
adult

light-morph
adult

light-morph
adult

dark-morph
adult

SHORT-TAILED HAWK

RED-TAILED HAWK
Common M158

Buteo jamaicensis (see also pp. 130 and 132)

19–22 in. (48–56 cm). The common conspicuous hawk of roadsides and woodland edges. When soaring, adults show *rufous* on topside of tail, pale pinkish below. Also note mottled *white patches* on scapulars. Overhead, a dependable mark on all but blackish birds is *dark patagial bar* on fore edge of wing. Immatures have brownish tail with narrow, dark banding. Underparts of typical eastern Red-taileds are "zoned" (light breast, dark *belly band*). Some birds of sw. TX ("Fuertes's" Red-tailed) lack belly band. On Great Plains, pale "Krider's" morph is found. There is much variation farther west, where Red-taileds tend to be darker. One might encounter the blackish "Harlan's" as well as rufous and dark brown birds. The latter usually have telltale rust on tail. **VOICE:** Asthmatic squeal, *keeer-r-r* (slurring downward). **SIMILAR SPECIES:** Rough-legged, Ferruginous, Swainson's, Red-shouldered, and Broad-winged hawks. **HABITAT:** Open country, woodlands, prairie groves, mountains, plains, roadsides.

"HARLAN'S" RED-TAILED HAWK
Uncommon

Buteo jamaicensis harlani (see also p. 132)

A variable, usually blackish race of Red-tailed. Similar to other dark-morph Red-taileds, but tail usually dirty white, with *longitudinal* mottling and freckling of gray, black, sometimes red, merging into dark subterminal band. Rare light morph has similar tail pattern, but body very pale and mottled, more like "Krider's" Red-tailed Hawk. **RANGE:** Breeds from cen. AK to nw. Canada. Winters primarily from Pacific Northwest diagonally to TX and lower Mississippi Valley.

"KRIDER'S" RED-TAILED HAWK
Uncommon

Buteo jamaicensis

A pale prairie morph of Red-tailed, with whitish tail that may be tinged with pale rufous. **RANGE:** Prairies and plains of Canada and n.cen. U.S. Winters south through plains to TX, LA.

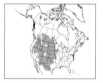

SWAINSON'S HAWK
Common M155

Buteo swainsoni (see also pp. 130 and 132)

19–21 in. (48–53 cm). A buteo of the plains. Slimmer than Red-tailed Hawk, with narrower, more pointed wings. When gliding, holds wings slightly above horizontal. When perched, *wingtips extend to tail tip.* In light and intermediate morphs, overhead, *pale wing linings contrast with dark flight feathers. Adult:* Typical adults have dark breastband; tail gray-brown above, often pale toward base; dark and rufous morph birds best identified by shape and shaded flight feathers. *Immature:* Variably streaked below, white band across rump; best identified by shape and wing pattern. Many subadults are distinctly pale-headed. **VOICE:** Shrill, plaintive whistle, *kreeeeeeer.* **SIMILAR SPECIES:** Swainson's wing shape distinctive for a buteo. Lacks white scapular patches of bulkier Red-tailed. In TX, see White-tailed Hawk. **HABITAT:** Plains, grasslands, agricultural land, open hills, sparse trees.

FERRUGINOUS HAWK
Uncommon M159

Buteo regalis (see also pp. 128 and 132)

23–24 in. (58–61 cm). A large buteo of plains. Note large bill, long gape line, *long tapered wings* with *pale panel* on upper surface of primaries, *mostly white tail. Adult:* Rufous above, mostly whitish head and breast, rufous wash on tail, rufous thighs form *dark V* on birds overhead. Dark morphs are rufous brown with whitish flight feathers and whitish tail. *Immatures:* Lack rufous tones; best identified by shape as well as wing and tail patterns. **SIMILAR SPECIES:** Red-tailed Hawk and dark-morph Rough-legged Hawk. **HABITAT:** Plains, grasslands, agricultural fields.

BUTEOS

rufous adult

Western juvenile

Eastern juvenile

dark adult

Western adult

Eastern adult

RED-TAILED HAWK

"KRIDER'S" juvenile

"HARLAN'S" adult

"Harlan's" adult

juvenile

light morph

adult

dark morph

adult light morph

SWAINSON'S HAWK

adult light morph

light morph

dark morph

FERRUGINOUS HAWK

CARACARAS AND FALCONS Family Falconidae

Caracaras are large, long-legged birds of prey, some with naked face. Sexes alike. **FOOD:** Our one U.S. species feeds mostly on carrion. **RANGE:** S. U.S. to Tierra del Fuego, Falklands. Falcons are streamlined birds of prey with pointed wings, longish tail. **FOOD:** Birds, rodents, reptiles, insects. **RANGE:** Almost worldwide.

CRESTED CARACARA   Uncommon, local M162
Caracara cheriway (see also p. 132)
23 in. (58 cm). A large, long-legged, big-headed, long-necked bird of prey, often seen feeding with vultures. *Adult: Black crest* and *red face* distinctive. In flight, underbody presents alternating areas of light and dark: white chest, black belly, and whitish, dark-tipped tail. Note combination of *pale wing patches, pale chest, and pale tail panel*, giving impression of "white at all four corners." *Immature:* Browner, streaked on breast. **VOICE:** Weird, guttural series of croaks and rattles. **HABITAT:** Prairies, rangeland, deserts.

GYRFALCON *Falco rusticolus* (see also p. 126)   Scarce M165
20–25 in. (51–64 cm). A very large Arctic falcon, larger and more robust and buteo-like than Peregrine Falcon; slightly broader tailed. On perched birds, wingtips do not reach near tail tip. Wingbeats deceptively slower. Thinner mustache. There are brown, gray, and white color morphs. Darker immature birds are more prone to wander south. **VOICE:** Harsh *kak-kak-kak* series. **SIMILAR SPECIES:** Peregrine Falcon smaller, slimmer, with dark hood and broad black mustache, more uniform underwing, and more tapered tail. Prairie Falcon slimmer, pale brown. See also Northern Goshawk. **HABITAT:** Arctic barrens, seacoasts, open mountains; in winter, open country, coastlines.

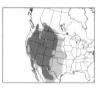

PRAIRIE FALCON *Falco mexicanus* (see also p. 126)   Uncommon M167
16–19 in. (41–50 cm). Like a sandy-colored Peregrine Falcon, with *white eyebrow stripe* and *narrower mustache*. In flight overhead, shows *blackish patches* in axillars ("wingpits") and inner coverts. **VOICE:** Generally silent. Harsh *kak-kak-kak* around nest. **SIMILAR SPECIES:** Peregrine has slaty or dark brown back, more black on face, different underwing pattern. Female Prairie Merlin (*richardsoni*) same color above but much smaller, lacks dark underwing patch. **HABITAT:** Open country, from alpine tundra to grasslands, prairies, agricultural land, deserts, marshes.

PEREGRINE FALCON *Falco peregrinus* (see also p. 126)   Uncommon M166
16–20 in. (41–51 cm). Formerly endangered; reintroduced in many regions. Size of a crow, but longer looking. Note *wide black mustache*. Known as a falcon by pointed wings, narrow tail, and quick, powerful wingbeats. Size and strong face pattern indicate this species. *Adult:* Slaty-backed, light-chested, barred and spotted below. Northwestern population, "Peale's" (*pealei*), breeding off s. AK and BC *darker* and more heavily marked on breast. Tundra-race (*tundrius*) adults have pale forehead and upper breast. *Immature:* Brown, heavily streaked below. **VOICE:** At eyrie, a repeated *we'chew;* a rapid *kek kek kek kek.* **SIMILAR SPECIES:** Merlin, Gyrfalcon. **HABITAT:** Nests on cliffs and ledges; open country, from mountains to coasts. Established as a reintroduced breeder (on building ledges and bridges) in many major cities in East and Midwest.

CARACARA AND LARGE FALCONS

juvenile

CRESTED
CARACARA

adults

PRAIRIE
FALCON

gray
morph

gray
morph

rown
norph

white
morph

brown
morph

GYRFALCON

PEREGRINE
FALCON

juvenile

Pacific
("Peale's")
adult

Tundra
adult

adults

AMERICAN KESTREL

Fairly common M163

Falco sparverius (see also p. 126)

9½–10½ in. (24–27 cm). A falcon the size of a large jay. No other *small hawk* has *rufous back or tail.* Male has blue-gray wings. Both sexes have black-and-white face with double mustache. *Hovers* for prey on rapidly beating wings, kingfisher-like. Sits fairly erect, occasionally lifting tail. **VOICE:** Rapid, high *klee klee klee* or *killy killy killy.* **SIMILAR SPECIES:** Merlin (which only rarely perches on wires). Sharp-shinned Hawk has rounded wings, gray or brown back and tail. Neither species hovers. **HABITAT:** Open country, farmland, wood edges, residential areas, dead trees, wires, roadsides.

MERLIN *Falco columbarius* (see also p. 126)

Uncommon M164

11–12 in. (28–31 cm). A small (slightly larger than jay-sized) falcon; suggests a miniature Peregrine Falcon, but with less distinct mustache. *Male:* Blue-gray above, with broad black bands on *gray tail. Female and immature:* Dusky brown, with banded tail; boldly streaked below. Prairie subspecies *(richardsoni)* paler gray or brown (color of a Prairie Falcon), lacks mustache. Coastal Northwest subspecies, "Black" *(suckleyi),* very dark, lacks light eyebrow stripe. **VOICE:** High, rapid *kee-kee-kee-kee.* **SIMILAR SPECIES:** Compared with American Kestrel, Merlin has broader-based wings, more boldly barred tail, and more heavily marked underparts (and underwing), lacks rusty color above and bold facial marks, and is faster flying. Sharp-shinned Hawk has rounded (not pointed) wings. See Peregrine and Prairie falcons. **HABITAT:** Open woods, cliffs, grasslands, tundra; in migration and winter, also open country, marshes, beaches, locally in neighborhoods.

EURASIAN KESTREL *Falco tinnunculus*

Vagrant

13½–14 in. (34–36 cm). Similar to American Kestrel, but slightly larger. *Adult male:* Dusky mustache on grayish head, fully spotted pale chestnut upperparts and wing coverts, dusky outer wing; gray rump and tail, tail ending in black, white-tipped band; and spotted buff underbody. *Female:* Rusty brown upperparts and inner wings, duskier outer wings, rusty tail and buff white underparts, strongly barred above and boldly spotted in lines below except on vent. *Immature:* Brighter than female, with paler background color; both show dark subterminal tail band. **RANGE:** Eurasian species. Casual vagrant to e. N. America (Atlantic Canada south to FL) and along West Coast from w. AK to CA.

EURASIAN HOBBY *Falco subbuteo*

Vagrant

12½–13 in. (31–33 cm). Most aerial of the falcons; sickle-shaped wings and short tail produce a swiftlike outline. Flight dashing, with rapid, clipped wingbeats; when patrolling, action slower, more rowing, recalling Peregrine Falcon; never hovers. *Adult:* Distinctly patterned, with dark slate mustache, cap, and upperparts contrasting with cream throat, heavily streaked underparts, chestnut thighs and vent, and darkly barred underwing. *Juvenile:* Lacks chestnut areas. **SIMILAR SPECIES:** Peregrine Falcon. **RANGE:** Eurasian species. Casual vagrant to w. AK; accidental in WA.

APLOMADO FALCON *Falco femoralis* (see also p. 126)

Rare, local

15–16½ in. (38–42 cm). A medium-sized falcon, a little smaller than Peregrine Falcon. *Long wings and tail.* Note *dark underwing* and *black belly,* contrasting with white or pale cinnamon breast. Thighs and undertail coverts orange-brown. **VOICE:** High-pitched whistled scream: *klee-klee-klee-klee!* **SIMILAR SPECIES:** Peregrine Falcon. **RANGE:** Formerly a very rare visitor from Mex., but population in U.S. growing because of reintroduction program in s. TX and s. NM. **HABITAT:** Arid brushy deserts and grasslands, yucca flats.

SMALL FALCONS

AMERICAN KESTREL

♀

♂

♀

♂

♂

♂

♂

MERLIN

Pacific
(Black)

Taiga

Prairie

RARE FALCONS

EURASIAN HOBBY

APLOMADO FALCON

EURASIAN KESTREL

juvenile

♀

♂

adult

adult
♂

Accipiters (bird hawks) have short rounded wings and a long tail. They fly with several rapid beats and a short glide. They are better adapted to hunting in the woodlands than most other hawks. Females are larger than males. Immatures (not shown) have a streaked breast.

COOPER'S HAWK *Accipiter cooperii* p. 114
Underparts rusty (adult). Tail rounded and tipped with broad white terminal band. Note head and neck projecting noticeably beyond leading edge of wing.

NORTHERN GOSHAWK *Accipiter gentilis* p. 114
Adult with bold facial pattern, underbody heavily barred with pale gray. Tail and wings broad.

SHARP-SHINNED HAWK *Accipiter striatus* p. 114
Small. When folded, tail square or notched, with narrow pale tip. Fanned tail slightly rounded. Note small head and short neck barely projecting beyond wing.

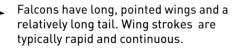

Falcons have long, pointed wings and a relatively long tail. Wing strokes are typically rapid and continuous.

PEREGRINE FALCON *Falco peregrinus* p. 122
Falcon shape; large; bold face pattern; longer wings than Merlin or Kestrel.

AMERICAN KESTREL *Falco sparverius* p. 124
Small; banded rufous tail. Paler underwing and less heavily marked underparts than Merlin.

MERLIN *Falco columbarius* p. 124
Small; heavily marked underparts and dark underwing; heavily banded tail.

GYRFALCON *Falco rusticolus* p. 122
Larger than Peregrine Falcon; without that bird's contrasting facial pattern, and with broader wings and tail. Varies in color from brown to gray to white.

APLOMADO FALCON *Falco femoralis* p. 124
Black belly band or vest, light chest, orange undertail. Tail barred with black.

PRAIRIE FALCON *Falco mexicanus* p. 122
Size of Peregrine Falcon. *Dark axillars* ("wingpits") and inner coverts.

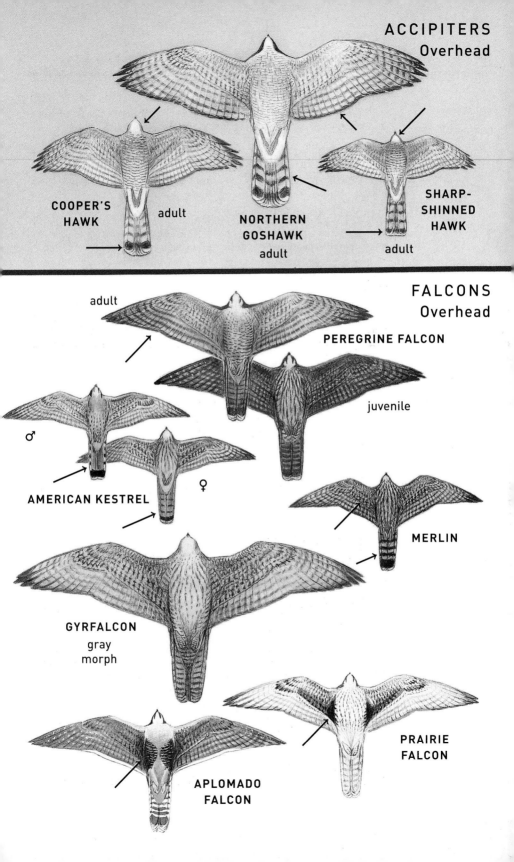

ACCIPITERS
Overhead

COOPER'S
HAWK
adult

NORTHERN
GOSHAWK
adult

SHARP-
SHINNED
HAWK
adult

FALCONS
Overhead

adult

PEREGRINE FALCON

juvenile

♂

AMERICAN KESTREL

♀

MERLIN

GYRFALCON
gray
morph

APLOMADO
FALCON

PRAIRIE
FALCON

FERRUGINOUS HAWK *Buteo regalis*   p. 120
Whitish underparts, with dark V formed by reddish thighs in adult. Wings and tail long for a buteo. A bird of western plains and open range.

GRAY HAWK *Buteo nitidus*   p. 116
Stocky. Broadly banded tail (suggestive of Broad-winged Hawk); adults have gray-barred underparts. Uncommon resident of Rio Grande Valley and se. AZ.

WHITE-TAILED HAWK *Buteo albicaudatus*   p. 116
Adult: Whitish underparts, gray head. White tail with black band near tip. Soars with marked dihedral. Resident of coastal prairie of TX.

NORTHERN HARRIER *Circus cyaneus*   p. 114
Male: Whitish wings with black tips and dark trailing edge. Gray hood.
Female: Brown, heavily streaked; note long, slim wings and tail.
Immature (not shown): Warm brown, unstreaked body, dark head. From above, all plumages have white rump.

WHITE-TAILED KITE *Elanus leucurus*   p. 112
Adult: Falcon-shaped. White body; whitish tail; dark underside to primaries.

MISSISSIPPI KITE *Ictinia mississippiensis*   p. 112
Falcon-shaped. *Adult:* Pale gray head, black tail, dark gray and blackish wings, gray body.
Immature: Streaked breast; banded square-tipped or notched tail.

Kites (except Snail Kite and Hook-billed Kite) are falcon-shaped but, unlike falcons, are buoyant gliders, not power fliers. All are southern.

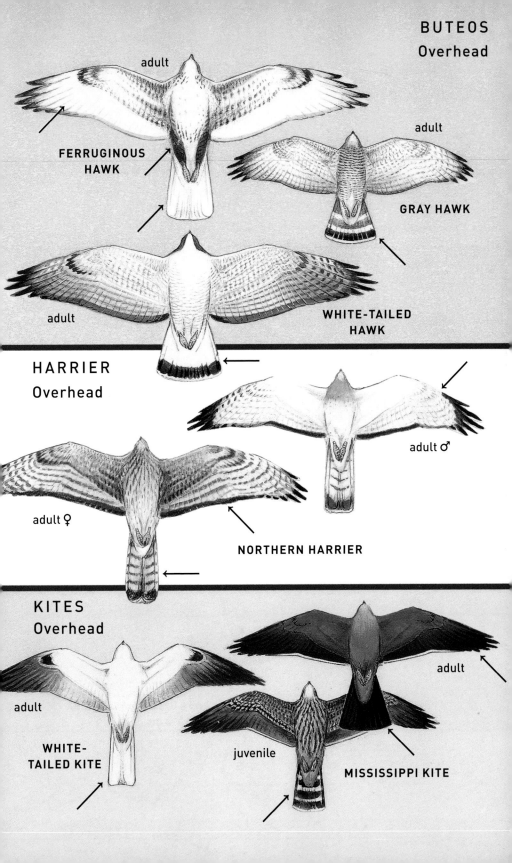

BUTEOS
Overhead

adult

FERRUGINOUS
HAWK

adult

GRAY HAWK

adult

WHITE-TAILED
HAWK

HARRIER
Overhead

adult ♂

adult ♀

NORTHERN HARRIER

KITES
Overhead

adult

adult

WHITE-
TAILED KITE

juvenile

MISSISSIPPI KITE

RED-TAILED HAWK *Buteo jamaicensis* p. 120
Dark patagial bar at fore edge of wing is best mark from below. *Adult:*
Light chest, streaked belly (often forming belly band); tail plain, with hint
of red and little or no banding.
Immature: Streaked below, has light tail banding.

SWAINSON'S HAWK *Buteo swainsoni* p. 120
Adult: Dark breast-band. Long, pointed, two-toned wings.
Immature: Similar, but has streaks on underbody.

RED-SHOULDERED HAWK *Buteo lineatus* p. 118
Adult: Tail strongly banded (white bands narrower than dark ones).
Strongly barred with rusty coloring on body and underwing coverts.
Immature: Chest and belly heavily streaked. Both immature and adult
show light crescent "window" on outer wings, longish tail.

BROAD-WINGED HAWK *Buteo platypterus* p. 118
Smaller and chunkier than Red-shouldered with shorter tail, more
pointed wings. *Adult:* Widely banded tail (white bands wider); underwing
pale with dark rear margin and tip.
Immature: Body usually streaked, tail narrowly banded. Pale underwings
may show lighter "window" near wingtips when molting in first spring.

ROUGH-LEGGED HAWK *Buteo lagopus* p. 118
Note black carpal patch contrasting with white flight feathers. Broad,
blackish band ("cummerbund") across belly is distinctive in female and
immature. Tail light, with broad, dark subterminal band. Adult male
darker chested, has multiple bands on tail, less bold belly patch.

Buteos are chunky, with broad wings and a broad, rounded tail.
They soar and wheel high in the air.

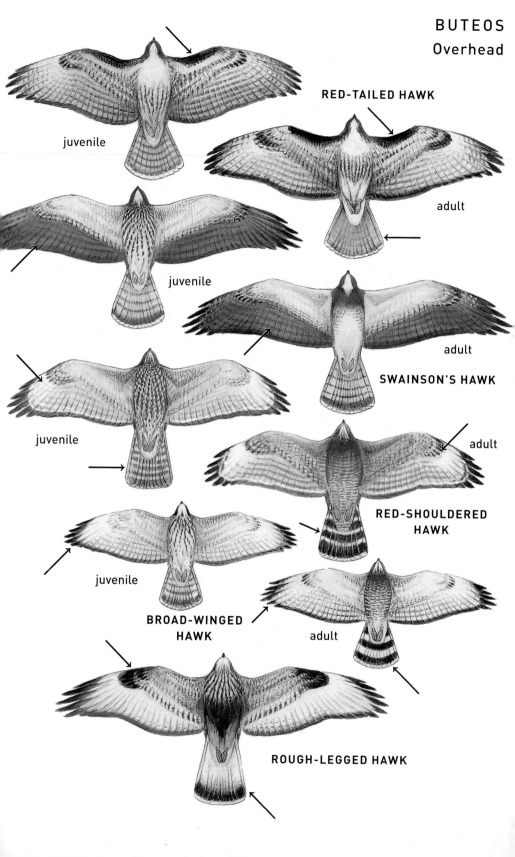

BUTEOS
Overhead

RED-TAILED HAWK

juvenile

adult

juvenile

adult

SWAINSON'S HAWK

juvenile

adult

RED-SHOULDERED HAWK

juvenile

BROAD-WINGED HAWK

adult

ROUGH-LEGGED HAWK

Dark Birds of Prey Overhead

CRESTED CARACARA *Caracara cheriway*   p. 122
Whitish chest, black belly, large *pale patches* in primaries, white tail with black band. Elongated neck, stiff-winged flight.

ROUGH-LEGGED HAWK *Buteo lagopus* (dark morph)   p. 118
Dark body and wing linings; *whitish flight feathers;* tail light from below, with one broad, *black terminal band* in female; additional bands in male.

FERRUGINOUS HAWK *Buteo regalis* (dark morph)   p. 120
Similar to dark-morph Rough-legged Hawk, but tail whitish, without dark banding. Note also white wrist marks, or "commas."

SWAINSON'S HAWK *Buteo swainsoni* (dark morph)   p. 120
In dark morph, fairly pointed wings are usually dark throughout, *including flight feathers;* tail narrowly banded, whitish undertail coverts. Rufous morph may be rustier, with lighter rufous wing linings.

RED-TAILED HAWK *Buteo jamaicensis* (dark morph)   p. 120
Typical chunky shape of Red-tailed; tail reddish above, pale tinged with rusty below; variable. Dark patagial bar on leading edge of wing obscured.

"HARLAN'S" RED-TAILED HAWK   p. 120
Buteo jamaicensis harlani (dark morph)
Similar to dark-morph Red-tailed Hawk. Breast mottled white; tail tends to be mottled with gray and whitish and with dusky subterminal band, lacks obvious red; primary tips barred dark and light.

BROAD-WINGED HAWK *Buteo platypterus* (dark morph)   p. 118
Typical size and shape of Broad-winged. Tail pattern and flight feathers as in light morph, but body and wing linings dark. Note whiter flight feathers than Short-tailed.

ZONE-TAILED HAWK *Buteo albonotatus* (immature)   p. 116
Slim and longish, *two-toned wings* (suggesting Turkey Vulture) with barred flight feathers. Several white bands on slim tail (only one visible on folded tail). Yellow legs.

SHORT-TAILED HAWK *Buteo brachyurus* (dark morph)   p. 118
Jet-black body and wing linings. Lightly banded tail; flight feathers more shaded than in dark Broad-wing.

HARRIS'S HAWK *Parabuteo unicinctus*   p. 116
Chocolate brown body, chestnut wing linings. Very broad white band at base of black tail, narrow white terminal band.

COMMON BLACK-HAWK *Buteogallus anthracinus*   p. 116
Thickset black wings; faint light patches near wingtips. Short, broad tail with broad white band at *midtail* and very broad black subterminal band. Whereas Zone-tailed Hawk seems to mimic Turkey Vulture, a deceptive ploy when it is hunting, chunkier Common Black-Hawk may be compared to Black Vulture.

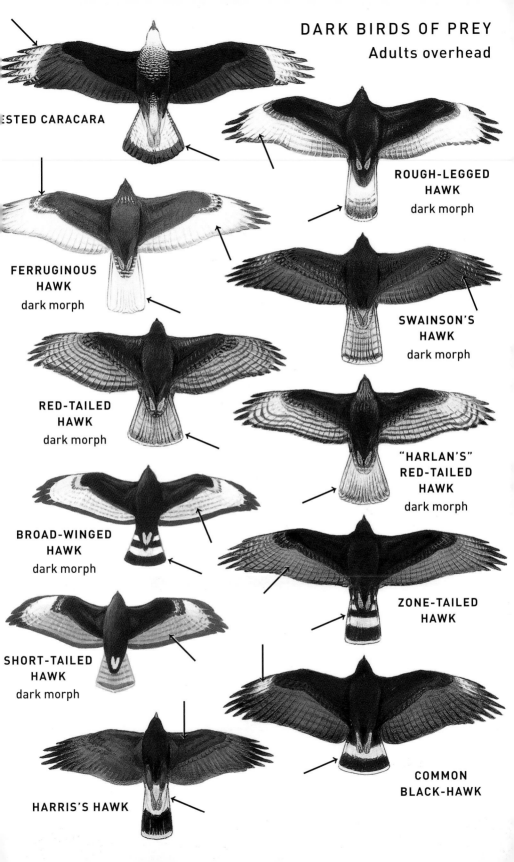

DARK BIRDS OF PREY
Adults overhead

ESTED CARACARA

ROUGH-LEGGED
HAWK
dark morph

FERRUGINOUS
HAWK
dark morph

SWAINSON'S
HAWK
dark morph

RED-TAILED
HAWK
dark morph

"HARLAN'S"
RED-TAILED
HAWK
dark morph

BROAD-WINGED
HAWK
dark morph

ZONE-TAILED
HAWK

SHORT-TAILED
HAWK
dark morph

COMMON
BLACK-HAWK

HARRIS'S HAWK

BALD EAGLE *Haliaeetus leucocephalus* p. 110
Adult: White head and tail.
Immature: Some white in wing linings, often on body.

GOLDEN EAGLE *Aquila chrysaetos* p. 110
Adult: Almost uniformly dark; wing linings dark.
Immature: White patch at base of primaries and tail; no white on body.

OSPREY *Pandion haliaetus* p. 110
White body and coverts; black wrist patch; crooked wing.

TURKEY VULTURE *Cathartes aura* p. 106
Mostly brownish black. Two-toned wings held in distinct dihedral. Small head, red in adult, gray in immature. Longish tail. Tips and teeters in flight.

BLACK VULTURE *Coragyps atratus* p. 106
Blackish overall. Silver wing patch. Wings held flat or in very slight dihedral. Rapid, shallow wingbeats. Stubby tail. Gray head.

Where the Bald Eagle, Turkey Vulture, and Osprey all are found, they can be separated at a great distance by their manner of soaring: the Bald Eagle with flat wings; the Turkey Vulture with a dihedral; the Osprey often with a gull-like kink or crook in its wings.

Turkey Vulture (p. 106)

Black Vulture (p. 106)

EAGLES, OSPREY, AND VULTURES
Overhead

BALD EAGLE
adult

Bald Eagle
juvenile

GOLDEN EAGLE
adult

Golden Eagle
juvenile

OSPREY
adult

Coots, Gallinules, and Rails Family Rallidae

Rails are rather hen-shaped marsh birds, many of secretive habits and mysterious voices, more often heard than seen. Flight is brief and reluctant, with legs dangling. Gallinules and coots are much easier to see; they swim and might be confused with small ducks except for smaller head, forehead shield, and chickenlike bill. They spend most of their time swimming but may also feed on shores. Often vocal, giving loud squawks, grunts, and peeps. **FOOD**: Aquatic plants, seeds, insects, frogs, crustaceans, mollusks. **RANGE**: Nearly worldwide.

AMERICAN COOT *Fulica americana*   Uncommon to common M176
15–15½ in. (38–39 cm). A slaty, ducklike bird with blackish head and neck, slate gray body, *white bill*, and divided white patch under tail. No side striping. Its big feet are lobed ("scallops" on toes). Gregarious. When swimming, pumps head back and forth; dabbles but also dives from surface. Taking off, it skitters, flight labored, big feet trailing beyond short tail, narrow white border showing along rear of wings. Aberrant birds may show some additional white or yellowish on forehead above bill. *Immature:* Slightly paler, with duller bill. Downy young has hairy, *orange-red* head and shoulders. **VOICE**: Grating *kuk-kuk-kuk-kuk; kakakakakaka;* etc.; also a measured *ka-ha, ha-ha;* various cackles, croaks. **SIMILAR SPECIES**: Common Moorhen slightly smaller, browner above, has thin white band on flanks, different-colored bill. Coots flock more on open water and land. **HABITAT**: Ponds, lakes, marshes; in winter, also fields, park ponds, lawns, salt bays.

COMMON MOORHEN *Gallinula chloropus*   Uncommon M175
14 in. (36 cm). Note adult's rather chickenlike *red bill with yellow tip, red forehead shield*, and white band on flanks. When walking, flicks white undertail coverts; while swimming, pumps head like a coot. *Immature:* Duller bill. **VOICE**: Croaking *kr-r-ruk*, repeated; a froglike *kup;* also *kek, kek, kek* (higher than coot's call); loud, complaining, henlike notes. **SIMILAR SPECIES**: American Coot, immature Purple Gallinule. **HABITAT**: Freshwater marshes, reedy ponds.

PURPLE GALLINULE *Porphyrio martinica*   Uncommon M174
13 in. (33 cm). Very colorful; swims, wades, and climbs bushes. *Adult:* Head and underparts *deep violet-purple*, back bronzy green. Shield on forehead *pale blue;* bill red with yellow tip. Legs *yellow,* conspicuous in flight. *Immature:* Buffy brown below, dark above tinged greenish; bill dark; sides unstriped. **VOICE**: Henlike cackling, *kek, kek, kek;* also guttural notes, sharp reedy cries. **SIMILAR SPECIES**: Common Moorhen has *red* frontal shield, lacks greenish plumage, has duller legs and white side stripe; young moorhen also has whitish side stripe. Young American Coot much darker overall, has pale bill. Purple Swamphen (*Porphyrio porphyrio,* not illustrated), introduced from Eurasia and becoming established in s. FL, is much larger and has red legs and a huge all-red bill and frontal shield. **HABITAT**: Freshwater swamps, marshes, ponds.

COOTS AND GALLINULES

coots skitter on takeoff

lobed foot of coot

juvenile

adult

coot chick

moorhen
chick

juvenile

adult

AMERICAN COOT

adult

juvenile

adult

COMMON MOORHEN

juvenile

adult

**PURPLE
GALLINULE**

VIRGINIA RAIL *Rallus limicola*   Fairly common M172

9½ in. (24 cm). A small rusty rail with gray cheeks, black bars on flanks, and long, slightly decurved, reddish bill with dark tip. Near size of meadowlark; only small rail with *long slender* bill. Juvenile in late summer shows much black. **VOICE:** Descending grunt, *wuk-wuk-wuk-wuk*, etc.; also *kidick, kidick,* etc.; various "kicking" and grunting sounds. **SIMILAR SPECIES:** Sora has small stubby bill, unbarred undertail coverts. Clapper and King rails much larger. **HABITAT:** Fresh and brackish marshes; in winter, also salt marshes.

KING RAIL *Rallus elegans*   Uncommon, secretive M171

15 in. (38 cm). A large rusty rail with long slender bill; twice the size of Virginia Rail, or about that of a small chicken. Similar to Clapper Rail, but note rusty/chestnut cheeks and black-and-white flanks, more rusty overall with *bolder back pattern* (blacker feathers with buffier edges); prefers fresh marshes. **VOICE:** Low, slow, grunting *bup-bup, bup-bup-bup,* etc., or evenly spaced *chuck-chuck-chuck* (deeper than Virginia Rail). **SIMILAR SPECIES:** Clapper Rail. Virginia Rail half the size, has slaty gray cheeks. *Note:* Hybrids between Clapper and King occur. **HABITAT:** Fresh and brackish marshes, rice fields, ditches, swamps. In winter, also salt marshes.

CLAPPER RAIL *Rallus longirostris*   Fairly common M170

14½ in. (37 cm). The large "marsh hen" of coastal marshes. Sometimes swims. Note henlike appearance; strong legs; long, slightly decurved bill; barred flanks; and white patch under short cocked tail, which it flicks nervously. Cheeks gray. Western birds have rusty orange underparts. **VOICE:** Clattering *kek-kek-kek-kek,* etc., or *cha-cha-cha,* etc. **SIMILAR SPECIES:** King Rail prefers fresh (sometimes brackish) marshes, has bolder pattern on back and flanks, rusty brown on wings. Its breast is cinnamon, but Clappers along Gulf Coast and in CA and Southwest show similar warm tawny tones. Clapper has grayer cheeks. Where these two rails occur in adjacent brackish marshes, they occasionally hybridize. **HABITAT:** Coastal populations in salt marshes; in interior Southwest, freshwater marshes.

LONG-BILLED RAILS

adult

juvenile

VIRGINIA RAIL

KING RAIL

Atlantic
Coast

Gulf Coast
and West

**CLAPPER
RAIL**

chick

Limpkin
(p. 100)
for comparison

SORA *Porzana carolina*   Fairly common M173
8½ in. (22 cm). Note *short yellow* bill. *Adult:* A small, plump, gray-brown rail with *black patch* on face and throat. Short, cocked tail reveals white or buff undertail coverts. *Immature:* Lacks dark throat patch and is browner. **VOICE:** Descending whinny, *whee-ee-ee-ee-ee-ee-e-e-e.* Also a plaintive whistled *keu-wee?* Clapping one's hands causes startled birds to utter a sharp *keek.* **SIMILAR SPECIES:** Immature may be confused with smaller and rarer Yellow Rail, which has large white wing patches and blacker-centered feathers above. Virginia Rail has slender bill. **HABITAT:** Freshwater marshes; in migration, also wet meadows; in winter, also salt marshes.

YELLOW RAIL *Coturnicops noveboracensis*   Scarce, secretive M168
7¼ in. (18 cm). Note *white wing patch* (in flight). A small buffy-and-black rail, suggesting a week-old chick. Bill very short, greenish or yellowish. Back dark, striped, barred, and checkered with buff, white, and black. *Mouselike; very difficult to see.* **VOICE:** Nocturnal ticking notes, often in long series: *tic-tic, tic-tic-tic, tic-tic, tic-tic-tic,* etc., in alternating groups of two and three. Compared to hitting two small stones together. **SIMILAR SPECIES:** Young Sora somewhat larger, buffier overall, lacks dark barring and checkering above, has thin pale trailing edge to wing. **HABITAT:** Grassy marshes, wet meadows; winters mostly in salt marshes and grain fields.

BLACK RAIL *Laterallus jamaicensis*   Scarce, local, secretive M169
6 in. (15 cm). A tiny blackish rail with small *black* bill; about the size of a young sparrow. Nape deep chestnut. *Very difficult to glimpse. Caution:* All young rails in downy plumage are black. **VOICE:** Male (mostly at night), *kiki-doo* or *kiki-krrr* (or *kitty go*). Also a growl. **HABITAT:** Salt marshes, freshwater marshes, grassy meadows.

JACANAS Family Jacanidae

Shorebird relatives that look like gallinules but walk like rails. Dark birds with very long toes perfect for walking over floating aquatic vegetation. Sexes alike. **FOOD:** Aquatic insects, seeds, and vegetation. **RANGE:** Pantropical.

NORTHERN JACANA *Jacana spinosa*   Vagrant
9½ in. (24 cm). This vagrant has spectacularly long toes for walking on lily pads. *Adult:* Chestnut body with dark head. Yellow bill and forehead frontal shield. Striking yellow primaries and secondaries in flight. Holds wings over head when it lands. *Immature:* Has white underparts, distinct line behind eye. **VOICE:** Rapid series of high, nasal notes: *jeek-jeek-jeek-jeek.* **RANGE:** Casual visitor from Mex. to TX; accidental in AZ. **HABITAT:** Frequents ponds with emergent vegetation, especially lily pads.

SHORT-BILLED RAILS AND JACANA

adult

immature

chick

SORA

YELLOW RAIL

immature

NORTHERN JACANA

adult

BLACK RAIL

Shorebirds

Many shorebirds (or "waders," as they are called in the Old World) are real puzzlers to the novice, and to many experienced birders as well! There are a dozen plovers in our area, and nearly 60 sandpipers and their allies. Most species have two or three different plumages: breeding adult, nonbreeding adult, and juvenal. Being able to properly age many species is an important part of correctly identifying them. Noting size, shape, and feeding style is also a critical part of the identification process.

Plovers are usually more compact and thicker necked than most sandpipers, with a pigeonlike bill and larger eyes. They run in short starts and stops.

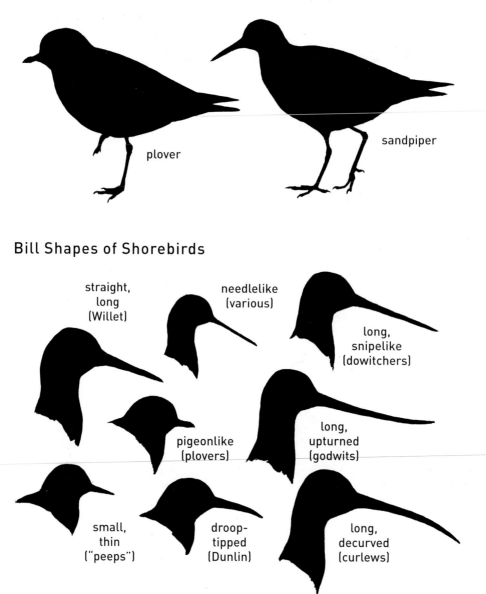

plover

sandpiper

Bill Shapes of Shorebirds

straight, long (Willet)

needlelike (various)

long, snipelike (dowitchers)

pigeonlike (plovers)

long, upturned (godwits)

small, thin ("peeps")

droop-tipped (Dunlin)

long, decurved (curlews)

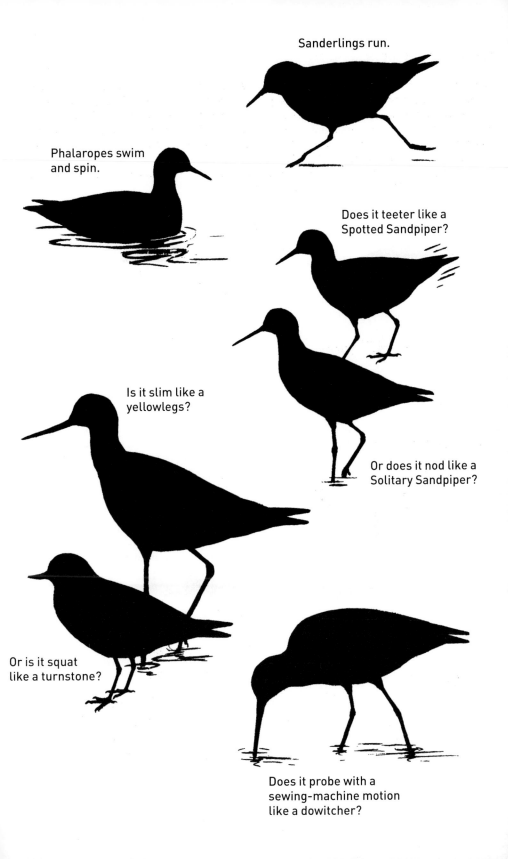

Sanderlings run.

Phalaropes swim and spin.

Does it teeter like a Spotted Sandpiper?

Is it slim like a yellowlegs?

Or does it nod like a Solitary Sandpiper?

Or is it squat like a turnstone?

Does it probe with a sewing-machine motion like a dowitcher?

PLOVERS Family Charadriidae

Wading birds, more compactly built and thicker necked than most sandpipers, with shorter, pigeonlike bill and larger eyes. Call notes assist identification. Unlike most sandpipers, plovers run in short starts and stops. Sexes alike or differ slightly. **FOOD:** Small marine life, insects, some vegetable matter. **RANGE:** Nearly worldwide.

BLACK-BELLIED PLOVER Common M180
Pluvialis squatarola (see also p. 168)
11½ in. (29 cm). A large plover. *Breeding adult:* Have *black face and breast (slightly duller in female)* and pale speckled back. *Nonbreeding adult and immature:* Look tan-gray but can be recognized as plovers by stocky shape, hunched posture, and short, pigeonlike bill. In flight, in any plumage, note *black wingpits* and white rump and tail. **VOICE:** Plaintive slurred whistle, *tlee-oo-eee* or *whee-er-ee* (middle note lower). **SIMILAR SPECIES:** American and Pacific golden-plovers slightly smaller and slimmer, smaller billed, buffier or more golden on at least some feathering, have more distinct supercilium, and *lack pattern of white in wings and tail.* Their wingpits are *gray,* not black. **HABITAT:** Mudflats, marshes, beaches, rocks, short-grass habitats; in summer, tundra.

AMERICAN GOLDEN-PLOVER Uncommon M181
Pluvialis dominica (see also p. 168)
10¼–10½ in. (26–27 cm). Size of Killdeer. Shows distinct wingtip extension of three to five primary tips, well beyond tail tip. *Breeding adult:* Dark, spangled above with *whitish and pale yellow spots;* underparts black (slightly mottled in female). *Broad white stripe* runs over eye and down sides of neck and breast. *Nonbreeding adult and juvenile:* Gray-brown, darker above than below, with distinct pale supercilium, dark crown. **VOICE:** Whistled *queedle* or *que-e-a* (dropping at end). **SIMILAR SPECIES:** Black-bellied Plover, Pacific Golden-Plover. **HABITAT:** Prairies, mudflats, shores, short-grass pastures, sod farms; in summer, tundra.

PACIFIC GOLDEN-PLOVER Uncommon, local M182
Pluvialis fulva (see also p. 168)
10–10¼ in. (25–26 cm). Very similar to American Golden-Plover. *Breeding adult:* White neck stripe *extends down to flanks* and there is more white on undertail coverts (but molting American Golden-Plovers may have this look). Golden spangles on back brighter. Bill slightly larger, legs slightly longer. Wingtip extension shows only one or two visible primary tips, and they barely extend beyond tail tip. *Nonbreeding adult and juvenile:* Also *more golden* above than other plovers, and juveniles may also be brightly washed with golden buff on face and breast. **VOICE:** Whistled *chu-wee* or *chu-wee-dle.* **HABITAT:** Same as American, though typically breeds in lower, wetter tundra.

MOUNTAIN PLOVER *Charadrius montanus* Scarce, local M188
9 in. (23 cm). White forehead and line over eye, contrasting with dark crown. In nonbreeding plumage, may be told from nonbreeding golden-plovers by tan-brown back devoid of mottling and by tan, unmarked breast. Has pale blue-gray legs, light wing stripe, and dark tail band. **VOICE:** Low whistle, variable. **SIMILAR SPECIES:** Killdeer, Black-bellied Plover, golden-plovers, Buff-breasted Sandpiper. **HABITAT:** Plowed fields, short-grass plains, dry sod farms.

nonbreeding

nonbreeding

breeding

juvenile

BLACK-BELLIED PLOVER

nonbreeding

n-
eeding

nonbreeding

breeding

AMERICAN GOLDEN-PLOVER

nonbreeding

breeding

nonbreeding

PACIFIC GOLDEN-PLOVER

MOUNTAIN PLOVER

breeding

COMMON RINGED PLOVER *Charadrius hiaticula* Rare, local
7½ in. (19 cm). A Eurasian species, very similar to Semipalmated Plover; best distinguished by *voice*. Slightly longer bill, darker cheeks. Lacks obvious orbital ring. Breeding adults have slightly bolder supercilium, wider breast-band. In all birds there is basal webbing between only two toes, but this is very difficult to see. VOICE: Softer, more minor *poo-eep* or *too-li*. RANGE: Breeds in e. Canadian Arctic and on St. Lawrence Is., AK; winters on Old World. Casual or accidental migrant elsewhere in N. America. HABITAT: Same as Semipalmated Plover.

SEMIPALMATED PLOVER Common M185
Charadrius semipalmatus (see also p. 168)
7¼ in. (18 cm). A small, plump, brown-backed plover, half the size of Killdeer, with *single dark breast-band*. *Adult:* Bill orangey with black tip or (nonbreeding) nearly all dark. Orangey orbital ring. Legs bright orange or yellow. *Juvenile:* Slightly browner above, and breast-band may be incomplete. VOICE: Plaintive, upward-slurred *chi-we* or *too-li*. SIMILAR SPECIES: Whereas Piping and Snowy plovers are pale — color of dry sand — Semipalmated is darker above, like wet sand or mud. Snowy Plover also has thinner bill, darker legs. HABITAT: Shores, tidal flats, wet fields; in summer, tundra.

PIPING PLOVER *Charadrius melodus* (see also p. 168) Uncommon M186
7¼ in. (18 cm). As pallid as a beach flea or sand crab — color of dry sand. Complete or incomplete dark ring around neck. Legs yellow or orange. *Breeding adult:* Bill has yellow-orange base, black tip. *Nonbreeding adult and juvenile:* Black on collar indistinct or lacking, bill all dark. Note tail pattern. Adults perform stiff-winged "bat-flight" on breeding territory. VOICE: Plaintive whistle: *peep-lo* (first note higher). SIMILAR SPECIES: Snowy and Semipalmated plovers. HABITAT: Sandy beaches, dry mudflats; in summer, also lakeshores and river islands.

SNOWY PLOVER Uncommon M183
Charadrius alexandrinus (see also p. 168)
6¼–6½ in. (16–17 cm). A pale plover of beaches and alkaline flats. *Male:* Has *slim black bill*, dark (sometimes pale) legs, and *dark ear patch. Female and juvenile:* May lack black in plumage. VOICE: Musical whistle, *pe-wee-ah* or *o-wee-ah*; also a low *prit*. SIMILAR SPECIES: Juvenile and nonbreeding Piping Plovers may also have dark (though stubbier) bill, but they have *white on rump*, visible in flight, and brighter legs. HABITAT: Beaches, sandy flats, alkaline lakeshores.

WILSON'S PLOVER Uncommon M184
Charadrius wilsonia (see also p. 168)
7¾–8 in. (19–20 cm). A "ringed" plover, larger than Semipalmated Plover, with *wider breast-band* and longer, *heavier black bill*. Legs pinkish gray. VOICE: Emphatic whistled *whit!* or *wheet!* HABITAT: Open beaches, tidal flats, sandy islands.

KILLDEER *Charadrius vociferus* (see also p. 168) Common M187
10½ in. (27 cm). The common, noisy plover of farm country and playing fields. Note *two black breast-bands* (chick has only one band and might be confused with Wilson's Plover). In flight or distraction display near nest, shows *rusty orange rump*, longish tail, white wing stripe. VOICE: Noisy, and often heard at night. Loud, insistent *kill-deeah*, repeated; plaintive *dee-ee* (rising), *dee-dee-dee*, etc. Also a low trill. SIMILAR SPECIES: Other banded plovers smaller, have single breast-band. HABITAT: Fields, airports, lawns, riverbanks, mudflats, shores.

BANDED PLOVERS

COMMON
RINGED
PLOVER

breeding

nonbreeding

breeding

SEMIPALMATED
PLOVER

nonbreeding

east-
and
y be
roken

breeding

PIPING PLOVER

non-
breeding

♂

breeding

SNOWY
PLOVER

♀

♂

WILSON'S
PLOVER

KILLDEER

chick

Common Ringed

Piping

Killdeer

Wilson's

wy

Semipalmated

OYSTERCATCHERS Family Haematopodidae

Large waders with long, laterally flattened, chisel-tipped, red bill. Sexes alike. **FOOD**: Mollusks, crabs, marine worms. **RANGE**: Widespread on coasts of world; inland in some areas of Europe and Asia.

AMERICAN OYSTERCATCHER *Haematopus palliatus* Fairly common M189
17½–18½ in. (44–47 cm). A very noisy, thickset, black-headed shorebird with dark back, white belly, and large white wing and tail patches. Outstanding feature is large straight red bill, flattened laterally. Legs pale pink. *Immature:* Bill dark-tipped. **VOICE**: Piercing *wheep!* or *kleep!*; a loud *pic, pic, pic.* **SIMILAR SPECIES**: Differs from Black Oystercatcher in having *white belly,* browner upperparts, white wing stripe and rump patch. Subspecies found in nw. Mex. *(frazari)* somewhat less clean-cut than birds in e. N. America; may have some dark spotting on upper breast. Also, hybrids between the two oystercatcher species occur, which show more extensive dark mottling on underparts and rump. See also Black Skimmer. **HABITAT**: Coastal beaches, tidal flats.

BLACK OYSTERCATCHER *Haematopus bachmani* Uncommon M190
17–17½ in. (43–44 cm). A large, heavily built, blackish shorebird with straight *orange-red bill,* flattened laterally. Thickish legs are pale pinkish. *Immature:* Bill dark-tipped. **VOICE**: Piercing, sharply repeated, whistled *wheep!* or *kleep!,* often in descending series. **SIMILAR SPECIES**: American Oystercatcher. **HABITAT**: Rocky coasts, sea islets.

STILTS AND AVOCETS Family Recurvirostridae

Slim waders with very long legs and very slender bill (bent upward in avocets). Sexes fairly similar. **FOOD**: Insects, crustaceans, other aquatic life. **RANGE**: N., Cen., and S. America, Africa, s. Eurasia, Australia, Pacific region.

BLACK-NECKED STILT *Himantopus mexicanus* Fairly common M191
14 in. (36 cm). A large, extremely slim wader; black above (female and immature tinged brown), white below. Note *extremely long pinkish red legs,* needlelike bill. In flight, black *unpatterned* wings contrast strikingly with white rump, tail, and underparts. **VOICE**: Sharp yipping: *kyip, kyip, kyip.* **SIMILAR SPECIES**: Nonbreeding American Avocet. **HABITAT**: Marshes, mudflats, pools, shallow lakes (fresh and alkaline), flooded fields.

AMERICAN AVOCET *Recurvirostra americana* Fairly common M192
18 in. (46 cm). A large, slim shorebird with very slender, *upturned bill,* more upturned in female. This and striking white-and-black pattern make this bird unique. In breeding plumage, head and neck pinkish tan or orangey buff; in nonbreeding plumage, this color replaced by pale gray. Avocets feed with scythelike sweep of head and bill. **VOICE**: Sharp *wheek* or *kleet,* excitedly repeated. **HABITAT**: Mudflats, shallow lakes, marshes, prairie ponds.

OYSTERCATCHERS, STILT, AND AVOCET

BLACK
OYSTERCATCHER

AMERICAN
OYSTERCATCHER

BLACK-NECKED
STILT

breeding

breeding

nonbreeding

AMERICAN
AVOCET

SANDPIPERS, PHALAROPES, AND ALLIES
Family Scolopacidae

Small to large shorebirds. Bills more slender than those of plovers. Sexes mostly similar, except in phalaropes (swimmers formerly regarded as a separate family). **FOOD:** Insects, crustaceans, mollusks, worms, etc. **RANGE:** Cosmopolitan.

WILLET *Tringa semipalmata* (see also p. 170)   Fairly common M197
15–16 in. (38–41 cm). Stockier than Greater Yellowlegs; has grayer look, heavier bill, blue-gray legs. In flight, note *striking black-and-white wing pattern*. At rest, this large wader is rather nondescript: gray above, somewhat mottled or barred below when breeding, unmarked in nonbreeding plumage. *Juvenile:* Browner above with some light buff spots. *Note:* Western breeding population larger, has longer, thinner bill and is paler overall than eastern breeding population. **VOICE:** Musical, repetitious *pill-will-willet* (in breeding season); a loud *kay-ee* (second note lower). Also a rapidly repeated *kip-kip-kip*, etc. In flight, *kree-ree-ree.* **SIMILAR SPECIES:** Greater Yellowlegs; see also dowitchers, Wandering Tattler (which is much smaller). **HABITAT:** Marshes, wet meadows, mudflats, beaches.

GREATER YELLOWLEGS   Common M196
Tringa melanoleuca (see also p. 172)
14 in. (36 cm). Note *bright yellow legs* (shared with next species). A slim gray sandpiper; back checkered with gray, black, and white. Often teeters body. In flight, appears *dark-winged* (no stripe), with *whitish rump and tail*. Bill long, *slightly upturned, paler at base*. Breeding adult heavily barred below. **VOICE:** Three-note strident whistle, *dear! dear! dear!* **SIMILAR SPECIES:** Lesser Yellowlegs, Willet. **HABITAT:** Marshes, mudflats, streams, ponds, flooded fields; in summer, wooded muskeg, spruce bogs.

LESSER YELLOWLEGS *Tringa flavipes* (see also p. 172)   Common M198
10½ in. (27 cm). Like Greater Yellowlegs, but smaller (obvious when both species are together). Lesser's shorter, slimmer, all-dark bill is *straight* and about *equal to length of head;* Greater's appears slightly uptilted, paler based, and longer than bird's head. Readily separated by voice. **VOICE:** *Yew* or *yu-yu* (usually one or two notes); less forceful than usual three-syllable call of Greater. **SIMILAR SPECIES:** Solitary and Stilt sandpipers, Wilson's Phalarope. Both yellowlegs species may swim briefly, like a phalarope. **HABITAT:** Marshes, mudflats, ponds, flooded fields; in summer, open, moist boreal woods and taiga.

SOLITARY SANDPIPER   Uncommon M194
Tringa solitaria (see also p. 172)
8½ in. (22 cm). Note *dark wings* and conspicuous *white sides of tail* (crossed by bold black bars). A dark-backed sandpiper, whitish below, with *light eye-ring* and greenish legs. Nods like a yellowlegs. Usually alone, seldom in groups. **VOICE:** *Peet!* or *peet-weet-weet!* (higher and more strident than Spotted Sandpiper's call). **SIMILAR SPECIES:** Lesser Yellowlegs has bright yellow (not greenish) legs, white (not dark) rump, is paler overall, lacks bold eye-ring. Spotted Sandpiper teeters, tail (not head) has white wedge at breast-side, different wing and tail patterns. **HABITAT:** Streamsides, wooded swamps and ponds, ditches, freshwater marshes.

STILT SANDPIPER *Calidris himantopus*   See p. 162
Nonbreeding: Long yellow-green legs, slight droop to bill, white rump; distinct light eyebrow (supercilium).

WILSON'S PHALAROPE *Phalaropus tricolor*   See p. 166
Nonbreeding: Straight needle bill, clear white underparts, pale gray back, dull yellow legs.

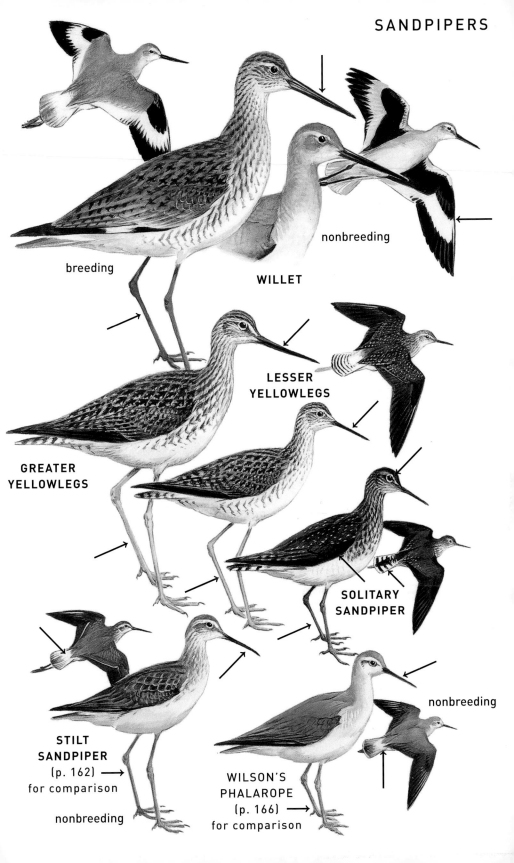

breeding

nonbreeding

WILLET

LESSER
YELLOWLEGS

GREATER
YELLOWLEGS

SOLITARY
SANDPIPER

STILT
SANDPIPER
(p. 162) ⟶
for comparison

nonbreeding

WILSON'S
PHALAROPE
(p. 166) ⟶
for comparison

nonbreeding

HUDSONIAN GODWIT *Limosa haemastica* (see also p. 170)   Scarce M202
15–15½ in. (38–39 cm). Rather large size and long, *slightly upturned* bill
mark this wader as a godwit; *blackish wing linings* proclaim it as this species. Black tail *ringed broadly with white.* Breeding: Male ruddy-breasted,
female duller. *Nonbreeding:* Both sexes gray-backed, pale-breasted. **VOICE:**
Tawit! (or *godwit!*); higher pitched than Marbled Godwit's call. **SIMILAR
SPECIES:** Bar-tailed Godwit has different wing and tail patterns; see Black-
tailed Godwit, a vagrant from Eurasia. **HABITAT:** Mudflats, prairie pools;
in summer, marshy taiga and tundra.

MARBLED GODWIT *Limosa fedoa* (see also p. 170)   Fairly common M204
17½–18½ in. (44–46 cm). Rich, mottled *buff brown* color identifies this
species. Underwing linings *cinnamon.* **VOICE:** Accented *kerwhit!* (*godwit!*);
also *raddica, raddica.* **SIMILAR SPECIES:** When head tucked in, may be difficult to tell from Long-billed Curlew except by leg color (blackish in godwit, blue-gray in curlew); in AK, see Bar-tailed Godwit. Hudsonian Godwit has white on wings and tail, blackish wing linings. **HABITAT:** Prairies,
pools, shores, mudflats, beaches.

LONG-BILLED CURLEW   Uncommon M201
Numenius americanus (see also p. 170)
22–24 in. (55–60 cm). Note *very long, sickle-shaped bill* (4–8½ in.;
10–21 cm). Larger than Whimbrel and more buffy overall; lacks distinct
dark crown stripes. Overhead shows *cinnamon wing linings.* In young
birds, bill may be scarcely longer than that of Whimbrel. **VOICE:** Loud *cur-
lee* (rising inflection); rapid, whistled *kli-li-li-li.* "Song" a trilled, liquid
curleeeeeeeeeuuu. **SIMILAR SPECIES:** Marbled Godwit. **HABITAT:** High
plains, rangeland; in winter, cultivated land, mudflats, beaches, salt marshes.

WHIMBREL *Numenius phaeopus* (see also p. 170)   Fairly common M200
17–18 in. (43–46 cm). A large gray-brown wader with long *decurved bill.*
Much grayer brown than Long-billed Curlew; bill shorter (2¾–4 in.;
7–10 cm); crown *striped.* **VOICE:** Five to seven short, rapid whistles: *hee-
hee-hee-hee-hee-hee.* **SIMILAR SPECIES:** Long-billed Curlew. **HABITAT:**
Mudflats, beaches, marshes, pastures, short-grass habitats; in summer,
tundra.

Basic Flight Patterns of Sandpipers

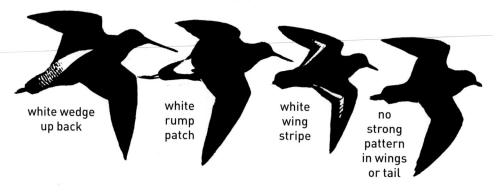

white wedge up back

white rump patch

white wing stripe

no strong pattern in wings or tail

LARGE SANDPIPERS

breeding

nonbreeding

nonbreeding

nonbreeding

HUDSONIAN GODWIT

breeding ♂

**MARBLED
GODWIT**

**LONG-BILLED
CURLEW**

WHIMBREL

WANDERING TATTLER *Tringa incana*   Uncommon M195
11 in. (28 cm). Recognized from other shorebirds that also inhabit rocks by *lack of pattern in flight.* Solid grayish above; light line over eye, dark line through it. Legs yellowish. Bobs and teeters like Spotted Sandpiper. *Breeding:* Underparts *barred. Nonbreeding:* Gray-chested, with no barring. **VOICE:** Clear *whee-he-he-he-he,* less sharp than Greater Yellowlegs, and all on same pitch; or *tweet-tweet-tweet,* similar to Spotted Sandpiper's call. **SIMILAR SPECIES:** Willet much larger, with very different wing pattern. In w. AK, see Gray-tailed Tattler. **HABITAT:** Rocky coasts, pebbly beaches, more rarely mudflats and sandy beaches. Nests near mountain streams above timberline.

SURFBIRD *Aphriza virgata*   Uncommon M207
10 in. (25 cm). A stocky, dark sandpiper of wave-washed rocks. Note conspicuous *white rump and tail tipped with broad black band;* legs *yellowish. Breeding:* Heavily streaked and spotted with blackish above and below; orangey scapulars. *Nonbreeding:* Solid gray above and across breast. Bill short, yellow at base. **VOICE:** Sharp *pee-weet* or *key-a-weet.* **SIMILAR SPECIES:** Rock Sandpiper smaller and slimmer, with longer, slimmer bill, different tail pattern. Black Turnstone smaller, darker, has slimmer bill, white stripe up back, and reddish brown legs. **HABITAT:** Rocky coasts; nests on mountain tundra.

ROCK SANDPIPER *Calidris ptilocnemis*   Uncommon M217
8¾–9¼ in. (22–24 cm). *Breeding:* Suggests a Dunlin, with rusty back, black splotch on breast (but Dunlin redder, with black splotch lower down, black legs). *Nonbreeding:* Similar to Purple Sandpiper of Atlantic Coast, but duller (more greenish yellow) legs and bill base. Slaty, with white belly, white wing stripe. Legs dull yellow or greenish. Pribilof Islands subspecies slightly larger and paler than other subspecies. **VOICE:** Flickerlike *du-du-du.* When breeding, a trill. **SIMILAR SPECIES:** Its rock-feeding associates, Black Turnstone and Surfbird, are plumper, have shorter bill, and show broad *white band* across base of tail. **HABITAT:** Rocky shores; nests on mossy tundra.

PURPLE SANDPIPER   Uncommon M216
Calidris maritima (see also p. 174)
9 in. (23 cm). Stocky, dark sandpipers on rocks, jetties, or breakwaters along our n. Atlantic Coast in winter are likely to be this hardy species. *Nonbreeding:* Slate gray with white belly. At close range, note short yellow-orange legs, dull orangish base of bill, and white eye-ring. *Breeding:* Much browner, more heavily streaked above and below with purplish sheen to some back feathers. **VOICE:** Low, scratchy *weet-wit* or *twit.* **SIMILAR SPECIES:** Nonbreeding Dunlin, also found roosting on jetties, has plain brown back and breast, black bill and legs. Nonbreeding Rock Sandpiper nearly identical but no range overlap. **HABITAT:** Wave-washed rocks, jetties, rarely sandy shoreline. Often quite tame. In summer, coastal tundra.

ROCK-LOVING SHOREBIRDS

WANDERING TATTLER

nonbreeding

breeding

SURFBIRD

breeding

nonbreeding

breeding

nonbreeding

ROCK SANDPIPER

breeding

nonbreeding

PURPLE SANDPIPER

RUDDY TURNSTONE Fairly common M205

Arenaria interpres (see also p. 168)

9½ in. (24 cm). A squat, robust, *orange-legged* shorebird, with *harlequin pattern. Breeding:* With russet back and curious face and breast pattern, bird is unique, but in flight it is even more striking. *Nonbreeding and juvenile:* Duller, but retain enough of basic pattern to be recognized. **VOICE:** Staccato *tuk-a-tuk* or *kut-a-kut;* also a single *kewk.* **SIMILAR SPECIES:** Black Turnstone. **HABITAT:** Beaches, mudflats, rocky shores, jetties; in summer, tundra.

BLACK TURNSTONE Fairly common M206

Arenaria melanocephala (see also p. 168)

9¼ in. (23 cm). A squat, blackish shorebird with blackish chest and white belly. In breeding plumage, oval white spot before eye, and white speckling. Flight pattern similar to Ruddy Turnstone's. Legs darkish. **VOICE:** Rattling call, higher and longer than that of Ruddy Turnstone. **SIMILAR SPECIES:** Nonbreeding Ruddy Turnstone has brighter legs, browner back, more rounded and less solid breast patches. Some juvenile Ruddy Turnstones are unusually dark. See also Surfbird. **HABITAT:** Strictly coastal. Rocky shores, surf-pounded islets, sometimes sandy beaches and mudflats. Nests on coastal tundra.

RED KNOT *Calidris canutus* (see also p. 174) Uncommon M208

10½ in. (27 cm). Larger than Sanderling. Stocky, with medium-length, straight bill and short legs. *Breeding:* Face and underparts *pale robin red;* back mottled with black, gray, and russet. *Nonbreeding:* A dumpy wader with washed-out gray look and mottled flanks; medium bill, pale rump, greenish legs. *Juvenile:* May show *pale feather edgings* above and pale buff wash on breast. **VOICE:** Low *knut;* also a low, mellow *tooit-wit* or *wah-quoit.* **SIMILAR SPECIES:** Dowitchers. **HABITAT:** Tidal flats, sandy beaches, shores; tundra when breeding.

SANDERLING *Calidris alba* (see also p. 174) Common M209

8 in. (20 cm). A plump, active sandpiper of outer beaches, where it chases retreating waves like a wind-up toy. Note bold *white wing stripe* in flight. *Breeding:* Bright rusty about head, back, and breast. *Nonbreeding:* The palest sandpiper; snowy white underparts, plain pale gray back, *black shoulders. Juvenile:* Differs from nonbreeding adults in having salt-and-pepper pattern on back and breast sides. **VOICE:** Short *kip* or *quit.* **SIMILAR SPECIES:** Western Sandpiper, Red-necked Stint. **HABITAT:** Beaches, mudflats, lakeshores; when nesting, stony tundra.

DUNLIN *Calidris alpina* (see also p. 174) Common M218

8½–8¾ in. (22–23 cm). Slightly larger than a peep or Sanderling, with *longish, droop-tipped bill.* Black legs. *Breeding: Rusty red above,* with *black patch on belly. Nonbreeding:* Unpatterned gray or gray-brown above, with *grayish wash across breast* (not clean white as in Sanderling or Western Sandpiper). *Juvenile* (this plumage rarely seen away from nesting areas): Rusty above, with buffy breast and suggestion of belly patch. **VOICE:** Nasal, rasping *cheezp* or *treezp.* **SIMILAR SPECIES:** Nonbreeding Sanderling and Western Sandpiper have clean white breast; Sanderling also paler above and has straighter bill; Western Sandpiper slightly smaller. See also Rock Sandpiper. **HABITAT:** Tidal flats, beaches, muddy pools; in summer, moist tundra.

SANDPIPERS

nonbreeding

nonbreeding

breeding

RUDDY TURNSTONE

BLACK TURNSTONE

breeding

nonbreeding

nonbreeding

juvenile

breeding

RED KNOT

juvenile

nonbreeding

SANDERLING

breeding

juvenile

nonbreeding

DUNLIN

breeding

Peeps

Collectively, the three common small sandpipers resident in N. America are nicknamed "peeps." Sometimes somewhat larger *Calidris* are also called peeps. In Old World, small peeps are called "stints."

LEAST SANDPIPER *Calidris minutilla* (see also p. 174)   Common M212
6 in. (15 cm). Distinguished from the other two common peeps by its slightly smaller size, *browner* look, and *yellowish or greenish*—not blackish—legs (but which might appear dark if caked in mud). *Bill slighter, finer, and slightly drooped at tip.* Adult: Mostly brownish (breeding) or brownish gray (nonbreeding). Juvenile: Much brighter, with extensive rufous on upperparts and buff wash across breast. **VOICE:** Thin *krreet, kreeeet.* **SIMILAR SPECIES:** Western and Semipalmated sandpipers have blackish legs, thicker-based bill, paler upperparts, and different voice; whitish breast in nonbreeding plumage. **HABITAT:** Mudflats, marshes, rain pools, shores, flooded fields; in summer, taiga wetlands.

SEMIPALMATED SANDPIPER   Common M210
Calidris pusilla (see also p. 174)
6¼ in. (16 cm). The "Semi" is a small black-legged peep with a *straight,* somewhat *tubular bill* of variable length. *Breeding:* Gray-brown above, many birds with a tinge of russet to cheeks and back; dark streaks on breast. *Nonbreeding:* Rarely seen in our area. Uniformly plain gray across upperparts. *Juvenile:* Breast washed with buff and with fine streaks on sides; scaly upperpart pattern with pale edges, tinged buff when fresh. **VOICE:** Call *chit* or *chirt* (lacks *ee* sound of Least and Western sandpipers). **SIMILAR SPECIES:** Typical Western Sandpiper (especially female) has *longer bill, slightly drooped* at tip. Breeding Western more rufous above, more heavily streaked below, particularly on flanks. Juvenile has rusty scapulars and slightly paler face. Least Sandpiper smaller, browner, and thinner billed; has *yellowish or greenish* legs; in nonbreeding plumage, has darker breast. **HABITAT:** Mudflats, marshes, shores, beaches; in summer, tundra.

WESTERN SANDPIPER *Calidris mauri*   Common M211
6½ in. (17 cm). Very similar to Semipalmated Sandpiper. Legs black. In typical adult female, bill distinctly thicker at base and *longer* than Semipalmated's and *droops near tip. Breeding: Heavily spotted* on breast and flanks; *rusty scapulars, crown, and ear patch. Nonbreeding:* Gray or graybrown above, perhaps the palest peep; unmarked whitish below. *Juvenile:* Buffy wash on breast; scaly upperparts, like juvenile Semipalmated but with distinct rusty scapulars. **VOICE:** Distinct high-pitched *jeet* or *cheet,* unlike lower, soft *chirt* of Semipalmated. **SIMILAR SPECIES:** Semipalmated and Least sandpipers, Dunlin. Because of their shorter bill, many male Westerns may be particularly difficult to separate from Semipalmated; see also voice. Semipalmated does not winter in our area, but Western does. **HABITAT:** Shores, beaches, mudflats, marshes; in summer, tundra.

SMALL "PEEP" SANDPIPERS

nonbreeding

juvenile

LEAST SANDPIPER

breeding

nbreeding

juvenile

breeding

SEMIPALMATED SANDPIPER

nbreeding ♀

juvenile

WESTERN SANDPIPER

breeding ♀

Least

Semipalmated

Western

WHITE-RUMPED SANDPIPER
Uncommon M213

Calidris fuscicollis (see also p. 174)
7½ in. (19 cm). Larger than Semipalmated Sandpiper, smaller than Pectoral Sandpiper. The only peep with completely *white rump*. At rest, this long-winged bird has *tapered* look, with *wingtips extending well beyond tail*. Distinct pale supercilium. *Breeding:* Some rusty on back. *Dark streaks and chevrons on sides extend to flanks.* Bill reddish at base of lower mandible. *Nonbreeding:* Gray upperparts and *breast, gray smudging down flanks,* bold *white eyebrow. Juvenile:* Rusty edges on crown and back. **VOICE:** High, thin, mouselike *jeet,* like two flint pebbles scraping. **SIMILAR SPECIES:** Long wings and very attenuated look shared only by Baird's Sandpiper among other peeps, but Baird's browner, has dark center to rump, lacks bold supercilium and dark streaks on flanks, and has much lower pitched call. **HABITAT:** Prairie pools, shores, mudflats, marshes; in summer, tundra.

BAIRD'S SANDPIPER *Calidris bairdii* (see also p. 174)   Uncommon M214
7½ in. (19 cm). Larger than Semipalmated or Western sandpiper, with more *long-winged, tapered look* (wings extend ½ in., 1 cm, beyond tail tip). *Breeding and juvenile:* Brown or *buff* across breast. Suggests large, long-winged Least Sandpiper with black legs. Back of juvenile has *scaled* look. **VOICE:** Call a low *kreep* or *kree;* a rolling trill. **SIMILAR SPECIES:** White-rumped and Pectoral sandpipers. Buff-breasted Sandpiper buffier below, without streaks, and has *yellowish* (not *blackish*) legs. **HABITAT:** Pond margins, grassy mudflats, shores, upper beaches; in summer, tundra.

PECTORAL SANDPIPER
Fairly common M215

Calidris melanotos (see also p. 172)
8¼–8¾ in. (21–23 cm). Medium sized (but variable); neck longer than in smaller peeps. Note that heavy breast streaks end rather *abruptly,* like a bib. Dark back lined with white. Wing stripe faint or lacking; crown variably rusty. Legs usually dull yellowish. Bill may be pale yellow-brown at base. *Juvenile:* Brighter upperparts and crown, buffy wash on breast under streaking. **VOICE:** Low, reedy *churrt* or *trrip, trrip.* **SIMILAR SPECIES:** Sharp-tailed, Baird's, and Least sandpipers. **HABITAT:** In migration, prairie pools, sod farms, muddy shores, fresh and tidal marshes; in summer, tundra.

SANDPIPERS

nonbreeding

breeding

**WHITE-RUMPED
SANDPIPER**

juvenile

breeding

BAIRD'S SANDPIPER

breeding ♂

juvenile

**PECTORAL
SANDPIPER**

breeding

SPOTTED SANDPIPER

Common M193

Actitis macularius (see also p. 174)
7½ in. (19 cm). The most widespread sandpiper along shores of small lakes and streams. Teeters rear body up and down nervously. Note *long tail. Breeding:* Note *round breast spots. Nonbreeding and juvenile:* No spots; brown above, with white line over eye. Dusky smudge enclosing white wedge near shoulder is a good aid. Flight distinctive: wings beat in a *shallow arc,* giving a stiff, bowed appearance. Underwing striped. **VOICE:** Clear *peet* or *peet-weet!* or *peet-weet-weet-weet-weet.* **SIMILAR SPECIES:** Solitary Sandpiper. **HABITAT:** Pebbly shores, ponds, streamsides, marshes; in winter, also seashores, rock jetties.

STILT SANDPIPER

Uncommon M219

Calidris himantopus (see also pp. 150 and 172)
8½ in. (22 cm). Slight *droop* to tip of bill. Legs long and greenish yellow. Feeds like a dowitcher (sewing-machine motion) but *tilts tail up* more than a dowitcher while feeding. *Breeding:* Heavily marked below with *transverse bars.* Note *rusty cheek patch. Nonbreeding:* Yellowlegs-like; gray above, white below; dark-winged and *white-rumped;* note more *greenish legs* and *white eyebrow. Juvenile:* Slight buffy wash to breast and pale edgings above. **VOICE:** Single *whu* (like Lesser Yellowlegs but lower, hoarser). **SIMILAR SPECIES:** Yellowlegs. Dowitchers pudgier, have longer, yellowish-based, less drooped bills, and in flight show white wedge up back. See also Curlew Sandpiper. **HABITAT:** Shallow pools, mudflats, marshes; in summer, tundra.

BUFF-BREASTED SANDPIPER

Scarce M220

Tryngites subruficollis (see also p. 172)
8¼ in. (21 cm). No other small shorebird is as *buffy* below (paling to whitish on undertail coverts). A tame, buffy bird, with erect stance, small head, short bill, and yellowish legs. Dark eye stands out on plain face. In flight or in "display," buff body contrasts with underwing (*white* with marbled tip). *Juvenile:* Scaly above, paler on belly (most fall birds along coasts are in this plumage). **VOICE:** Low, trilled *pr-r-r-reet.* Sharp *tik.* **SIMILAR SPECIES:** Juvenile Ruff. **HABITAT:** Dry dirt, sand, and short-grass habitats, including drying lakeshores, pastures, sod farms; in summer, drier tundra ridges.

UPLAND SANDPIPER

Uncommon M199

Bartramia longicauda (see also p. 172)
12 in. (30–31 cm). A "pigeon-headed" brown sandpiper; larger than Killdeer. Short bill, *small head,* shoe-button eye, thin neck, and *long tail* are helpful points. Often perches with erect posture on fenceposts and poles; on alighting, holds wings elevated. **VOICE:** Mellow, whistled *kip-ip-ip-ip,* often heard at night. Song a weird windy whistle: *whooooleeeeee, wheeloooooooooo.* **SIMILAR SPECIES:** Buff-breasted Sandpiper, yellowlegs. **HABITAT:** Grassy prairies, open meadows, fields, airports, sod farms.

SANDPIPERS

nonbreeding

breeding

SPOTTED SANDPIPER

juvenile

nonbreeding

breeding

STILT
SANDPIPER

UPLAND
SANDPIPER

BUFF-
BREASTED
SANDPIPER

AMERICAN WOODCOCK

Fairly common but secretive M224

Scolopax minor (see also p. 172)

11 in. (28 cm). A woodland-loving shorebird. Near size of Northern Bobwhite, with extremely long bill and large bulging eyes placed high on head. Rotund, almost neckless, with leaflike brown camouflage pattern, broadly barred crown. When flushed, produces whistling sound with wings. **VOICE:** At dusk in spring, a nasal *beezp* (suggesting nighthawk). Aerial "song" a chipping trill made by wings as bird ascends, changing to a bubbling twittering on descent. **HABITAT:** Wet thickets, moist woods, brushy swamps. Spring courtship by male is a crepuscular display ("sky dance") high over semiopen fields, pastures.

WILSON'S SNIPE

Fairly common M223

Gallinago delicata (see also p. 172)

10¼–10½ in. (26–27 cm). A tight-sitting bog and wet-field prober; on nesting grounds may be seen standing on posts. Note *extremely long bill*. Brown, with *buff stripes on back* and a *striped head*. When flushed, flies off in *zigzag*, showing *short rusty orange tail* and uttering rasping note. **VOICE:** When flushed, a rasping *scaip*. Song a measured *chip-a, chip-a, chip-a*, etc. In high aerial display, a winnowing *huhuhuhuhuhuhu*. **SIMILAR SPECIES:** Dowitchers. **HABITAT:** Marshes, bogs, ditches, wet fields and meadows.

SHORT-BILLED DOWITCHER

Common M221

Limnodromus griseus (see also p. 174)

11–11¼ in. (27–28 cm). A snipelike bird of open mudflats. Note very long bill, sewing-machine feeding motion, and, in flight, *long white wedge up back*. *Breeding:* Underparts rich rusty with some barring on flanks. Underbelly in Atlantic subspecies *(griseus)* shows extensive white, which helps separate from lookalike Long-billed Dowitcher. Bill length not a dependable mark for separation. Pacific Coast subspecies *(caurinus)* also has extensive white on belly. Great Plains *(hendersoni)* more extensively rusty below but color paler orange than Long-billed and fades toward belly. *Nonbreeding:* Gray. *Juvenile:* Brighter upperparts, buff wash to neck and breast; *patterned tertial feathers* an important distinction from juvenile Long-billed. **VOICE:** Staccato *tu-tu-tu;* pitch of Lesser Yellowlegs. **SIMILAR SPECIES:** Long-billed Dowitcher, Stilt Sandpiper. In nonbreeding plumage, see Red Knot. **HABITAT:** Mudflats, tidal marshes, pond edges. More frequent on large tidal mudflats than Long-billed Dowitcher. In summer, taiga and tundra.

LONG-BILLED DOWITCHER

Common M222

Limnodromus scolopaceus (see also p. 174)

11½ in. (29 cm). When feeding, shows more round-bodied profile than Short-billed; dark tail bars average wider; bill averages longer—but bill lengths of the two dowitchers overlap, so only extreme birds are distinctive. *Breeding:* Underparts *evenly bright rusty to lower belly* (white or very pale lower belly in Short-billed Dowitcher), with dark spotting on neck and barring on sides. Dark bars on tail broader, giving tail a darker look. *Nonbreeding:* Averages darker than Short-billed with smoother gray breast and darker centers to scapulars. *Juvenile: Solid gray tertials with pale fringe;* Short-billed has *internal rusty markings* similar to "tiger barring." **VOICE:** Single sharp, high *keek,* occasionally given in twos or threes. **SIMILAR SPECIES:** The two dowitcher species are most easily separated by voice. **HABITAT:** Mudflats, shallow pools, marshes; when breeding, tundra. More partial to fresh water than Short-billed, but extensive overlap.

SNIPELIKE WADERS

AMERICAN
WOODCOCK

winnowing
display
flight

WILSON'S
SNIPE

SHORT-
BILLED
DOWITCHER

juvenile

nonbreeding

coastal
breeding

snipe

central
breeding

juvenile

non-
breeding

breeding

LONG-BILLED
DOWITCHER

probing

PHALAROPES

Sandpipers with lobed toes; equally at home wading or swimming. Placed by some taxonomists in a family of their own, Phalaropodidae. When feeding, phalaropes often spin like tops, rapidly dabbling at disturbed water for plankton, brine shrimp, and other marine invertebrates; mosquito larvae; and insects. Females slightly larger and more colorful than males. **RANGE:** Two of the three species are circumpolar, wintering at sea; the other species breeds in N. American interior, winters in S. America.

WILSON'S PHALAROPE
Fairly common M225

Phalaropus tricolor (see also p. 150 and p. 172)
9¼ in. (23½ cm). This trim phalarope is plain-winged (no stripe), with white rump. In addition to spinning in water, may also feed by dashing about on shorelines. *Breeding:* Female unique, with *broad black face and neck stripe blending into cinnamon.* Male duller, with just a wash of cinnamon on sides of neck and white spot on hindneck. *Nonbreeding:* Suggests Lesser Yellowlegs (plain wings, white rump), but whiter below, with no breast streaking; bill *needlelike;* legs greenish or straw colored. *Juvenile:* Shows buffy and brown pattern above, buffy wash on breast. **VOICE:** Low nasal *wurk;* also *check, check, check.* **SIMILAR SPECIES:** Other two phalaropes show white wing stripe, dark central tail, and bolder dark patch through eye. See also yellowlegs, which may swim for brief periods of time. **HABITAT:** Shallow lakes, freshwater marshes, pools, shores, mudflats; in migration, also salt marshes.

RED-NECKED PHALAROPE
Common offshore, scarce inland M226

Phalaropus lobatus (see also p. 174)
7¾ in. (20 cm). A shorebird far out to sea is most likely a phalarope. This is usually the more common of the two "sea snipes" and the one more likely to occur inland as well. Note dark patch through eye and needlelike black bill. *Breeding:* Female gray above, with *rufous chestnut on neck,* white throat and eyebrow. Male duller, but similar in pattern. *Nonbreeding:* Both sexes gray above with whitish streaks, white below. *Juvenile:* Has distinct buff stripes on back. **VOICE:** Sharp *kit* or *whit,* similar to call of Sanderling. **SIMILAR SPECIES:** Red Phalarope. **HABITAT:** Ocean, bays, lakes, ponds; in summer, tundra.

RED PHALAROPE
Uncommon offshore, very rare onshore M227

Phalaropus fulicarius (see also p. 174)
8¼–8½ in. (21–22 cm). Seagoing habits and buoyant swimming (like a tiny gull) distinguish this as a phalarope. *Breeding:* Female has deep *reddish underparts, white face,* and mostly yellow bill. Male duller. *Nonbreeding:* Both sexes plain gray above, white below; in flight suggest Sanderling, but with *dark patch* through eye. Bill mostly dark with small pale base. *Juvenile:* Has peach-buff wash on neck; acquires adult's pale gray back-feathering quickly. **VOICE:** *Whit* or *kit,* higher than Red-necked Phalarope's call. **SIMILAR SPECIES:** Red-necked Phalarope slightly smaller, has more needlelike bill; nonbreeding birds darker gray above with thin pale back stripes. Slightly thicker bill of Red Phalarope may have small yellowish base. **HABITAT:** More strictly pelagic than Red-necked. In summer, tundra.

PHALAROPES

breeding ♀

nonbreeding

juvenile

nonbreeding

breeding ♂

WILSON'S PHALAROPE

alaropes spin

RED-NECKED PHALAROPE

breeding ♀

nonbreeding

juvenile

nonbreeding

breeding ♂

breeding ♀

nonbreeding

RED PHALAROPE

juvenile

nonbreeding

breeding ♂

lobed foot of phalarope

Plovers and Turnstone in Flight

Learn their distinctive flight calls.

PIPING PLOVER *Charadrius melodus*   p. 146
Pale sand color above, wide black tail spot, whitish rump.
Call a plaintive whistle, *peep-lo* (first note higher).

SNOWY PLOVER *Charadrius alexandrinus*   p. 146
Pale sand color above; tail with dark center, white sides; rump not white.
Call a musical whistle, *pe-wee-ah* or *o-wee-ah.*

SEMIPALMATED PLOVER *Charadrius semipalmatus*   p. 146
Mud brown above; dark tail with white borders.
Call a plaintive upward-slurred *chi-we* or *too-li.*

WILSON'S PLOVER *Charadrius wilsonia*   p. 146
Similar in pattern to Semipalmated; larger with big bill.
Call an emphatic whistled *whit!* or *wheet!*

KILLDEER *Charadrius vociferus*   p. 146
Tawny orange rump, longish tail.
Noisy; a loud *kill-deeah* or *killdeer;* also *dee-dee-dee,* etc.

BLACK-BELLIED PLOVER *Pluvialis squatarola*   p. 144
Breeding: Black below, white undertail coverts.
Year-round: Black wingpits, white in wing and tail.
Call a plaintive slurred whistle, *tlee-oo-eee* or *whee-er-ee.*

AMERICAN GOLDEN-PLOVER *Pluvialis dominica*   p. 144
Breeding: Black below, black undertail coverts.
Nonbreeding: Speckled brown above, grayish below.
Year-round: Underwing grayer than Black-bellied Plover's; no black in wingpits.
Call a querulous whistled *queedle* or *que-e-a.*

PACIFIC GOLDEN-PLOVER *Pluvialis fulva* (not shown)   p. 144
Like American, but breeding birds show some white along flanks and undertail; nonbreeding birds more gold-washed on face.
Call a loud, whistled *chu-whee* or *chu-wee-dle.*

RUDDY TURNSTONE *Arenaria interpres*   p. 156
Harlequin pattern distinctive.
Call a low chuckling *tuk-a-tuk* or *kut-a-kut.*

BLACK TURNSTONE *Arenaria melanocephala* (not shown)   p. 156
Boldly patterned in black and white. Fairly similar to nonbreeding Ruddy Turnstone, but brown replaced by black.
Call a short series of rattling notes.

PLOVERS AND
TURNSTONE

PIPING
PLOVER

SNOWY
PLOVER

SEMIPALMATED
PLOVER

WILSON'S
PLOVER

KILLDEER

breeding

non-
breeding

BLACK-BELLIED
PLOVER

onbreeding

nonbreeding

breeding

nonbreeding

American
Golden-Plover

AMERICAN
GOLDEN-PLOVER

RUDDY TURNSTONE

breeding

LARGE WADERS IN FLIGHT

Learn to know their flight calls, which are distinctive.

HUDSONIAN GODWIT *Limosa haemastica*　　　　　　　　p. 152
Upturned bill, white wing stripe, ringed tail. Blackish wing linings.
Flight call *tawit!*, higher pitched than Marbled Godwit's.

WILLET *Tringa semipalmata*　　　　　　　　　　　　　p. 150
Contrasty black, gray, and white wing pattern. Overhead, wing pattern is
even more striking.
Flight call a whistled one- to three-note *kree-ree-ree.*

MARBLED GODWIT *Limosa fedoa*　　　　　　　　　　　p. 152
Long upturned bill, tawny brown color. Cinnamon wing linings.
Flight call an accented *kerwhit!* (or *godwit!*).

WHIMBREL *Numenius phaeopus*　　　　　　　　　　　p. 152
Decurved bill, gray-brown overall color, striped crown. Grayer than next
species, lacks cinnamon wing linings.
Flight call five to seven short, rapid whistles: *hee-hee-hee-hee-hee-hee.*

LONG-BILLED CURLEW *Numenius americanus*　　　　　p. 152
Very long, sicklelike bill; no head striping. Bright cinnamon wing linings.
Juvenile's bill shorter but note head patterns.
Flight call a rapid, whistled *kli-li-li-li.*

LARGE
WADERS

♀
HUDSONIAN
GODWIT

breeding

nonbreeding

WILLET

nonbreeding

MARBLED
GODWIT

WHIMBREL

juvenile
Long-billed Curlew

LONG-BILLED CURLEW

Snipelike Waders and Sandpipers in Flight

These species and those on the next plate show their basic flight patterns. Most of these have unpatterned wings, lacking a pale stripe. All are shown in full color on other plates. Learn their distinctive flight calls.

WILSON'S SNIPE *Gallinago delicata*   p. 164
Long bill, pointed wings, rusty orange tail, zigzag flight.
Flight call, when flushed, a rasping *scaip.*

AMERICAN WOODCOCK *Scolopax minor*   p. 164
Long bill, rounded wings, chunky shape. Wings whistle in flight.
At dusk, aerial flight "song."

SOLITARY SANDPIPER *Tringa solitaria*   p. 150
Very dark unpatterned wings (underwing dark also—pale in yellowlegs),
conspicuous bars on white sides of tail.
Flight call *peet!* or *peet-weet-weet!* (higher than Spotted Sandpiper's).

LESSER YELLOWLEGS *Tringa flavipes*   p. 150
Similar to Greater Yellowlegs, but smaller, with smaller bill.
Flight call *yew* or *yu-yu* (rarely three), softer than Greater's call.

GREATER YELLOWLEGS *Tringa melanoleuca*   p. 150
Plain unpatterned wings, whitish rump and tail, long bill.
Flight call a forceful three-note whistle, *dear! dear! dear!*

WILSON'S PHALAROPE *Phalaropus tricolor*   p. 166
Nonbreeding: Suggests Lesser Yellowlegs; smaller, whiter, bill needlelike.
Flight call a low nasal *wurk.*

STILT SANDPIPER *Calidris himantopus*   p. 162
Suggests Lesser Yellowlegs, but legs greenish yellow, bill longer and
drooped.
Flight call a single *whu,* lower than Lesser Yellowlegs'.

UPLAND SANDPIPER *Bartramia longicauda*   p. 162
Brown; small head, long tail.
Often flies "on tips of wings," like Spotted Sandpiper.
Flight call a mellow whistled *kip-ip-ip-ip.*

BUFF-BREASTED SANDPIPER *Tryngites subruficollis*   p. 162
Buff below, contrasting with white wing linings; plain upperparts.
Flight call a low, trilled *pr-r-r-reet;* usually silent.

PECTORAL SANDPIPER *Calidris melanotos*   p. 160
Like an oversized Least Sandpiper. Wing stripe faint or lacking.
Flight call a low, reedy *churrt* or *trrip, trrip.*

SNIPELIKE WADERS AND SANDPIPERS IN FLIGHT

WILSON'S SNIPE

AMERICAN WOODCOCK

SOLITARY SANDPIPER

GREATER YELLOWLEGS

LESSER YELLOWLEGS

WILSON'S PHALAROPE

nonbreeding

STILT SANDPIPER

nonbreeding

UPLAND SANDPIPER

BUFF-BREASTED SANDPIPER

PECTORAL SANDPIPER

DOWITCHERS *Limnodromus* spp.   p. 164
Long bill, long wedge of white up back.
Flight call of Short-billed Dowitcher a staccato mellow *tu-tu-tu;* that of
Long-billed Dowitcher a single sharp *keek,* occasionally given in twos or
threes and uttered repeatedly by feeding birds (unlike Short-billed).

DUNLIN *Calidris alpina*   p. 156
Nonbreeding: Slightly larger than peeps, darker than Sanderling.
Flight call a nasal rasping *cheezp* or *treezp.*

RED KNOT *Calidris canutus*   p. 156
Nonbreeding: Washed-out gray look, pale rump.
Flight call a low *knut.*

PURPLE SANDPIPER *Calidris maritima*   p. 154
Slaty color.
Flight call a low *weet-wit* or *twit.*

WHITE-RUMPED SANDPIPER *Calidris fuscicollis*   p. 160
White rump; only peep so marked, but beware partial or poor views of
other peep, all of which have mostly white rumps with narrow dark bar.
Flight call a mouselike squeak, *jeet.*

CURLEW SANDPIPER *Calidris ferruginea*   p. 182
Nonbreeding: Suggests Dunlin, but rump white.

RUFF *Philomachus pugnax*   p. 182
If seen well, oval white patch on each side of dark tail distinctive.
Usually silent.

SPOTTED SANDPIPER *Actitis macularius*   p. 162
Shallow wing stroke gives stiff, bowed effect; longish tail.
Flight call a clear *peet* or *peet-weet.*

SANDERLING *Calidris alba*   p. 156
The most contrasting wing stripe of any small shorebird.
Flight call a sharp metallic *kip* or *quit.*

RED PHALAROPE *Phalaropus fulicarius*   p. 166
Nonbreeding: Paler above than Red-necked Phalarope; bill slightly thicker.

RED-NECKED PHALAROPE *Phalaropus lobatus*   p. 166
Nonbreeding: Sanderling-like, but with dark eye patch.
Flight call (both pelagic phalaropes) a sharp *kit* or *whit.*

LEAST SANDPIPER *Calidris minutilla*   p. 158
Very small, brown with short wings and tail; faint wing stripe.
Flight call a thin *krreet, krreet.*

SEMIPALMATED SANDPIPER *Calidris pusilla*   p. 158
Grayer than Least Sandpiper.
Flight call a soft *chit* or *chirt* (lacks *ee* sound of Least).

BAIRD'S SANDPIPER *Calidris bairdii*   p. 160
Larger and longer winged than above two. Size of White-rumped Sand-
piper, but rump dark.
Flight call a low, raspy *kreep* or *kree.*

SANDPIPERS AND PHALAROPES

nonbreeding

SHORT-BILLED DOWITCHER
Long-billed has
similar pattern

nonbreeding

RED KNOT

DUNLIN
nonbreeding

nonbreeding

**PURPLE
SANDPIPER**

**WHITE-RUMPED
SANDPIPER**

**CURLEW
SANDPIPER**

nonbreeding

RUFF

nonbreeding

SPOTTED SANDPIPER

nonbreeding

SANDERLING

nonbreeding

**RED
PHALAROPE**

nonbreeding

**RED-NECKED
PHALAROPE**

LEAST SANDPIPER

**SEMIPALMATED
SANDPIPER**

**BAIRD'S
SANDPIPER**

NORTHERN LAPWING *Vanellus vanellus*　　　　Vagrant
12–12½ in. (30–32 cm). A distinctive round-winged plover with unique long wispy crest. **RANGE:** Casual European vagrant, mostly in late fall and early winter, from Atlantic Canada south to mid-Atlantic states; accidental farther south and west. **HABITAT:** Farmland, marshes, mudflats.

LESSER SAND-PLOVER (MONGOLIAN PLOVER)　　　　Vagrant
Charadrius mongolus
7½ in. (19 cm). Asian. Slightly larger and larger-billed than Semipalmated Plover. *Breeding:* Very distinctive, with *broad rufous breast-band.* Female duller. *Nonbreeding and juvenile:* Breastband gray-brown; no white collar. **VOICE:** Calls include a ploverlike whistle and a rolling trill. **RANGE:** Rare but regular migrant on Aleutians and Bering Sea islands. Casual vagrant from mainland AK to CA, accidental farther east.

EUROPEAN GOLDEN-PLOVER *Pluvialis apricaria*　　　　Vagrant
11 in. (28 cm). Very similar to American and Pacific golden-plovers but shows *white* underwings. Breeding adult has white along flanks and undertail like Pacific but is larger-bodied, smaller-billed. **VOICE:** Melodic drawn-out whistle. **SIMILAR SPECIES:** American and Pacific golden-plovers. **RANGE:** Very rare spring vagrant to NL, casual elsewhere in Maritimes.

EURASIAN DOTTEREL *Charadrius morinellus*　　　　Vagrant
8¼–8½ in. (21–22 cm). Narrow white stripe crossing midbreast identifies this dark plover. Broad *white eyebrow stripes* join in broad V on nape. **VOICE:** Repeated piping, *titi-ri-titi-ri,* running into a trill. **RANGE:** Very rare Asian visitor to w. AK, casual farther south along Pacific Coast. A few pairs may breed locally on high tundra of nw. AK.

SPOTTED REDSHANK *Tringa erythropus*　　　　Vagrant
12½ in. (32 cm). A slender, long-legged, long-billed shorebird. *Breeding: Sooty black,* with small white speckles on back and wings, making bird appear a trifle paler above. Long legs *dark red;* long black bill *reddish basally,* has *slight droop at tip. Nonbreeding and juvenile:* Gray and somewhat yellowlegs-like, but legs *orange-red,* bill *orange-red* basally. In flight, shows *long white wedge* on back, white underwing. **VOICE:** Sharp, whistled *tcheet,* with rising inflection. **RANGE:** Casual Eurasian visitor; records widely scattered.

COMMON GREENSHANK *Tringa nebularia*　　　　Vagrant
13½ in. (34 cm). Size and shape of Greater Yellowlegs, but legs *dull greenish* (not bright yellow). Wedgelike white rump patch runs up back, as in a dowitcher. **VOICE:** Ringing, whistled *tew tew tew,* similar to Greater Yellowlegs. **RANGE:** Eurasian species; annual visitor on w. AK islands, accidental elsewhere.

WOOD SANDPIPER *Tringa glareola*　　　　Very rare
8 in. (20 cm). Shape of Solitary Sandpiper, but has pale (not dark) underwings. Pale supercilium. Upperparts slightly paler and browner, *heavily spotted* with pale buff. Rump patch *white* (Solitary has dark rump). Legs dull yellow. Overall, looks very short in rear. **VOICE:** Sharp, high *chew-chew-chew* or *chiff-chiff-chiff.* **RANGE:** Regular migrant on Aleutians and Bering Sea islands, accidental elsewhere.

RARE SHOREBIRDS

NORTHERN LAPWING

breeding

LESSER SAND-PLOVER

breeding

breeding

nonbreeding

breeding

EUROPEAN GOLDEN-PLOVER

breeding ♀

juvenile

EURASIAN DOTTEREL

nonbreeding

non-
eding

SPOTTED REDSHANK

breeding

COMMON GREENSHANK

nonbreeding

WOOD SANDPIPER

breeding

BAR-TAILED GODWIT
Rare, local M203

Limosa lapponica
16–17 in. (41–44 cm). Alaskan birds have *mottled rump* and *whitish tail* crossed by narrow dark bars. European birds have whiter rump. *Breeding:* Male rich *reddish orange,* particularly on head and underparts. Female duller. *Nonbreeding:* Both sexes grayish above, white below. *Juvenile:* Underparts washed buffy, back with neat buff-and-black pattern. **VOICE:** Flight call a harsh *kirrick;* alarm a shrill *krick.* **SIMILAR SPECIES:** Marbled and Hudsonian godwits. Bar-tailed has slightly shorter bill and legs, underwing dusky. **RANGE:** Nests in w. AK; vagrant on both West and East coasts. **HABITAT:** Mudflats, shores, tundra.

BLACK-TAILED GODWIT *Limosa limosa*
Vagrant

16½ in. (42 cm). This elegant Eurasian godwit resembles Hudsonian Godwit (white rump, white wing stripe, black tail), but bill straighter. In breeding plumage, has chestnut head and neck, black-and-white barred belly. Best field distinction in all plumages is *white* underwing linings in Black-tailed, *black* in Hudsonian. **VOICE:** Flight call a clear *reeka-reeka-reeka.* **RANGE:** Casual visitor to both AK and East Coast. **HABITAT:** Large lakes with muddy shores.

"EURASIAN" WHIMBREL *Numenius phaeopus*
Vagrant

Two subspecies of Whimbrel from Eurasia occur as very rare visitors in N. America. Asian race *variegatus* is a rare but regular migrant in w. AK; casual farther south along Pacific Coast. European race *phaeopus* is a casual visitor along Atlantic Coast. Both differ from N. American Whimbrel by showing mostly *white rump* (slightly mottled in *variegatus*) and whiter underwing. **VOICE:** Calls similar to N. American Whimbrel.

BRISTLE-THIGHED CURLEW *Numenius tahitiensis*
Rare, local

17½–18 in. (44–46 cm). Very similar to Whimbrel, but *tawnier,* especially about *tail and unbarred rump.* Breast less streaked. Call very different. **VOICE:** Slurred *chi-u-it* (Inuit name) or *whee-oo-wheep;* suggests call of Black-bellied Plover. Also a wolf whistle–like *whee-wheeo.* **RANGE:** Nests locally in w. AK; accidental farther south. **HABITAT:** In summer, tundra; in winter, reefs and beaches.

ESKIMO CURLEW *Numenius borealis*
Probably extinct

14 in. (36 cm). Last documented record in early 1960s. Much smaller than Whimbrel. Bill shorter, thinner, only slightly curved. More patterned above than Whimbrel; more like Long-billed Curlew, with strong buff interspersed with black. Linings of raised wing cinnamon-buff with unbarred primaries. Legs slate gray. **VOICE:** Call has been variously described as *tee-dee-dee* or repeated *tee-dee* or a note suggestive of Common Tern. **SIMILAR SPECIES:** Upland Sandpiper, Little Curlew. **HABITAT:** Open grasslands, coastal areas; in summer, tundra.

LITTLE CURLEW *Numenius minutus*
Vagrant

12 in. (30 cm). The tiniest curlew. Bill *short and gently decurved.* Breast washed with buff, finely streaked. At rest, wingtips even with tail tip (extend beyond tail in Eskimo Curlew); note difference in *underwing* (pale buff, not cinnamon) and *flanks* (lightly barred, not heavy chevrons). **RANGE:** Asian species; casual along West Coast.

RARE SHOREBIRDS

European nonbreeding

Alaskan nonbreeding

BAR-TAILED GODWIT

nonbreeding

nonbreeding

juvenile

breeding

nonbreeding

BLACK-TAILED GODWIT

breeding

BRISTLE-THIGHED CURLEW

"Eurasian"

WHIMBREL

LITTLE CURLEW

underwing

ESKIMO CURLEW

underwing

COMMON SANDPIPER *Actitis hypoleucos*   Vagrant
8 in. (20 cm). At all seasons resembles nonbreeding Spotted Sandpiper (no spots). Best feature is *longer tail.* At rest, wingtips of Common reach only halfway to tail tip, those of Spotted closer to tip. Common has grayer legs, longer white wing stripe. **VOICE:** In flight, *twee-see-see,* thinner than Spotted's call. **RANGE:** Rare but regular, mostly in spring, on Aleutians and Bering Sea islands.

TEREK SANDPIPER *Xenus cinereus*   Vagrant
9 in. (23 cm). Note *upturned bill* and short *orange-yellow legs, jagged black stripe* along scapulars. Often bobs like Spotted Sandpiper. In flight, wing has dark leading edge and broad *white band* at rear. **VOICE:** Fluty *dudududu* or sharp piping, *twita-wit-wit-wit.* **RANGE:** Very rare in w. AK islands, accidental farther south.

LITTLE STINT *Calidris minuta*   Vagrant
6 in. (15 cm). Size of Semipalmated Sandpiper, but bill slightly finer. *Breeding:* Rusty orange above and on breast. Similar to some Red-necked Stints, but body less elongated, legs longer, and *dark breast markings washed with orange. Juvenile:* Like juvenile Semipalmated Sandpiper, but with longer wingtip projection, bold white V on mantle, black-centered wing coverts and tertials. **VOICE:** Sanderling-like *tit.* **RANGE:** Widespread casual visitor, mostly to coasts.

RED-NECKED STINT *Calidris ruficollis*   Rare visitor and breeder, local
6¼ in. (17 cm). A rare but regular visitor, recognized in breeding plumage by *bright rusty head and neck, bordered below by dark streaks. Juvenile:* Has long wingtip projection like Little Stint but contrasting rusty upper scapulars like juvenile Western. **VOICE:** Short, clipped *chit,* or *chit chit,* suggesting Semipalmated Sandpiper. **RANGE:** Rare but regular migrant in w. AK, where very rare breeder; casual migrant elsewhere in N. America.

GRAY-TAILED TATTLER *Tringa brevipes*   Rare visitor, local
10 in. (25 cm). Very similar to Wandering Tattler; best told by voice. *Breeding:* Compared with Wandering, barring on underparts finer and less extensive; supercilium somewhat bolder. *Juvenile:* Gray-tailed has more extensive whitish spots and notches to scapulars, coverts, and tertials than Wandering, is slightly paler gray above (sometimes tinged brownish), and flanks paler. **VOICE:** Up-slurred whistle, *too-weet?* or *tu-whip?*, with accent on second syllable. **RANGE:** Asian species, regular visitor to w. AK islands, accidental elsewhere.

TEMMINCK'S STINT *Calidris temminckii*   Vagrant
6¼ in. (16 cm). A brownish gray stint with *irregular black spots* on scapulars. Has *elongated, crouching look; short dull yellow legs.* In flight, shows *white outer tail feathers.* **VOICE:** In flight, a dry *trree,* often repeated in cricketlike trill. **SIMILAR SPECIES:** Least and Baird's sandpipers. **RANGE:** Very rare visitor to w. AK islands, accidental farther south.

LONG-TOED STINT *Calidris subminuta*   Vagrant
6 in. (15 cm). Much like Least Sandpiper, but *brighter* above, with more erect stance, *longer legs* and *toes,* dark forehead. May suggest miniature Sharp-tailed Sandpiper. **VOICE:** Purring *prrp.* **RANGE:** Rare but regular migrant on w. AK islands, accidental farther south.

TEREK SANDPIPER

breeding

juvenile

COMMON SANDPIPER

breeding Spotted Sandpiper (p. 162)
for comparison

Wandering Tattler
(p. 154)
for comparison

nonbreeding

breeding

LITTLE
STINT

breeding

breeding

GRAY-TAILED
TATTLER

early spring
(breeding)

RED-NECKED
STINT

juvenile

juvenile

breeding

TEMMINCK'S
STINT

breeding

LONG-TOED
STINT

SHARP-TAILED SANDPIPER *Calidris acuminata*   Rare to casual visitor
8½ in. (22 cm). Similar to Pectoral Sandpiper, but shows bolder whitish supercilium and brighter rusty crown. Most birds in N. America are juveniles, which have rich *orangey buff breast*, finely streaked on sides only. Breeding adults have heavy *dark chevrons* extending to flanks. Crissum streaked. In no plumage is there as sharp a demarcation between white belly and streaked breast as in Pectoral. **VOICE:** Trilled *prreeet* or *trrit-trrit*, sometimes twittered. **SIMILAR SPECIES:** Juvenile Ruff. **RANGE:** Asian species. Regular fall migrant in w. AK, casual in spring and along Pacific Coast, accidental elsewhere. **HABITAT:** Marshy and grassy borders of wetlands, muddy shores, wet pastures; in summer, tundra.

CURLEW SANDPIPER   Very rare visitor
Calidris ferruginea (see also p. 174)
8½–8¾ in. (21–22 cm). A Eurasian species with slim downcurved bill, blackish legs, and white rump in flight. *Breeding:* Male variably rich rufous red; female duller with thin pale barring. *Nonbreeding:* Resembles Dunlin, but slightly longer legged, bolder pale supercilium; bill curved slightly throughout; whitish rump. *Juvenile:* Buff edges on feathers of back give it a very scaly look; breast washed with buff. Similar to juvenile Stilt Sandpiper, but Curlew's legs black rather than greenish, and bill curves downward throughout its length. **VOICE:** Liquid *chirrip.* **SIMILAR SPECIES:** In breeding plumage, see also Red Knot. **RANGE:** Very rare but annual migrant along East Coast, casual inland and along West Coast. **HABITAT:** Marshy pools, mudflats; in summer, tundra.

RUFF *Philomachus pugnax* (see also p. 174)   Very rare visitor
Male (Ruff) 12–13 in. (30–32 cm); female (known informally as Reeve) 9 in. (23 cm). *Breeding male:* Unique, with erectile *ruffs* and *ear tufts* that may be black, brown, rufous, buff, white, or barred, in various combinations. Legs may be greenish, yellow, or orange. Bill color also variable. *Breeding female:* Smaller than male; lacks ruffs, breast *heavily blotched* with dark. *Nonbreeding:* Rather plain, with short bill, small head, thick neck, mottling of gray across breast. Note *erect stance* and (in flight) *oval white patch* on each side of dark tail. *Juvenile:* Buffy below, very scaly on back. **VOICE:** Often silent; flight call a low *too-i* or *tu-whit.* **SIMILAR SPECIES:** Juvenile Sharp-tailed Sandpiper. Adult Buff-breasted Sandpiper. **RANGE:** Breeds in Eurasia. Very rare but regular migrant along both coasts and in Great Lakes region; casual elsewhere inland. **HABITAT:** Marshes, tundra in summer. Mudflats, marshes, coastal pools, wet agricultural fields in migration.

COMMON SNIPE *Gallinago gallinago*   Rare, local visitor
10½ in. (27 cm). Compared with Wilson's Snipe, has paler underwing, bolder white trailing edge to secondaries, weaker flank barring, slightly buffier overall color, and lower-pitched winnowing in flight display. **RANGE:** Eurasian species. Regular visitor to w. AK islands. **HABITAT:** Similar to Wilson's Snipe.

RARE SHOREBIRDS

juvenile

SHARP-TAILED SANDPIPER

breeding

nonbreeding

breeding dress of ♂ variable

♂

♂

nonbreeding

nonbreeding ♀

juvenile ♂

CURLEW SANDPIPER

breeding

RUFF

breeding ♀

COMMON SNIPE

GULLS Family Laridae

Long-winged swimming birds with superb flight. Most are more robust, wider winged, and longer legged than terns, and most have slightly hooked bills. Tails square or rounded (terns usually have forked tail). Gulls seldom dive (most terns hover, then plunge head-first). FOOD: Omnivorous; marine life, plant and animal food, refuse, carrion. RANGE: Nearly worldwide.

AGING GULLS

It is often important to determine the age of a gull before identifying it. Knowing what a gull looks like in both its adult and first-year (also often referred to as "first-winter") plumages is helpful in identifying the bird to species in its intermediate stages.

SEQUENCE OF PLUMAGES IN A TWO-YEAR GULL

On the top of the opposite page, the Bonaparte's Gull illustrates the transition of plumages from first year to adult. Species in this category are mostly smaller gulls, including Bonaparte's, Black-headed, Little, Ross's, Sabine's, and Ivory gulls, and Red-legged Kittiwake.

SEQUENCE OF PLUMAGES IN A THREE-YEAR GULL

In the middle of the opposite page, the Ring-billed Gull, widespread and abundant both coastally and inland, illustrates the transition of plumages from first year to adult. Species in this category are mostly medium-sized gulls, including Ring-billed, Laughing, Franklin's, and Mew gulls and Black-legged Kittiwake. The larger Yellow-footed Gull is also a three-year species.

SEQUENCE OF PLUMAGES IN A FOUR-YEAR GULL

On the bottom of the opposite page, the Herring Gull, a widespread species, illustrates the transition of plumages from first year to adult. Species in this category are most of the larger gulls, including California, Herring, Lesser Black-backed, Great Black-backed, Slaty-backed, Western, Glaucous-winged, Glaucous, Iceland, and Thayer's gulls. These species attain full maturity in 3½ to 4½ years. Surprisingly, the medium-sized Heermann's Gull is also a four-year species.

In this field guide, intended for identification on the species level, no other four-year gull receives similarly full treatment. That is the province of a larger handbook or text specifically on gulls. For in-depth analysis of other species, consult the *Peterson Reference Guide to Gulls of the Americas,* which focuses on the details and intricacies of gull identification.

Caution: There is extensive variation within species (particularly the immatures), resulting from several factors including dimorphism (males are larger than females), molt, variation in wear and bleaching, albinism, and other factors. In addition, hybridization is a regular phenomenon among most four-year species. Even expert birders leave some gulls unidentified.

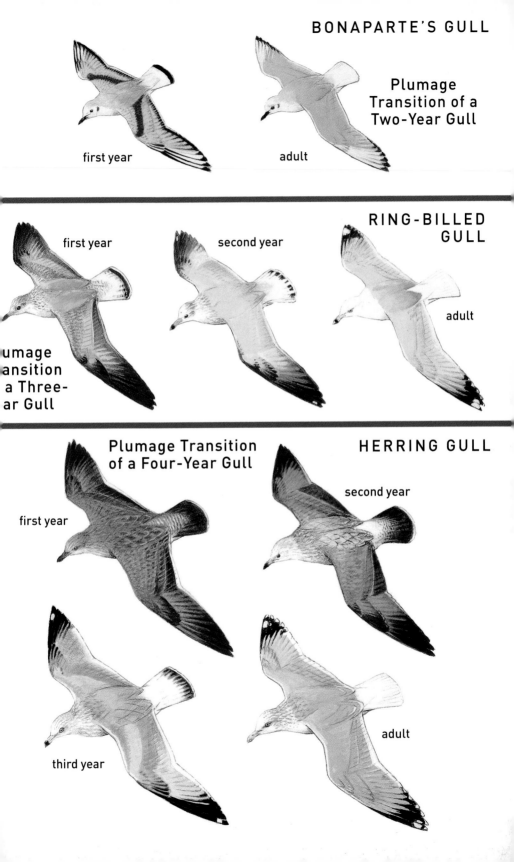

BONAPARTE'S GULL

Plumage Transition of a Two-Year Gull

first year

adult

RING-BILLED GULL

first year

second year

adult

umage ansition a Three-ar Gull

Plumage Transition of a Four-Year Gull

HERRING GULL

first year

second year

third year

adult

LAUGHING GULL *Larus atricilla* Common M228

16–16½ in. (41–42 cm). A small coastal gull named for its call. *Dark mantle blends into black wingtips.* Bold white trailing edge to dark wing. Head *black* in breeding plumage; pale in nonbreeding plumage, with dark gray smudge across eye and nape. Bill longish, often with slight droop to tip; reddish when breeding, mostly dark when not breeding. *Immature:* See p. 194. **VOICE:** Nasal *ha-a* and strident laugh, *ha-ha-ha-ha-ha-haah-haah-haah*, etc. **SIMILAR SPECIES:** Franklin's Gull slightly smaller, shorter billed, rounder headed, shorter winged, has broader white eye-arcs, paler underwing, and *different wingtip pattern.* Bonaparte's Gull smaller still, with very different wing pattern. **HABITAT:** Salt marshes, coastlines, parks, farm fields.

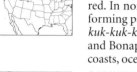

FRANKLIN'S GULL *Larus pipixcan* Fairly common M229

14½–15 in. (37–38 cm). Note *white band* near wingtip, separating black from gray. In breeding plumage, head black; breast has rosy bloom; bill red. In nonbreeding plumage, head paler but with dark cheeks and nape forming partial hood; bill mostly dark. *Immature:* See p. 194. **VOICE:** Shrill *kuk-kuk-kuk;* also mewing, laughing cries. **SIMILAR SPECIES:** Laughing and Bonaparte's gulls. **HABITAT:** Prairies, inland marshes, lakes; in winter, coasts, ocean.

SABINE'S GULL *Xema sabini* Scarce M247

13½–14 in. (34–36 cm). A small, *ternlike* gull with slightly *forked tail.* Note *bold upperwing pattern* of black outer primaries and *triangular white wing patch.* Bill black with *yellow tip;* legs dark. Full slaty hood of breeding plumage may be held well into fall; in nonbreeding plumage, a dusky wash. *Immature:* See p. 194. **VOICE:** Various grating or buzzy ternlike calls, given mostly on breeding grounds. **SIMILAR SPECIES:** Bonaparte's and Laughing gulls, Black-legged Kittiwake. **HABITAT:** Ocean; nests on tundra pools.

BLACK-HEADED GULL *Larus ridibundus* Rare M231

15¾–16 in. (40–41 cm). This Eurasian species regularly visits coastal N. America. Similar in pattern to Bonaparte's Gull and often associates with it or with Ring-billed Gull. Slightly larger than Bonaparte's; mantle slightly paler; shows much *blackish gray on underside of primaries;* bill *dark red,* not black. In nonbreeding plumage, loses dark brown hood and has black ear spot. *Immature:* See p. 194. **VOICE:** Harsh *kerrr.* **HABITAT:** Same as Little and Bonaparte's gulls; also beaches, lawns.

BONAPARTE'S GULL *Larus philadelphia* Common M232

13–13½ in. (33–34 cm). A petite, almost ternlike gull. Note *wedge of white* on *fore edge* of wing. Legs red to pinkish; bill small, black. In breeding plumage, head blackish. In nonbreeding plumage, head whitish with *black ear spot. Immature:* See p. 194. Also see Sequence of Plumages in a Two-Year Gull, p. 184. **VOICE:** Nasal, grating *cheeer* or *cherr.* Some calls ternlike. **SIMILAR SPECIES:** Franklin's, Black-headed, and Little gulls. **HABITAT:** Ocean, bays, lakes, sewage-treatment ponds; in summer, muskeg.

LITTLE GULL *Larus minutus* Rare M230

11 in. (28 cm). This rare visitor is the smallest gull; usually associates with Bonaparte's Gull. Note *blackish undersurface* of *rather rounded wing* and absence of black above. Legs red. In breeding plumage, head black, bill dark red, breast may be washed rosy. In nonbreeding plumage, head *dark-capped, black ear spot,* bill black. *Immature:* See p. 194. **VOICE:** Series of one- or two-syllable *key* notes. **SIMILAR SPECIES:** Bonaparte's Gull. **HABITAT:** Lakes, rivers, bays, coastal waters, sewage-treatment ponds; often with Bonaparte's Gulls.

SMALL HOODED GULLS
Adults

nonbreeding

LAUGHING
GULL

breeding

FRANKLIN'S
GULL

nonbreeding

breeding

SABINE'S GULL

nonbreeding

breeding

BLACK-HEADED
GULL

nonbreeding

breeding

BONAPARTE'S
GULL

nonbreeding

breeding

nonbreeding

LITTLE GULL

breeding

HEERMANN'S GULL *Larus heermanni*   Common M233
19 in. (48 cm). The easiest gull in West to identify. *In all plumages, has black legs and feet.* Adult has *dark gray body, black tail* with thin white tip, whitish head, *red bill with black tip.* In fall and early winter, white head becomes gray. A few birds have white patches on upperwing. *Immature:* See p. 194. **VOICE:** Whining *whee-ee;* also a repeated *cow-auk.* **SIMILAR SPECIES:** May be confused with jaegers because of Heermann's habit of chasing other birds for food, overall dark coloration, and occasional adult with white wing patch. **HABITAT:** Ocean and immediate coastlines, including parks.

CALIFORNIA GULL *Larus californicus*   Common M236
21–21½ in. (53–55 cm). Resembles smaller Ring-billed Gull (both may have yellow or yellowish green legs) or larger Herring Gull, but note darker mantle and *darker eye.* Shows more white in wingtips than Ring-billed does. In nonbreeding plumage, head streaked or mottled brownish, dark spot on bill may extend to upper mandible, legs slightly duller. *Immature:* See p. 196. **VOICE:** Like Herring Gull's but higher, more hoarse. **HABITAT:** Ocean and coasts, lakes, farms, dumps, urban centers.

RING-BILLED GULL *Larus delawarensis*   Common M235
17–17½ in. (43–45 cm). Similar to Herring Gull, but smaller, more buoyant, and dovelike. A small gull, with *pale eye* and *light gray mantle* (similar to Herring's); *legs yellow or greenish yellow* (may be duller in nonbreeding plumage). Note complete *black ring* encircling bill. In nonbreeding plumage, shows some fine dark streaking on head. *Immature:* See p. 194. Also see Sequence of Plumages in a Three-Year Gull, p. 184. **VOICE:** Higher pitched than Herring Gull's. **SIMILAR SPECIES:** Mew Gull lacks bold blackish bill ring, has darker mantle, dark eye, and, in nonbreeding plumage, more extensive dark mottling on head and neck. Also see immature Mew Gull. **HABITAT:** Lakes, bays, coasts, piers, dumps, plowed fields, sewage outlets, shopping malls, fast-food restaurants.

MEW GULL *Larus canus*   Common M234
16–17 in. (41–44 cm). Slightly smaller than Ring-billed Gull, with more greenish yellow legs and small, short, *unmarked greenish yellow bill.* (Birds in full breeding condition have yellow bill and legs.) *Darkish eye. Mantle medium gray, noticeably darker than Ring-billed's.* Mew shows larger white "mirrors" in its black wingtips than either California or Ring-billed gull. *Immature:* See p. 194. **VOICE:** Low, mewing *queeu* or *meeu.* Also *hiyah-hiyah-hiyah,* etc., higher than voice of other gulls. **SIMILAR SPECIES:** Immature Ring-billed Gull; adult Black-legged Kittiwake. **HABITAT:** In winter, ocean, coastlines, parks, dumps, wet fields, tidal rivers; in summer, lakes, taiga, tundra.

BLACK-LEGGED KITTIWAKE *Rissa tridactyla*   Uncommon M248
16–17 in. (41–43 cm). A small, buoyant oceanic gull. Wingtips lack white spots and are *solid black,* almost *straight across,* as if dipped in ink. Bill small, pale yellow, and unmarked. Legs and feet *black. Eyes dark.* In nonbreeding plumage, rear head and nape dusky. *Immature:* See p. 194. **VOICE:** At nesting colony, a raucous *kaka-week* or *kitti-waak.* **SIMILAR SPECIES:** Mew, Ring-billed, and Sabine's gulls; in w. AK, Red-legged Kittiwake. **HABITAT:** Chiefly oceanic; rarely on beaches, casual inland. Nests on sea cliffs.

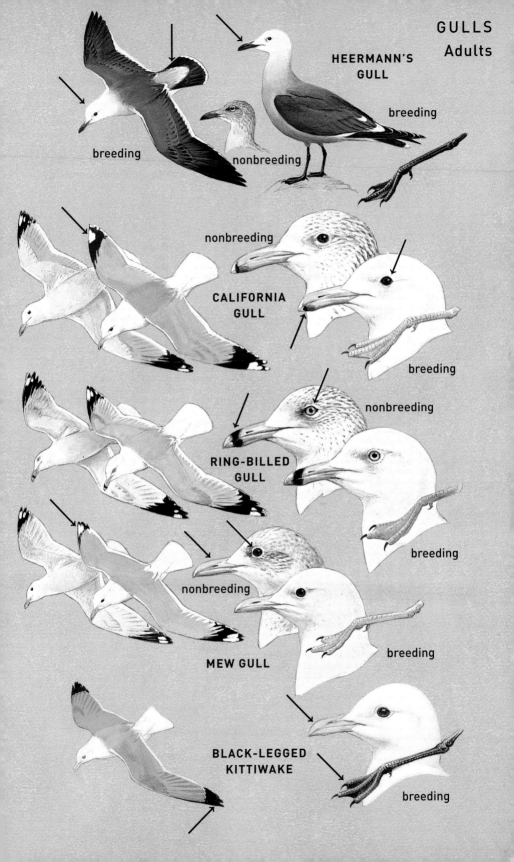

GULLS
Adults

HEERMANN'S
GULL

breeding

breeding

nonbreeding

CALIFORNIA
GULL

nonbreeding

breeding

RING-BILLED
GULL

nonbreeding

breeding

MEW GULL

nonbreeding

breeding

BLACK-LEGGED
KITTIWAKE

breeding

HERRING GULL
Common in East, uncommon in West M237

Larus argentatus

24–25 in. (61–64 cm). A widespread (though less numerous in West than in East), fairly large gull. Regularly hybridizes with Glaucous-winged Gull in AK. *Pale gray* mantle, *pinkish* legs, *pale eye*. Outer primaries *black* with white spots or "mirrors." Bill yellow with red spot on lower mandible. In nonbreeding plumage, head and neck streaked or mottled with brownish. *Immature:* See p. 196. Also see Sequence of Plumages in a Four-Year Gull, p. 184. **VOICE:** A loud *hiyak . . . hiyak . . . hyiah-hyak* or *yuk-yuk-yuk-yuk-yuckle-yuckle.* Mewing squeals. Anxiety call *gah-gah-gah.* **SIMILAR SPECIES:** Thayer's and California gulls. Latter darker mantled, has dark eye, greenish yellow legs. **HABITAT:** Ocean, coasts, bays, beaches, lakes, dams, piers, farmland, dumps.

THAYER'S GULL *Larus thayeri*
Scarce M238

23–24 in. (58–61 cm). Formerly thought to be a race of Herring Gull. Now designated as a full species, but regarded by some as a subspecies of Iceland Gull. Very similar to Herring Gull. Typical adult has *pale to dark brown* eyes, *only a thin trailing edge of black* on *grayish* underside of primaries, slightly darker mantle, slightly deeper pink legs, and somewhat slighter bill, often with greenish-tinged base. In nonbreeding plumage, head and neck streaked or mottled with brownish. *Immature:* See p. 198. **VOICE:** Similar to Herring Gull. **SIMILAR SPECIES:** Iceland Gull; Glaucous-winged × Western gull hybrid larger, has larger, thicker bill. **HABITAT:** Similar to Herring Gull.

GLAUCOUS-WINGED GULL *Larus glaucescens*
Locally common M244

25–26 in. (63–66 cm). A *very large pinkish-legged* gull, with large bill, pale gray mantle, and *medium gray* primaries. *Immature:* See p. 198. Hybridizes with Western Gull where their ranges overlap in Pacific Northwest, and with Herring Gull in AK. **VOICE:** Low *kak-kak-kak;* a low *wow;* a high *keer, keer.* **SIMILAR SPECIES:** Adult Glaucous Gull has whitish primaries, thinner bill, paler eye. See also Western, Thayer's, and Herring gulls. **HABITAT:** Ocean, coastlines, parks, dumps, lakeshores.

GLAUCOUS GULL *Larus hyperboreus*
Uncommon M245

27–28 in. (68–72 cm). A large, chalky white gull with pinkish legs. Note "frosty" wingtips. Has pale gray mantle and *unmarked white outer primaries. Light eye. Immature:* See p. 198. **VOICE:** Much like Herring Gull's. **SIMILAR SPECIES:** Iceland Gull, but that species is smaller than Herring Gull; also, Iceland's bill is smaller, head rounder, and wings proportionately longer and narrower. Breeding adult Iceland has narrow red eye-ring (Glaucous, yellow), but this is hard to see. See also Glaucous-winged Gull. **HABITAT:** Mainly coastal; a few inland at large lakes and dumps.

ICELAND GULL *Larus glaucoides*
Uncommon M239

22–23 in. (56–60 cm). A pale ghostly gull, slightly smaller than Herring Gull. Mantle pale gray; primaries whitish and extending *well beyond tail. Immature:* See p. 198. "Kumlien's" Gull *(Larus glaucoides kumlieni),* the subspecies that breeds in e. Arctic Canada, is the one seen in U.S.; has gray or dark markings, variable in extent, toward tips of whitish primaries (not black with white "mirrors" as in Herring Gull). **VOICE:** Similar to Herring Gull but higher pitched; rarely heard away from breeding grounds. **SIMILAR SPECIES:** Glaucous Gull larger, has larger bill, shorter primary extension. Adult Thayer's Gull has slightly darker mantle, blacker primaries, dark eye. **HABITAT:** Ocean, coastlines, dumps.

GULLS
Adults

HERRING GULL

nonbreeding

breeding

THAYER'S GULL

nonbreeding

breeding

GLAUCOUS-WINGED GULL

nonbreeding

breeding

GLAUCOUS GULL

breeding

nonbreeding

breeding

ICELAND GULL

"Kumlien's" (typical)

pale extreme

WESTERN GULL *Larus occidentalis*   Locally common M243
25–26 in. (64–66 cm). A large, large-billed gull. Note *very dark* back and wings (called *"mantle"*) contrasting with snowy underparts. Legs and feet dull pinkish. Northern race (cen. CA to WA) has paler mantle, but it is still noticeably darker than that of California Gull. Southern race is blacker backed and paler eyed, appears cleaner headed in winter. *Immature:* See p. 196. *Note:* There is much hybridization with Glaucous-winged Gull where their breeding ranges overlap. Hybrids have intermediate mantle and wingtip coloration. They are found in winter south to cen. CA, with a few inland as well. **VOICE:** Guttural *kuk kuk kuk;* also *whee whee whee* and *ki-aa.* **SIMILAR SPECIES:** Glaucous-winged and Herring gulls. **HABITAT:** Offshore and coastal waters, beaches, piers, city waterfronts, parks, lower reaches of tidal rivers.

YELLOW-FOOTED GULL *Larus livens*   Uncommon, very local M242
27 in. (69 cm). In U.S., this species found regularly only at Salton Sea. This large gull closely resembles Western Gull, but adult has *yellow* (not pinkish) legs and feet and slightly thicker bill. It matures in its third year, not fourth as Western Gull does. *Immature:* Brown juvenile has whitish belly and by first winter already has some black on back. Yellow legs and feet are attained by second winter. **VOICE:** Deeper than Western's. **HABITAT:** Same as Western Gull.

GREAT BLACK-BACKED GULL *Larus marinus*   Common M246
29–30 in. (73–76 cm). Largest gull in the world, with broad wings and heavy body and bill. Black back and wings, snow-white underparts, no head streaking in winter. Legs and feet *pale* pinkish. *Immature:* See p. 196. **VOICE:** Harsh deep seal-like *kyow* or *owk.* **SIMILAR SPECIES:** Lesser Black-backed and Slaty-backed gulls. **HABITAT:** Mainly coastal waters, estuaries, dumps; a few well inland on large lakes and rivers.

LESSER BLACK-BACKED GULL *Larus fuscus*   Scarce M240
21–22½ in. (53–57 cm). Similar to Great Black-backed Gull but smaller (smaller than Herring Gull) and slimmer, with longer wings and smaller bill. Distinguished by yellowish (not pink) legs and slate gray (not black) mantle. Extensive head and neck streaking or mottling in nonbreeding plumage. Pale eye. Oblong red spot on bill. *Immature:* See p. 196. **VOICE:** Harsh *kyah.* **SIMILAR SPECIES:** Great Black-backed Gull. **HABITAT:** Same as Herring Gull.

GULLS
Dark-backed Adults

southern

WESTERN
GULL

northern

YELLOW-
FOOTED GULL

LESSER BLACK-
BACKED GULL

Great Black-backed Gull

among the gulls on this plate, only
Lesser Black-backed shows heavy
head streaking in nonbreeding plumage

GREAT BLACK-BACKED GULL

Immature Gulls

Immatures of many gull species are more difficult to identify than adults. They are usually darkest the first year and lighter the second, when some species start to show their adult eye and back color. Larger species do not develop their full adult plumage until the third or fourth year. (See pp. 184–85.) Identify mainly by pattern, size, and structure. The most typical plumages are shown here; intermediate and successive stages can be expected, but because of variables such as stage of molt, wear, age, individual variation, hybridization, and occasional albinism, some birds may remain a mystery even to the expert.

LAUGHING GULL *Larus atricilla*   Adult, p. 186
A three-year gull. *Juvenile:* Dark brown with black tail, white rump, and *broad white* trailing edge of wing. *First year:* Neck and back become extensively smudged with gray. *Second year:* Similar to nonbreeding adult, but with trace of black in tail. **SIMILAR SPECIES:** Franklin's Gull.

FRANKLIN'S GULL *Larus pipixcan*   Adult, p. 186
A three-year gull. *First year:* Similar to first-year Laughing Gull, but more petite with *smaller and straighter bill, blackish extensive half-hood, white neck, incomplete tail band* (outermost tail feather *white*), whitish breast, paler underside to primaries. *Second year:* Close to second winter Laughing but with blackish half hood, pale underside to primaries.

BLACK-HEADED GULL *Larus ridibundus*   Adult, p. 186
A two-year gull. *First year:* Similar to first-year Bonaparte's Gull but slightly larger; bill longer, *orange to red* at base, black at tip; *sooty underwing;* broad dusky trailing edge to upperwing.

BONAPARTE'S GULL *Larus philadelphia*   Adult, p. 186.
A two-year gull. Petite, ternlike. *First year:* Note dark ear spot, narrow black tail band, neat dark trailing edge to wings, and pattern of black and white in outer primaries. Pale underwing. See Sequence of Plumages in a Two-Year Gull, p. 184.

LITTLE GULL *Larus minutus*   Adult, p. 186
A two-year gull. *First year:* Slightly smaller than Bonaparte's Gull, with *blacker M pattern* across back and wings, *white trailing edge* to wings, *dusky cap.*

SABINE'S GULL *Xema sabini*   Adult, p. 186
A two-year gull. *Juvenile:* Dark grayish brown on back, but with adult's bold *triangular wing pattern.* Note also *forked* tail.

HEERMANN'S GULL *Larus heermanni*   Adult, p. 188
A four-year gull. Readily told by *black legs and feet* and overall *dark brown or sooty gray color.* Note two-toned bill.

BLACK-LEGGED KITTIWAKE *Rissa tridactyla*   Adult, p. 188
A three-year gull. *First year:* Note *dark bar on nape* (held into early winter), *black M across back and wings;* tail may seem notched. White trailing edge to wings.

MEW GULL *Larus canus*   Adult, p. 188
A three-year gull. *First year:* Smaller than Ring-billed with shorter, slimmer bill, rounder head, browner primaries, broader tail band and heavily mottled tail coverts, darker gray back, dark belly smudge.

RING-BILLED GULL *Larus delawarensis*   Adult, p. 188
A three-year gull. *First year:* Usually *bicolored (pinkish-based) bill,* mostly whitish underneath and on rump and upper tail, *pale gray back.* Subterminal tail band narrow and usually well defined; contrasty wing pattern. **SIMILAR SPECIES:** Mew and California gulls.

SMALL GULLS
Immatures

juvenile

first winter

juvenile

LAUGHING GULL

first winter

Laughing
Gull

Franklin's Gull

first year

first year

RANKLIN'S GULL

BLACK-
EADED GULL

first year

BONAPARTE'S
GULL

first year

LITTLE
GULL

first year

SABINE'S GULL

juvenile

first year

HEERMANN'S GULL

first year

second
year

BLACK-LEGGED
KITTIWAKE

first year

first year

first year

RING-BILLED
GULL

MEW GULL

WESTERN GULL *Larus occidentalis*　　　　　　　　　Adult, p. 192
A four-year gull. Compared with first-year Herring Gull, first-year Western is larger, larger-billed, sootier brown, lacks pale inner primaries.

CALIFORNIA GULL *Larus californicus*　　　　　　　　Adult, p. 188
A four-year gull. *First year:* Like Herring Gull, but slightly smaller, with smaller bicolored bill. In flight, shows double dark bar on wing and lacks pale area on inner primaries. *Second year:* Legs and bill base often dull gray-green-blue. Much like first-winter Ring-billed Gull, but somewhat larger, retains dark eye, darker gray on back, and tail mostly dark rather than with only a dark subterminal band.

LESSER BLACK-BACKED GULL *Larus fuscus*　　　　　Adult, p. 192
A four-year gull. Smaller, slimmer than Herring Gull. *First year:* Like miniature first-year Great Black-backed but with broader tail band, darker wings, more heavily streaked breast; colder brown than Herring with white tail base, paler head and underparts, darker wings.

HERRING GULL *Larus argentatus*　　　　　　　　　　Adult, p. 190
A four-year gull. *First year:* Brownish overall, with brownish black wingtips and dark brown tail; only all-brown gull commonly seen in the East. Often shows much mottling or checkering on upperwing coverts and rump. *Pale area on inner primaries visible in flight.* Bill all dark at first, becoming paler at base later. *Second and third years:* Head and underparts whiter; eye pale; back pale gray; rump white; bill pale, dark-tipped. See Sequence of Plumages in a Four-Year Gull, p. 184.

GREAT BLACK-BACKED GULL *Larus marinus*　　　　Adult, p. 192
A four-year gull. *First year:* Larger and more salt-and-pepper patterned than first-year Herring Gulls. They show more contrast, being paler on head, rump, and underparts. Pale belly contrasts with dark underwing. More checkered looking than Herring. *Second year:* The "saddle-back" pattern is suggested; they may resemble later immature stages of Herring Gull, but back darker, head and bill larger.

second year

first year

LARGE GULLS
Dark
Immatures

first year

second year

WESTERN GULL

first year

second year

first year

California Gull

first year

**ESSER BLACK-
BACKED GULL**

first year

**GREAT BLACK-
BACKED GULL**

first year

**HERRING
GULL**

second year

CALIFORNIA GULL

first year

HERRING GULL

first year

second year

THAYER'S GULL *Larus thayeri*   Adult, p. 190

A four-year gull. *First year:* Tan-brown and checkered; similar to juvenile Herring Gull but lighter; primaries paler, usually *light tan-brown* (not brownish black) *with pale edges to tips; bill entirely or almost entirely blackish, more petite; underside of primaries pale.* Often shows dark smudge through eye. *Second year:* Paler and grayer; primaries gray-brown with darker outer webs.

ICELAND GULL *Larus glaucoides*   Adult, p. 190

Sequence of plumages similar to Glaucous Gull's, but Iceland is smaller (smaller than Herring Gull) with smaller bill and proportionately longer wings (projecting beyond tail at rest). Bill of most first-year Iceland Gulls mostly dark, only very rarely as sharply demarcated as in Glaucous. Most birds show a hint of a tail band as well as some dark in outer primaries, both lacking in Glaucous; darkest birds approach Thayer's in appearance.

GLAUCOUS GULL *Larus hyperboreus*   Adult, p. 190

A four-year gull. *First year:* Recognized by its large size, pale tan or off-whitish (particularly by late winter) coloration, and unmarked *frosty primaries,* a shade lighter than rest of wing. Brownish barring on undertail coverts and mottling in wing coverts and tail. Bill *pale pinkish* with dark tip—*sharply demarcated. Second year:* Pale gray back and pale eye acquired.

GLAUCOUS-WINGED GULL *Larus glaucescens*   Adult, p. 190

A four-year gull. Variable. Size of Herring Gull, and with similar sequence of plumages (see p. 196), but primaries are close to same tone as rest of wing, not markedly darker as in Western and Herring gulls, or paler or translucent as in Glaucous Gull. Hybrids with Western or Herring gulls have intermediate-colored primaries. Worn Glacous-wingeds in spring and summer may appear very white, but lack clean-cut two-toned bill and tan mottling to wing- and undertail coverts of Glaucous.

LARGE GULLS
Pale Immatures

THAYER'S GULL

second year

first year

first year

first year

ICELAND GULL

third year

Glaucous Gull
first year

Iceland Gull
first year

second year

first year

GLAUCOUS GULL

second year

first year

first year

second year

GLAUCOUS-WINGED GULL

BLACK-TAILED GULL *Larus carassirostris*   Vagrant
18–18½ in. (46–47 cm). Slightly larger than Ring-billed Gull, and with slightly longer wings and bill. Adult has red tip to black-banded bill, slate gray mantle, and wide black subterminal band on tail. **RANGE:** Casual visitor from e. Asia, with widely scattered records across much of N. America.

YELLOW-LEGGED GULL *Larus cachinnans*   Vagrant
24–24½ in. (61–63 cm). This native of s. Europe was recently split from Herring Gull. Very similar to Herring Gull, but bill slightly stouter, adult's mantle slightly *darker gray,* and head flatter and only *finely streaked on crown* in nonbreeding plumage. Orbital ring red, and red spot on bill slightly larger. *Yellow legs* of adult usually distinctive, but beware some Herring Gulls that show yellowish tones to legs in late winter and early spring. **RANGE:** Casual visitor to Atlantic Seaboard, with most records to date from NL. **HABITAT:** Similar to Herring Gull.

SLATY-BACKED GULL *Larus schistisagus*   Scarce, local M241
25–26 in. (64–67 cm). Any large, very dark backed gull in Bering Sea is likely to be this Asian species. Adult similar to Western Gull, but with slightly slimmer bill, paler eye, deeper pinkish feet, *extensive head streaking, and dusky mark through eye in nonbreeding plumage.* Note how broad white trailing edge of wing invades outer wing, forming *thin white bar* crossing dark primaries (best seen across underwing). Primaries *gray* beneath. **SIMILAR SPECIES:** Siberian subspecies of Herring Gull *(vegae),* found in same areas of w. AK, is darker mantled than typical N. American Herring Gull. **RANGE:** Regular visitor to w. AK, casual across much of the rest of N. America. **HABITAT:** Seacoasts, beaches, dumps.

RED-LEGGED KITTIWAKE *Rissa brevirostris*   Uncommon, very local M249
15 in. (38 cm). *Adult:* Similar to Black-legged Kittiwake but smaller, with *darker gray mantle* (very noticeable when both species seen together); *shorter bill and rounder head* give it a more dove-headed look; legs *bright red.* Has similar wing pattern above (although white trailing edge broader); *darkish gray underwing. Immature:* Wing pattern more similar to Sabine's Gull; tail lacks black terminal band. Legs duller than in adult. **VOICE:** High-pitched *tuu-WEE* near nesting colony. **HABITAT:** Open ocean, where it often forages at night. Nests in colonies on steep, rocky ocean cliffs.

ROSS'S GULL *Rhodostethia rosea*   Very rare M250
13–13½ in. (33–35 cm). A rare Arctic gull of drift ice. Note *wedge-shaped tail, medium gray wing linings,* and *small black bill.* A two-year gull. *Breeding:* Rosy blush on underparts, *fine black collar. Nonbreeding:* Rosy blush duller or lacking, lacks black collar, may be washed with gray. *First winter:* Similar in pattern to immature Black-legged Kittiwake or Little Gull, but intermediate in size and note *wedge-shaped tail* (not square or notched) and *gray* linings of underwing; lacks dark nape of young kittiwake. **HABITAT:** Arctic waters, tundra in summer.

IVORY GULL *Pagophila eburnea*   Very rare, threatened M251
17 in. (43 cm). A declining species of Arctic pack ice. Most individuals that wander south of normal range are immatures. A two-year gull. *Adult:* The only all-white gull with black legs. Pigeon sized with dovelike head; wings long, flight ternlike. Bill greenish with yellow tip. *Immature:* White, with dark *smudge on face,* a *sprinkling of black spots* above, black spots on primary tips, and narrow black tip to tail. Legs and feet black, a distinction from all other white gulls. **HABITAT:** Open Arctic waters near pack ice.

RARE GULLS

LACK-
AILED
GULL

onbreeding

YELLOW-
LEGGED GULL

nonbreeding

SLATY-BACKED
GULL

breeding

breeding

RED-LEGGED
KITTIWAKE

nonbreeding

breeding

first year

ROSS'S
GULL

nonbreeding

breeding

adult

first year

IVORY GULL

TERNS Subfamily Sterninae

Graceful waterbirds, more streamlined than gulls; wings more pointed, tail usually forked. Bill sharp-pointed, often tilted toward water when bird is flying. Most terns are whitish with black cap; in nonbreeding plumage, black of forehead replaced by white. Sexes alike. Terns often hover and plunge headfirst for fish. Normally do not swim (gulls do). **FOOD:** Small fish, marine life, large insects. **RANGE:** Almost worldwide.

FORSTER'S TERN *Sterna forsteri*   Common M263
14½ in. (37 cm). Very similar to Common Tern, but adult Forster's paler; all adults have frosty wingtips (lighter than rest of wing; darkening in Common). Whitish below in all plumages, lacking gray wash of breeding Common. Tail grayer; bill slightly thicker and more orange than red. Nonbreeding adult and immature have isolated *black mask* and lack dark carpal ("shoulder") bar of Common in similar plumages. See also Arctic Tern. **VOICE:** Harsh, nasal *za-a-ap* and nasal *kyarr*. **HABITAT:** Fresh and salt marshes, lakes, bays, beaches, nearshore ocean; nests in marshes.

COMMON TERN *Sterna hirundo*   Uncommon to common M261
14 in. (36 cm). A graceful, small, black-capped, slim bird with deeply forked tail. *Breeding adult:* Pearl gray mantle and black cap; bill red with black tip; feet orange-red. Similar to Forster's Tern, but several outer primaries form *dark wedge on upperwing, grayer below, bill slightly smaller and redder, legs shorter. Nonbreeding adult and immature:* Cap, nape, and bill blackish. *Show dark shoulder (carpal) bar.* Asian subspecies *(longipennis)*, a very rare visitor in w. AK, darker, with *black bill* in breeding plumage and *blackish legs and feet.* **VOICE:** Drawling *kee-arr* (downward inflection); also *kik-kik-kik;* a quick *kirri-kirri.* **HABITAT:** Lakes, ocean, bays, marshes, beaches; nests colonially on sandy beaches and small islands.

ARCTIC TERN *Sterna paradisaea*   Uncommon M262
15 in. (38 cm). A pelagic (seagoing) tern. Similar to Forster's and particularly Common terns. Bill and neck shorter, head rounder. *Legs shorter.* Overhead, note *translucent* effect of primaries and *narrow* black trailing edge; from above, secondaries pale. *Breeding adult:* Bill usually *blood red* to tip, uniform pale gray upperwing, extensive wash of *gray below,* setting off white cheeks. (*Caution:* Breeding Common Terns are fairly similar below.) *Nonbreeding and juvenile:* Like Common, but black on head slightly more extensive, shoulder bar somewhat *weaker, secondaries whitish,* and same structural differences as in breeding. **VOICE:** *Kee-yak,* similar to Common Tern's cry, but less slurred, higher. A high *keer-keer* is characteristic. **HABITAT:** Open ocean, coasts, islands; in summer, also taiga lakes, tundra.

ROSEATE TERN *Sterna dougallii*   Scarce, local M260
15½ in. (39 cm). Similar to Common Tern, but much paler overall, with longer tail points. *At rest, tail extends well beyond wingtips.* In spring and summer, *thin, long black bill sets it apart from similar terns,* all of which have reddish bill at that time of year. When breeding, Roseate may acquire rosy blush to breast and varying amounts of red at base of bill; then rely on other points such as *more shallow wingbeats* and *different call* to separate from Common. *Immature:* Back of juvenile shows pattern of coarse crescents. Secondaries pale (darker in Common). **VOICE:** Rasping *ka-a-ak;* a soft two-syllable *chu-ick* or *chiv-ick.* **HABITAT:** Salt bays, estuaries, ocean.

SMALLER TERNS

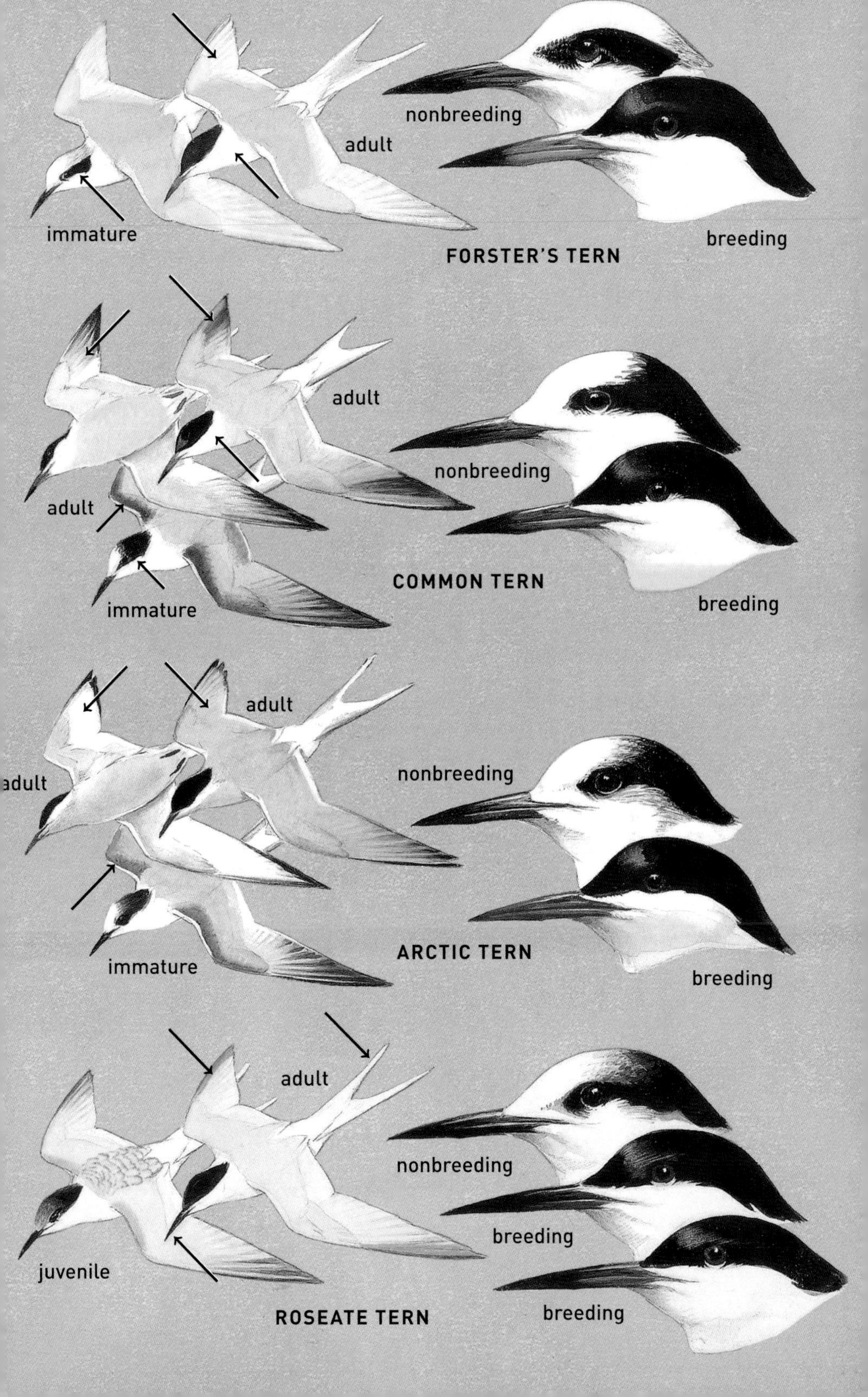

FORSTER'S TERN

nonbreeding
adult
immature
breeding

COMMON TERN

adult
adult
immature
nonbreeding
breeding

ARCTIC TERN

adult
adult
immature
nonbreeding
breeding

ROSEATE TERN

adult
juvenile
nonbreeding
breeding
breeding

SANDWICH TERN *Thalasseus sandvicensis*   Fairly common M265

15–15½ in. (38–40 cm). Larger than Common Tern. Note *long black bill with yellow tip* "as though dipped in mustard." Bill of young can be mostly black or mostly yellow. Dark outer primaries. *Adult:* All-black cap in breeding plumage, white forehead in nonbreeding plumage; feathers on back of crown elongated, forming crest. Legs black. **VOICE:** Grating *kirrick* (higher than Gull-billed Tern's *kay-weck*). **SIMILAR SPECIES:** Gull-billed Tern has stout black bill. **HABITAT:** Coastal waters, jetties, beaches. Often seen with Royal Tern.

ELEGANT TERN *Thalasseus elegans*   Locally common M266

17 in. (43 cm). This Mexican species has recently expanded its breeding range to include San Diego and Orange counties in CA. North of there it should be looked for primarily between midsummer and late fall. In size, slightly smaller than Royal Tern. Bill orange or orange-yellow, proportionately *longer, more slender,* and slightly droopier than deeper orange bill of Royal. Elegant's black crown extends farther down nape. In nonbreeding plumage, dark of head *includes eye.* **VOICE:** Nasal *karrik* or *kerr-rik.* **SIMILAR SPECIES:** Royal and Caspian terns. **HABITAT:** Ocean, coasts, beaches, salt bays.

ROYAL TERN *Thalasseus maximus*   Common M264

20 in. (51 cm). A large tern, slimmer than Caspian, with large *orange* bill (Caspian's bill heavier, redder, and has dark mark near tip). Tail forked. Although some Royal Terns in spring show solid black crown, for most of year they have *much white on forehead,* black crown feathers forming a crest. In nonbreeding plumage, black feathers behind eye usually *do not encompass eye* as they do in nonbreeding Elegant Tern. Dusky upperside and *pale underside to primaries,* opposite of Caspian. **VOICE:** Sonorous *karr-rik,* mellower (slower and lower-pitched) than Elegant or Sandwich; also *kaak* or *kak.* **SIMILAR SPECIES:** Caspian and Elegant terns. **HABITAT:** Ocean, coasts, beaches, salt bays. More closely tied to coastal waters than Caspian, which is common inland.

CASPIAN TERN *Hydroprogne caspia*   Uncommon M258

21 in. (53 cm). Large size and *stout reddish bill with small dark mark near tip* set Caspian apart from all other terns. Tail of Caspian *shorter;* head and bill larger, crest shorter. Royal's forehead is usually *clear white* (in adult nonbreeding plumage, Caspian has *streaked* forehead). Caspian shows obvious *grayish black on undersurface of primaries, but pale upper surface.* Caspian ranges inland, Royal does not. **VOICE:** Raspy, low *kraa-uh* or *karr,* also repeated *kak;* juveniles give whistled *wheee-oo.* **SIMILAR SPECIES:** Royal and Elegant terns. **HABITAT:** Large lakes, rivers, coastal waters, beaches, bays.

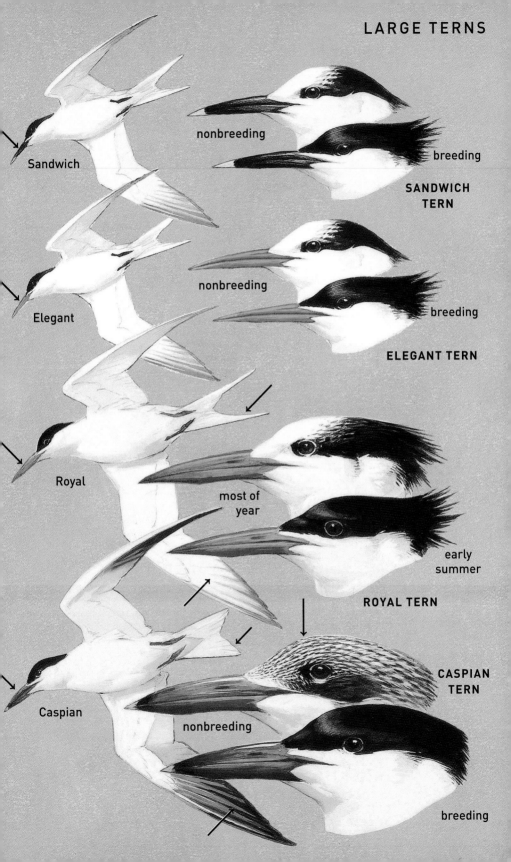

LARGE TERNS

nonbreeding

Sandwich

breeding

SANDWICH TERN

nonbreeding

Elegant

breeding

ELEGANT TERN

Royal

most of year

early summer

ROYAL TERN

Caspian

nonbreeding

CASPIAN TERN

breeding

GULL-BILLED TERN *Gelochelidon nilotica*   Uncommon M257
14 in. (36 cm). Note *stout black* bill. Stockier and paler than Common Tern; tail much less forked; feet *black*. In nonbreeding plumage, head white with smudgy dark ear patch, pale dusky on nape; suggests a small gull with notched tail. *Immature:* Similar to nonbreeding adult. This tern plucks food from water's surface and often hawks for insects over marshes and fields, swooping (rarely diving) after prey. **VOICE:** *Kay-weck, kay-weck;* also a throaty, rasping *za-za-za.* **SIMILAR SPECIES:** Sandwich Tern, mid-sized gulls. **HABITAT:** Marshes, fields, coastal bays.

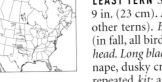

LEAST TERN *Sternula antillarum*   Locally common M256
9 in. (23 cm). A *very small,* pale tern, with rapid wingbeats (quicker than other terns). *Breeding adult:* Dark-tipped *yellow bill, yellow legs and feet* (in fall, all birds may have dark bill, but feet show yellow), and *white forehead. Long black wedge on outer wing. Immature:* Dark bill, dark cheek and nape, dusky crown, dark shoulder (carpal) bar, duller legs. **VOICE:** Sharp, repeated *kit;* a harsh, squealing *zree-eek* or *k-zeek;* also a rapid *kitti-kitti-kitti.* **SIMILAR SPECIES:** Forster's Tern. **HABITAT:** Beaches, bays, ponds, large rivers, sandbars.

ALEUTIAN TERN *Onychoprion aleuticus*   Scarce, local M255
13½–14 in. (34–36 cm). A lead-colored tern of Alaskan coastal waters. Told from Arctic Tern by its *blackish bill and legs, clean-cut white forehead, dark bar along underside of secondaries.* Lead gray body and mantle contrast with white tail. *Juvenile:* Boldly edged with rusty orange above; legs orangey red. **VOICE:** Three-syllable whistle, suggesting a shorebird or House Sparrow. **HABITAT:** Open ocean; summers/nests along AK coast on islands, sandbars.

BLACK TERN *Chlidonias niger*   Uncommon M259
9½–9¾ in. (24–25 cm). A black-bodied tern. Short tail only slightly forked. *Breeding adult:* Head and underparts (except undertail coverts) *black; back, wings, and tail dark gray;* wing linings whitish. *Nonbreeding adult:* By midsummer, molting birds are mottled, with black largely replaced by white. Note pied head, with dark smudge from crown to ear coverts and on sides of breast. *Immature:* Similar to nonbreeding adult. **VOICE:** Sharp *kik, keek,* or *klea.* **SIMILAR SPECIES:** White-winged Tern. **HABITAT:** Freshwater marshes, lakes; in migration, also coastal waters, including open ocean.

WHITE-WINGED TERN *Chlidonias leucopterus*   Vagrant
9¼–9½ in. (23–24 cm). *Breeding: Underwing lining black, upperwing mostly white,* tail paler. *Nonbreeding:* Paler than Black Tern; lacks dark shoulder spot. **RANGE:** Vagrant from Eurasia. Widespread eastern sightings; a few in West.

TERNS

Gull-billed

nonbreeding

breeding

GULL-BILLED TERN

immature

adult

nonbreeding

breeding

LEAST TERN

nonbreeding

breeding

ALEUTIAN TERN

breeding

nonbreeding

BLACK TERN

breeding

nonbreeding

nonbreeding

WHITE-WINGED TERN

breeding

BROWN NODDY *Anous stolidus*   Uncommon, local M252
15–15½ in. (38–40 cm). A sooty brown tern with *whitish cap.* Wedge-shaped tail. Immature has duller cap. **VOICE:** Ripping *karrrk* or *arrrrowk;* a harsh *eye-ak.* **SIMILAR SPECIES:** Black Noddy occurs occasionally with Brown Noddies at Dry Tortugas, FL. **HABITAT:** Warm ocean waters.

BLACK NODDY *Anous minutus*   Very rare visitor
13½ in. (34 cm). A rare but almost annual spring visitor to Dry Tortugas, FL, and casual visitor to TX. Slightly smaller and slimmer than Brown Noddy, with thinner and proportionately *longer bill,* darker body, and more extensive and *sharply defined white cap.* Most birds seen in U.S. are one-year-olds, which show worn, brownish wing coverts. **VOICE:** Variety of chatters, croaks, and bill rattles. **SIMILAR SPECIES:** Brown Noddy. **HABITAT:** Tropical islands.

SOOTY TERN *Onychoprion fuscatus*   Uncommon, local M253
16 in. (41 cm). *Adult:* A cleanly patterned tern, black above and white below. Cheeks and patch on forehead white; bill and feet black. *Immature:* Dark brown; back spotted with white; note forked tail. **VOICE:** Nasal *wide-a-wake* or *wacky-wack.* **SIMILAR SPECIES:** Bridled Tern. **HABITAT:** Warm ocean waters.

BRIDLED TERN *Onychoprion anaethetus*   Uncommon, local M254
15 in. (38 cm). A tern of warm oceans and, after hurricanes, farther north. **VOICE:** Mostly silent; sometimes gives a soft, nasal *wheeep.* **SIMILAR SPECIES:** Resembles Sooty Tern, but back brownish, not blackish; *note whitish collar separating black cap from back;* white forehead patch extends behind eye (in Sooty, to above eye). Sooty also has more limited white in tail and *darker underside of primaries.* **HABITAT:** Warm ocean waters, usually well offshore.

SKIMMERS Subfamily Rynchopinae

Slim, short-legged relatives of gulls and terns. Scissorlike red bill; *lower mandible longer than upper.* **FOOD:** Small fish, crustaceans. **RANGE:** Coasts, ponds, marshes, beaches, rivers of warmer parts of world.

BLACK SKIMMER *Rhynchops niger*   Locally common M267
18–18½ in. (46–47 cm). More slender than a gull, with very long wings. Skims low, dipping lower mandible in water, snapping shut when it comes in contact with a food item. (Forages mostly at night.) *Adult:* Black above; white face and underparts. Bright red bill (tipped with black) is long and flat vertically; *lower mandible juts a third beyond upper.* Reddish legs. *Immature:* Brownish and speckled above, bill smaller, bill and legs duller. **VOICE:** Soft, short, barking notes. Also *kaup, kaup.* **HABITAT:** Bays, marshes, beaches, protected ocean waters.

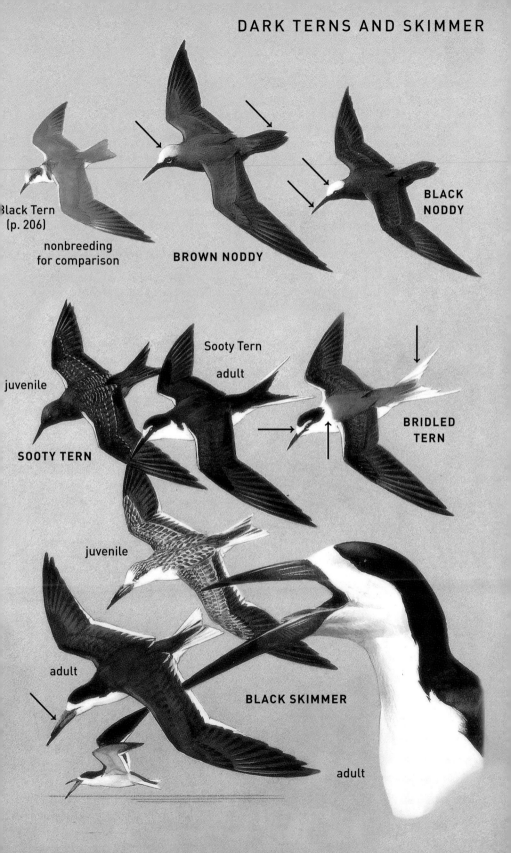

DARK TERNS AND SKIMMER

Black Tern
(p. 206)

nonbreeding
for comparison

BROWN NODDY

BLACK
NODDY

juvenile

Sooty Tern

adult

SOOTY TERN

BRIDLED
TERN

juvenile

adult

BLACK SKIMMER

adult

SKUAS AND JAEGERS Family Stercorariidae

Falconlike seabirds that harass gulls and terns, forcing them to disgorge or drop their food. Light, intermediate, and dark morphs exist in at least two species; all have flash of white in primaries. Adult jaegers have two projecting central tail feathers, which are sometimes broken or missing. Young birds lack these feathers. Separating jaegers in most plumages can be very difficult. Skuas are larger, lack tail points, and are broader winged. Sexes alike. **FOOD:** In Arctic, lemmings, eggs, young birds. At sea, food taken from other birds or from water. **RANGE:** Seas of world, breeding in subpolar regions.

SOUTH POLAR SKUA *Stercorarius maccormicki*   Scarce M269
21 in. (53 cm). Near size of Herring Gull, but stockier, with deep-chested, hunch-backed look. Dark, with short, slightly wedge-shaped tail and *conspicuous white wing patch at base of primaries visible on both upper- and underwing.* "Blond" morph has *pale head and underparts* contrasting with darker wings; dark morph uniform gray-brown with *paler nape.* **SIMILAR SPECIES:** Great Skua; dark jaegers (particularly Pomarine Jaeger) may lack tail points, but skuas larger, their wings wider, and they have more striking white wing patches.

GREAT SKUA *Stercorarius skua*   Scarce M268
22–23 in. (56–58 cm). Note conspicuous white wing patch visible on both upper- and underwing. Near size of Herring Gull, but stockier. Dark brown, with rusty and streaked upperparts and short, slightly wedge-shaped tail. Flight strong and swift; harasses other seabirds. **SIMILAR SPECIES:** Dark jaegers may lack distinctive tail-feather extensions. However, skuas' wings wider, less falconlike, white wing patches more striking both above and below, and flight more powerful. Very much like South Polar Skua but averages larger and heavier-billed. Note *warmer brown color, dark cap, less distinct pale nape,* and more *streaked appearance* to upperparts.

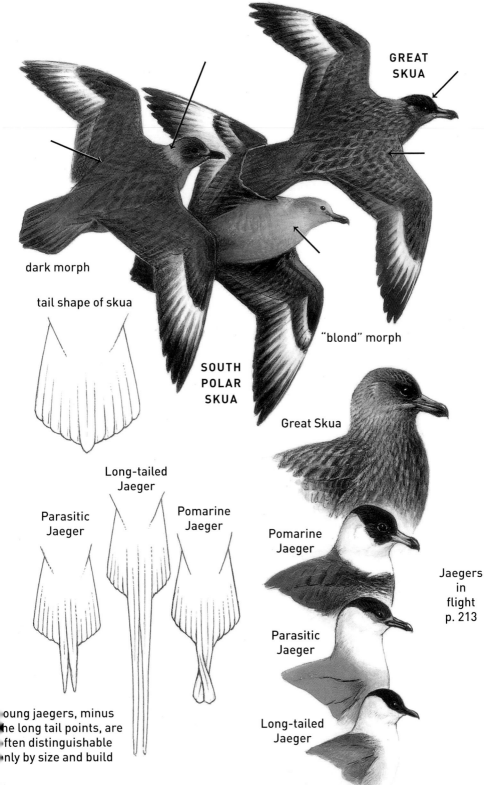

GREAT
SKUA

dark morph

tail shape of skua

"blond" morph

SOUTH
POLAR
SKUA

Great Skua

Long-tailed
Jaeger

Parasitic
Jaeger

Pomarine
Jaeger

Pomarine
Jaeger

Parasitic
Jaeger

Long-tailed
Jaeger

Jaegers
in
flight
p. 213

oung jaegers, minus
he long tail points, are
ften distinguishable
nly by size and build

PARASITIC JAEGER *Stercorarius parasiticus*   Uncommon M271
17–19 in. (44–49 cm). This is the jaeger most frequently seen from shore.
Flies with strong, falconlike wing strokes. Like other jaegers, it shows
white wing-flash. *Adult:* Dark crown, pale underparts. Sharp tail points
project up to 3½ in. (9 cm). Shows small *pale spot* above base of bill. Varies from light to dark morphs. *Juvenile:* Juvenile jaegers show heavy barring, especially on underwing. Juvenile Parasitic is usually *warmer brown*
than other juvenile jaegers, often with *more distinct white patch on upperwing.* Up close, look for *streaked head* and *pale-edged primary tips.* **SIMI-
LAR SPECIES:** Pomarine and Long-tailed jaegers, Heermann's Gull (which
also often harasses terns, small gulls). **HABITAT:** Primarily ocean, regularly
seen from shore; in summer, tundra.

POMARINE JAEGER *Stercorarius pomarinus*   Uncommon M270
19–21 in. (48–53 cm). Like Parasitic Jaeger, but slightly heavier with more
gull-like flight style. *Adult: Broad and twisted* central tail feathers project
2–7 in. (5–18 cm). Dark cap extends *farther down* through face to "jowls."
Bill heavy and *pink-based;* breast band *darker* and more barred than in
Parasitic. *Juvenile:* Plumage variable, but compared with juvenile Parasitic
it lacks warm tones, and very short central tail feathers are blunt-tipped.
Look for white-based primary coverts creating *double white flash* on
underwing. **HABITAT:** Open ocean, seen from shore in small numbers; in
summer, tundra.

LONG-TAILED JAEGER *Stercorarius longicaudus*   Scarce M272
17–22 in. (44–56 cm). The smallest, slimmest jaeger with buoyant, ternlike flight style. *Adults:* Paler and grayer above than other jaegers with distinctly *two-toned upperwing* in flight; *long tail streamers* project 3–6 in.
(8–15 cm); black cap neat and *sharply defined; no breast band;* almost *no
white in wings. Juvenile:* Varies from light to dark morph. All show very
limited white on upperwing (two or three primary shafts), *stubby bill,* and
longer, blunter-tipped central tail feathers than other juvenile jaegers.
Light morph has distinctvely *pale grayish head and breast* and extensively
white belly. Dark morph cold gray-brown and often with pale nape and
pale lower breast patch. **HABITAT:** Open ocean; tundra in summer. Most
pelagic of the jaegers.

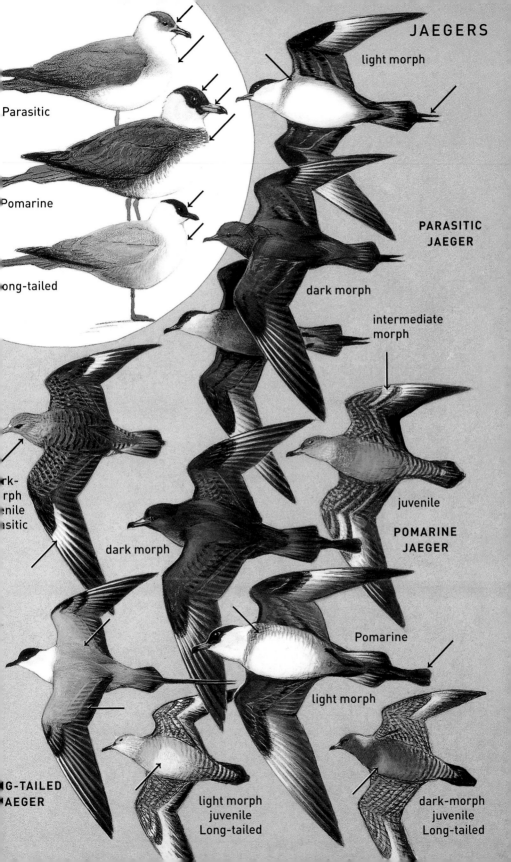

JAEGERS

Parasitic

Pomarine

ong-tailed

light morph

PARASITIC
JAEGER

dark morph

intermediate
morph

rk-
rph
nile
sitic

dark morph

juvenile

POMARINE
JAEGER

Pomarine

light morph

G-TAILED
AEGER

light morph
juvenile
Long-tailed

dark-morph
juvenile
Long-tailed

AUKS, MURRES, AND PUFFINS Family Alcidae

The northern counterparts of penguins, but alcids can fly, beating their small narrow wings in a whir, often veering. They have short neck and pointed, stubby, or deep and laterally compressed bill. Alcids swim and dive expertly. Most species nest on sea cliffs or in burrows, often in crowded colonies, and most winter on open ocean. Mostly silent away from breeding grounds. Sexes alike. **FOOD:** Fish, squid, zooplankton. **RANGE:** N. Atlantic, N. Pacific, and Arctic oceans.

RAZORBILL *Alca torda*   Uncommon M276
17 in. (43 cm). Size of a small duck. Black above and white below; characterized by rather heavy head, thick neck, and flat bill crossed midway by a white mark. On water, cocked-up pointed tail is often characteristic. **VOICE:** Weak whirring whistle; a deep growling *hey Al.* **SIMILAR SPECIES:** Nonbreeding face pattern suggests Common Murre. Bill of immature Razorbill is smaller than adult's and lacks white mark (hence resembling a murre's), but it is stubby and rounded enough to suggest bird's identity as an auk. See also Long-tailed Duck. **HABITAT:** Nests on rocky offshore islands. Forages in coastal waters.

THICK-BILLED MURRE *Uria lomvia*   Scarce M275
18 in. (46 cm). Similar to Common Murre, but a bit *blacker above*. Bill slightly shorter, thicker, with *whitish line along gape*. Overall a bit stockier. White of foreneck forms inverted V. In nonbreeding plumage, dark on head extends *well below eye;* no dark line through white ear coverts. White bill mark less evident. **VOICE:** Guttural calls and moans, hence the name "murre." **SIMILAR SPECIES:** Common Murre. **HABITAT:** Nests on coastal cliff ledges. Spends nonbreeding season on offshore ocean waters.

COMMON MURRE *Uria aalge*   Fairly common West, uncommon East M274
17–17½ in. (43–45 cm). Size of a small duck, with slender pointed bill. *Breeding:* Head, neck, back, and wings dark, *tinged brownish;* underparts, wing linings, and line on rear edge of wing white. *Dusky markings on flanks* on some birds. *Nonbreeding:* Similar, but throat and cheeks white. *Black mark extends from eye to cheek* (see also Razorbill). Murres often raft on water, fly in lines, stand erect on sea cliffs. Chicks in Pacific may be mistaken for Xantus's Murrelet. Bridled morph occurs within regular plumage in N. Atlantic and AK. **SIMILAR SPECIES:** Thick-billed Murre, Razorbill, Long-tailed Duck. **HABITAT:** Same as Thick-billed Murre, but regularly seen from shore throughout year along Pacific Coast.

ALCIDS (AUKS)

immature

breeding

RAZORBILL

nonbreeding

nonbreeding

COMMON

THICK-BILLED MURRE

breeding

nonbreeding

breeding

COMMON
breeding

COMMON MURRE

THICK-BILLED
breeding

bridled
morph

RAZORBILL

breeding

Great Auk
extinct 1844

DOVEKIE *Alle alle* — Scarce M273

8–8¼ in. (20–21 cm). A very small alcid (by far the smallest in East), about the size of European Starling. Chubby and seemingly neckless, with very stubby bill. In flight, flocks bunch tightly, starlinglike. Contrasting alcid pattern — black above, white below. Black-hooded in breeding plumage, white-chested in nonbreeding plumage. **VOICE:** Shrill chatter. Noisy on nesting grounds. **SIMILAR SPECIES:** In AK, Parakeet Auklet slightly larger and with larger bill, less clean-cut, and lacks white line on rear edge of wing. See nonbreeding Least Auklet. **HABITAT:** Nests in high Arctic on coastal cliffs. Winters at sea in N. Atlantic.

BLACK GUILLEMOT *Cepphus grylle* — Fairly common M277

13 in. (33 cm). *Breeding:* Midsized black bird with large white wing patch, bright red feet, and pointed bill. Inside of mouth red. *Nonbreeding:* Pale with whitish underparts and barred back. Wings black with white patch as in summer. *Immature:* Darker above than nonbreeding adult, with dingier, mottled wing patch. **VOICE:** Wheezy or hissing *peeee;* very high pitched. **SIMILAR SPECIES:** No other Atlantic alcid has white wing patch (although others show a narrow line of white on trailing edge of wing). In winter, much larger White-winged Scoter (with white wing patch) is black, whereas Black Guillemot is usually whitish. Wing patch of White-winged Scoter is positioned at rear of wing. In nw. AK, compare with Pigeon Guillemot. Black Guillemot's white wing patch lacks dark bar; underwing linings *white* with thin dark border (at least half dusky in Pigeon). Nonbreeding and juvenile Black Guillemots paler than most, but not all, Pigeon Guillemots. **HABITAT:** Inshore ocean waters; breeds in small groups or singly in holes in ground or under rocks on rocky shores, islands. Less pelagic than most other alcids.

ATLANTIC PUFFIN *Fratercula arctica* — Uncommon M290

12½ in. (32 cm). Colorful triangular bill is most striking feature of chunky little "Sea Parrot." On the wing, it is a stubby, short-necked, thick-headed bird with buzzy flight. No white border on wing. *Breeding:* Upperparts black, underbody white, cheeks pale gray; triangular bill broadly tipped with red. Feet bright orange. *Nonbreeding:* Cheeks grayer; bill smaller, duller, but obviously a puffin. *Immature:* Bill much smaller, mostly dark, but both mandibles well curved. Chunky shape and gray cheeks are unmistakably those of a puffin. **VOICE:** Usually silent. When nesting, a low, growling *ow* or *arr.* **SIMILAR SPECIES:** Immature may be mistaken for young Razorbill, but note gray cheeks, all-dark underwing. **HABITAT:** Very rarely seen from shore except near breeding colonies.

ATLANTIC ALCIDS
(AUKS)

DOVEKIE

nonbreeding

breeding

nonbreeding

breeding

nonbreeding

breeding

BLACK GUILLEMOT

breeding

immature

nonbreeding

ATLANTIC PUFFIN

breeding
adults

Black Guillemot
breeding

Dovekie
breeding

Atlantic Puffin

TUFTED PUFFIN *Fratercula cirrhata*   Uncommon M292
15–16 in. (38–40 cm). A stocky, dark seabird with massive bill. *Breeding:*
Blackish, with *large, triangular, orange-red* bill; white face; and *long,
curved, ivory yellow ear tufts.* Feet orange. *Nonbreeding:* White face and ear
tufts much reduced (a trace of dull buffy-yellowish); duller orange-red
bill not as triangular as in summer. *Immature:* Body grayer, bill smaller,
with no red. **VOICE:** Throaty growling in nesting colony; silent at sea. **SIMI-
LAR SPECIES:** Compare immature with Rhinoceros Auklet. **HABITAT:**
Same as Horned Puffin.

HORNED PUFFIN *Fratercula corniculata*   Fairly common, local M291
15 in. (38 cm). A puffin with *clear white underparts* and broad black collar.
Feet bright orange. *Breeding:* Cheeks *white,* with small, dark erectile horn
above each eye. Bill massive, *triangular,* laterally flat; *yellow with red tip.*
Nonbreeding: Cheeks dusky; bill blackish with red tip. *Immature:* Resembles nonbreeding adult with dusky cheeks, but bill smaller and all dark.
VOICE: Low, growling *arrr.* **SIMILAR SPECIES:** Atlantic Puffin; separated by
range. **HABITAT:** Nests on rocky ocean cliffs. Forages in offshore waters.

PIGEON GUILLEMOT *Cepphus columba*   Fairly common M278
13½ in. (34 cm). *Breeding:* A small, black, pigeonlike waterbird, with large
white wing patches (subdivided by variable black bar or wedge, sometimes
rather indistinct), *red feet,* pointed black bill, orange-red mouth lining,
and mostly dark or dirty underwing. *Nonbreeding:* Pale with white underparts and blackish wings with large white patches as in summer. *Juvenile:*
Similar to nonbreeding adult, but white wing patches mottled; underwing
may have center third or more pale. **VOICE:** Feeble wheezy or hissing whistle, *peeeee.* **SIMILAR SPECIES:** Marbled Murrelet, Black Guillemot. **HABI-
TAT:** Inshore ocean waters; less pelagic than most other alcids.

RHINOCEROS AUKLET *Cerorhinca monocerata*   Uncommon M289
15 in. (38 cm). A dark stubby seabird. *Breeding* (plumage acquired in late
winter): *White mustache,* narrow *white plume* behind eye, *short erect horn*
at base of yellowish bill. *Nonbreeding:* Note size and *uniform dark color
with paler lower vent.* White plumes shorter, horn absent. *Immature:* Similar to nonbreeding adult, with smaller, darker bill. **VOICE:** Wide array of
barks, growls, groans. **SIMILAR SPECIES:** Cassin's Auklet, immature Tufted
Puffin. **HABITAT:** Nests colonially in burrows on islands. Found in both
inshore and offshore ocean waters.

ature

TUFTED
PUFFIN

on-
eding

breeding

Black Guillemot
(p. 216)
for comparison

immature

nonbreeding

HORNED
PUFFIN

breeding

PIGEON
GUILLEMOT

immature

nonbreeding

breeding

RHINOCEROS AUKLET

Tufted
Puffin

Horned
Puffin

breeding
Tufted Puffin

Horned Puffin

breeding

fted Puffin

reeding

Horned Puffin

breeding

Rhinoceros
Auklet

breeding

PACIFIC ALCIDS

LONG-BILLED MURRELET *Brachyramphus perdix* Vagrant
10–11 in. (25–28 cm). *Breeding:* Paler brown than Marbled Murrelet; *white throat. Nonbreeding:* Like Marbled, but *lacks white collar* and shows two small pale *oval patches* on nape. **RANGE AND HABITAT:** Casual visitor (mostly between late summer and early winter) from Asia to West Coast and at lakes, reservoirs, and rivers far inland all the way to Atlantic Coast.

MARBLED MURRELET Uncommon, threatened M279
Brachyramphus marmoratus
9¾–10 in. (24–25 cm). *Breeding: Dark brown; heavily mottled* on underparts. The only alcid south of AK so colored (in AK, see Kittlitz's Murrelet). *Nonbreeding:* A small neckless-looking seabird, dark above and white below, with *strip of white on scapulars,* white collar. **VOICE:** Sharp *keer, keer* or lower *kee.* **SIMILAR SPECIES:** Nonbreeding Pigeon Guillemot slightly larger, and white patch is on wing, not scapulars. See Long-billed Murrelet. **HABITAT:** Coastal ocean waters, bays. Breeds short distance inland, mainly high on limbs of mossy old-growth conifers if available.

KITTLITZ'S MURRELET *Brachyramphus brevirostris* Scarce, local M280
9¼–9½ in. (23–24 cm). *Breeding:* Buffy or tan overall, *mottled and freckled with white* above, giving a pale look. *Nonbreeding:* Similar to Marbled Murrelet, but *white on face surrounds eyes.* White outer tail feathers in all plumages. **SIMILAR SPECIES:** Marbled Murrelet, nonbreeding Pigeon Guillemot. **HABITAT:** Glacial waters; nests presumably on barren slopes above timberline in coastal mountains.

XANTUS'S MURRELET Uncommon, local M281
Synthliboramphus hypoleucus
9½–9¾ in. (24–25 cm). A small brown-black and white alcid with solid dark back. Suggests a miniature murre. Very similar to Craveri's Murrelet, but with white wing linings. *Scrippsi* race is regular breeding subspecies in CA. *Hypoleucus* subspecies of Baja CA, a very rare late-summer and fall visitor north to BC, has white arc around eye.

CRAVERI'S MURRELET *Synthliboramphus craveri* Rare, local M282
9¼–9½ in. (23–24 cm). Very similar to Xantus's Murrelet, but with *black partial collar* on breast, slight black chin (below bill), and *dusky* (not white) underwing linings. Bill very slightly longer. **HABITAT:** Breeds on offshore islands.

ANCIENT MURRELET *Synthliboramphus antiquus* Scarce M283
10 in. (25 cm). In all plumages, *gray back contrasts with black cap. Breeding:* Note sharply cut *black throat patch* and *white stripe over eye.* Bill yellow. *Nonbreeding:* Weaker head stripe. **SIMILAR SPECIES:** Other similarly sized alcids lack back/crown contrast. **HABITAT:** Breeds on rocky and debris-strewn slopes.

MURRELETS

LONG-BILLED MURRELET

nonbreeding

MARBLED MURRELET

reeding
adult

KITTLITZ'S MURRELET

reeding
adult

XANTUS'S MURRELET

northern
(*scrippsi*)

nset above
ft, southern
ypoleucus)

CRAVERI'S MURRELET

reeding
adult

ANCIENT MURRELET

CRESTED AUKLET *Aethia cristatella* Fairly common, local M288
9½–10½ in. (24–27 cm). A droll auklet of Bering Sea. *Adult:* Completely slate gray, darker on back; thin white plume behind eye. In breeding plumage, stubby bill is *bright orange* and a curious crest *curls forward* over bill. In nonbreeding plumage, orange gape on bill is lost and crest is shorter. *Immature:* Paler gray overall, with dark bill. **VOICE:** Doglike bark in nesting colony. **SIMILAR SPECIES:** Whiskered and Cassin's auklets. **HABITAT:** Nests on remote islands and coastal areas of Bering Sea. Forages in open ocean.

WHISKERED AUKLET *Aethia pygmaea* Scarce, local M287
7¾–8 in. (20 cm). Similar to slightly larger Crested Auklet, but in addition to curled black plume on forehead, this bird has *three thin white plumes* (whiskers) on each side of face. In nonbreeding plumage, plumes shorter. At all times has *pale lower belly and undertail coverts.* **HABITAT:** Tidal rips, rocky coasts.

PARAKEET AUKLET *Aethia psittacula* Uncommon, local M285
10 in. (25 cm). A small alcid with *stubby, red bill* (like colorful bill of a parakeet) and whitish underparts. *Breeding:* Entire head black, with thin white plume behind eye. *Nonbreeding and immature:* Mostly whitish underneath, and bill shows less red. **VOICE:** At nesting colony, a high whinny. **SIMILAR SPECIES:** Crested Auklet entirely dark. Least Auklet much smaller. **HABITAT:** Offshore occurs singly or in small groups (not in large flocks like other small alcids); nests in scattered pairs or in colonies on sea cliffs and rubble slopes.

LEAST AUKLET *Aethia pusilla* Fairly common, local M286
6–6¼ in. (15–16 cm). The tiniest alcid; chubby, neckless. Black above, white below. In flight, a whirring ping-pong ball. In breeding plumage, dark band across upper breast. Tiny size and small stubby bill separate it from other alcids except Dovekie. **VOICE:** High-pitched chattering in colony. **SIMILAR SPECIES:** Dovekie. **HABITAT:** Nests on remote rocky islands in colonies with other auklets. Forages in open ocean.

CASSIN'S AUKLET *Ptychoramphus aleuticus* Fairly common M284
9 in. (23 cm). A small stubby seabird; entirely dark gray except for white crescent above eye and white belly; note pale spot at base of lower mandible. **VOICE:** Usually silent. In nesting colony, a series of harsh *kueek-kueek* notes. **SIMILAR SPECIES:** In winter, all other small alcids in its range show much more white. See Rhinoceros Auklet. **HABITAT:** Nests on sea cliffs. Forages in open ocean.

CRESTED AUKLET

WHISKERED AUKLET

PARAKEET AUKLET

LEAST AUKLET

nonbreeding
adult

breeding
adult

**CASSIN'S
AUKLET**

adult

PIGEONS AND DOVES Family Columbidae

Plump, fast-flying birds with small head and low, cooing voice; nod their head as they walk. Two types: (1) birds with fanlike tails (e.g., Rock Pigeon) and (2) smaller birds with rounded or pointed tail (e.g., Mourning Dove). Sexes mostly similar. **FOOD:** Seeds, waste grain, fruit, insects. **RANGE:** Nearly worldwide in tropical and temperate regions.

BAND-TAILED PIGEON *Patagioenas fasciata* Fairly common M296
14½–15 in. (37–38 cm). Heavily built; might be mistaken for Rock Pigeon except for its woodland habitat and tendency to alight in trees. Note *broad pale band* across end of tail; *white band* on nape. Feet *yellow*. Bill *yellow* with *dark tip*. **VOICE:** Hollow owl-like *oo-whoo* or *whoo-oo-whoo*, repeated. **SIMILAR SPECIES:** Rock Pigeon. **HABITAT:** Oak canyons, foothills, chaparral, mountain forests; also some residential areas, parks.

RED-BILLED PIGEON *Patagioenas flavirostris* Scarce, local M295
14–14½ in. (36–37 cm). A large all-dark pigeon (in good light deep maroon), including underbelly. Bill red with yellowish tip. Shy, mostly arboreal. Recent decline in numbers. **VOICE:** *Whoo, whoo, whooooo.* **SIMILAR SPECIES:** Rock Pigeon. **HABITAT:** Riparian woodlands with tall trees and brush.

WHITE-CROWNED PIGEON Uncommon, local M294
Patagioenas leucocephala
13½ in. (34 cm). A stocky, shy pigeon completely dark except for immaculate white crown. **VOICE:** Low owl-like *wof, wof, wo, co-woo.* **SIMILAR SPECIES:** Rock Pigeon. **HABITAT:** Mangrove keys, thickets, hardwood hammocks. Perches on power lines, treetops.

AFRICAN COLLARED-DOVE *Streptopelia roseogrisea* Exotic
12 in. (30 cm). Escaped cage bird. Formerly known as Ringed Turtle-Dove *(S. risoria)*. A very pale dove with dark bill and eye and black partial collar. In flight, white tail tip obvious. **VOICE:** Soft series of two-syllable cooing notes. **SIMILAR SPECIES:** Eurasian Collared-Dove darker overall, with medium gray undertail coverts, darker primaries, and *three*-syllable notes. Hybrids with Eurasians occur mixed in with pure birds in the wild. **HABITAT:** Urban areas, suburban yards, power lines, feeders.

EURASIAN COLLARED-DOVE Locally common, exotic M297
Streptopelia decaocto
12½–13 in. (32–33 cm). Recent colonizer of N. America from Caribbean but native to Eurasia; rapidly increasing and spreading. Slightly chunkier than Mourning Dove, *paler beige,* and with *square-cut tail.* Note *narrow black ring on hindneck. Grayish undertail coverts.* Three-toned wing pattern in flight. **VOICE:** *Three*-noted *coo-COOO-cup.* **SIMILAR SPECIES:** African Collared-Dove. **HABITAT:** Towns, field edges, cultivated land.

SPOTTED DOVE *Streptopelia chinensis* Uncommon, local, exotic M298
12 in. (30–31 cm). Note *broad collar of black and white spots* on hindneck. A bit larger than Mourning Dove; tail rounded with much white in corners. *Juvenile:* Lacks collar, but can be told by shape of spread tail. **VOICE:** *Coo-who-coo;* resembles cooing of White-winged Dove. **SIMILAR SPECIES:** Mourning Dove. **RANGE:** Introduced from Asia, formerly widespread in s. CA, now much reduced. **HABITAT:** Residential areas, parks.

ROCK PIGEON (ROCK DOVE, DOMESTIC PIGEON) Common, exotic M293
Columba livia
12½ in. (32 cm). Typical birds are gray with *whitish rump, two black wing bars,* and broad, dark tail band. Domestic stock or feral birds may have many color variants. **VOICE:** Soft, gurgling *coo-roo-coo.* **SIMILAR SPECIES:** Band-tailed Pigeon. **HABITAT:** Cities, farms, cliffs, bridges.

PIGEONS AND DOVES

BAND-TAILED PIGEON

RED-BILLED PIGEON

WHITE-CROWNED PIGEON

AFRICAN COLLARED-DOVE

plumages variable

RASIAN LARED-DOVE

ROCK PIGEON

SPOTTED DOVE

typical form

WHITE-WINGED DOVE *Zenaida asiatica*   Common M299

11½–12 in. (29–30 cm). A dove of desert, readily known by *white wing patches, large when bird is in flight, narrow when at rest.* Otherwise similar to Mourning Dove, but tail *rounded* and tipped with broad white corners, bill slightly longer, eye orangey red. **VOICE:** Harsh cooing, *who cooks for you?;* also, *ooo-uh-CUCK oo.* Sounds vaguely like crowing of a young rooster. **SIMILAR SPECIES:** Mourning and White-tipped doves. **HABITAT:** River woods, mesquite, saguaros, desert oases, groves, towns, feeders.

MOURNING DOVE *Zenaida macroura*   Common M300

12 in. (30–31 cm). The common widespread wild dove. Brown; smaller and slimmer than Rock Pigeon. Note *pointed tail* with large white spots. **VOICE:** Hollow, mournful *coah, cooo, coo, cooo.* At a distance, only the three *coo*s are audible. **SIMILAR SPECIES:** White-winged Dove. **HABITAT:** Farms, towns, open woods, fields, scrub, roadsides, grasslands, feeders.

WHITE-TIPPED DOVE *Leptotila verreauxi*   Uncommon, local M304

11½ in. (29 cm). Large stocky dove with broad, dark wings. Short tail has *white corners.* Body pale, underwings cinnamon. Spends a good deal of time on ground. Flies fast through woods. **VOICE:** Long, drawn-out, hollow *who — whooooooooo.* **SIMILAR SPECIES:** White-winged and Mourning doves. **HABITAT:** Often seen walking in shadows of brushy tangles or dense woods.

RUDDY GROUND-DOVE *Columbina talpacoti*   Rare M303

6½–6¾ in. (16–17 cm). This rare but regular visitor (and very rare breeder) to border states from Mex. is similar to Common Ground-Dove but is slightly larger, longer tailed, and longer billed; has *dark, grayish base* to bill; *lacks all scaliness.* Has *blackish* spots and streaks on wing coverts and *scapulars. Male:* Washed rufous. *Female and immature:* Plain brown and gray. *Caution:* A bright male Common Ground-Dove may be misidentified as a Ruddy. **VOICE:** Cooing similar to Common Ground-Dove's, but faster and more repetitive: *pity-you pity-you pity you.* **SIMILAR SPECIES:** Inca Dove, Common Ground-Dove. **HABITAT:** Farms, livestock pens, fields, brushy areas. Often found with Inca Dove and Common Ground-Dove.

COMMON GROUND-DOVE *Columbina passerina*   Uncommon M302

6¼–6½ in. (15–16 cm). A very small dove. Note *stubby black tail,* scaly breast, pinkish or orangey base of bill, and rounded wings that flash *rufous* in flight, *bronzy* spots and streaks on wing coverts. Feet yellow or pink. Adult male's body washed pinkish. **VOICE:** Soft, monotonously repeated *woo-oo, woo-oo,* etc. May sound monosyllabic — *wooo,* with rising inflection. **SIMILAR SPECIES:** Inca Dove, Ruddy Ground-Dove. **HABITAT:** Farms, orchards, brushy areas, roadsides.

INCA DOVE *Columbina inca*   Fairly common M301

8¼–8½ in. (21–22 cm). A very small, slim dove with *scaly* look. *Rufous* in primaries (as in ground-doves), but has *longer tail* with *white sides.* **VOICE:** Monotonous *coo-hoo* or *no-hope.* **SIMILAR SPECIES:** Common Ground-Dove has short tail without obvious white, lacks scaling on back. **HABITAT:** Towns, parks, farms.

DOVES

PASSENGER
PIGEON
extinct
1914

WHITE-
WINGED
DOVE

MOURNING
DOVE

WHITE-TIPPED DOVE

INCA DOVE

RUDDY
GROUND-DOVE
adult ♂

COMMON
GROUND-DOVE

PARAKEETS AND PARROTS Family Psittacidae

Noisy and gaudily colored. Compact, short-necked birds with stout, hooked bill. Parakeets smaller, with long, pointed tail. Feet zygodactyl (two toes fore, two aft). **RANGE:** Worldwide in Tropics and subtropics. Several exotic species have been released or have escaped, especially around Miami.

MONK PARAKEET *Myiopsitta monachus*　　　　Locally fairly common
(Argentina) 11 in. (28 cm). Pale gray face and chest, buff band across belly. Established in spots from CT to FL and west to IL and TX. Massive nest of sticks (only parrot to build a stick nest), with several compartments. Raucous calls. Comes to feeders.

GREEN PARAKEET *Aratinga holochlora*　　　　Locally established
10–12 in. (25–30 cm). *Aratinga* parakeets have long pointed tails, so are readily separable from chunkier square-tailed parrots. This, the largest (size of Mourning Dove), is green above, yellow-green below. **VOICE:** Sharp, squeaky notes, shrill noisy chatter. **RANGE AND HABITAT:** Tropical Mex. to s. Nicaragua. Resident populations established in some residential areas of s. Rio Grande Valley in TX.

RED-CROWNED PARROT *Amazona viridigenalis*　　　　Locally established
12 in. (30 cm). Large, with red crown (reduced in first year), blue nape, red wing panels. Established in several southern cities, including Los Angeles, from introductions. S. TX residents may be from Mexican population.

BLACK-HOODED PARAKEET *Nandayus nenday*
(S. America) 12 in. (30 cm). Locally established on west coast of FL.

ROSE-RINGED PARAKEET *Psittacula krameri*
(Africa, India) 16 in. (41 cm). A few in suburbs on coastal slopes of s. CA.

MITRED PARAKEET *Aratinga mitrata*
(S. America) 15 in. (38 cm). Found in Los Angeles area and s. FL.

WHITE-WINGED PARAKEET *Brotogeris versicolurus*　　　　Local
(S. America) 9 in. (23 cm). Locally established in Miami area. Now outnumbered by Yellow-chevroned Parakeet.

YELLOW-CHEVRONED PARAKEET *Brotogeris chiriri*
(S. America) 9 in. (23 cm). Found in s. FL and CA.

BUDGERIGAR *Melopsittacus undulatus*　　　　Local
(Australia) 7 in. (18 cm). Variable. Usually green; a small minority may be blue, yellow, or white. Thousands were established along west coast of FL; lesser numbers on southeast coast of FL. Recent years have seen dramatic decline. Escapees seen in many areas.

LILAC-CROWNED PARROT *Amazona finschi*
(Mex.) 12½–13½ in. (30–34 cm). Like first-year Red-crowned but darker. Red forehead, *lilac* crown, longer tail. A few live in Los Angeles area and s. TX.

YELLOW-HEADED PARROT *Amazona oratrix*
(Mex. and Belize) 14–15 in. (36–38 cm). Escapees found in several areas; established locally in Los Angeles region, also in s. FL and s. TX.

RED-LORED PARROT *Amazona autumnalis*
(Cen. and S. America) 12–13 in. (30–33 cm). Small numbers seen in TX, CA, FL.

WHITE-FRONTED PARROT *Amazona albifrons*
(Cen. America) 9–10 in. (23–25 cm). Found in small numbers in FL and CA.

PARAKEETS AND PARROTS

CAROLINA
PARAKEET
extinct 1920s

MONK
PARAKEET

GREEN
PARAKEET

RED-CROWNED
PARROT

UNESTABLISHED EXOTICS

BLACK-HOODED
PARAKEET

BUDGERIGAR

MITRED
PARAKEET

WHITE-
WINGED
PARAKEET

YELLOW-
CHEVRONED
PARAKEET

some
individuals
may be blue
or yellow

ROSE-RINGED
PARAKEET

LILAC-
CROWNED
PARROT

YELLOW-
HEADED
PARROT

RED-LORED
PARROT

WHITE-
FRONTED
PARROT

Cuckoos, Roadrunners, and Anis
Family Cuculidae

Slender, long-tailed birds; feet zygodactyl (two toes forward, two backward). Sexes alike. **FOOD**: Cuckoos eat caterpillars, other insects; roadrunners eat reptiles, rodents, large insects, small birds; anis eat seeds, fruit. **RANGE**: Warm and temperate regions of world. N. American cuckoos are not parasitic.

YELLOW-BILLED CUCKOO *Coccyzus americanus*   Fairly common M305
12 in. (30–31 cm). Known as a cuckoo by slim sinuous look, brown back, and white underparts; as this species by *rufous* in wings, *large white* spots at tips of dark undertail feathers, and *yellow* lower mandible on slightly curved bill. **VOICE**: Song a rapid throaty *ka-ka-ka-ka-ka-ka-ka-ka-ka-ka-ka-ka-kow-kow-kowlp-kowlp — kowlp — kowlp* (slowing toward end). **SIMILAR SPECIES**: Black-billed Cuckoo. **HABITAT**: Riparian woodlands (particularly cottonwoods).

MANGROVE CUCKOO *Coccyzus minor*   Uncommon, local M306
12 in. (30–31 cm). Similar to Yellow-billed Cuckoo (both found in s. FL), but belly creamy buff; no rufous in wing. Note black ear patch. **VOICE**: Accelerating series of guttural notes, almost like grunts: *unh unh unh unh unh unh aanngg aanngg*. Final two notes longer. **SIMILAR SPECIES**: Other cuckoos, especially Yellow-billed. **HABITAT**: Mangroves, hardwood forests.

BLACK-BILLED CUCKOO *Coccyzus erythropthalmus*   Uncommon M307
11½–12 in. (29–30 cm). *Adult:* Similar to Yellow-billed Cuckoo, but *bill dark gray to blackish;* narrow *red orbital ring. No rufous in wing;* undertail spots small. *Immature:* Has yellow orbital ring and may have small amount of rufous in wing; thus more like Yellow-billed Cuckoo, but has *all-dark bill.* **VOICE**: Fast, rhythmic *cucucu, cucucu, cucucu,* etc. The grouped rhythm (three or four) is typical, but often employs irregular cadences. May sing at night. **HABITAT**: Wood edges, groves, thickets.

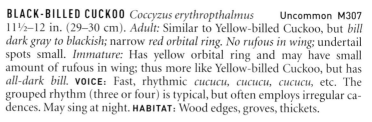

GROOVE-BILLED ANI *Crotophaga sulcirostris*   Uncommon, local M310
13–13½ in. (33–34 cm). Very similar to Smooth-billed but bill has fine grooves (lacking in juvenile) and less arched ridge. **VOICE**: Repeated *whee-o* or *tee-ho,* first note slurring up. **HABITAT**: Thickets, open woodlands.

SMOOTH-BILLED ANI *Crotophaga ani*   Scarce, local M309
14–14½ in. (35–37 cm). A coal black, grackle-sized bird with long loose-jointed tail, short wings, and *huge bill with high curved ridge* and noticeable angle to lower mandible (giving it puffinlike profile). Flight weak; alternately flaps and sails. Often moves in groups. **VOICE**: Whining whistle. Querulous *que-lick.* **SIMILAR SPECIES**: Groove-billed Ani grackles. **HABITAT**: Brushy edges, thickets. Recent major population declines in FL.

GREATER ROADRUNNER *Geococcyx californianus*   Fairly common M308
22–23 in. (56–58 cm). The familiar cuckoo that runs on ground (tracks show two toes forward, two backward). A large, slender, streaked bird, with long, white-edged tail; shaggy crest; long legs. White crescent on wing (visible when spread). **VOICE**: Six to eight low, dovelike *coo*s, descending in pitch. **SIMILAR SPECIES**: Thrashers in same habitat are also streaky and brown but are much smaller. **HABITAT**: Deserts, open country with scattered cover, chaparral, brush.

CUCKOOS, ETC.

YELLOW-BILLED
CUCKOO

adults

MANGROVE
CUCKOO

immature

BLACK-
BILLED
CUCKOO

adult

GROOVE-
BILLED
ANI

SMOOTH-
BILLED ANI

GREATER
ROADRUNNER

Owls
Families Tytonidae (Barn Owls) and Strigidae (Typical Owls)

Chiefly nocturnal birds of prey, with large heads and flattened faces forming facial disk; large, forward-facing eyes; hooked bill and claws; usually feathered feet (outer toe reversible). Flight noiseless, mothlike. Some species have "horns," or ear tufts. Sexes similar; female larger. **FOOD:** Rodents, birds, reptiles, fish, large insects. **RANGE:** Nearly worldwide.

SHORT-EARED OWL *Asio flammeus*   Uncommon M327
15 in. (38 cm). An owl of open country; often abroad by day, particularly at dawn and dusk or when cloudy. Often tussles with Northern Harrier. Streaked, tawny brown color and irregular flopping flight identify it. Large buffy wing patches show in flight, along with black carpal ("wrist") patch. *Dark facial disk* emphasizes yellow eyes. **VOICE:** Emphatic, sneezy bark: *kee-yow!, wow!,* or *waow!* **SIMILAR SPECIES:** Long-eared Owl somewhat similar in flight, but with jerkier wing action. **HABITAT:** Grasslands, fresh and salt marshes, dunes, tundra. Roosts on ground, rarely in and under trees. Winter range and numbers vary from year to year.

BARN OWL *Tyto alba*   Uncommon M311
16 in. (41 cm). A long-legged, knock-kneed, pale, monkey-faced owl. *White heart-shaped face and dark eyes;* no ear tufts. Distinguished in flight as an owl by large head and mothlike flight; as this species by unstreaked whitish, buff, or pale cinnamon underparts (ghostly at night) and warm brown back. **VOICE:** Shrill, rasping hiss or snore: *kschh* or *shiiish.* **SIMILAR SPECIES:** Short-eared Owl streaked, has darker face and underparts, *yellow* eyes. **HABITAT:** Open country, groves, farms, barns, towns, cliffs.

LONG-EARED OWL *Asio otus*   Uncommon M326
15 in. (38 cm). A slender, crow-sized owl with long ear tufts. Usually seen "frozen" close to trunk of a tree. Much smaller than Great Horned Owl; underparts streaked *lengthwise*, not barred crosswise. Ears *closer together, erectile* much black around eyes. **VOICE:** One or two long *hooos*; usually silent. Also a catlike whine and doglike bark. **SIMILAR SPECIES:** In flight, similar to Short-eared Owl, which has more mothlike, meandering flight. See Great Horned Owl. **HABITAT:** Coniferous and deciduous woodlands, desert groves. Often roosts in groups in nonbreeding season. Hunts over open country.

GREAT HORNED OWL *Bubo virginianus*   Common M316
21–22 in. (54–56 cm). A *very large* owl with ear tufts, or "horns." Heavily *barred* beneath; conspicuous *white throat bib.* In flight, as large as our larger hawks; looks neckless, large-headed. Varies regionally from very dark to rather pale. Often active just before dark. **VOICE:** Male usually utters five or six resonant hoots: *hu-hu-hu-hu, hoo! hoo!* Female's hoots slightly higher pitched than male's, in shorter sequence. Young birds make catlike screams, especially when begging or when separated from adults in late summer and fall. **SIMILAR SPECIES:** Long-eared Owl smaller (crow-sized in flight), with lengthwise streaking rather than crosswise barring beneath; ears closer together; lacks white bib. **HABITAT:** Forests, woodlots, deserts, residential areas, open country.

SHORT-EARED
OWL

BARN
OWL

female
(male is whiter below)

LONG-EARED
OWL

subarctic

GREAT HORNED OWL

typical

SPOTTED OWL *Strix occidentalis* Scarce M323
17½–18 in. (45–46 cm). A large, dark brown forest owl with puffy round head. Large *dark eyes* (all other large N. American owls except Barn and Barred owls have yellow eyes) and *heavily spotted chest and barred belly* identify this endangered bird, which in many areas may eventually be displaced by Barred Owl. **VOICE:** High-pitched hoots, like barking of a small dog; usually in groups of three *(hoo, hoo-hoo)* or four *(hoo, who-who-whooo)*. Also a longer series of rapid hoots in crescendo, and a rising whistle. **SIMILAR SPECIES:** See Barred Owl. **HABITAT:** In north, mature old-growth forests; in south, more varied habitats, including conifers, mixed woods, wooded canyons.

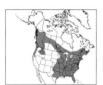

BARRED OWL *Strix varia* Fairly common M324
20–21 in. (51–53 cm). A large, brown, puffy-headed woodland owl with large, moist *brown* eyes. Barred *across* chest and streaked *lengthwise* on belly; this combination separates it from Spotted Owl. **VOICE:** Usually eight accented hoots, in two groups of four: *hoohoo-hoohoo, hoohoohoo-HOOaaw.* The *aaw* at end is characteristic. Sometimes rendered as *who cooks for you, who cooks for you-all.* Also simply a *hoo-aww.* **SIMILAR SPECIES:** Other large owls, except Barn and Spotted, have yellow eyes. **HABITAT:** Woodlands, wooded river bottoms, wooded swamps.

GREAT GRAY OWL *Strix nebulosa* Scarce M325
26–28 in. (67–73 cm). Our largest N. American owl; very tame. Dusky gray, heavily striped *lengthwise* on underparts. Round-headed, without ear tufts; large, *strongly lined facial disk* dwarfs *yellow* eyes. Note *black chin spot* bordered by two broad white patches like *white mustaches.* Tail long for an owl. An irruptive species. Invades to the south one year, then may be rare for several years. **VOICE:** Deep *whoo-hoo-hoo.* Also deep single *whoo*s. **SIMILAR SPECIES:** Barred and Spotted owls much smaller. **HABITAT:** Coniferous forests, adjacent meadows, bogs. Often hunts by day, particularly in winter.

SNOWY OWL *Bubo scandiacus* Scarce M317
22–24 in. (56–61 cm). An irruptive, large, mostly *white*, Arctic, day-flying owl; variably flecked or barred with dusky. Round head, *yellow eyes.* Adult males much whiter than females and young birds. **VOICE:** Usually silent. Flight call when breeding a loud, repeated *krow-ow;* also a repeated *rick.* **SIMILAR SPECIES:** Barn Owl whitish on underparts only; much smaller and has dark eyes. Many young owls are whitish when in down. See Gyrfalcon (white morph). **HABITAT:** Prairies, fields, marshes, beaches; in summer, Arctic tundra. Perches on dunes, posts, haystacks, ground in open country, sometimes buildings. Has cyclic winter irruptions southward into U.S.

LARGE OWLS
Without ear tufts

SPOTTED OWL

BARRED OWL

Spotted

Barred

GREAT GRAY OWL

SNOWY OWL

WESTERN SCREECH-OWL *Megascops kennicottii*   Fairly common M313
8½ in. (22 cm). A widespread small owl with conspicuous ear tufts. Yellow eyes. Usually *gray* overall, but n. Great Basin population has two color morphs, *gray* and *brown*. Birds in northwestern humid regions are *usually* darker brown; those in arid regions paler, grayer. Bill dark with pale tip. **VOICE:** Series of hollow whistles on one pitch, running into a tremolo (rhythm of a small ball bouncing to a standstill). **SIMILAR SPECIES:** Eastern Screech-Owl has paler bill; best told by voice. See Whiskered Screech-Owl. Flammulated Owl smaller, plumage tinged rusty, has dark eyes. **HABITAT:** Wooded canyons, farm groves, shade trees, well-vegetated residential areas, pinyon-juniper and cactus woodlands.

WHISKERED SCREECH-OWL *Megascops trichopsis* Uncommon, local M315
7¼–7½ in. (18–19 cm). Very similar to Western Screech-Owl. Has large white spots on scapulars, coarser black spots on underparts, longer facial bristles, *yellow-green bill, smaller legs and feet.* Readily identified by voice. **VOICE:** *Boo-boo, booboo-boo-boo, booboo-boo-boo,* etc.; arrangement of this "code" may vary. At times a repeated, four-syllable *chooyoo-coo-cooo,* vaguely suggestive of White-winged Dove. **SIMILAR SPECIES:** Western Screech-Owl. **HABITAT:** Canyons, pine-oak woods, sycamores; typically at higher elevation than Western Screech-Owl.

FLAMMULATED OWL *Otus flammeolus*   Uncommon M312
6–7 in. (15–18 cm). Smaller than a screech-owl. *Our only small owl with dark eyes.* Largely gray, with *tawny scapulars* and inconspicuous ear tufts. Southern birds rustier. **VOICE:** Mellow *hoot* (also *hoo-hoot* or *hu-hu, hoot*), low in pitch for so small an owl; repeated steadily at intervals of two or three seconds. Ventriloquial. **SIMILAR SPECIES:** Screech-owls. **HABITAT:** Open pine and fir forests in mountains and canyons.

EASTERN SCREECH-OWL *Megascops asio*   Common M314
8½ in. (22 cm). The only small eastern owl with ear tufts. Two color morphs: red and gray. No other owl is bright foxy red. Young birds may lack conspicuous ear tufts. **VOICE:** Mournful whinny or wail; tremulous, *descending* in pitch. Sometimes a series of notes on one pitch. **SIMILAR SPECIES:** Like Western Screech-Owl, but separated by voice and, usually, range. Bill paler (greenish, versus gray-black in Western). Also differs in having bright *red-brown* morph. **HABITAT:** Deciduous woodlands, shade trees.

ELF OWL *Micrathene whitneyi*   Uncommon M321
5¾ in. (15 cm). A tiny, small-headed, short-tailed, earless owl. Underparts softly striped with rusty; eyebrows white. Hides by day in woodpecker holes in saguaros, telephone poles, or trees. Found at night by call. **VOICE:** Rapid, high-pitched *whi-whi-whi-whi-whi-whi* or *chewk-chewk-chewk-chewk,* etc., often becoming higher and more yipping or puppylike, and chattering in middle of series. **SIMILAR SPECIES:** Western Screech-Owl. **HABITAT:** Saguaro and mesquite woodlands and deserts, wooded canyons.

SMALL OWLS

Northwest

gray morph

WESTERN SCREECH-OWL

FLAMMULATED OWL

WHISKERED SCREECH-OWL

red morph

red morph

EASTERN SCREECH-OWL

gray morph

ELF OWL

BURROWING OWL *Athene cunicularia*　　　　　Uncommon M322
9½ in. (24 cm). A small owl of open country, often seen by day standing erect on ground or low perches. Note *long legs*. Barred and spotted, with white chin stripe, round head. Bobs and bows when agitated. **VOICE:** Rapid, chattering *quick-quick-quick*. At night, a mellow *co-hoo*, higher than Mourning Dove's *coo*. Young in burrow rattle like rattlesnake to deter predators. **HABITAT:** Open grasslands, unplowed prairies, farmland, airfields, golf courses. Nests in burrows in ground or in pipes.

NORTHERN HAWK OWL *Surnia ulula*　　　　　Scarce M318
16 in. (41 cm). A medium-sized day-flying owl, with *long, rounded tail* and *barred underparts*. Often *perches at tip of tree* and jerks tail like a kestrel. Shrikelike, it flies low, rising abuptly to perch. **VOICE:** Falconlike chattering *kikikiki*, and kestrel-like *illy-illy-illy-illy*. Also a harsh scream. **HABITAT:** Open coniferous forests, birch scrub, tamarack bogs, muskeg, field edges. Sporadically appears south of normal range.

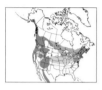

NORTHERN SAW-WHET OWL *Aegolius acadicus*　　Uncommon M329
8 in. (20 cm). A very tame little owl; smaller than a screech-owl, without ear tufts. Underparts have blotchy, reddish brown streaks. Bill black. Forehead streaked white. *Juvenile:* Chocolate brown in summer, with conspicuous white eyebrows; belly *tawny ocher*. **VOICE:** Song a mellow, whistled note repeated in endless succession, often 100 to 130 times per minute: *too, too, too, too*, etc. Longer and faster than in Northern Pygmy-Owl, which is also more apt to vary tempo. Also raspy, squirrel-like yelps. **SIMILAR SPECIES:** Boreal Owl. **HABITAT:** Coniferous and mixed woods, swamps.

BOREAL OWL *Aegolius funereus*　　　　　Scarce M328
10 in. (25 cm). A small, flat-headed, earless owl of northern and high-elevation coniferous forests. Tame. Similar to Northern Saw-whet Owl, but a bit larger; facial disk pale grayish white, *framed with black;* bill pale horn color or *yellowish;* forehead *thickly spotted* with white. *Juvenile:* Similar to young Northern Saw-whet, but duskier; eyebrows grayish; belly obscurely blotched. **VOICE:** "Song" an accelerating series of hoots, similar to a winnowing snipe; call includes a raspy *skew*. **SIMILAR SPECIES:** Northern Saw-whet Owl. **HABITAT:** Forests primarily of spruce, fir, and lodgepole pine; muskeg. Sporadically appears south of normal range, in east.

NORTHERN PYGMY-OWL *Glaucidium gnoma*　　Uncommon M319
6¾–7 in. (17–18 cm). *Black patches* on each side of hindneck suggest "eyes on back of the head." A very small, earless owl; warm or gray brown, with *sharply streaked underparts* and *rather long tail barred with white*. Frequently heard calling or seen flying in daytime, particularly early and late. Often mobbed by birds. Spotted head is proportionately smaller than that of Northern Saw-whet Owl or screech-owls. Tail often held at perky angle. **VOICE:** Single mellow whistle, *hoo*, repeated in well-spaced series every two or three seconds. Also a rolling series, ending with two or three deliberate notes: *too-too too-too-too-too-too-too-took-took-took*. Birds in se. AZ mountain canyons double the *hoos*. **SIMILAR SPECIES:** Ferruginous Pygmy-Owl, Northern Saw-whet Owl. **HABITAT:** Open coniferous and mixed woods, wooded canyons.

FERRUGINOUS PYGMY-OWL *Glaucidium brasilianum*　Scarce M320
6½–6¾ in. (16–17 cm). Hunts by day, particularly early and late. Often mobbed by birds. Streaking on breast *brownish* rather than black; crown has fine pale streaks (not dots). Tail *rusty, barred with black*. **VOICE:** *Chook* or *took;* sometimes repeated monotonously two or three times per second. Calls both in day and at night. **SIMILAR SPECIES:** Northern Pygmy-Owl (note habitat). **HABITAT:** In s. TX, mesquite and subtropical woods; in s. AZ, saguaro desert.

NORTHERN HAWK OWL

BURROWING
OWL

juvenile

NORTHERN
SAW-WHET OWL

adult

BOREAL
OWL

gray
morph

FERRUGINOUS
PYGMY-OWL

NORTHERN
PYGMY-OWL

note "eye
pattern" on
nape

GOATSUCKERS (NIGHTJARS) Family Caprimulgidae

Nocturnal birds with ample tail, large eyes, tiny bill, large bristled gape, and very short legs. By day, they rest on limbs or on ground, camouflaged by their "dead-leaf" pattern. Best identified at night by voice. **FOOD**: Nocturnal insects. **RANGE**: Nearly worldwide in temperate and tropical land regions.

COMMON NIGHTHAWK
Uncommon to fairly common M331

Chordeiles minor
9½ in. (24 cm). A slim-winged, gray-brown bird, often seen high in air; flies with easy strokes, changing gear to quicker erratic strokes. Prefers dusk, but may be abroad at midday. Note *broad white bar* across pointed wing. Barred white-and-gray undertail coverts. Male has white bar across notched tail and white throat. At rest, *tertial feathers extend well past white wing patch;* wingtips extend to or beyond tail tip. **VOICE**: Nasal *peer* or *pee-ik*. In aerial display, male dives, then zooms up sharply with sudden deep whir of wings. **SIMILAR SPECIES**: Antillean Nighthawk regular in FL Keys; best distinguished by voice. Lesser Nighthawk's white on wing closer to tip, wings more bluntly tipped; most are browner and less barred than Common. **HABITAT**: Open country from mountains to lowlands; open pine woods; sagebrush; often seen in air over cities, towns. Also over ponds. Sits on ground, posts, rails, roofs, limbs.

LESSER NIGHTHAWK *Chordeiles acutipennis*
Fairly common M330

8½–9 in. (21–23 cm). Slightly smaller than Common Nighthawk; white bar (*buffy* in female) *closer to tip of wing* (at rest, this bar even with or slightly beyond tips of tertial feathers). More extensive brown spotting on inner primaries. Undertail coverts browner, less sharply barred. Readily identified by odd calls. Does not power-dive. **VOICE**: Low *chuck chuck* and soft purring or whinnying sound, much like trilling of a toad. **SIMILAR SPECIES**: Common Nighthawk. **RANGE**: A few may wander east along Gulf Coast as far as FL. **HABITAT**: Lowlands; arid scrub, dry grasslands, farm fields, deserts, dirt roads. Also seen in air over ponds. Sits on branches and ground.

ANTILLEAN NIGHTHAWK *Chordeiles gundlachii*
Scarce, local

8–8½ in. (20–22 cm). This W. Indian species is a regular late-spring and summer visitor to FL Keys and Dry Tortugas. Somewhat tawnier and smaller than Common Nighthawk, but readily distinguished from it only by call. **VOICE**: Katydid-like *killy-kadick* or *pity-pit-pit*. **SIMILAR SPECIES**: Common and Lesser nighthawks. **HABITAT**: Open fields, suburban areas.

NIGHTHAWKS

COMMON
NIGHTHAWK

LESSER
NIGHTHAWK

ANTILLEAN
NIGHTHAWK

BUFF-COLLARED NIGHTJAR *Caprimulgus ridgwayi*   Rare, local M335
8¾–9 in. (22–23 cm). Similar to Whip-poor-will, but with *buff or tawny collar* across hindneck. Best told by voice. **VOICE:** Staccato, cricketlike notes, terminating with longer, strongly accented phrase, *cuk-cuk-cuk-cuk-cuk-cuk-cuk-cukacheea.* **SIMILAR SPECIES:** Common Poorwill, Whip-poor-will. **RANGE:** Annual spring and summer visitor to se. AZ. **HABITAT:** Rocky slopes and washes near mesquite or junipers.

COMMON POORWILL *Phalaenoptilus nuttallii*   Uncommon M333
7½–7¾ in. (19–20 cm). Best known by its night cry in arid hills. Appears smaller than a nighthawk, has shorter, more rounded wings (*no white bar*), and short, rounded tail has *white corners.* Short wings and tail give it a *compact look* at rest. **VOICE:** At night, a loud, repeated *poor-will* or *poor-jill.* **SIMILAR SPECIES:** Whip-poor-will. **HABITAT:** Dry or rocky hills, including open pine forests, sagebrush, juniper, and chaparral; roadsides.

WHIP-POOR-WILL *Caprimulgus vociferus*   Uncommon M336
9½–9¾ in. (24–25 cm). A voice in the night woods, this species is more often heard than seen. When flushed by day, flits away on rounded wings, like a large brown moth. Male shows large *white tail patches;* in female these are buffy. At rest, tail extends beyond wings, unlike nighthawk's. Note *black throat* and *broad black crown stripe.* **VOICE:** At night, a rolling, tiresomely repeated *WHIP poor-WEEL,* or *purple-rib,* etc. Birds in Southwest give much burrier song. **SIMILAR SPECIES:** Common Poorwill, Chuck-will's-widow. **HABITAT:** Drier second-growth woodlands, especially oak and pine.

CHUCK-WILL'S-WIDOW *Caprimulgus carolinensis*   Uncommon M334
12 in. (30 cm). Similar to Whip-poor-will; larger, much browner, with *brown* (not blackish) throat and *streaked crown.* Identify by size (flat, bull-headed appearance), brownish look; more restricted white areas in tail of male; also by voice, range. **VOICE:** Call four-syllable *chuck-will-widow* (less vigorous than effort of Whip-poor-will); *chuck* often very low and difficult to hear. **SIMILAR SPECIES:** Whip-poor-will, Common Poorwill. **HABITAT:** Pine and mixed forests, river woodlands, groves.

COMMON PAURAQUE *Nyctidromus albicollis*   Uncommon, local M332
11 in. (28 cm). Larger than Whip-poor-will. Dark brown, with long, round wings and tail. Flight floppy with deep wingbeats. Note *broad white band* across pointed wing of male (female's wing bars buffy). *White in tail feathers is obvious.* At rest, note *pale-edged scapulars.* Recognized by its call. **VOICE:** A hoarse slurred whistle: *purr-WEE-eeerr.* **SIMILAR SPECIES:** Other nightjars. **HABITAT:** Dense brushy woodlands.

GOATSUCKERS

BUFF-COLLARED NIGHTJAR

COMMON
POORWILL

WHIP-POOR-WILL

CHUCK-WILL'S-WIDOW

COMMON PAURAQUE

HUMMINGBIRDS Family Trochilidae

The smallest birds. Iridescent, with needlelike bill for sipping nectar. Jewel-like gorget (throat feathers) adorns most adult males; in poor light, however, iridescence may not show and throat will appear dark. Hummingbirds hover when feeding; their wing motion is so rapid that wings appear as a blur. They can fly backward. Pugnacious. Vocal differences can be important identification aids. **FOOD:** Nectar (red flowers favored), small insects, spiders. **RANGE:** W. Hemisphere; majority in Tropics.

RUBY-THROATED HUMMINGBIRD
Fairly common M348
Archilochus colubris
3¾ in. (10 cm). *Male: Fiery red throat,* iridescent green back, forked tail. *Female:* Lacks red throat; tail blunt, with white spots. *The only widespread species in East;* several other hummers may turn up as strays, especially in Southeast states in fall and winter. **VOICE:** Male's wings hum in courtship display. Chase calls high, squeaky. Other call a soft *chew.* **SIMILAR SPECIES:** Male Broad-tailed Hummingbird lacks forked tail, typically makes wing-trill sound. Female and immature similar to Black-chinned Hummingbird but have *crown and back brighter green,* bill slightly shorter, underparts whiter, pump tail less. *Outermost primary narrower and straighter at tip, more club-shaped in Black-chinned.* Adult male Black-chinned has shallower tail fork than male Ruby-throated (both look black-throated in poor light). See also Anna's and Costa's hummingbirds. Some day-flying sphinx moths (Sphingidae) might be mistaken for hummers. **HABITAT:** Flowers, gardens, wood edges, over streams.

COSTA'S HUMMINGBIRD *Calypte costae*
Uncommon M351
3½ in. (9 cm). *Male:* Note *purple* or *amethyst* throat and crown. Feathers of gorget *project* markedly at sides. **VOICE:** Series of ticking notes. Male in display, a rising *zing.* **SIMILAR SPECIES:** Female very similar to female Black-chinned Hummingbird, but duller green above, shorter bill and tail, *voices differ.* Female Anna's Hummingbird slightly larger, more mottled, less clean-cut below. **HABITAT:** Deserts, coastal sage scrub, chaparral, arid hillsides, feeders.

BLACK-CHINNED HUMMINGBIRD
Fairly common M349
Archilochus alexandri
3¾ in. (10 cm). *Male:* Note *black throat* and conspicuous white collar. Blue-violet of lower throat shows only in certain lights. *Caution:* Throat of other hummers may look black until it catches the light. *Female:* Very difficult to separate from female Ruby-throated Hummingbird in field. **VOICE:** Like Ruby-throated. **SIMILAR SPECIES:** Ruby-throated, Costa's, and Anna's hummingbirds. **HABITAT:** Riparian woodlands, wooded canyons, semiarid country, chaparral, suburbs, feeders.

ANNA'S HUMMINGBIRD *Calypte anna*
Common M350
4 in. (10 cm). *Male:* The only U.S. hummer with rose *red crown.* Throat rose red. *Female:* Slightly larger than other West Coast hummers. Overall a bit drabber or "messier" than similar species, grayer below, with more heavily spotted throat than female Costa's or Black-chinned hummingbird; often with small, red, central throat patch. The only hummingbird commonly found along Pacific Coast in midwinter. **VOICE:** Feeding call *chick.* Chase call a raspy chatter. Song (from a perch) squeaking, grating notes. When diving in its aerial "pendulum display," male makes *sharp popping sound* at bottom of arc. **SIMILAR SPECIES:** Black-chinned and Costa's hummingbirds. Vocal differences important. **HABITAT:** Gardens, parks, feeders, chaparral, open woods.

♂

RUBY-THROATED HUMMINGBIRD

♂

♀

sphinx moths resemble hummingbirds

♂

♀

♂

♀

COSTA'S HUMMINGBIRD

BLACK-CHINNED HUMMINGBIRD

♂

♀

ANNA'S HUMMINGBIRD

BROAD-TAILED HUMMINGBIRD Fairly common M353
Selasphorus platycercus
4 in. (10 cm). *Male:* Known by sound of its wings, a *shrill trilling (except when in molt).* Crown and back green; throat bright *rose red,* greenish on sides. *Female:* Slightly larger and larger-tailed than female Black-chinned Hummingbird; sides tinged with buffy; touch of rufous at basal corners of tail. **VOICE:** Produces a variety of vocal and nonvocal sounds. *Chi-che-wee chi-chewee* often given in flight. Male's wings produce distinctive high trill. Call a sharp *chit!* **SIMILAR SPECIES:** Female Calliope Hummingbird smaller, with smaller bill; at rest *wingtips extend beyond short, square-cut tail.* Female Rufous Hummingbird has slightly smaller tail, usually more sharply defined rufous on sides, and usually more rufous in tail. Male Ruby-throated Hummingbird smaller with forked tail. **HABITAT:** Mountains and canyons; common at feeders.

RUFOUS HUMMINGBIRD *Selasphorus rufus* Common M354
3¾ in. (9–10 cm). *Male:* No other N. American hummingbird has *rufous back.* Upperparts bright red-brown; throat flaming orange-red. Aerial display is a closed ellipse, slowing on return climb. *Female and immature:* Green-backed; dull *rufous on sides and at base of outer tail feathers* (visible when tail fully spread). Adult females often have a few patchy orange-red feathers on throat. **VOICE:** Produces a variety of vocal and nonvocal sounds. Aggressive flight call a buzzy *zap* followed by sputtering notes, or *zeee chippity chippity.* Displaying male utters low hum. Male's wings make high trill in flight. **SIMILAR SPECIES:** Allen's, Calliope, and Broad-tailed hummingbirds. **HABITAT:** Wooded or brushy areas, parks, gardens, feeders; in southbound migration, also mountain meadows.

ALLEN'S HUMMINGBIRD *Selasphorus sasin* Uncommon M355
3¾ in. (9–10 cm). *Male:* Like Rufous Hummingbird (*rufous* sides, rump, tail, and cheeks; fiery throat), but back *green.* (*Note:* Some adult Rufous have a mix of green and rufous.) *Female and immature:* Not safely distinguishable in field from female Rufous (when measured in the hand, Allen's has narrower outermost tail feathers). **VOICE:** Flight call similar to that of Rufous. Aerial display of male unlike that of Rufous. Starts "pendulum display" in a shallow arc and after several swoops goes into steep climb and swoops back, with an air-splitting *vrrrip.* **SIMILAR SPECIES:** May be inseparable in field from female and immature Rufous. Adult male and some molting young male Rufous have largely or entirely rufous back. See also female Broad-tailed and Calliope hummingbirds. **HABITAT:** Wooded or brushy canyons, riparian woodlands, parks, gardens, feeders; in southbound migration, also mountain meadows.

CALLIOPE HUMMINGBIRD *Stellula calliope* Uncommon M352
3¼ in. (8 cm). The smallest hummer normally found in U.S. and Canada. *Adult male: Throat with purple-red rays on white background* (may be folded like a dark inverted V on white throat); the only U.S. hummingbird with this effect. *Female and immature:* Similar to female Broad-tailed and Rufous hummingbirds (which have buffy sides, some rufous at base of tail), but Calliope *shorter tailed (wingtips extend beyond square-tipped tail at rest),* slightly smaller, and shorter billed; rust on sides paler, face pattern shows dark and pale spots in front of eye, weak pale line over base of bill. **VOICE:** High-pitched chips and buzzes in series. **HABITAT:** Mountains and canyons, feeders; in migration, also lowlands.

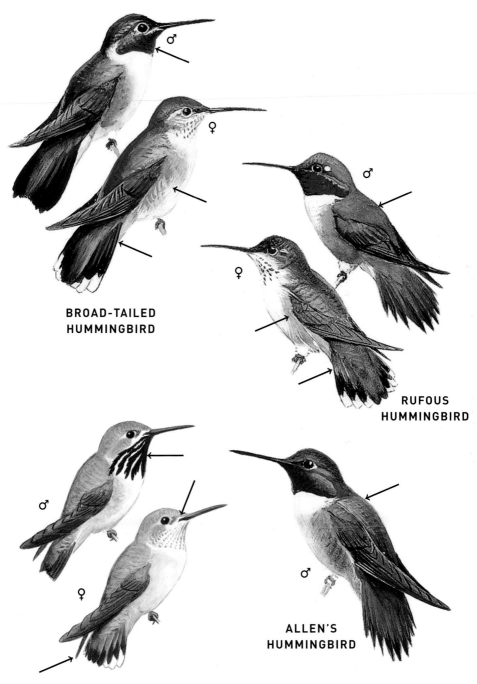

BROAD-TAILED
HUMMINGBIRD

RUFOUS
HUMMINGBIRD

CALLIOPE HUMMINGBIRD

ALLEN'S
HUMMINGBIRD

BROAD-BILLED HUMMINGBIRD
Uncommon, local M341

Cynanthus latirostris
4 in. (10 cm). *Male:* Dark green above and below, with *blue throat* (bird may look all black at a distance or in poor light). Bill *reddish* with black tip. Tail notched and *bluish black,* often flicked when hovering. *Female:* Identified by combination of *dull orange-red base to bill* (often restricted to lower mandible), *dark tail,* and *unmarked, pearly gray* throat; thin white line behind eye. Voice important. **VOICE:** Distinctive rough chattering. **SIMILAR SPECIES:** White-eared Hummingbird. **HABITAT:** Desert canyons, mountain slopes, riparian woodlands, agaves, mesquite, feeders.

VIOLET-CROWNED HUMMINGBIRD *Amazilia violiceps* Scarce, local M344

4½ in. (11 cm). A medium-sized hummer with *immaculate white underparts, including throat;* bill *red* with dark tip. Sexes similar, but *crown violet-blue* in male, *dull greenish blue* in female and immature. No iridescent gorget on male. **VOICE:** Aggressive call a series of squeaky notes. Call note *chak.* **SIMILAR SPECIES:** Anna's Hummingbird. **HABITAT:** Riparian woodlands, lower canyons, sycamores, agaves, feeders.

BUFF-BELLIED HUMMINGBIRD
Uncommon, local M343

Amazilia yucatanensis
4¼ in. (11 cm). Note combination of buff underparts, rufous tail, and green throat. Bill orange-red with dark tip. Sexes similar. **VOICE:** Call a surprisingly loud *smak smak smak.* Aggressive flight call an unmusical buzz: *chr chr chr chr chr.* **SIMILAR SPECIES:** Extremely rare Berylline Hummingbird similar in appearance but does not overlap in range. **HABITAT:** Open woodlands, gardens, feeders.

BLUE-THROATED HUMMINGBIRD
Uncommon M345

Lampornis clemenciae
5 in. (13 cm). Note large tail with *large white patches. Male:* A very large hummingbird, with black and white stripes about eye and light *blue throat;* big black tail with large white patches at corners. *Female:* Large, with *evenly gray* underparts, white marks on face, and big, blue-black tail with *large white corners,* as in male. **VOICE:** Call a distinctive squeaking *seek.* **SIMILAR SPECIES:** Magnificent Hummingbird. **HABITAT:** Near wooded streams in mountain canyons; feeders.

MAGNIFICENT HUMMINGBIRD *Eugenes fulgens*
Uncommon M346

5¼ in. (13 cm). *Male:* A very large hummingbird with *blackish belly, bright green throat,* and *purple crown.* Looks all black at a distance. Wingbeats discernible; sometimes the bird briefly glides on set wings. *Female:* Large; greenish above, washed with greenish or dusky below. **VOICE:** Call a thin, sharp *chip;* distinctive. **SIMILAR SPECIES:** Told from female Blue-throated Hummingbird by voice, more mottled underparts, short eye stripe, and dark greenish tail with obscure pale corners. **HABITAT:** Mountain glades, pine-oak woods, canyons, feeders.

HUMMINGBIRDS

VIOLET-CROWNED
HUMMINGBIRD

BROAD-BILLED
HUMMINGBIRD

BUFF-BELLIED
HUMMINGBIRD

BLUE-THROATED
HUMMINGBIRD

MAGNIFICENT
HUMMINGBIRD

GREEN VIOLET-EAR *Colibri thalassinus* Vagrant
4¾ in. (12 cm). A large, dark hummingbird. Sexes mostly similar. Green
with violet ear patch, bluish tail. Bill long and slightly decurved. **VOICE:**
Song and call a series of dry *chip*s. **SIMILAR SPECIES:** Broad-billed and
Magnificent hummingbirds. **RANGE AND HABITAT:** Widespread, mostly
summer stray from Mex., most records from TX. In U.S. almost always
seen at feeders.

GREEN-BREASTED MANGO *Anthracothorax prevostii* Vagrant
4¾ in. (12 cm). Large, with long downcurved bill. *Adult male:* Dark emerald green above with velvety black throat edged in emerald. Center of
belly deep blue-green. Tail purple. *Female:* Paler green back, light underparts with irregular dark stripe from throat to belly. Dusky tail. *Immature
male* (which accounts for most sightings north of border): Very similar to
female, but lacks stripe on chin. **VOICE:** Call a high-pitched *tzat.* Song a
metallic series of two-part notes. **SIMILAR SPECIES:** Other all-dark hummingbirds. **RANGE AND HABITAT:** Stray from Mex., primarily to s. TX, and
almost always at feeders.

WHITE-EARED HUMMINGBIRD *Hylocharis leucotis* Rare M342
3¾ in. (10 cm). A rare but regular summer visitor to s. AZ mountains.
Male: Bill short, orangey red, with black tip; *broad white stripe behind eye.*
Underparts dark greenish, throat blue and green, crown purple. *Female:*
Orangey red bill, bold white stripe behind eye. Note small *green spots* on
throat. **VOICE:** Makes a variety of thin chips, sometimes in rapid series.
SIMILAR SPECIES: Female Broad-billed Hummingbird often mistaken for
rarer White-eared (reddish-based bill and pronounced white eye stripe),
but note *vocal differences* and Broad-billed's slightly longer bill, slightly
shorter white eyebrow, more forked tail, and evenly gray throat and underparts. **HABITAT:** Montane pine-oak woods near streams; feeders.

BERYLLINE HUMMINGBIRD *Amazilia beryllina* Rare
4¼ in. (11 cm). *Male: Glittering green* on underparts; *deep rich rufous* in
wings, rump, and tail. Bill partly red. *Female:* Duller; belly gray. **VOICE:** All
vocal sounds very scratchy and buzzy. **SIMILAR SPECIES:** Buff-bellied
Hummingbird. **RANGE AND HABITAT:** Mexican species; rare visitor and casual breeder in oak-clad mountain canyons of se. AZ, often at feeders.

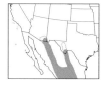

LUCIFER HUMMINGBIRD *Calothorax lucifer* Scarce, local M347
3½ in. (9 cm). A small hummingbird. Note pronounced *decurved bill.*
Male: Purple throat, rusty or buffy sides. No purple on crown (as in Costa's
Hummingbird); tail *deeply forked,* often folded. *Female: Decurved bill, underparts extensively buff,* rufous at base of outer tail feathers. **VOICE:** Series
of dry twitters. Male in courtship display makes "playing-card shuffle"
sound. **SIMILAR SPECIES:** Black-chinned Hummingbird may show slight
curve to bill. **HABITAT:** Arid slopes, agaves, feeders.

PLAIN-CAPPED STARTHROAT *Heliomaster constantii* Vagrant
5 in. (13 cm). A large, *long-billed* hummer, with red throat, *white facial
stripes, white rump.* **VOICE:** Variety of strong *chips* given singly or in series.
SIMILAR SPECIES: Magnificent and Anna's hummingbirds. **RANGE AND
HABITAT:** Mexican species, casual visitor at lower elevations in s. AZ, usually at feeders.

RARE HUMMINGBIRDS

♂

♀

♂

**GREEN
VIOLET-EAR**

**GREEN-BREASTED
MANGO**

♂

♀

**WHITE-EARED
HUMMINGBIRD**

♀

♂

**BERYLLINE
HUMMINGBIRD**

adult

♂

♀

tail may
fold in a
spikelike
point

**LUCIFER
HUMMINGBIRD**

**PLAIN-CAPPED
STARTHROAT**

SWIFTS Family Apodidae

Swallowlike, but structurally distinct, with flat skull and all four toes pointing forward. Flight very rapid, "twinkling," sailing between spurts; narrow wings often stiffly bowed. **FOOD:** Flying insects. **RANGE:** Nearly worldwide.

VAUX'S SWIFT *Chaetura vauxi*   Uncommon M339
4¾ in. (12 cm). A small, dark, swallowlike bird with no apparent tail (unless spread). Between spurts of rapid wingbeats, glides with wings *bowed* in a *crescent*. Twinkling flight style marks it as a swift; range, small size, and dingy underparts as this species. **VOICE:** High-pitched, rapid ticking or chippering notes, often run into an insectlike trill. **SIMILAR SPECIES:** Very difficult to separate from Chimney Swift (very rare in West), which is slightly larger and longer winged, has darker throat and rump, and louder chippering call. **HABITAT:** Open sky over woodlands, lakes, and rivers; nests in tree cavities, more rarely chimneys.

CHIMNEY SWIFT *Chaetura pelagica*   Common M338
5¼ in. (13 cm). Like a cigar with wings. A blackish swallowlike bird with long, slightly curved, stiff wings and stubby tail. Rapid, twinkling wingbeats interspersed with bowed-winged glides. **VOICE:** Loud, rapid ticking or twittering notes. **SIMILAR SPECIES:** This is only eastern swift. In West, see Vaux's Swift. Also see swallows. **HABITAT:** Open sky, especially over cities, towns; nests and roosts in chimneys (originally in large hollow trees and cliff crevices).

BLACK SWIFT *Cypseloides niger*   Uncommon, local M337
7¼ in. (18 cm). A large *blackish* swift with notched tail (sometimes fanned). At close range, a touch of white on forehead. Slower wingbeats than in other U.S. swifts. **VOICE:** Sharp *plik-plik-plik-plik-plik*, etc., rarely heard away from nest site. **SIMILAR SPECIES:** Vaux's Swift much smaller. **HABITAT:** Open sky; favors mountain country, coastal cliffs; nests on sea cliffs and behind waterfalls.

WHITE-THROATED SWIFT *Aeronautes saxatalis*   Uncommon M340
6½ in. (17 cm). Known from other N. American swifts by its contrasting *black-and-white pattern*. In poor light look for long slim tail. **VOICE:** Shrill, excited *jejejejeje*, in descending scale. **SIMILAR SPECIES:** Other swifts and swallows. **HABITAT:** Open sky. Breeds mainly in dry mountains, canyons, cliffs; locally on sea cliffs.

TROGONS Family Trogonidae

Solitary, brightly colored forest and woodland birds with short neck, stubby bill, long tail, and very small feet. Erect when perched. May remain motionless for long periods. Flutter when plucking berries. **FOOD:** Small fruit, insects. **RANGE:** Mainly tropical parts of world.

EARED QUETZAL (EARED TROGON) *Euptilotis neoxenus*   Very rare
13½–14 in. (35–36 cm). Note *black bill*, *lack of white breast band*, and mostly *white* underside of blue tail. "Ears" of male inconspicuous. **VOICE:** High-pitched, rising squeal; series of whistled notes. **RANGE AND HABITAT:** Very rare visitor from Mex., mostly in late summer and fall, to mountains and canyons in se. AZ, casual to cen. AZ.

ELEGANT TROGON *Trogon elegans*   Uncommon, local M356
12–12½ in. (31–32 cm). Note *geranium red belly, white breast band,* yellow bill, and *finely barred underside of tail* (coppery above). Female has *white mark* on cheek. **VOICE:** Series of low, coarse notes, suggesting a hen turkey: *kowm kowm kowm kowm kowm kowm* or *koa, koa, koa,* etc. **HABITAT:** Mountain forests, pine-oak and sycamore canyons.

SWIFTS

Roosting
Swifts

WHITE-
THROATED
SWIFT

CHIMNEY
SWIFT

BLACK
SWIFT

VAUX'S
SWIFT

TROGONS

♀

♂

♀

♂

ELEGANT
TROGON

EARED
QUETZAL

KINGFISHERS Family Alcedinidae

Solitary birds with large head, long pointed bill, and small syndactyl feet (two toes partially joined). Most are fish eaters, perching above water or hovering and plunging headfirst. **FOOD**: Mainly fish; some species eat insects, lizards. **RANGE**: Almost worldwide.

GREEN KINGFISHER *Chloroceryle americana*   Uncommon, local **M359**
8½–8¾ in. (22 cm). Kingfisher shape, small size; flight buzzy, direct. Upperparts deep green with white spots; collar and underparts white, sides spotted. *Male*: Has *rusty* breast-band. *Female*: Has one or two greenish bands. (The reverse is true in Belted Kingfisher: female has rusty band.) **VOICE**: Sharp clicking, *tick tick tick;* also a sharp squeak. **SIMILAR SPECIES**: Belted Kingfisher. **HABITAT**: Small rivers and streams with clear water.

RINGED KINGFISHER *Ceryle torquatus*   Uncommon, local **M357**
16 in. (41 cm). Larger than Belted Kingfisher; bill very large. *Male*: Has entirely chestnut breast and belly. *Female*: Has broad blue-gray band across breast, separated from chestnut belly by narrow white line. **VOICE**: Rusty *cla-ack* or *wa-ak* or rolling rattle after a loud *chack*. **SIMILAR SPECIES**: Belted Kingfisher. **HABITAT**: Slow rivers, marshes.

BELTED KINGFISHER *Ceryle alcyon*   Fairly common **M358**
13 in. (33 cm). Hovering on rapidly beating wings in readiness for the plunge, or flying with uneven wingbeats (as if changing gear), rattling as it goes, Belted Kingfisher is easily recognized. Perched, it is big-headed and big-billed, larger than a robin. *Male*: Blue-gray above, with ragged bushy crest and broad gray breast-band. *Female*: Has an additional rusty breast-band. **VOICE**: Loud dry rattle. **SIMILAR SPECIES**: Ringed Kingfisher in TX. **HABITAT**: Streams, lakes, bays, coasts; nests in banks, perches on wires.

KINGFISHERS

♀

♂

GREEN KINGFISHER

RINGED KINGFISHER

♀

male entirely
chestnut below

hovering

♀

plunging

BELTED KINGFISHER

♂

WOODPECKERS AND ALLIES Family Picidae

Chisel-billed, wood-boring birds with strong zygodactyl feet (usually two toes front, two rear), remarkably long tongue, and stiff spiny tail that acts as prop for climbing. Flight usually undulating. **FOOD:** Tree-boring insects; some species eat ants, flying insects, berries, acorns, sap. **RANGE:** Most wooded parts of world; absent in Australian region, Madagascar, most oceanic islands.

RED-HEADED WOODPECKER
Uncommon M361

Melanerpes erythrocephalus
9¼ in. (24 cm). *Adult:* A black-backed woodpecker with *entirely red* head (other woodpeckers may have patch of red). Back *solid black,* rump white. Large, square *white patches* conspicuous on wing (making lower back look white when bird is on a tree). Sexes similar. *Immature:* Dusky-headed; wing patches mottled with dark. **VOICE:** Loud *queer* or *queeah.* **SIMILAR SPECIES:** Red-bellied Woodpecker has partially red head. **HABITAT:** Groves, farm country, shade trees in towns, large scattered trees.

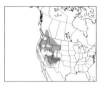

LEWIS'S WOODPECKER *Melanerpes lewis*
Uncommon M360

10¾–11 in. (27–28 cm). A large, dark woodpecker with extensive *pinkish red belly.* Has *wide gray collar* and dark red face patch. Sexes similar. Has straight *crowlike flight;* flycatching habit. **VOICE:** Usually silent. Occasionally a harsh *churr* or *chee-ur.* **SIMILAR SPECIES:** Red-headed and Acorn woodpeckers. **HABITAT:** Open, burned, or logged forests, usually of ponderosa pine or oak, river groves, oak savanna.

ACORN WOODPECKER *Melanerpes formicivorus*
Common M362

9 in. (23 cm). Social, usually found in clans. Note *clownish black, white, and red head pattern.* A black-backed woodpecker showing conspicuous white rump and *white wing patches* in flight. Both sexes have whitish eyes, red on crown. Stores acorns in holes drilled in bark and wooden building sides. **VOICE:** *Whack-up, whack-up, whack-up,* or *ja-cob, ja-cob.* **HABITAT:** Oak woods, mixed oak-pine forests, foothills.

RED-BELLIED WOODPECKER *Melanerpes carolinus*
Common M365

9¼ in. (24 cm). *Adult:* A *zebra-backed* woodpecker with *red cap, white rump.* Red covers both crown and nape in male, *only nape in female. Juvenile:* Also zebra-backed, but has brown head, devoid of red. **VOICE:** Call *kwirr, churr,* or *chaw;* also *chiv, chiv.* Also a muffled flickerlike series. **SIMILAR SPECIES:** Golden-fronted and Red-headed woodpeckers. **HABITAT:** Woodlands, groves, orchards, towns, feeders.

GILA WOODPECKER *Melanerpes uropygialis*
Fairly common M363

9¼ in. (24 cm). *Male:* Note *round red cap.* A zebra-backed woodpecker; in flight, shows *white wing patch.* Head and underparts gray-brown. *Female:* Similar, but without red cap. **VOICE:** Rolling *churr* and a sharp *pit* or *yip.* **SIMILAR SPECIES:** Ladder-backed Woodpecker has striped face, lacks white wing patch. See female Williamson's Sapsucker. **HABITAT:** Desert washes, saguaros, riparian woodlands, towns.

GOLDEN-FRONTED WOODPECKER *Melanerpes aurifrons*
Common M364

9½ in. (25 cm). *Male:* Note *multicolored head* (yellow near bill, poppy red on crown, orange nape). A zebra-backed woodpecker with light underparts and white rump. Shows white wing patch in flight. *Female:* Lacks red crown patch. *Immature:* Lacks color patches on head. **VOICE:** Tremulous *churrrr;* flickerlike *kek-kek-kek-kek.* **SIMILAR SPECIES:** Red-bellied Woodpecker. **HABITAT:** Mesquite, woodlands, groves.

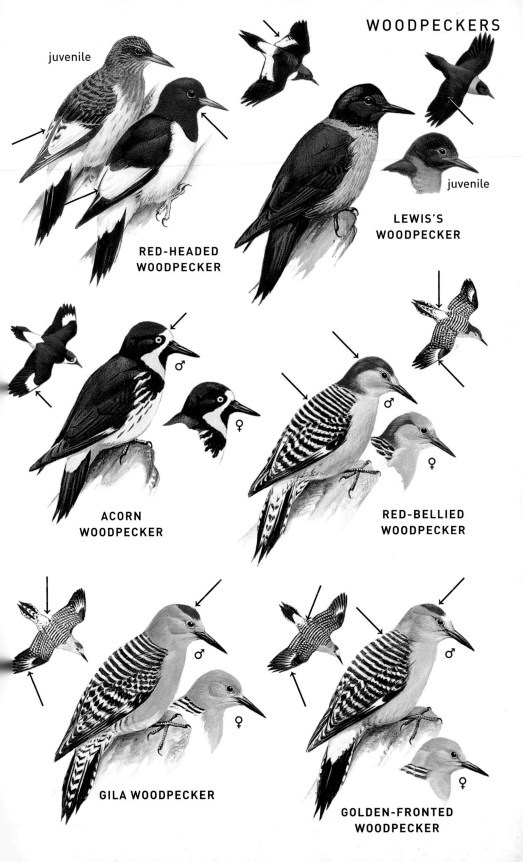

WOODPECKERS

juvenile

RED-HEADED WOODPECKER

LEWIS'S WOODPECKER

juvenile

♂ ♀

ACORN WOODPECKER

♂ ♀

RED-BELLIED WOODPECKER

♂ ♀

GILA WOODPECKER

♂ ♀

GOLDEN-FRONTED WOODPECKER

NORTHERN FLICKER *Colaptes auratus* Common M379

12–12½ in. (30–32 cm). In flight, note conspicuous *white rump.* This and barred *brown back* mark bird as a flicker. Close up, it shows *black patch* across chest. Flight undulating. Often hops awkwardly on ground, feeding on ants. Two basic subspecies groups are recognized: "Yellow-shafted" Flicker, the Northern and eastern form, has *golden yellow* underwings and tail. *Red crescent* on nape; *gray crown; tan-brown cheeks;* male has *black* mustache. "Red-shafted" Flicker, the widespread western form, has underwing and undertail *salmon red.* Both sexes lack red crescent on nape; have *brownish crown* and *gray cheeks;* male has *red* mustache. Where ranges overlap (western edge of plains), intergrades occur. VOICE: Loud *wick wick wick wick wick,* etc. Also a loud *klee-yer* and a squeaky *flick-a, flick-a,* etc. (see also Pileated Woodpecker). SIMILAR SPECIES: Gilded Flicker. HABITAT: Open forests, woodlots, towns.

GILDED FLICKER *Colaptes chrysoides* Uncommon, local M380

11–11½ in. (28–29 cm). Some overlap with Northern Flicker. Wing and tail linings usually *yellow,* crown mustard brown, male has *red* mustache. Black breast patch slightly thicker, dark barring on back slightly narrower. VOICE: Same as Northern Flicker's, but slightly higher pitched. HABITAT: Cactus deserts, riparian woodland corridors.

WILLIAMSON'S SAPSUCKER *Sphyrapicus thyroideus* Uncommon M366

9 in. (23 cm). *Male:* Black crown, *black back, long white shoulder patch,* white rump. Note white facial stripes, *red throat, yellow belly. Female:* Very different looking: a brownish *zebra-backed* woodpecker with white rump, *barred sides, brown head,* yellow belly. VOICE: Nasal *cheeer.* Drum is several rapid thumps followed by three or four slow, accented thumps. SIMILAR SPECIES: Female told from Gila Woodpecker by medium brown head, barred sides, yellow belly, and usually habitat. HABITAT: Coniferous forests, rarely other types of trees.

RED-BREASTED SAPSUCKER *Sphyrapicus ruber* Uncommon M369

8½ in. (22 cm). Note *entirely red head and breast, sapsucker wing stripe.* Northern birds have blacker back, less white and black in face than birds from CA. Hybridizes regularly with Red-naped Sapsucker. VOICE: Similar to Red-naped Sapsucker. SIMILAR SPECIES: Hybrid Red-naped × Red-breasted sapsuckers have more black and white on face (but some southern Red-breasteds quite similar) and mix of black and red on breast. HABITAT: Coniferous and mixed woods, groves.

RED-NAPED SAPSUCKER *Sphyrapicus nuchalis* Fairly common M368

8½ in. (22 cm). Sapsuckers drill orderly rows of small holes in trees for sap and the insects it attracts. Note *longish sapsucker wing patch* and *striped head.* Very similar to Yellow-bellied but note *red nape.* Black frame around throat *broken* toward rear. Female shows both red and white on throat. Hybridizes with Red-breasted Sapsucker. VOICE: Nasal mewing note, *cheerrrr;* drum is several rapid thumps followed by several slow, rhythmic thumps; similar to Yellow-bellied and Red-breasted sapsuckers. SIMILAR SPECIES: Yellow-bellied Sapsucker. HABITAT: Coniferous, mixed, and deciduous woodlands; in summer, particularly aspen groves.

YELLOW-BELLIED SAPSUCKER *Sphyrapicus varius* Fairly common M367

8½ in. (22 cm). *Adult:* Note sapsucker wing stripe, red forehead. Male has all-red throat, female white. VOICE: Similar to Red-naped Sapsucker. SIMILAR SPECIES: Red-naped Sapsucker. HABITAT: Coniferous, mixed, and deciduous woods, shade trees.

♀

"Red-shafted"

"Red-shafted"

"Yellow-shafted"

"Red-shafted"

♂

"Yellow-shafted"

Gilded Flicker

NORTHERN FLICKER

GILDED FLICKER

♂

♂

"Red-shafted"

immature

♂

♂

WILLIAMSON'S SAPSUCKER

♀

southern

juvenile

RED-BREASTED SAPSUCKER

northern

♀

♂

♂

juvenile

♀

RED-NAPED SAPSUCKER

YELLOW-BELLIED SAPSUCKER

NUTTALL'S WOODPECKER *Picoides nuttallii*   Fairly common M371
7½ in. (19 cm). The only black-and-white zebra-backed woodpecker with *black-and-white-striped face* normally found *in far west*. Male has red crown. **VOICE:** High-pitched whinny or rattle. Call a low *pa-teck,* lower and raspier than that of Ladder-backed Woodpecker. **SIMILAR SPECIES:** Ladder-backed Woodpecker inhabits more arid country; range barely overlaps (hybrids are known); has thicker white stripes on face and back. See Downy Woodpecker. **HABITAT:** Riparian, canyon, and mixed montane woodlands, particularly those with oaks.

LADDER-BACKED WOODPECKER *Picoides scalaris*   Fairly common M370
7¼ in. (18 cm). The only black-and-white zebra-backed woodpecker with *black-and-white-striped face* in more arid country *east of Sierra Nevada*. Male has red crown. **VOICE:** Rattling series, *chikikikikikikikikik,* diminishing. Call a sharp *pick* or *chik* (like Downy Woodpecker). **SIMILAR SPECIES:** Nuttall's Woodpecker. **HABITAT:** Deserts, canyons, pinyon-juniper, riparian woodlands, arid brush.

HAIRY WOODPECKER *Picoides villosus*   Fairly common M373
9–9¼ in. (23–24 cm). Note *white* back and *large* bill. Downy and Hairy woodpeckers are almost identical in pattern, checkered and spotted with black and white; males with small red patch on back of head, females without. Hairy is like an exaggerated Downy, especially its bill. *Juvenile:* May show orangey crown patch. **VOICE:** Kingfisher-like rattle, run together more than that of Downy. Call a sharp *peek!* (Downy says *pick*.) **SIMILAR SPECIES:** Downy Woodpecker. American Three-toed Woodpecker has some barring on back and barred sides. **HABITAT:** Forests, woodlands, shade trees, suet feeders.

DOWNY WOODPECKER *Picoides pubescens*   Common M372
6½–6¾ in. (17 cm). Note *white back* and *small bill*. This industrious bird is like a small edition of Hairy Woodpecker. Outer tail feathers spotted, red nape patch of male in unbroken square. Amount of white spotting in wings varies regionally, as it does in Hairy. **VOICE:** Rapid whinny of notes, descending in pitch. Call a flat *pick,* not as sharp as Hairy's *peek!* **SIMILAR SPECIES:** Hairy Woodpecker has clean white outer tail feathers. Ladder-backed Woodpecker has similar call. **HABITAT:** Forests, woods, residential areas, suet feeders, even corn and cattail stems.

AMERICAN THREE-TOED WOODPECKER *Picoides dorsalis*   Scarce M377
8½–8¾ in. (22 cm). Males of this and the next species are our only woodpeckers that normally have *yellow cap*. Both have *barred sides*. This species is distinguished by irregular white patch on back (Rockies) or *bars* (farther north). Female lacks yellow cap and suggests Downy or Hairy woodpecker, but note *barred sides*. **VOICE:** A level-pitched whinny and a flat *pyik*. **SIMILAR SPECIES:** Black-backed Woodpecker, Hairy Woodpecker. **HABITAT:** Coniferous forests, particularly where deadwood is present.

BLACK-BACKED WOODPECKER *Picoides arcticus*   Scarce M378
9½ in. (24 cm). Note combination of *solid black back* and *barred sides*. Male has *yellow cap*. This and preceding species (both have three toes) inhabit boreal and montane forests; their presence can be detected by patches of bark scaled from dead conifers. **VOICE:** Low flat *kuk* or *puk* and a short buzzy call. **SIMILAR SPECIES:** American Three-toed and Hairy woodpeckers. **HABITAT:** Coniferous forests, particularly where deadwood is present.

WOODPECKERS

NUTTALL'S WOODPECKER

♂ ♀

LADDER-BACKED WOODPECKER

♂ ♀

East

Northwest

Rockies

♂ ♂ ♂ ♀

HAIRY WOODPECKER

Northwest

Rockies

♂ ♂ ♀

DOWNY WOODPECKER

Rockies

North

♀ ♂ ♂

AMERICAN THREE-TOED WOODPECKER

♂ ♀

BLACK-BACKED WOODPECKER

ARIZONA WOODPECKER *Picoides arizonae*   Uncommon, local M374
7½ in. (19 cm). A dark, *brown-backed* woodpecker with *white-striped face;* spotted and barred below. Male has red nape patch. The only U.S. woodpecker with *solid brown* back. **VOICE:** Sharp *spik;* a hoarse whinny. Fairly similar to Hairy Woodpecker's calls. **SIMILAR SPECIES:** Northern Flicker has *barred brown back,* white rump, is larger. Also see Ladder-backed, Downy, and Hairy woodpeckers. **HABITAT:** Canyon woodlands of oak, juniper, and pine-oak.

RED-COCKADED WOODPECKER *Picoides borealis*   Rare, local M375
8½ in. (22 cm). Zebra-backed, with black cap. White cheek is obvious field mark. Male's tiny red cockade hard to see. Endangered. **VOICE:** Rough rasping *sripp* or *zhilp* (suggests flock note of young starling). Sometimes a higher *tsick.* Forms colonial "clans." **SIMILAR SPECIES:** Downy and Hairy woodpeckers. **HABITAT:** Open pine woodlands that have trees with heartwood disease. Red-cockaded numbers continue to decline.

WHITE-HEADED WOODPECKER *Picoides albolarvatus*   Uncommon M376
9¼ in. (23 cm). Our only woodpecker with *white head.* Male has red patch on nape; otherwise black overall, with large white patch in primaries. No white on rump (as in Acorn Woodpecker). **VOICE:** Sharp, *doubled ki-dik,* sometimes rapidly repeated, *chick-ik-ik-ik;* also a rattle similar to Downy Woodpecker's. **SIMILAR SPECIES:** Downy and Hairy woodpecker calls are *single, not double,* notes. **HABITAT:** Mountain pine forests, particularly ponderosa, Jeffrey, and sugar pines.

PILEATED WOODPECKER *Dryocopus pileatus*   Uncommon M381
16½–17 in. (42–44 cm). A spectacular black, *crow-sized* woodpecker, with flaming red *crest.* Female has blackish forehead, lacks red on mustache. Great size, sweeping wingbeats, and flashing white underwing coverts identify Pileated in flight. Large foraging pits in dead or dying trees — large *oval* or *oblong* holes — indicate its presence. **VOICE:** Call resembles a flicker, but louder, irregular: *kik-kik-kikkik-kik-kik,* etc. Also a more ringing, hurried call that may rise or fall slightly in pitch and volume. **SIMILAR SPECIES:** Ivory-billed Woodpecker (possibly extinct). **HABITAT:** Coniferous, mixed, and hardwood forests; woodlots.

IVORY-BILLED WOODPECKER *Campephilus principalis*   Possibly extinct
19–19½ in. (40–50 cm). Separated from Pileated Woodpecker by its slightly larger size, ivory white bill, large white wing patch visible at rest, and all-white underwing pattern with black line through it. Female has black crest. **VOICE:** Call unlike that of Pileated: a single loud tooting note constantly uttered as bird forages — a sharp nasal *kent* suggesting to some a big nuthatch. Audubon wrote it as *pait,* resembling high false note of a clarinet. Drum is a quick double knock, unique among North American woodpeckers. **SIMILAR SPECIES:** Pileated Woodpecker. **RANGE:** Throughout the Southeast. Reports persist, but the last universally accepted sightings were in the 1940s. **HABITAT:** Bottomland hardwood forests, wooded bayous and swamps.

WOODPECKERS

ARIZONA
WOODPECKER

♂

♀

RED-COCKADED
WOODPECKER

♂

PILEATED
WOODPECKER

♀

♂

WHITE-HEADED
WOODPECKER

♂

♀

IVORY-BILLED
WOODPECKER

♂

below

above

Pileated
below

TYRANT FLYCATCHERS Family Tyrannidae

New World Flycatchers, or Tyrant Flycatchers, make up the largest family of birds in the world, with approximately 425 known species. They are found chiefly in the Neotropics. A large number are very similar and require attention to fine points to separate them. Most species perch quietly, sitting upright on exposed branches, and sally forth to snap up insects. Bill flattened, with bristles at base. **FOOD:** Mainly flying insects. Some species also eat fruit in winter. **RANGE:** New World; majority in Tropics.

OLIVE-SIDED FLYCATCHER *Contopus cooperi*   Uncommon M383
7½ in. (19 cm). A stout, large-headed flycatcher; often perches on dead snags at tops of trees. Note large bill and *dark chest patches* separated by narrow strip of white (like unbuttoned vest). A *cottony tuft* may poke from behind wing (often not visible). **VOICE:** Call a two- or three-note *pip-pip-pip*. Song a spirited whistle, *I SAY there* or *Quick three beers!*, middle note highest, last one sliding. **SIMILAR SPECIES:** Wood-pewees, Greater Pewee. **HABITAT:** Coniferous forests, bogs, burns. In migration, usually seen on dead branches at tips of trees.

GREATER PEWEE *Contopus pertinax*   Uncommon, local M384
7¾ in. (20 cm). Resembles Olive-sided Flycatcher, but more obvious crest, breast more uniformly gray with *no white stripe* down center. *Lower mandible brighter and more extensively orangey.* **VOICE:** Thin, plaintive whistle, *ho-say, re-ah* or *ho-say, ma-re-ah* (nickname, "José María"). Call *pip-pip.* **SIMILAR SPECIES:** Western Wood-Pewee. **HABITAT:** Pine and pine-oak forests of mountains, canyons.

WESTERN WOOD-PEWEE *Contopus sordidulus*   Fairly common M385
6¼ in. (16 cm). A dusky, sparrow-sized flycatcher with two narrow wing bars but *no eye-ring.* Often appears "vested" below (with "top button buttoned"). Some fresh fall birds tinged yellow on belly. Bill shows small amount of pale on lower mandible. **VOICE:** Nasal *peeyee* or *peeeer.* **SIMILAR SPECIES:** Eastern Wood-Pewee. Olive-sided Flycatcher larger, more strongly "vested," different voice. Lack of any tail flicking, and calls, distinguish wood-pewees from *Empidonax* flycatchers, most of which also have eye-ring. **HABITAT:** Pine-oak forests, open conifers, canyon and riparian woodlands.

EASTERN WOOD-PEWEE *Contopus virens*   Fairly common M386
6¼ in. (16 cm). About the size of Eastern Phoebe, but with *two narrow wing bars, no eye-ring,* and variably pale orangish lower mandible. *Slightly larger* than *Empidonax* flycatchers, but with no eye-ring; wings extend farther down tail; *does not flick tail.* Very similar to Western Wood-Pewee, but slightly greener above and paler below (vest "not buttoned"); best distinguished by voice, range. **VOICE:** Sweet plaintive whistle, *pee-a-wee,* slurring down, then up. Also *pee-ur,* slurring down, and a *chip.* **SIMILAR SPECIES:** Western Wood-Pewee. Eastern Phoebe lacks wing bars; bobs tail downward. **HABITAT:** Woodlands, groves.

NORTHERN BEARDLESS-TYRANNULET   Uncommon, local M382
Camptostoma imberbe
4¼ in. (11 cm). A very small, nondescript flycatcher that may suggest a kinglet, Bell's Vireo, or immature Verdin. Grayish olive, with *slight crested* look. *Dull wing bars* and indistinct pale supercilium. Distinguished from *Empidonax* flycatchers by its smaller size, smaller head, and stubby bill, and voice. **VOICE:** Thin *peeee-yuk.* A gentle, descending *ee, ee, ee, ee, ee.* **SIMILAR SPECIES:** Buff-breasted Flycatcher, *Empidonax* flycatchers. **HABITAT:** Lowland woods, mesquite, stream thickets, lower canyons. Builds a globular nest with entrance on side.

FLYCATCHERS

OLIVE-SIDED
FLYCATCHER

GREATER PEWEE

WESTERN WOOD-PEWEE

EASTERN WOOD-PEWEE

NORTHERN
BEARDLESS-TYRANNULET

EMPIDONAX FLYCATCHERS

Several small, drab flycatchers share the characters of light eye-ring and two pale wing bars. When breeding, some of these birds may be separated by habitat and manner of nesting. Voice is *always* the best means of identification. Silent individuals are very tough to identify, so many may have to be let go simply as "empids." Distinguishing characters to emphasize are subtle and include size and shape of bill and color of lower mandible; shape and boldness of eye-ring; pattern of underparts; primary (wingtip) projection; tail length; direction of tail wag; habitat; and calls.

ACADIAN FLYCATCHER *Empidonax virescens*   Fairly common M388
5¾ in. (15 cm). A *greenish Empidonax* with *pale* underparts, thin eye-ring, thin, *long* bill with pale lower mandible. **VOICE:** "Song" a sharp explosive *pit-see!* or *wee-see!* (sharp upward inflection); also a sharp *peet.* **SIMILAR SPECIES:** Other eastern empids. **HABITAT:** Shady deciduous forests, ravines, swampy woods, beech and hemlock groves.

YELLOW-BELLIED FLYCATCHER *Empidonax flaviventris* Uncommon M387
5½ in. (14 cm). Yellowish underparts (including *throat*) separate this from all other empids except Cordilleran and Pacific-slope flycatchers. (*Caution:* All other empids may show yellow belly but *not throat.*) **VOICE:** Song a simple, spiritless *chi-lek;* also a rising *chu-wee,* whistled *chew.* **SIMILAR SPECIES:** Among other Eastern empids, only Acadian is so green above but Acadian has *white* throat and *paler,* less olive washed underparts. Cordilleran and Pacific-slope flycatchers slightly browner, with peaked head; *teardrop-shaped eye-ring,* often broken above eye; duller wings. **HABITAT:** In summer, boreal forests, muskeg, bogs.

LEAST FLYCATCHER *Empidonax minimus*   Fairly common M391
5¼ in. (13 cm). A small empid, *grayish* above and *pale* below with *bold white eye-ring,* short wingtip projection, and short, wide-based bill. Whitish wing bars on mostly blackish wing. Actively flicks tail. **VOICE:** Emphatic, sharply snapped *che-bek!* Call a sharp, dry *whit.* **SIMILAR SPECIES:** Alder Flycatcher is browner above with bigger bill, longer wingtips, and weaker eye-ring. Hammond's and Dusky flycatchers have darker throat and underparts, duller wings. Hammond's also has *thinner, darker bill,* more teardrop-shaped eye-ring, and longer wingtips. **HABITAT:** Deciduous and mixed woodlands, poplars, aspens.

WILLOW FLYCATCHER *Empidonax traillii*   Fairly common M390
5¾ in. (15 cm). Alder and Willow flycatchers (formerly lumped as one species) are almost identical in appearance, a bit larger, longer billed, and browner than Least Flycatcher. They may be separated from each other mainly by voice and breeding habitat. Willow averages paler and browner (less olive) than Alder and shows little or no eye-ring (weak to moderately bold in Alder). **VOICE:** Song a sneezy *fitz-bew,* unlike *fee-BE-o* of Alder. Call a soft *whit.* **HABITAT:** Bushes, willow thickets, etc.; often in drier situations (brushy fields, upland copses, etc.) than Alder, but found side by side in some areas.

ALDER FLYCATCHER *Empidonax alnorum*   Fairly common M389
5¾ in. (15 cm). The northern counterpart of Willow Flycatcher, with which it was formerly lumped as Traill's Flycatcher. Safely separated only by voice. (See Willow Flycatcher.) **VOICE:** Song an accented *fee-BE-o* or *rree-BE-o.* Call *kep* or *pit.* **HABITAT:** Willows, alders, brushy swamps, swales. Usually in moister areas than Willow.

EMPIDONAX FLYCATCHERS

Empidonax flycatchers are best identified by voice. Breeding habitat is also a helpful clue.

it-see!

chi-lek

[de]ciduous woods, esp. [be]ech trees; wooded [sw]amps; s. and cen. U.S.

coniferous woods, bogs; Canada, n. edge of U.S.

ACADIAN [F]LYCATCHER

[gre]ener than Least, [Al]der, or Willow

YELLOW-BELLIED FLYCATCHER

throat and breast washed with yellow

LEAST FLYCATCHER

che-BEK or *chebek*

farms, orchards, groves, open woods; n. U.S. and Canada

grayest of the group

fitz-bew

fee-bee'-o

[sun] and dry thickets, brushy [pas]tures, old orchards, [mead]ows; n. and cen. U.S.

WILLOW FLYCATCHER

alder swamps, wet thickets, usually near water; n. U.S., Canada

ALDER FLYCATCHER

BUFF-BREASTED FLYCATCHER *Empidonax fulvifrons* Scarce, local M397
5 in. (13 cm). Easily distinguished from the other empids by its small size and *rich buffy breast*. **VOICE:** Accented *chee-lik*. Call a dry *pit* or *whit*. **SIMILAR SPECIES:** Northern Beardless-Tyrannulet. **HABITAT:** High-elevation canyons, open pine forests.

PACIFIC-SLOPE FLYCATCHER *Empidonax difficilis*   Uncommon M395
5½ in. (14 cm). This species and Cordilleran Flycatcher were formerly considered conspecific, as Western Flycatcher. Silent birds are impossible to tell apart with certainty. Voice and range are best identification clues. Pacific-slope Flycatcher slightly less colorful than Cordilleran. Both species have *yellowish* underparts, *including throat*. Other empids in their ranges may have wash of yellow, especially in fall, but their throats are gray or whitish. Eye-ring of Pacific-slope and Cordilleran is *teardrop-shaped and broken above*. **VOICE:** Song of both species a thin, squeaky *pit-PEET SWEEE;* variable. Call an upslurred *tsueet*. **SIMILAR SPECIES:** Cordilleran and Yellow-bellied flycatchers. **HABITAT:** In summer, riparian, mixed, or coniferous woodlands.

CORDILLERAN FLYCATCHER *Empidonax occidentalis*   Uncommon M396
5½ in. (14 cm). This species and Pacific-slope Flycatcher were split from a single species, Western Flycatcher. Silent birds are impossible to tell apart with certainty. Identify by voice and range. **VOICE:** Song of both species a thin, squeaky *pit-PEET SWEEE;* variable. Call a two-noted *soo-seet*. **SIMILAR SPECIES:** Pacific-slope and Yellow-bellied flycatchers. Other empids have white or gray throats. **HABITAT:** In summer, riparian, mixed, or coniferous woodlands; shaded canyons, often with rock walls.

HAMMOND'S FLYCATCHER *Empidonax hammondii*   Uncommon M392
5½ in. (14 cm). Both Hammond's and Dusky flycatchers breed in coniferous and mixed woods, with Hammond's preferring a more closed canopy. Hammond's has more *teardrop-shaped eye-ring;* slightly *shorter and thinner bill* (almost kingletlike) with mostly *dark lower mandible;* is more prone to flick wings; has slightly shorter tail and longer wings. In late summer and fall it molts *before* migrating and is more olive and yellowish below with grayer throat. **VOICE:** Song typically three-parted and similar to that of Dusky Flycatcher but slightly lower pitched. Abrupt *tse-beek*. Call a sharp, thin *peep* or *peek*. **SIMILAR SPECIES:** Dusky and Least flycatchers. **HABITAT:** Woodlands with coniferous component; in migration through lowlands, other trees, thickets.

DUSKY FLYCATCHER *Empidonax oberholseri*   Uncommon M394
5¾ in. (15 cm). Very similar to Hammond's Flycatcher; see that account for subtle differences. **VOICE:** Three-part song ends in a high *preet*. Call a dry *whit*. **SIMILAR SPECIES:** Least, Hammond's, and Gray flycatchers. **HABITAT:** Breeds in open pine forests, montane chaparral with scattering of trees, brushy meadow and stream edges.

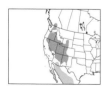

GRAY FLYCATCHER *Empidonax wrightii*   Uncommon M393
6 in. (15 cm). Similar to Dusky and Hammond's flycatchers, but in spring and summer even grayer overall, lower mandible mostly pinkish. In fall and early winter, trace of yellow below, olive above. Has habit of *first wagging its tail downward* like a phoebe, then bringing it back up (all other empids *flick tail upward*). *Direction of tail wag best noted immediately after bird lands*. **VOICE:** Two-syllable *chewip* or *cheh-we*. Call a dry *whit*. **SIMILAR SPECIES:** Other empids. **HABITAT:** Dry pine forests with sagebrush, pinyon-juniper; in winter, willows, mesquite. Often drops to ground to grab prey.

WESTERN *EMPIDONAX* FLYCATCHERS

Empidonax flycatchers are best identified by voice. Breeding habitat is also a helpful clue.

BUFF-BREASTED FLYCATCHER
oak-pine canyons; AZ, NM

PACIFIC-SLOPE FLYCATCHER and CORDILLERAN FLYCATCHER
moist woods, groves, shady canyons

heeLIK *CHEWW* *zvREET*

pit-PEET *swEEE*

PIT-ik

RI-drt *PRRDT*

chVREE

SEE-pik

HAMMOND'S FLYCATCHER
closed-canopy coniferous forests

chwEEP *CHI-wik*

DUSKY FLYCATCHER
montane chaparral, open coniferous woodlands

GRAY FLYCATCHER
sagebrush, pinyon-juniper

MISCELLANEOUS FLYCATCHERS

BLACK PHOEBE *Sayornis nigricans* Fairly common M398
6¾–7 in. (17–18 cm). Our only *black-breasted* flycatcher; belly white. Has typical phoebe tail-bobbing habit. *Immature:* Wing bars cinnamon-buff. **VOICE:** Thin, strident *fi-bee, fi-bee,* rising then dropping; also a sharp slurred *chip.* **SIMILAR SPECIES:** Eastern Phoebe, juncos (which are ground-loving birds). **HABITAT:** Streams, walled canyons, farmyards, towns, parks; usually near water.

EASTERN PHOEBE *Sayornis phoebe* Fairly common M399
7 in. (18 cm). Note *downward tail-bobbing.* A grayish, sparrow-sized fly-catcher *without eye-ring or strong wing bars* (thin buff wing bars on im-mature); small, *all-dark bill* and dark head; yellowish belly in fall. **VOICE:** Song a well-enunciated *phoe-be* or *fi-bree* (second note alternately higher or lower). Call a sharp *chip.* **SIMILAR SPECIES:** Eastern Wood-Pewee and smaller *Empidonax* flycatchers have conspicuous wing bars; bills partly yellowish or horn colored on lower mandible. All *Empidonax* except Gray Flycatcher flick tail *upward.* **HABITAT:** Streamsides, bridges, farms, road-sides, towns.

SAY'S PHOEBE *Sayornis saya* Fairly common M400
7½ in. (19 cm). A midsized, brownish flycatcher with contrasty black tail and pale *orange-buff belly.* **VOICE:** Plaintive, down-slurred *pweer* or *pee-ee.* **SIMILAR SPECIES:** Ash-throated and Dusky-capped flycatchers, Eastern Phoebe. **HABITAT:** Open country, scrub, canyons, ranches, parks.

VERMILION FLYCATCHER *Pyrocephalus rubinus* Uncommon M401
6 in. (15 cm). *Adult male:* Crown (often raised in slight bushy crest) and underparts *flaming vermilion;* upperparts brown and tail blackish. *Imma-ture male:* Breast whitish, with some streaks; crown, belly, and undertail coverts washed with vermilion. *Female:* Breast whitish, narrowly streaked; belly washed with pinkish or yellowish. **VOICE:** *P-p-pit-zee* or *pit-a-zee.* **SIMILAR SPECIES:** Female told from Say's Phoebe by shorter tail, pale su-percilium, and dusky streaks on breast. See also male Scarlet Tanager (which has scarlet back and black wings). **HABITAT:** Moist areas in arid country, such as streams, ponds, pastures, golf courses, ranches.

GREAT KISKADEE *Pitangus sulphuratus* Fairly common, local M406
9¾ in. (25 cm). A large, *big-headed* flycatcher, like Belted Kingfisher in ac-tions, even catching small fish. Note *striking head pattern,* rufous wings and tail, *yellow underparts and crown.* **VOICE:** Loud *kiss-ka-dee;* also a loud *reea.* Often heard before it is seen. **SIMILAR SPECIES:** Tropical and Couch's kingbirds, which share this kiskadee's limited range. **HABITAT:** Woodlands and brushy edges, usually near water.

SULPHUR-BELLIED FLYCATCHER Uncommon, local M407
Myiodynastes luteiventris
8½ in. (22 cm). A large flycatcher with *bright rufous tail* and dark patch through eye; underparts *pale yellowish, with black streaks.* No other U.S. flycatcher is streaked *above and below.* **VOICE:** High, penetrating *kee-ZEE ick! kee-ZEE ick!* (like squeezing a bathroom rubber duckie). **HABITAT:** Midelevation canyons, often with sycamores.

FLYCATCHERS

BLACK PHOEBE

EASTERN PHOEBE

SAY'S PHOEBE

immature ♂

adult ♂

adult ♀

immature ♀

VERMILION FLYCATCHER

GREAT KISKADEE

SULPHUR-BELLIED FLYCATCHER

BROWN-CRESTED FLYCATCHER *Myiarchus tyrannulus* Uncommon M405
8¾ in. (22 cm). Similar to Ash-throated Flycatcher, but larger, with noticeably larger bill. Underparts brighter yellow. Tail rusty, a bit less so than in Ash-throated. Voice important. **VOICE:** Sharp *whit* and rolling, throaty *purreeer*. Voice much more vigorous and raucous than Ash-throated's. **SIMILAR SPECIES:** Great Crested Flycatcher. **HABITAT:** In Southwest, sycamore-dominated canyons, cottonwood groves, saguaros. In TX, woodlands and well-vegetated residential areas.

GREAT CRESTED FLYCATCHER *Myiarchus crinitus*   Fairly common M404
8½–8¾ in. (21–22 cm). A kingbird-sized flycatcher with cinnamon wings and tail, dark olive back, *mouse gray breast,* and bright yellow belly. Often erects bushy crest. Note *strongly contrasting tertial pattern* and pink-based bill. **VOICE:** Loud whistled *wheeep!* Also a rolling *prrrrreet!* **SIMILAR SPECIES:** Brown-crested Flycatcher equal in size but has all-dark bill, paler gray breast, paler yellow belly, less contrasting tertials. Ash-throated Flycatcher has grayer back, much paler below. Vocal differences important. **HABITAT:** Woodlands, groves.

DUSKY-CAPPED FLYCATCHER   Uncommon, local M402
Myiarchus tuberculifer
7 in. (18 cm). Similar to Ash-throated Flycatcher, but slightly smaller overall with proportionately larger bill; cap and throat darker, belly brighter yellow, and *almost no rusty* in tail. Voice distinctive. **VOICE:** Mournful, down-slurred whistle, *pweeeur.* **HABITAT:** Pine-oak and deciduous canyons.

LA SAGRA'S FLYCATCHER *Myiarchus sagrae*   Vagrant
7¼–7½ in. (19 cm). Very rare visitor to FL from W. Indies. Similar to Ash-throated Flycatcher, but has only a *hint of yellow on belly. Tail brownish, not rufous.* Short primaries. Often "droopy" posture. **VOICE:** High, rapid double *wick-wick.* **SIMILAR SPECIES:** Great Crested and Ash-throated flycatchers. **HABITAT:** Shrubby coastal woods.

ASH-THROATED FLYCATCHER   Fairly common M403
Myiarchus cinerascens
8–8¼ in. (20–21 cm). A medium-sized flycatcher, smaller than a kingbird, with two wing bars, *whitish* throat, *pale* gray breast, *pale yellowish belly,* and *rufous* tail. Head slightly bushy. Except for prairie and southwest border areas, this is normally the only flycatcher in West with rusty tail. **VOICE:** *Prrt;* also a rolling *chi-queer* or *prit-wheer.* **SIMILAR SPECIES:** Great Crested, Brown-crested, and Dusky-capped flycatchers; Say's Phoebe. **HABITAT:** Semiarid country, deserts, brush, mesquite, pinyon-juniper, chaparral, open woods.

MYIARCHUS FLYCATCHERS
Most have extensively rusty tails

OWN-CRESTED
FLYCATCHER

GREAT
CRESTED
FLYCATCHER

DUSKY-CAPPED
FLYCATCHER

ASH-THROATED
FLYCATCHER

LA SAGRA'S
FLYCATCHER

KINGBIRDS

WESTERN KINGBIRD *Tyrannus verticalis*   Common M412
8¾ in. (22 cm). The most widespread kingbird in West. Note *pale gray head and breast,* white throat, *yellowish belly.* Western's *black tail* has *narrow white edges.* **VOICE:** Shrill, bickering calls; a sharp *kip* or *whit-ker-whit;* dawn song *pit-PEE-tu-whee.* **SIMILAR SPECIES:** Eastern, Cassin's, Couch's, and Tropical kingbirds. **HABITAT:** Farms, shelterbelts, semiopen country, roadsides, fences, wires.

EASTERN KINGBIRD *Tyrannus tyrannus*   Common M413
8½ in. (22 cm). The *white band* across tail tip marks Eastern Kingbird. Red crown mark is concealed and rarely seen. Often seems to fly quiveringly on tips of wings. Harasses crows, hawks. **VOICE:** Rapid sputter of high, bickering electric-shock notes: *dzee-dzee-dzee,* etc., and *kit-kit-kitter-kitter,* etc. Also a nasal *dzeep.* **SIMILAR SPECIES:** Gray Kingbird. **HABITAT:** Wood edges, river groves, farms, shelterbelts, roadsides, fences, wires.

CASSIN'S KINGBIRD   Uncommon to fairly common M410
Tyrannus vociferans
9 in. (23 cm). Like Western Kingbird, but *darker head and chest contrast with whitish chin and upper throat,* darker olive-gray back; *no distinct white sides* on dark brown (not truly black) tail, which may be *lightly tipped with gray-buff.* Wing coverts often edged in pale gray. **VOICE:** Low, nasal *queer, chi-queer,* or *chi-beer;* also an excited *ki-ki-ki-dear, ki-dear, ki-dear.* **SIMILAR SPECIES:** Some worn Western Kingbirds may lack white sides on tail, but head, breast, and back *paler, lack contrasty pale chin* and pale edges to wing coverts, and have *different call.* In much of interior, Cassin's prefers higher elevations. **HABITAT:** Semiopen country, pine-oak mountains, pinyon-juniper, ranch groves, eucalyptus.

THICK-BILLED KINGBIRD *Tyrannus crassirostris*   Scarce, local M411
9½ in. (24 cm). A large kingbird with *oversized bill;* differs from similar kingbirds in having extensive *dark cap.* Entirely dark tail. *Adult:* Upperparts *brownish,* underparts *whitish* with pale yellow wash on belly. *Fall adult and immature:* May be quite yellow below. **VOICE:** Quick, shrill *brrr-zee* or *kut'r-eet.* **SIMILAR SPECIES:** Bright, fresh fall birds told from Tropical Kingbird by bill size, dark head. **HABITAT:** Riparian woodlands, particularly sycamores.

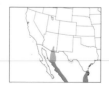

TROPICAL KINGBIRD *Tyrannus melancholicus*   Uncommon, local M408
9¼ in. (23 cm). Nearly identical to Couch's Kingbird. Both species similar to Western and Cassin's kingbirds, but *bill larger and longer,* tail *notched* and *brownish;* bright yellow on underparts *includes breast.* **VOICE:** Insect-like twittering. **SIMILAR SPECIES:** See Couch's Kingbird. **HABITAT:** Groves along streams and ponds, open areas with scattered trees and short cut grass (golf courses, ball fields, etc.).

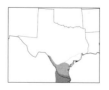

COUCH'S KINGBIRD *Tyrannus couchii*   Fairly common, local M409
9¼ in. (23 cm). Very similar to Tropical Kingbird and best distinguished by voice. Couch's has slightly shorter, thicker bill and brighter green back. **VOICE:** Nasal *queer* or *beeer* (suggests Common Pauraque). Also a sharp *kip.* **SIMILAR SPECIES:** Tropical Kingbird. **HABITAT:** Open wooded and brushy areas with large trees; most common in native habitat.

KINGBIRDS

WESTERN
KINGBIRD

EASTERN
KINGBIRD

CASSIN'S
KINGBIRD

THICK-
BILLED
KINGBIRD

fall

TROPICAL
KINGBIRD

COUCH'S
KINGBIRD

Tropical

MORE TYRANT FLYCATCHERS AND BECARD

FORK-TAILED FLYCATCHER *Tyrannus savana*   Vagrant
14½–16 in. (37–41 cm). Vagrant from Tropics. Told from Scissor-tailed Flytcatcher by *black cap,* white flanks and underwing. Black tail not rigid in flight. *Immature:* Much shorter tail; might be confused with Eastern Kingbird. **VOICE:** Mechanical-sounding *tik-tik-tik.* **SIMILAR SPECIES:** Scissor-tailed Flycatcher. **RANGE:** Normal range from Mex. to S. America. Vagrant to U.S. and Canada; records widespread but predominantly in the East and in fall. **HABITAT:** Open fields, pastures with scattered trees, wires.

SCISSOR-TAILED FLYCATCHER *Tyrannus forficatus*   Common M415
13–15 in. (33–38 cm). A beautiful bird, pale pearly gray, with *extremely long, scissorlike tail* that is usually folded. Flanks orange-buff, wing linings salmon pink. *Immature:* Shorter tail and duller sides may suggest Western Kingbird. Hybrids are known. **VOICE:** Harsh *keck* or *kew;* a repeated *ka-leep;* also shrill, kingbirdlike bickerings and stutterings. **SIMILAR SPECIES:** Western Kingbird, Fork-tailed Flycatcher. **HABITAT:** Semiopen country, ranches, farms, roadsides, fences, wires.

GRAY KINGBIRD *Tyrannus dominicensis*   Fairly common, local M414
9 in. (23 cm). Resembles Eastern Kingbird, but larger and much paler. Conspicuously *notched tail* has no white band. *Very large bill* gives large-headed look. Dark ear patch. **VOICE:** Rolling *pi-teer-rrry* or *pe-cheer-ry.* **SIMILAR SPECIES:** Eastern Kingbird. **HABITAT:** Roadsides, wires, mangroves, edges.

ROSE-THROATED BECARD *Pachyramphus aglaiae*   Rare, local M416
7¼ in. (18 cm). Big-headed and thick-billed. *Male:* Dark gray above, pale to dusky below, with *blackish cap and cheeks* and lovely *rose-colored throat* (lacking in some males). *Female:* Brown above, with *dark cap* and *light buffy collar* around nape. Underparts strong buff. **VOICE:** Thin, slurred whistle, *seeoo.* **SIMILAR SPECIES:** Kingbirds, Say's Phoebe. **HABITAT:** Riparian woodlands, particularly sycamores.

FLYCATCHERS

FORK-TAILED
FLYCATCHER

SCISSOR-TAILED
FLYCATCHER

♂

adult

immature

ROSE-THROATED
BECARD

♀

♂

GRAY
KINGBIRD

SHRIKES Family Laniidae

Songbirds with hook-tipped bill. Shrikes perch watchfully on bush tops, treetops, wires; often impale prey on thorns, barbed wire. **FOOD:** Insects, lizards, small rodents, small birds. **RANGE:** Widespread in Old World; two species breed in N. America.

NORTHERN SHRIKE *Lanius excubitor*   Scarce M418
10–10¼ in. (25–26 cm). This denizen of North is an irregular winter visitor south of Canadian border. Similar to Loggerhead Shrike, but paler; note *narrower dark mask with more white around eye, faintly barred* breast, and longer, more hooked bill with *pale base. Juvenile:* Plumage held throughout first winter; *brown,* with weak mask and extensive *fine barring* below. **VOICE:** Song a disjointed, thrasherlike succession of harsh notes and musical notes. Call *shek-shek;* a grating *jaaeg.* **SIMILAR SPECIES:** Loggerhead Shrike, Northern Mockingbird. **HABITAT:** Semiopen country with lookout posts; in summer, taiga, muskeg, tundra.

LOGGERHEAD SHRIKE *Lanius ludovicianus*   Uncommon to rare M417
9 in. (23 cm). Big head, slim tail; gray, black, and white, with *black mask, short hooked bill.* Sits quietly on wires or bush tops; flies low with flickering flight showing white patches in wings, then swoops up to perch. *Juvenile:* Shows faint barring below *briefly in late summer.* **VOICE:** Song consists of harsh, deliberate notes and phrases, repeated 3 to 20 times, suggesting mockingbird's song; *queedle, queedle,* over and over, or *tsurp-see, tsurp-see.* Call *shack shack* or *jeeer jeeer.* **SIMILAR SPECIES:** Northern Shrike. Northern Mockingbird lacks dark mask and hooked bill. **HABITAT:** Semiopen country with lookout posts: wires, fences, trees, shrubs.

VIREOS Family Vireonidae

Small olive- or gray-backed birds, much like wood-warblers, usually less active. Bill slightly thicker, with more curved ridge and small hook to tip. May be divided into those with wing bars (and "spectacles") and those without (these have eye stripes). **FOOD:** Mostly insects, also fruit in winter. **RANGE:** Canada to Argentina.

BELL'S VIREO *Vireo bellii*   Uncommon M420
4¾ in. (12 cm). Small, nondescript. Usually stays concealed in dense cover. Thin, pale, broken eye-ring and loral stripe. One or two weak wing bars. Southwestern birds are grayer, flick tail like gnatcatchers; eastern birds are green on back, yellow on flanks, pump tail like Palm Warbler. **VOICE:** Sings as if through clenched teeth; husky phrases at short intervals: *cheedle cheedle chee? cheedle cheedle chew!* **SIMILAR SPECIES:** Warbling Vireo has plain wings, bold eyebrow. Immature White-eyed Vireo has bolder wing bars, yellow lores. Gray Vireo slightly larger with complete eye-ring; note voice and habitat. **HABITAT:** Willows, streamsides, hedgerows, mesquite.

BLACK-CAPPED VIREO *Vireo atricapilla*   Scarce, local, endangered M421
4½ in. (11 cm). Small and sprightly; cap *glossy black* in male, slate gray in female. Note wing bars, white spectacles, *red* eyes. **VOICE:** Song hurried, harsh; phrases remarkable for restless, almost angry quality. Call a harsh *chit-ah.* **SIMILAR SPECIES:** Blue-headed and Cassin's vireos larger with dark eyes. **HABITAT:** Oak scrub, brushy hills, rocky canyons. Often hard to see.

WHITE-EYED VIREO *Vireo griseus*   Fairly common M419
5 in. (13 cm). Distinctive combination of *yellow spectacles, whitish throat.* Also note wing bars, yellowish sides, white eye (dark in immature). Somewhat skulking. **VOICE:** Song a sharply enunciated *CHICK-a-per-weeoo-CHICK.* Variable; usually starts and ends with *chick.* **SIMILAR SPECIES:** Bell's Vireo. **HABITAT:** Wood edges, brush, brambles, dense undergrowth.

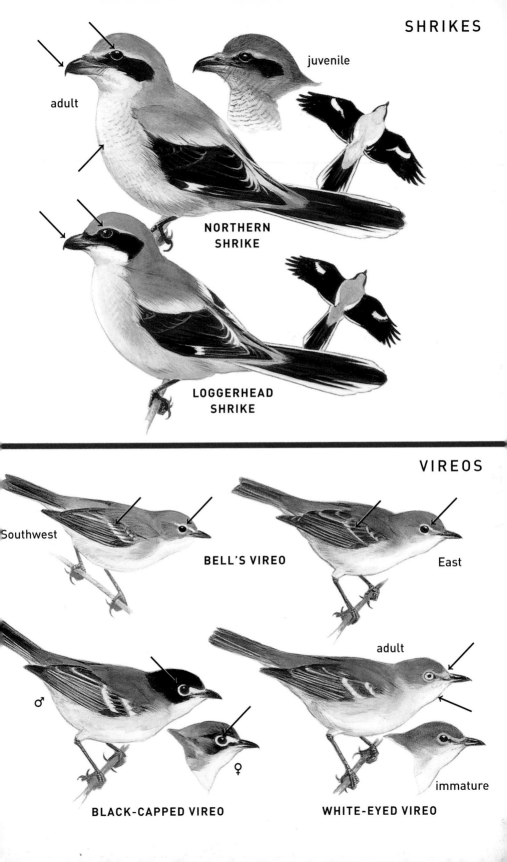

SHRIKES

adult

juvenile

NORTHERN SHRIKE

LOGGERHEAD SHRIKE

VIREOS

Southwest

BELL'S VIREO

East

♂

BLACK-CAPPED VIREO

♀

adult

immature

WHITE-EYED VIREO

BLUE-HEADED VIREO *Vireo solitarius*　　Fairly common M426
5¼ in. (14 cm).The northern/eastern representative of the "Solitary Vireo" complex. Note *sharply demarcated* blue-gray cap, *bright white* spectacles and throat, *bright green* back, yellowish wash to side. **VOICE:** Song of burry phrases with deliberate pauses between; sweet and high pitched: *wee-ay, chweeo, chuweep* (slower than Red-eyed Vireo with fewer notes per phrase). Also gives a whiny chatter. **SIMILAR SPECIES:** Cassin's Vireo. **HABITAT:** Coniferous, mixed, and deciduous woods.

CASSIN'S VIREO *Vireo cassinii*　　Uncommon M425
5¼ in. (14 cm). The Pacific/northwest representative of the "Solitary Vireo" complex. Greener back and more yellowish sides than Plumbeous. Duller overall with less contrasting face pattern than Blue-headed. **VOICE:** Song of slurred phrases with deliberate pauses between, *wee-ay, chweeo, chuweep.* Also gives a whiny chatter. **SIMILAR SPECIES:** Some worn, dull Blue-headeds can be difficult to separate from bright Cassin's, and some dull Cassin's are difficult to separate from Plumbeous. See also Gray and Bell's vireos. **HABITAT:** Coniferous, mixed, and deciduous woods.

PLUMBEOUS VIREO *Vireo plumbeus*　　Uncommon M424
5½ in. (15 cm). The Rocky Mountain/Great Basin representative of the "Solitary Vireo" complex. Although their nesting ranges barely overlap, all three species may occur together on migration. Mostly gray above, whitish below, with grayish or grayish olive wash to sides of breast and variable wash of gray or yellow on flanks. **VOICE:** Song of slurred phrases with deliberate pauses between. Blue-headed Vireo's phrases sweeter. Cassin's and Plumbeous vireos have burrier, slurred phrases, e.g., *wee-ay, chweeo, chuweep.* (Plumbeous is slowest, burriest.) All three species give a whiny chatter. **SIMILAR SPECIES:** Blue-headed and Cassin's vireos. Some dull Cassin's are difficult to separate from Plumbeous. See also Gray Vireo. **HABITAT:** Coniferous, mixed, and deciduous woods.

YELLOW-THROATED VIREO *Vireo flavifrons*　　Fairly common M423
5½ in. (14 cm). Bright yellow throat, yellow spectacles, and white wing bars. Olive back contrasts with gray rump. **VOICE:** Song similar to Blue-headed Vireo's, but lower pitched with *burry quality;* swings back and forth with phrases that sound like *ee-yay, three-eight.* **SIMILAR SPECIES:** Pine Warbler has some dusky streaks below, white tail spots, smaller bill. **HABITAT:** Deciduous woodlands, shade trees, particularly oaks.

GRAY VIREO *Vireo vicinior*　　Scarce M422
5½ in. (14 cm). This plain, gray-backed vireo of arid mountains has *complete, narrow, white eye-ring* and only *one faint wing bar.* Though drab, it has character, flipping tail like a gnatcatcher. **VOICE:** Song similar to Plumbeous Vireo's, but sweeter, more rapid, in regular series. **SIMILAR SPECIES:** Plumbeous Vireo stockier, has shorter tail that is not flipped, bold spectacles rather than just eye-ring, and two, thicker wing bars. See Bell's Vireo. **HABITAT:** Pinyon-juniper woodlands, brushy slopes, chamise-dominated chaparral, scrub oak.

HUTTON'S VIREO *Vireo huttoni*　　Fairly common M427
5 in. (13 cm). A chunky olive-brown vireo with bold wing bars. Note *incomplete eye-ring,* broken *above,* and large light loral spot. **VOICE:** Buzzy, rising *zu-weep* or falling *zee-ur,* oft-repeated; a hoarse, deliberate *day dee dee.* **SIMILAR SPECIES:** Ruby-crowned Kinglet smaller with skinny black legs, quicker movements, black "highlight bar" behind wing bars. **HABITAT:** Woodlands, parks, particularly with oaks.

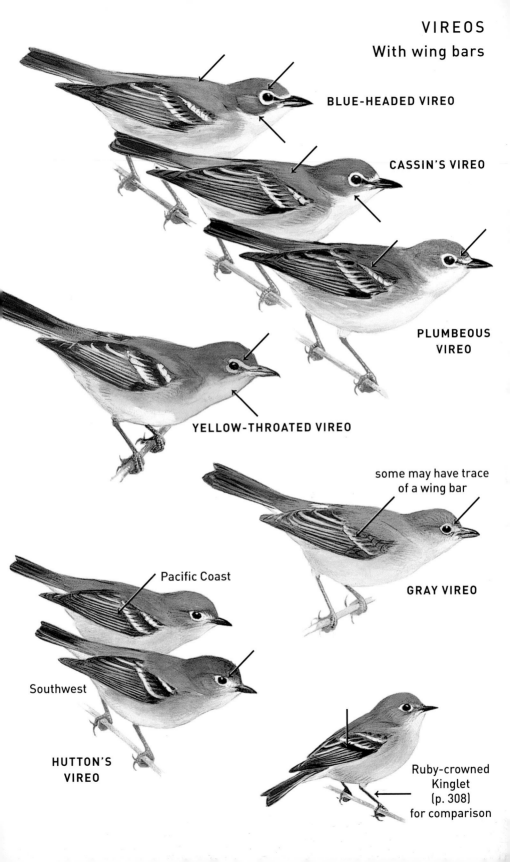

VIREOS
With wing bars

BLUE-HEADED VIREO

CASSIN'S VIREO

PLUMBEOUS VIREO

YELLOW-THROATED VIREO

some may have trace of a wing bar

GRAY VIREO

Pacific Coast

Southwest

HUTTON'S VIREO

Ruby-crowned Kinglet (p. 308) for comparison

YELLOW-GREEN VIREO *Vireo flavoviridis* Very rare, local
6–6¼ in. (15–16 cm). This tropical species is very similar to Red-eyed Vireo, but has *strong yellow tones* on sides, flanks, and undertail coverts; back *yellower* green; head stripes *less distinct;* bill slightly *longer* and paler. (Immature Red-eyed Vireos may have yellow on flanks and undertail coverts.) **VOICE:** Song slower than Red-eyed's, suggestive of House Sparrow. **RANGE:** Rare summer resident in lower Rio Grande Valley, TX. Casual farther north in TX and in s. AZ; casual fall vagrant in coastal CA. **HABITAT:** Deciduous woods.

RED-EYED VIREO *Vireo olivaceus* Common M430
6 in. (15 cm). Note *gray cap* contrasting with olive back, and strong, *black-bordered white eyebrow stripe (supercilium).* Red iris may not be obvious at a distance. Iris is brown in immature birds in fall. **VOICE:** Song is abrupt, robinlike phrases, monotonous. Call a nasal, whining *chway.* **SIMILAR SPECIES:** Warbling Vireo slightly smaller, duller and less contrasty above, with pale lores and arching supercilium. See Yellow-green and Black-whiskered vireos, both scarce and local. **HABITAT:** Deciduous woodlands, shade trees, groves.

BLACK-WHISKERED VIREO *Vireo altiloquus* Uncommon, local M431
6¼ in. (16 cm). Narrow dark whisker on each side of throat. Otherwise similar to Red-eyed Vireo, but duller overall, particularly head pattern, and more brownish olive above, with slightly longer bill. **VOICE:** Song slightly slower than Red-eyed's. **HABITAT:** Mangroves, subtropical hardwoods.

WARBLING VIREO *Vireo gilvus* Fairly common M428
5½ in. (14 cm). One of the widespread vireos that lack wing bars. In this *very plain* species, note *whitish breast, pale lores,* and *lack of black borders* on eyebrow stripe that arches slightly above dark eye. Back tinged dull greenish. Immature and Western birds have more yellow on sides. **VOICE:** Song distinctive: a languid warble, unlike broken phrases of other vireos; suggests Purple Finch's song, but less spirited, with burry undertone. Call a wheezy querulous *twee* and short *vit.* **SIMILAR SPECIES:** Philadelphia Vireo yellowish on throat and breast, as bright in middle as on sides, has slate gray line through lores. Red-eyed Vireo larger, greener above, and has bolder eyebrow stripe. See also Tennessee Warbler. **HABITAT:** Deciduous and mixed woods, aspen groves, cottonwoods, riparian woodlands, shade trees.

PHILADELPHIA VIREO *Vireo philadelphicus* Uncommon M429
5¼ in. (13 cm). This smallish vireo has a face pattern reminiscent of Warbling Vireo, but with more distinct dark eye line (including lores), slightly greener back, and single faint wing bar. Underparts pale and vary from a small wash of pale yellow on lower throat and upper breast in duller adults to more extensive yellow in bright immatures. **VOICE:** Song very similar to Red-eyed Vireo's; higher, slower. Call, a quick, husky *niff-niff-niff-niff.* **SIMILAR SPECIES:** Bright Warbling Vireos in fall tinged green above and have yellow on sides, but that yellow is *dull or lacking in center of breast and throat;* also *lack Philadelphia's dark line through lores.* Different song. Tennessee Warbler slightly smaller, has finer bill, clear white (not yellow) undertail coverts, blackish rather than blue-gray legs. **HABITAT:** Second-growth woodlands, poplars, willows, alders.

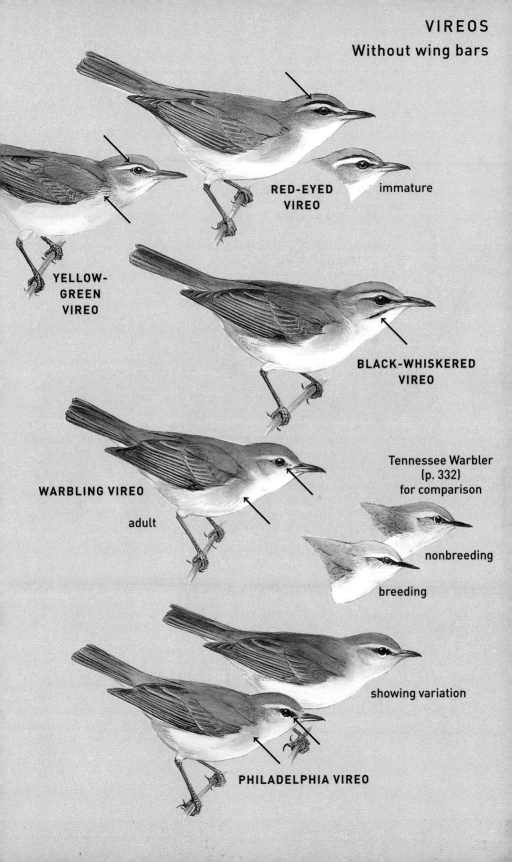

VIREOS
Without wing bars

RED-EYED
VIREO

immature

YELLOW-
GREEN
VIREO

BLACK-WHISKERED
VIREO

WARBLING VIREO

adult

Tennessee Warbler
(p. 332)
for comparison

nonbreeding

breeding

showing variation

PHILADELPHIA VIREO

JAYS, CROWS, AND ALLIES Family Corvidae

Large perching birds with strong, longish bill, nostrils covered by forward-pointing bristles. Crows and ravens are very large and black. Jays are often colorful (usually blue). Magpies are black and white, with long tail. Sexes alike. Most immatures resemble adults. **FOOD:** Almost anything edible. **RANGE:** Worldwide except s. S. America, some islands, Antarctica.

FLORIDA SCRUB-JAY *Aphelocoma coerulescens*   Uncommon, local M437
11–11¼ in. (29 cm). Look for this *crestless* jay in FL in stretches of oak scrub. Note *whitish forehead, pale* gray-brown back, solid blue wings and tail (no white markings). **VOICE:** Rough, rasping *kwesh . . . kwesh.* Also a low, rasping *zhreek* or *zhrink.* **SIMILAR SPECIES:** Blue Jay, often present in same localities in FL, has crest and bold white spotting on wings and tail. **HABITAT:** Mainly scrub, low oaks.

WESTERN SCRUB-JAY *Aphelocoma californica*   Common M439
11–11¼ in. (29 cm). *Crestless* with blue head, wings, and tail, *brownish* back, white throat with *necklace.* **VOICE:** Rough, rasping *kwesh . . . kwesh.* Also a harsh *shreck-shreck-shreck-shreck* and a rasping *zhreek, zhreek.* **SIMILAR SPECIES:** Mexican Jay. **HABITAT:** Oaks, pine-oak, oak-chaparral of foothills and lower mountains, riparian woodlands, pinyon-juniper, residential areas, parks.

ISLAND SCRUB-JAY   Uncommon, local M438
Aphelocoma insularis (not shown)
12½–13 in. (31–33 cm). Recently elevated to full species status. Found only on Santa Cruz I. off coast of s. CA, most restricted range of any species in N. America. **VOICE:** Same as Western Scrub-Jay. **SIMILAR SPECIES:** Almost identical to Pacific Coast Western Scrub-Jay (no range overlap), but slightly larger and larger billed, deeper blue, darker cheek. **HABITAT:** Woodlands and scrubby habitat.

MEXICAN JAY   Fairly common, local M440
Aphelocoma ultramarina
11½ in. (29 cm). A blue crestless jay of Southwest. Resembles Western Scrub-Jay, but *more uniform;* back and breast grayer. *No strong contrast* between throat and breast. Also *lacks narrow whitish line over eye.* In AZ, juveniles may have partly yellow bill. **VOICE:** Rough, querulous *wink? wink?* or *zhenk?* **SIMILAR SPECIES:** Western Scrub-Jay. **HABITAT:** Pine-oak and oak-juniper woodlands.

BLUE JAY *Cyanocitta cristata*   Common M434
11 in. (28 cm). A showy, noisy, *crested jay;* larger than a robin. Bold *white spots on wings and tail;* whitish or dull gray underparts; *black necklace.* **VOICE:** Harsh slurring *jeeah* or *jay;* a musical *queedle, queedle;* also many other notes. Mimics calls of Red-shouldered and Red-tailed hawks. **SIMILAR SPECIES:** Florida Scrub-Jay, Steller's. **HABITAT:** Oak and pine woods, suburban gardens, groves, towns, feeders.

STELLER'S JAY *Cyanocitta stelleri*   Common M433
11½ in. (29 cm). In coniferous woodlands between Rockies and Pacific, this is the resident jay with a crest. Foreparts *blackish;* rear parts (wings, tail, belly) *deep blue.* Some interior birds have white eyebrow. **VOICE:** Loud *shook-shook-shook* or *shack-shack-shack* or *wheck-wek-wek-wek-wek* or *kwesh kwesh kwesh;* harsh *jjaairr* and many other notes. Frequently mimics hawks. **SIMILAR SPECIES:** Other "blue jays" show some white below. **HABITAT:** Coniferous and pine-oak forests; also some residential areas, feeders.

JAYS

FLORIDA
SCRUB-JAY

interior

Pacific
Coast

WESTERN
SCRUB-JAY

AZ juvenile

MEXICAN
JAY

BLUE JAY

STELLER'S
JAY

PINYON JAY *Gymnorhinus cyanocephalus* Uncommon M441
10½ in. (27 cm). Looks *like a small dull blue crow,* but nearer size of a robin, though chunkier, with long, sharp bill. Readily told from other jays by its short tail, uniform pale blue coloration, and crowlike flight. Pinyon Jays are gregarious, often gathering in large noisy flocks and walking about like small crows. **VOICE:** Nuthatchlike *nasal* cawing, *kaa-ah* or *karn-ah* (descending inflection); has mewing effect. Also jaylike notes; chattering. **SIMILAR SPECIES:** Other western jays. **HABITAT:** Primarily pinyon-juniper; also dry, open ponderosa and Jeffrey pine woodlands; ranges into sagebrush.

CLARK'S NUTCRACKER *Nucifraga columbiana* Fairly common M442
12 in. (30–31 cm). Built like a small crow, with *light gray* or tan-gray body and large *white patches* in black wings and tail. If these patches are seen, it should be confused with no other bird of high mountains. Long bill. Tame birds often can be fed by hand. **VOICE:** Flat, drawn-out, grating *caw, khaaa* or *khraa.* **SIMILAR SPECIES:** Gray Jay has shorter bill, lacks white patches. **HABITAT:** Coniferous forests in mountains as high as near tree line; mountain resorts.

GRAY JAY *Perisoreus canadensis* Uncommon M432
11¼–11½ in. (28–29 cm). A large, fluffy, gray bird of cool northern forests; larger than a robin. Called "Whiskey Jack" by woodsmen. *Adult: Black patch* or partial cap across back of head and *white forehead* (or crown); suggests a huge overgrown chickadee. *Juvenile: Dark sooty,* almost blackish; only distinguishing mark is *whitish whisker.* Pacific Coast and far northern birds have dark on heads. Rocky Mt. birds have mostly white heads. **VOICE:** Soft *whee-ah;* also many other notes, some harsh. **SIMILAR SPECIES:** Clark's Nutcracker. **HABITAT:** Spruce and fir forests. Becomes tame around campgrounds, picnic areas.

GREEN JAY *Cyanocorax yncas* Fairly common, local M435
10½ in. (27 cm). Unmistakable. The *only green-colored jay. Black throat, violet crown.* Often seen in noisy flocks. **VOICE:** Four or more harsh notes given rapidly: *cheek, cheek, cheek, cheek.* Also a variety of jaylike croaks and squeaks. **HABITAT:** Dense cover in scrubby woods. Visits feeders for fruit and seeds.

BROWN JAY *Cyanocorax morio* Rare, local M436
16½–17 in. (42–43 cm). A very large jay with *brown upperparts and pale belly.* Adult has dark bill; juvenile has yellow bill. In flight, pale belly stands out. **VOICE:** Very loud *chaa-chaa-chaa* repeated over and over. Flocks can make a loud noise. **HABITAT:** Dense scrub and brushy woods.

JAYS

PINYON
JAY

CLARK'S
NUTCRACKER

adult

North and
Pacific

GRAY
JAY

Rockies

GREEN JAY

Gray Jay

juvenile

BROWN JAY

CHIHUAHUAN RAVEN *Corvus cryptoleucus* Fairly common M448
19–19½ in. (48–50 cm). Slightly larger than American Crow; a small raven of arid plains and deserts. Flies with typical flat-winged glide of a raven; has somewhat wedge-shaped tail. White feather bases on neck and breast sometimes show when feathers are ruffled by the wind, hence former name White-necked Raven. **VOICE:** Hoarse *kraak,* flatter and higher than Common Raven's. **SIMILAR SPECIES:** Difficult to tell from Common Raven, particularly when separate, but slightly smaller and tail slightly less wedge-shaped, calls higher pitched, and bristles extend farther down upper mandible. **HABITAT:** Arid and semiarid scrub and grasslands, deserts, yucca, mesquite, towns, dumps.

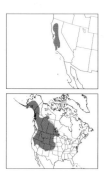

COMMON RAVEN *Corvus corax* Common M449
23½–24 in. (59–61 cm). Note *wedge-shaped tail.* Much larger than American Crow; has heavier voice and is not inclined to be as gregarious, often solitary or in family groups. More hawklike in flight, it alternates flapping and sailing, gliding on flat, somewhat sweptback wings (crow glides much less and with slight upward dihedral). When bird is perched and not too distant, note "goiter" look created by shaggy throat feathers and heavier "Roman-nose" bill. **VOICE:** Croaking *cr-r-ruck* or *prruk;* also a metallic *tok.* **SIMILAR SPECIES:** Chihuahuan Raven. **HABITAT:** Boreal and mountain forests, desert lowlands (particularly in winter), cliffs, tundra, towns, dumps.

YELLOW-BILLED MAGPIE *Pica nuttalli* Fairly common, local M444
16½–17 in. (42–43 cm). Similar to Black-billed Magpie, but *bill yellow.* At close range shows crescent of bare yellow skin below eye. **VOICE:** Similar to Black-billed Magpie's *maag?,* etc. **HABITAT:** Oak savanna, riparian groves, ranches, farms. Usually in small to medium-sized flocks.

BLACK-BILLED MAGPIE *Pica hudsonia* Fairly common M443
18½–19½ in. (47–49 cm); tail 9½–12 in. (24–30 cm). A large, slender, *black-and-white bird,* with *long, graduated tail.* In flight, iridescent greenish black tail streams behind and large *white patches flash in wings.* **VOICE:** Harsh, rapid *queg queg queg queg* or *wah-wah-wah.* Also a querulous, nasal *maag?* or *aag-aag?* **SIMILAR SPECIES:** Yellow-billed Magpie; ranges do not overlap, although escapees may occur. **HABITAT:** Rangeland, brushy country, conifers, streamsides, forest edges, farms. Often in flocks.

MAGPIES AND RAVENS

may show white on nape when feathers are ruffled

CHIHUAHUAN RAVEN

ravens have wedge-shaped tails

COMMON RAVEN

YELLOW-BILLED MAGPIE

American Crow

BLACK-BILLED MAGPIE

FISH CROW *Corvus ossifragus*   Fairly common **M447**
15¼–15½ in. (38–39 cm). Slightly smaller and more delicately propor-
tioned than American Crow. Tail slightly longer and wings slightly more
tapered. *Best identified by voice,* as measurements of the two species
broadly overlap. **VOICE:** Short nasal *car* or *ca.* Most distinctive is *two-
syllable ca-ha.* (American Crow utters *caw.*) Some calls of young American Crows may sound like those of Fish Crows. **SIMILAR SPECIES:** American Crow larger, has different call. **HABITAT:** Often near tidewater, river
valleys, lakes. Also farm fields, wood edges, towns and cities, dumps.

TAMAULIPAS CROW *Corvus imparatus*   Rare, local
14¼–14½ in. (36–37 cm). A small crow with small bill, long tail, and slim
wings. Glossier colored than other crows. **VOICE:** A "stressed" voice (a
harsh, froglike *awwwk*). **SIMILAR SPECIES:** In its range this is the only
small crow—next larger all-black corvid is Chihuahuan Raven. **RANGE:**
Found irregularly near Brownsville, TX. **HABITAT:** Arid scrub, mesquite
thickets; also ranches, dumps.

AMERICAN CROW *Corvus brachyrhynchos*   Common **M445**
17–17½ in. (43–45 cm). A large, chunky, ebony bird. Completely black;
glossed with purplish in strong sunlight. Bill and feet strong and black.
Often gregarious. **VOICE:** Loud *caw, caw, caw* or *cah* or *kahr.* **SIMILAR SPE-
CIES:** Fish Crow is smaller with longer, slimmer tail, more tapered wings;
most readily distinguished by voice. Common Raven larger, has wedge-
shaped tail, more sweptback wings, different call. See also Chihuahuan
Raven, Northwestern Crow. **HABITAT:** Woodlands, farms, fields, river
groves, shores, towns, dumps.

NORTHWESTERN CROW *Corvus caurinus*   Uncommon, local **M446**
16 in. (41 cm). This small beachcombing crow of Northwest is very similar to American Crow but is slightly smaller and has slightly quicker wingbeats. It replaces the latter on the narrow northwestern coastal strip. There
is apparently integration with American Crow in Puget Sound area; hence
some believe they may be conspecific. **VOICE:** *Khaaa* or *khaaw.* Usually
more resonant than American Crow's *caw.* Also, *cowp-cowp-cowp.* **SIMI-
LAR SPECIES:** American Crow. **HABITAT:** Near tidewater, shores, coastal
towns.

CROWS

TAMAULIPAS
CROW

FISH CROW

NORTHWESTERN
CROW

AMERICAN
CROW

Fish Crow

American Crow

Tamaulipas
Crow

SWALLOWS Family Hirundinidae

Slim, streamlined form and graceful flight characterize these sparrow-sized birds. Pointed wings; short bill with very wide gape; tiny feet. **FOOD**: Mostly flying insects. **RANGE**: Worldwide except for polar regions, some islands.

TREE SWALLOW *Tachycineta bicolor*　　　Common M452
5¾ in. (15 cm). *Adult: Male steely blue, tinged green, above; white below.* Female slightly duller than male. *Juvenile:* Dusky gray-brown back and dusky smudge across breast. Tree Swallows have distinctly notched tail; glide in circles, ending glide with quick flaps and a short climb. **VOICE**: Rich *cheet* or *chi-veet;* a liquid twitter, *weet, trit, weet,* etc. **SIMILAR SPECIES**: May be confused with Violet-green Swallow (white or light brown above eye, more obvious white patches on sides of rump), Northern Rough-winged Swallow (dingy throat, different flight style), or Bank Swallow (bolder dark breast-band than juvenile Tree, smaller overall, browner above). All species also have different calls. **HABITAT**: Open country near water, marshes, meadows, streams, lakes, wires. Fall premigratory flocks roost in reeds. Nests in holes in trees, birdhouses.

BANK SWALLOW *Riparia riparia*　　　Fairly common M455
5 in. (12 cm). *Our smallest swallow. Brown-backed with slightly darker wings and paler rump.* Note distinct *dark breast-band.* White of throat *curls up behind ear. Wingbeats rapid and shallow.* **VOICE**: Dry, trilled chitter or rattle, *brrt* or *trr-tri-tri.* **SIMILAR SPECIES**: Northern Rough-winged Swallow and juvenile Tree Swallow. When perched in mixed-species flocks, Bank's smaller size stands out. **HABITAT**: Near water; fields, marshes, lakes. Nests colonially in dirt and sand banks.

NORTHERN ROUGH-WINGED SWALLOW　　　Fairly common M454
Stelgidopteryx serripennis
5¼ in. (12 cm). *Adult: Brown-backed;* does not show contrast above that Bank Swallow does; *throat and upper breast dusky;* no breast-band. Flight more languid; wings pulled back at end of stroke. *Juvenile:* Has cinnamon-rusty wing bars. **VOICE**: Call a low, liquid *trrit,* lower and less grating than Bank Swallow's. **SIMILAR SPECIES**: Bank Swallow and juvenile Tree Swallow. **HABITAT**: Near streams, lakes, rivers. Nests in banks, pipes, and crevices, but not colonially as Bank Swallow does.

VIOLET-GREEN SWALLOW *Tachycineta thalassina*　　Fairly common M453
5¼ in. (13 cm). Note *white patches that almost meet* over base of tail. *Male:* Dark and shiny above; adults glossed with beautiful *green on back and purple on rump and uppertail;* clear white below. *White of face partially encircles eye. Female and immature:* Somewhat duller above, and white above eye tinged grayish or brownish. **VOICE**: A twitter; a thin *ch-lip* or *chew-chit;* rapid *chit-chit-chit wheet, wheet.* **SIMILAR SPECIES**: Separated from Tree Swallow by pale feathering above eye, greener back, white patches on sides of rump, slightly smaller size, and shorter wings. See also White-throated Swift. **HABITAT**: Widespread when foraging. Nests in holes in cliffs and in trees in open forests, foothill woods, mountains, canyons, towns.

SWALLOWS

nests in tree holes or nest boxes

adult

TREE SWALLOW

juvenile

Bank Swallow colony

BANK SWALLOW

NORTHERN ROUGH-WINGED SWALLOW

VIOLET-GREEN SWALLOW

adult

Violet-green

Northern Rough-winged

Tree

Cliff (p. 294)

Barn (p. 294)

Purple Martin (p. 294)

Bank

Swallows on a wire

PURPLE MARTIN Fairly common in East, uncommon and local in West M451
Progne subis
8 in. (20 cm). The largest N. American swallow. *Male:* Uniformly blue-black *above and below;* no other swallow is dark-bellied. *Female and juvenile:* Light-bellied; throat and breast grayish, often with faint gray collar. Glides in circles, alternating quick flaps and glides; often spreads tail. **VOICE:** Throaty and rich *tchew-wew,* etc., or *pew, pew.* Song gurgling, ending in a succession of rich, low guttural notes. **SIMILAR SPECIES:** Tree and Violet-green swallows, much smaller than female Purple Martin, are cleaner white below. In flight, male martin might be confused with European Starling. **HABITAT:** Towns, farms, open or semiopen country, often near water. In East, nests exclusively in human-supplied martin houses. In West, uses cavities in trees (e.g., sycamores, ponderosa pines), posts, and, in s. AZ, saguaros; rarely martin houses.

CAVE SWALLOW *Petrochelidon fulva* Uncommon M457
5½ in. (14 cm). Similar to Cliff Swallow (rusty rump, square-cut tail), but face colors reversed: *throat and cheeks buffy* (not dark), forehead *dark chestnut* (not pale, although Cliff Swallows in Southwest have chestnut forehead). *Buff color sets off dark mask and cap.* **VOICE:** Clear, sweet *weet* or *cheweet;* a loud, accented *chu, chu.* **SIMILAR SPECIES:** Cliff Swallow; Cave has buffier throat and face, more deeply colored rump, different call. **HABITAT:** Open country. Cuplike nest placed in caves, culverts, and under bridges; nests colonially.

CLIFF SWALLOW Common in West, uncommon in East M456
Petrochelidon pyrrhonota
5½ in. (14 cm). Note *rusty* or *buffy rump.* Overhead, appears square-tailed, with dark throat patch. Glides in a long ellipse, ending each glide with a roller coaster–like climb. **VOICE:** *Zayrp;* a low *chur.* Alarm call *keer!* Song consists of creaking notes and guttural gratings; harsher than Barn and Cave swallows' songs. **SIMILAR SPECIES:** Barn and Cave swallows. **HABITAT:** Open to semiopen land, farms, cliffs, lakes. Nests colonially on cliffs, barn sides, under eaves and bridges; rarely on trees. Builds mud jug, or gourdlike, nest. Barn and Cave swallows build cuplike open nest; and Barn Swallows often but not always nest *inside* the barn.

BARN SWALLOW *Hirundo rustica* Common M458
6¾ in. (17 cm). Our only swallow that is truly *swallow-tailed;* also the only one with *white tail spots. Adult:* Blue-black above; cinnamon-buff below, with darker throat. *Immature:* More whitish below. Flight direct, close to ground; wingtips pulled back at end of stroke; not much gliding. **VOICE:** Soft *vit* or *kvik-kvik, vit-vit.* Also *szee-szah* or *szee.* Anxiety call a harsh, irritated *ee-tee* or *keet.* Song a long, musical twitter interspersed with guttural notes. **SIMILAR SPECIES:** Most other N. American swallows have notched (not deeply forked) tail. Cliff Swallow is colonial, building mud jugs under eaves or cliffs. See Cave Swallow. **HABITAT:** Open or semiopen land; farms, fields, marshes, lakes; often perches on wires; usually near habitation. Builds *cuplike nest inside* barns or under eaves, not in tight colonies like Cliff Swallow.

SWALLOWS

martin house

PURPLE MARTIN

♂

♀

CAVE SWALLOW

CLIFF SWALLOW

Southwest

juglike nests under eaves or on cliffs; colonial

nests on beams inside barns

juvenile

BARN SWALLOW

LARKS Family Alaudidae

Brown terrestrial birds with long hind claws. Gregarious in nonbreeding season, when they may be joined by longspurs and Snow Buntings. Larks often sing in high display flights. **FOOD:** Seeds, insects. **RANGE:** Mainly Old World.

HORNED LARK *Eremophila alpestris*   Uncommon to common M450
7–7¼ in. (18–19 cm). *Male:* Note head pattern. A brown ground bird, larger than a sparrow, with *black mustache,* two small *black "horns"* (not always noticeable), and black breast splotch. *Walks,* does not hop. Overhead, pale with *black* tail; folds wings after each beat. Varies from paler to darker races. *Female and immature:* Duller. *Juvenile:* Very different, *streaked below.* **VOICE:** Song tinkling, irregular, high-pitched, often prolonged; from ground or in air. Call a clear *tsee-titi.* **SIMILAR SPECIES:** Juvenile sometimes misidentified as Sprague's Pipit. **HABITAT:** Prairies, shortgrass and dirt fields, golf courses, airports, shores, tundra.

SKY LARK (EURASIAN SKYLARK) *Alauda arvensis*   Scarce, local
7¼ in. (19 cm). Slightly larger than a sparrow; brown, strongly streaked; underparts buff white; breast streaked. *Trailing edge of broad-based wing and sides of tail white.* Short *crest.* **VOICE:** Call a clear, liquid *chir-r-up.* Song, in hovering flight, high-pitched, with long-sustained runs and trills. **SIMILAR SPECIES:** Juvenile Horned Lark, pipits. **RANGE:** Introduced birds from Europe are resident on s. Vancouver I., BC. Vagrants from Asia reach w. AK islands. **HABITAT:** Open country, fields, airports.

BUSHTITS Family Aegithalidae

Very small, drab-gray birds with long tail. Nearly always found in flocks except during breeding season, often mixing with small birds of other species. Only representative in N. America of this Old World family. **FOOD:** Insects. **RANGE:** From sw. BC to s. Guatemala.

BUSHTIT *Psaltriparus minimus*   Common M472
4½ in. (11 cm). A very small, plain bird that, except briefly during nesting season, moves from bush to tree in *straggling flocks,* conversing in light gentle notes. Other species, such as warblers, may join these flocks. Nondescript; gray back, pale underparts, brownish crown and cheeks, stubby bill, longish tail. Females have yellow eyes. Birds in Rockies and Great Basin have gray crown. Males of form known as "Black-eared" Bushtit in s. NM (San Luis Mts.) and w. TX (Davis and Chisos mts.) have black or black-flecked cheeks. **VOICE:** Insistent light *tsits,* *pits,* and *clenks.* **SIMILAR SPECIES:** Verdin, Wrentit. **HABITAT:** Oak scrub, chaparral, mixed woods, pinyon-juniper, parks, residential areas.

VERDIN Family Remizidae

Small, very active, pale gray desert birds with short, rounded tail and tiny pointed bill. Most often heard before they are seen. Found singly or in pairs, not flocks. Build large spherical nest for roosting. **FOOD:** Insects, fruit, berries. **RANGE:** Desert regions of sw. N. America.

VERDIN *Auriparus flaviceps*   Fairly common M471
4½ in. (11 cm). Tiny. *Adult:* Gray, with *yellowish head, rufous bend of wing* (often hidden). *Juvenile:* Just plain gray. **VOICE:** Insistent *see-lip.* Rapid chipping. Song a three-note whistle, *tsee see-see.* **SIMILAR SPECIES:** Bushtit longer tailed than immature Verdin; does not usually live in desert lowlands. See also Lucy's Warbler, Northern Beardless-Tyrannulet. **HABITAT:** Brushy desert and semiarid lowlands, mesquite.

LARKS

towering
flight

overhead

prairie

juvenile

SKY LARK

adult

northern

adult

**HORNED
LARK**

BUSHTIT AND VERDIN

Pacific
Coast

adult

VERDIN

terior

emales have
ellow eyes

BUSHTIT

juvenile ♂
"Black-eared"

juvenile

CHICKADEES AND TITMICE Family Paridae

Small, plump, small-billed birds. Acrobatic when feeding. Sexes usually alike. Often found in mixed-species flocks during nonbreeding season with other parids, kinglets, warblers, etc. **FOOD:** Insects, seeds, acorn mast, berries; at feeders, suet, sunflower seeds. **RANGE:** Widespread in N. America, Eurasia, Africa.

CAROLINA CHICKADEE *Poecile carolinensis*   Common M459
4¾ in. (12 cm). Very similar to Black-capped Chickadee and best distinguished by range and voice. **VOICE:** "Chickadee" call of this species is higher pitched and more rapid than that of Black-capped. Whistled song is a four-syllable *fee-bee, fee-bay.* **SIMILAR SPECIES:** Black-capped Chickadee is slightly larger with cleaner white rear edge of cheek patch and more prominent white edging in wings (particularly the wing coverts). Hybrids are known. In some winters, Black-cappeds penetrate southward into range of Carolina. **HABITAT:** Mixed and deciduous woods; willow thickets, shade trees, residential areas, feeders.

BLACK-CAPPED CHICKADEE *Poecile atricapillus*   Common M460
5–5¼ in. (12–13 cm). This small, tame acrobat can be separated from other widespread chickadees except Carolina by its *solid black cap* in conjunction with *gray back* and buffy sides. **VOICE:** Clearly enunciated *chick-a-dee-dee-dee.* Song a clear whistle, *fee-bee-ee* or *fee-bee,* first note higher. **SIMILAR SPECIES:** Carolina Chickadee. **HABITAT:** Mixed and deciduous woods; willow thickets, shade trees, residential areas, feeders.

CHESTNUT-BACKED CHICKADEE *Poecile rufescens*   Fairly common M463
4¾ in. (12 cm). The cap, bib, and white cheeks indicate a chickadee; the *chestnut back and rump,* this species. Sides *chestnut* (or *gray* in race found along coast of cen. CA). **VOICE:** Hoarser and more rapid than Black-capped Chickadee, e.g., *sick-a-see-see.* No whistled song. **HABITAT:** Moist coniferous forests, oaks, willows, shade trees, parks.

MOUNTAIN CHICKADEE *Poecile gambeli*   Fairly common M461
5¼ in. (13 cm). Similar to Black-capped Chickadee, but black of cap interrupted by *white line over eye.* **VOICE:** Song a clear whistled *fee-bee-bee* or *fee-ee-bee-bee,* first note(s) usually higher; also *tsick-a-zee-zee-zee,* huskier than Black-capped's, and a rolling *deedleedleoo.* **HABITAT:** Mountain forests, conifers; irregularly moves to lower elevations in winter.

GRAY-HEADED CHICKADEE (SIBERIAN TIT)   Rare, local M465
Poecile cincta
5½ in. (14 cm). This subarctic chickadee can be separated from Boreal Chickadee by its *grayer cap* and *more extensive white cheek.* **VOICE:** Peevish *dee-deer* or *chee-ee.* **HABITAT:** Spruce forests, particularly at border with streamside willow and alder thickets and cottonwoods.

MEXICAN CHICKADEE *Poecile sclateri*   Uncommon, local M462
5 in. (13 cm). Similar to Black-capped Chickadee, but *black of throat more extensive,* spreading across upper breast. Note *dark gray sides.* Lacks whitish supercilium of Mountain Chickadee. The only chickadee in its local U.S. range. **VOICE:** Nasal and husky for a chickadee: a low *dzay-dzeee.* **HABITAT:** Montane coniferous forests; sometimes moves to lower canyons in winter.

BOREAL CHICKADEE *Poecile hudsonica*   Uncommon M464
5½ in. (14 cm). Note *dull brown cap,* rich brown to pinkish brown flanks, extensively *grayish cheeks.* **VOICE:** Wheezy *chick-che-day-day;* notes slower, more raspy and drawling than lively *chick-a-dee-dee-dee* of Black-capped Chickadee. **SIMILAR SPECIES:** Gray-headed Chickadee. **HABITAT:** Coniferous forests, evergreen plantations.

CHICKADEES

CAROLINA
CHICKADEE

BLACK-CAPPED
CHICKADEE

CHESTNUT-BACKED
CHICKADEE

Rockies

cen. CA
coast

MOUNTAIN
CHICKADEE

GRAY-HEADED
CHICKADEE

MEXICAN
CHICKADEE

BOREAL
CHICKADEE

BLACK-CRESTED TITMOUSE

Fairly common M470

Baeolophus atricristatus
6¼ in. (16 cm). A small gray bird with *black crown and crest*. Forehead and underparts pale, sides rusty. Juveniles have mostly gray crest briefly in summer. **VOICE:** Chickadee-like calls. Song a whistled *peter peter peter peter* or *hear hear hear hear*. Varied. **SIMILAR SPECIES:** Tufted Titmouse has plain gray crest and black forehead. Bridled Titmouse has harlequin face pattern. **HABITAT:** Woodlands, canyons, towns, feeders.

TUFTED TITMOUSE *Baeolophus bicolor*

Common M469

6¼ in. (16 cm). A small, gray, *mouse-colored bird with tufted crest. Flanks rusty buff*. Plain face, large black eyes. Very inquisitive and loudly vocal. **VOICE:** Clear whistled chant: *peter, peter, peter* or *here, here, here, here*. Calls similar to those of chickadees, but more drawling, nasal, wheezy, and complaining. **SIMILAR SPECIES:** Other titmice, chickadees. **HABITAT:** Woodlands, shade trees, groves, residential areas, feeders.

OAK TITMOUSE *Baeolophus inornatus*

Fairly common M467

5¾ in. (15 cm). This is the sole titmouse west of Sierra Nevada. Very like Juniper Titmouse, but slightly browner. Plain Titmouse was split into Oak and Juniper titmice. **VOICE:** Call a scratchy *sissi-chee*. Song a whistled *weety weety* or *tee-wit tee-wit tee-wit;* highly variable. **SIMILAR SPECIES:** Other titmice, but separated by range. **HABITAT:** Oak and oak-pine woods; locally in riparian woodlands, shade trees, residential areas.

JUNIPER TITMOUSE *Baeolophus ridgwayi*

Uncommon M468

5¾ in. (15 cm). Birds bearing the name "titmouse" are our only *small,* gray-backed birds with pointed crest. Juniper and Oak titmice were once combined as a single species, Plain Titmouse. The two are very similar, although Juniper is slightly grayer. **VOICE:** Call more rapid than Oak's, *si-dee-dee-dee-dee.* **SIMILAR SPECIES:** Juniper Titmice reported from Big Bend and Edwards Plateau areas of TX are probably young Black-crested Titmice, which have short gray crest. **HABITAT:** Pinyon-juniper and oak-juniper woodlands.

BRIDLED TITMOUSE *Baeolophus wollweberi*

Fairly common M466

5¼ in. (13 cm). Crest and black-and-white *"bridled" face* identify this small gray titmouse of Southwest. **VOICE:** Similar to other titmice and chickadees, but higher and faster. Song a repeated two-syllable phrase. **SIMILAR SPECIES:** Black-crested Titmouse. **HABITAT:** Oak, pine-oak, and sycamore canyons, riparian woodlands, feeders.

TITMICE

TUFTED
TITMOUSE

BLACK-
CRESTED
TITMOUSE

JUNIPER
TITMOUSE

OAK
TITMOUSE

BRIDLED
TITMOUSE

Mountain Chickadee
(p. 298)
for comparison

NUTHATCHES Family Sittidae

Small, stubby tree climbers with strong, woodpecker-like bill and strong feet. Short, square-cut tail is not braced like a woodpecker's tail during climbing. Nuthatches habitually go down trees headfirst. Sexes similar, or mostly so. **FOOD:** Bark insects, seeds, nuts; attracted to feeders by suet, sunflower seeds. **RANGE:** Most of N. Hemisphere.

WHITE-BREASTED NUTHATCH *Sitta carolinensis*   Common M474
5¾ in. (15 cm). This, the most widespread nuthatch, is known by its *black cap* (gray in female) and beady black eye on white face. Undertail coverts chestnut. **VOICE:** Song a rapid series of low, nasal, whistled notes on one pitch: *whi, whi, whi, whi, whi, whi* or *who, who, who,* etc. Notes of birds in interior West higher pitched and given in rapid series. Call a distinctive nasal *yank, yank, yank;* also a nasal *tootoo.* **SIMILAR SPECIES:** Red-breasted Nuthatch. **HABITAT:** Forests, woodlots, groves, river woods, shade trees; visits feeders.

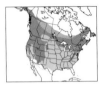

RED-BREASTED NUTHATCH *Sitta canadensis*   Common M473
4½ in. (11 cm). A small nuthatch with *broad black line* through eye and white line above it. Underparts washed with rusty (deeper in male). **VOICE:** Call higher, more nasal than White-breasted Nuthatch, *ank* or *enk,* sounding like a baby nuthatch or tiny tin horn. **SIMILAR SPECIES:** Pygmy and Brown-headed nuthatches have gray-brown or brown crown, lack white supercilium, have very different calls. **HABITAT:** Coniferous forests; in winter, also other trees, feeders.

PYGMY NUTHATCH *Sitta pygmaea*   Fairly common M475
4¼ in. (11 cm). A very small, pine-loving nuthatch, with *gray-brown cap coming down to eye* and a whitish spot on nape. Usually roams about in little flocks. **VOICE:** High, piping *peep-peep* or *pit-pi-dit-pi-dit.* Also a high *ki-dee;* incessant, sometimes becoming an excited chatter. Often heard before it is seen. **SIMILAR SPECIES:** Brown-headed Nuthatch. **HABITAT:** Favors ponderosa, Jeffrey, and Monterey pines, Douglas-fir.

BROWN-HEADED NUTHATCH *Sitta pusilla*   Uncommon M476
4½ in. (11 cm). A small nuthatch of southern pinelands. Smaller than White-breasted Nuthatch, with brown cap coming down to eye and a usually pale or whitish spot on nape. Travels in groups. **VOICE:** Sounds like a toy rubber mouse: a high, rapid *kit-kit-kit;* also a squeaky piping *ki-day* or *ki-dee-dee,* constantly repeated, sometimes becoming an excited twitter or chatter. **SIMILAR SPECIES:** Other nuthatches, Brown Creeper. **HABITAT:** Open pine woods.

CREEPERS Family Certhiidae

Small, slim, stiff-tailed birds, with slender, slightly curved bill used to probe bark of trees. **FOOD:** Bark insects. **RANGE:** Cooler parts of N. Hemisphere.

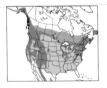

BROWN CREEPER *Certhia americana*   Uncommon M477
5¼ in. (13 cm). A very small, slim, camouflaged tree climber. Brown above, whitish below, with *slender decurved bill* and *stiff* tail, which is used as a brace during climbing. Ascends trees spirally from base, hugging bark closely. **VOICE:** Call a single high, thin *seee,* similar to quick three-note call (*see-see-see*) of Golden-crowned Kinglet. Song a high, thin, sibilant *see-ti-wee-tu-wee* or *trees, trees, trees, see the trees.* **SIMILAR SPECIES:** Pygmy and Brown-headed nuthatches. **HABITAT:** Nests in variety of coniferous and mixed woodlands; in nonbreeding season, also in deciduous woods, groves, shade trees.

NUTHATCHES AND CREEPER

WHITE-BREASTED NUTHATCH

♀

♂

BROWN CREEPER

♀

♂

RED-BREASTED NUTHATCH

PYGMY NUTHATCH

BROWN-HEADED NUTHATCH

WRENS Family Troglodytidae

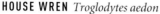

Mostly small, energetic brown birds; stumpy, with slim, slightly curved bill; tail often cocked. **FOOD:** Insects, spiders. **RANGE:** N., Cen., and S. America; one (Winter Wren) also in Eurasia.

HOUSE WREN *Troglodytes aedon*   Common M483
4½–4¾ in. (11–12 cm). A small, energetic, gray-brown wren with light eye-ring and no strong eyebrow stripe. **VOICE:** Stuttering, gurgling song rises in a musical burst, then falls at end; calls a rolled *prrrr* and harsh *cheh, cheh.* **SIMILAR SPECIES:** Winter Wren. **HABITAT:** Open woods, thickets, towns, gardens; often nests in bird boxes.

WINTER WREN *Troglodytes troglodytes*   Uncommon M484
4 in. (10 cm). A very small, round, dark wren, told from House Wren by its smaller size, *much stubbier tail*, stronger eyebrow, and *dark, heavily barred belly*. Often bobs body and flicks wings. Mouselike and secretive; stays near ground. **VOICE:** Song a rapid succession of high tinkling warbles, trills. Call a hard, two-syllable *timp-timp* (suggests Wilson's Warbler) west of Rockies, or *kip-kip* (suggests Song Sparrow) east of Rockies. **SIMILAR SPECIES:** House Wren and other small wrens. **HABITAT:** Dense, shaded woodland underbrush, ferns, fallen trees; in summer, also coniferous forests.

BEWICK'S WREN   Common in West, scarce in East M482
Thryomanes bewickii
5¼ in. (13 cm). Note longish tail with *white corners* and bold *white eyebrow stripe*. Mouse brown above. **VOICE:** Song suggests Song Sparrow's, but thinner, starting on two or three high notes, dropping lower, ending on a thin trill; calls sharp *vit, vit* and buzzy *dzzzzzt.* **SIMILAR SPECIES:** Some Carolina Wrens have limited buff below. **HABITAT:** Thickets, underbrush, gardens; often nests in bird boxes.

CAROLINA WREN *Thryothorus ludovicianus*   Common M481
5½ in. (14 cm). A large wren, near size of a sparrow. *Warm rusty brown* above, variably buff below; conspicuous *white eyebrow stripe*. **VOICE:** Two- or three-syllable chant. Variable; *tea-kettle, tea-kettle, tea kettle,* or *chirpity, chirpity, chirpity, chirp.* Variety of chips and churrs. **SIMILAR SPECIES:** Bewick's and Marsh wrens. **HABITAT:** Tangles, undergrowth, gardens; often nests in bird boxes.

SEDGE WREN *Cistothorus platensis*   Uncommon, secretive M485
4½ in. (11 cm). Stubbier than Marsh Wren; buffier, with *buffy* undertail coverts, *barred wings*, and *finely streaked* crown. **VOICE:** Song a dry staccato chattering: *chap chap chap chap chap chap chap chapper-rrrrr.* Call a single or double *chap,* like first note of song. **SIMILAR SPECIES:** House Wren. **HABITAT:** Grassy and sedgy marshes and meadows.

MARSH WREN *Cistothorus palustris*   Fairly common M486
5 in. (13 cm). *White stripes on back* and white eyebrow stripe identify this marsh dweller. **VOICE:** Song reedy, gurgling, often ending in a guttural rattle: *cut-cut-turrrrrrrrr-ur;* often heard at night. Call a low *tsuck-tsuck.* **SIMILAR SPECIES:** Sedge Wren. **HABITAT:** Fresh and brackish marshes (cattail, tule, bulrush); in winter, also salt marshes.

HOUSE
WREN

WINTER
WREN

BEWICK'S
WREN

CAROLINA
WREN

SEDGE
WREN

MARSH
WREN

CANYON WREN *Catherpes mexicanus*   Fairly common M480
5¾–6 in. (15 cm). Note *white bib*. Rusty, with dark rufous brown belly contrasting with white breast and throat. Long, slightly decurved bill. **VOICE:** Gushing cadence of clear, curved notes tripping down scale; *te-you, te-you, tew tew*. Or *tee tee tee tee tew tew tew tew*. Call a shrill *beet*. **SIMILAR SPECIES:** Rock and Bewick's wrens. **HABITAT:** Cliffs, canyons, rockslides, stone buildings.

ROCK WREN *Salpinctes obsoletus*   Fairly common M479
6 in. (15 cm). A gray western wren with *finely streaked breast*, rusty rump, and *buffy terminal tail band*. Frequently bobs. **VOICE:** Song a harsh chant. A loud dry trill; also *ti-keer*. **SIMILAR SPECIES:** Canyon Wren. **HABITAT:** Rocky slopes, canyons, rubble.

CACTUS WREN *Campylorhynchus brunneicapillus*   Fairly common M478
8½ in. (22 cm). A very large wren of arid country. Distinguished from other N. American wrens by *much larger size and heavy spotting*, which in adults gathers into *a cluster on upper breast*. White supercilium, chestnut cap. Spotted outer tail feathers. **VOICE:** Monotonous *chu-chu-chu-chu* or *chug-chug-chug-chug*, on one pitch, gaining speed. **SIMILAR SPECIES:** Smaller wrens, Sage Thrasher. **HABITAT:** Arid areas of cactus, mesquite, yucca.

BABBLERS Family Timaliidae

Long-tailed denizens of brushy cover. This Old World family is represented in N. America by just one species. **FOOD:** Insects, fruit. **RANGE:** Widespread in temperate and tropical Old World.

WRENTIT *Chamaea fasciata*   Fairly common M508
6½ in. (17 cm). Heard far more often than seen. *Long*, rounded, slightly cocked tail and obscurely streaked breast help identify this small, drab bird, which can be seen as it slips through brush. *Eye distinctly pale*. Bill short. Behavior wrenlike. Slight pinkish cast on breast. Southern birds grayer overall, northern ones browner. **VOICE:** Song (heard year-round) consists of staccato ringing notes on one pitch; starting deliberately, running into a trill—like a bouncing ball. Female gives slower, double-note version. Call a soft *prr*. **SIMILAR SPECIES:** Bushtit much smaller, usually travels in flocks. **HABITAT:** Chaparral, coastal sage scrub, brush, parks, garden shrubs.

DIPPERS Family Cinclidae

Plump, stub-tailed; like very large wrens. Solitary or in family groups. Dippers dive and swim underwater, where they walk on bottom. **FOOD:** Insects, larvae, aquatic invertebrates, small fish. **RANGE:** Eurasia, w. N. America, Andes of S. America.

AMERICAN DIPPER *Cinclus mexicanus*   Uncommon M487
7½ in. (19 cm). A chunky, *slate-colored* bird of rushing mountain streams. Shaped like a wren (size of a small thrush); *tail stubby*. Legs pale, *eyelids white*. Note bobbing motions, slaty color, flashing eyelid. Dives, submerges. *Juvenile:* Has pale bill. **VOICE:** Call a sharp, buzzy *zeet*. Song clear and ringing, mockingbird-like in form (much repetition of notes), but higher, more wrenlike. **SIMILAR SPECIES:** Wrens. **HABITAT:** Fast-flowing streams in mountains and canyons; more rarely pond edges. Nests under bridges, behind waterfalls. Some birds move to lower elevations in winter.

WRENS, WRENTIT, AND DIPPER

CANYON WREN

ROCK WREN

juvenile

CACTUS WREN

adult

WRENTIT

northern

southern

adult

AMERICAN DIPPER

juvenile

KINGLETS Family Regulidae

Tiny active birds with small slender bill, short tail, bright crown. In nonbreeding season, often found in mixed-species flocks with chickadees and warblers. **FOOD:** Insects, larvae. **RANGE:** N. America.

RUBY-CROWNED KINGLET *Regulus calendula*   Common M489
4¼ in. (11 cm). A tiny, stub-tailed, olive-gray birdlet, smaller than most warblers, *flicks wings constantly.* Note bold wing bars bordered behind by *black "highlight bar,"* broken white eye-ring. Male has *scarlet crown patch* (usually concealed; erect when excited). **VOICE:** Husky *ji-dit.* Song is three or four high notes, several lower notes, and a chant, *tee tee tee-tew tew tew — ti-didee, ti-didee, ti-didee.* **SIMILAR SPECIES:** Golden-crowned Kinglet, Hutton's Vireo, Orange-crowned Warbler. **HABITAT:** In summer, coniferous forests; in migration and winter, variety of other woodlands.

GOLDEN-CROWNED KINGLET *Regulus satrapa*   Fairly common M488
4 in. (10 cm). Tiny olive-gray bird, smaller than warblers. Note *boldly striped face,* wing bars. Flicks wings, though less emphatically than Ruby-crowned Kinglet. **VOICE:** High, wiry *see-see-see.* Song a series of high thin notes, ascending, then dropping into a little chatter. **SIMILAR SPECIES:** Ruby-crowned Kinglet. **HABITAT:** Conifers; in winter, also other trees.

OLD WORLD WARBLERS AND GNATCATCHERS
Family Sylviidae

Active birds with slender bill. Gnatcatchers have long, mobile tail. **FOOD:** Insects, larvae. **RANGE:** Worldwide.

BLUE-GRAY GNATCATCHER *Polioptila caerulea*   Fairly common M491
4½ in. (11 cm). A tiny, slim mite, blue-gray above, whitish below, with narrow *white eye-ring. Long tail* is *mostly white underneath* and often flipped about and cocked. **VOICE:** Call a thin, peevish *zpee;* often doubled, *zpee-zee.* Song a thin, squeaky, wheezy, bubbly series of notes, easily overlooked. **SIMILAR SPECIES:** Other gnatcatchers. **HABITAT:** Dry, open woods in West; swampier woods in East; also brushy habitats in winter.

BLACK-CAPPED GNATCATCHER *Polioptila nigriceps*   Rare, local
4¼ in. (11 cm). This visitor to se. AZ has recently become a very local breeder there. Note *largely white undertail* (largely black in Black-tailed Gnatcatcher) and *long bill.* Breeding male has *black cap;* female and winter male lack black cap but former shows browner wash to back and wings than Blue-gray Gnatcatcher. **VOICE:** Rough *meeeer.* **SIMILAR SPECIES:** Blue-gray Gnatcatcher. **HABITAT:** Brushy washes and streamside habitat in desert.

BLACK-TAILED GNATCATCHER *Polioptila melanura*   Uncommon M493
4½ in. (11 cm). Similar to Blue-gray Gnatcatcher, but breeding male has *black cap,* both sexes have darker underparts, underside of tail *largely black.* **VOICE:** Call a thin harsh *chee,* repeated two or three times; soft *chip-chip-chip* series. **SIMILAR SPECIES:** California Gnatcatcher. **HABITAT:** Desert brush, ravines, dry washes, mesquite.

CALIFORNIA GNATCATCHER *Polioptila californica*   Scarce, local M492
4½ in. (11 cm). Formerly regarded as a subspecies of Black-tailed Gnatcatcher. No range overlap. Dull *gray below,* tinged buff-brown on wings and flanks, less white on undertail than Black-tailed Gnatcatcher. **VOICE:** Kittenlike *meew,* rising then falling; harsher *jih-jih-jih.* **SIMILAR SPECIES:** See Blue-gray Gnatcatcher. **HABITAT:** Restricted to coastal sage scrub. Endangered.

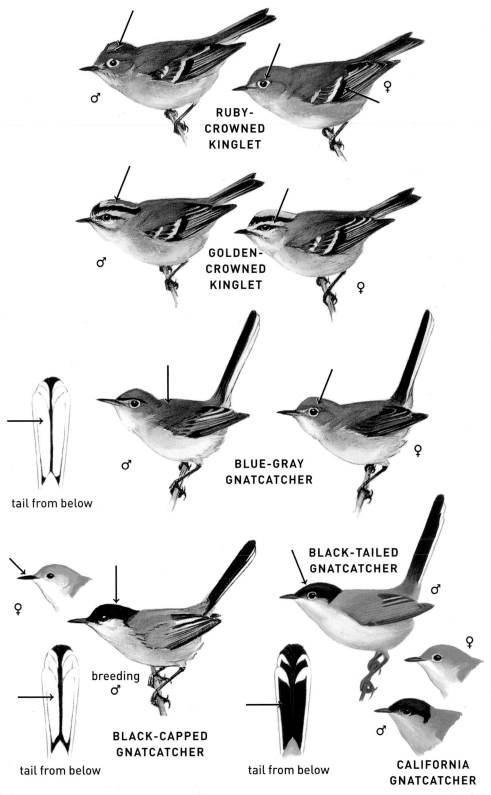

KINGLETS AND GNATCATCHERS

♂ ♀
RUBY-
CROWNED
KINGLET

♂ ♀
GOLDEN-
CROWNED
KINGLET

tail from below

♂ ♀
BLUE-GRAY
GNATCATCHER

BLACK-TAILED
GNATCATCHER
♂

♀

breeding
♂

tail from below

BLACK-CAPPED
GNATCATCHER

tail from below

♀

♂
CALIFORNIA
GNATCATCHER

DUSKY WARBLER *Phylloscopus fuscatus*   Vagrant
5¼ in. (13 cm). A small, plain Old World warbler; *brown above, no wing bars.* Whitish below, with *buffy eyebrow,* flanks, and undertail coverts. **VOICE:** Call a hard *tik.* **SIMILAR SPECIES:** Arctic Warbler. **RANGE:** Asian species; casual vagrant to AK and CA, mostly in fall. **HABITAT:** Thick, scrubby cover.

ARCTIC WARBLER *Phylloscopus borealis*   Uncommon, local M490
5 in. (13 cm). A small, plain, Old World warbler; bill and legs slightly thicker than in wood-warblers. Dull greenish above, whitish below; light eyebrow; *single narrow whitish wing bar;* pale or dusky legs. Fresh birds in fall are brighter green above, yellowish below. Sexes similar. **VOICE:** Song a monotonous series of buzzy notes; call a buzzy *tsik.* **SIMILAR SPECIES:** Orange-crowned and Tennessee warblers. **HABITAT:** Willow and alder scrub.

ACCENTORS Family Prunellidae

Eurasian family of attractive birds in genus *Prunella* that appear thrushlike but are more closely related to pipits. Only one species occurs in N. America, and it does so only as a vagrant. **FOOD:** Insects, seeds, fruit. **RANGE:** Palearctic regions of world.

SIBERIAN ACCENTOR *Prunella montanella*   Vagrant
5½ in. (14 cm). *Dark cheeks; bright ocher-buff eyebrow; bright ocher-buff throat and underparts;* plum brown upperparts. Sides streaked; bill *warblerlike.* **VOICE:** Call a thin, high-pitched *sree* given in series. **RANGE:** Primarily a very rare fall visitor to St. Lawrence I., casual to other Bering Sea islands. Accidental at several seasons to mainland AK, BC, WA, ID, MT. **HABITAT:** Thickets.

THRUSHES Family Turdidae

Large-eyed, slender-billed, usually strong-legged songbirds. Most species that bear the name "thrush" are brown-backed with spotted breasts. Robins and bluebirds, etc., suggest their relationship through their speckle-breasted young. Thrushes are often fine singers. **FOOD:** Insects, worms, snails, berries, fruit. **RANGE:** Nearly worldwide.

BLUETHROAT *Luscinia svecica*   Scarce, local M494
5½ in. (14 cm). A small, sprightly bird; often cocks tail. Skulking, except for singing male. When tail slightly spread, shows *chestnut base.* Distinct pale supercilium. *Male: Blue throat* (partially blue in nonbreeding plumage) with *reddish patches. Female:* Whitish throat with *dark necklace.* **VOICE:** Call a sharp *tac* and a soft *wheet;* often a cricketlike note. Song composed of repetitious notes, musical and varied. **SIMILAR SPECIES:** Siberian Rubythroat. **HABITAT:** Dwarf willows and alders, thick brush.

SIBERIAN RUBYTHROAT *Luscinia calliope*   Vagrant
6 in. (15 cm). Brown above; white eyebrow and whiskers. *Male: Ruby red throat,* gray breast. *Female:* White throat, light brown sides. **VOICE:** Series of chattering notes. Call a sharp *chak.* **SIMILAR SPECIES:** Bluethroat. **RANGE:** Asian species; very rare vagrant to w. AK. **HABITAT:** Thickets.

NORTHERN WHEATEAR *Oenanthe oenanthe*   Uncommon, local M495
5¾ in. (15 cm). A small, dapper bird of Arctic barrens, particularly rocky areas and roadsides, fanning its tail and bobbing. Note *white rump and sides of tail.* Black on tail forms *broad inverted T. Breeding male:* Pale gray back, black wings, and *black ear patch. Female and nonbreeding:* Buffier, with brown back, reduced black in face. **VOICE:** Call a hard *chak-chak* or *chack-weet, weet-chack.* **SIMILAR SPECIES:** Mountain Bluebird, Horned Lark. **HABITAT:** Open, stony areas; in summer, rocky tundra.

ARCTIC
WARBLER

DUSKY
WARBLER

♀

breeding ♂

♂

SIBERIAN
RUBYTHROAT

BLUETHROAT

SIBERIAN
ACCENTOR

breeding ♂

nonbreeding

NORTHERN WHEATEAR

EASTERN BLUEBIRD *Sialia sialis* Fairly common M496
7 in. (18 cm). A blue bird with *rusty red breast;* appears round-shouldered when perched. Female duller than male; has rusty throat and breast, *white* belly. *Juvenile:* Speckle-breasted. **VOICE:** Call a musical *chur-wi.* Song three or four gurgling notes. **SIMILAR SPECIES:** Western Bluebird, but *throat rusty,* not blue. Belly and undertail *whiter,* not as gray. Western Bluebird usually has some rust color on back. Fresh female and immature Mountain Bluebirds may have warm buff wash on throat and breast, but flanks not as bright, and they are longer winged and slightly longer billed. **HABITAT:** Open country with scattered trees; farms, roadsides. Often nests in bluebird boxes.

WESTERN BLUEBIRD *Sialia mexicana* Fairly common M497
7 in. (18 cm). Appears round-shouldered when perched. *Male:* Head, wings, and tail *blue;* breast and back *rusty red.* (In some birds, back is partially or wholly blue.) *Throat blue. Female:* Paler, duller, with rusty breast, *grayish* throat and belly. *Juvenile:* Speckle-breasted, grayish, devoid of red, but with some telltale blue in wings and tail. **VOICE:** Short *pew* or *mew.* Also a hard, chattering note. **SIMILAR SPECIES:** Eastern Bluebird. Fresh female and immature Mountain Bluebirds have buff wash on breast, but flanks duller, blue typically slightly paler, and bill and wings slightly longer. **HABITAT:** Scattered trees, open pine forests, oak savanna, farms; in winter, semiopen terrain, pinyon-juniper, mistletoe, mesquite, parks, golf courses, desert edges. Nests in cavities, including nest boxes.

MOUNTAIN BLUEBIRD *Sialia currucoides* Fairly common M498
7¼–7½ in. (18–19 cm). *Male: Turquoise blue,* paler below; belly whitish. No rusty. *Female and immature:* Dull brownish gray, with touch of pale blue on rump, tail, and wings. **VOICE:** Low *chur* or *vhew.* Song a short, subdued warble. **SIMILAR SPECIES:** Has straighter posture than female Western and Eastern bluebirds, with slightly longer bill and tail. Warm-colored birds in fresh plumage lack rusty-colored flanks. Like other bluebirds, often forms flocks in winter, but Mountain Bluebird flocks often very large, and this species more apt to be seen hovering over fields in search of prey. **HABITAT:** Open country with some trees; in winter, also treeless terrain. Often nests in bluebird boxes.

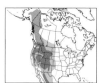

TOWNSEND'S SOLITAIRE *Myadestes townsendi* Uncommon M499
8½ in. (22 cm). A slim gray bird with *white eye-ring, white sides on tail,* and *buffy wing patches.* Pattern in wing and tail gives it a not-too-remote resemblance to Northern Mockingbird, but note eye-ring, darker breast, and especially buff wing patches. *Juvenile:* Dark overall with light spots and scaly belly. **VOICE:** Song a rich warbling. Call a high-pitched *eek,* like a squeaky bicycle wheel. **SIMILAR SPECIES:** Northern Mockingbird, shrikes. **HABITAT:** Variety of coniferous forests almost to tree line, rocky cliffs; in winter, particularly fond of junipers, also chaparral, open woods. Nests on ground.

juvenile

♂

WESTERN
BLUEBIRD

♀

♂

EASTERN
BLUEBIRD

♂

juvenile

♀

MOUNTAIN
BLUEBIRD

TOWNSEND'S
SOLITAIRE

VEERY *Catharus fuscescens*   Fairly common M500

7 in. (18 cm). Note *uniform rusty brown* cast above and grayish flanks. No strong eye-ring (may have dull whitish ring) on grayish face. Of all our brown thrushes, this is the least spotted (spots often indistinct). **VOICE:** Song liquid, breezy, ethereal, wheeling downward: *vee-ur, vee-ur, veer, veer.* Call a down-slurred *phew* or *view.* **SIMILAR SPECIES:** Easily confused with russet-backed race of Swainson's Thrush (Pacific Coast states), but latter has distinct buffy eye-ring or spectacles, more spotting on breast, browner sides and flanks, and different vocalizations. Also Gray-cheeked Thrush. **HABITAT:** Moist deciduous woods, willow and alder thickets along streams and meadows in pine forests.

SWAINSON'S THRUSH *Catharus ustulatus*   Fairly common M503

7 in. (18 cm). This spotted thrush is marked by its conspicuous *buffy eye-ring* or *spectacles,* buff on cheeks and upper breast. Interior and eastern forms are dull *olivey brown* above; subspecies in Pacific Coast region much more *russet.* **VOICE:** Song is breezy, flutelike phrases, each phrase sliding *upward.* Call a liquid *whit* or *foot.* Migrants at night (in sky) give a short whistled *quee.* **SIMILAR SPECIES:** Gray-cheeked Thrush has thin, often *incomplete* grayish eye-ring on *grayish face.* Young Hermit Thrush may have buff-tinged eye-ring, but all Hermits show *contrasty rufous tail, no buffy* on breast, regularly *flick wings and raise tail,* and *vocalizations differ.* See Veery. **HABITAT:** Moist spruce and fir forests, riparian woodlands; in migration, other woods.

BICKNELL'S THRUSH *Catharus bicknelli*   Scarce, local M502

6½–6¾ in. (17 cm). Slightly smaller than Gray-cheeked Thrush, upperparts *warmer brown, tail dull chestnut,* breast *washed with buffy,* lower mandible more than half yellow (less than half in Gray-cheeked). Legs more dusky than toes (uniform pale in Gray-cheeked). **VOICE:** Melodic flutelike rolling from high to low to high, *whee-toolee-weee,* rising at close (falling in Gray-cheeked). **SIMILAR SPECIES:** Gray-cheeked and Hermit thrushes. **HABITAT:** Breeds in stunted mountain fir forests of Northeast to shoreline in Maritimes. In migration, forests.

GRAY-CHEEKED THRUSH *Catharus minimus*   Uncommon M501

7–7¼ in. (17–18 cm). A dull, "cold-colored," *gray-brown,* furtive thrush, distinguished from Swainson's by its *grayish cheeks, grayish,* less conspicuous, often broken eye-ring. *Little or no buffy on breast.* **VOICE:** Song thin and nasal, downward, suggesting Veery's: *whee-wheeoo-titi-wheew.* Call a downward *pheu.* **SIMILAR SPECIES:** Other thrushes. **HABITAT:** Boreal forests, tundra willow and alder scrub; in migration, other woodlands.

HERMIT THRUSH *Catharus guttatus*   Fairly common M504

6¾ in. (17 cm). A spot-breasted brown thrush with *rufous* tail. When perched, it has habit of *flicking wings* and of *cocking tail and dropping it slowly.* Different subspecies groups vary in exact color of back and flanks, some being warmer, others grayer. **VOICE:** Call a low *chuck;* also a scolding *tuk-tuk-tuk* and a rising, whiny *pay.* Song clear, ethereal, flutelike; three or four phrases at *different pitches,* each with a *long introductory note.* **SIMILAR SPECIES:** Swainson's and Gray-cheeked thrushes. Some Fox Sparrows have rusty tail and are found in same habitat, but they are heavily streaked rather than spotted and have conical bill. **HABITAT:** Coniferous or mixed woods; in winter, woods, thickets, chaparral, parks, gardens.

SPOTTED THRUSHES

VEERY

Pacific Coast

East and interior West

SWAINSON'S THRUSH

BICKNELL'S THRUSH

GRAY-CHEEKED THRUSH

tail-lifting

interior West

HERMIT THRUSH

Pacific Coast and East

AMERICAN ROBIN *Turdus migratorius*   Common M506
10 in. (25 cm). A very familiar bird; often seen on lawns, with an erect
stance, giving short runs then pauses. Recognized by dark gray back and
brick red breast. Dark stripes on white throat. On male, head and tail
blackish, underparts solid, deep reddish; those colors duller on female. *Juvenile:* Has speckled breast, but rusty wash identifies it. **VOICE:** Song a clear
caroling; short phrases, rising and falling, often prolonged. Calls *tyeep* and
tut-tut-tut. **SIMILAR SPECIES:** Varied Thrush (in West), Clay-colored and
Rufous-backed robins (both rare). **HABITAT:** Wide variety of habitats, including towns, parks, lawns, farmland, shade trees, many types of forests
and woodlands; in winter, also berry-producing trees.

VARIED THRUSH *Ixoreus naevius*   Uncommon M507
9½ in. (24 cm). Similar to American Robin, but with *orangish eye stripe,*
orange wing bars, and *orange bar on underwing* visible in flight. *Male:*
Blue-gray above, with wide *black breast-band. Female:* Duller gray above,
with *gray breast-band. Juvenile:* Breast-band imperfect or speckled. **VOICE:**
Song a long, eerie, quavering, whistled note, followed, after a pause, by
one on a lower or higher pitch. Call a liquid *chup.* **SIMILAR SPECIES:** Orangey wing bars and eye stripe, and a breast-band, distinguish it from
a robin, with which it only rarely mingles. **HABITAT:** Thick, wet coniferous and mixed forests; in winter, also other moist, dense woods, ravines,
thickets.

WOOD THRUSH *Hylocichla mustelina*   Fairly common M505
7¾ in. (20 cm). *Rusty-headed.* Smaller than a robin; plumper than other
brown thrushes, distinguished by deepening rufous about head, *streaked*
gray cheeks, white eye-ring, and *rounder, bolder,* more numerous *breast*
spots. **VOICE:** Song with rounder phrases than other thrushes. Listen for
flutelike *ee-o-lay.* Occasional guttural notes are distinctive. Call a rapid
pip-pip-pip-pip. **SIMILAR SPECIES:** Other brown thrushes, juvenile American Robin. **HABITAT:** Mainly deciduous woodlands, cool moist glades.

juvenile

AMERICAN ROBIN

♀

♂

♂

♀

juvenile

VARIED
THRUSH

juvenile

WOOD THRUSH

FIELDFARE *Turdus pilaris*   Vagrant
10 in. (25 cm). Robinlike, with heavily marked tawny breast. *Back rusty, contrasting with gray head and rump, dark tail.* **VOICE:** Harsh, chattering *tchak-tchak-tchak* and a quiet *see.* Song a rapid mix of feeble squeaking, chuckling notes, often given in flight. **SIMILAR SPECIES:** Juvenile American Robin, Redwing (vagrant), other spot-breasted thrushes. **RANGE:** Eurasian species; most N. American records from Northeast in winter. **HABITAT:** Open country, fields, hedgerows, residential areas.

REDWING *Turdus iliacus*   Vagrant
8¼ in. (21 cm). Named for its rust-colored wing linings (most visible in flight). Broad *pale eyebrow, heavily streaked below.* Bill two-toned, black at tip, yellow at base. **VOICE:** Flight call a thin, high, reedy *seeeh.* **SIMILAR SPECIES:** Fieldfare (vagrant), juvenile American Robin. **RANGE:** Eurasian species; most N. American records from Northeast in winter. **HABITAT:** Semi-open country and young woodlands.

RUFOUS-BACKED ROBIN *Turdus rufopalliatus*   Rare visitor
9¼ in. (24 cm). This very rare Mexican winter visitor is like a pale American Robin (extensive cinnamon underparts; grayish head, wings, and tail), but with orangier tinge below, *rufous back,* and *no white around eye.* More heavily streaked throat. *Orangier bill.* A timid skulker. **VOICE:** Call a soft whistled *teeww.* Song a mellow series of warbles, each repeated two or more times. **SIMILAR SPECIES:** American Robin. **RANGE:** Most records from AZ, but also recorded west to CA, north to UT, and east to s. TX. **HABITAT:** Woods and thickets, often near water.

CLAY-COLORED ROBIN *Turdus grayi*   Scarce, local
9 in. (23 cm). Scarce resident of southernmost TX. Warm brown above, dull tan on chest, paling to light tawny buff on belly. Throat streaked with light brown, not black. **VOICE:** Lower-pitched, simpler version of American Robin's song. **SIMILAR SPECIES:** Brown thrushes (which are smaller and less like American Robin). **HABITAT:** Tropical woodlands and well-vegetated residential areas.

AZTEC THRUSH *Ridgwayia pinicola*   Vagrant
9¼ in. (24 cm). A robinlike thrush with *dark hood,* white belly, white rump. Wings strikingly *patched with white. Male:* Blackish on head, breast, and back. *Female:* Brownish. Often sits still for long periods. **VOICE:** Nasal, wheezy *wheeeah.* Often silent. **SIMILAR SPECIES:** Northern Mockingbird, juvenile Spotted Towhee. **RANGE:** Casual late-summer visitor from Mex. to se. AZ and w. TX. **HABITAT:** Mixed montane woodlands, especially pine-oak forests.

RARE THRUSHES

FIELDFARE

REDWING

UFOUS-BACKED
ROBIN

CLAY-COLORED
ROBIN

AZTEC
THRUSH

MOCKINGBIRDS AND THRASHERS Family Mimidae

Often called "mimic thrushes." Excellent songsters; some mimic other birds. Strong-legged; usually longer tailed than true thrushes, bill usually longer and more decurved. **FOOD**: Insects, fruit. **RANGE**: New World.

LONG-BILLED THRASHER
Fairly common, local M513
Toxostoma longirostre
11½ in. (29 cm). *Duller brown* above than Brown Thrasher, breast stripes *blacker, cheeks grayer;* bill longer, slightly more curved, and all dark. **VOICE**: Song similar to Brown Thrasher's, but more jumbled. Call a harsh *tchuk.* **SIMILAR SPECIES**: Curve-billed Thrasher. **HABITAT**: Brush, mesquite.

BROWN THRASHER *Toxostoma rufum*
Fairly common M512
11½ in. (29 cm). Slimmer but longer than a robin; *bright rufous* above, *heavily streaked* below. Note *wing bars,* slightly curved bill, long tail, and yellow eyes. **VOICE**: Song a succession of deliberate notes and phrases resembling Gray Catbird's song, but each phrase usually *in pairs.* Call a harsh *chack!* **SIMILAR SPECIES**: The various brown thrushes have shorter tails, lack wing bars, are spotted (not striped), and have brown (not yellow) eyes. In s. TX see Long-billed Thrasher. **HABITAT**: Thickets, brush.

SAGE THRASHER *Oreoscoptes montanus*
Uncommon M511
8½ in. (22 cm). A bit smaller than a robin. Gray-backed, with heavily streaked breast, white wing bars, and *white tail corners.* Eyes pale yellow, duller in immature. Small size, shorter tail, *shorter bill,* and *striped breast* distinguish it from other western thrashers. Streaking may be muted in worn plumage in late summer. **VOICE**: Song is clear, ecstatic warbled phrases, sometimes repeated in thrasher fashion; more often continuous, suggestive of Black-headed Grosbeak. Call a blackbirdlike *chuck.* **SIMILAR SPECIES**: Cactus Wren, Bendire's Thrasher, juvenile Northern Mockingbird. **HABITAT**: Sagebrush, mesas; in winter, also deserts.

GRAY CATBIRD *Dumetella carolinensis*
Common M509
8¾ in. (23 cm). Slate gray; slim. Note *black cap. Chestnut undertail coverts* (may not be noticeable). Flips tail jauntily. **VOICE**: *Catlike mewing;* distinctive. Also a grating *tcheck-tcheck.* Song is disjointed notes and phrases; not repetitious, compared with other mimids. **SIMILAR SPECIES**: Northern Mockingbird. **HABITAT**: Riparian undergrowth, brush.

BAHAMA MOCKINGBIRD *Mimus gundlachii*
Vagrant
11 in. (28 cm). Chunkier than Northern Mockingbird and overall browner with *less white in tail* and *no white in wings.* Dark streaks on flanks, belly, and neck give this species a thrasherlike appearance. **VOICE**: Song simpler than Northern's, with two-syllable phrases. Call a sharp *tchak,* like Northern's but harsher. **RANGE**: Straggler to s. FL from Caribbean. **HABITAT**: A skulker in deep brushy cover.

NORTHERN MOCKINGBIRD *Mimus polyglottos*
Common M510
10 in. (25 cm). A familiar and conspicuous species. Gray; slimmer, longer tailed than a robin. Note *large white patches* on wings and tail, prominent in flight. **VOICE**: Song a varied, prolonged succession of notes and phrases, may be repeated a half-dozen times or more before changing. Often heard at night. Many mockingbirds are excellent mimics of other species. Call a loud *tchack;* also *chair.* **SIMILAR SPECIES**: Shrikes have dark facial masks. Sage Thrasher looks similar to juvenile mockingbird but has distinct streaks, not spots, and lacks large white flashes in tail and wings. See Bahama Mockingbird. **HABITAT**: Towns, parks, gardens, farms, roadsides, thickets.

THRASHERS AND
MOCKINGBIRDS

LONG-BILLED
THRASHER

BROWN
THRASHER

SAGE
THRASHER

BAHAMA
MOCKINGBIRD

GRAY
CATBIRD

NORTHERN
MOCKINGBIRD

wing-flashing

juvenile

shrike (p. 278)
for comparison

CALIFORNIA THRASHER *Toxostoma redivivum*   Fairly common M516
12 in. (31 cm). A large, brownish thrasher, with *pale cinnamon belly and undertail coverts;* tail long; bill long and *sickle-shaped.* Eyes dark brown. It is the only thrasher of this type in CA west of deserts (except locally where Le Conte's Thrasher overlaps). **VOICE:** Call a dry *chak,* also a sharp *g-leek.* Song a long, sustained series of notes and phrases, some musical, some harsh. Phrases may be *repeated* once or twice, but not several times as in Northern Mockingbird; song more leisurely than Mocker's. **SIMILAR SPECIES:** Crissal Thrasher very similar but has deeper chestnut undertail coverts; ranges do not overlap. **HABITAT:** Chaparral, coastal sage scrub, thickets, parks, gardens.

CRISSAL THRASHER *Toxostoma crissale*   Uncommon M517
11½ in. (29 cm). A *rather dark* thrasher of desert, with long, *deeply curved bill.* Note dark *chestnut undertail coverts* (or "crissum"), darker than in other thrashers. No breast spots. Eyes dull yellowish. **VOICE:** Song sweeter and less spasmodic than in other thrashers. Call *pichoory* or *chideary,* repeated two or three times. **SIMILAR SPECIES:** California Thrasher. **HABITAT:** Dense brush along desert streams, mesquite thickets, willows, locally at higher elevations in manzanita, scrub oak.

LE CONTE'S THRASHER *Toxostoma lecontei*   Uncommon M518
11 in. (28 cm). A *very pale* thrasher of driest deserts. Shows contrastingly *darker tail.* Salmon-rust undertail coverts. Eyes dark and stand out on plain face. Rather shy. Runs long distances on ground. **VOICE:** Song (Jan.–Apr.) similar to songs of most other thrashers. Call *ti-reep,* rising on second syllable. **SIMILAR SPECIES:** Crissal and California thrashers much darker overall. Sage Sparrow also runs on desert floor with tail cocked up, but much smaller and very differently plumaged. **HABITAT:** Desert flats with sparse bushes, mostly saltbush (*Atriplex*) or creosote bush.

CURVE-BILLED THRASHER *Toxostoma curvirostre*   Fairly common M515
11 in. (28 cm). This, the most common desert thrasher, can be told from others that have *well-curved* bill by *mottled breast.* Some individuals have narrow white wing bars. Eyes pale orange. *Juvenile:* Yellow eyes, somewhat straighter bill. **VOICE:** Call a sharp, liquid *whit-wheet!* (like a whistle to attract attention). Song a musical series of notes and phrases, almost grosbeaklike in quality but faster. Not much repetition. **SIMILAR SPECIES:** Bendire's Thrasher has *shorter, straighter bill, with slight paling at base,* is slightly browner overall, breast spots more triangular (except when worn), different call. **HABITAT:** Deserts, arid brush, lower canyons, ranch yards.

BENDIRE'S THRASHER *Toxostoma bendirei*   Uncommon, local M514
9¾ in. (25 cm). Of the various drab desert thrashers, this one may be known by its *shorter, more robinlike bill* (lower mandible quite straight), with paler (horn-colored or pale gray) base. Breast lightly spotted. Eyes usually *yellow.* **VOICE:** Song a *continuous,* clear, double-note warble, not broken into phrases. Call a soft *tirup.* **SIMILAR SPECIES:** Curve-billed Thrasher. *Caution:* Young Curve-billed may have a bill as short as Bendire's, and yellow eyes. Worn Sage Thrasher has much shorter, straighter bill. **HABITAT:** Deserts, yuccas, dry brushy farmland.

THRASHERS

CALIFORNIA
THRASHER

CRISSAL
THRASHER

LE CONTE'S
THRASHER

CURVE-BILLED
THRASHER

TX and
NM

AZ

BENDIRE'S THRASHER

PIPITS AND WAGTAILS Family Motacillidae

Pipits are streaked brown ground birds with white outer tail feathers, long hind claws, thin bill. They walk briskly instead of hopping, and most wag their tail. Wagtails are widespread in the Old World, with two species breeding eastward into AK. Long tails are wagged constantly; flight undulating. **FOOD:** Insects, seeds. **RANGE:** Nearly worldwide.

AMERICAN PIPIT *Anthus rubescens*   Fairly common M523
6½ in. (17 cm). A *slim-billed, sparrowlike* bird of open country. *Bobs tail almost constantly* as it *walks.* Underparts buffy or off-whitish with streaks; *outer tail feathers white;* legs blackish to dusky pinkish. Asian subspecies *(japonicus),* rare but regular mostly in fall in w. AK and casual farther south, more boldly streaked below, has brighter pinkish legs. **VOICE:** Call a thin *jeet* or *jee-eet.* In aerial song flight, *chwee chwee chwee chwee chwee chwee chwee.* **SIMILAR SPECIES:** Red-throated and Sprague's pipits. Savannah and Vesper sparrows have thicker bills, do not wag tails. **HABITAT:** In summer, Arctic and alpine tundra; in migration and winter, fields, short-grass habitats, shores.

SPRAGUE'S PIPIT *Anthus spragueii*   Uncommon M524
6½ in. (17 cm). A furtive species, often hard to see well. Note *pinkish legs.* Buffy below, with *striped back* and white outer tail feathers. *Plain buffy face with beady dark eye.* More solitary than American Pipit. When flushed, often towers high, then drops like a rock back to ground. Does *not* wag tail. **VOICE:** Sings high in air; a sweet, thin jingling series, descending in pitch: *shiing-a-ring-a-ring-a-ring-a.* When flushed, often gives a distinctive *squeet* or *squeet-squeet* call. **SIMILAR SPECIES:** American Pipit told by its facial and upperpart patterns, darker legs, tail wagging, and voice. See juvenile Horned Lark. **HABITAT:** Short- to medium-grass prairies and fields.

RED-THROATED PIPIT *Anthus cervinus*   Rare, local M522
6 in. (15 cm). Rare Pacific Coast visitor. A few nest in w. AK. *Adult:* Breeding male has *pinkish red face and breast;* less extensive in female and non-breeding male. *Immature: Heavily streaked below; bold striping on back,* pinkish legs. **VOICE:** Call a high, thin *speee* and a hoarse *tzeez.* **SIMILAR SPECIES:** American Pipit lacks pale stripes on back, is less heavily marked below, has duskier legs, different call. **HABITAT:** In summer, hillside tundra; in migration, same as American Pipit but usually with a bit more cover; migrants often found in flocks of American Pipits.

WHITE WAGTAIL *Motacilla alba*   Rare, local M521
7¼ in. (18 cm). Note bold head pattern, gray back, and white wing patches. "Black-backed" Wagtail *(M. a. lugens),* formerly considered a full species, has *black back* and *white chin* in breeding plumage (dark gray back in nonbreeding), *more white in wings.* **VOICE:** Call a lively *tchizzik,* also an abrupt *tchik.* **SIMILAR SPECIES:** Some immature Eastern Yellow Wagtails are off-white below, but have less white in face and wings; slightly shorter tail; different call. **HABITAT:** Tundra, open country, shorelines.

EASTERN YELLOW WAGTAIL   Uncommon, local M520
Motacilla tschutschensis
6½ in. (17 cm). This species of AK and northeasternmost Asia was recently split from Yellow Wagtail *(M. flava)* of the remainder of Eurasia. *Adult:* Variably *yellow below. Immature:* Dull whitish below, some tinged yellow; throat outlined in dark. **VOICE:** Call a buzzy *tsoueep.* Song *tsip-tsip-tsipsi.* **SIMILAR SPECIES:** Dull immature in flight might be confused with White Wagtail. Buzzy flight call similar to Red-throated Pipit's. **HABITAT:** Willow scrub on tundra, marshy country, shorelines.

PIPITS AND WAGTAILS

breeding

AMERICAN PIPIT

nonbreeding

American and Red-throated pipits wag their tails

SPRAGUE'S PIPIT

Sprague's overhead

towering flight

SPRAGUE'S PIPIT

breeding ♀

RED-THROATED PIPIT

immature

breeding ♂

nonbreeding

breeding ♂

WHITE WAGTAIL

"Black-backed"

breeding ♂

breeding ♂

EASTERN YELLOW WAGTAIL

WAXWINGS Family Bombycillidae

Pointed crest may be raised or lowered. Waxy red tips on secondaries in most individuals. Gregarious. **FOOD:** Berries, insects. **RANGE:** N. Hemisphere.

BOHEMIAN WAXWING *Bombycilla garrulus*   Uncommon, irregular **M525**
8¼ in. (21 cm). Similar to Cedar Waxwing (yellow tip on tail), but larger and grayer, with *no yellow on belly;* wings with strong white or *white and yellow* markings, warmer brown to face. Note *deep rusty* undertail coverts (white in Cedar Waxwing). Often travels in large nomadic flocks. Shape in flight very starlinglike. **VOICE:** *Zreee,* rougher than thin note of Cedar Waxwing. **HABITAT:** In summer, boreal forests, muskeg; in winter, widespread in search of berries, especially in towns where plantings and fruiting trees attract them.

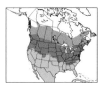

CEDAR WAXWING *Bombycilla cedrorum*   Common **M526**
7¼ in. (18 cm). Note *yellow band* at tip of tail. A sleek, crested, brown bird, larger than House Sparrow. Adults usually have *waxy red tips* on secondaries. *Juvenile:* Grayer, with blurry streaks below. Waxwings are gregarious in nonbreeding season, flying and feeding in compact flocks. Although berry eaters, they often indulge in flycatching. **VOICE:** High, thin lisp or *zeee;* sometimes slightly trilled. **SIMILAR SPECIES:** Differs from Bohemian Waxwing in having yellow on belly, *white* (not rusty) undertail coverts, fewer markings on wings. Flocking behavior and silhouette in flight reminiscent of European Starling. **HABITAT:** Open woodlands, streamside willows and alders, orchards; in winter, widespread, including towns, fruiting trees and bushes; nomadic.

BULBULS Family Pycnonotidae

Native to Old World. One species introduced in FL. **FOOD:** Insects, fruit.

RED-WHISKERED BULBUL *Pycnonotus jocosus*   Uncommon, local
7 in. (18 cm). Note black crest, red cheek patch, black half-collar, and red undertail coverts. **VOICE:** Noisy chattering. **SIMILAR SPECIES:** Phainopepla, waxwings. **RANGE:** This native of se. Asia was established locally in s. Miami, FL, in early 1960s, where it still forms a small breeding population. **HABITAT:** Heavy vegetation in suburban neighborhoods.

SILKY-FLYCATCHERS Family Ptilogonatidae

Slim, crested, waxwinglike birds. **FOOD:** Berries, insects. **RANGE:** Sw. U.S. to Panama.

PHAINOPEPLA *Phainopepla nitens*   Uncommon **M527**
7¾ in. (20 cm). Both sexes are sleek, crested, with red eye. *Male: Glossy black* with conspicuous *white wing patches* in flight. *Female: Dark gray;* wing patches light, not as conspicuous as male's. Eats berries but also catches insects. **VOICE:** Call a soft, rising *wurp* and harsher *churrrr.* Song a weak, casual warble, wheezy and disconnected. **SIMILAR SPECIES:** Cedar Waxwing browner than female Phainopepla, has yellow tail band, lacks pale wing patches. Northern Mockingbird (white wing patches) lacks crest and has much white in tail. **HABITAT:** Desert scrub, mesquite, mistletoe (especially), oak foothills, pepper trees.

juvenile

CEDAR
WAXWING

BOHEMIAN WAXWING

adult

RED-WHISKERED
BULBUL

♂

♀

PHAINOPEPLA

STARLINGS Family Sturnidae

A varied family; some blackbirdlike. Sharp-billed, usually short-tailed. Gregarious. **FOOD**: Insects, seeds, berries. **RANGE**: Widespread in Old World. Introduced in New World.

EUROPEAN STARLING *Sturnus vulgaris*　　　　Common M519
8½ in. (22 cm). Introduced from Europe in 1890. A gregarious, garrulous "blackbird"; shape of a meadowlark with *short tail* and *sharply pointed bill*. In flight, has *triangular wings;* flies swiftly and directly. *Breeding:* Plumage iridescent, bill *yellow. Nonbreeding: Heavily speckled with white,* bill dark. *Immature:* Dusky gray-brown, a bit like a female cowbird, but tail shorter, bill longer. **VOICE**: Harsh *tseeeer;* a whistled *whooee.* Also clear whistles, clicks, chuckles; often mimics other birds. **SIMILAR SPECIES**: Cedar Waxwing, in flight. **HABITAT**: Cities, suburbs, parks, feeders, farms, livestock pens, open groves, fields. Has had substantial negative impact on several native cavity-nesting species.

HILL MYNA *Gracula religiosa*　　　　Uncommon, local
10½ in. (27 cm). *Glossy black* body, orange bill, yellow face wattles and legs. *White wing patches* stand out in flight. Sexes alike. **VOICE**: Squawks, buzzes, whistles; excellent mimic. **SIMILAR SPECIES**: European Starling. **RANGE**: Exotic from Asia, established in s. FL. **HABITAT**: Lush suburban neighborhoods and parks.

COMMON MYNA *Acridotheres tristis*　　　　Common, local
10 in. (25 cm). A *brown-bodied* relative of European Starling, with black head and *white undertail.* Bill, face, and legs bright yellow. **VOICE**: Starlinglike gurgles, squeaks, and cackles. **SIMILAR SPECIES**: European Starling. **RANGE**: Introduced from s. Asia. Widespread and increasing in s. and cen. FL. **HABITAT**: Urban and suburban habitats.

OLIVE WARBLER Family Peucedramidae

Formerly considered a wood-warbler but now placed in its own family. Young males may take two full years to reach adult plumage. Longer winged than wood-warblers, and tail deeply notched. **FOOD**: Insects. **RANGE**: Pine and oak forests at higher elevations from se. AZ and sw. NM to Nicaragua.

OLIVE WARBLER *Peucedramus taeniatus*　　　　Uncommon, local M528
5¼ in. (13 cm). *Male:* Note *orange-brown head and chest* and *black ear patch. Female:* Duller crown tinged olive, breast yellowish. Ear patch dusky. *Immature:* Like female, but may lack most yellow. All plumages show *deeply notched tail* and bold wing bars with *white patch at base of primaries.* **VOICE**: Song a ringing *peter peter peter peter,* variable. Call a rich *kew.* **SIMILAR SPECIES**: Female Grace's and Pine warblers. Male Western Tanager much larger with black wings. **HABITAT**: Pine and fir forests of high mountains.

STARLING, MYNAS, AND OLIVE WARBLER

breeding

juvenile

nonbreeding

EUROPEAN STARLING

HILL MYNA

COMMON MYNA

♂

OLIVE WARBLER

♀

WOOD-WARBLERS Family Parulidae

Active, brightly colored birds, usually smaller than sparrows, with thin, needle-pointed bill. The majority have some yellow in plumage. **FOOD:** Mainly insects though many species also eat fruit in fall and winter. **RANGE:** AK and Canada to n. Argentina.

BACHMAN'S WARBLER *Vermivora bachmanii* Probably extinct
4¾ in. (12 cm). *Male: Face and underparts yellow;* bib and crown black (suggests a small Hooded Warbler with incomplete hood). *Female:* Lacks black bib; forehead yellow; crown and cheek grayish; eye-ring yellow. Bill thin and *downcurved.* **VOICE:** Song a rapid series of flat mechanical buzzes rendered on one pitch: *bzz-bzz-bzz-bzz-bzz-bzz-bzz-bzz,* also given in flight. **SIMILAR SPECIES:** Female may resemble female Yellow Warbler but note more decurved bill and lack of yellow edging in wings and tail; female Wilson's lacks gray head and white undertail. **RANGE:** Former resident of Southeast; last definite record in 1962. **HABITAT:** Swampy areas, canebrakes.

GOLDEN-WINGED WARBLER *Vermivora chrysoptera* Uncommon M530
4¾ in. (12 cm). Gray above, white below. *Male:* The only warbler with combination of *yellow wing patch* and *black throat.* Note yellow forecrown, black *ear patch,* whitish underparts. *Female:* Ear and throat patches grayer. **VOICE:** Song a buzzy note followed by one to three on a lower pitch: *bee-bz-bz-bz.* (Blue-winged Warbler sings a lazier *beee-bzzz.*) Call like Blue-winged's. **SIMILAR SPECIES:** "Brewster's," "Lawrence's," and Blue-winged warblers. **HABITAT:** Open woodlands, swampy edges, brushy clearings, undergrowth. Declining in many northeastern and southern areas.

"BREWSTER'S" WARBLER Scarce
Golden-winged and Blue-winged warblers hybridize where their ranges overlap, producing two basic types, "Lawrence's" and "Brewster's" warblers ("Brewster's" is the more frequent hybrid and more variable). Typical "Brewster's" is like Blue-winged with whitish underparts. Some have white wing bars, others yellow; some are tinged with yellow below. Black eye mark and white or largely white (not solid yellow) underparts are diagnostic. **VOICE:** May sing like either parent. **HABITAT:** Same as Blue-winged and Golden-winged warblers.

"LAWRENCE'S" WARBLER Rare
Recessive hybrid of Blue-winged × Golden-winged warbler combination. Yellow below like Blue-winged, but with black head pattern of Golden-winged. Note black ear patch. **VOICE:** Like either Golden-winged or Blue-winged. **HABITAT:** Same as Blue-winged and Golden-winged warblers.

BLUE-WINGED WARBLER *Vermivora pinus* Fairly common M529
4¾ in. (12 cm). Note *narrow black line through eye.* Face and underparts yellow; wings *with two white bars.* Female averages duller than male. **VOICE:** Song a buzzy *beeee-bzzz,* as if inhaled and exhaled. Call a sharp *tsik.* **SIMILAR SPECIES:** "Brewster's," "Lawrence's," Prothonotary, Golden-winged, and Yellow warblers. **HABITAT:** Field edges, undergrowth, bushy edges, woodland openings.

♀ BACHMAN'S WARBLER ♂

♂ "LAWRENCE'S" WARBLER

♀ GOLDEN-WINGED WARBLER ♂

"BREWSTER'S" WARBLER ♂

♂ BLUE-WINGED WARBLER

TENNESSEE WARBLER *Vermivora peregrina*   Fairly common M531
4¾ in. (12 cm). Note short tail, *bold eyebrow, white undertail coverts.*
Breeding male: Pale gray head contrasting with greenish back. *Female and*
immature: Washed with greenish on head, yellow on breast; often showing a trace of a single wing bar. **VOICE:** Song staccato, three-part: *ticka ticka*
ticka ticka, swit swit, chew-chew-chew-chew-chew. Call a sweet *chip.* **SIMI-**
LAR SPECIES: Orange-crowned Warbler. Warbling and Philadelphia vireos slightly larger and thicker billed, duller on back. **HABITAT:** Deciduous
and mixed forests; in migration, variety of woodlands.

COLIMA WARBLER *Vermivora crissalis*   Scarce, local M535
5¾ in. (15 cm). Found in high Chisos Mts. in w. TX. Drab, with *yellow*
rump and undertail coverts. Larger than Virginia's Warbler; sides *brown-*
ish; lacks yellow on breast. **VOICE:** Song a trill, like Chipping Sparrow or
Orange-crowned Warbler, but more musical and ending in two lower
notes. **SIMILAR SPECIES:** Lucy's and Virginia's warblers. **HABITAT:** Oak-
pine canyons.

ORANGE-CROWNED WARBLER Common in West, uncommon in East M532
Vermivora celata
5 in. (13 cm). Usually drab *olive green* with *yellow undertail coverts* and
blurry breast streaking. Subspecies vary in brightness: some quite drab and
gray-headed, others brighter yellow-green. "Orange" of crown seldom
visible. **VOICE:** Song a colorless trill, becoming weaker toward end. Often
changes pitch, rising or dropping slightly. Call a sharp *stik.* **SIMILAR SPE-**
CIES: Nonbreeding Tennessee Warbler has white undertail coverts, shorter
tail, brighter green above, lacks dusky breast streaks. See Yellow and Wilson's warblers. **HABITAT:** Open woodlands, brushy clearings, willows,
chaparral, parks, gardens.

NASHVILLE WARBLER *Vermivora ruficapilla*   Uncommon M533
4¾ in. (12 cm). Note *white eye-ring* in combination with *yellow* throat.
Head gray, contrasting with olive green back. No wing bars. Underparts
bright yellow with white vest. Regularly bobs tail. **VOICE:** Song two-part:
seebit, seebit, seebit, seebit, titititi (ends like Chipping Sparrow's song).
Call a sharp *pink.* **SIMILAR SPECIES:** Connecticut Warbler is larger, be-
haves very differently (*walks* on limbs and ground, does *not* flutter about
actively), and has grayish or brownish throat. Some dull Nashvilles in fall
can look almost as dull as Virginia's, but always have *yellow on throat.*
HABITAT: Open mixed woods with undergrowth, forest edges, bogs; in
migration, also brushy areas.

VIRGINIA'S WARBLER *Vermivora virginiae*   Uncommon M534
4¾ in. (12 cm). *Male:* A slim *gray* warbler with *yellowish rump* and *bright*
yellow undertail coverts, white eye-ring, rufous spot on crown (usually
concealed), and touch of yellow on breast. Flicks or jerks tail. *Female:*
Duller. *Immature:* Lacks yellow on breast, but always has *contrasting yel-*
low undertail coverts. **VOICE:** Song loose, colorless notes on nearly the same
pitch: *chlip-chlip-chlip-chlip-chlip-wick-wick.* Call a sharp *pink,* like Nashville and Lucy's warblers. **SIMILAR SPECIES:** Nashville and Lucy's warblers.
HABITAT: Oak canyons, brushy slopes, pinyon-juniper.

LUCY'S WARBLER *Vermivora luciae*   Uncommon M536
4¼ in. (11 cm). A small desert warbler; known by its *chestnut rump patch.*
Dull white eye-ring, small patch of chestnut on crown (difficult to see).
Immature: May show touch of peach-buff on breast. **VOICE:** High *weeta*
weeta weeta che che che che, on two pitches. Call a sharp *pink,* like Virginia's Warbler. **SIMILAR SPECIES:** Virginia's and Colima (rare) warblers.
HABITAT: Mesquite along desert streams and washes; willows, cottonwoods.

WARBLERS

TENNESSEE WARBLER

immature

breeding ♂

♀

immature   eastern

ORANGE-CROWNED WARBLER

COLIMA WARBLER

NASHVILLE WARBLER

♀

♂

VIRGINIA'S WARBLER

♀

♂

LUCY'S WARBLER

♀

♂

NORTHERN PARULA *Parula americana*   Fairly common M537

4½ in. (11 cm). A small, short-tailed warbler, *pale bluish above*, with yellow throat and breast and two white wing bars. Suffused *greenish patch* on back. Distinct *broken white eye-ring*. Adult male has *dark breast-band;* immature lacks breast-band, has greenish wash on head. **VOICE:** Song a buzzy trill that climbs scale and trips over the top: *zeeeeeeeee-up*. Also *zh-zh-zh-zheeeeee*. **SIMILAR SPECIES:** Tropical Parula of s. TX has dark face mask, no eye-ring. **HABITAT:** Breeds mainly in humid woods where either *Usnea* lichen or Spanish moss hangs from trees (occasionally in some woods where neither is found).

TROPICAL PARULA *Parula pitiayumi*   Rare, local M538

4½ in. (11 cm). Similar in size and habits to Northern Parula, but limited in range to s. TX, near Rio Grande. Dark head and *black face, lacks white eye-ring*. Two bold white wing bars. Lacks distinct color bands across chest (like adult male Northern Parula has). **VOICE:** Like Northern Parula's. **SIMILAR SPECIES:** Northern Parula. **HABITAT:** Breeds mainly in humid woods near water, usually where Spanish moss hangs from trees.

YELLOW WARBLER *Dendroica petechia*   Common M539

5 in. (13 cm). No other warbler is so extensively yellow. Even *tail spots are yellow* (other warblers have white tail spots or none). Male has *rusty breast streaks* (in female, these are faint or lacking). Note dark beady eye. *Immature:* Lacks breast streaks; some individuals may be quite dull, with bright yellow restricted to lower vent and undertail coverts. May show some very faint dusky breast streaks. All show *yellow edgings to wing and tail.* **VOICE:** Song a bright cheerful *tsee-tsee-tsee-tsee-titi-wee* or *weet weet weet weet tsee-tsee wew.* Variable. Call a soft, slurred, rich *chip.* **SIMILAR SPECIES:** Shorter tailed than Wilson's Warbler and brighter yellow individuals of Orange-crowned Warbler, with yellow tail spots. Note vocal differences. **HABITAT:** Riparian woodlands and understory, swamp edges, particularly alders and willows; also parks, gardens.

CHESTNUT-SIDED WARBLER   Fairly common M540
Dendroica pensylvanica

5 in. (13 cm). Usually holds tail cocked up at an angle. *Breeding:* Identified by combination of *yellow crown, chestnut sides. Nonbreeding:* Lime greenish above, whitish below; narrow white eye-ring, *two pale yellow* wing bars. Adults retain some chestnut; immatures do not. **VOICE:** Song similar to Yellow Warbler's: *see see see see Miss BEECHer* or *please please pleased to MEETcha,* last note dropping. Call a rich, slurred *chip,* like Yellow Warbler's. **HABITAT:** Undergrowth, overgrown field edges, small trees.

MAGNOLIA WARBLER *Dendroica magnolia*   Fairly common M541

5 in. (13 cm). The "black-and-yellow warbler." *Breeding male:* Upperparts blackish, with large white patches on wings and tail; underparts yellow, with heavy black stripes. Note black tail crossed midway by *broad white band* (from beneath, tail is white with broad black tip). *Female and nonbreeding male:* Duller. *Immature:* Has weak stripes on sides, but tail pattern distinctive; often shows thin, weak grayish band across upper breast. **VOICE:** Song suggests Yellow Warbler's but is shorter: *weeta weeta weetsee* (last note rising); or a Hooded Warbler–like *weeta weeta wit-chew.* Call an odd nasal note. **SIMILAR SPECIES:** Yellow-rumped and Black-throated Green warblers. **HABITAT:** Low conifers; in migration, a variety of woodlands.

WARBLERS

♀

NORTHERN
PARULA

♂

TROPICAL
PARULA

♂

♀

YELLOW
WARBLER

♂

breeding
♀

CHESTNUT-SIDED
WARBLER

breeding
♂

breeding
♀

MAGNOLIA
WARBLER

breeding
♂

CAPE MAY WARBLER *Dendroica tigrina*　　　　Uncommon M542
5 in. (13 cm). *Breeding male:* Note *chestnut* cheeks. Yellow below, striped with black; rump yellow, crown black. *Female and nonbreeding:* Lack chestnut cheeks; duller, breast often whitish, streaked. Note dull *patch of yellow behind ear, yellowish rump,* and *one wing bar bolder than the other.* Immature female distinctly *gray.* **VOICE:** Song a very high, thin *seet seet seet seet.* May be confused with song of Bay-breasted or Black-and-white warbler. **SIMILAR SPECIES:** Dull birds in nonbreeding plumage may be confused with Yellow-rumped Warbler but have small pale patch behind ear; duller, greenish yellow rump; and shorter tail. **HABITAT:** Spruce forests; often searches out isolated spruce and fir trees in migration, also broadleaf trees.

BLACK-THROATED BLUE WARBLER　　　　Fairly common M543
Dendroica caerulescens
5¼ in. (13 cm). *Male:* Clean-cut; upperparts *deep blue;* throat and sides *black,* belly white; wing with white spot. *Female:* Olive-brown–backed, with light line over eye and small *white wing spot.* Immature female may lack this white "pocket handkerchief," but note *dark cheek.* **VOICE:** Song a husky, lazy *zur, zur, zur, zreee* or *beer, beer, bree* (ending higher). Call a hard *thip,* similar to call of Dark-eyed Junco. **HABITAT:** Understory of deciduous and mixed woodlands.

YELLOW-RUMPED WARBLER *Dendroica coronata*　　　Common M544
5½ in. (14 cm). Includes "Audubon's" and "Myrtle" warblers, two subspecies groups formerly considered separate species. Note bright *yellow rump* and call. *Breeding male:* Blue-gray above; heavy black breast patch (like an inverted U); crown and side patches yellow. "Audubon's" (breeds w. U.S., sw. Canada); differs from "Myrtle" (breeds AK, much of Canada, e. U.S.) in having *yellow throat* (which does not extend back below cheek, as white does in "Myrtle"), large white wing patches, no white supercilium. *Breeding female:* Duller. *Nonbreeding:* More brownish above; whitish below, streaked; throat yellowish (sometimes dim) in "Audubon's"; *rump yellow.* **VOICE:** Variable song, juncolike but two-part, rising or dropping in pitch, *seet-seet-seet-seet-seet, trrrrrrrr.* Call a loud *check* ("Myrtle") or higher *tchip* ("Audubon's"). **SIMILAR SPECIES:** Cape May and Magnolia warblers. **HABITAT:** Coniferous forests. In migration and winter, varied; open woods, brush, thickets, parks, gardens, even upper beaches.

BLACK-THROATED GRAY WARBLER　　　　Fairly common M545
Dendroica nigrescens
5 in. (13 cm). *Male:* Gray above, with black throat, cheek, and crown separated by *white.* Small *yellow spot in lores.* *Female:* *Slaty* crown and cheek; dusky or light throat; loral spot duller yellow. *Immature:* May be tinged brownish above; loral spot pale. **VOICE:** Song a buzzy chant, "full of Zs," *zeedle zeedle zeedle ZEETche* (next-to-last or last note higher). Call a dull *tup.* **SIMILAR SPECIES:** Suggests Black-and-white Warbler, but lacks white stripes on back and crown, does not crawl around on branches and limbs. **HABITAT:** Nests in oaks, pinyon-juniper, mixed woods.

breeding

♀

CAPE MAY WARBLER

breeding

♂

♀

BLACK-THROATED BLUE WARBLER

♂

immature

breeding

♂

"Myrtle" Warbler

♀

YELLOW-RUMPED WARBLER

breeding

BLACK-THROATED GRAY WARBLER

breeding

♂

♀

"Audubon's" Warbler

♂

immature

♂

♀

GOLDEN-CHEEKED WARBLER *Dendroica chrysoparia* Scarce, local M546
5¼ in. (14 cm). Breeds in Ashe Juniper hills of Edwards Plateau, TX. *Male:*
Similar to Black-throated Green Warbler, but with *black back* and blacker
line through eye. *Female:* Similar to female Black-throated Green, but
back darker olive with dusky streaks, belly snowy white (lacking tinge of
yellow on flanks). **VOICE:** Song a hurried *tweeah, tweeah, tweesy* or *bzzzz,
laysee, daysee.* Call like Black-throated Green's. **SIMILAR SPECIES:** Black-
throated Green, Hermit, and Townsend's warblers. **HABITAT:** Junipers,
oaks; also streamside trees.

HERMIT WARBLER *Dendroica occidentalis* Uncommon M549
5 in. (13 cm). *Male:* Note bright *yellow face* set off by *black throat and nape*
and dark gray back. *Female:* Black of throat much reduced or wanting,
but plain-looking yellow face, gray back, and *unstreaked* underparts identify it. **VOICE:** Song three high lisping notes followed by two abrupt lower
ones: *sweety, sweety, sweety, CHUP CHUP* or *seedle, seedle, seedle, CHUP
CHUP.* Call a flat *tip* (like Townsend's Warbler's). **SIMILAR SPECIES:**
Townsend's Warbler has dark cheek patches, olive back, extensive yellow
below. Hybrid Townsend's × Hermit warblers occur regularly. East of
Rockies, see Black-throated Green Warbler. **HABITAT:** Coniferous forests;
in migration, coniferous and deciduous woods.

TOWNSEND'S WARBLER *Dendroica townsendi* Fairly common M548
5 in. (13 cm). *Male:* Easily distinguished by *black-and-yellow pattern of
head,* with *blackish cheek patch; underparts yellow,* with heavily striped
sides. *Female and immature:* Throat largely yellow, not black; may be
known by *well-defined dark cheek patch, bordered by yellow* as in male.
VOICE: Song like Black-throated Gray Warbler's but higher: *dzeer dzeer
dzeer tseetsee* or *weazy, weazy, seesee.* Call a soft, flat *tip.* **SIMILAR SPECIES:**
Hermit Warbler, with which Townsend's sometimes hybridizes, lacks distinct dark cheek and crown, has duller back. See Black-throated Green
Warbler. **HABITAT:** Tall conifers, cool fir forests; in migration and winter,
also oaks, riparian woodlands, parks, gardens.

BLACK-THROATED GREEN WARBLER Fairly common M547
Dendroica virens
5 in. (13 cm). *Male:* Bright *yellow face* is framed by black throat and olive
green crown. *Female and immature:* Recognized by yellow face; much less
black on throat; unmarked olive green back. All birds show small yellow
spot on rear flank. **VOICE:** Lisping, weezy or buzzy *zoo zee zoo zoo zee* or *zee
zee zee zee zoo zee; zee* notes on same pitch, *zoo* notes lower. Call a flat *tip*
or *tup.* **SIMILAR SPECIES:** Townsend's Warbler has darker cheek, darker
above, yellow on lower breast. Hermit Warbler has yellow on crown, lacks
eye stripe; back gray; no black stripes on sides. Golden-cheeked Warbler
rare and very local, has black line through eye. **HABITAT:** Mainly coniferous or mixed woods; in migration, variety of woodlands.

BLACKBURNIAN WARBLER *Dendroica fusca* Fairly common M550
5 in. (13 cm). The "fire throat." *Breeding male:* Black and white, with *flame
orange* on head and throat. *Female and nonbreeding:* Paler orange (adult
female and immature male) or yellowish (immature female) on throat;
dark cheek patch. Note head stripes, *pale back stripes.* **VOICE:** Song *zip zip
zip titi tseeeeee,* ending on a very high, up-slurred note (inaudible to some
ears). Also a two-part *teetsa teetsa teetsa teetsa zizizizizi,* more like Nashville Warbler. Call a rich *chip.* **SIMILAR SPECIES:** Yellow-rumped ("Audubon's"), Yellow-throated, and Cerulean warblers. **HABITAT:** Woodlands; in
summer, conifers.

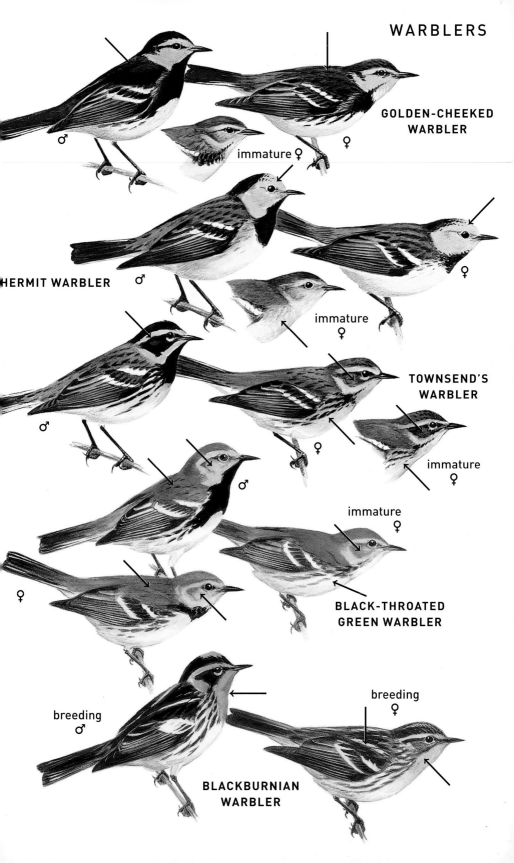

WARBLERS

**GOLDEN-CHEEKED
WARBLER**

♂

immature ♀

♀

HERMIT WARBLER   ♂

immature
♀

♀

**TOWNSEND'S
WARBLER**

♂

immature
♀

♀

immature
♀

♂

immature
♀

♀

**BLACK-THROATED
GREEN WARBLER**

breeding
♂

breeding
♀

**BLACKBURNIAN
WARBLER**

PINE WARBLER *Dendroica pinus*   Common M553
5½ in. (14 cm). All plumages show dark cheeks, blurry streaking at breast-sides, unstreaked back, and white tail spots. *Male:* Yellow-breasted, with olive green back, *white wing bars. Female:* Duller; brownish olive above; immature females often obscure. **VOICE:** Song a trill on one pitch like Chipping Sparrow's song, but more musical, slower. Call a sweet *chip.* **SIMILAR SPECIES:** Nonbreeding Blackpoll and Bay-breasted warblers. **HABITAT:** Pine woods. In winter sometimes in fields with bluebirds.

PRAIRIE WARBLER *Dendroica discolor*   Fairly common M555
4¾ in. (12 cm). This warbler *bobs its tail* (as does Palm Warbler); under-parts yellow, paling on undertail coverts; black stripes *confined to sides; two black face marks,* one through eye, one below. At close range, chestnut marks may be seen on back of male (reduced in female). **VOICE:** Song a thin *zee zee zee zee zee zee zee zee,* ascending the chromatic scale. Call a sharp *tschip.* **SIMILAR SPECIES:** Pine, Palm, and Yellow warblers. **HABITAT:** Brushy pastures, low pines, mangroves.

PALM WARBLER *Dendroica palmarum*   Common M556
5¼ in. (14 cm). Note constant *bobbing* of tail. Both sexes brownish or ol-ive above; yellowish or dirty white below, narrowly streaked; *bright yellow undertail coverts,* white spots in tail corners. In breeding plumage has *chestnut cap.* Two subspecies: Eastern breeders show more yellow below and on eyebrow; western breeders duller, may have yellow restricted to undertail coverts in fall. **VOICE:** Song weak, repetitious notes: *zhe-zhe-zhe-zhe-zhe-zhe.* Call a distinctive sharp *tsup.* **SIMILAR SPECIES:** Yellow-rumped and Prairie warblers. **HABITAT:** In summer, wooded borders of muskeg, bogs. In migration and winter, low trees, bushes, weedy fields. A ground-loving warbler.

YELLOW-THROATED WARBLER *Dendroica dominica* Fairly common M551
5½ in. (14 cm). A gray-backed warbler with *yellow throat.* Black eye mask, white wing bars, black stripes on sides. Sexes similar. Creeps about branches of trees. "Sutton's" Warbler is a very rare hybrid of Yellow-throated Warbler and Northern Parula. **VOICE:** Song a series of clear slurred notes dropping slightly in pitch: *tee-ew, tew, tew, tew, tew, tew wi* (last note rising). Call a rich *chip.* **SIMILAR SPECIES:** Grace's and female Blackburnian warblers. **HABITAT:** Open woodlands, especially sycamores, live oaks, pines. In winter, almost always in palms.

KIRTLAND'S WARBLER *Dendroica kirtlandii*   Rare, local M554
5¾ in. (15 cm). Bluish gray above, *streaked with black;* yellow below, with black spots or streaks confined to sides. *Male:* Has *blackish mask. Female:* Duller, lacks mask; immature female browner. Persistently wags tail (as does Prairie Warbler). **VOICE:** Song, loud and low-pitched for a *Dendroica,* resembles Northern Waterthrush's song. Typical song starts with three or four low staccato notes, continues with rapid ringing notes on higher pitch, and ends abruptly. **SIMILAR SPECIES:** Yellow-rumped, Yellow-throated, and Magnolia warblers. **HABITAT:** Groves of young jack pines 5 to 18 ft. high with ground cover of blueberries, bearberry, or sweet fern. Habitat succession and Brown-headed Cowbird are having an impact on endangered Kirtland's population.

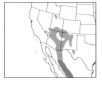

GRACE'S WARBLER *Dendroica graciae*   Uncommon M552
5 in. (13 cm). *Gray-backed, with yellow throat and upper breast,* two wing bars, *yellowish eyebrow stripe,* dark streaks on sides. **VOICE:** *Cheedle cheedle che che che che* (ends in a trill). Call a soft, sweet *chip.* **SIMILAR SPECIES:** Yellow-rumped ("Audubon's") Warbler. Yellow-throated Warbler, a va-grant in West, has white patch behind ear, blacker facial pattern. **HABITAT:** Pine-oak forests of canyons and mountains.

immature
♀

PINE WARBLER

♂

♀

PRAIRIE WARBLER

♂

non-
breeding

breeding
♂

western

PALM WARBLER

breeding
♂

eastern

"SUTTON'S" WARBLER

YELLOW-THROATED WARBLER

♂

KIRTLAND'S WARBLER

GRACE'S WARBLER

BAY-BREASTED WARBLER *Dendroica castanea*   Uncommon M557
5½ in. (14 cm). *Breeding male:* Dark looking, with *chestnut throat, upper breast,* and sides. Note *buff patch* on neck. *Breeding female:* Paler, with whitish throat. *Nonbreeding:* Olive green above; two white wing bars; pale *buff breast, flanks,* and *undertail coverts, dark feet; no streaks on back or breast.* **VOICE:** High, sibilant *tees teesi teesi;* resembles song of Black-and-white Warbler, but thinner, shorter, more on one pitch. Call a sharp *chip,* like Blackpoll Warbler's. **SIMILAR SPECIES:** See nonbreeding Blackpoll and Pine warblers. **HABITAT:** Woodlands; in summer, conifers.

BLACK-AND-WHITE WARBLER *Mniotilta varia*   Common M560
5¼ in. (13 cm). *Creeping along trunks* and branches of trees, this warbler is *striped lengthwise with black and white* and has striped crown, white stripes on back. *Male:* Black throat partly or mostly lost in winter. *Female and immature:* Paler cheek, fainter streaks below, and buffy wash on flanks. **VOICE:** Song a thin *weesee weesee weesee weesee;* suggests one of American Redstart's songs, but higher pitched and longer. A second, more rambling song drops in pitch midway. Call a sharp *chip.* **SIMILAR SPECIES:** Blackpoll and Black-throated Gray warblers. **HABITAT:** Woods.

BLACKPOLL WARBLER *Dendroica striata*   Common M558
5½ in. (14 cm). *Breeding male:* A striped gray warbler with *black cap, white cheeks, distinct pale legs. Breeding female: Greenish gray above,* whitish below, *streaked. Nonbreeding:* Olive above, greenish yellow below, *faintly streaked* on back and on breast; two wing bars; *whitish undertail coverts;* usually *pale legs* (or at least *feet*). **VOICE:** Song a thin, deliberate, mechanical *zi-zi-zi-zi-zi-zi-zi-zi-zi* on one pitch, becoming stronger, then diminishing. Call a sharp *chip.* **SIMILAR SPECIES:** Breeding Black-and-white Warbler has white stripe through crown and on back, different behavior. Nonbreeding Bay-breasted Warbler lacks streaking on breast and flanks, has buff wash on flanks and undertail coverts, and dark feet. See also Pine Warbler. **HABITAT:** Conifers; in migration, broadleaf trees.

CERULEAN WARBLER *Dendroica cerulea*   Uncommon M559
4¾ in. (12 cm). A small, short-tailed warbler, often high up in large trees. *Male: Blue* above, white below. Note *narrow black band* across chest. *Female:* Dull blue (mostly restricted to crown and rump) and *olive green above,* whitish below; two white wing bars, *broad whitish eyebrow. Immature:* Like a dull female; washed with pale yellow on breast. **VOICE:** Buzzy notes on same pitch, followed by longer note on a higher pitch: *zray zray z-z-z zeeeee.* Call a rich, slurred *chip.* **SIMILAR SPECIES:** Female suggests Tennessee Warbler, but latter has no wing bars; also nonbreeding Blackpoll Warbler, but greener above, whitish below, with more conspicuous eyebrow. Dull female Blackburnian Warbler has streaked back pattern. See also female Black-throated Gray Warbler. **HABITAT:** High in deciduous forests, especially in river valleys and ridges.

AMERICAN REDSTART *Setophaga ruticilla*   Common M561
5¼ in. (13 cm). Butterfly-like; actively flitting, with drooping wings and spread tail. *Adult male:* Black; *bright orange patches* on wings and tail. *Female:* Gray-olive above; *yellow flash patches* on wings and tail. *Immature male:* Like female, but tinged with orange on chest patches, sometimes with black splotches on face. **VOICE:** Songs (often alternated) *zee zee zee zee zwee* (last note higher), *tsee tsee tsee tsee tsee-o* (last syllable dropping), and *teetsa teetsa teetsa teetsa teet* (notes paired). Call a slurred, rich *chip.* **HABITAT:** Second-growth woods, riparian woodlands.

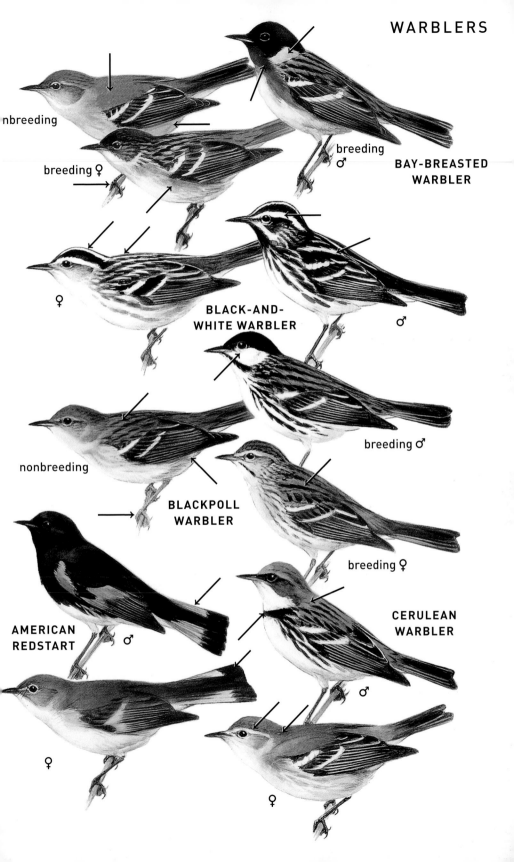

WARBLERS

nbreeding

breeding ♂

breeding ♀

BAY-BREASTED WARBLER

♀

♂

BLACK-AND-WHITE WARBLER

breeding ♂

nonbreeding

BLACKPOLL WARBLER

breeding ♀

AMERICAN REDSTART

♂

CERULEAN WARBLER

♀

♂

♀

SWAINSON'S WARBLER *Limnothlypis swainsonii*   Uncommon M564
5½ in. (14 cm). A skulker, difficult to see. Long bill. Olive-brown above and plain buffy white below, with *brown crown* and *light eyebrow stripe*. Sexes alike. **VOICE:** Song suggests Louisiana Waterthrush's, but shorter (five notes: two slurred notes, two lower notes, and a higher note): *wee-wee-chip-poor-will*. Call a sharp, loud *chip*. **SIMILAR SPECIES:** Ovenbird, Worm-eating Warbler, waterthrushes. **HABITAT:** Cane thickets, swamps, stream bottoms, thick woodland brush; locally in rhododendron-hemlock tangles in Appalachians.

WORM-EATING WARBLER *Helmitheros vermivorum*   Uncommon M563
5¼ in. (13 cm). An unobtrusive forager of wooded slopes and thick understory. Often probes dead-leaf clusters. *Dull olive*, with *black stripes on buffy head*. Breast *rich buff*. Sexes alike. **VOICE:** Song a series of thin dry notes; resembles trill or rattle of Chipping Sparrow, but thinner, more rapid, and insectlike. Call a flat *chip*, also a distinctive *zeet-zeet* in flight. **SIMILAR SPECIES:** Ovenbird, Swainson's Warbler, waterthrushes. **HABITAT:** Wooded hillsides, undergrowth, ravines.

OVENBIRD *Seiurus aurocapilla*   Common M565
6 in. (15 cm). When breeding, more often heard than seen. Usually seen walking on leafy floor of woods. Suggests a small thrush, but *striped* rather than spotted beneath. *Orangish patch on crown bordered by blackish stripes*. *White eye-ring*. **VOICE:** Song an emphatic *TEACHer, TEACHer, TEACHer,* etc., in crescendo. In some areas, monosyllabic, *TEACH, TEACH, TEACH,* etc. Call a loud, sharp *tshuk*. **SIMILAR SPECIES:** Waterthrushes. See also spotted thrushes (p. 314). **HABITAT:** Near or on ground in leafy and pine-oak woods; in migration, also thickets.

LOUISIANA WATERTHRUSH *Seiurus motacilla*   Uncommon M567
6 in. (15 cm). Similar to Northern Waterthrush, but underparts *white on breast, pinkish buff on flanks and undertail coverts*. Bill slightly larger. *Eyebrow stripe pure white and flares noticeably behind eye*. Throat usually *lacks stripes*. Legs pinkish. **VOICE:** Song musical and ringing; three clear slurred whistles, followed by a jumble of twittering notes dropping in pitch. **SIMILAR SPECIES:** Some nonbreeding Northern Waterthrushes (particularly western form, *S. n. notabilis*) have whitish eyebrow stripe. Northern has small spots or stripes on throat and ground color of underparts is *even-toned* (yellow to off-white), not bicolored like Louisiana. Song of Swainson's Warbler somewhat similar. **HABITAT:** Streams, brooks, ravines, wooded swamps.

NORTHERN WATERTHRUSH *Seiurus noveboracensis*   Common M566
5¾ in. (15 cm). Suggests a small thrush. *Walks* along water's edge and *teeters* like a Spotted Sandpiper. Brown-backed, with *striped* underparts, strong eyebrow stripe; both eyebrow and underparts vary from whitish to pale yellow. *Throat striped*. **VOICE:** Call a sharp *chink*. Song a vigorous, rapid *twit twit twit sweet sweet sweet chew chew chew* (*chews* drop in pitch). **SIMILAR SPECIES:** Louisiana Waterthrush, Ovenbird. **HABITAT:** Swamps, bogs, wet woods with standing water, streamsides, pond shores; in migration, also marsh edges, puddles, mangroves.

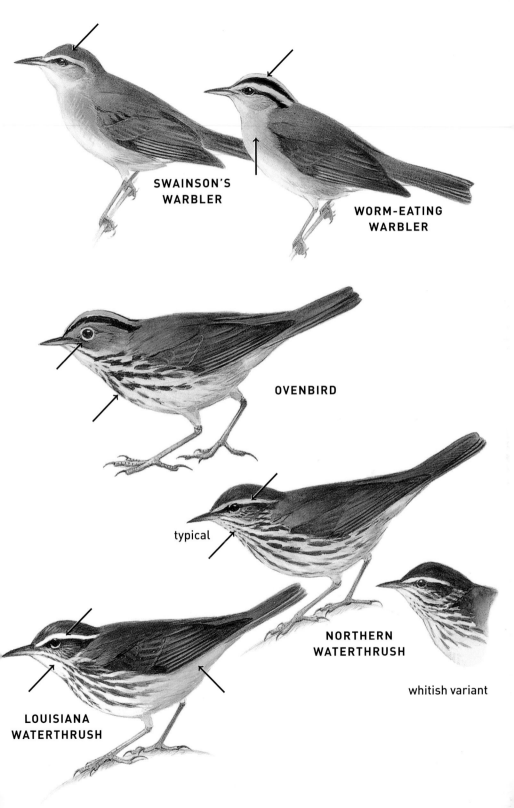

SWAINSON'S
WARBLER

WORM-EATING
WARBLER

OVENBIRD

typical

NORTHERN
WATERTHRUSH

whitish variant

LOUISIANA
WATERTHRUSH

PROTHONOTARY WARBLER *Protonotaria citrea*   Fairly common M562
5½ in. (14 cm). A golden bird of wooded swamps. *Male:* Entire head and breast deep *yellow to orangey.* Wings blue-gray *with no bars. Female:* Duller. **VOICE:** Song *zweet zweet zweet zweet zweet zweet,* on one pitch. Call a loud *seep.* **SIMILAR SPECIES:** Yellow and Blue-winged warblers. **HABITAT:** Wooded swamps, backwaters, river edges.

KENTUCKY WARBLER *Oporornis formosus*   Uncommon M568
5¼ in. (13 cm). Note *broad black sideburns* extending down from eye and *yellow spectacles.* Sexes similar, though female and immature slightly duller. Learn song; 10 Kentuckies are heard for every 1 seen. **VOICE:** Song a rapid rolling chant, *tory-tory-tory-tory* or *churry-churry-churry-churry,* suggestive of Carolina Wren, but less musical (two-syllable rather than three-syllable). Call a rich, low *tup.* **SIMILAR SPECIES:** Common Yellowthroat lacks spectacles. See also Hooded Warbler. **HABITAT:** Woodland undergrowth.

CONNECTICUT WARBLER *Oporornis agilis*   Uncommon M569
5¾–6 in. (15 cm). Shy and skulking. Similar to MacGillivray's and Mourning warblers, but slightly larger; note *walking behavior*—on limbs and ground—and *complete white eye-ring, long undertail coverts* reaching almost to tail tip. *Breeding:* Hood gray in male, gray-brown in female. *Nonbreeding female and immature:* Duller, with brownish hood, paler throat. **VOICE:** Repetitious *chip-chup-ee, chip-chup-ee, chip-chup-ee, chip* or *sugartweet, sugar-tweet, sugar-tweet.* **SIMILAR SPECIES:** Breeding Mourning Warbler lacks eye-ring (but immature has slightly broken one). Male has black throat. Also, Connecticut walks, Mourning hops. Nashville Warbler also has eye-ring, but is smaller, has yellow throat, and is a more active feeder. See also MacGillivray's Warbler. **HABITAT:** Poplar bluffs, muskeg, mixed woods; in migration, undergrowth. Feeds mostly on ground.

MOURNING WARBLER *Oporornis philadelphia*   Uncommon M570
5¼ in. (13 cm). Shy and skulking. Olive above, yellow below, with slate gray head encircling head and neck. *Male:* Has irregular black bib. *Female and immature:* May have thin, light eye-ring that is barely broken, typically not thicker eye-arcs of MacGillivray's Warbler, but this difference may be minimal. Some breeding females and most nonbreeding birds show yellow wash on throat, sometimes extending through middle breast and resulting in bird *not* appearing "hooded." Yellow undertail coverts of medium length of the three similar *Oporornis* warblers. **VOICE:** Song *chirry, chirry, chorry, chorry* (*chorry* lower). Considerable variation. Call a hard, buzzy, wrenlike *chack.* **SIMILAR SPECIES:** MacGillivray's and Connecticut warblers; both are skulkers. **HABITAT:** Thickets, undergrowth.

MACGILLIVRAY'S WARBLER *Oporornis tolmiei*   Uncommon M571
5¼ in. (13 cm). *Male:* Olive above, yellow below, with *slate gray hood* (blackish lores and upper breast) completely encircling head and neck. *Partial white eye-ring is broken fore and aft, forming crescent shapes. Female:* Similar, but hood paler, washed out on throat. *Immature:* Like a dull female. **VOICE:** Song a rolling *chiddle-chiddle-chiddle, turtle-turtle,* last notes dropping; or *sweeter-sweeter-sweeter, sugar-sugar.* Call a low, hard *chik,* given often. **SIMILAR SPECIES:** Immature told from young Mourning Warbler in fall by *grayish white,* not yellowish, throat and by complete pale grayish breast-band. Some Orange-crowned Warblers also have grayish head contrasting with olivey yellow body and pale, broken eye-ring; but they are shaped and behave differently, are duller yellow, and have blurry breast streaks. See voice. **HABITAT:** Low dense undergrowth; shady thickets.

WARBLERS

PROTHONOTARY
WARBLER

♀   ♂

KENTUCKY
WARBLER

CONNECTICUT
WARBLER

immature

Nashville Warbler
(p. 332)
for comparison

♂

♀

MOURNING
WARBLER

immature
♀

♀

♂

♀

immature
♀

MACGILLIVRAY'S
WARBLER

GRAY-CROWNED YELLOWTHROAT *Geothlypis poliocephala* **Vagrant**
5½ in. (14 cm). Male has partial mask *not extending to forehead or cheeks; gray crown*. Both sexes have *thick bill* with *pale lower mandible;* broken white eye-ring. **VOICE:** Burbling warble. Call *chlee-dee*. **SIMILAR SPECIES:** Common Yellowthroat slightly smaller, and slightly smaller billed. **RANGE:** Very rare visitor from Mex. to s. TX, where formerly bred. **HABITAT:** Reeds and weedy vegetation near water.

COMMON YELLOWTHROAT *Geothlypis trichas* **Common M572**
5 in. (13 cm). Wrenlike. *Male: Black (Lone Ranger) mask,* yellow throat and upper breast. *Female and immature:* Olive-brown, with rich yellow throat, duller below, but brighter yellow undertail coverts; lack or have only a suggestion of black mask. **VOICE:** Bright rapid chant, *witchity-witchity-witchity-witch;* sometimes *witchy-witchy-witchy-witch*. Call a husky *tchep*. **SIMILAR SPECIES:** Female and immature distinguished from immature *Oporornis* warbler by whitish belly, smaller size. **HABITAT:** Swamps, marshes, wet thickets, woodland edges.

WILSON'S WARBLER **Common in West, uncommon in East M574**
Wilsonia pusilla
4¾ in. (12 cm). Note longish tail, dark beady eye. *Male:* Golden yellow with *round black cap. Female:* May show trace of cap (on forecrown). *Immature:* Some lack even suggestion of dark cap; they are golden-looking birds with yellow stripe above *beady eye* and *yellow lores*. Constantly moving and flitting about. **VOICE:** Song a thin, rapid little chatter, dropping in pitch at end: *chi chi chi chi chi chet chet*. Call a flat *timp*. **SIMILAR SPECIES:** Female Hooded Warbler has white spots on tail, dark lores. Yellow Warbler has yellow spots on shorter tail, yellow edging in wings. See also Orange-crowned Warbler. Vocal differences important. **HABITAT:** Thickets and trees along streams, moist tangles, low shrubs, willows, alders.

HOODED WARBLER *Wilsonia citrina* **Fairly common M573**
5¼ in. (13 cm). *Male: Black hood* or cowl encircles yellow face and forehead. *Female:* Lacks hood, although yellow face may be sharply outlined (adults); aside from *white tail spots,* may lack other distinctive marks. **VOICE:** Song a loud whistled *weeta wee-tee-o*. Also other arrangements; slurred *tee-o* is a clue. Call a sharp *chink,* like waterthrushes or California Towhee. **SIMILAR SPECIES:** Female and immature Wilson's Warbler lack tail spots and any suggestion of Hooded's face pattern. **HABITAT:** Wooded undergrowth, laurels, wooded swamps.

CANADA WARBLER *Wilsonia canadensis* **Uncommon M575**
5¼ in. (13 cm). The "necklaced warbler." *Male: Solid gray above;* bright yellow below, with *necklace of short black stripes;* white vent. *Female and immature:* Similar; necklace fainter, upperparts may be washed with brownish. All have *spectacles of white eye-ring and yellow loral stripe*. No white in wings or tail. **VOICE:** Song a staccato burst, irregularly arranged. *Chip, chupety swee-ditchety*. Call *tchip*. **SIMILAR SPECIES:** Magnolia, Yellow-throated, and Grace's warblers. **HABITAT:** Forest undergrowth, shady thickets.

WARBLERS

GRAY-CROWNED
YELLOWTHROAT

♀
♂

COMMON
YELLOWTHROAT

♂

♀

WILSON'S
WARBLER

♀

♂

HOODED
WARBLER

♀

♂

CANADA
WARBLER

♀

♂

RED-FACED WARBLER *Cardellina rubrifrons*   Uncommon, local M576
5½ in. (14 cm). The only U.S. warbler with *bright red face*. Has gray back, black patch on head, and white nape. Females and immatures only slightly duller than adult male. **VOICE:** Clear, sweet song, similar to Yellow Warbler. Call a sharp *chip* or *chup.* **SIMILAR SPECIES:** Painted Redstart has overlapping range in Southwest. **HABITAT:** Open fir and pine-oak forests in upper canyons, mountains.

PAINTED REDSTART *Myioborus pictus*   Uncommon M577
5¾ in. (15 cm). Beautiful; postures with half-spread wings and tail, showing off *large white patches*. Black head and upperparts; *large bright red patch* on lower breast and belly. White crescent under eye. Also called Painted Whitestart. *Juvenile:* Lacks red. **VOICE:** Song a repetitious *weeta weeta weeta wee* or *weeta weeta chilp chilp chilp.* Call *clee-ip*, suggesting a siskin, not warbler. **SIMILAR SPECIES:** Red-faced Warbler, American Redstart. **HABITAT:** Pine-oak canyons and mountains; comes to sugar-water feeders.

GOLDEN-CROWNED WARBLER *Basileuterus culicivorus*   Vagrant
5 in. (13 cm). Yellow crown and gray eyebrow stripe bordered by black. Broken eye-ring. Dusky yellow below. Drab olive above. **VOICE:** Song a series of slurred whistles. Call a short, sharp *tuk.* **SIMILAR SPECIES:** Common Yellowthroat, Orange-crowned Warbler. **RANGE:** Casual stray from Mex. to s. TX. **HABITAT:** Dense woodland understory.

RUFOUS-CAPPED WARBLER *Basileuterus rufifrons*   Very rare visitor
5 in. (13 cm). *Rufous cap and cheek* separated by white eyebrow stripe. Throat and upper breast bright yellow, upperparts olive. Long, spindly tail often held cocked up at angle. **VOICE:** Accelerating series of whistled, musical chips and warbles. Call *tick.* **SIMILAR SPECIES:** Common Yellowthroat. **RANGE:** Very rare visitor from Mex. to s. AZ and TX. **HABITAT:** Thick brush, oak woodlands near water.

YELLOW-BREASTED CHAT *Icteria virens*   Uncommon M578
7½ in. (19 cm). Our largest warbler with *heavy bill* and *long tail.* Note *white* spectacles, *bright yellow* throat and breast. No wing bars. Habitat and voice suggest a thrasher or mockingbird. **VOICE:** Repeated whistles, alternating with harsh notes and soft *caws.* Suggests Northern Mockingbird, but repertoire more limited; much longer pauses between phrases. Single notes: *whoit, kook, zhairr*, etc. Often sings in short, awkward courtship display flight. **SIMILAR SPECIES:** Common Yellowthroat (much smaller). **HABITAT:** Brushy tangles, briars, stream thickets.

juvenile

adult

RED-FACED
WARBLER

PAINTED
REDSTART

RUFOUS-
CAPPED
WARBLER

GOLDEN-
CROWNED
WARBLER

YELLOW-
BREASTED
CHAT

♂

Common Yellowthroat
(p. 348)
for comparison

FALL WARBLERS

Most of these have streaks or wing bars.

RUBY-CROWNED KINGLET *Regulus calendula* p. 308
(Not a warbler.) Broken eye-ring, pale wing bars, wing-flicking behavior.

CHESTNUT-SIDED WARBLER *Dendroica pensylvanica* p. 334
Immature: Green above, grayish-white below; eye-ring; tail cocked at angle.

PINE WARBLER *Dendroica pinus* p. 340
Immatures differ from Blackpoll and Bay-breasted warblers in heavier bill, less contrasting wing patterns, darker cheeks. Also note dark legs, unstreaked back, white undertail coverts.

BAY-BREASTED WARBLER *Dendroica castanea* p. 342
Note dark legs and feet, buff undertail coverts, unstreaked breast. Adult may retain a wash of rust or "bay" on flanks. See Blackpoll Warbler.

BLACKPOLL WARBLER *Dendroica striata* p. 342
Very similar to Bay-breasted Warbler, but slimmer. Note streaked back and breast, white (not buff) undertail coverts; pale yellowish legs and especially feet.

NORTHERN PARULA *Parula americana* p. 334
Immature: Small and short-tailed. Combination of bluish head, broken eye-ring, and yellow throat; wing bars.

MAGNOLIA WARBLER *Dendroica magnolia* p. 334
Immature: Broad white band at midtail. Note yellow rump. Faint dusky band across yellow breast. Side streaking.

PRAIRIE WARBLER *Dendroica discolor* p. 340
Immature: Jaw stripe, side streaks. Bobs tail.

YELLOW WARBLER *Dendroica petechia* p. 334
Yellow edging to wings and tail. Beady dark eye. Some females and immatures are so dusky that they may resemble Orange-crowned Warbler.

BLACKBURNIAN WARBLER *Dendroica fusca* p. 338
Immature: Yellow or yellow-orange throat, dark cheek; broad supercilium, pale back stripes. Obvious wing bars.

BLACK-THROATED GREEN WARBLER *Dendroica virens* p. 338
Immature: Dusky outline frames yellow cheek. Plain greenish back.

PALM WARBLER *Dendroica palmarum* p. 340
Brownish back, yellowish undertail coverts. Bobs tail.

YELLOW-RUMPED WARBLER *Dendroica coronata* p. 336
Immature: Bright yellow rump, streaked back; brownish above.

CAPE MAY WARBLER *Dendroica tigrina* p. 336
Immature: Streaked breast, greenish yellow rump. Immature female very gray (not brownish like Yellow-rumped).

RUBY-CROWNED
KINGLET

CHESTNUT-SIDED
WARBLER

SELECTED FALL
WARBLERS
with streaks
or wing bars

♂

♀

not a warbler

immature

PINE WARBLER

immature

BLACKPOLL
WARBLER

PINE WARBLER

BAY-
BREASTED
WARBLER

immature
♀

immature

MAGNOLIA
WARBLER

immature
♀

PRAIRIE
WARBLER

NORTHERN
PARULA

YELLOW
WARBLER

immature

immature

immature ♀

BLACKBURNIAN
WARBLER

BLACK-
THROATED
GREEN
WARBLER

nmature

PALM
WARBLER
western

immature
♀

YELLOW-
RUMPED
WARBLER

immature ♀

CAPE MAY
WARBLER

Fall Warblers

Most of these lack streaks or wing bars.

ORANGE-CROWNED WARBLER *Vermivora celata* p. 332
Dingy breast with faint dusky streaks, yellow undertail coverts, faint eye line. Immature of northern and eastern subspecies *(celata)* greenish drab overall, barely paler below. Some birds often quite gray; other, more western subspecies, brighter yellow.

TENNESSEE WARBLER *Vermivora peregrina* p. 332
Similar to Orange-crowned Warbler but has white undertail coverts; more conspicuous eyebrow stripe; greener look above; paler underparts, with no hint of streaks; trace of a light wing bar; shorter tail. Note also needle-thin bill.

PHILADELPHIA VIREO *Vireo philadelphicus* p. 282
(Not a warbler.) "Vireo" song and actions. Note also thicker vireo bill. Compare with female Tennessee Warbler.

HOODED WARBLER *Wilsonia citrina* p. 348
Immature female: Yellow eyebrow stripe, mostly yellow cheeks, dark lores, bold white tail spots. (Immature male resembles adult male.)

WILSON'S WARBLER *Wilsonia pusilla* p. 348
Immature: Beady dark eye. Smaller and slimmer than Hooded Warbler with yellow lores, mostly olive cheeks, slimmer tail with no white.

BLACK-THROATED BLUE WARBLER *Dendroica caerulescens* p. 336
Female: Dark cheek, white wing spot ("handkerchief"). Some immature females lack this white spot and may suggest Tennessee Warbler, but note dark cheek and duller (browner olive) back. (Immature male resembles adult male.)

CONNECTICUT WARBLER *Oporornis agilis* p. 346
Immature: Large size. Brownish hood; complete, bold, eye-ring. Walks.

MOURNING WARBLER *Oporornis philadelphia* p. 346
Immature and fall female: Suggestion of hood; broken eye-ring. Brighter yellow below than Connecticut Warbler, including often on throat, contrary to grayish white throat of MacGillivray's Warbler.

NASHVILLE WARBLER *Vermivora ruficapilla* p. 332
Yellow throat (may be dull) and undertail coverts, white eye-ring, grayish crown and nape. Short tail, which it bobs.

COMMON YELLOWTHROAT *Geothlypis trichas* p. 348
Female: Yellow throat, breast, and undertail coverts; brownish sides; white belly.

PROTHONOTARY WARBLER *Protonotaria citrea* p. 346
Female: Dull golden head tinged greenish on crown in some immatures; dark eye stands out on plain face. Gray wings, white undertail, long bill.

CANADA WARBLER *Wilsonia canadensis* p. 348
Immature: Lores yellow, eye-ring white. Solid gray above, yellow below, trace of necklace.

SELECTED FALL WARBLERS
without streaks
or wing bars

PHILADELPHIA
VIREO
not a
warbler

immature

ORANGE-
CROWNED
WARBLER

TENNESSEE
WARBLER

WILSON'S
WARBLER

immature
♀

HOODED
WARBLER

♀

♀

adult
♀

BLACK-
THROATED
BLUE
WARBLER

immature

immature

mmature

NNECTICUT
WARBLER

MOURNING
WARBLER

NASHVILLE
WARBLER

♀

♀

♀

immature

PROTHONOTARY
WARBLER

CANADA
WARBLER

COMMON
YELLOWTHROAT

TANAGERS Family Thraupidae

Male tanagers are brightly colored; females of our species are greenish to grayish above, yellow below, suggesting large, thick-billed warblers or orioles. The rather stout bills are notched. **FOOD:** Insects, fruit. **RANGE:** New World, most species in Tropics.

HEPATIC TANAGER *Piranga flava*   Uncommon, local **M579**
8 in. (20 cm). *Male:* Darker than Summer Tanager; orange-red, *brightest on crown and throat*, with *dark ear patch, dark bill, grayish flanks. Female:* Dull yellowish and gray, but shares male's pattern with dusky gray bill, cheeks, and flanks; yellow on throat may be tinged orange. **VOICE:** Song very similar to Black-headed Grosbeak's. Call a single *chuck.* **SIMILAR SPECIES:** Summer Tanager. **HABITAT:** Nests in open mountain and canyon woodlands with oaks, pines.

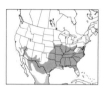

SUMMER TANAGER *Piranga rubra*   Fairly common **M580**
7¾ in. (20 cm). *Male: Rose red all over,* with *pale* bill. *Female:* Olive above, *mustard yellow* below; pale bill. Young males acquiring adult plumage may be patched with red, yellow, and green; some adult females have orangey undertail coverts. **VOICE:** Call a staccato *pi-tuk* or *pik-i-tuk-i-tuk.* Song robinlike phrases, richer and less nasal than Western Tanager's. **SIMILAR SPECIES:** Male Northern Cardinal has crest, black face. Female Scarlet Tanager is more yellow-green in color and has darker wings and smaller, duskier bill. Hepatic Tanager has darker bill, grayish cheek, grayish flanks; brightest on crown and throat. **HABITAT:** Riparian woodlands, oaks.

SCARLET TANAGER *Piranga olivacea*   Fairly common **M581**
7 in. (18 cm). *Breeding male: Flaming scarlet,* with *jet-black* wings and tail. *Female, immature, and nonbreeding male: Greenish olive* above, variably *yellowish* below; dark *brownish or blackish wings;* normally no wing bars, but young birds may have single faint bar. Molting male patched with red. **VOICE:** Song four or five short phrases, robinlike but hoarse (suggesting a robin with a sore throat): *hurry-worry-flurry-blurry.* Call *chip-burr.* **SIMILAR SPECIES:** Summer and Western tanagers, Northern Cardinal. **HABITAT:** Deciduous and mixed forests, shade trees, especially oaks. Often stays high and is overlooked.

WESTERN TANAGER *Piranga ludoviciana*   Fairly common **M582**
7¼ in. (18 cm). Our only tanager with *strong wing bars. Male:* Yellow with black back, wings, and tail, two wing bars, and *reddish head.* Red is much reduced in fall and winter. *Female and immature:* Variably yellow below, with white belly but yellow undertail coverts; dull olive above, dull grayish "saddle" may be apparent on back, white wing bars thinner than male's. **VOICE:** Song is short phrases; similar to American Robin's in form, but less sustained, hoarser. Calls a dry *pr-tee* or *pri-ti-tic* and breathy *whee?* **SIMILAR SPECIES:** Resembles female orioles, but tail shorter, bill stouter. Worn birds in late summer may have very faint wing bars and might be confused with Scarlet Tanager. **HABITAT:** Nests in open coniferous or mixed forests; widespread in migration; a few winter in blooming eucalyptus in CA.

FLAME-COLORED TANAGER *Piranga bidentata*   Vagrant
7¼ in. (18 cm). *Male: Fire red* with *streaked back, dark ear patch,* two white wing bars, and white tips on tertials. Dark tail tipped at corners with white. *Female:* Looks like female Western Tanager, but note *streaked back, dark cheek patch,* pale tips on tertials and tail, and dark bill. Hybrids are known. **VOICE:** Husky and burry series of phrases, like a slowed-down Western Tanager. **RANGE:** Casual spring and summer visitor from Mex. to mountains of se. AZ; accidental to TX. **HABITAT:** Pine-oak forests.

TANAGERS

HEPATIC TANAGER

♀

♂

♂ immature

SUMMER TANAGER

♂ immature changing to adult

♀

♂

♂ changing

nonbreeding ♂

breeding ♂

SCARLET TANAGER

♀

♂ orange variant

FLAME-COLORED TANAGER

♀

♂

breeding ♂

WESTERN TANAGER

♀

♂ nonbreeding

WESTERN SPINDALIS *Spindalis zena*   Vagrant
6¾ in. (17 cm). Formerly known as Stripe-headed Tanager. This boldly
marked species is our smallest tanager. *Male:* Bold black-and-white head
stripes and shoulder patch stand out. Body burnt orange, back color varies by subspecies from black to green. *Female:* Plain gray-brown overall
with pale wing spot; differentiated from other drab birds by thick tanager
bill and size. **VOICE:** Series of thin high notes, *tzee-tzee-tzee,* often given
with buzzy phrase toward end. **SIMILAR SPECIES:** Female may be confused
with female Brown-headed Cowbird. **RANGE:** Very rare visitor to s. FL
from W. Indies. **HABITAT:** Brushy woodlands, fruit trees.

BANANAQUIT Family Coerebidae

The Bananaquit is currently "homeless" taxonomically, although the species is likely most
closely related to several tropical Emberizids. **FOOD:** Nectar, insects. **RANGE:** New World
tropical areas centered on Caribbean.

BANANAQUIT *Coereba flaveola*   Vagrant
4½ in. (11 cm). A small, short-tailed bird with decurved bill and bold
white supercilium. *Adult:* Dark above, white below with white throat and
yellow wash across belly. *Juvenile:* Paler overall. **VOICE:** Explosive series of
buzzy notes and sneezy squeaks. **SIMILAR SPECIES:** Female Black-throated
Blue Warbler, nuthatches. **RANGE:** Very rare visitor to s. FL from W. Indies.
HABITAT: Open brushy areas, nectar- and fruit-bearing trees.

EMBERIZIDS: SPARROWS, OLD WORLD BUNTINGS, AND RELATIVES
Family Emberizidae

This large family of songbirds, whose taxonomic relationships are incompletely under-
stood, comprises species with short conical bills, such as seedeaters, towhees, sparrows,
longspurs, and Old World buntings. **FOOD:** Seeds, insects, fruit, varying seasonally.
RANGE: Worldwide.

WHITE-COLLARED SEEDEATER *Sporophila torqueola*   Scarce, local **M583**
4½ in. (11 cm). Tiny, with stubby bill. *Male:* Dark cap, incomplete light
collar, white wing spot. Variable. *Female:* Buffy with eye-ring, wing bars.
VOICE: High, then low *sweet, sweet, sweet, cheer, cheer, cheer.* Call a high
wink. **HABITAT:** Tall, thick stands of grass and other similar deep cover.

OLIVE SPARROW *Arremonops rufivirgatus*   Uncommon, local **M584**
6¼ in. (16 cm). Olive above, gray below with two dull brown stripes
on crown. **VOICE:** Song composed of dry notes on one pitch going into
Chipping Sparrow–like rattle; reminiscent of Field Sparrow. Call a sharp
chip like Orange-crowned Warbler; also a hissing trill. **HABITAT:** Bushy
thickets.

GREEN-TAILED TOWHEE *Pipilo chlorurus*   Fairly common **M585**
7¼ in. (18 cm). A slender finchlike bird, known by its *rufous cap,* conspicuous *white throat,* black mustache, gray chest, and plain *olive green upperparts,* brightest on wings and tail. **VOICE:** Call a catlike mewing note. Song
variable; opening with sweet notes, followed by burry notes: *weet-churr-
cheeeeee-churr.* **HABITAT:** Brushy mountain slopes, open pine woods with
brushy understory, sage, montane chaparral; in winter, also brushy riparian woods.

MISCELLANEOUS PASSERINES

BANANAQUIT

adult

♂

♀

WESTERN SPINDALIS

♀

♂

WHITE-COLLARED SEEDEATER

OLIVE SPARROW

GREEN-TAILED TOWHEE

EASTERN TOWHEE *Pipilo erythrophthalmus*   Fairly common M587

8 in. (20–21 cm). Smaller and more slender than a robin; rummages among leaf litter. Readily recognized by rufous sides. *Male:* Head and upperparts black; sides rufous rust, belly white. Flashes large white patches at tail corners. Eye usually red (but white in birds of s. Atlantic Coast and FL). *Female:* Similar, but brown where male is black. *Juvenile:* Streaked below like a large sparrow, but with diagnostic towhee wing and tail pattern. **VOICE:** Song *drink-your-tea*, last syllable higher, wavering. Call a loud *chewink!* Southern white-eyed race gives a more slurred *shrink* or *zree*; song *cheet cheet cheeeeee*. **SIMILAR SPECIES:** Spotted Towhee. **HABITAT:** Open woods, undergrowth, brushy edges, hedgerows, feeders.

SPOTTED TOWHEE *Pipilo maculatus*   Common M586

8 in. (20–21 cm). Formerly lumped with Eastern Towhee, this species is also readily recognized by *rufous sides*. *Male:* Head and chest black; sides rufous red, belly white, *back heavily spotted with white* (amount varying geographically). Flashes *large white patches* in tail corners. Eye fiery red. *Female:* Similar, but black replaced by dusky grayish black to brownish black—also varying geographically. *Juvenile:* Streaked below, like a large sparrow, but with flash pattern in tail. **VOICE:** Song a drawn-out, buzzy *chweeeeee*. Sometimes *chup chup chup zeeeeeee;* variable. Call a catlike *gueeee?* or (Southwest mountains) rising and falling *chreeeer*. **SIMILAR SPECIES:** Eastern Towhee overlaps slightly on Great Plains in winter; lacks white spotting on back, shows small white patch at base of primaries; female is dark chocolate brown. Call might be confused with one call of Hermit Thrush. **HABITAT:** Open woods, undergrowth, chaparral, brushy edges, gardens.

CANYON TOWHEE *Pipilo fuscus*   Uncommon M588

8¾ in. (22 cm). Slightly paler and grayer than California Towhee, with rufous crown, faint dusky necklace, and dark spot on breast. **VOICE:** Very different from California Towhee. Call an odd *shed-lp* or *kedlp*. Song an accelerating string of call notes. **HABITAT:** Brushy areas in canyons and deserts, residential areas, feeders.

CALIFORNIA TOWHEE *Pipilo crissalis*   Common M589

9 in. (23 cm). A common, dull brown, ground-loving bird, with moderately long dark tail; suggests a very plain, slim, overgrown sparrow. Note pale *rusty undertail coverts* and streaked buffy or rusty throat. **VOICE:** Call a metallic *chink*. Song a rapid *chink-chink-ink-ink-ink-ink-ink-ink* on one pitch; often ends in trill. **SIMILAR SPECIES:** Canyon and Abert's towhees (but ranges do not overlap with California). California Thrasher larger, with long, slim, curved bill. **HABITAT:** Brushy areas, chaparral, coastal sage scrub, canyons, gardens.

ABERT'S TOWHEE *Pipilo aberti*   Uncommon M590

9½ in. (24 cm). A desert species, similar to California Towhee, but note *blackish facial patch embracing base of bill*. Entire underparts buffy brown, sometimes appearing washed with cinnamon or pinkish buff; rustier on undertail coverts. **VOICE:** Call a sharp *peek* and high squeal. Song a rapid series of high *peek* and lower *tuk* notes. **SIMILAR SPECIES:** California and Canyon towhees. **HABITAT:** Riparian scrub, desert brush, mesquite, parks.

TOWHEES

♂
white-
eyed form

♀

juvenile

**EASTERN
TOWHEE**

♂

♂

juvenile

SPOTTED TOWHEE

♀

CALIFORNIA TOWHEE

NYON
WHEE

**ABERT'S
TOWHEE**

RUFOUS-WINGED SPARROW *Aimophila carpalis*   Scarce, local M591
5¾ in. (15 cm). An AZ specialty. Suggests Chipping Sparrow, but plumper bodied, tail not notched. *Double black "whiskers,"* rufous eye line, gray stripe through rufous crown. *Rufous shoulder* not easily seen. **VOICE:** Song one or two sweet introductory notes and a rapid series of musical chips on one pitch. **SIMILAR SPECIES:** Rufous-crowned and Field sparrows. **HABITAT:** Desert grasslands, thorn brush, desert hackberry, mesquite.

RUFOUS-CROWNED SPARROW *Aimophila ruficeps*   Uncommon M595
6 in. (15 cm). A dark sparrow with plain dusky breast, rufous cap and line behind eye, and rounded tail. Note *black whiskers* bordering throat and *distinct circular whitish eye-ring.* Seen singly or in pairs. **VOICE:** Song stuttering, gurgling, suggesting a thin, weak House Wren song. Call *dear, dear, dear.* **SIMILAR SPECIES:** Chipping Sparrow. **HABITAT:** Grassy or rocky slopes with sparse low bushes; open pine-oak woods.

BOTTERI'S SPARROW *Aimophila botterii*   Uncommon, local M594
6 in. (15 cm). Nondescript. Has buffy breast, plain brown tail lacking white corners. *Best told by voice.* Bill slightly curved on upper edge. **VOICE:** Song a constant tinkling and "pitting," sometimes running into a dry trill on same pitch. Very unlike song of Cassin's Sparrow. **SIMILAR SPECIES:** Cassin's Sparrow, breeding in same habitat, is almost identical, but grayer, has faint dusky streaks on flanks, small white corners to tail, straighter upper edge to bill; upperparts often look spotted (streaked in Botteri's). **HABITAT:** Desert grasslands and bunch grass (particularly sacaton grass).

CASSIN'S SPARROW *Aimophila cassinii*   Fairly common M592
6 in. (15 cm). A large, drab sparrow of open arid country; underparts dingy without markings, or with faint streaking on flanks. Upperparts often appear more spotted than streaked. *Pale or whitish corners* on *rounded,* gray-brown tail. *Best clue is song.* **VOICE:** Song one or two short notes, a high sweet trill, and two lower notes: *ti ti tseeeeeee tay tay.* Often "skylarks" in air, giving trill at climax; Botteri's Sparrow does not skylark. **SIMILAR SPECIES:** Botteri's Sparrow. Savannah Sparrow also has yellow lore spots but is streakier overall, and shorter tailed, than Cassin's. **HABITAT:** Desert grasslands and semiarid prairies, bushes.

BACHMAN'S SPARROW *Aimophila aestivalis*   Scarce M593
6 in. (15 cm). In dry open pine woods with grass and palmetto scrub of South, this shy sparrow flushes reluctantly, then drops back into cover. A large sparrow, with long, rounded tail. Striped with reddish brown above, washed with dingy buff across plain breast, with gray bill. **VOICE:** Song variable; usually a clear liquid whistle followed by loose trill or warble on a different pitch, e.g., *seeeee, slip slip slip slip slip.* **SIMILAR SPECIES:** Field Sparrow smaller, with pink bill. Grasshopper Sparrow lives in meadows, has light crown stripe and short tail. Juvenile Bachman's suggests Lincoln's Sparrow, which would not be in South in summer and has eye-ring and streaked buffy breast. **HABITAT:** Open pine or oak woods, palmetto scrub.

RUFOUS-WINGED
SPARROW

RUFOUS-
CROWNED
SPARROW

BOTTERI'S
SPARROW

CASSIN'S
SPARROW

BACHMAN'S
SPARROW

LARK SPARROW *Chondestes grammacus*   Fairly common M604

6½ in. (17 cm). *Adult:* Note *black tail with much white at corners;* also single dark *central breast spot* on clean grayish white underparts, and *quail-like head pattern,* with *chestnut ear patch* and striped crown. *Immature:* Head pattern duller, but still clearly of this species; a few dusky streaks on breast sides. **VOICE:** A broken song; clear notes and trills with pauses between, characterized by buzzing and churring passages. Call a sharp *tsip.* **SIMILAR SPECIES:** Vesper Sparrow. **HABITAT:** Open country with bushes, trees; pastures, farms, roadsides.

SAGE SPARROW *Amphispiza belli*   Uncommon M606

6–6¼ in. (15–16 cm). A gray sparrow of arid brush. Note combination of *single breast spot* and *heavy dark "whiskers" on each side of throat. Gray head contrasts with browner back and wing.* Dark cheek, *white eye-ring,* touch of whitish over eye. Long tail often *flicked and waved* about. *Often seen running on ground, with tail held high, like a miniature thrasher.* "Bell's" Sparrow, a subspecies resident west of Sierra Nevada in CA, is darker, with heavier black whiskers. **VOICE:** Song four to seven mechanically delivered notes, *tsit-tsoo-tseee-tsay* (third note highest). Or *tsit, tsit, tsi you, tee a-tee.* Twittering call. **SIMILAR SPECIES:** See juvenile Black-throated Sparrow. **HABITAT:** Sage and saltbush flats; in winter, also creosote bush. "Bell's" found in dry brushy foothills, chaparral.

BLACK-THROATED SPARROW *Amphispiza bilineata* Fairly common M605

5½ in. (14 cm). *Adult:* Note face pattern. A pretty, gray, desert sparrow, with *white face stripes* and *jet-black throat and chest.* White corners to *distinct black tail. Juvenile:* Seen into fall; *lacks* black throat but has similar cheek pattern and broad white supercilium; breast weakly streaked. **VOICE:** Song a sweet *cheet cheet cheeeeeee* (two short, clear opening notes and a fine trill on lower or higher pitch); calls are light tinkling notes. **SIMILAR SPECIES:** Juveniles somewhat resemble Sage Sparrow but have bolder supercilium and contrastingly black tail (with more white at corners). **HABITAT:** Arid brush, creosote-bush and cactus deserts, juniper hillsides.

FIVE-STRIPED SPARROW   Very rare, local M596
Aimophila quinquestriata

6 in. (15 cm). A rare Mexican sparrow. *Dusky,* with *five white stripes* on head (white throat, eyebrow, and jaw line) and single black spot on dark gray breast. **VOICE:** High-pitched, watery phrases, each note repeated several times, like a thrasher does. Call a sharp *tchak!* **SIMILAR SPECIES:** Black-throated and Sage sparrows. **HABITAT:** Dense shrubs on dry canyon slopes, rocky arid hillsides.

BLACK-CHINNED SPARROW *Spizella atrogularis*   Uncommon M602

5¾ in. (15 cm). A small, slim, somewhat juncolike sparrow (with no white in tail); has streaked brown back, but *head and underparts medium gray. Breeding male:* Small *pinkish bill* encircled by *black chin* and facial patch. *Female and nonbreeding male:* Lack black face. Can be told by *unmarked gray head and breast, pinkish bill,* striped brown back. **VOICE:** Song a sweet series of notes on about same pitch, or descending slightly; starts with several high, thin, clear notes and ends in rough trill, *sweet, sweet, sweet, weet-trrrrrrr.* **SIMILAR SPECIES:** Black-throated Sparrow, juncos. **HABITAT:** Brushy mountain slopes, open chaparral, juniper; winters on rocky, brushy canyon slopes, usually in flocks.

SPARROWS

adult

juvenile

LARK SPARROW

"Bell's" (coastal)

SAGE SPARROW

juvenile

adult

adult

BLACK-
THROATED
SPARROW

adult

adult

FIVE-STRIPED
SPARROW

juvenile

♂

♀

BLACK-CHINNED
SPARROW

AMERICAN TREE SPARROW *Spizella arborea*   Fairly common M597
6¼ in. (16 cm). Note *dark "stickpin,"* on breast, and *red-brown cap. Bill dark above, yellow below;* white wing bars; rufous wash on flanks. **VOICE:** Song sweet, variable, opening on one or two high, clear notes. Call *tseet;* feeding call a musical *teelwit.* **SIMILAR SPECIES:** Field and Chipping sparrows. **HABITAT:** Arctic and taiga scrub, willow thickets; in winter, brushy roadsides, weedy edges, freshwater marshes (particularly with cattails), feeders.

CHIPPING SPARROW *Spizella passerina*   Common M598
5½ in. (14 cm). *Breeding:* A small, slim, long-tailed, plain-breasted sparrow with bright *rufous cap, black eye line, white eyebrow. Nonbreeding:* Duller; note *dark eyeline, dirty grayish breast, gray rump. Juvenile:* Shows fine streaks on breast, rump not as gray; this plumage may be held until midautumn in western birds. **VOICE:** Song a dry chipping rattle on one pitch. Call a thin *tseet.* **SIMILAR SPECIES:** Clay-colored and Brewer's sparrows. Also Rufous-winged and Swamp sparrows. **HABITAT:** Open woods, especially pine, oak; orchards, farms, towns, lawns, feeders. Often forms flocks in fall and winter.

FIELD SPARROW *Spizella pusilla*   Fairly common M601
5¾ in. (15 cm). A small, slim, rusty-capped sparrow. Note *pink bill,* white eye-ring, plain buffy breast; rusty upperparts, and weak face striping. *Juvenile:* Has finely streaked breast, but this plumage not held long. **VOICE:** Song opens on deliberate, sweet, slurring notes, speeding into a trill (which ascends, descends, or stays on same pitch). Call *tseew.* **SIMILAR SPECIES:** American Tree, Chipping, and Brewer's sparrows. **HABITAT:** Overgrown fields, pastures, brush, feeders.

CLAY-COLORED SPARROW *Spizella pallida*   Fairly common M599
5½ in. (14 cm). Like a pale, nonbreeding Chipping Sparrow, but buffier, with *pale lores, sharply outlined ear patch,* more contrasting gray nape, bolder white mustache, *browner rump,* whiter underparts. **VOICE:** Unbirdlike; three or four low, flat buzzes: *bzzz, bzzz, bzzz.* Call a thin *tseet,* like Chipping's but higher. **SIMILAR SPECIES:** See also Brewer's Sparrow. **HABITAT:** Scrub, brushy prairies, jack pines, weedy areas.

SWAMP SPARROW *Melospiza georgiana*   Fairly common M619
5¾ in. (15 cm). A rather plump, dark, *rusty-winged* sparrow with tawny flanks and *broad black back striping. Adult:* White throat, rusty cap, blue-gray neck and breast. *Immature:* Blackish or dark rust crown, *olive-gray neck and breast;* dim flank streaking. **VOICE:** Song a loose trill, similar to Chipping Sparrow's but slower, sweeter, and stronger. Call a hard *cheep,* similar to Black or Eastern phoebe. **SIMILAR SPECIES:** Song Sparrow slightly larger, has *heavier breast streaks,* lacks tawny flanks. Lincoln's Sparrow has buff breast with fine sharp streaks. Chipping, Field, and American Tree sparrows are longer tailed and have wing bars. **HABITAT:** Nests in freshwater marshes with bushes, cattails, sedges, willows; winters in marshes, pond edges, moist brushy areas, weedy ditches.

BREWER'S SPARROW *Spizella breweri*   Fairly common M600
5½ in. (14 cm). A small, slim, pale, *nondescript* sparrow of sagebrush and desert scrub. Resembles Chipping and Clay-colored sparrows. Note pale lores, brownish rump, pale *eye-ring,* and *lack of white central crown stripe.* "Timberline" subspecies has slightly bolder plumage; nests near tree line in n. Rockies of Canada and extreme e. AK. **VOICE:** Song long, musical buzzy trills on different pitches; canarylike. Call a thin *tsee.* **SIMILAR SPECIES:** Chipping and Clay-colored sparrows. **HABITAT:** Nests in sagebrush, saltbush; winters in brushy plains and deserts, weedy fields. "Timberline" Sparrow nests near tree line, mostly in stunted willow.

SPARROWS

breeding

nonbreeding

juvenile

AMERICAN
TREE
SPARROW

CHIPPING SPARROW

nonbreeding

breeding

CLAY-COLORED SPARROW

juvenile

FIELD
SPARROW

adult

BREWER'S SPARROW

SWAMP
SPARROW

immature

adult

SAVANNAH SPARROW *Passerculus sandwichensis*   Common M608
5½–5¾ in. (14–15 cm). This streaked, open-country sparrow suggests a small Song Sparrow, but it usually has *yellowish on front of eyebrow (may be lacking or difficult to see in some birds); whitish stripe through crown; short,* notched tail; pinker legs. Noting tail notch and length is an identification aid when flushing sparrows. "Large-billed" Savannah Sparrow is scarce and local post-breeding visitor to Salton Sea and coastal s. CA from w. Mex. Has larger, paler bill and pale but warm-toned brownish body. "Belding's" Savannah Sparrow is one of several very dark subspecies that are permanent residents in coastal salt marshes of CA; threatened. "Ipswich" race birds (breeding on Sable I., NS and wintering along Atlantic Coast) are paler overall and slightly larger. **VOICE:** Song a lisping, buzzy *tsit-tsit-tsit, tseeee-tsaaay* (last note lower). Call a light *tsu.* **SIMILAR SPECIES:** Song Sparrow's tail longer, rounded. See also Vesper Sparrow. Song similar to Grasshopper Sparrow's except for Savannah's lower last note. **HABITAT:** Open fields, farms, meadows, salt marshes, prairies, dunes.

GRASSHOPPER SPARROW *Ammodramus savannarum*   Uncommon M609
5 in. (13 cm). A small-bodied, large- and flat-headed, short- and sharp-tailed sparrow of taller grasslands. Crown with pale median stripe; *yellow lores; whitish eye-ring;* note relatively *unstriped buffy breast.* Yellow bend in wing hard to see. Flight feeble. *Juvenile:* Has dusky streaks on sides. **VOICE:** Very thin, dry, insectlike *pi-tup zeeeeeeeeeeee.* **SIMILAR SPECIES:** Le Conte's Sparrow has longer, bolder, orangier eyebrow; bolder side streaking. Grasshopper's song fairly similar to Savannah Sparrow's. **HABITAT:** Grasslands, hayfields, pastures, prairies.

HENSLOW'S SPARROW *Ammodramus henslowii*   Scarce, secretive M611
5 in. (13 cm). A secretive sparrow of fields, easily overlooked were it not for its odd song. Short-tailed and flat-headed, with large pale bill; finely striped across breast. Striped olive-colored head in conjunction with reddish wings help identify it. Also note double mustache stripes and spots behind "ear." **VOICE:** Song a poor vocal effort: a hiccuping *tsi-lick.* May sing on quiet, windless nights. **SIMILAR SPECIES:** Grasshopper Sparrow. Young Henslow's Sparrow (summer) is practically without breast streaks, thus resembles adult Grasshopper. Conversely, young Grasshopper has breast streaks, but lacks adult Henslow's olive and russet tones. **HABITAT:** Very specific. Partially overgrown fields with certain plant development of exacting components. Disappearing from many former haunts. Winters in dense cover in southern pine forests.

BAIRD'S SPARROW *Ammodramus bairdii*   Scarce, local, secretive M610
5½ in. (14 cm). An elusive, skulking prairie sparrow. Light breast crossed by *narrow band* of fine black streaks. Head ocher-buff, streaked. Key mark is broad *ocher* median crown stripe. *Double mustache stripes.* Flat head. Hard to see well except when singing. *Juvenile:* Pale edges form scaly pattern above. **VOICE:** Song begins with two or three high musical *zips,* ends with trill on lower pitch; more musical than Savannah Sparrow. **SIMILAR SPECIES:** Savannah Sparrow has more extensive streaking below, narrow white median crown stripe, and lacks dark marks at rear of auriculars and double mustache stripes. See Henslow's Sparrow. **HABITAT:** Native prairies, scattered bushes used as song perches.

STREAK-BREASTED GRASS SPARROWS

"Belding's"

typical

"Large-billed"

SAVANNAH SPARROW

"Ipswich"

adult

juvenile

GRASSHOPPER SPARROW

HENSLOW'S SPARROW

juvenile

adult

BAIRD'S SPARROW

NELSON'S SHARP-TAILED SPARROW   Uncommon M613
Ammodramus nelsoni
5 in. (13 cm). A shy marshland skulker with three widely separated breeding populations. Note bright *orange on face,* completely surrounding gray ear patch. *Breast warm buff with faint blurry streaks,* stronger streaks on flanks. Gray central crown and *unmarked gray nape.* Back sharply striped with white. Birds of New England and Maritimes grayer with less distinct stripes. **VOICE:** Song a buzzy, two-part *shleeee-tup.* **SIMILAR SPECIES:** Saltmarsh Sharp-tailed Sparrow has heavier breast streaking and any orange on breast is *paler* than orange on face (breast and face equally bright in Nelson's). Le Conte's Sparrow has white median crown stripe, purplish chestnut streaks on nape. **HABITAT:** In summer, prairie and coastal marshes, muskeg; in winter, coastal marshes.

SALTMARSH SHARP-TAILED SPARROW   Uncommon M614
Ammodramus caudacutus
5¼ in. (13 cm). A short-tailed, often shy sparrow of coastal marshes. Note deep ocher yellow or orange of face, which completely surrounds gray ear patch. Distinct streaks on mostly whitish or light buff breast, flat-headed appearance. **VOICE:** Song a weak varied jumble of buzzy hisses and clicks; not distinctly two-part like Nelson's. **SIMILAR SPECIES:** Nelson's Sharp-tailed and Le Conte's sparrows. Juvenile Seaside Sparrow in late summer is much like Saltmarsh Sharp-tailed. Savannah Sparrow has yellow in lores only, has notched tail. **HABITAT:** Coastal salt marshes.

LE CONTE'S SPARROW *Ammodramus leconteii*   Uncommon M612
5 in. (13 cm). A skulking sharp-tailed sparrow of prairie marshes, boggy fields. Note *bright orange* eyebrow and buffy breast (with streaks *confined to sides*). Other points are *purplish chestnut streaks on nape,* white median crown stripe, strong stripes on back. **VOICE:** Song two extremely thin, grasshopper-like hisses. **SIMILAR SPECIES:** Nelson's Sharp-tailed Sparrow. Grasshopper Sparrow has yellow in front of eye only and faint side streaks, if any. **HABITAT:** Grassy marshes, tallgrass fields, weedy hayfields.

SEASIDE SPARROW *Ammodramus maritimus*   Fairly common M615
6 in. (15 cm). A dark, *gray* sparrow of salt marshes, with short *yellow area above lores. Whitish throat* and white above dark malar. Shares marshes with both sharp-tailed sparrows. "Cape Sable" Seaside Sparrow is an endangered subspecies confined to s. FL (the only Seaside that breeds there); more greenish than typical birds with *much heavier streaking.* **VOICE:** Song *cutcut ZHE-eeeeeeee;* much stronger than Saltmarsh Sharp-tailed Sparrow. Call *chack.* **HABITAT:** Salt marshes.

MARSH SPARROWS

SALTMARSH SHARP-TAILED SPARROW

NELSON'S HARP-TAILED SPARROW

coastal

interior

LE CONTE'S SPARROW

juvenile

adult

SEASIDE SPARROW

"Cape Sable"

FOX SPARROW *Passerella iliaca*   Uncommon M616

7 in. (18 cm). A large, plump sparrow; most subspecies have *rusty rump and tail*. Action towhee-like, kicking among dead leaves and other ground litter. *Breast heavily streaked* with triangular spots; these often cluster in large blotch on upper breast. Fox Sparrows vary widely. Many subspecies; can be roughly divided into four basic types, with breeding range noted: (1) "Red" subspecies: bright rusty with rusty back stripes (northern and eastern); (2) "Sooty" subspecies: dusky or sooty head, back (unstreaked), and upper breast (Northwest coast); (3) "Slate-colored" subspecies: gray-headed and gray-backed (unstreaked), yellowish-based bill (Rockies, Great Basin); and (4) "Thick-billed" subspecies: similar to 3 but large-billed (southern Cascades, CA mountains). In fall and winter, some of these types intermingle. **VOICE:** Song brilliant and musical; a varied arrangement of short clear notes and sliding whistles. Call varies by type, a sharp *chink* (type 4) to flatter *chup*. **SIMILAR SPECIES:** Hermit Thrush has reddish tail but lacks streaks on back, is thin-billed, spotted, not striped. **HABITAT:** Wooded undergrowth, brush, feeders.

SONG SPARROW *Melospiza melodia*   Common M617

5¾–6½ in. (15–17 cm). This common midsized sparrow has a *long rounded tail* and *heavy breast streaks* that merge into a *large central spot*. Broad grayish eyebrow. *Juvenile:* More finely streaked, often lacks central spot. Song Sparrows vary widely in color and size, as shown opposite. Many different subspecies are recognized by taxonomists. **VOICE:** Song a variable series of notes, some musical, some buzzy; usually starts with three or four bright repetitious notes, *sweet sweet sweet*, etc. Call a low, nasal *tchep*. **SIMILAR SPECIES:** Savannah Sparrow more of a field bird; often shows yellowish over eye, has shorter notched tail, pinker legs. See Lincoln's and Swamp sparrows. **HABITAT:** Thickets, brush, marshes, roadsides, gardens, feeders.

LINCOLN'S SPARROW   Fairly common in West, uncommon in East M618
Melospiza lincolnii

5¾ in. (15 cm). A somewhat skulking species, prefers to be near cover. Similar to Song Sparrow, but smaller and trimmer, side of face grayer, sharp breast streaks *much finer* and overlay band of *creamy buff* that contrasts with whitish belly and throat; also has narrow whitish eye-ring and buffy mustache. **VOICE:** Song sweet and gurgling; suggests both House Wren and Purple Finch; starts with low passages, rises abruptly, drops. Calls a hard *tik* and buzzy *zzzeeet*. **SIMILAR SPECIES:** Immature Swamp Sparrow has duller breast, with blurry streaks and rustier wing. **HABITAT:** Willow and alder thickets, muskeg, brushy bogs; in winter, thickets, bushes, gardens, sometimes feeders.

VESPER SPARROW *Pooecetes gramineus*   Uncommon M603

6¼ in. (16 cm). *White outer tail feathers* are conspicuous when bird flies. Otherwise suggests slightly largish Savannah Sparrow or grayish Song Sparrow, but has *whitish eye-ring*. Bend of wing chestnut (*often difficult to see*). Note white male's stripe and lack of central crown stripe. **VOICE:** Song throatier than Song Sparrow's; usually begins with two clear minor notes, followed by two higher ones. **SIMILAR SPECIES:** Savannah Sparrow lacks white outer tail feathers and distinct eye-ring. Other sparrowlike field birds with white tail-sides or corners include pipits, longspurs, juncos, and Lark Sparrow. **HABITAT:** Meadows and prairies with scattered trees or bushes (such as sage), roadsides, farm fields.

STREAKED
SPARROWS

"Red" (North and East)

"Slate-colored"
(Rockies)

"Thick-billed"
(CA)

"Sooty"
rthwest
coast)

FOX SPARROW

AK

Southwest

East

(typical)

SONG SPARROW

NCOLN'S
PARROW

VESPER
SPARROW

WHITE-THROATED SPARROW   Common in East, rare in West M620
Zonotrichia albicollis

6¾ in. (17 cm). *Breeding:* A gray-breasted sparrow with white throat and yellow above the lores. Bill grayish. Polymorphic; some adults have black and white head stripes, others brown and tan. *Nonbreeding:* Somewhat duller; darker head stripes varying shades of black, brown, tan. *Immature:* May be somewhat streaked on breast; throat duller. **VOICE:** Song several clear pensive whistles, easily imitated; one or two clear notes, followed by three quavering notes on a different pitch. Call a thin, slurred *tseet;* also a hard *chink.* **SIMILAR SPECIES:** White-crowned Sparrow. **HABITAT:** Thickets, brush, undergrowth of coniferous and mixed woodlands. Visits feeders, preferring to stay on ground.

WHITE-CROWNED SPARROW   Common in West, uncommon in East M622
Zonotrichia leucophrys

7 in. (18 cm). This species comprises multiple subspecies, which exhibit variation in color of lores (whitish or black) and bill (orangey, pinkish, or yellowish). *Adult:* Clear grayish breast, puffy crown *striped with black and white. Immature:* Head stripes dark red-brown and light buff. **VOICE:** Song one or more clear, plaintive whistles (similar to White-throated Sparrow), followed by husky trilled whistles. Variable; many local dialects. Call a sharp *pink.* **SIMILAR SPECIES:** White-throated Sparrow browner, has well-defined white throat, yellow spot before eye, grayish bill. Immature Golden-crowned Sparrow slightly larger, has *duskier bill and underparts,* more muted head pattern, *dull yellowish forehead.* "Gambel's" subspecies nests on western tundra. They have orange bills and pale lores. **HABITAT:** Brush, forest edges, thickets, chaparral, gardens, parks; in winter, also farms, desert washes, feeders.

GOLDEN-CROWNED SPARROW   Fairly common M623
Zonotrichia atricapilla

7¼ in. (18 cm). Similar to White-crowned Sparrow, but without white head stripes; instead, adult has *dull yellow central crown stripe,* bordered broadly with black. Dusky bill. Immature birds and some nonbreeding adults may look like large female House Sparrows but are longer tailed and darker, usually with dull yellow suffusion on forehead. **VOICE:** Song three to five high whistled notes of plaintive minor quality, coming down scale, *oh-dear-me.* Sometimes a faint trill. Call a sharp *tsew.* **SIMILAR SPECIES:** White-crowned Sparrow. **HABITAT:** Boreal and subalpine scrub, willow thickets, stunted spruces; in winter, similar to that of White-crowned (with which it is often found in mixed flocks), but Golden-crowned favors denser shrubs, particularly chaparral.

HARRIS'S SPARROW *Zonotrichia querula*   Uncommon M621

7½ in. (19 cm). Large; size of Fox Sparrow. *Breeding adult: Black crown, face, and bib encircling pink bill. Nonbreeding adult:* Black crown scaled with gray, cheeks mostly tan-brown. *Immature:* Has *white on throat,* less black on crown, buffy brown on rest of head; blotched and streaked on breast. **VOICE:** Song has quavering quality of White-throated Sparrow: clear whistles on same pitch, or one or two at one pitch, the rest slightly lower; general effect *minor.* Alarm call *wink.* **HABITAT:** Stunted boreal forests; in winter, brush, hedgerows, open woods. May mix with White-crowned Sparrows in nonbreeding season.

SPARROWS

tan-striped morph

immature

white-striped morph

WHITE-THROATED SPARROW

WHITE-CROWNED SPARROW

"Gambel's"

immature

immature

adult

GOLDEN-CROWNED SPARROW

breeding adult

adult

immature

HARRIS'S SPARROW

DARK-EYED JUNCO *Junco hyemalis*   Common M624

6–6½ in. (15–16 cm). This hooded sparrow is characterized by *white outer tail feathers* that flash conspicuously as it flies away. Bill and belly usually whitish. Male may have dark hood; female and immature duller. Juvenile in summer finely streaked on breast, hence its white outer tail feathers might even suggest Vesper Sparrow. *Note:* Until 1970s this species was divided into four full species in N. America. Some have gray sides, others rusty or pinkish. They are now lumped as one highly complex species. Intergrades are known. Treated separately, the main subspecies groups are known as follows.

"Oregon" Junco is generally the most widespread subspecies in West. Male has *rusty brown back* with *blackish hood* and *buffy or rusty sides*. Female duller, but note contrast between paler gray hood and brown back, convex shape to lower border of hood.

"Pink-sided" Junco is found from the Rockies westward, south of AK. Has a pale gray hood, pink flanks, and black lores.

"Gray-headed" Junco occurs in Great Basin and s. Rockies. Rufous patch on back of otherwise pale to medium gray plumage, with *gray sides* and *gray head, dark lores*. Breeders in Southwest have bicolored bill.

"Slate-colored" Junco is most northern and eastern form, wintering mainly east of Rockies, sparingly westward. A gray junco with *gray back,* white belly. Female and immature duller gray tinged brownish. The more uniform coloration, lacking rusty areas, is distinctive. Some particularly brownish young birds may be confused with "Oregon" Junco.

"White-winged" Junco breeds in Black Hills region. A large, pale form with gray back; usually has *two whitish wing bars* and exhibits considerably more white in tail (four outer feathers on each side). *Note:* Some "Slate-colored" Juncos can show thin, weak wing bars.

VOICE: Song a loose trill, suggestive of Chipping Sparrow but more musical. Call a light *smack;* also clicking or twittering notes. **HABITAT:** Coniferous and mixed woods. In nonbreeding season, open woods, undergrowth, roadsides, brush, parks, gardens, feeders; usually in flocks, in West sometimes containing multiple subspecies.

YELLOW-EYED JUNCO *Junco phaeonotus*   Uncommon, local M625

6¼ in. (16 cm). Our only junco with *yellow eyes,* which give it a somewhat fierce look. Otherwise like "Gray-headed" Junco except that rufous on back *extends onto wing.* Walks rather than hops. **VOICE:** Song musical, unjunco-like; more complicated, three-part: *chip chip chip, wheedle wheedle, che che che che che.* **HABITAT:** Coniferous forests, pine-oak woods; in winter, some come down to slightly lower elevations in canyons, including at feeders.

DARK-EYED JUNCO

♀

♂

juvenile

"Oregon"

Rockies/Great Basin

"Gray-headed"

♂

"Pink-sided"

♂ Southwest

"Slate-colored"

♀

♂

"White-winged"

♂

♂

YELLOW-EYED JUNCO

LAPLAND LONGSPUR Uncommon to fairly common M627

Calcarius lapponicus

6¼ in. (16 cm). Lapland Longspurs — like Horned Larks, pipits, and other longspurs — are birds of open country; in flight, they appear to have shorter tail. In nonbreeding season, longspurs are often found in flocks of larks. *Breeding male: Black face outlined with white* is distinctive. Rusty collar. *Nonbreeding male:* Sparse black streaks on sides, dull rusty nape, and smudge across breast help identify it. *Breeding female:* Resembles nonbreeding male. *All nonbreeding plumages:* Note *dark frame to rear cheek, rufous brown wing coverts,* tail pattern. **VOICE:** In flight, a dry rattle, also a musical *teew;* when perched, a soft *pee-dle.* Song in display flight is vigorous, musical. **SIMILAR SPECIES:** Smith's Longspur buffier below; note face pattern. Other longspurs have more white in tail. American Pipit and Horned Lark have thin bill, different plumage. **HABITAT:** In summer, tundra; in winter, fields, prairies, shores.

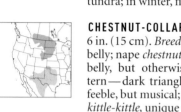

CHESTNUT-COLLARED LONGSPUR *Calcarius ornatus* Uncommon M629

6 in. (15 cm). *Breeding male:* Solid *black* below, except on throat and lower belly; nape *chestnut. Female and nonbreeding:* Adult males show dull black belly, but otherwise all are sparrowlike; best field mark is tail pattern — dark triangle on white tail — and flight call. **VOICE:** Song short, feeble, but musical; suggests Western Meadowlark. Call a finchlike *ji-jiv* or *kittle-kittle,* unique among longspurs. **SIMILAR SPECIES:** McCown's Longspur. **HABITAT:** Plains, native-grass prairies; generally prefers some cover, and winter flocks may disappear in grass until flushed.

MCCOWN'S LONGSPUR *Calcarius mccownii* Uncommon, local M626

6 in. (15 cm). *Breeding male:* Crown and patch on breast black, tail largely white. Hindneck *gray* (brown or chestnut in other longspurs). *Female and nonbreeding male:* Rather plain; note tail pattern (inverted T of black on white) and *swollen-looking, fleshy bill.* Some birds are especially *plain looking,* reminiscent of female House Sparrow. **VOICE:** Song in display flight is clear sweet warbles, suggestive of Lark Bunting. Call a dry rattle, softer than Lapland Longspur's. Also a soft *pink.* **SIMILAR SPECIES:** Breeding male Chestnut-collared Longspur has chestnut collar, black belly; nonbreeding birds darker, more heavily marked below, have slightly smaller and darker bill, different call. **HABITAT:** Plains, prairies, short-grass and dirt fields.

SMITH'S LONGSPUR *Calcarius pictus* Scarce, local M628

6¼ in. (16 cm). This secretive longspur prefers enough grassy cover to disappear in. It is *warm buff on entire underparts.* Tail edged with white, as in Vesper Sparrow and Lapland Longspur. *Breeding male: Deep buff;* ear patch with *white spot,* strikingly outlined by *black triangle. Female and nonbreeding:* Less distinctive; *buffy breast* lightly streaked; small pale spot on side of neck; some males may show white shoulder patch. **VOICE:** Rattling or clicking notes in flight (has been likened to winding of a cheap watch). Song sweet, warblerlike, terminating in *WEchew.* Does not sing in flight. **SIMILAR SPECIES:** Lapland and Chestnut-collared longspurs, Vesper Sparrow, Sprague's Pipit. **HABITAT:** Prairies, fields, airports; in summer, tundra with scattered bushes.

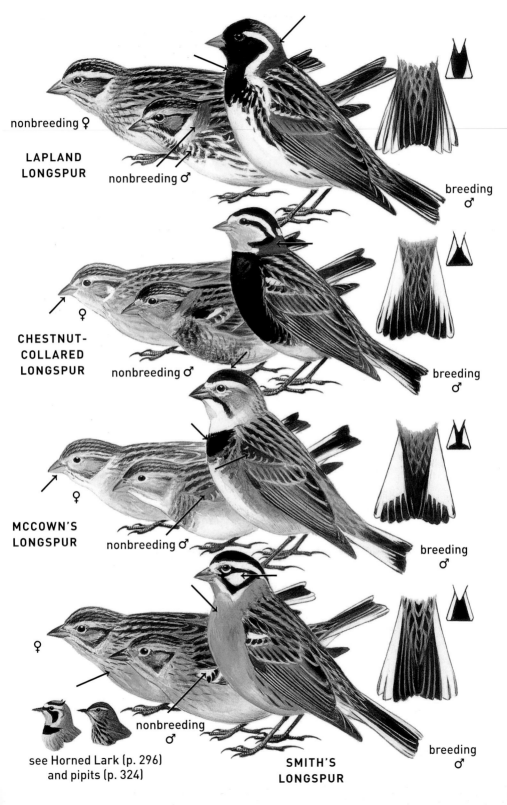

nonbreeding ♀

**LAPLAND
LONGSPUR**

nonbreeding ♂

breeding
♂

**CHESTNUT-
COLLARED
LONGSPUR**

♀

nonbreeding ♂

breeding
♂

**MCCOWN'S
LONGSPUR**

♀

nonbreeding ♂

breeding
♂

♀

nonbreeding
♂

see Horned Lark (p. 296)
and pipits (p. 324)

**SMITH'S
LONGSPUR**

breeding
♂

SNOW BUNTING *Plectrophenax nivalis*   Uncommon **M630**
6¾ in. (17 cm). Snow Buntings often swirl over snowy fields or dunes in flocks, sometimes mixed with Horned Larks or Lapland Longspurs. No other N. American songbird (except McKay's Bunting) shows so much white. In winter some individuals, especially females and immatures, may look quite brown, but when they fly their flashing *white wing patches* identify them. Overhead, Snow Bunting looks almost entirely white, whereas American Pipit and Horned Lark are mostly black-tailed. Breeding male has black back, contrasting with white head and underparts. **VOICE:** Call a sharp, whistled *teer* or *tew;* also a rough, purring *brrt*, both similar to Lapland Longspur's calls. Song a musical *ti-ti-chu-ree,* repeated. **SIMILAR SPECIES:** In w. AK, see McKay's Bunting. Albino landbirds—such as juncos—are sometimes mistaken for Snow Buntings. **HABITAT:** Prairies, fields, dunes, shores. In summer, tundra.

MCKAY'S BUNTING *Plectrophenax hyperboreus*   Scarce, local **M631**
7 in. (18 cm). A specialty of w. AK, breeding regularly only on St. Matthew and Hall Is. *Breeding male:* Almost pure white, except for ends of primaries and scapulars and near tips of central tail feathers. *Breeding female:* Shows some dark on back. *Nonbreeding:* Both sexes have light touches of warm tan-brown above, but less than in Snow Bunting. Wings and tail show more white. Hybridizes with Snow Bunting. **VOICE:** Song of male said to suggest American Goldfinch. **SIMILAR SPECIES:** Breeding male Snow Bunting has *black* back. Female and winter Snow Buntings browner; note coloration and pattern of tail, rump, and back. **HABITAT:** Tundra, barrens, shores; in nonbreeding season, often in mixed flocks with Snow Buntings.

RUSTIC BUNTING *Emberiza rustica*   Vagrant
5¾–6 in. (16 cm). A *rusty,* sparrowlike bird with *rusty* breast-band and *dark cheek outlined in white.* Head slightly crested, bill pink. *Breeding male:* Black head markings. *Female and immature:* Light spot on brown cheek patch, rusty brown sides and rump. **VOICE:** Short, musical jumble of notes, ending on down-slurred *chew.* **SIMILAR SPECIES:** Little Bunting. **RANGE:** Regular Asian stray to w. AK islands, casual farther south.

BRAMBLING   Vagrant
Fringilla montifringilla (Family Fringillidae, p. 400)
6¼ in. (16 cm). *Tawny* or *orangey buff* breast and shoulders, *whitish rump distinctive in flight. Breeding male:* Black head and back. *Female and nonbreeding:* Gray cheek (with dark markings in male) bordered by dark, flanks streaked or spotted. **VOICE:** Call a rising, whiny *zweee;* in flight, a distinctive nasal, hollow *eck.* **SIMILAR SPECIES:** This rarely seen species might be confused with more common N. American birds, including Orchard Oriole, Black-headed Grosbeak, and Spotted or Eastern towhee. **RANGE:** Eurasian species; regular on w. AK islands, casual but widespread records elsewhere in N. America.

BUNTINGS AND BRAMBLING

nonbreeding ♂

nonbreeding ♀

Snow
Bunting

SNOW BUNTING

breeding ♂

♀

Snow
Bunting

♂

breeding ♂

breeding
♀

McKay's
Bunting

♂

MCKAY'S
BUNTING

nonbreeding ♂

breeding ♂

♀

breeding ♂

USTIC BUNTING

nonbreeding
♂

BRAMBLING

CARDINALS, BUNTINGS, AND ALLIES
Family Cardinalidae

Medium-sized songbirds with heavy, seed-crushing bills. Includes the crested cardinals, heavy-billed grosbeaks, and smaller *Passerina* buntings and grosbeak. **FOOD:** Seeds, fruit, insects. **RANGE:** New World.

ROSE-BREASTED GROSBEAK
Pheucticus ludovicianus   Fairly common M634

8 in. (20 cm). *Adult male:* Black and white, with large triangle of rose red on breast and thick pale bill. In flight, pattern of black and white flashes across upperparts. Wing linings rose pink. *Immature male:* In first-autumn plumage similar to female, but has touch of red on buffier breast. *Female:* Streaked, like a large sparrow or female Purple Finch; recognized by large grosbeak bill, broad white wing bars, striped crown, and broad white eyebrow stripe. Wing linings yellow. **VOICE:** Song consists of rising and falling passages; resembles American Robin's song, but given with more feeling (as if a robin had taken voice lessons). Call a squeaky, metallic *kick* or *eek*. **SIMILAR SPECIES:** Female told from female Purple Finch by larger size, boldly striped head, obvious wing bars, and pink bill. Differs from female and immature Black-headed Grosbeak in having *heavily streaked* breast, paler bill. **HABITAT:** Deciduous woods, orchards, groves, thickets, sometimes at feeders in spring.

BLACK-HEADED GROSBEAK
Pheucticus melanocephalus   Fairly common M635

8¼ in. (21 cm). A stocky bird, larger than a sparrow, with outsized bill. *Male:* Breast, collar, and rump *dull orange-brown*. Otherwise, black head and bold black-and-white wing and tail pattern are similar to those of its eastern counterpart, Rose-breasted Grosbeak. In nonbreeding plumage, head appears somewhat striped. *Female and immature:* Largely brown, with sparrowlike streaks above; head strongly patterned with light stripes and dark ear patch. Breast strongly *washed with yellow-buff, ocher-buff, or butterscotch;* dark streaks on sides *fine,* nearly absent across middle of chest. Wing linings yellow. *Maxilla dark.* **VOICE:** Song consists of rising and falling passages; resembles American Robin's song, but more fluent and mellow. Call a flat *ik* or *eek*. **SIMILAR SPECIES:** Rose-breasted Grosbeak. Rarely hybridizes with Rose-breasted where ranges come into contact. **HABITAT:** Deciduous and riparian woods.

CRIMSON-COLLARED GROSBEAK   *Rhodothraupis celaeno*   Vagrant
8½ in. (22 cm). *Male:* A blackish grosbeak with *dark red collar and underparts* encircling throat and chest. Red underparts often spotted or blotched with black. *Female and immature:* Similar to male, but *yellowish green* replaces red. **VOICE:** Song similar to Black-headed Grosbeak; a hoarse, bouncy warble, ending in up-slurred note: *zwee!* **SIMILAR SPECIES:** Female tanagers and orioles. **RANGE:** Mexican species, casual visitor (mostly in winter) to s. TX. **HABITAT:** Brushy woods, second growth.

YELLOW GROSBEAK   *Pheucticus chrysopeplus*   Vagrant
9¼ in. (24 cm). Size and shape of Black-headed Grosbeak. *Male:* Golden yellow and black, suggesting overblown goldfinch except for large, blackish grosbeak bill. *Female:* Duller, with streaked back and crown. **VOICE:** Rich, whistly warble, similar to Black-headed Grosbeak: *cheer-reah, churr-weoh.* **SIMILAR SPECIES:** Evening and Black-headed grosbeaks. **RANGE:** Mexican species, casual visitor to southwestern states. **HABITAT:** Deciduous woods, often near water.

GROSBEAKS

breeding ♂

ROSE-
BREASTED
GROSBEAK

breeding ♂

♀

BLACK-HEADED
GROSBEAK

♀

CRIMSON-COLLARED
GROSBEAK

♀

♂

♂

♀

YELLOW GROSBEAK

NORTHERN CARDINAL *Cardinalis cardinalis*   Common M632
8¾ in. (22 cm). *Male:* An *all-red* bird with pointed *crest* and black patch at base of heavy, *triangular reddish bill. Female:* Buff brown, with some red on wings and tail. *Crest, dark face,* and *heavy reddish orange bill* distinctive. *Juvenile:* Similar to female, but with blackish bill. **VOICE:** Song is clear, slurred whistles, repeated. Several variations: *what-cheer cheer cheer,* etc.; *whoit whoit whoit* or *birdy birdy birdy,* etc.; usually two-part. Call a short, sharp *tik.* **SIMILAR SPECIES:** Pyrrhuloxia. Male Summer and Hepatic tanagers, also all red, lack cardinal's crest. **HABITAT:** Woodland edges, thickets, deserts, towns, gardens, feeders.

PYRRHULOXIA *Cardinalis sinuatus*   Fairly common M633
8¾ in. (22 cm). *Male:* A *slender, gray and red bird,* with *long, spiky crest* and *pale yellowish,* stubby, almost parrotlike bill (strongly curved upper mandible). *Female:* Has gray back, buff breast, and touch of red in wings. Always note spiky crest and *stubby yellow bill.* **VOICE:** Song a clear *quink quink quink quink quink,* on one pitch; also a slurred, whistled *what-cheer, what-cheer,* etc., usually not two-part like Northern Cardinal's song. **SIMILAR SPECIES:** Best told from Northern Cardinal by bill color and shape, also by grayer color overall and spiky crest. **HABITAT:** Mesquite, thorn scrub, deserts, feeders.

BLUE GROSBEAK *Passerina caerulea*   Uncommon M636
6¾ in. (17 cm). *Adult male:* Deep *dull blue,* with thick bill, *two broad rusty or chestnut wing bars.* Often *flips or twitches tail. Immature male:* A mixture of brown and blue. *Female:* About size of Brown-headed Cowbird; warm brown, slightly lighter below, with two *rusty buff wing bars;* rump or tail may be tinged with blue. **VOICE:** Warbling song, phrases rising and falling; suggests Purple or House finch, but slower, more guttural. Call a sharp *chink,* in flight a flat *bzzzt.* **SIMILAR SPECIES:** Female and immature Indigo Bunting also warm brown and have buffy, though weaker, wing bars, but they are smaller, and smaller billed. **HABITAT:** Thickets, hedgerows, riparian undergrowth, brushy hillsides, weedy ditches.

RED AND BLUE FINCHES

NORTHERN CARDINAL

♂

♀

juvenile

PYRRHULOXIA

♂

♀

BLUE GROSBEAK

♂

♀

INDIGO BUNTING *Passerina cyanea*   Common M638

5½ in. (14 cm). *Male:* A small finch, *rich deep blue all over.* In first spring, blue is duller and blotchy. Nonbreeding male more like brown female, but usually with some blue in wings and tail. *Female and immature:* A small, medium to warm brown finch; breast slightly paler with faint *blurry* streaks; buffy wing bars weak or lacking. May hybridize with Lazuli Bunting where ranges overlap. Like Blue Grosbeak, may flick or jerk tail sideways. **VOICE:** Song lively, high, and strident; measured phrases, usually paired: *sweet-sweet, chew-chew,* etc. Call a sharp, thin *spit* and a dry buzz (in flight). **SIMILAR SPECIES:** Blue Grosbeak (larger) has rusty wing bars. Female and immature Lazuli Bunting have slightly duller brown upperparts; more distinct, whitish wing bars; and unstreaked breast (except for juveniles, whose streaks are finer and sharper than Indigo's broader, blurrier streaks). **HABITAT:** Overgrown brushy fields, riparian thickets, bushy wood edges.

BLUE BUNTING *Cyanocompsa parellina*   Vagrant

5½ in. (14 cm). *Male:* Deep blue-black; brighter blue on crown, shoulders, and rump. *Female:* Richer brown than female Indigo Bunting; no bars or streaks; *bill blacker.* **VOICE:** Song a high and sweet jumble of warbled phrases. Call a metallic *chink!* **SIMILAR SPECIES:** Indigo Bunting, Blue Grosbeak. **RANGE:** Mexican visitor, casual to s. TX, mostly in winter. **HABITAT:** Brushy woods with dense cover.

LAZULI BUNTING *Passerina amoena*   Fairly common M637

5½ in. (14 cm). *Breeding male:* A small, turquoise blue finch with burnt orangey breast and white belly, suggesting a bluebird, but with *two white wing bars.* *Nonbreeding male:* Brownish tips to feathers mute some of blue. *Female and immature:* A small finch with unstreaked plain brown back and two pale wing bars (stronger than in female Indigo Bunting); often a trace of blue in wings and tail; breast washed with buff is typically unstreaked except in juvenile, which may retain fine, sharp streaks into fall. Hybrids are regular where range overlaps that of Indigo. **VOICE:** Song similar to Indigo Bunting's, but faster. Calls similar. **SIMILAR SPECIES:** Female Indigo Bunting has less pronounced wing bars, is richer brown above, usually shows faint blurry streaks on breast. **HABITAT:** Open brush, grassy hillsides with scattered bushes, riparian shrubs, grassy patches in chaparral, weedy fields and ditches.

PAINTED BUNTING *Passerina ciris*   Uncommon M640

5½ in. (14 cm). The most gaudily colored N. American songbird. This small finch is size of Chipping Sparrow. *Male:* A patchwork of *blue-violet* on head, *green* on back, *red* on rump and underparts, red orbital ring. *Female and immature: Electric green above,* paling to lemon yellow below; *no other small finch is so green.* *Juvenile:* Grayer above with only tinge of green, duller below. **VOICE:** Song a wiry warble; suggests Warbling Vireo. Call a sharp *chip.* **HABITAT:** Riparian undergrowth, brushy hedgerows, woodland edges, stands of weedy grass.

VARIED BUNTING *Passerina versicolor*   Scarce, local M639

5½ in. (14 cm). *Male:* A small dark finch with plum purple body (looks black at a distance). Crown, face, and rump blue, with *bright red patch on nape;* colored like an Easter egg. *Female:* A small, plain *gray-brown* finch with lighter underparts. *No strong wing bars, breast streaks, or distinctive marks of any kind.* **VOICE:** Song thin, bright, more distinctly phrased, less warbled than Painted Bunting's; notes not as paired as Lazuli Bunting's. **SIMILAR SPECIES:** Female Indigo Bunting warmer brown, with hint of blurry breast streaks. **HABITAT:** Riparian thickets, mesquite and other scrub in washes and lower canyons.

BLUE FINCHES, ETC.

breeding ♂

molting ♂

♀

INDIGO BUNTING

♂

BLUE BUNTING

♀

LAZULI BUNTING

breeding ♂

♂

♀

VARIED BUNTING

♀

♂

PAINTED BUNTING

DICKCISSEL *Spiza americana* (Family Cardinalidae) **Fairly common M641**
6¼ in. (16 cm). A grass- and farmland bird; migrants often travel in large
flocks. Sings from fenceposts and wires. *Male:* Suggests a miniature meadowlark (black bib, yellow chest). Has chestnut shoulder patch. In fall, bib
obscure. *Female and immature:* Much like female House Sparrow, but
with bolder stripe over eye (often tinged yellowish), touch of yellow on
breast, and blue-gray bill. **VOICE:** Song a staccato *dick-ciss-ciss-ciss* or
chup-chup-klip-klip-klip. Call a short, hard buzz, often given in flight. **SIM-
ILAR SPECIES:** Meadowlarks, female House Sparrow. **HABITAT:** Alfalfa and
other fields, meadows, prairies, weedy patches.

LARK BUNTING   **Fairly common M607**
Calamospiza melanocorys (Family Emberizidae)
7 in. (18 cm). A plump, short-tailed prairie bird. Gregarious in nonbreeding season. Note rather *heavy, blue-gray bill. Breeding male: Black,* with
large white wing patches. Female, immature, and nonbreeding male: Brown,
streaked; pattern suggests female Purple Finch. Adult males retain some
black on face, wings, and belly. All show *whitish* or *buffy white wing patches*
and *tail corners.* **VOICE:** Song, given in display flight, composed of cardi-
nal-like slurs, unmusical chatlike *chugs,* piping whistles and trills; each
note repeated 3 to 11 times. Call a flat, mellow *heew.* **SIMILAR SPECIES:**
Male Bobolink has yellow nape patch and white rump. Leucistic blackbirds—those showing odd patches of white in plumage, including
wings—may be confused with male Lark Bunting. **HABITAT:** Plains, prairies; in winter, also weedy desert lowlands and farm fields.

BLACKBIRDS AND ORIOLES Family Icteridae

Varied color patterns; sharp bills. Some black and iridescent; orioles are highly colored.
Sexes unlike. **FOOD:** Insects, fruit, seeds, waste grain, small aquatic life. **RANGE:** New
World; most in Tropics.

EASTERN MEADOWLARK   **Uncommon to fairly common M645**
Sturnella magna
9½ in. (24 cm). In grassy country, a chunky, brown, starling-shaped bird.
When flushed, shows conspicuous white sides on short tail. Several shallow, snappy wingbeats alternate with short glides—like a Spotted Sandpiper. When bird perches on a post, chest shows bright yellow crossed by
black V. Walking, it flicks tail open and shut. Subspecies found in e. N.
America are warmer, darker brown above, with blacker crown, buffier
flanks. Southwestern subspecies—"Lilian's" Meadowlark—paler overall,
with more white in tail. **VOICE:** Song composed of two clear, slurred whistles, musical and pulled out, *tee-yah, tee-yair* (last note slurred and descending). Call a rasping or buzzy *dzrrt;* also a guttural chatter. **SIMILAR
SPECIES:** Western Meadowlark, Dickcissel. **HABITAT:** Open fields and pastures, meadows, prairies, marsh edges; "Lilian's" partial to grasslands.

WESTERN MEADOWLARK *Sturnella neglecta*   **Fairly common M646**
9½ in. (24 cm). Nearly identical to Eastern Meadowlark, but paler above
and on flanks; yellow of throat invades malar area behind bill. Crown
stripes paler, more streaked with buff; wingbeats floppier, more Starlinglike; in the Southwest, "Lilian's" Eastern Meadowlarks are just as pale as
Westerns but show much more white in the tail. Best identified by call
note. **VOICE:** Song variable; 7 to 10 flutelike notes, gurgling and double-
note, unlike clear whistles of Eastern Meadowlark. Calls *chupp* or *chuck*
and a dry rattle. **SIMILAR SPECIES:** Eastern Meadowlark. **HABITAT:** Grasslands, cultivated fields and pastures, meadows, prairies, marsh edges.

OPEN FIELD BIRDS

breeding ♂

DICKCISSEL

♀

nonbreeding

Bobolink (p. 390) for comparison

breeding ♂

♀

(nonbreeding ♂ similar)

LARK BUNTING

EASTERN MEADOWLARK

WESTERN MEADOWLARK

RED-WINGED BLACKBIRD *Agelaius phoeniceus*   Common M643
8½–8¾ in. (22 cm). *Adult male:* Black, with *bright red or orange-red epaulets,* most conspicuous in breeding display. Much of the time red is concealed and only yellowish or off-whitish margin shows. *Immature male:* Sooty brown, mottled (like female), but with red shoulders. *Female:* Brownish, with sharply pointed bill, "blackbird" appearance, and *well-defined dark streaking* below; may have pinkish tinge to throat. Gregarious, traveling and roosting in flocks during nonbreeding season. "Bicolored" subspecies in cen. CA. **VOICE:** Calls a loud *check* and a high, slurred *tee-err.* Song a liquid, gurgling *konk-la-ree* or *o-ka-lay.* **SIMILAR SPECIES:** Other blackbird species, especially Tricolored Blackbird. **HABITAT:** Breeds in marshes, brushy swamps, fields, pastures, roadsides; forages also in cultivated land, feedlots, towns, feeders, etc.

TRICOLORED BLACKBIRD *Agelaius tricolor*   Uncommon, local M644
8½–8¾ in. (22 cm). *Male:* Similar to Red-winged Blackbird, but shoulder patch darker red, with conspicuous *white margin.* (*Note:* Some male Red-wingeds have whitish margins as well.) Overall plumage slightly glossier. *Female:* Darker than most races of Red-winged, particularly on belly, and never shows pinkish on throat, but difficult to identify. See voice. Highly gregarious. Nests in dense colonies often numbering in the hundreds or thousands, whereas Red-winged is territorial. In nonbreeding season, may segregate by sex. **VOICE:** More nasal than Red-winged: *on-ke-kaangh.* A nasal *kemp.* **SIMILAR SPECIES:** Red-winged Blackbird. **HABITAT:** Nests in cattail or tule marshes; forages in fields, farms, feedlots, park lawns.

YELLOW-HEADED BLACKBIRD   Fairly common M647
Xanthocephalus xanthocephalus
9–9¾ in. (23–25 cm). Gregarious. *Adult male:* A robin-sized blackbird, with *yellow or orange-yellow head and breast;* in flight, shows *white wing patch.* *Female and immature male:* Smaller (female) and browner; most of yellow confined to throat and chest; lower breast streaked with white; white wing patch restricted or lacking. **VOICE:** Song consists of low, hoarse rasping notes produced with much effort; suggests rusty hinges. Call a low *kruck* or *kack.* **HABITAT:** Nests in freshwater marshes. Forages in farm fields, open country, feedlots. Often associates with other blackbirds in mixed flocks in fall and winter.

BOBOLINK *Dolichonyx oryzivorus*   Fairly common M642
7 in. (18 cm). *Breeding male:* Our only songbird that is *solid black below and largely white above,* suggesting a dress suit on backward. Has buff-yellow nape. Birds in fresh plumage in spring show extensive brownish tips to dark feathering. *Female and nonbreeding male:* A bit larger than House Sparrow; rich buff-yellow, with dark striping on crown and back. Bill more like a sparrow's than a blackbird's. Note pointed tail feathers. **VOICE:** Song, in hovering flight and quivering descent, ecstatic and bubbling: starts with low, reedy notes and rollicks upward. Flight call a clear *ink,* often heard overhead in migration. **SIMILAR SPECIES:** Male Lark Bunting has white confined to wings. Female Red-winged Blackbird heavily striped below; longer bill, less buff-yellow overall. **HABITAT:** Hayfields, moist meadows, marsh edges.

ICTERIDS
(BLACKBIRDS, ETC.)

red epaulets
hidden

♂

♀

D-WINGED
LACKBIRD

♂

immature ♂
Red-winged
Blackbird

"Bicolored"

♂

♀

TRICOLORED
BLACKBIRD

Tricolored
Blackbird

♂

♀

YELLOW-HEADED
BLACKBIRD

breeding

♂

♀

nonbreeding

BOBOLINK

COMMON GRACKLE *Quiscalus quiscula*   Common M650

12½ in. (32 cm). *Male:* A large, *iridescent,* yellow-eyed blackbird, larger than a robin, with long, wedge-shaped or *keel-shaped (when breeding) tail.* In good light, iridescent purple-blue on head. *Female:* Somewhat smaller and duller, with less wedge-shaped tail. *Juvenile:* Sooty, with dark eyes. "Bronzed" Grackle (New England and west of Appalachians; deep bronze on back and belly) and "Purple" Grackle (seaboard south of New England; greener tinge to back) are separate, identifiable subspecies. **VOICE:** Call *chuck* or *chack.* "Song" a split rasping note. **SIMILAR SPECIES:** Boat-tailed and Great-tailed grackles, Brewer's Blackbird. **HABITAT:** Cropland, towns, parks, feeders, groves; swampy woods; often nests in conifers.

BOAT-TAILED GRACKLE *Quiscalus major*   Fairly common, local M651

Male 16½ in. (42 cm); female 14½ in. (37 cm). *Male:* A very large blackbird; larger than Common Grackle, with longer, more ample tail. More rounded head than other grackles. Males of Atlantic Coast (except in FL) have yellow eyes; those of Gulf region and FL have brown eyes, but some may have dull yellowish eyes. *Female:* Smaller than male; much browner than female Common Grackle and with pale brownish breast. **VOICE:** Harsh *check check check;* harsh whistles and clucks. **SIMILAR SPECIES:** LA westward, see Great-tailed Grackle. **HABITAT:** Largely resident near salt water along coasts, marshes; more widespread habitats in FL.

GREAT-TAILED GRACKLE *Quiscalus mexicanus*   Common M652

Male 18 in. (46 cm); female 15 in. (38 cm). Like several other blackbirds, often found in large flocks. *Male:* A very large, purple-glossed blackbird, distinctly larger than Common Grackle and with longer, more ample tail. *Female:* Smaller than male; dark gray-brown above, warm brown below. Adults of both sexes have yellow eyes. **VOICE:** Harsh *check check check;* also a high *kee-kee-kee-kee.* Shrill, discordant notes, whistles, and clucks. A rapid, upward-slurring *ma-ree.* **SIMILAR SPECIES:** Common Grackle (smaller). Boat-tailed Grackle slightly smaller, with dark eyes (where ranges overlap), rounder crown (male), and slightly shorter, more rounded tail. **HABITAT:** Groves, farms, feedlots, towns, city parks, parking lots.

♂

♂

COMMON
GRACKLE

♀

"Purple"

♂
Atlantic
Coast

"Bronzed"

♀

FL and
Gulf Coast

♂

♂

BOAT-TAILED
GRACKLE

♂

♀

GREAT-TAILED
GRACKLE

RUSTY BLACKBIRD *Euphagus carolinus*   Uncommon M648
9 in. (23 cm). Rusty only in fall and winter; otherwise suggests Brewer's Blackbird. *Breeding male:* A medium-sized blackbird with pale yellow eye. Black head may show faint *greenish* gloss (not purplish). *Breeding female:* Slate colored, with *light eye. Nonbreeding and immature:* Variably *washed with rusty,* including *rusty edgings to flight feathers, buffy eyebrow, narrow dark patch through eye;* males *barred* below, have pale gray rump. **VOICE:** Call *chack.* "Song" a split creak, like a rusty hinge: *kush-a-lee,* alternating with *ksh-lay.* **SIMILAR SPECIES:** Brewer's Blackbird, Common Grackle. **HABITAT:** River groves, wooded swamps, muskeg, pond edges.

BREWER'S BLACKBIRD *Euphagus cyanocephalus*   Common M649
9 in. (23 cm). A common and familiar blackbird in w. N. America. *Male:* All black, with whitish eye; in good light, *purplish* reflections may be seen on head and neck, with some greenish reflections on body. *Female:* Brownish gray, with *dark* eye. **VOICE:** Song a harsh, wheezy, creaking *ksh-eee.* Call *chack.* **SIMILAR SPECIES:** Breeding male Rusty Blackbird flatter black with dull *greenish* head reflections (hard to see); bill slightly longer. Female Rusty has *light* eye. Unlike Rusty (both sexes), adult Brewer's remain in same plumage year-round and do not acquire a rusty look in fall and winter. See also Brown-headed Cowbird. **HABITAT:** Fields, mountain meadows, prairies, farms, feedlots, towns, parks, lawns, shopping malls, parking lots.

BROWN-HEADED COWBIRD *Molothrus ater*   Common M655
7½ in. (19 cm). A rather small blackbird with short, sparrowlike bill. *Male:* Black with *brown head (may appear all black in poor light). Female:* Gray-brown with lighter throat; note short *finchlike bill. Juvenile:* Paler than female. Buffy gray, with soft breast streaking and pale scaling (edges) above; this plumage held into early fall. Often seen being fed by smaller birds whose nests have been parasitized. Young males in fall molt patterned with splotches of tan and black. When flocking with other blackbirds, cowbirds look smaller and feed on ground with tails lifted high. **VOICE:** Flight call *weee-titi* (high whistle, two lower notes). Song a bubbly and creaky *glug-glug-gleeee.* Call *chuck.* **SIMILAR SPECIES:** Gray-brown female can be told from female Brewer's and Rusty blackbirds by its *stubby bill* and smaller size. Juvenile starling has longer bill, shorter tail. Juvenile cowbirds are often misidentified as nonblackbirds. **HABITAT:** In nesting season, where passerine nest-hosts are numerous, a variety of forests and woodlands; also farms, fields, feedlots, roadsides, towns, parks, lawns, feeders. Parasitizes a wide variety of smaller bird nests. Never builds its own nest.

BRONZED COWBIRD *Molothrus aeneus*   Fairly common M654
8½–8¾ in. (21–22 cm). *Male:* Slightly larger and more *bull-headed* than Brown-headed Cowbird. Does *not* have brown head. Bill longer. *Red eye* can be seen only at close range. In breeding season, has conspicuous *ruff* on nape. *Female:* Smaller nape ruff; dark gray overall, darker than female Brown-headed. **VOICE:** High-pitched mechanical creakings. Male's display very animated. **SIMILAR SPECIES:** Other cowbirds. **HABITAT:** Cropland, brush, semiopen country, feedlots.

SHINY COWBIRD *Molothrus bonariensis*   Scarce, local M653
7½ in. (19 cm). *Male:* Same size as Brown-headed Cowbird, but black with overall violet gloss, thin pointed bill. *Female:* Warm brown, slightly thinner, blacker bill compared with Brown-headed. **VOICE:** Series of liquid burbles, ending in thin whistled note. **SIMILAR SPECIES:** Other cowbirds. **RANGE:** An invader to s. FL since 1985. Scattered records from as far north as NB and west to OK. **HABITAT:** Agricultural areas, disturbed habitats, suburban lawns.

ICTERIDS (BLACKBIRDS, ETC.)

breeding ♂

breeding ♀

RUSTY BLACKBIRD

nonbreeding ♂

♀

BREWER'S BLACKBIRD

variant immature ♂

♂

BROWN-HEADED COWBIRD

♂

♀

juvenile

molting immature ♂

♀

♂

BRONZED COWBIRD

♂

SHINY COWBIRD

ORCHARD ORIOLE *Icterus spurius* — Fairly common M656

7–7¼ in. (18 cm). A small, short- and straight-billed oriole. Often flicks tail sideways. *Male:* All dark; rump and underparts *deep chestnut. Female and immature:* Olive or greenish gray above, yellowish below; two white wing bars. First-spring male has black bib down to chest. **VOICE:** Song a fast-moving outburst interspersed with piping whistles and guttural notes. Suggests Purple or House finch. A strident slurred *wheeer!* at or near end is distinctive. Call a soft *chuck.* **SIMILAR SPECIES:** Some female and immature Baltimore Orioles have black throat (as do immature male Orchards), but are slightly larger and more orange. Female Scarlet and Summer tanagers lack wing bars, have different bill shape. Females and immatures difficult to tell from young Hooded Orioles but note Hooded's more curved bill, longer tail, and weaker wing bars. See voice. **HABITAT:** Wood edges, orchards, shade trees; more likely than other orioles to be seen in brushy areas.

BALTIMORE ORIOLE *Icterus galbula* — Fairly common M662

8¼–8½ in. (21–22 cm). *Adult male:* Flame orange and black, with solid black head, orange sides to tail. *Female and immature:* Olive-brown above, burnt orange-yellow below; two white wing bars. Many adult females have traces of black on head, suggesting hood of male. Some immature females very dull, with grayer back, limited orange (mostly on plain face and breast), and whitish vent; much like female Bullock's Oriole. **VOICE:** Song rich, piping whistles. Call a low, whistled *hewli.* Chatter call not as rough as Bullock's. **SIMILAR SPECIES:** Female Orchard Oriole greener than female Baltimore. Dull female Baltimore much like female Bullock's, but latter has more distinct dark eye line and yellowish supercilium, plain gray back lacking dark scalloping, and yellowish rather than orange undertail coverts. **HABITAT:** Open deciduous woods, elms, shade trees.

BULLOCK'S ORIOLE *Icterus bullockii* — Fairly common M658

8¼–8½ in. (21–22 cm). *Adult male:* Note *orange cheeks* and *dark eye line, large white wing patches,* and *black-tipped tail. Female:* Dark eye line, yellowish supercilium, plain gray back, *whitish belly. Immature male:* Similar to female, but slightly more orange and has black goatee. May hybridize with Baltimore Oriole. **VOICE:** Accented double notes and one or two piping notes. Calls include a rough chatter and low *churp.* **SIMILAR SPECIES:** Baltimore Oriole; also Hooded and Orchard orioles. **HABITAT:** Deciduous and riparian woods, oaks, shade trees, ranch yards; small numbers winter in blooming eucalyptus in CA.

SPOT-BREASTED ORIOLE *Icterus pectoralis* — Uncommon, local M659

9¼–9½ in. (24 cm). Note *orange crown,* black bib, and black spots on sides of breast. Much white in wing. **VOICE:** Song a long, melodic series of whistles, slower than other orioles. **SIMILAR SPECIES:** Baltimore Oriole. Spot-breasted Oriole has orange crown. **HABITAT:** Flowering trees, residential areas.

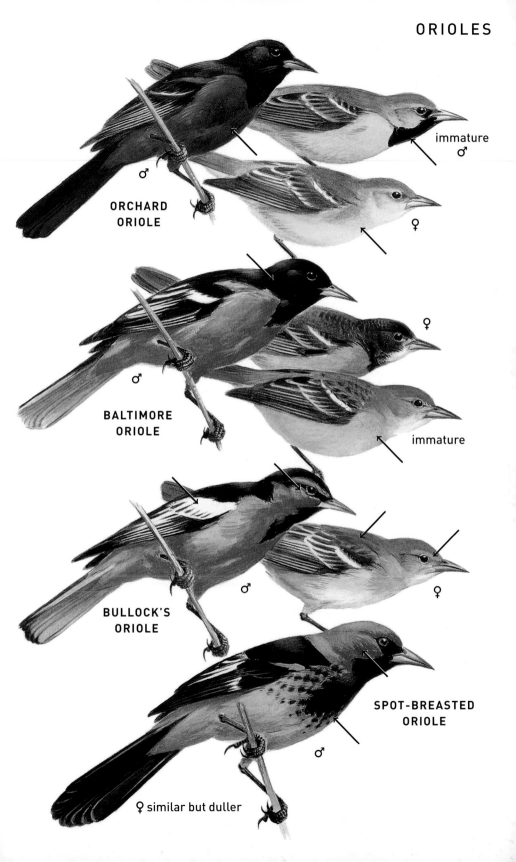

ORIOLES

ORCHARD
ORIOLE

♂

immature
♂

♀

BALTIMORE
ORIOLE

♂

♀

immature

BULLOCK'S
ORIOLE

♂

♀

SPOT-BREASTED
ORIOLE

♂

♀ similar but duller

HOODED ORIOLE *Icterus cucullatus*   Fairly common M657

7½–8 in. (19–20 cm). *Male:* Orange and black, with black throat and *orange crown*. In winter, back obscurely scaled. *Female:* Similar to female Bullock's Oriole, but bill longer, slightly curved; more extensively yellow below; back olive-gray; head and tail more yellowish. Call different. *Immature:* Like female, with slightly shorter bill; much like female Orchard Oriole. **VOICE:** Song consists of rambling, grating notes and piping whistles: *chut chut chut whew whew;* opening notes throaty. Call an up-slurred, whistled *eek* or *wheenk*. **SIMILAR SPECIES:** Orchard and Scott's orioles. **HABITAT:** Open woods, shade trees, towns, gardens, palms.

ALTAMIRA ORIOLE *Icterus gularis*   Uncommon, local M660

10 in. (25 cm). Similar to male Hooded Oriole, but larger, with thicker bill. Upper wing bar yellow or orange, not white. Sexes similar. **VOICE:** Song disjointed whistled notes. A harsh "fuss" note. **SIMILAR SPECIES:** Other orange orioles. **HABITAT:** Scrubby woodlands, often near water. Its name, in Spanish, means "look high." And this is often where this species is found — in treetops.

STREAK-BACKED ORIOLE *Icterus pustulatus*   Vagrant

8¼ in. (21 cm). Breeding adult has *streaked back*. Much white in wing. Otherwise resembles Hooded Oriole or perhaps immature male Bullock's Oriole. *Male:* Basically yellow-orange, head much deeper orange. *Female:* Duller, back more olivaceous, but streaking still obvious. **VOICE:** Rich warble, similar to Baltimore or Bullock's oriole. **SIMILAR SPECIES:** Adult male Hooded Oriole in winter shows crescent-shaped dark edges to back feathers, not streaks, and bill not as thick at base. **RANGE:** Very rare visitor from Mex., mostly in fall and winter, to AZ; casual west to CA and east to TX. **HABITAT:** Arid scrub, woodland edges.

AUDUBON'S ORIOLE *Icterus graduacauda*   Uncommon, local M661

9½ in. (24 cm). A yellow oriole with black wings, head, and tail. Yellowish back distinctive. Other male orioles have black back. Sexes similar, but female duller. **VOICE:** Disjointed notes suggesting a child learning to whistle. **SIMILAR SPECIES:** Scott's Oriole. Green Jay at a distance looks yellow with a black head. **HABITAT:** Riparian woods.

SCOTT'S ORIOLE *Icterus parisorum*   Uncommon M663

8¾–9 in. (22–23 cm). *Adult male:* Solid black head and back and *lemon yellow* pattern distinguish it. *Female:* More greenish yellow below and more olivey gray and streaked above than other female orioles. Many have black on throat and face. **VOICE:** Song composed of rich fluty whistles; suggests Western Meadowlark. Call a harsh *chuck*. **SIMILAR SPECIES:** Female Hooded and Bullock's orioles. **HABITAT:** Dry woods and scrub in desert mountains, yucca forests, Joshua trees, pinyon-juniper, sugar-water feeders. Also eucalyptus and date palms in winter.

ORIOLES

immature ♂

♂

♀

HOODED ORIOLE

ALTAMIRA ORIOLE

♂

STREAK-BACKED ORIOLE

AUDUBON'S ORIOLE

♀

♂

immature

SCOTT'S ORIOLE

Fringilline and Cardueline Finches and Allies Family Fringillidae

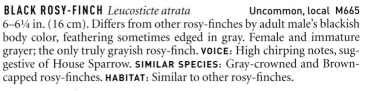

These birds have a seed-cracking bill, relatively short, notched tail, and somewhat undulating flight. Sexes usually unlike. Tend to be more arboreal than sparrows. **FOOD**: Seeds, insects, small fruit. **RANGE**: Worldwide.

BLACK ROSY-FINCH *Leucosticte atrata*   Uncommon, local M665
6–6¼ in. (16 cm). Differs from other rosy-finches by adult male's blackish body color, feathering sometimes edged in gray. Female and immature grayer; the only truly grayish rosy-finch. **VOICE**: High chirping notes, suggestive of House Sparrow. **SIMILAR SPECIES**: Gray-crowned and Brown-capped rosy-finches. **HABITAT**: Similar to other rosy-finches.

BROWN-CAPPED ROSY-FINCH   Uncommon, local M666
Leucosticte australis
6–6¼ in. (16 cm). The plainest rosy-finch. Like Gray-crowned, but male has more restricted gray on head, darker crown. Female and immature much drabber than male. **VOICE**: High chirping notes, suggestive of House Sparrow. **SIMILAR SPECIES**: Gray-crowned and Black rosy-finches. **HABITAT**: Similar to other rosy-finches.

GRAY-CROWNED ROSY-FINCH *Leucosticte tephrocotis*   Uncommon M664
6–8 in. (16–20 cm). A large sparrow-sized bird of high snowfields and maritime tundra; it walks, not hops. Several subspecies; vary in size and amount of gray on head. *Male: Dark brown*, with *pinkish wash* on belly, wings, and rump. *Light gray patch* on back of head; in some subspecies cheeks also gray. *Female and immature:* Duller; gray patch reduced or almost wanting. "Hepburn's" subspecies breeds in western mountains from AK and YT south to Cascades. Widespread in winter. **VOICE**: High chirping notes, suggestive of House Sparrow. **SIMILAR SPECIES**: Black and Brown-capped rosy-finches. **HABITAT**: Rocky summits, alpine cirques and snowfields; also rocky islands (off AK); winters in open country at mid- and lower elevations, regular at feeders in mountain towns.

WHITE-WINGED CROSSBILL *Loxia leucoptera* Uncommon, irregular M672
6½ in. (17 cm). All plumages show *crossed mandibles, bold white wing bars,* and white tertial tips. *Male: Dull rose pink. Female and immature:* Olive-gray, with yellowish rump. *Juvenile:* Heavily streaked. **VOICE**: Calls a liquid *peet* and a dry *chif-chif.* Song a succession of loud trills on different pitches. **SIMILAR SPECIES**: Red Crossbill may show a single weak wing bar, but not two broad ones, and it lacks white tips to tertials. **HABITAT**: Spruce and fir forests, hemlocks; very rarely at feeders.

RED CROSSBILL *Loxia curvirostra*   Uncommon, irregular M671
5¾–7 in. (14–17 cm). This erratic wanderer has a heavy head and short tail. Note *crossed mandibles* and *plain wings.* The sound when it cracks cones of evergreens often betrays its presence. Usually found in *flocks. Male: Dull red,* brighter on rump. Subadult males are more orange. *Female and immature:* Dull olive-gray to mustard yellow; yellowish on rump. *Juvenile:* Streaked above and below, suggesting a large Pine Siskin; note bill. Many subspecies vary slightly in bill size, body size, and color; most readily distinguished by flight call. **VOICE**: Call a hard *jip-jip* or *kip-kip-kip* (in some populations, *kwit-kwit* or *kewp-kewp*). Song consists of finchlike warbled passages, *jip-jip-jip-jeeaa-jeeaa;* trills, *chips.* **SIMILAR SPECIES**: White-winged Crossbill has white wing bars in all plumages. **HABITAT**: Variety of conifers; rarely at feeders. Erratic and irruptive wanderings, especially in winter.

ROSY-FINCHES AND CROSSBILLS

BLACK ROSY-FINCH

BROWN-CAPPED ROSY-FINCH

Immature

♀

♂

♂

"Hepburn's"

Gray-crowned Rosy-Finch

Pribilofs
♂

♂

GRAY-CROWNED ROSY-FINCH

♂

♀

WHITE-WINGED CROSSBILL

♀

♂

RED CROSSBILL

COMMON REDPOLL *Carduelis flammea*　　　Uncommon, irregular M673

5¼ in. (13 cm). Note *bright red forehead* and *black chin* of this little winter finch. Male has *pink breast;* female lacks this. Usually found in flocks. **VOICE:** In flight, a rattling *chet-chet-chet.* Song a trill, followed by the rattling *chet-chet-chet.* **SIMILAR SPECIES:** Hoary Redpoll, Pine Siskin. Male House and Purple finches larger, redder, have red rump; lack black chin. **HABITAT:** Birches, tundra scrub. In winter, weeds, brush, thistle feeders.

HOARY REDPOLL *Carduelis hornemanni*　　　Rare, irregular M674

5¼–5½ in. (13–14 cm). In nonbreeding season, often found in flocks of Common Redpolls. *Very similar.* Look for a "frostier" bird, with whiter rump containing *little or no streaking.* Also note *stubbier bill* and lighter streaking on flanks and undertail coverts. Some individuals *very difficult to identify.* **VOICE:** In flight, a rattling *chet-chet-chet.* Song a trill, followed by the rattling *chet-chet-chet.* **SIMILAR SPECIES:** Common Redpoll, Pine Siskin. **HABITAT:** Birches, tundra scrub. In winter, weeds, brush, feeders.

HOUSE FINCH *Carpodacus mexicanus*　　　Common M670

5¾–6 in. (14–15 cm). Slimmer than Purple or Cassin's finch with longer, more square-tipped tail. *Male:* Breast, forehead, stripe over eye, and rump vary from *red to orange to almost deep yellow* (diet related). Note *dark streaks* on sides and belly. *Female:* Streaked brown; separated from slightly larger female Purple and Cassin's finches by its smaller head, bill, and *bland face.* **VOICE:** Song bright, loose, and disjointed; often ends in nasal *wheer.* Call suggests a House Sparrow's *chirp,* but more musical. **SIMILAR SPECIES:** Purple and Cassin's finches. **HABITAT:** Cities, suburbs, farms. Bacterial infection of eyes has reduced numbers in some areas.

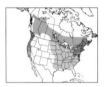

PURPLE FINCH *Carpodacus purpureus*　　　Uncommon M668

6 in. (15 cm). Like a sparrow dipped in raspberry juice. *Adult male:* Dull rose red, brightest on head, chest, and rump. Flanks unstreaked. *Female and immature:* Heavily streaked, brown; similar to female House Finch, but note *broad dark jaw stripe,* dark *ear patch,* broad light stripe behind eye, more deeply notched tail, undertail coverts with few or no streaks. **VOICE:** Song a fast lively warble; call a dull, flat, metallic *pik* or *tick.* **SIMILAR SPECIES:** Cassin's and House finches. East of Rockies, see Rosebreasted Grosbeak. **HABITAT:** Woods, groves, suburbs, feeders.

CASSIN'S FINCH *Carpodacus cassinii*　　　Fairly common M669

6¼ in. (16 cm). *Adult male:* Very similar to Purple Finch, but red of breast paler; *red crown patch contrasts abruptly* with brown of nape; bill has straighter ridge. *Female and immature:* Whiter underparts, sharper streaking above and below, streaked undertail coverts, pale eye-ring, and bill shape distinguish it from Purple Finch. **VOICE:** Song flutier and more varied than Purple's. Call a musical *chidiup.* **HABITAT:** Conifers in mountains; some move to lower elevations in winter.

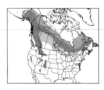

PINE GROSBEAK *Pinicola enucleator*　　　Scarce, irregular M667

8¾–9 in. (23 cm). Near size of a robin; a large, tame finch with dark, stubby bill, longish tail. Flight undulating. May be seen on dirt roads eating grit. *Adult male:* Dull *rose red,* wings dark with *two white wing bars. Female:* Gray, with two white wing bars; head and rump tinged with dull mustard yellow. *Immature male:* Similar to gray female, but with touch of russet on head and rump. **VOICE:** Song a rich, rapid warbling. Call a musical *chee-vli* in West; *pe-pew-pew* in East. **SIMILAR SPECIES:** Crossbills, Purple Finch. **HABITAT:** Conifers, particularly lodgepole pines, larches; in winter, also mixed woods, crabapples and other fruiting trees, ashes. Much less irruptive in West than in East.

RED FINCHES, ETC.

orange
variant

♂

♀

♂

HOUSE FINCH

COMMON
REDPOLL

♀

♂

HOARY
REDPOLL

♂

♀

PURPLE
FINCH

♂

♂

♀

CASSIN'S
FINCH

♂

♀

PINE GROSBEAK

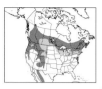

EVENING GROSBEAK

Uncommon, irregular M679

Coccothraustes vespertinus

8 in. (20 cm). Size of a starling. A *chunky, short-tailed* finch with *very large, pale, conical bill* (sometimes tinged greenish). *Male:* Dull yellow, with darker head, *yellow eyebrow,* and black-and-white wings; suggests an overgrown American Goldfinch. *Female:* Silver gray, with enough yellow, black, and white to be recognized. Gregarious. In flight, overall shape and *large white wing patches* identify this species. **VOICE:** Song a short, uneven warble. Also a ringing, finchlike *clee-ip;* a high, clear *thew.* **SIMILAR SPECIES:** American Goldfinch (much smaller), female crossbills. **HABITAT:** Coniferous and mixed forests; in winter, box elders, fruiting shrubs, feeders.

AMERICAN GOLDFINCH *Carduelis tristis*

Common M678

5 in. (13 cm). Goldfinches are distinguished from other small, olive-yellow birds (warblers, etc.) by their short, conical bill and behavior. *Breeding male:* A small yellow bird with *black forehead and wings;* tail also black; bill pale. *Breeding female:* Dull yellow-olive; darker above, with blackish wings and conspicuous wing bars. *Nonbreeding:* Both sexes much like breeding female, but gray-brown; yellow on throat, bill dark. **VOICE:** Song clear, light, canary-like. In undulating flight, each dip is punctuated by *ti-DEE-di-di* or *per-chik-o-ree* or *po-ta-to-chip.* **SIMILAR SPECIES:** Lesser and Lawrence's goldfinches, Pine Siskin. Yellow Warbler yellowish all over, including wings and tail. **HABITAT:** Patches of thistles and weeds, dandelions on lawns, sweet-gum balls, roadsides, open woods, edges; in winter, also feeders, where often in flocks.

LESSER GOLDFINCH *Carduelis psaltria*

Fairly common M676

4½ in. (11 cm). *Male:* A very small finch with *black cap,* black or greenish back, and yellow underparts; white on wings. Black cap retained in winter. Males of subspecies *psaltria* (s. Rockies) have *black* back; males of western subspecies *hesperophilus* have *greenish* back. Some birds have mottled back. *Female:* Similar to nonbreeding American Goldfinch, but usually yellower below, has *less contrasting wing bars, yellowish* (not white) *undertail coverts,* and *dark rump.* Calls differ. **VOICE:** Sweet, plaintive, whiny notes, *tee-yee* (rising) and *tee-yer* (dropping). Song more phrased than American Goldfinch's; will imitate some other bird calls. **SIMILAR SPECIES:** American Goldfinch. **HABITAT:** Open brushy and weedy country, open woods, wooded streams, towns, parks, gardens, feeders.

LAWRENCE'S GOLDFINCH

Uncommon, irregular M677

Carduelis lawrencei

4¾ in. (12 cm). Known in all plumages by *large amount of yellow in wings.* *Male:* Has bold *black face* (including chin). *Female and immature:* Very *plain and gray.* **VOICE:** Song similar to Lesser Goldfinch's, but with high tinkling notes and even more mimicry. Call distinctive: *tink-oo,* syllables emphasized equally. **SIMILAR SPECIES:** Other goldfinches. **HABITAT:** Oak-pine and riparian woodland edges, chaparral, ranch yards, parks; often found near isolated water sources such as stream pools, stock tanks.

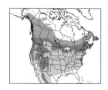

PINE SISKIN *Carduelis pinus*

Fairly common, irregular M675

5 in. (13 cm). Size of a goldfinch. A small, dark, *heavily streaked* finch with deeply notched tail, sharply pointed bill. *A touch of yellow in wings* and at *base of tail* (not always evident). Often first detected by voice, flying over. **VOICE:** Call a loud *chlee-ip;* also a light *tit-i-tit;* a buzzy *shreeeee.* Song suggests goldfinch, but coarser, wheezy. **SIMILAR SPECIES:** Nonbreeding American Goldfinch lacks streaks. Female House Finch has stubbier bill, less notch in tail. Common Redpoll has red forehead. All lack yellow in wings and tail. **HABITAT:** Conifers, mixed woods, alders, sweet-gum balls, weedy areas, feeders.

YELLOW FINCHES, ETC.

♂

♀

EVENING GROSBEAK

nonbreeding ♂

breeding ♂

♀

AMERICAN
GOLDFINCH

♂

♀

black-backed

green-backed

LESSER
GOLDFINCH

♀

♂

♂

♀

PINE
SISKIN

LAWRENCE'S
GOLDFINCH

OLD WORLD SPARROWS Family Passeridae

Old World sparrows differ from our native sparrows (which are in the Emberizidae family) in several subtle ways, including having a more curved culmen (ridge on bill). The introduced and widespread House Sparrow is the best-known species. **FOOD:** Mainly insects, seeds. **RANGE:** Widespread in Old World, two species introduced in New World.

HOUSE SPARROW *Passer domesticus*   Common M680
6¼ in. (16 cm). Introduced from Europe in 1840. Familiar to many people. Sooty city birds often bear little resemblance to clean country males with *black throat, white cheeks, chestnut nape.* Much plainer female and young lack black throat, have dingy breast, and dull eye stripe *behind eye only;* note *single bold wing bar.* **VOICE:** Hoarse *chirp* and *shillip* notes, also a rising *sweep.* **SIMILAR SPECIES:** Female Dickcissel, buntings, sparrows, Eurasian Tree Sparrow. **HABITAT:** Cities, towns, farms, feeders.

EURASIAN TREE SPARROW *Passer montanus*   Uncommon, local
6 in. (15 cm). Both sexes resemble male House Sparrow, but black throat patch smaller. Key mark is *black ear spot.* Crown brown. **VOICE:** Higher pitched than House Sparrow's. A metallic *chik* or *chup,* a repeated *chit-tchup.* In flight, a hard *tek, tek.* **SIMILAR SPECIES:** House Sparrow. **RANGE:** Introduced from Europe around St. Louis in 1870. Some northward expansion since then. Accidental to NE, NB, MN. **HABITAT:** Farmland, weedy patches, locally in residential areas, feeders.

EUROPEAN GOLDFINCH *Carduelis carduelis* (Family Fringillidae)
5½ in. (14 cm). Occasional reports, mostly at feeders. Assumed to be all or almost all escaped captive birds. Note red face, yellow wing patches.

WEAVERS Family Ploceidae

Old World family including weavers and bishops. Escaped captives established very locally in s. CA and possibly very locally elsewhere. **FOOD:** Seeds, insects. **RANGE:** Native to Old World. Several species introduced.

ORANGE BISHOP *Euplectes franciscanus*   Uncommon, local
4¼ in. (10 cm). This small member of the weaver finch family is native to Africa but has been introduced in CA, Puerto Rico, and Bermuda. There is a local established population in Los Angeles area. Short tail, large head, large bill. *Breeding male: Bright reddish body; black face, bill, belly. Female and nonbreeding male:* Similar to female House Sparrow or Grasshopper Sparrow, but with larger, *paler bill, short tail.*

ESTRILDID FINCHES Family Estrildidae

Old World family represented in N. America by escaped cage birds, including Nutmeg Mannikin.

NUTMEG MANNIKIN *Lonchura punctulata*   Uncommon, local
4½ in. (11 cm). A small, dark finch, native to se. Asia but introduced to CA and s. FL. Established very locally in moderate numbers in s. CA. *Adult:* Dark, *cocoa brown* body, large dark bill, brown *belly checked with white.* Sexes similar. *Juvenile:* Pale brown overall, bill dark.

INTRODUCED FINCHLIKE BIRDS

EURASIAN TREE SPARROW

♂

♀

HOUSE SPARROW

juvenile

Brown-headed Cowbird (p. 394) for comparison

♀

EUROPEAN GOLDFINCH

♀

ORANGE BISHOP

breeding ♂

NUTMEG MANNIKIN

adult

MAPS

LIFE LIST

INDEX

RANGE MAPS

The maps on the following pages are approximate, giving the general outlines of the range of each species. Within these broad outlines may be many gaps — areas ecologically unsuitable for the species. A Marsh Wren must have a marsh, a Ruffed Grouse a woodland or a forest. Certain species may be extremely local or sporadic for reasons that may or may not be clear. Some birds are extending their ranges, a few explosively. Others are declining or even disappearing from large areas where they were formerly found. Winter ranges are often not as definite as breeding ranges. A species may exist at a very low density near the northern limits of its winter range, surviving through December in mild seasons but often succumbing to the bitter conditions of January and February. Varying weather conditions and food supplies from year to year may result in substantial variations in winter bird populations.

The maps are specific only for the area covered by this field guide. The Mallard, for example, is found over a large part of the globe. The map shows only its range in North America.

The maps are based on data culled from many publications (particularly from monographs detailing the status and distribution of a state or province's avifauna, as well as from breeding bird atlases), from such journals as *North American Birds* (formerly *American Birds* and *Audubon Field Notes*), and from communication with many state and provincial experts from throughout North America.

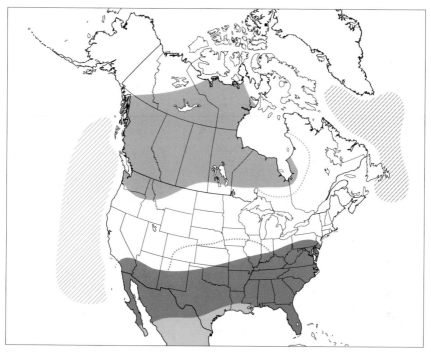

Many maps include comments on population increases and declines, extralimital occurrences, and regular winter or summer ranges outside North America. Migration routes are not depicted in these maps, but side notes sometimes include information on migration. Maps are likewise not filled in with solid color if the species is considered rare, very rare, casual, accidental, and/or a vagrant. Migrants can often be found in suitable habitat in those areas that lie between summering/breeding areas and wintering/nonbreeding areas.

Key to Range Maps

- **Red**: summer range
- **Blue**: winter range
- **Purple**: year-round range
- **Red dash line**: approximate limits of irregular summer range and/ or post-breeding dispersal
- **Blue dash line**: approximate limits of irregular winter range
- **Purple dash line**: approximate limits of irregular year-round range
- **Striped area**: pelagic range

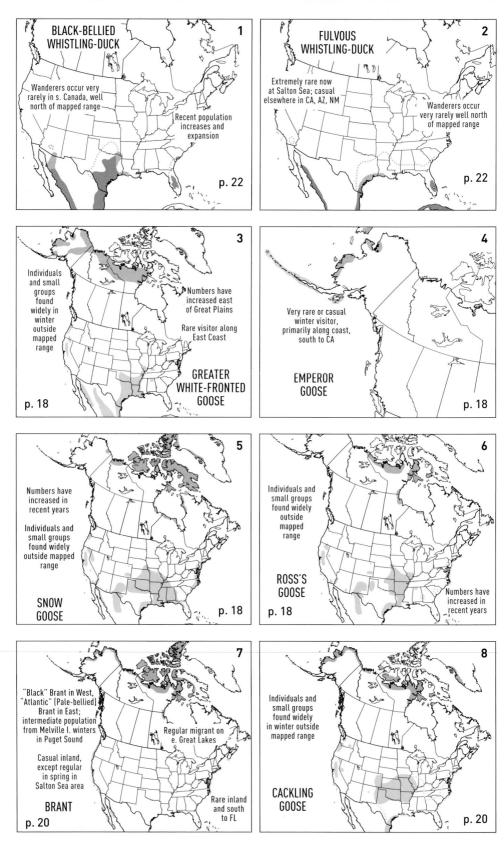

1 BLACK-BELLIED WHISTLING-DUCK

Wanderers occur very rarely in s. Canada, well north of mapped range

Recent population increases and expansion

p. 22

2 FULVOUS WHISTLING-DUCK

Extremely rare now at Salton Sea; casual elsewhere in CA, AZ, NM

Wanderers occur very rarely well north of mapped range

p. 22

3 GREATER WHITE-FRONTED GOOSE

Individuals and small groups found widely in winter outside mapped range

Numbers have increased east of Great Plains

Rare visitor along East Coast

p. 18

4 EMPEROR GOOSE

Very rare or casual winter visitor, primarily along coast, south to CA

p. 18

5 SNOW GOOSE

Numbers have increased in recent years

Individuals and small groups found widely outside mapped range

p. 18

6 ROSS'S GOOSE

Individuals and small groups found widely outside mapped range

Numbers have increased in recent years

p. 18

7 BRANT

"Black" Brant in West, "Atlantic" (Pale-bellied) Brant in East; intermediate population from Melville I. winters in Puget Sound

Casual inland, except regular in spring in Salton Sea area

Regular migrant on e. Great Lakes

Rare inland and south to FL

p. 20

8 CACKLING GOOSE

Individuals and small groups found widely in winter outside mapped range

p. 20

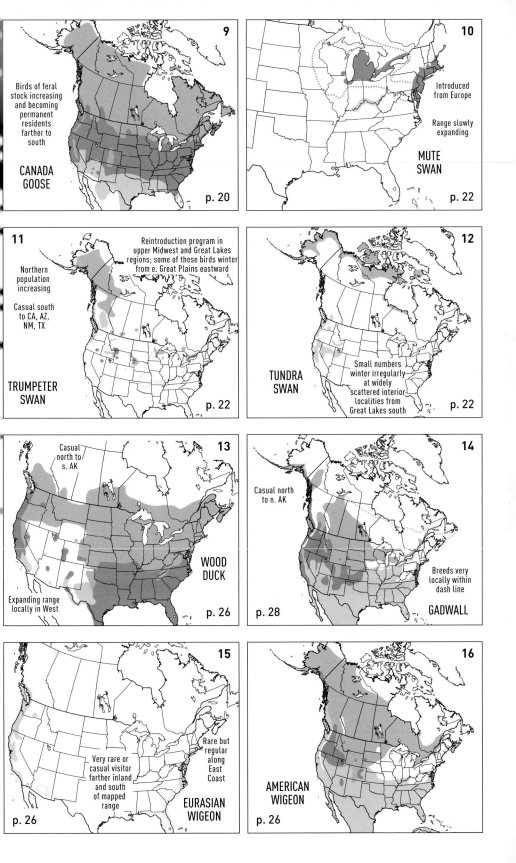

9

Birds of feral stock increasing and becoming permanent residents farther to south

CANADA GOOSE

p. 20

10

Introduced from Europe

Range slowly expanding

MUTE SWAN

p. 22

11

Northern population increasing

Casual south to CA, AZ, NM, TX

Reintroduction program in upper Midwest and Great Lakes regions; some of these birds winter from e. Great Plains eastward

TRUMPETER SWAN

p. 22

12

Small numbers winter irregularly at widely scattered interior localities from Great Lakes south

TUNDRA SWAN

p. 22

13

Casual north to s. AK

Expanding range locally in West

WOOD DUCK

p. 26

14

Casual north to n. AK

Breeds very locally within dash line

p. 28

GADWALL

15

Very rare or casual visitor farther inland and south of mapped range

Rare but regular along East Coast

p. 26

EURASIAN WIGEON

16

AMERICAN WIGEON

p. 26

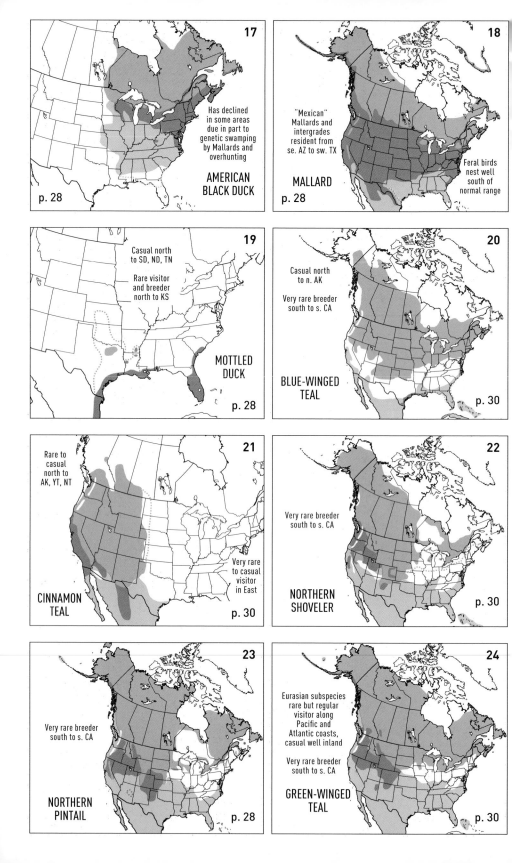

17

Has declined in some areas due in part to genetic swamping by Mallards and overhunting

AMERICAN BLACK DUCK
p. 28

18

"Mexican" Mallards and intergrades resident from se. AZ to sw. TX

Feral birds nest well south of normal range

MALLARD
p. 28

19

Casual north to SD, ND, TN

Rare visitor and breeder north to KS

MOTTLED DUCK
p. 28

20

Casual north to n. AK

Very rare breeder south to s. CA

BLUE-WINGED TEAL
p. 30

21

Rare to casual north to AK, YT, NT

Very rare to casual visitor in East

CINNAMON TEAL
p. 30

22

Very rare breeder south to s. CA

NORTHERN SHOVELER
p. 30

23

Very rare breeder south to s. CA

NORTHERN PINTAIL
p. 28

24

Eurasian subspecies rare but regular visitor along Pacific and Atlantic coasts, casual well inland

Very rare breeder south to s. CA

GREEN-WINGED TEAL
p. 30

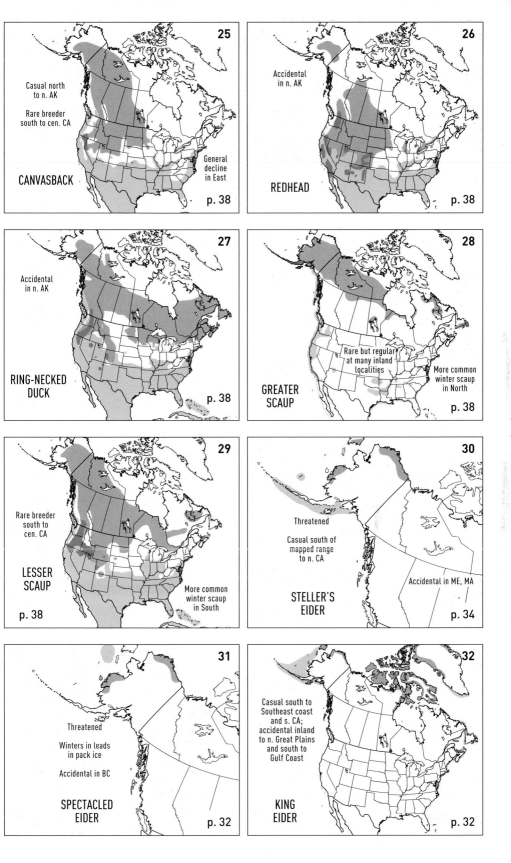

25
Casual north to n. AK

Rare breeder south to cen. CA

General decline in East

CANVASBACK
p. 38

26
Accidental in n. AK

REDHEAD
p. 38

27
Accidental in n. AK

RING-NECKED DUCK
p. 38

28
Rare but regular at many inland localities

More common winter scaup in North

GREATER SCAUP
p. 38

29
Rare breeder south to cen. CA

More common winter scaup in South

LESSER SCAUP
p. 38

30
Threatened

Casual south of mapped range to n. CA

Accidental in ME, MA

STELLER'S EIDER
p. 34

31
Threatened

Winters in leads in pack ice

Accidental in BC

SPECTACLED EIDER
p. 32

32
Casual south to Southeast coast and s. CA; accidental inland to n. Great Plains and south to Gulf Coast

KING EIDER
p. 32

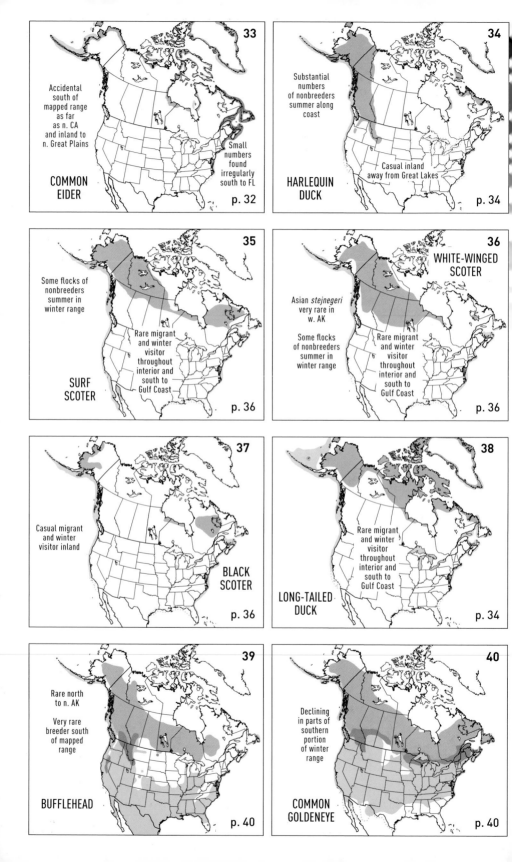

33

Accidental south of mapped range as far as n. CA and inland to n. Great Plains

Small numbers found irregularly south to FL

COMMON EIDER

p. 32

34

Substantial numbers of nonbreeders summer along coast

Casual inland away from Great Lakes

HARLEQUIN DUCK

p. 34

35

Some flocks of nonbreeders summer in winter range

Rare migrant and winter visitor throughout interior and south to Gulf Coast

SURF SCOTER

p. 36

36

WHITE-WINGED SCOTER

Asian *stejnegeri* very rare in w. AK

Some flocks of nonbreeders summer in winter range

Rare migrant and winter visitor throughout interior and south to Gulf Coast

p. 36

37

Casual migrant and winter visitor inland

BLACK SCOTER

p. 36

38

Rare migrant and winter visitor throughout interior and south to Gulf Coast

LONG-TAILED DUCK

p. 34

39

Rare north to n. AK

Very rare breeder south of mapped range

BUFFLEHEAD

p. 40

40

Declining in parts of southern portion of winter range

COMMON GOLDENEYE

p. 40

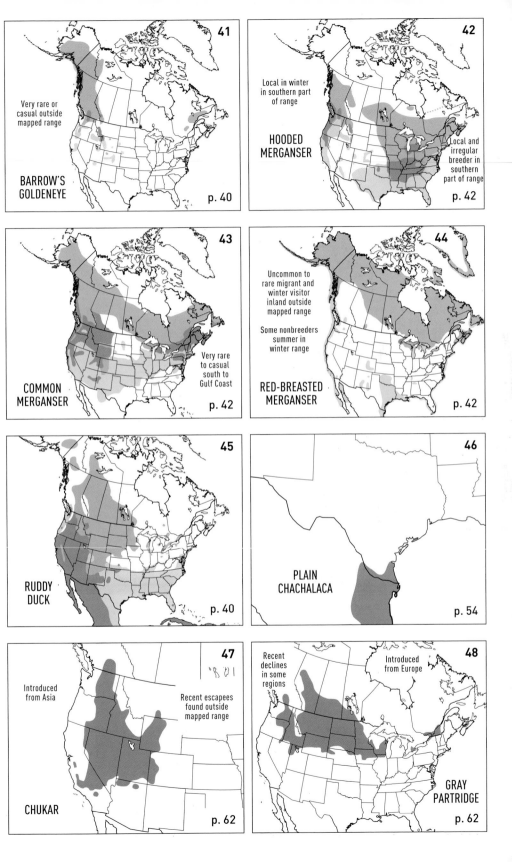

41

Very rare or
casual outside
mapped range

BARROW'S
GOLDENEYE

p. 40

42

Local in winter
in southern part
of range

HOODED
MERGANSER

Local and
irregular
breeder in
southern
part of range

p. 42

43

COMMON
MERGANSER

Very rare
to casual
south to
Gulf Coast

p. 42

44

Uncommon to
rare migrant and
winter visitor
inland outside
mapped range

Some nonbreeders
summer in
winter range

RED-BREASTED
MERGANSER

p. 42

45

RUDDY
DUCK

p. 40

46

PLAIN
CHACHALACA

p. 54

47

Introduced
from Asia

Recent escapees
found outside
mapped range

CHUKAR

p. 62

48

Recent
declines
in some
regions

Introduced
from Europe

GRAY
PARTRIDGE

p. 62

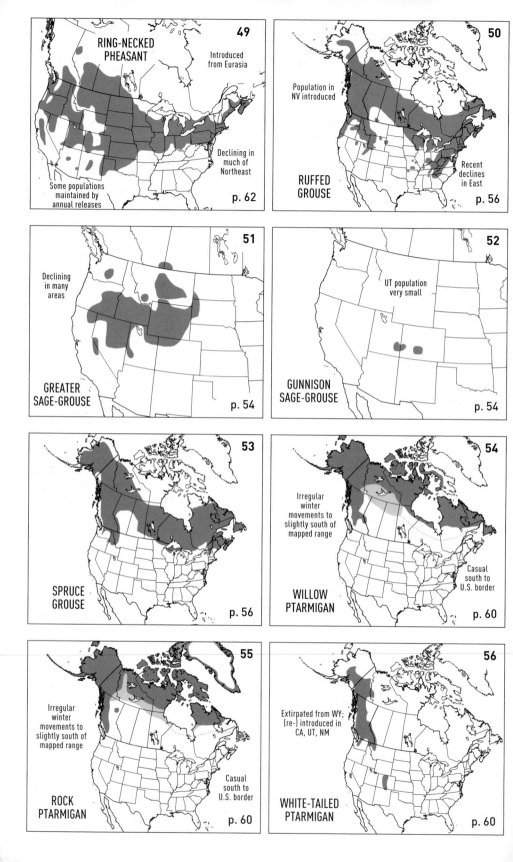

49 RING-NECKED PHEASANT
Introduced from Eurasia
Declining in much of Northeast
Some populations maintained by annual releases
p. 62

50 RUFFED GROUSE
Population in NV introduced
Recent declines in East
p. 56

51 GREATER SAGE-GROUSE
Declining in many areas
p. 54

52 GUNNISON SAGE-GROUSE
UT population very small
p. 54

53 SPRUCE GROUSE
p. 56

54 WILLOW PTARMIGAN
Irregular winter movements to slightly south of mapped range
Casual south to U.S. border
p. 60

55 ROCK PTARMIGAN
Irregular winter movements to slightly south of mapped range
Casual south to U.S. border
p. 60

56 WHITE-TAILED PTARMIGAN
Extirpated from WY; (re-) introduced in CA, UT, NM
p. 60

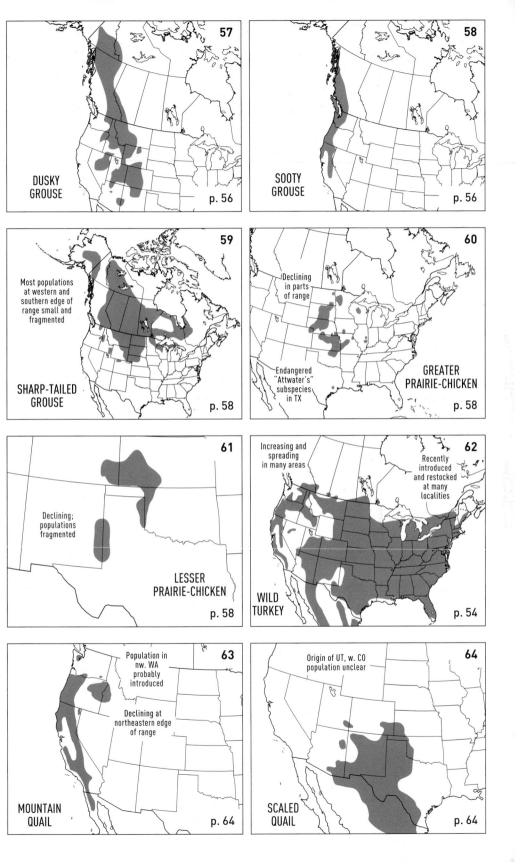

57
DUSKY GROUSE
p. 56

58
SOOTY GROUSE
p. 56

59
Most populations at western and southern edge of range small and fragmented
SHARP-TAILED GROUSE
p. 58

60
Declining in parts of range
Endangered "Attwater's" subspecies in TX
GREATER PRAIRIE-CHICKEN
p. 58

61
Declining; populations fragmented
LESSER PRAIRIE-CHICKEN
p. 58

62
Increasing and spreading in many areas
Recently introduced and restocked at many localities
WILD TURKEY
p. 54

63
Population in nw. WA probably introduced
Declining at northeastern edge of range
MOUNTAIN QUAIL
p. 64

64
Origin of UT, w. CO population unclear
SCALED QUAIL
p. 64

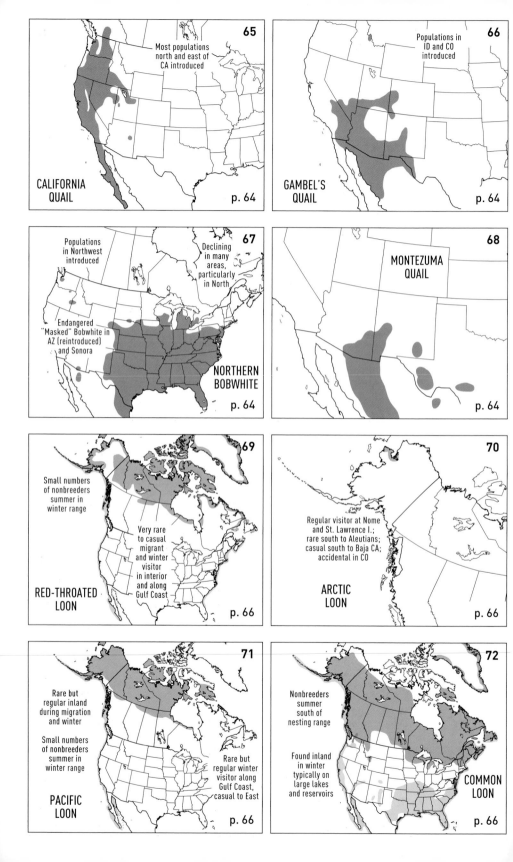

65
CALIFORNIA QUAIL
p. 64
Most populations north and east of CA introduced

66
GAMBEL'S QUAIL
p. 64
Populations in ID and CO introduced

67
NORTHERN BOBWHITE
p. 64
Populations in Northwest introduced
Declining in many areas, particularly in North
Endangered "Masked" Bobwhite in AZ (reintroduced) and Sonora

68
MONTEZUMA QUAIL
p. 64

69
RED-THROATED LOON
p. 66
Small numbers of nonbreeders summer in winter range
Very rare to casual migrant and winter visitor in interior and along Gulf Coast

70
ARCTIC LOON
p. 66
Regular visitor at Nome and St. Lawrence I.; rare south to Aleutians; casual south to Baja CA; accidental in CO

71
PACIFIC LOON
p. 66
Rare but regular inland during migration and winter
Small numbers of nonbreeders summer in winter range
Rare but regular winter visitor along Gulf Coast, casual to East

72
COMMON LOON
p. 66
Nonbreeders summer south of nesting range
Found inland in winter typically on large lakes and reservoirs

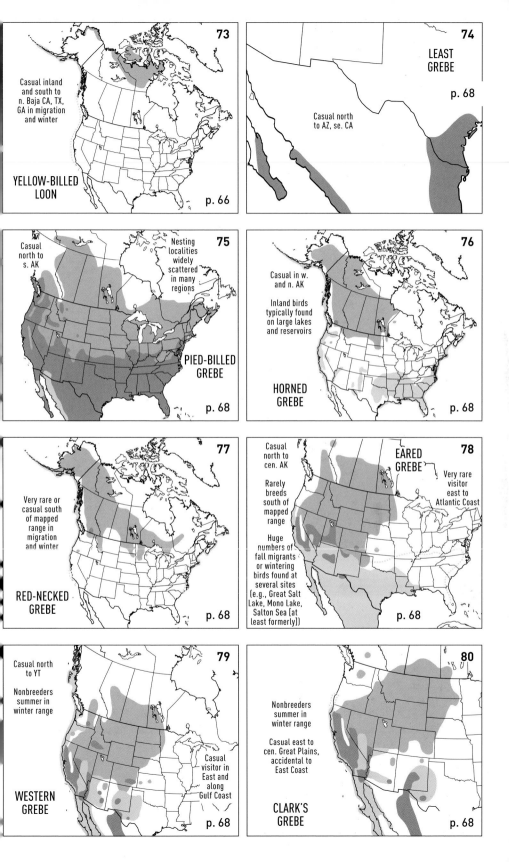

73 Casual inland and south to n. Baja CA, TX, GA in migration and winter

YELLOW-BILLED LOON

p. 66

74 LEAST GREBE

p. 68

Casual north to AZ, se. CA

75 Nesting localities widely scattered in many regions

Casual north to s. AK

PIED-BILLED GREBE

p. 68

76 Casual in w. and n. AK

Inland birds typically found on large lakes and reservoirs

HORNED GREBE

p. 68

77 Very rare or casual south of mapped range in migration and winter

RED-NECKED GREBE

p. 68

78 EARED GREBE

Casual north to cen. AK

Rarely breeds south of mapped range

Huge numbers of fall migrants or wintering birds found at several sites (e.g., Great Salt Lake, Mono Lake, Salton Sea [at least formerly])

Very rare visitor east to Atlantic Coast

p. 68

79 Casual north to YT

Nonbreeders summer in winter range

Casual visitor in East and along Gulf Coast

WESTERN GREBE

p. 68

80 Nonbreeders summer in winter range

Casual east to cen. Great Plains, accidental to East Coast

CLARK'S GREBE

p. 68

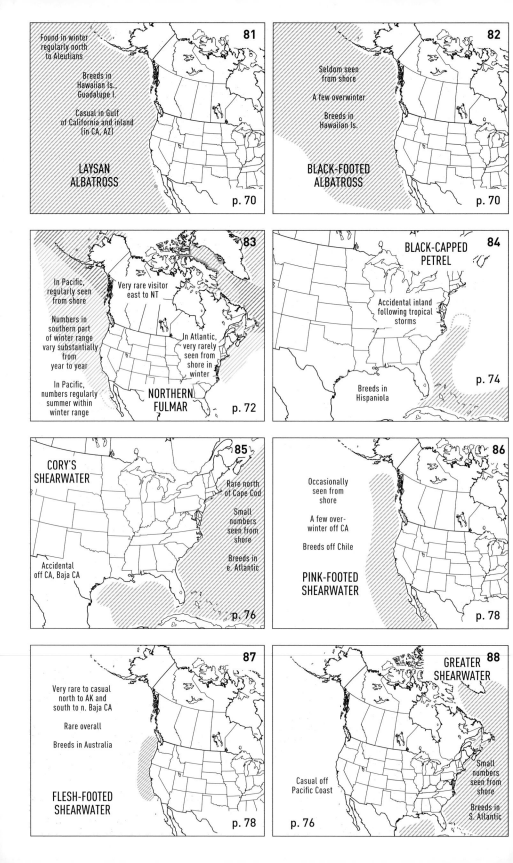

81
Found in winter regularly north to Aleutians

Breeds in Hawaiian Is., Guadalupe I.

Casual in Gulf of California and inland (in CA, AZ)

LAYSAN ALBATROSS

p. 70

82
Seldom seen from shore

A few overwinter

Breeds in Hawaiian Is.

BLACK-FOOTED ALBATROSS

p. 70

83
In Pacific, regularly seen from shore

Very rare visitor east to NT

Numbers in southern part of winter range vary substantially from year to year

In Atlantic, very rarely seen from shore in winter

In Pacific, numbers regularly summer within winter range

NORTHERN FULMAR

p. 72

84
BLACK-CAPPED PETREL

Accidental inland following tropical storms

Breeds in Hispaniola

p. 74

85
CORY'S SHEARWATER

Rare north of Cape Cod

Small numbers seen from shore

Breeds in e. Atlantic

Accidental off CA, Baja CA

p. 76

86
Occasionally seen from shore

A few over-winter off CA

Breeds off Chile

PINK-FOOTED SHEARWATER

p. 78

87
Very rare to casual north to AK and south to n. Baja CA

Rare overall

Breeds in Australia

FLESH-FOOTED SHEARWATER

p. 78

88
GREATER SHEARWATER

Small numbers seen from shore

Breeds in S. Atlantic

Casual off Pacific Coast

p. 76

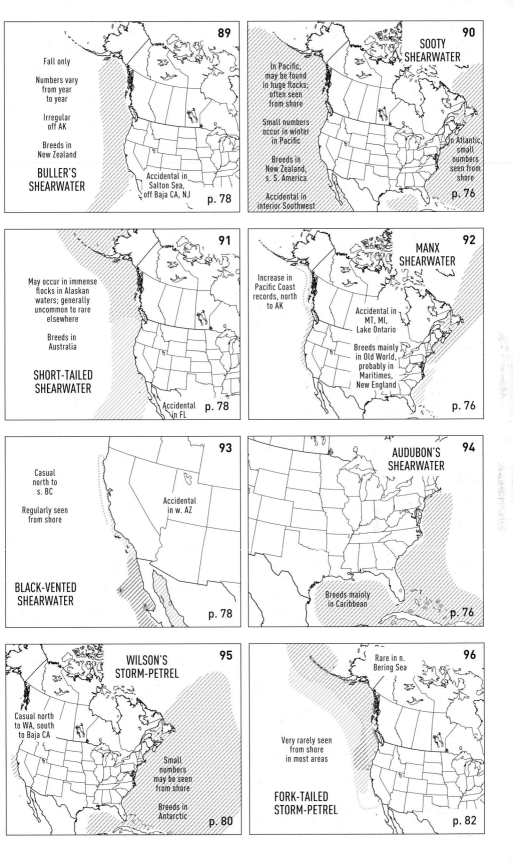

89

Fall only

Numbers vary from year to year

Irregular off AK

Breeds in New Zealand

BULLER'S SHEARWATER

Accidental in Salton Sea, off Baja CA, NJ

p. 78

90

SOOTY SHEARWATER

In Pacific, may be found in huge flocks; often seen from shore

Small numbers occur in winter in Pacific

Breeds in New Zealand, s. S. America

Accidental in interior Southwest

In Atlantic, small numbers seen from shore

p. 76

91

May occur in immense flocks in Alaskan waters; generally uncommon to rare elsewhere

Breeds in Australia

SHORT-TAILED SHEARWATER

Accidental in FL

p. 78

92

MANX SHEARWATER

Increase in Pacific Coast records, north to AK

Accidental in MT, MI, Lake Ontario

Breeds mainly in Old World, probably in Maritimes, New England

p. 76

93

Casual north to s. BC

Regularly seen from shore

Accidental in w. AZ

BLACK-VENTED SHEARWATER

p. 78

94

AUDUBON'S SHEARWATER

Breeds mainly in Caribbean

p. 76

95

WILSON'S STORM-PETREL

Casual north to WA, south to Baja CA

Small numbers may be seen from shore

Breeds in Antarctic

p. 80

96

Rare in n. Bering Sea

Very rarely seen from shore in most areas

FORK-TAILED STORM-PETREL

p. 82

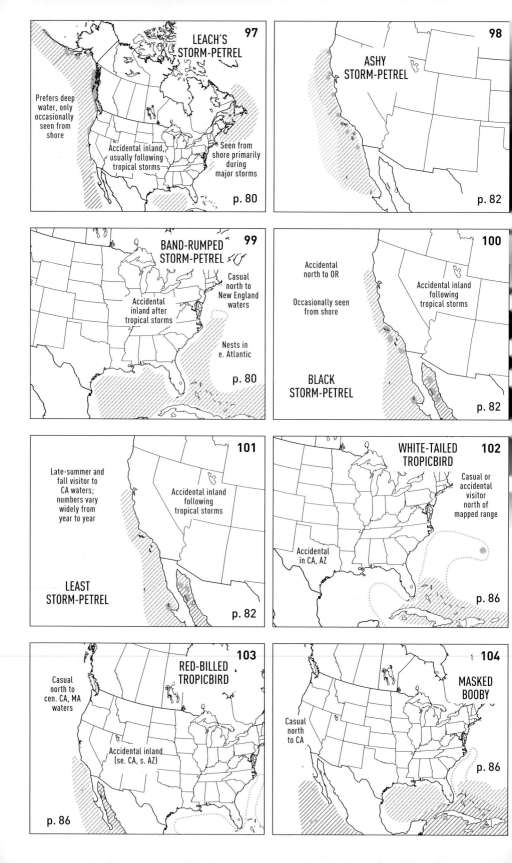

97 LEACH'S STORM-PETREL

Prefers deep water, only occasionally seen from shore

Accidental inland, usually following tropical storms

Seen from shore primarily during major storms

p. 80

98 ASHY STORM-PETREL

p. 82

99 BAND-RUMPED STORM-PETREL

Casual north to New England waters

Accidental inland after tropical storms

Nests in e. Atlantic

p. 80

100 BLACK STORM-PETREL

Accidental north to OR

Occasionally seen from shore

Accidental inland following tropical storms

p. 82

101 LEAST STORM-PETREL

Late-summer and fall visitor to CA waters; numbers vary widely from year to year

Accidental inland following tropical storms

p. 82

102 WHITE-TAILED TROPICBIRD

Casual or accidental visitor north of mapped range

Accidental in CA, AZ

p. 86

103 RED-BILLED TROPICBIRD

Casual north to cen. CA, MA waters

Accidental inland (se. CA, s. AZ)

p. 86

104 MASKED BOOBY

Casual north to CA

p. 86

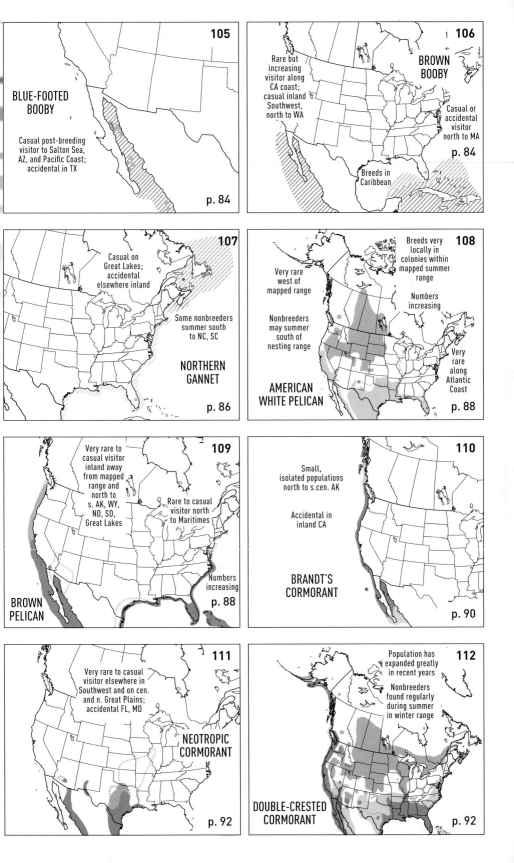

BLUE-FOOTED BOOBY — 105

Casual post-breeding visitor to Salton Sea, AZ, and Pacific Coast; accidental in TX

p. 84

BROWN BOOBY — 106

Rare but increasing visitor along CA coast; casual inland Southwest, north to WA

Casual or accidental visitor north to MA

Breeds in Caribbean

p. 84

NORTHERN GANNET — 107

Casual on Great Lakes; accidental elsewhere inland

Some nonbreeders summer south to NC, SC

p. 86

AMERICAN WHITE PELICAN — 108

Breeds very locally in colonies within mapped summer range

Very rare west of mapped range

Numbers increasing

Nonbreeders may summer south of nesting range

Very rare along Atlantic Coast

p. 88

BROWN PELICAN — 109

Very rare to casual visitor inland away from mapped range and north to s. AK, WY, ND, SD, Great Lakes

Rare to casual visitor north to Maritimes

Numbers increasing

p. 88

BRANDT'S CORMORANT — 110

Small, isolated populations north to s.cen. AK

Accidental in inland CA

p. 90

NEOTROPIC CORMORANT — 111

Very rare to casual visitor elsewhere in Southwest and on cen. and n. Great Plains; accidental FL, MD

p. 92

DOUBLE-CRESTED CORMORANT — 112

Population has expanded greatly in recent years

Nonbreeders found regularly during summer in winter range

p. 92

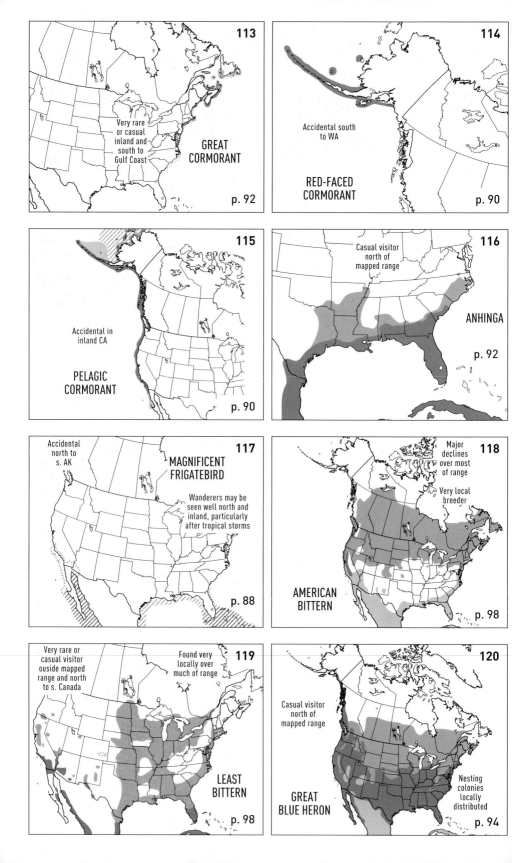

113
Very rare or casual inland and south to Gulf Coast
GREAT CORMORANT
p. 92

114
Accidental south to WA
RED-FACED CORMORANT
p. 90

115
Accidental in inland CA
PELAGIC CORMORANT
p. 90

116
Casual visitor north of mapped range
ANHINGA
p. 92

117
Accidental north to s. AK
MAGNIFICENT FRIGATEBIRD
Wanderers may be seen well north and inland, particularly after tropical storms
p. 88

118
Major declines over most of range
Very local breeder
AMERICAN BITTERN
p. 98

119
Very rare or casual visitor ouside mapped range and north to s. Canada
Found very locally over much of range
LEAST BITTERN
p. 98

120
Casual visitor north of mapped range
Nesting colonies locally distributed
GREAT BLUE HERON
p. 94

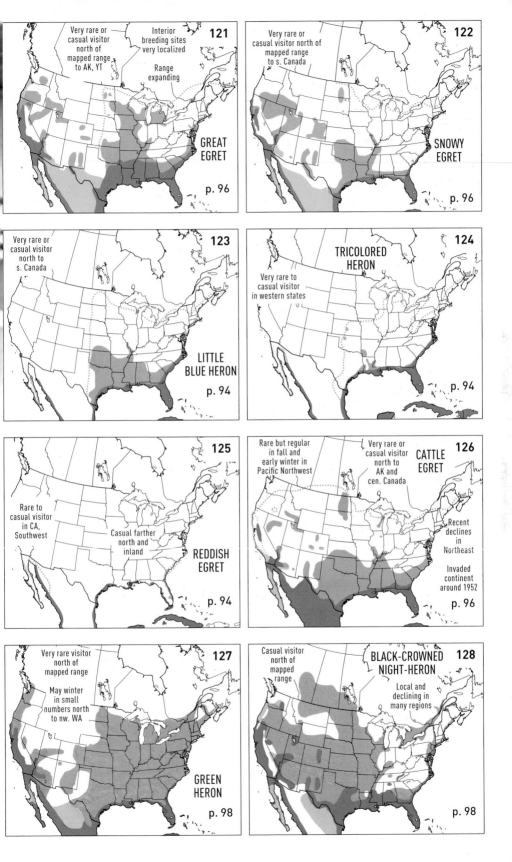

121

Very rare or casual visitor north of mapped range to AK, YT

Interior breeding sites very localized

Range expanding

GREAT EGRET

p. 96

122

Very rare or casual visitor north of mapped range to s. Canada

SNOWY EGRET

p. 96

123

Very rare or casual visitor north to s. Canada

LITTLE BLUE HERON

p. 94

124

TRICOLORED HERON

Very rare to casual visitor in western states

p. 94

125

Rare to casual visitor in CA, Southwest

Casual farther north and inland

REDDISH EGRET

p. 94

126

Rare but regular in fall and early winter in Pacific Northwest

Very rare or casual visitor north to AK and cen. Canada

CATTLE EGRET

Recent declines in Northeast

Invaded continent around 1952

p. 96

127

Very rare visitor north of mapped range

May winter in small numbers north to nw. WA

GREEN HERON

p. 98

128

Casual visitor north of mapped range

BLACK-CROWNED NIGHT-HERON

Local and declining in many regions

p. 98

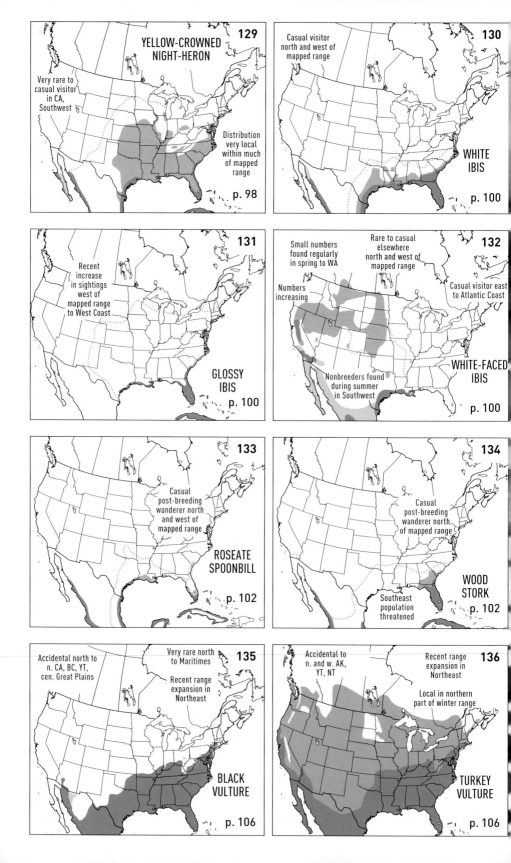

YELLOW-CROWNED NIGHT-HERON 129

Very rare to casual visitor in CA, Southwest

Distribution very local within much of mapped range

p. 98

130

Casual visitor north and west of mapped range

WHITE IBIS

p. 100

131

Recent increase in sightings west of mapped range to West Coast

GLOSSY IBIS

p. 100

132

Small numbers found regularly in spring to WA

Rare to casual elsewhere north and west of mapped range

Numbers increasing

Casual visitor east to Atlantic Coast

Nonbreeders found during summer in Southwest

WHITE-FACED IBIS

p. 100

133

Casual post-breeding wanderer north and west of mapped range

ROSEATE SPOONBILL

p. 102

134

Casual post-breeding wanderer north of mapped range

WOOD STORK

Southeast population threatened

p. 102

135

Accidental north to n. CA, BC, YT, cen. Great Plains

Very rare north to Maritimes

Recent range expansion in Northeast

BLACK VULTURE

p. 106

136

Accidental to n. and w. AK, YT, NT

Recent range expansion in Northeast

Local in northern part of winter range

TURKEY VULTURE

p. 106

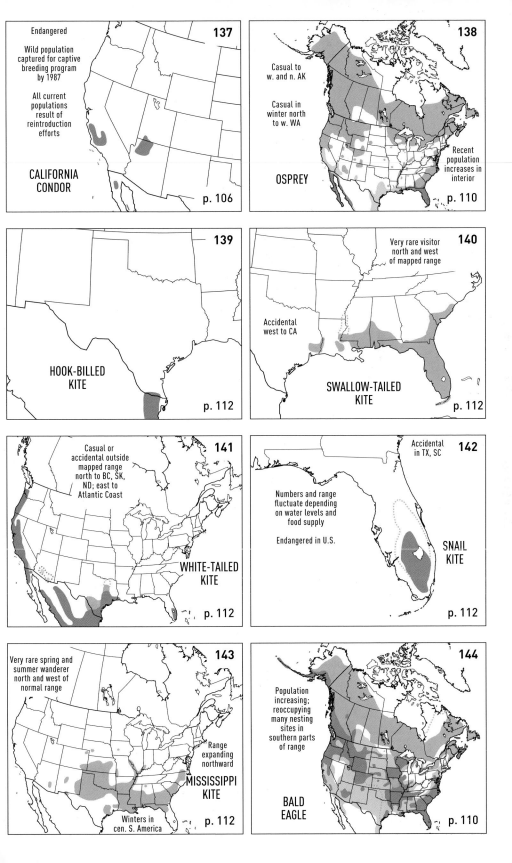

137 Endangered

Wild population captured for captive breeding program by 1987

All current populations result of reintroduction efforts

CALIFORNIA CONDOR

p. 106

138 Casual to w. and n. AK

Casual in winter north to w. WA

Recent population increases in interior

OSPREY

p. 110

139 HOOK-BILLED KITE

p. 112

140 Very rare visitor north and west of mapped range

Accidental west to CA

SWALLOW-TAILED KITE

p. 112

141 Casual or accidental outside mapped range north to BC, SK, ND; east to Atlantic Coast

WHITE-TAILED KITE

p. 112

142 Accidental in TX, SC

Numbers and range fluctuate depending on water levels and food supply

Endangered in U.S.

SNAIL KITE

p. 112

143 Very rare spring and summer wanderer north and west of normal range

Range expanding northward

MISSISSIPPI KITE

Winters in cen. S. America

p. 112

144 Population increasing; reoccupying many nesting sites in southern parts of range

BALD EAGLE

p. 110

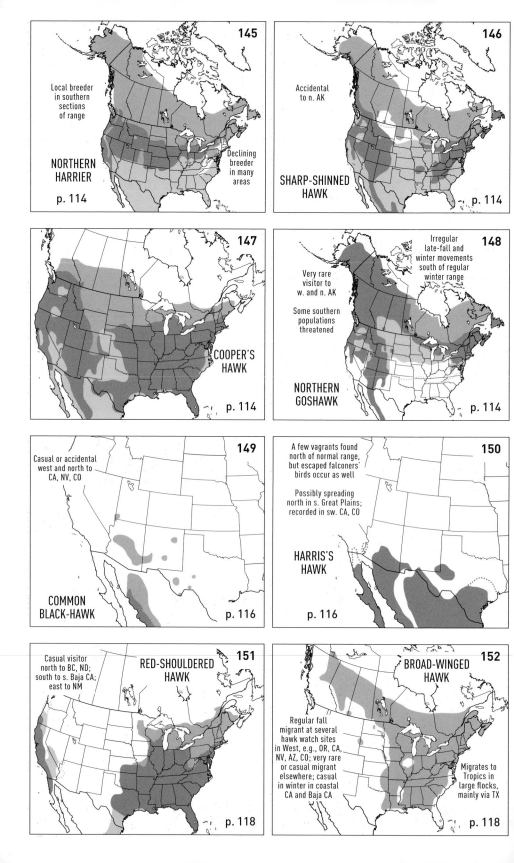

145

Local breeder in southern sections of range

Declining breeder in many areas

NORTHERN HARRIER

p. 114

146

Accidental to n. AK

SHARP-SHINNED HAWK

p. 114

147

COOPER'S HAWK

p. 114

148

Irregular late-fall and winter movements south of regular winter range

Very rare visitor to w. and n. AK

Some southern populations threatened

NORTHERN GOSHAWK

p. 114

149

Casual or accidental west and north to CA, NV, CO

COMMON BLACK-HAWK

p. 116

150

A few vagrants found north of normal range, but escaped falconers' birds occur as well

Possibly spreading north in s. Great Plains; recorded in sw. CA, CO

HARRIS'S HAWK

p. 116

151

Casual visitor north to BC, ND; south to s. Baja CA; east to NM

RED-SHOULDERED HAWK

p. 118

152

BROAD-WINGED HAWK

Regular fall migrant at several hawk watch sites in West, e.g., OR, CA, NV, AZ, CO; very rare or casual migrant elsewhere; casual in winter in coastal CA and Baja CA

Migrates to Tropics in large flocks, mainly via TX

p. 118

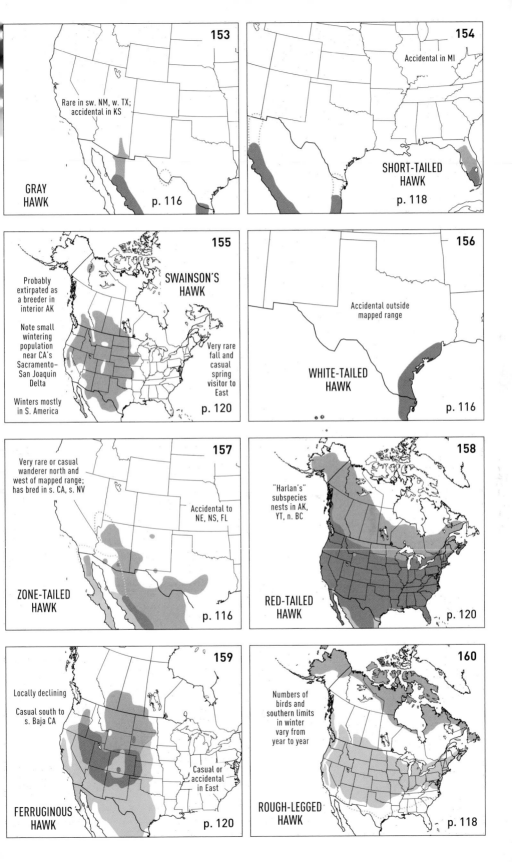

153
GRAY HAWK
Rare in sw. NM, w. TX; accidental in KS
p. 116

154
SHORT-TAILED HAWK
Accidental in MI
p. 118

155
SWAINSON'S HAWK
Probably extirpated as a breeder in interior AK
Note small wintering population near CA's Sacramento–San Joaquin Delta
Winters mostly in S. America
Very rare fall and casual spring visitor to East
p. 120

156
WHITE-TAILED HAWK
Accidental outside mapped range
p. 116

157
ZONE-TAILED HAWK
Very rare or casual wanderer north and west of mapped range; has bred in s. CA, s. NV
Accidental to NE, NS, FL
p. 116

158
RED-TAILED HAWK
"Harlan's" subspecies nests in AK, YT, n. BC
p. 120

159
FERRUGINOUS HAWK
Locally declining
Casual south to s. Baja CA
Casual or accidental in East
p. 120

160
ROUGH-LEGGED HAWK
Numbers of birds and southern limits in winter vary from year to year
p. 118

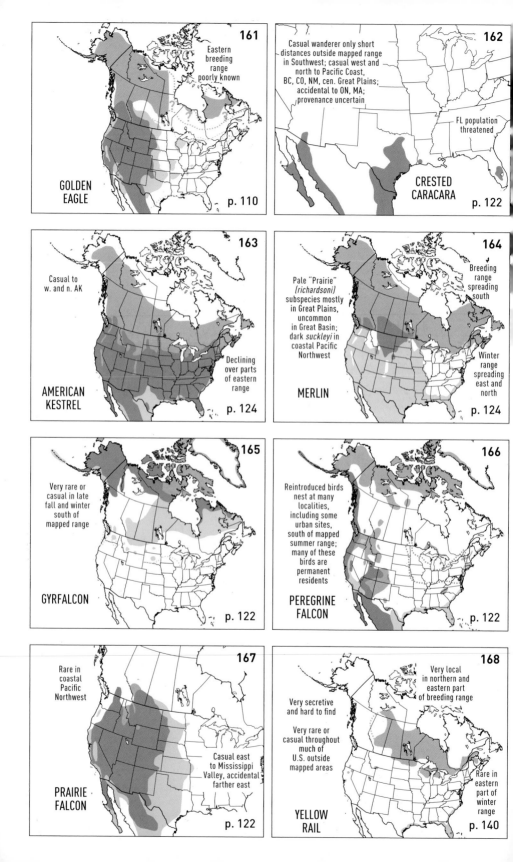

161

Eastern breeding range poorly known

GOLDEN EAGLE
p. 110

162

Casual wanderer only short distances outside mapped range in Southwest; casual west and north to Pacific Coast, BC, CO, NM, cen. Great Plains; accidental to ON, MA; provenance uncertain

FL population threatened

CRESTED CARACARA
p. 122

163

Casual to w. and n. AK

Declining over parts of eastern range

AMERICAN KESTREL
p. 124

164

Breeding range spreading south

Pale "Prairie" (*richardsoni*) subspecies mostly in Great Plains, uncommon in Great Basin; dark *suckleyi* in coastal Pacific Northwest

Winter range spreading east and north

MERLIN
p. 124

165

Very rare or casual in late fall and winter south of mapped range

GYRFALCON
p. 122

166

Reintroduced birds nest at many localities, including some urban sites, south of mapped summer range; many of these birds are permanent residents

PEREGRINE FALCON
p. 122

167

Rare in coastal Pacific Northwest

Casual east to Mississippi Valley, accidental farther east

PRAIRIE FALCON
p. 122

168

Very local in northern and eastern part of breeding range

Very secretive and hard to find

Very rare or casual throughout much of U.S. outside mapped areas

Rare in eastern part of winter range

YELLOW RAIL
p. 140

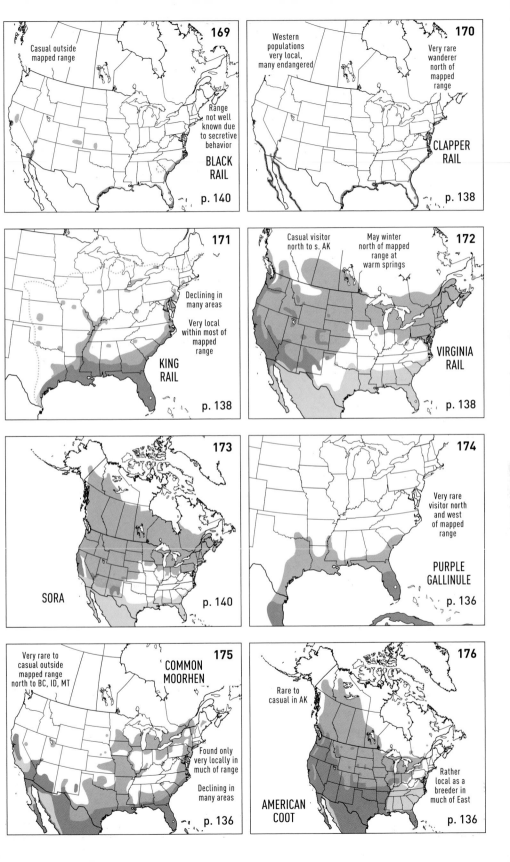

169

Casual outside mapped range

Range not well known due to secretive behavior

BLACK RAIL

p. 140

170

Western populations very local, many endangered

Very rare wanderer north of mapped range

CLAPPER RAIL

p. 138

171

Declining in many areas

Very local within most of mapped range

KING RAIL

p. 138

172

Casual visitor north to s. AK

May winter north of mapped range at warm springs

VIRGINIA RAIL

p. 138

173

SORA

p. 140

174

Very rare visitor north and west of mapped range

PURPLE GALLINULE

p. 136

175

Very rare to casual outside mapped range north to BC, ID, MT

COMMON MOORHEN

Found only very locally in much of range

Declining in many areas

p. 136

176

Rare to casual in AK

Rather local as a breeder in much of East

AMERICAN COOT

p. 136

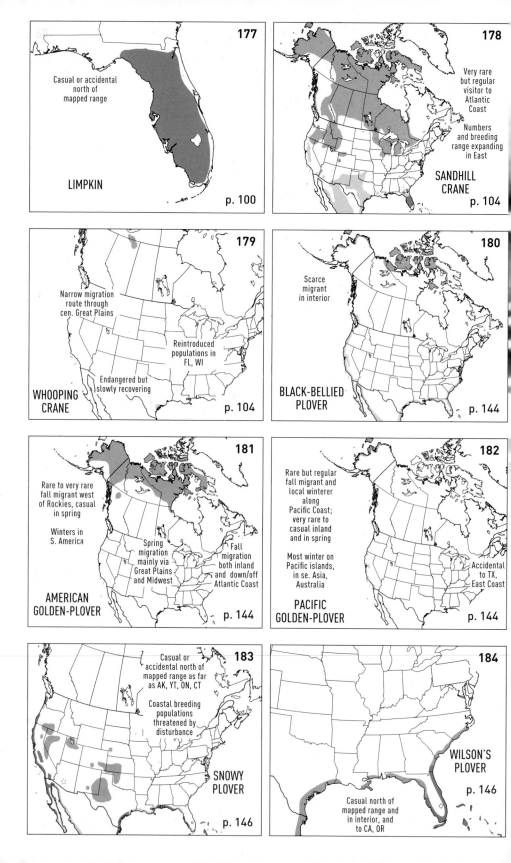

177

Casual or accidental north of mapped range

LIMPKIN

p. 100

178

Very rare but regular visitor to Atlantic Coast

Numbers and breeding range expanding in East

SANDHILL CRANE

p. 104

179

Narrow migration route through cen. Great Plains

Reintroduced populations in FL, WI

Endangered but slowly recovering

WHOOPING CRANE

p. 104

180

Scarce migrant in interior

BLACK-BELLIED PLOVER

p. 144

181

Rare to very rare fall migrant west of Rockies, casual in spring

Winters in S. America

Spring migration mainly via Great Plains and Midwest

Fall migration both inland and down/off Atlantic Coast

AMERICAN GOLDEN-PLOVER

p. 144

182

Rare but regular fall migrant and local winterer along Pacific Coast; very rare to casual inland and in spring

Most winter on Pacific islands, in se. Asia, Australia

Accidental to TX, East Coast

PACIFIC GOLDEN-PLOVER

p. 144

183

Casual or accidental north of mapped range as far as AK, YT, ON, CT

Coastal breeding populations threatened by disturbance

SNOWY PLOVER

p. 146

184

WILSON'S PLOVER

p. 146

Casual north of mapped range and in interior, and to CA, OR

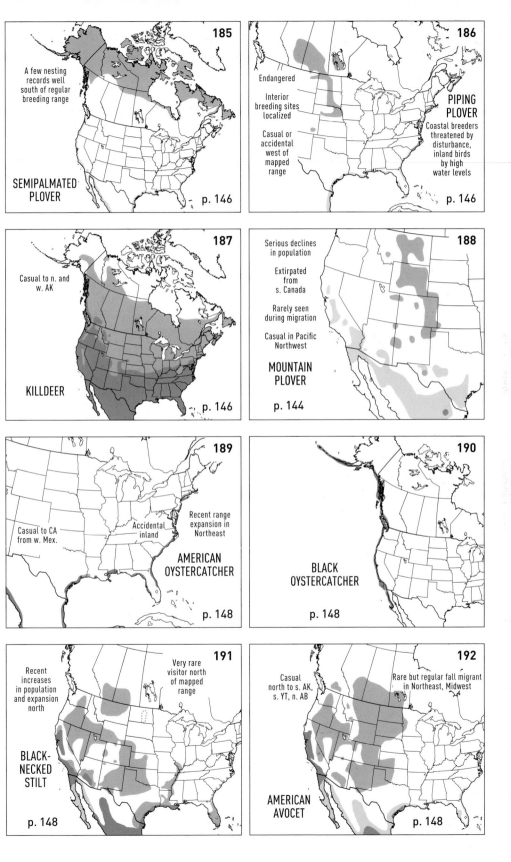

185

A few nesting records well south of regular breeding range

SEMIPALMATED PLOVER

p. 146

186

Endangered

Interior breeding sites localized

Casual or accidental west of mapped range

PIPING PLOVER

Coastal breeders threatened by disturbance, inland birds by high water levels

p. 146

187

Casual to n. and w. AK

KILLDEER

p. 146

188

Serious declines in population

Extirpated from s. Canada

Rarely seen during migration

Casual in Pacific Northwest

MOUNTAIN PLOVER

p. 144

189

Casual to CA from w. Mex.

Accidental inland

Recent range expansion in Northeast

AMERICAN OYSTERCATCHER

p. 148

190

BLACK OYSTERCATCHER

p. 148

191

Recent increases in population and expansion north

Very rare visitor north of mapped range

BLACK-NECKED STILT

p. 148

192

Casual north to s. AK, s. YT, n. AB

Rare but regular fall migrant in Northeast, Midwest

AMERICAN AVOCET

p. 148

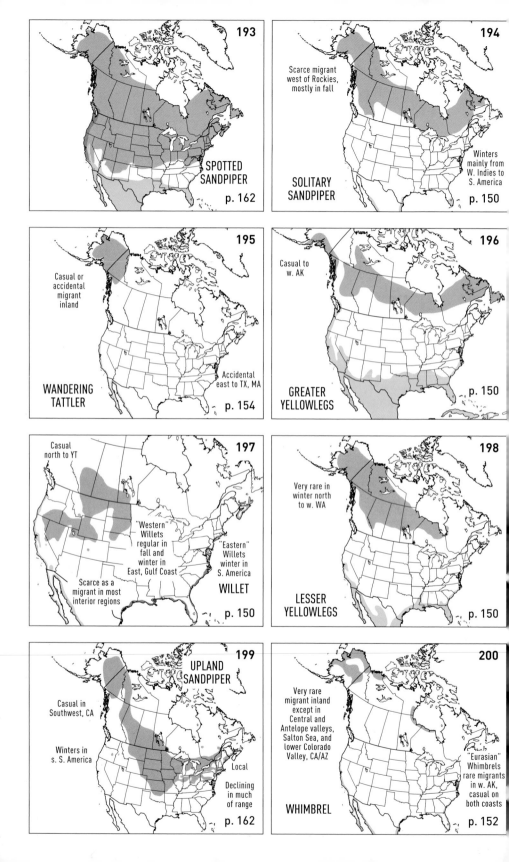

193
SPOTTED
SANDPIPER
p. 162

194
Scarce migrant
west of Rockies,
mostly in fall

Winters
mainly from
W. Indies to
S. America

SOLITARY
SANDPIPER
p. 150

195
Casual or
accidental
migrant
inland

Accidental
east to TX, MA

WANDERING
TATTLER
p. 154

196
Casual to
w. AK

GREATER
YELLOWLEGS
p. 150

197
Casual
north to YT

"Western"
Willets
regular in
fall and
winter in
East, Gulf Coast

"Eastern"
Willets
winter in
S. America

Scarce as a
migrant in most
interior regions

WILLET
p. 150

198
Very rare in
winter north
to w. WA

LESSER
YELLOWLEGS
p. 150

199
UPLAND
SANDPIPER

Casual in
Southwest, CA

Winters in
s. S. America

Local

Declining
in much
of range

p. 162

200
Very rare
migrant inland
except in
Central and
Antelope valleys,
Salton Sea, and
lower Colorado
Valley, CA/AZ

"Eurasian"
Whimbrels
rare migrants
in w. AK,
casual on
both coasts

WHIMBREL
p. 152

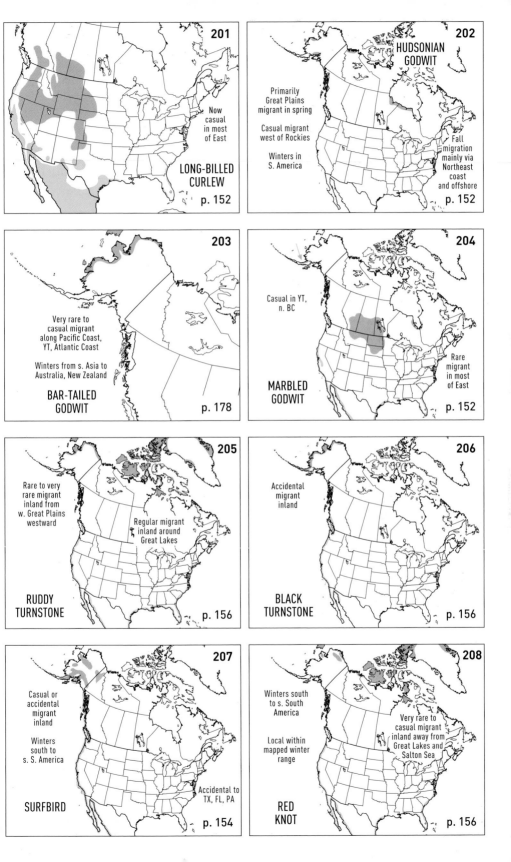

201
Now casual in most of East

LONG-BILLED CURLEW
p. 152

202
HUDSONIAN GODWIT

Primarily Great Plains migrant in spring

Casual migrant west of Rockies

Winters in S. America

Fall migration mainly via Northeast coast and offshore

p. 152

203
Very rare to casual migrant along Pacific Coast, YT, Atlantic Coast

Winters from s. Asia to Australia, New Zealand

BAR-TAILED GODWIT
p. 178

204
Casual in YT, n. BC

Rare migrant in most of East

MARBLED GODWIT
p. 152

205
Rare to very rare migrant inland from w. Great Plains westward

Regular migrant inland around Great Lakes

RUDDY TURNSTONE
p. 156

206
Accidental migrant inland

BLACK TURNSTONE
p. 156

207
Casual or accidental migrant inland

Winters south to s. S. America

SURFBIRD

Accidental to TX, FL, PA
p. 154

208
Winters south to s. South America

Local within mapped winter range

Very rare to casual migrant inland away from Great Lakes and Salton Sea

RED KNOT
p. 156

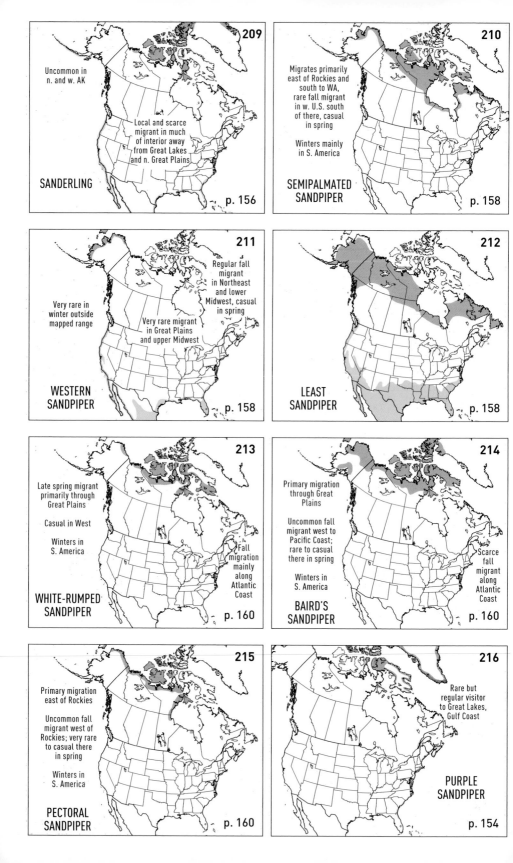

209

Uncommon in n. and w. AK

Local and scarce migrant in much of interior away from Great Lakes and n. Great Plains

SANDERLING

p. 156

210

Migrates primarily east of Rockies and south to WA, rare fall migrant in w. U.S. south of there, casual in spring

Winters mainly in S. America

SEMIPALMATED SANDPIPER

p. 158

211

Regular fall migrant in Northeast and lower Midwest, casual in spring

Very rare in winter outside mapped range

Very rare migrant in Great Plains and upper Midwest

WESTERN SANDPIPER

p. 158

212

LEAST SANDPIPER

p. 158

213

Late spring migrant primarily through Great Plains

Casual in West

Winters in S. America

Fall migration mainly along Atlantic Coast

WHITE-RUMPED SANDPIPER

p. 160

214

Primary migration through Great Plains

Uncommon fall migrant west to Pacific Coast; rare to casual there in spring

Winters in S. America

Scarce fall migrant along Atlantic Coast

BAIRD'S SANDPIPER

p. 160

215

Primary migration east of Rockies

Uncommon fall migrant west of Rockies; very rare to casual there in spring

Winters in S. America

PECTORAL SANDPIPER

p. 160

216

Rare but regular visitor to Great Lakes, Gulf Coast

PURPLE SANDPIPER

p. 154

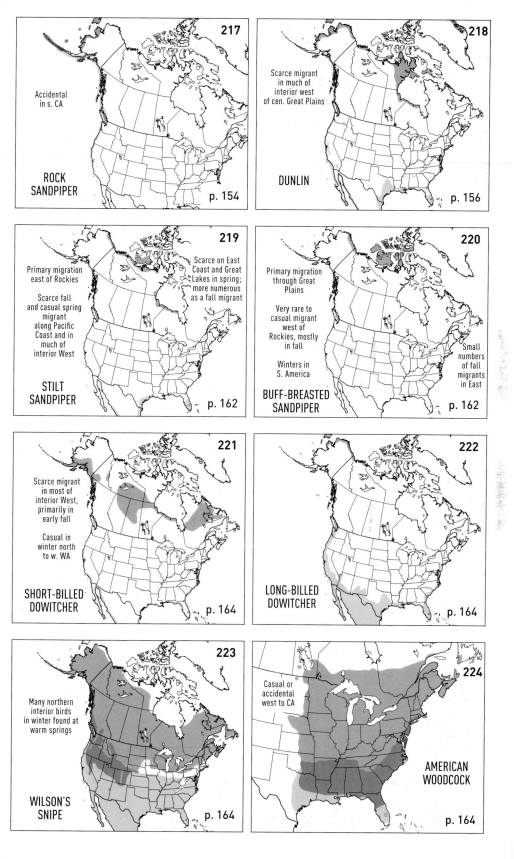

217

Accidental
in s. CA

ROCK
SANDPIPER

p. 154

218

Scarce migrant
in much of
interior west
of cen. Great Plains

DUNLIN

p. 156

219

Primary migration
east of Rockies

Scarce fall
and casual spring
migrant
along Pacific
Coast and in
much of
interior West

Scarce on East
Coast and Great
Lakes in spring;
more numerous
as a fall migrant

STILT
SANDPIPER

p. 162

220

Primary migration
through Great
Plains

Very rare to
casual migrant
west of
Rockies, mostly
in fall

Winters in
S. America

Small
numbers
of fall
migrants
in East

BUFF-BREASTED
SANDPIPER

p. 162

221

Scarce migrant
in most of
interior West,
primarily in
early fall

Casual in
winter north
to w. WA

SHORT-BILLED
DOWITCHER

p. 164

222

LONG-BILLED
DOWITCHER

p. 164

223

Many northern
interior birds
in winter found at
warm springs

WILSON'S
SNIPE

p. 164

224

Casual or
accidental
west to CA

AMERICAN
WOODCOCK

p. 164

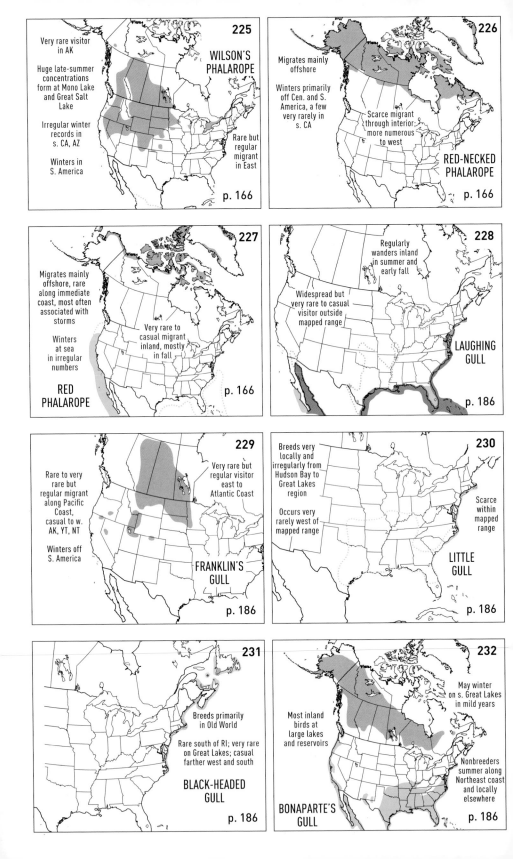

225
WILSON'S PHALAROPE

Very rare visitor in AK

Huge late-summer concentrations form at Mono Lake and Great Salt Lake

Irregular winter records in s. CA, AZ

Winters in S. America

Rare but regular migrant in East

p. 166

226
RED-NECKED PHALAROPE

Migrates mainly offshore

Winters primarily off Cen. and S. America, a few very rarely in s. CA

Scarce migrant through interior; more numerous to west

p. 166

227
RED PHALAROPE

Migrates mainly offshore, rare along immediate coast, most often associated with storms

Winters at sea in irregular numbers

Very rare to casual migrant inland, mostly in fall

p. 166

228
LAUGHING GULL

Regularly wanders inland in summer and early fall

Widespread but very rare to casual visitor outside mapped range

p. 186

229
FRANKLIN'S GULL

Rare to very rare but regular migrant along Pacific Coast, casual to w. AK, YT, NT

Winters off S. America

Very rare but regular visitor east to Atlantic Coast

p. 186

230
LITTLE GULL

Breeds very locally and irregularly from Hudson Bay to Great Lakes region

Occurs very rarely west of mapped range

Scarce within mapped range

p. 186

231
BLACK-HEADED GULL

Breeds primarily in Old World

Rare south of RI; very rare on Great Lakes; casual farther west and south

p. 186

232
BONAPARTE'S GULL

May winter on s. Great Lakes in mild years

Most inland birds at large lakes and reservoirs

Nonbreeders summer along Northeast coast and locally elsewhere

p. 186

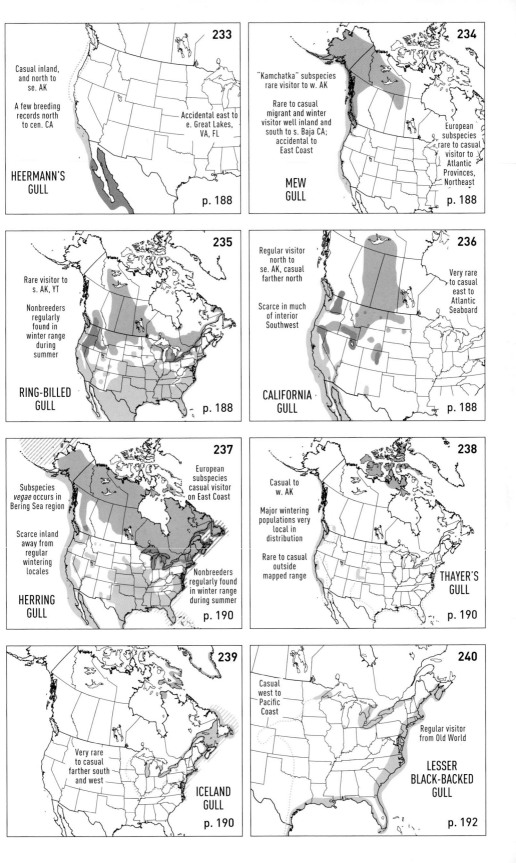

233

Casual inland, and north to se. AK

A few breeding records north to cen. CA

Accidental east to e. Great Lakes, VA, FL

HEERMANN'S GULL

p. 188

234

"Kamchatka" subspecies rare visitor to w. AK

Rare to casual migrant and winter visitor well inland and south to s. Baja CA; accidental to East Coast

European subspecies rare to casual visitor to Atlantic Provinces, Northeast

MEW GULL

p. 188

235

Rare visitor to s. AK, YT

Nonbreeders regularly found in winter range during summer

RING-BILLED GULL

p. 188

236

Regular visitor north to se. AK, casual farther north

Scarce in much of interior Southwest

Very rare to casual east to Atlantic Seaboard

CALIFORNIA GULL

p. 188

237

Subspecies *vegae* occurs in Bering Sea region

Scarce inland away from regular wintering locales

European subspecies casual visitor on East Coast

Nonbreeders regularly found in winter range during summer

HERRING GULL

p. 190

238

Casual to w. AK

Major wintering populations very local in distribution

Rare to casual outside mapped range

THAYER'S GULL

p. 190

239

Very rare to casual farther south and west

ICELAND GULL

p. 190

240

Casual west to Pacific Coast

Regular visitor from Old World

LESSER BLACK-BACKED GULL

p. 192

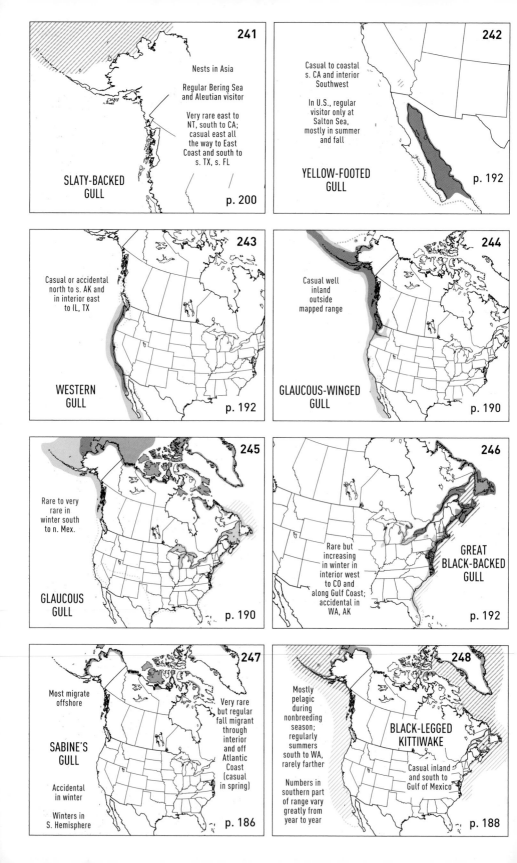

241

Nests in Asia

Regular Bering Sea and Aleutian visitor

Very rare east to NT, south to CA; casual east all the way to East Coast and south to s. TX, s. FL

SLATY-BACKED GULL

p. 200

242

Casual to coastal s. CA and interior Southwest

In U.S., regular visitor only at Salton Sea, mostly in summer and fall

YELLOW-FOOTED GULL

p. 192

243

Casual or accidental north to s. AK and in interior east to IL, TX

WESTERN GULL

p. 192

244

Casual well inland outside mapped range

GLAUCOUS-WINGED GULL

p. 190

245

Rare to very rare in winter south to n. Mex.

GLAUCOUS GULL

p. 190

246

Rare but increasing in winter in interior west to CO and along Gulf Coast; accidental in WA, AK

GREAT BLACK-BACKED GULL

p. 192

247

Most migrate offshore

Very rare but regular fall migrant through interior and off Atlantic Coast (casual in spring)

SABINE'S GULL

Accidental in winter

Winters in S. Hemisphere

p. 186

248

Mostly pelagic during nonbreeding season; regularly summers south to WA, rarely farther

Numbers in southern part of range vary greatly from year to year

BLACK-LEGGED KITTIWAKE

Casual inland and south to Gulf of Mexico

p. 188

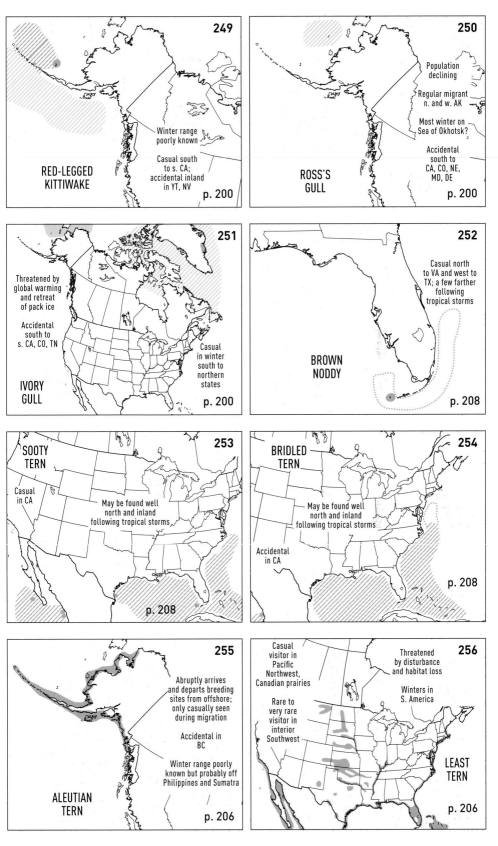

249 RED-LEGGED KITTIWAKE
Winter range poorly known
Casual south to s. CA; accidental inland in YT, NV
p. 200

250 ROSS'S GULL
Population declining
Regular migrant n. and w. AK
Most winter on Sea of Okhotsk?
Accidental south to CA, CO, NE, MD, DE
p. 200

251 IVORY GULL
Threatened by global warming and retreat of pack ice
Accidental south to s. CA, CO, TN
Casual in winter south to northern states
p. 200

252 BROWN NODDY
Casual north to VA and west to TX; a few farther following tropical storms
p. 208

253 SOOTY TERN
Casual in CA
May be found well north and inland following tropical storms
p. 208

254 BRIDLED TERN
May be found well north and inland following tropical storms
Accidental in CA
p. 208

255 ALEUTIAN TERN
Abruptly arrives and departs breeding sites from offshore; only casually seen during migration
Accidental in BC
Winter range poorly known but probably off Philippines and Sumatra
p. 206

256 LEAST TERN
Casual visitor in Pacific Northwest, Canadian prairies
Threatened by disturbance and habitat loss
Winters in S. America
Rare to very rare visitor in interior Southwest
p. 206

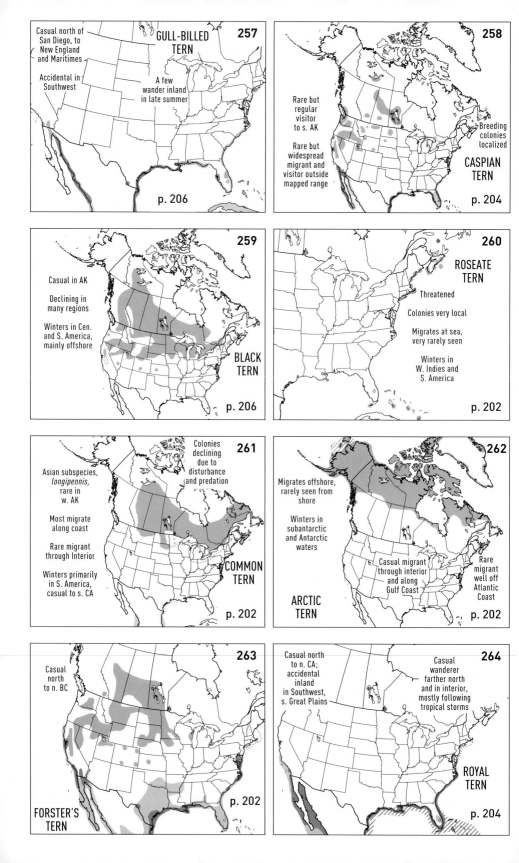

257 GULL-BILLED TERN
Casual north of San Diego, to New England and Maritimes
Accidental in Southwest
A few wander inland in late summer
p. 206

258 CASPIAN TERN
Rare but regular visitor to s. AK
Rare but widespread migrant and visitor outside mapped range
Breeding colonies localized
p. 204

259 BLACK TERN
Casual in AK
Declining in many regions
Winters in Cen. and S. America, mainly offshore
p. 206

260 ROSEATE TERN
Threatened
Colonies very local
Migrates at sea, very rarely seen
Winters in W. Indies and S. America
p. 202

261 COMMON TERN
Colonies declining due to disturbance and predation
Asian subspecies, *longipennis*, rare in w. AK
Most migrate along coast
Rare migrant through Interior
Winters primarily in S. America, casual to s. CA
p. 202

262 ARCTIC TERN
Migrates offshore, rarely seen from shore
Winters in subantarctic and Antarctic waters
Casual migrant through interior and along Gulf Coast
Rare migrant well off Atlantic Coast
p. 202

263 FORSTER'S TERN
Casual north to n. BC
p. 202

264 ROYAL TERN
Casual north to n. CA; accidental inland in Southwest, s. Great Plains
Casual wanderer farther north and in interior, mostly following tropical storms
p. 204

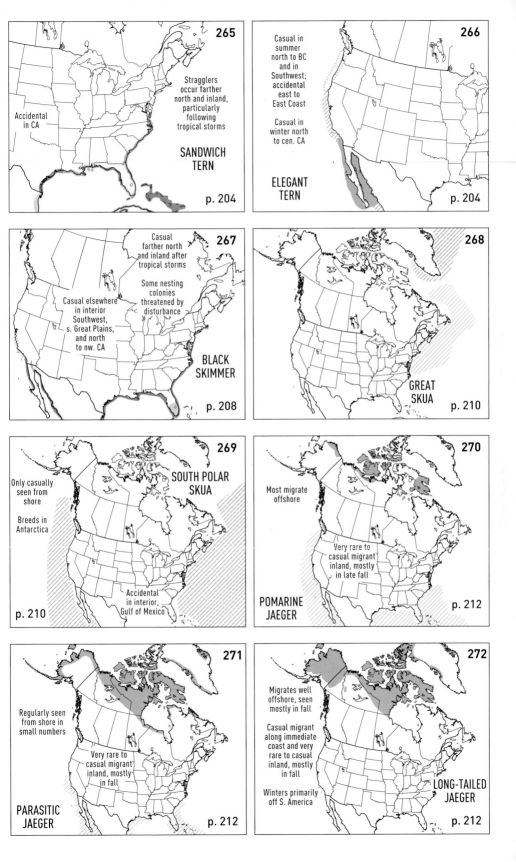

265

Accidental in CA

Stragglers occur farther north and inland, particularly following tropical storms

SANDWICH TERN

p. 204

266

Casual in summer north to BC and in Southwest; accidental east to East Coast

Casual in winter north to cen. CA

ELEGANT TERN

p. 204

267

Casual farther north and inland after tropical storms

Some nesting colonies threatened by disturbance

Casual elsewhere in interior Southwest, s. Great Plains, and north to nw. CA

BLACK SKIMMER

p. 208

268

GREAT SKUA

p. 210

269

Only casually seen from shore

Breeds in Antarctica

SOUTH POLAR SKUA

Accidental in interior, Gulf of Mexico

p. 210

270

Most migrate offshore

Very rare to casual migrant inland, mostly in late fall

POMARINE JAEGER

p. 212

271

Regularly seen from shore in small numbers

Very rare to casual migrant inland, mostly in fall

PARASITIC JAEGER

p. 212

272

Migrates well offshore, seen mostly in fall

Casual migrant along immediate coast and very rare to casual inland, mostly in fall

Winters primarily off S. America

LONG-TAILED JAEGER

p. 212

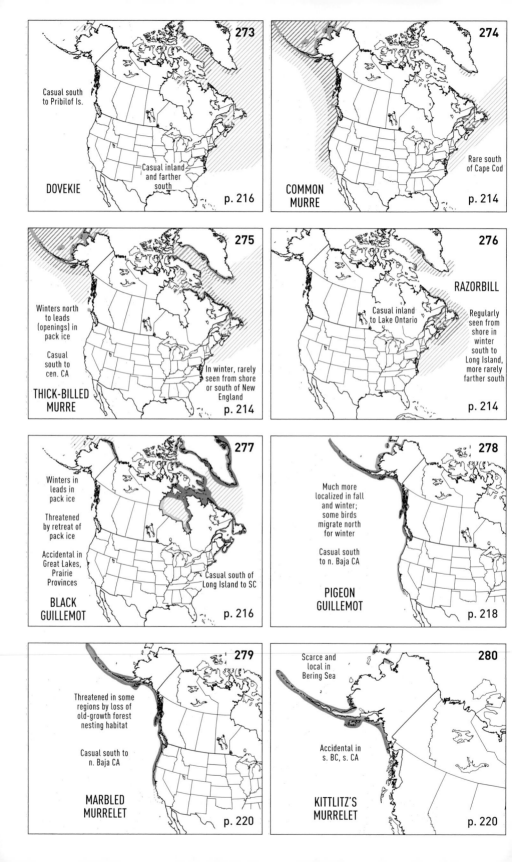

273

Casual south
to Pribilof Is.

Casual inland
and farther
south

DOVEKIE
p. 216

274

Rare south
of Cape Cod

COMMON
MURRE
p. 214

275

Winters north
to leads
(openings) in
pack ice

Casual
south to
cen. CA

In winter, rarely
seen from shore
or south of New
England

THICK-BILLED
MURRE
p. 214

276

RAZORBILL

Casual inland
to Lake Ontario

Regularly
seen from
shore in
winter
south to
Long Island,
more rarely
farther south

p. 214

277

Winters in
leads in
pack ice

Threatened
by retreat of
pack ice

Accidental in
Great Lakes,
Prairie
Provinces

Casual south of
Long Island to SC

BLACK
GUILLEMOT
p. 216

278

Much more
localized in fall
and winter;
some birds
migrate north
for winter

Casual south
to n. Baja CA

PIGEON
GUILLEMOT
p. 218

279

Threatened in some
regions by loss of
old-growth forest
nesting habitat

Casual south to
n. Baja CA

MARBLED
MURRELET
p. 220

280

Scarce and
local in
Bering Sea

Accidental in
s. BC, s. CA

KITTLITZ'S
MURRELET
p. 220

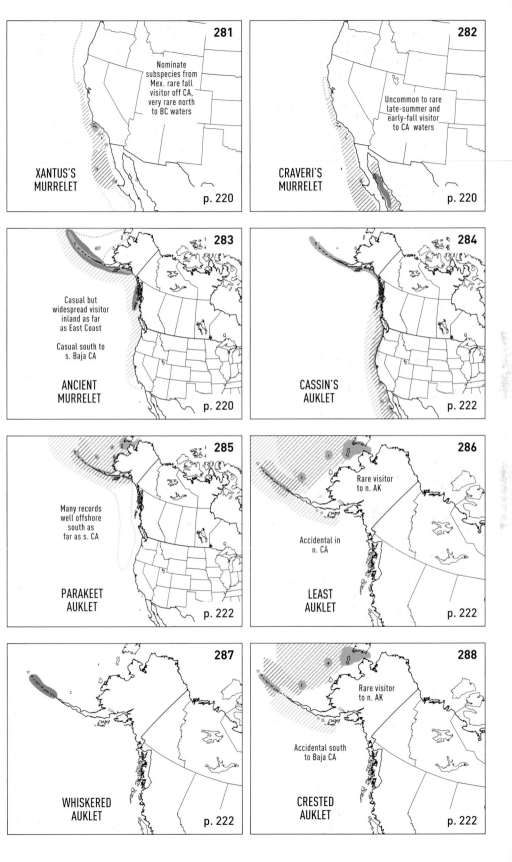

281

Nominate subspecies from Mex. rare fall visitor off CA, very rare north to BC waters

XANTUS'S
MURRELET

p. 220

282

Uncommon to rare late-summer and early-fall visitor to CA waters

CRAVERI'S
MURRELET

p. 220

283

Casual but widespread visitor inland as far as East Coast

Casual south to s. Baja CA

ANCIENT
MURRELET

p. 220

284

CASSIN'S
AUKLET

p. 222

285

Many records well offshore south as far as s. CA

PARAKEET
AUKLET

p. 222

286

Rare visitor to n. AK

Accidental in n. CA

LEAST
AUKLET

p. 222

287

WHISKERED
AUKLET

p. 222

288

Rare visitor to n. AK

Accidental south to Baja CA

CRESTED
AUKLET

p. 222

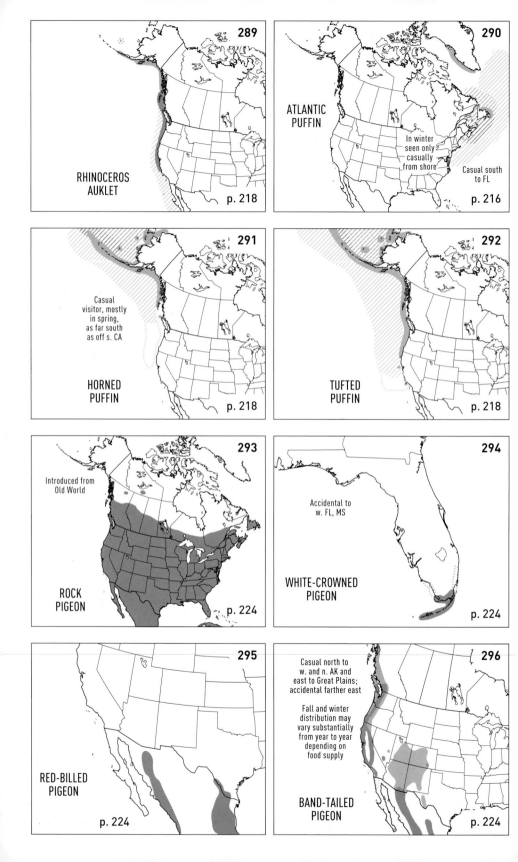

289
RHINOCEROS
AUKLET
p. 218

290
ATLANTIC
PUFFIN
In winter
seen only
casually
from shore
Casual south
to FL
p. 216

291
Casual
visitor, mostly
in spring,
as far south
as off s. CA
HORNED
PUFFIN
p. 218

292
TUFTED
PUFFIN
p. 218

293
Introduced from
Old World
ROCK
PIGEON
p. 224

294
Accidental to
w. FL, MS
WHITE-CROWNED
PIGEON
p. 224

295
RED-BILLED
PIGEON
p. 224

296
Casual north to
w. and n. AK and
east to Great Plains;
accidental farther east

Fall and winter
distribution may
vary substantially
from year to year
depending on
food supply

BAND-TAILED
PIGEON
p. 224

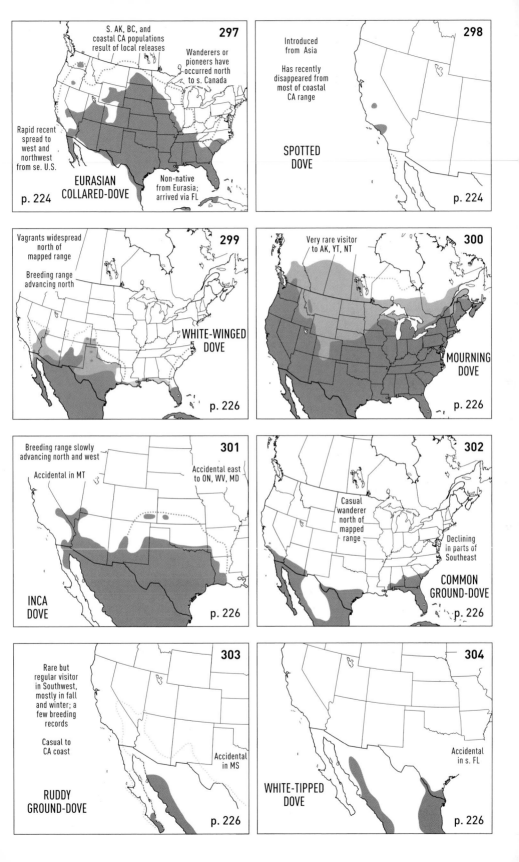

297
S. AK, BC, and coastal CA populations result of local releases

Wanderers or pioneers have occurred north to s. Canada

Rapid recent spread to west and northwest from se. U.S.

EURASIAN COLLARED-DOVE

Non-native from Eurasia; arrived via FL

p. 224

298
Introduced from Asia

Has recently disappeared from most of coastal CA range

SPOTTED DOVE

p. 224

299
Vagrants widespread north of mapped range

Breeding range advancing north

WHITE-WINGED DOVE

p. 226

300
Very rare visitor to AK, YT, NT

MOURNING DOVE

p. 226

301
Breeding range slowly advancing north and west

Accidental in MT

Accidental east to ON, WV, MD

INCA DOVE

p. 226

302
Casual wanderer north of mapped range

Declining in parts of Southeast

COMMON GROUND-DOVE

p. 226

303
Rare but regular visitor in Southwest, mostly in fall and winter; a few breeding records

Casual to CA coast

Accidental in MS

RUDDY GROUND-DOVE

p. 226

304
Accidental in s. FL

WHITE-TIPPED DOVE

p. 226

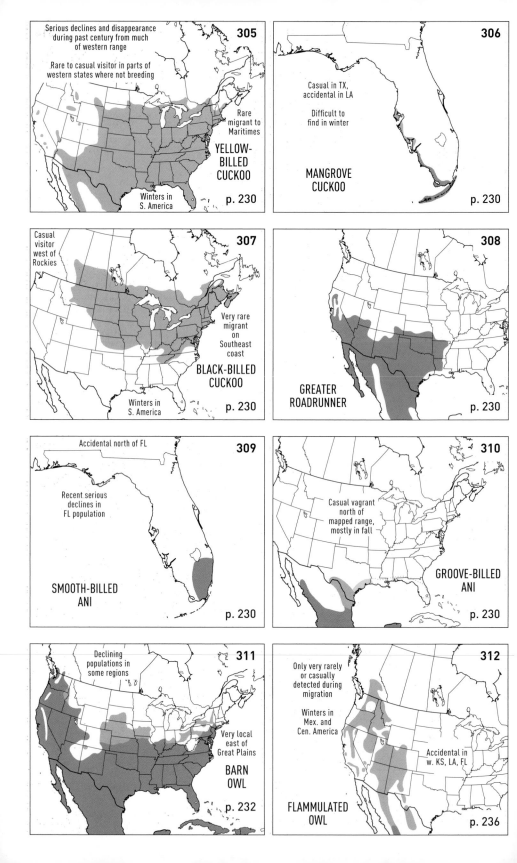

305 Serious declines and disappearance during past century from much of western range

Rare to casual visitor in parts of western states where not breeding

Rare migrant to Maritimes

YELLOW-BILLED CUCKOO

Winters in S. America

p. 230

306 Casual in TX, accidental in LA

Difficult to find in winter

MANGROVE CUCKOO

p. 230

307 Casual visitor west of Rockies

Very rare migrant on Southeast coast

BLACK-BILLED CUCKOO

Winters in S. America

p. 230

308 **GREATER ROADRUNNER**

p. 230

309 Accidental north of FL

Recent serious declines in FL population

SMOOTH-BILLED ANI

p. 230

310 Casual vagrant north of mapped range, mostly in fall

GROOVE-BILLED ANI

p. 230

311 Declining populations in some regions

Very local east of Great Plains

BARN OWL

p. 232

312 Only very rarely or casually detected during migration

Winters in Mex. and Cen. America

Accidental in w. KS, LA, FL

FLAMMULATED OWL

p. 236

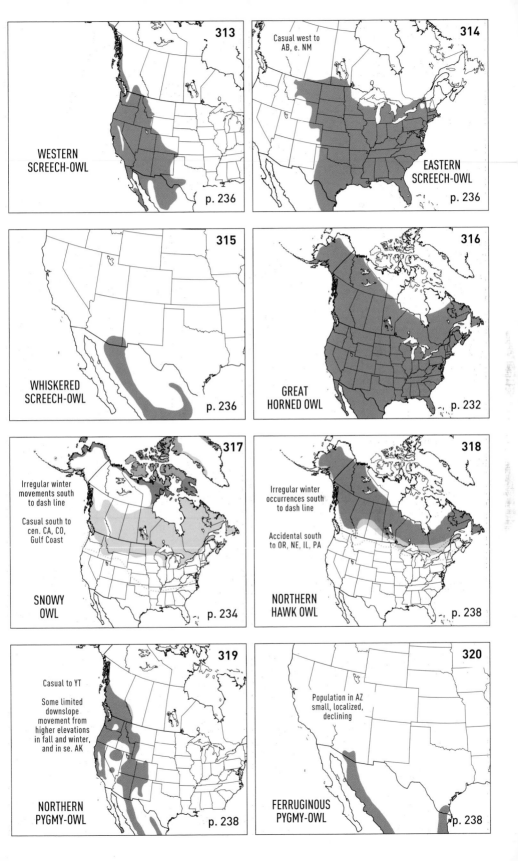

313

WESTERN
SCREECH-OWL

p. 236

314

Casual west to
AB, e. NM

EASTERN
SCREECH-OWL

p. 236

315

WHISKERED
SCREECH-OWL

p. 236

316

GREAT
HORNED OWL

p. 232

317

Irregular winter
movements south
to dash line

Casual south to
cen. CA, CO,
Gulf Coast

SNOWY
OWL

p. 234

318

Irregular winter
occurrences south
to dash line

Accidental south
to OR, NE, IL, PA

NORTHERN
HAWK OWL

p. 238

319

Casual to YT

Some limited
downslope
movement from
higher elevations
in fall and winter,
and in se. AK

NORTHERN
PYGMY-OWL

p. 238

320

Population in AZ
small, localized,
declining

FERRUGINOUS
PYGMY-OWL

p. 238

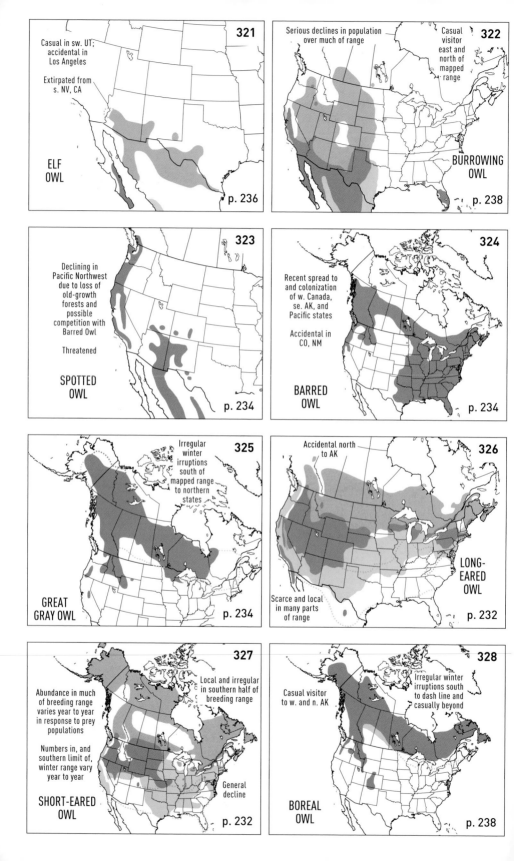

321 ELF OWL — p. 236

Casual in sw. UT; accidental in Los Angeles

Extirpated from s. NV, CA

322 BURROWING OWL — p. 238

Serious declines in population over much of range

Casual visitor east and north of mapped range

323 SPOTTED OWL — p. 234

Declining in Pacific Northwest due to loss of old-growth forests and possible competition with Barred Owl

Threatened

324 BARRED OWL — p. 234

Recent spread to and colonization of w. Canada, se. AK, and Pacific states

Accidental in CO, NM

325 GREAT GRAY OWL — p. 234

Irregular winter irruptions south of mapped range to northern states

326 LONG-EARED OWL — p. 232

Accidental north to AK

Scarce and local in many parts of range

327 SHORT-EARED OWL — p. 232

Abundance in much of breeding range varies year to year in response to prey populations

Numbers in, and southern limit of, winter range vary year to year

Local and irregular in southern half of breeding range

General decline

328 BOREAL OWL — p. 238

Casual visitor to w. and n. AK

Irregular winter irruptions south to dash line and casually beyond

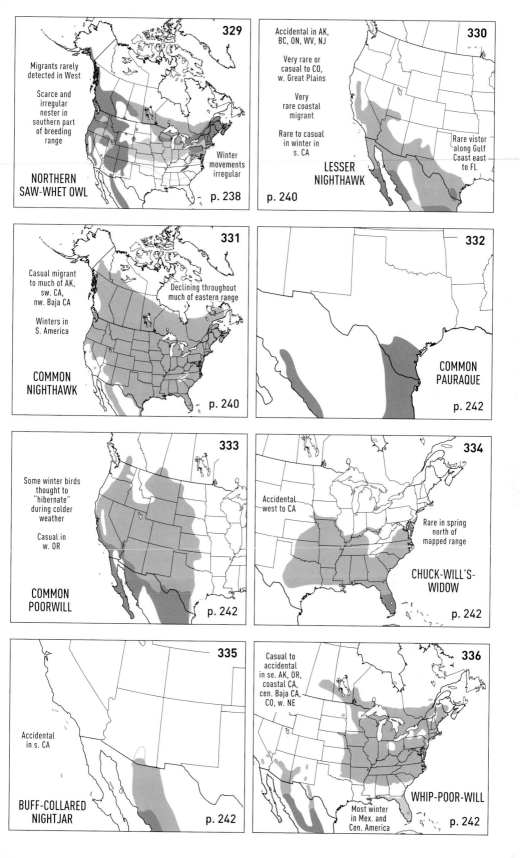

329

Migrants rarely detected in West

Scarce and irregular nester in southern part of breeding range

Winter movements irregular

NORTHERN SAW-WHET OWL

p. 238

330

Accidental in AK, BC, ON, WV, NJ

Very rare or casual to CO, w. Great Plains

Very rare coastal migrant

Rare to casual in winter in s. CA

Rare vistor along Gulf Coast east to FL

LESSER NIGHTHAWK

p. 240

331

Casual migrant to much of AK, sw. CA, nw. Baja CA

Winters in S. America

Declining throughout much of eastern range

COMMON NIGHTHAWK

p. 240

332

COMMON PAURAQUE

p. 242

333

Some winter birds thought to "hibernate" during colder weather

Casual in w. OR

COMMON POORWILL

p. 242

334

Accidental west to CA

Rare in spring north of mapped range

CHUCK-WILL'S-WIDOW

p. 242

335

Accidental in s. CA

BUFF-COLLARED NIGHTJAR

p. 242

336

Casual to accidental in se. AK, OR, coastal CA, cen. Baja CA, CO, w. NE

Most winter in Mex. and Cen. America

WHIP-POOR-WILL

p. 242

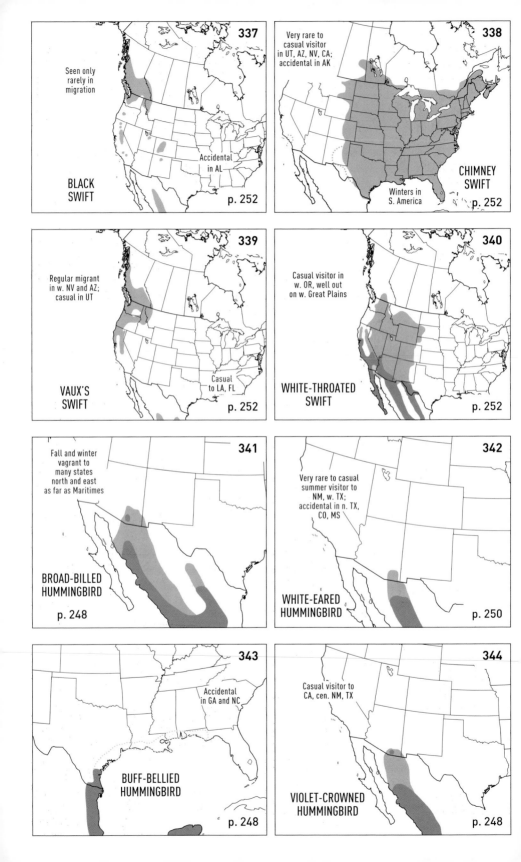

337

Seen only rarely in migration

Accidental in AL

BLACK SWIFT

p. 252

338

Very rare to casual visitor in UT, AZ, NV, CA; accidental in AK

Winters in S. America

CHIMNEY SWIFT

p. 252

339

Regular migrant in w. NV and AZ; casual in UT

Casual to LA, FL

VAUX'S SWIFT

p. 252

340

Casual visitor in w. OR, well out on w. Great Plains

WHITE-THROATED SWIFT

p. 252

341

Fall and winter vagrant to many states north and east as far as Maritimes

BROAD-BILLED HUMMINGBIRD

p. 248

342

Very rare to casual summer visitor to NM, w. TX; accidental in n. TX, CO, MS

WHITE-EARED HUMMINGBIRD

p. 250

343

Accidental in GA and NC

BUFF-BELLIED HUMMINGBIRD

p. 248

344

Casual visitor to CA, cen. NM, TX

VIOLET-CROWNED HUMMINGBIRD

p. 248

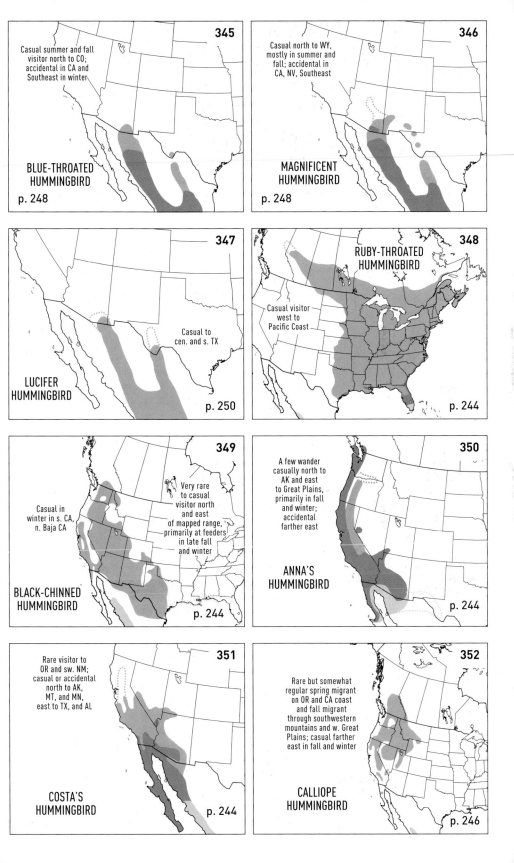

345

Casual summer and fall visitor north to CO; accidental in CA and Southeast in winter

BLUE-THROATED HUMMINGBIRD
p. 248

346

Casual north to WY, mostly in summer and fall; accidental in CA, NV, Southeast

MAGNIFICENT HUMMINGBIRD
p. 248

347

Casual to cen. and s. TX

LUCIFER HUMMINGBIRD
p. 250

348

RUBY-THROATED HUMMINGBIRD

Casual visitor west to Pacific Coast

p. 244

349

Very rare to casual visitor north and east of mapped range, primarily at feeders in late fall and winter

Casual in winter in s. CA, n. Baja CA

BLACK-CHINNED HUMMINGBIRD
p. 244

350

A few wander casually north to AK and east to Great Plains, primarily in fall and winter; accidental farther east

ANNA'S HUMMINGBIRD
p. 244

351

Rare visitor to OR and sw. NM; casual or accidental north to AK, MT, and MN, east to TX, and AL

COSTA'S HUMMINGBIRD
p. 244

352

Rare but somewhat regular spring migrant on OR and CA coast and fall migrant through southwestern mountains and w. Great Plains; casual farther east in fall and winter

CALLIOPE HUMMINGBIRD
p. 246

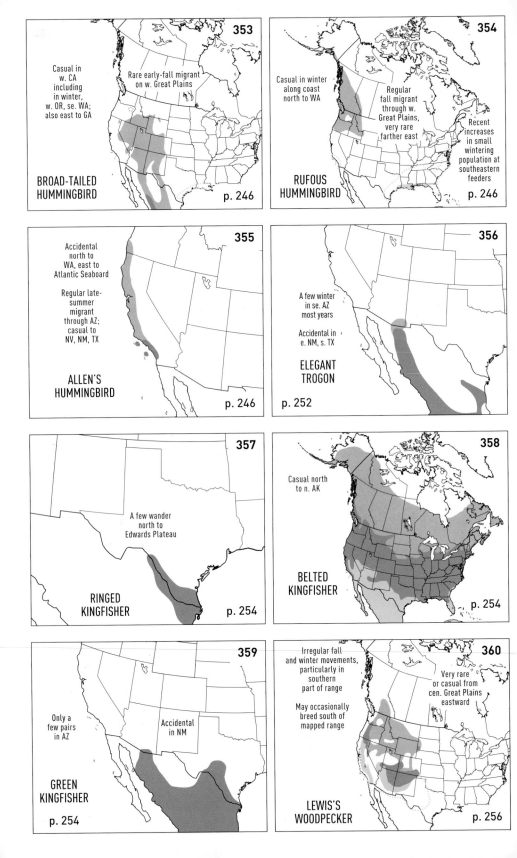

353

Casual in w. CA including in winter, w. OR, se. WA; also east to GA

Rare early-fall migrant on w. Great Plains

BROAD-TAILED HUMMINGBIRD

p. 246

354

Casual in winter along coast north to WA

Regular fall migrant through w. Great Plains, very rare farther east

Recent increases in small wintering population at southeastern feeders

RUFOUS HUMMINGBIRD

p. 246

355

Accidental north to WA, east to Atlantic Seaboard

Regular late-summer migrant through AZ; casual to NV, NM, TX

ALLEN'S HUMMINGBIRD

p. 246

356

A few winter in se. AZ most years

Accidental in e. NM, s. TX

ELEGANT TROGON

p. 252

357

A few wander north to Edwards Plateau

RINGED KINGFISHER

p. 254

358

Casual north to n. AK

BELTED KINGFISHER

p. 254

359

Only a few pairs in AZ

Accidental in NM

GREEN KINGFISHER

p. 254

360

Irregular fall and winter movements, particularly in southern part of range

May occasionally breed south of mapped range

Very rare or casual from cen. Great Plains eastward

LEWIS'S WOODPECKER

p. 256

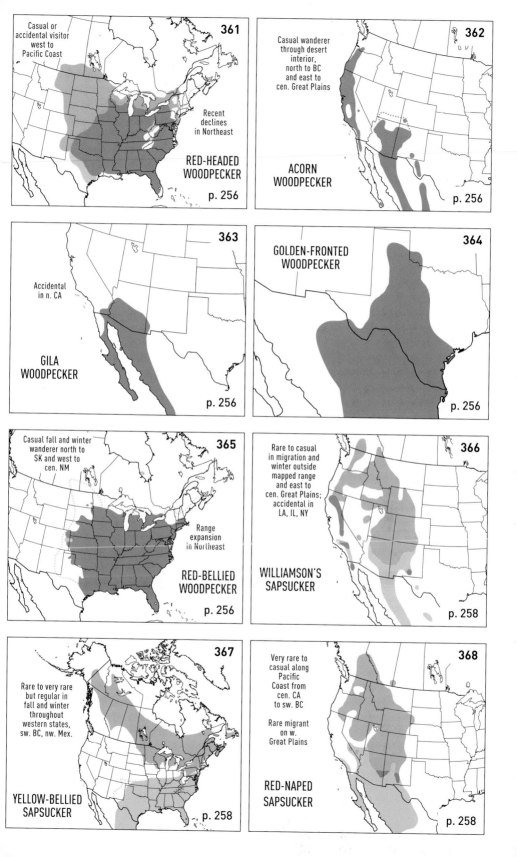

361

Casual or accidental visitor west to Pacific Coast

Recent declines in Northeast

RED-HEADED WOODPECKER

p. 256

362

Casual wanderer through desert interior, north to BC and east to cen. Great Plains

ACORN WOODPECKER

p. 256

363

Accidental in n. CA

GILA WOODPECKER

p. 256

364

GOLDEN-FRONTED WOODPECKER

p. 256

365

Casual fall and winter wanderer north to SK and west to cen. NM

Range expansion in Northeast

RED-BELLIED WOODPECKER

p. 256

366

Rare to casual in migration and winter outside mapped range and east to cen. Great Plains; accidental in LA, IL, NY

WILLIAMSON'S SAPSUCKER

p. 258

367

Rare to very rare but regular in fall and winter throughout western states, sw. BC, nw. Mex.

YELLOW-BELLIED SAPSUCKER

p. 258

368

Very rare to casual along Pacific Coast from cen. CA to sw. BC

Rare migrant on w. Great Plains

RED-NAPED SAPSUCKER

p. 258

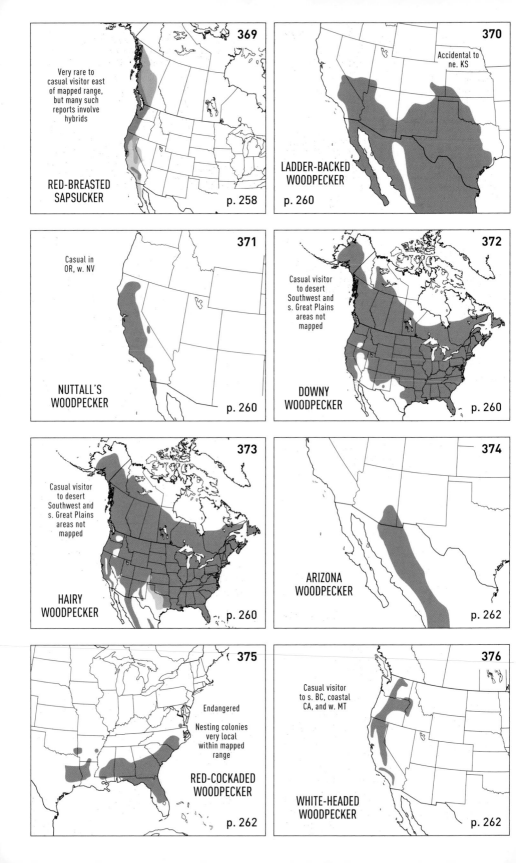

369

Very rare to
casual visitor east
of mapped range,
but many such
reports involve
hybrids

RED-BREASTED
SAPSUCKER

p. 258

370

Accidental to
ne. KS

LADDER-BACKED
WOODPECKER

p. 260

371

Casual in
OR, w. NV

NUTTALL'S
WOODPECKER

p. 260

372

Casual visitor
to desert
Southwest and
s. Great Plains
areas not
mapped

DOWNY
WOODPECKER

p. 260

373

Casual visitor
to desert
Southwest and
s. Great Plains
areas not
mapped

HAIRY
WOODPECKER

p. 260

374

ARIZONA
WOODPECKER

p. 262

375

Endangered

Nesting colonies
very local
within mapped
range

RED-COCKADED
WOODPECKER

p. 262

376

Casual visitor
to s. BC, coastal
CA, and w. MT

WHITE-HEADED
WOODPECKER

p. 262

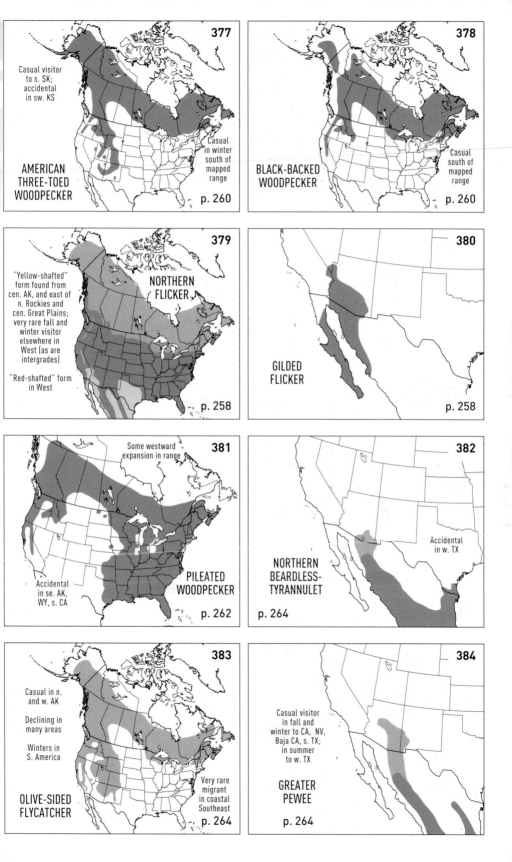

377

Casual visitor to s. SK; accidental in sw. KS

Casual in winter south of mapped range

AMERICAN THREE-TOED WOODPECKER

p. 260

378

Casual south of mapped range

BLACK-BACKED WOODPECKER

p. 260

379

"Yellow-shafted" form found from cen. AK, and east of n. Rockies and cen. Great Plains; very rare fall and winter visitor elsewhere in West (as are intergrades)

"Red-shafted" form in West

NORTHERN FLICKER

p. 258

380

GILDED FLICKER

p. 258

381

Some westward expansion in range

Accidental in se. AK, WY, s. CA

PILEATED WOODPECKER

p. 262

382

Accidental in w. TX

NORTHERN BEARDLESS-TYRANNULET

p. 264

383

Casual in n. and w. AK

Declining in many areas

Winters in S. America

Very rare migrant in coastal Southeast

OLIVE-SIDED FLYCATCHER

p. 264

384

Casual visitor in fall and winter to CA, NV, Baja CA, s. TX; in summer to w. TX

GREATER PEWEE

p. 264

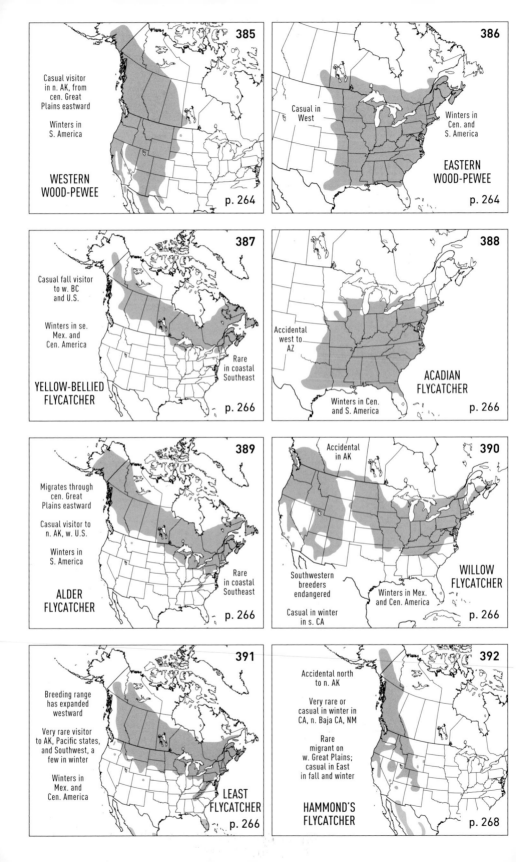

385

Casual visitor in n. AK, from cen. Great Plains eastward

Winters in S. America

WESTERN WOOD-PEWEE

p. 264

386

Casual in West

Winters in Cen. and S. America

EASTERN WOOD-PEWEE

p. 264

387

Casual fall visitor to w. BC and U.S.

Winters in se. Mex. and Cen. America

Rare in coastal Southeast

YELLOW-BELLIED FLYCATCHER

p. 266

388

Accidental west to AZ

Winters in Cen. and S. America

ACADIAN FLYCATCHER

p. 266

389

Migrates through cen. Great Plains eastward

Casual visitor to n. AK, w. U.S.

Winters in S. America

Rare in coastal Southeast

ALDER FLYCATCHER

p. 266

390

Accidental in AK

Southwestern breeders endangered

Casual in winter in s. CA

Winters in Mex. and Cen. America

WILLOW FLYCATCHER

p. 266

391

Breeding range has expanded westward

Very rare visitor to AK, Pacific states, and Southwest, a few in winter

Winters in Mex. and Cen. America

LEAST FLYCATCHER

p. 266

392

Accidental north to n. AK

Very rare or casual in winter in CA, n. Baja CA, NM

Rare migrant on w. Great Plains; casual in East in fall and winter

HAMMOND'S FLYCATCHER

p. 268

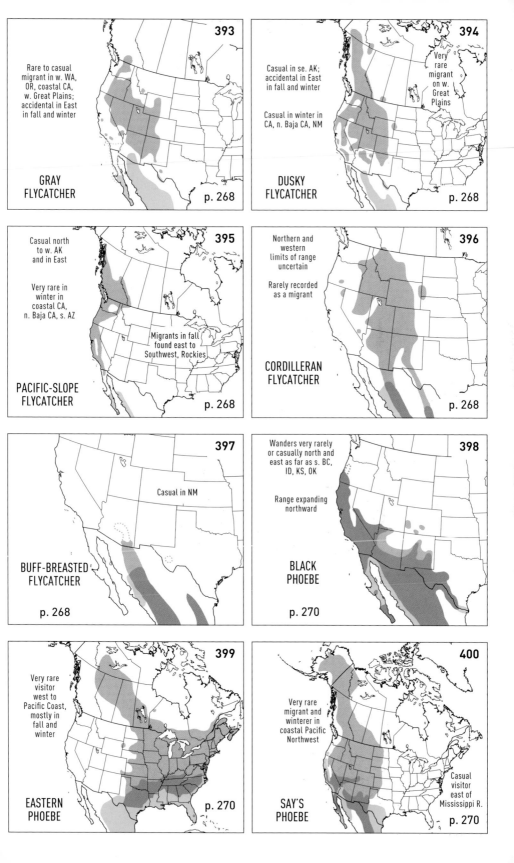

393

Rare to casual migrant in w. WA, OR, coastal CA, w. Great Plains; accidental in East in fall and winter

GRAY FLYCATCHER

p. 268

394

Casual in se. AK; accidental in East in fall and winter

Casual in winter in CA, n. Baja CA, NM

Very rare migrant on w. Great Plains

DUSKY FLYCATCHER

p. 268

395

Casual north to w. AK and in East

Very rare in winter in coastal CA, n. Baja CA, s. AZ

Migrants in fall found east to Southwest, Rockies

PACIFIC-SLOPE FLYCATCHER

p. 268

396

Northern and western limits of range uncertain

Rarely recorded as a migrant

CORDILLERAN FLYCATCHER

p. 268

397

Casual in NM

BUFF-BREASTED FLYCATCHER

p. 268

398

Wanders very rarely or casually north and east as far as s. BC, ID, KS, OK

Range expanding northward

BLACK PHOEBE

p. 270

399

Very rare visitor west to Pacific Coast, mostly in fall and winter

EASTERN PHOEBE

p. 270

400

Very rare migrant and winterer in coastal Pacific Northwest

Casual visitor east of Mississippi R.

SAY'S PHOEBE

p. 270

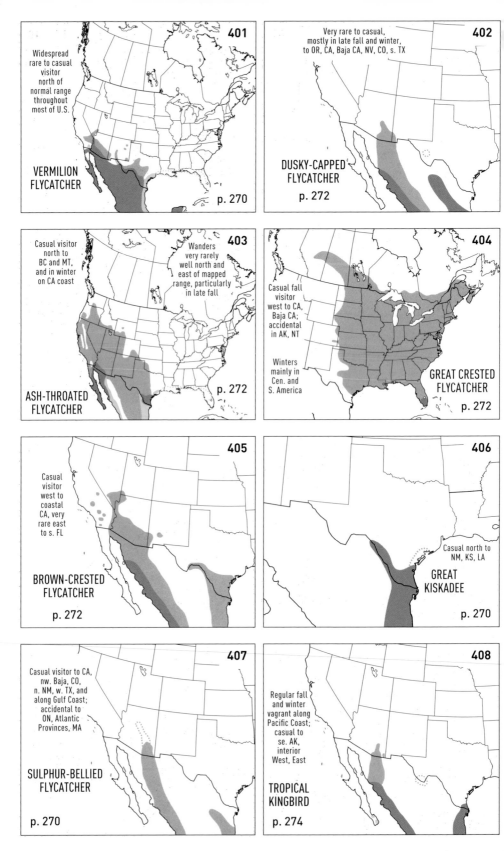

401

Widespread rare to casual visitor north of normal range throughout most of U.S.

VERMILION FLYCATCHER

p. 270

402

Very rare to casual, mostly in late fall and winter, to OR, CA, Baja CA, NV, CO, s. TX

DUSKY-CAPPED FLYCATCHER

p. 272

403

Casual visitor north to BC and MT, and in winter on CA coast

Wanders very rarely well north and east of mapped range, particularly in late fall

ASH-THROATED FLYCATCHER

p. 272

404

Casual fall visitor west to CA, Baja CA; accidental in AK, NT

Winters mainly in Cen. and S. America

GREAT CRESTED FLYCATCHER

p. 272

405

Casual visitor west to coastal CA, very rare east to s. FL

BROWN-CRESTED FLYCATCHER

p. 272

406

Casual north to NM, KS, LA

GREAT KISKADEE

p. 270

407

Casual visitor to CA, nw. Baja, CO, n. NM, w. TX, and along Gulf Coast; accidental to ON, Atlantic Provinces, MA

SULPHUR-BELLIED FLYCATCHER

p. 270

408

Regular fall and winter vagrant along Pacific Coast; casual to se. AK, interior West, East

TROPICAL KINGBIRD

p. 274

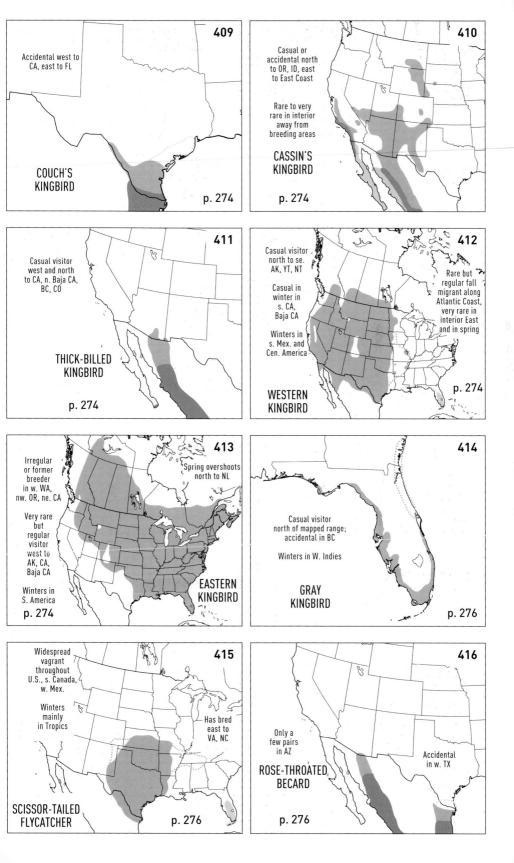

409

Accidental west to CA, east to FL

COUCH'S KINGBIRD

p. 274

410

Casual or accidental north to OR, ID, east to East Coast

Rare to very rare in interior away from breeding areas

CASSIN'S KINGBIRD

p. 274

411

Casual visitor west and north to CA, n. Baja CA, BC, CO

THICK-BILLED KINGBIRD

p. 274

412

Casual visitor north to se. AK, YT, NT

Casual in winter in s. CA, Baja CA

Winters in s. Mex. and Cen. America

Rare but regular fall migrant along Atlantic Coast, very rare in interior East and in spring

WESTERN KINGBIRD

p. 274

413

Irregular or former breeder in w. WA, nw. OR, ne. CA

Very rare but regular visitor west to AK, CA, Baja CA

Winters in S. America

Spring overshoots north to NL

EASTERN KINGBIRD

p. 274

414

Casual visitor north of mapped range; accidental in BC

Winters in W. Indies

GRAY KINGBIRD

p. 276

415

Widespread vagrant throughout U.S., s. Canada, w. Mex.

Winters mainly in Tropics

Has bred east to VA, NC

SCISSOR-TAILED FLYCATCHER

p. 276

416

Only a few pairs in AZ

Accidental in w. TX

ROSE-THROATED BECARD

p. 276

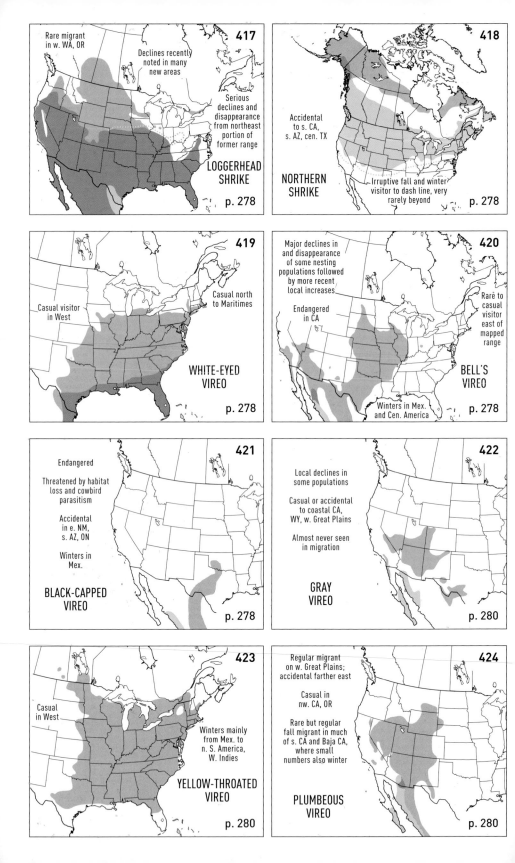

417
Rare migrant in w. WA, OR
Declines recently noted in many new areas
Serious declines and disappearance from northeast portion of former range
LOGGERHEAD SHRIKE
p. 278

418
Accidental to s. CA, s. AZ, cen. TX
Irruptive fall and winter visitor to dash line, very rarely beyond
NORTHERN SHRIKE
p. 278

419
Casual visitor in West
Casual north to Maritimes
WHITE-EYED VIREO
p. 278

420
Major declines in and disappearance of some nesting populations followed by more recent local increases
Endangered in CA
Rare to casual visitor east of mapped range
Winters in Mex. and Cen. America
BELL'S VIREO
p. 278

421
Endangered
Threatened by habitat loss and cowbird parasitism
Accidental in e. NM, s. AZ, ON
Winters in Mex.
BLACK-CAPPED VIREO
p. 278

422
Local declines in some populations
Casual or accidental to coastal CA, WY, w. Great Plains
Almost never seen in migration
GRAY VIREO
p. 280

423
Casual in West
Winters mainly from Mex. to n. S. America, W. Indies
YELLOW-THROATED VIREO
p. 280

424
Regular migrant on w. Great Plains; accidental farther east
Casual in nw. CA, OR
Rare but regular fall migrant in much of s. CA and Baja CA, where small numbers also winter
PLUMBEOUS VIREO
p. 280

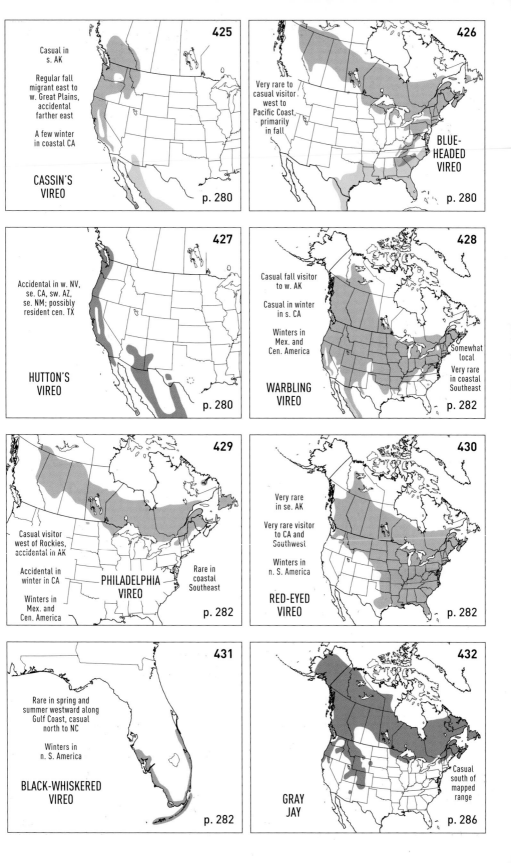

425

Casual in
s. AK

Regular fall
migrant east to
w. Great Plains,
accidental
farther east

A few winter
in coastal CA

CASSIN'S
VIREO

p. 280

426

Very rare to
casual visitor
west to
Pacific Coast,
primarily
in fall

BLUE-
HEADED
VIREO

p. 280

427

Accidental in w. NV,
se. CA, sw. AZ,
se. NM; possibly
resident cen. TX

HUTTON'S
VIREO

p. 280

428

Casual fall visitor
to w. AK

Casual in winter
in s. CA

Winters in
Mex. and
Cen. America

Somewhat
local

Very rare
in coastal
Southeast

WARBLING
VIREO

p. 282

429

Casual visitor
west of Rockies,
accidental in AK

Accidental in
winter in CA

Winters in
Mex. and
Cen. America

PHILADELPHIA
VIREO

Rare in
coastal
Southeast

p. 282

430

Very rare
in se. AK

Very rare visitor
to CA and
Southwest

Winters in
n. S. America

RED-EYED
VIREO

p. 282

431

Rare in spring and
summer westward along
Gulf Coast, casual
north to NC

Winters in
n. S. America

BLACK-WHISKERED
VIREO

p. 282

432

Casual
south of
mapped
range

GRAY
JAY

p. 286

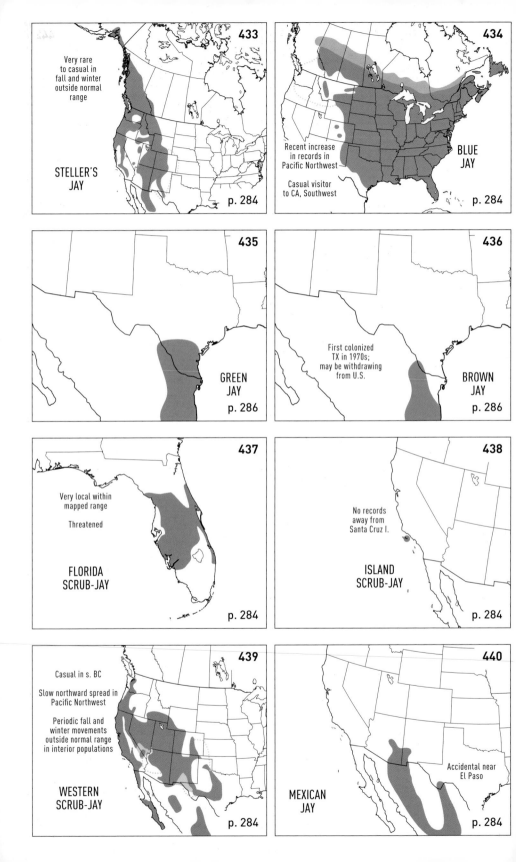

433 STELLER'S JAY — Very rare to casual in fall and winter outside normal range — p. 284

434 BLUE JAY — Recent increase in records in Pacific Northwest — Casual visitor to CA, Southwest — p. 284

435 GREEN JAY — p. 286

436 BROWN JAY — First colonized TX in 1970s; may be withdrawing from U.S. — p. 286

437 FLORIDA SCRUB-JAY — Very local within mapped range — Threatened — p. 284

438 ISLAND SCRUB-JAY — No records away from Santa Cruz I. — p. 284

439 WESTERN SCRUB-JAY — Casual in s. BC — Slow northward spread in Pacific Northwest — Periodic fall and winter movements outside normal range in interior populations — p. 284

440 MEXICAN JAY — Accidental near El Paso — p. 284

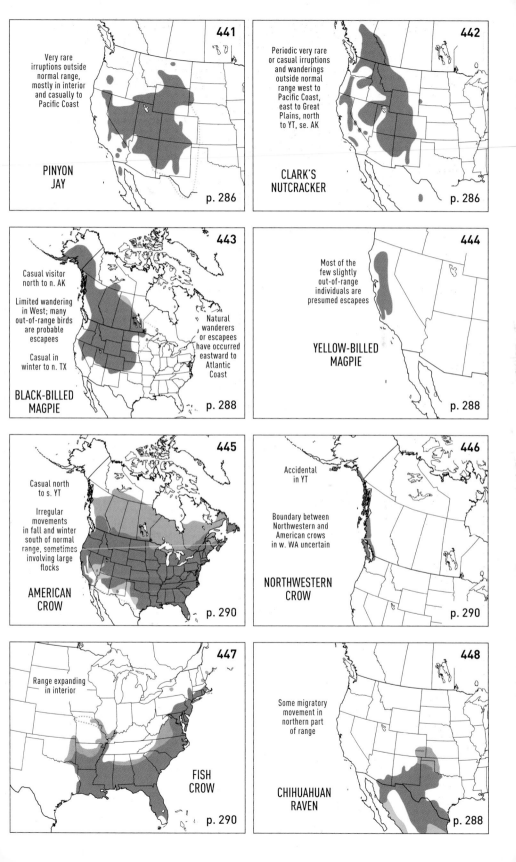

441

Very rare irruptions outside normal range, mostly in interior and casually to Pacific Coast

PINYON JAY

p. 286

442

Periodic very rare or casual irruptions and wanderings outside normal range west to Pacific Coast, east to Great Plains, north to YT, se. AK

CLARK'S NUTCRACKER

p. 286

443

Casual visitor north to n. AK

Limited wandering in West; many out-of-range birds are probable escapees

Casual in winter to n. TX

Natural wanderers or escapees have occurred eastward to Atlantic Coast

BLACK-BILLED MAGPIE

p. 288

444

Most of the few slightly out-of-range individuals are presumed escapees

YELLOW-BILLED MAGPIE

p. 288

445

Casual north to s. YT

Irregular movements in fall and winter south of normal range, sometimes involving large flocks

AMERICAN CROW

p. 290

446

Accidental in YT

Boundary between Northwestern and American crows in w. WA uncertain

NORTHWESTERN CROW

p. 290

447

Range expanding in interior

FISH CROW

p. 290

448

Some migratory movement in northern part of range

CHIHUAHUAN RAVEN

p. 288

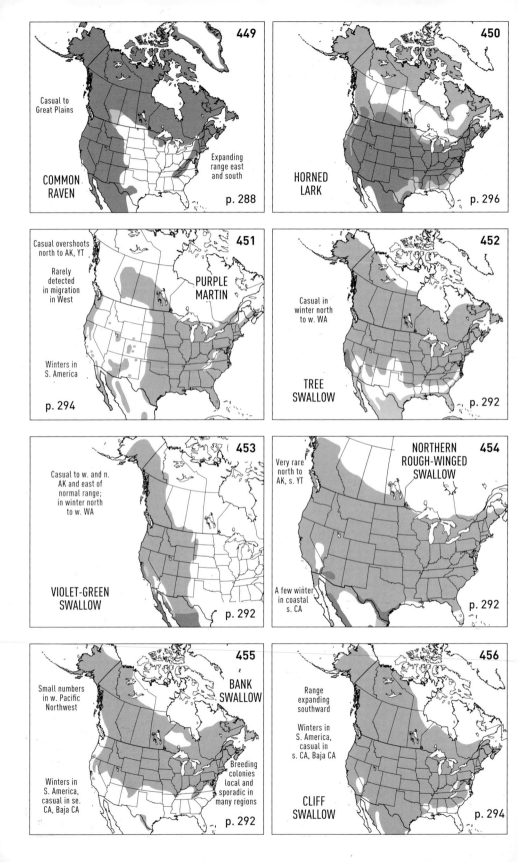

449

Casual to
Great Plains

Expanding
range east
and south

COMMON
RAVEN

p. 288

450

HORNED
LARK

p. 296

451

Casual overshoots
north to AK, YT

Rarely
detected
in migration
in West

PURPLE
MARTIN

Winters in
S. America

p. 294

452

Casual in
winter north
to w. WA

TREE
SWALLOW

p. 292

453

Casual to w. and n.
AK and east of
normal range;
in winter north
to w. WA

VIOLET-GREEN
SWALLOW

p. 292

454

NORTHERN
ROUGH-WINGED
SWALLOW

Very rare
north to
AK, s. YT

A few winter
in coastal
s. CA

p. 292

455

Small numbers
in w. Pacific
Northwest

BANK
SWALLOW

Breeding
colonies
local and
sporadic in
many regions

Winters in
S. America,
casual in se.
CA, Baja CA

p. 292

456

Range
expanding
southward

Winters in
S. America,
casual in
s. CA, Baja CA

CLIFF
SWALLOW

p. 294

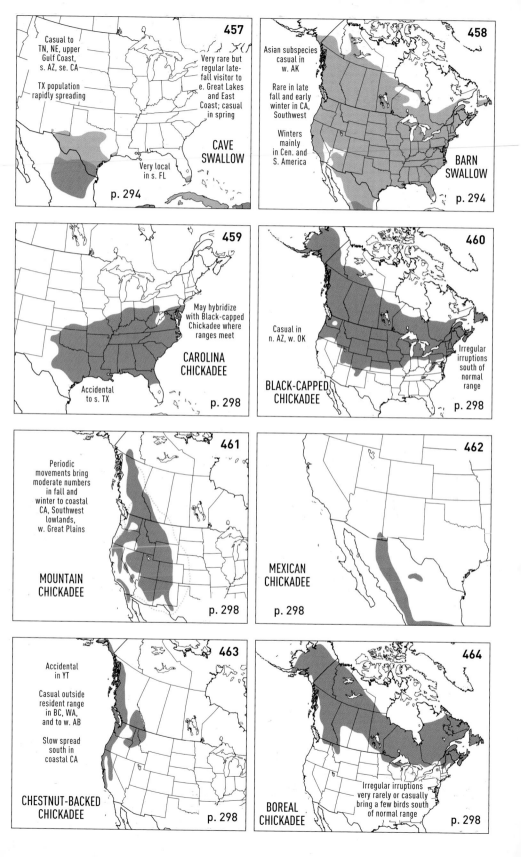

457

Casual to TN, NE, upper Gulf Coast, s. AZ, se. CA

TX population rapidly spreading

Very rare but regular late-fall visitor to e. Great Lakes and East Coast; casual in spring

Very local in s. FL

CAVE SWALLOW

p. 294

458

Asian subspecies casual in w. AK

Rare in late fall and early winter in CA, Southwest

Winters mainly in Cen. and S. America

BARN SWALLOW

p. 294

459

May hybridize with Black-capped Chickadee where ranges meet

Accidental to s. TX

CAROLINA CHICKADEE

p. 298

460

Casual in n. AZ, w. OK

Irregular irruptions south of normal range

BLACK-CAPPED CHICKADEE

p. 298

461

Periodic movements bring moderate numbers in fall and winter to coastal CA, Southwest lowlands, w. Great Plains

MOUNTAIN CHICKADEE

p. 298

462

MEXICAN CHICKADEE

p. 298

463

Accidental in YT

Casual outside resident range in BC, WA, and to w. AB

Slow spread south in coastal CA

CHESTNUT-BACKED CHICKADEE

p. 298

464

Irregular irruptions very rarely or casually bring a few birds south of normal range

BOREAL CHICKADEE

p. 298

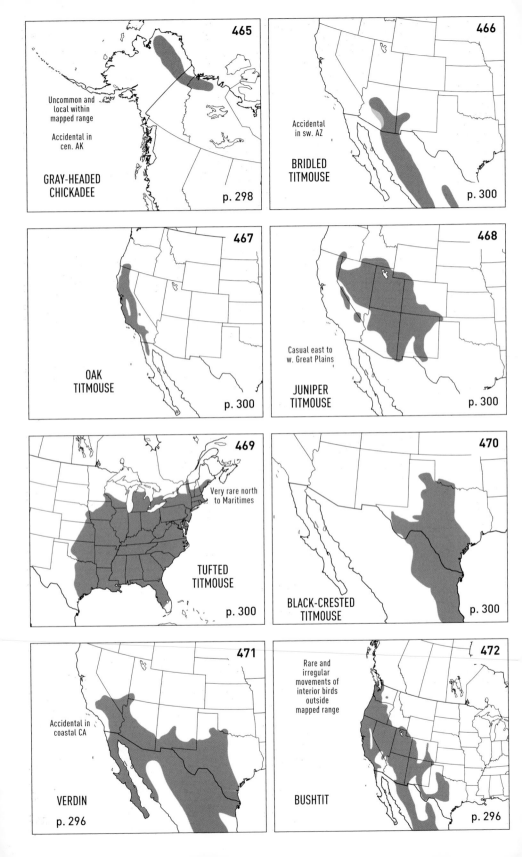

465
Uncommon and
local within
mapped range

Accidental in
cen. AK

GRAY-HEADED
CHICKADEE
p. 298

466
Accidental
in sw. AZ

BRIDLED
TITMOUSE
p. 300

467
OAK
TITMOUSE
p. 300

468
Casual east to
w. Great Plains

JUNIPER
TITMOUSE
p. 300

469
Very rare north
to Maritimes

TUFTED
TITMOUSE
p. 300

470
BLACK-CRESTED
TITMOUSE
p. 300

471
Accidental in
coastal CA

VERDIN
p. 296

472
Rare and
irregular
movements of
interior birds
outside
mapped range

BUSHTIT
p. 296

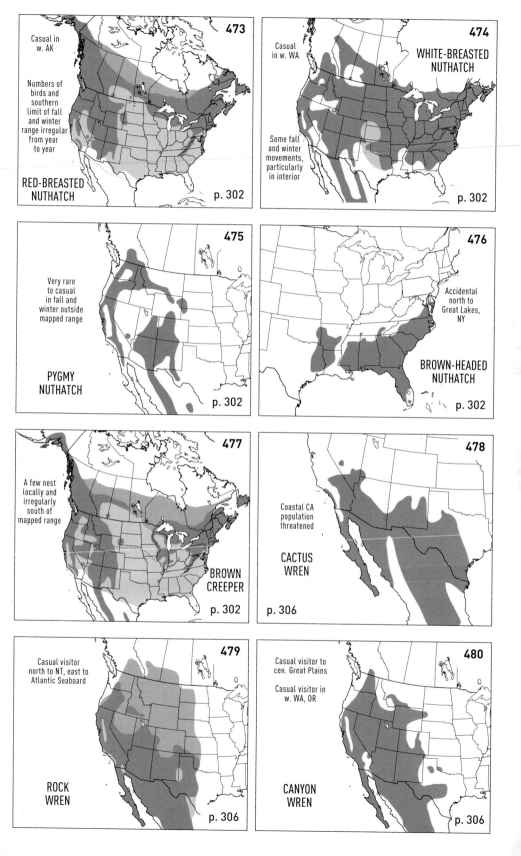

473

Casual in w. AK

Numbers of birds and southern limit of fall and winter range irregular from year to year

RED-BREASTED NUTHATCH

p. 302

474

WHITE-BREASTED NUTHATCH

Casual in w. WA

Some fall and winter movements, particularly in interior

p. 302

475

Very rare to casual in fall and winter outside mapped range

PYGMY NUTHATCH

p. 302

476

Accidental north to Great Lakes, NY

BROWN-HEADED NUTHATCH

p. 302

477

A few nest locally and irregularly south of mapped range

BROWN CREEPER

p. 302

478

Coastal CA population threatened

CACTUS WREN

p. 306

479

Casual visitor north to NT, east to Atlantic Seaboard

ROCK WREN

p. 306

480

Casual visitor to cen. Great Plains

Casual visitor in w. WA, OR

CANYON WREN

p. 306

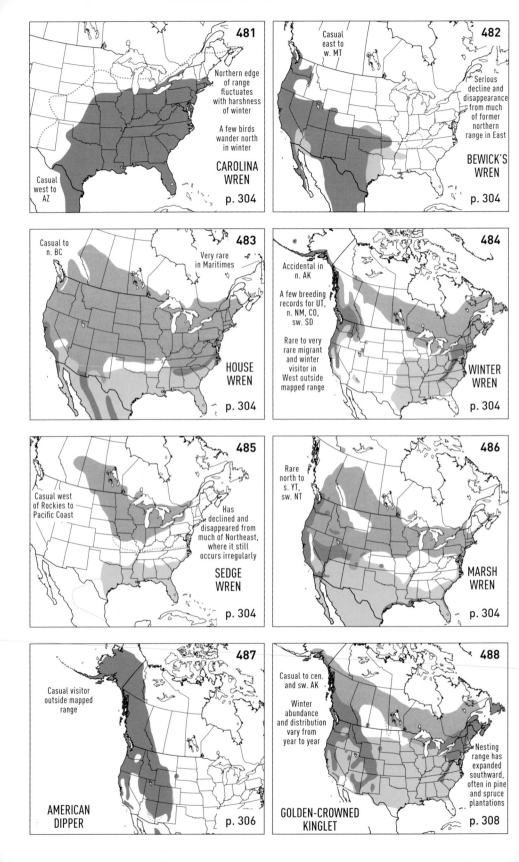

481

Northern edge of range fluctuates with harshness of winter

A few birds wander north in winter

CAROLINA WREN

Casual west to AZ

p. 304

482

Casual east to w. MT

Serious decline and disappearance from much of former northern range in East

BEWICK'S WREN

p. 304

483

Casual to n. BC

Very rare in Maritimes

HOUSE WREN

p. 304

484

Accidental in n. AK

A few breeding records for UT, n. NM, CO, sw. SD

Rare to very rare migrant and winter visitor in West outside mapped range

WINTER WREN

p. 304

485

Casual west of Rockies to Pacific Coast

Has declined and disappeared from much of Northeast, where it still occurs irregularly

SEDGE WREN

p. 304

486

Rare north to s. YT, sw. NT

MARSH WREN

p. 304

487

Casual visitor outside mapped range

AMERICAN DIPPER

p. 306

488

Casual to cen. and sw. AK

Winter abundance and distribution vary from year to year

Nesting range has expanded southward, often in pine and spruce plantations

GOLDEN-CROWNED KINGLET

p. 308

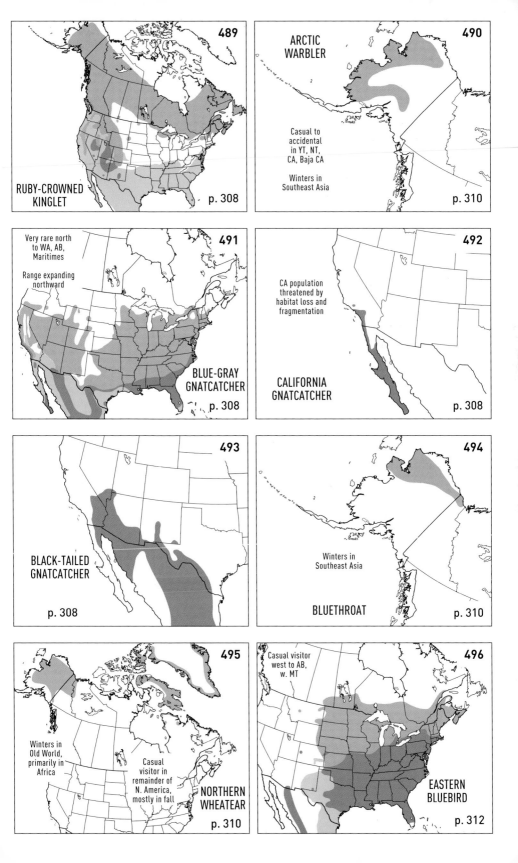

489
RUBY-CROWNED KINGLET
p. 308

490
ARCTIC WARBLER
Casual to accidental in YT, NT, CA, Baja CA
Winters in Southeast Asia
p. 310

491
Very rare north to WA, AB, Maritimes
Range expanding northward
BLUE-GRAY GNATCATCHER
p. 308

492
CA population threatened by habitat loss and fragmentation
CALIFORNIA GNATCATCHER
p. 308

493
BLACK-TAILED GNATCATCHER
p. 308

494
Winters in Southeast Asia
BLUETHROAT
p. 310

495
Winters in Old World, primarily in Africa
Casual visitor in remainder of N. America, mostly in fall
NORTHERN WHEATEAR
p. 310

496
Casual visitor west to AB, w. MT
EASTERN BLUEBIRD
p. 312

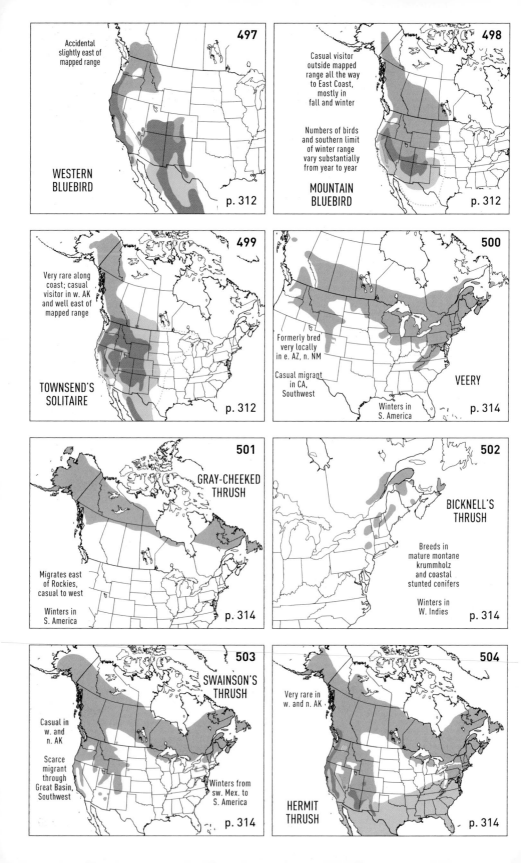

497 — **WESTERN BLUEBIRD** — p. 312
Accidental slightly east of mapped range

498 — **MOUNTAIN BLUEBIRD** — p. 312
Casual visitor outside mapped range all the way to East Coast, mostly in fall and winter

Numbers of birds and southern limit of winter range vary substantially from year to year

499 — **TOWNSEND'S SOLITAIRE** — p. 312
Very rare along coast; casual visitor in w. AK and well east of mapped range

500 — **VEERY** — p. 314
Formerly bred very locally in e. AZ, n. NM

Casual migrant in CA, Southwest

Winters in S. America

501 — **GRAY-CHEEKED THRUSH** — p. 314
Migrates east of Rockies, casual to west

Winters in S. America

502 — **BICKNELL'S THRUSH** — p. 314
Breeds in mature montane krummholz and coastal stunted conifers

Winters in W. Indies

503 — **SWAINSON'S THRUSH** — p. 314
Casual in w. and n. AK

Scarce migrant through Great Basin, Southwest

Winters from sw. Mex. to S. America

504 — **HERMIT THRUSH** — p. 314
Very rare in w. and n. AK

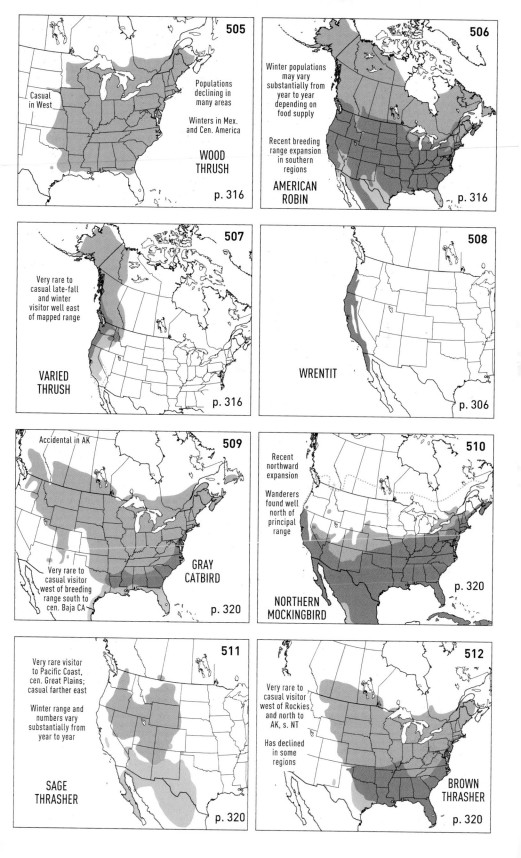

505

Casual in West

Populations declining in many areas

Winters in Mex. and Cen. America

WOOD THRUSH

p. 316

506

Winter populations may vary substantially from year to year depending on food supply

Recent breeding range expansion in southern regions

AMERICAN ROBIN

p. 316

507

Very rare to casual late-fall and winter visitor well east of mapped range

VARIED THRUSH

p. 316

508

WRENTIT

p. 306

509

Accidental in AK

Very rare to casual visitor west of breeding range south to cen. Baja CA

GRAY CATBIRD

p. 320

510

Recent northward expansion

Wanderers found well north of principal range

NORTHERN MOCKINGBIRD

p. 320

511

Very rare visitor to Pacific Coast, cen. Great Plains; casual farther east

Winter range and numbers vary substantially from year to year

SAGE THRASHER

p. 320

512

Very rare to casual visitor west of Rockies and north to AK, s. NT

Has declined in some regions

BROWN THRASHER

p. 320

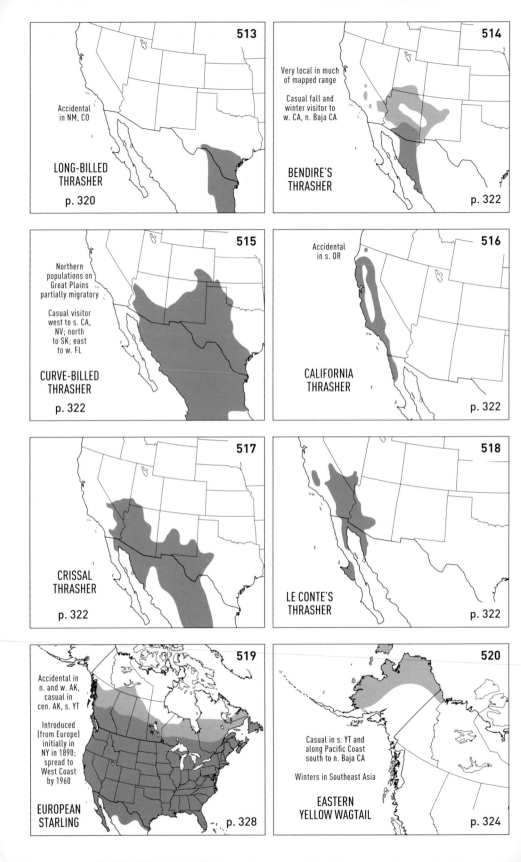

513

Accidental in NM, CO

LONG-BILLED THRASHER

p. 320

514

Very local in much of mapped range

Casual fall and winter visitor to w. CA, n. Baja CA

BENDIRE'S THRASHER

p. 322

515

Northern populations on Great Plains partially migratory

Casual visitor west to s. CA, NV; north to SK; east to w. FL

CURVE-BILLED THRASHER

p. 322

516

Accidental in s. OR

CALIFORNIA THRASHER

p. 322

517

CRISSAL THRASHER

p. 322

518

LE CONTE'S THRASHER

p. 322

519

Accidental in n. and w. AK, casual in cen. AK, s. YT

Introduced (from Europe) initially in NY in 1890; spread to West Coast by 1960

EUROPEAN STARLING

p. 328

520

Casual in s. YT and along Pacific Coast south to n. Baja CA

Winters in Southeast Asia

EASTERN YELLOW WAGTAIL

p. 324

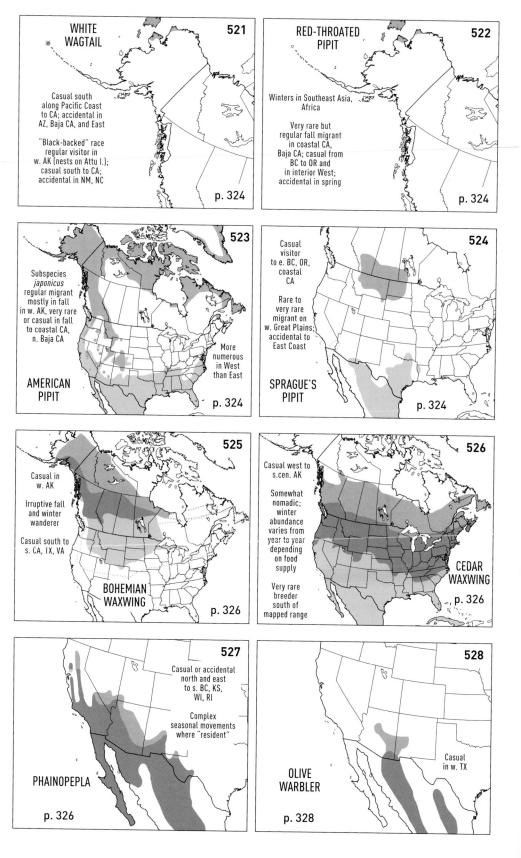

WHITE WAGTAIL — 521

Casual south along Pacific Coast to CA; accidental in AZ, Baja CA, and East

"Black-backed" race regular visitor in w. AK (nests on Attu I.); casual south to CA; accidental in NM, NC

p. 324

RED-THROATED PIPIT — 522

Winters in Southeast Asia, Africa

Very rare but regular fall migrant in coastal CA, Baja CA; casual from BC to OR and in interior West; accidental in spring

p. 324

AMERICAN PIPIT — 523

Subspecies *japonicus* regular migrant mostly in fall in w. AK, very rare or casual in fall to coastal CA, n. Baja CA

More numerous in West than East

p. 324

SPRAGUE'S PIPIT — 524

Casual visitor to e. BC, OR, coastal CA

Rare to very rare migrant on w. Great Plains; accidental to East Coast

p. 324

BOHEMIAN WAXWING — 525

Casual in w. AK

Irruptive fall and winter wanderer

Casual south to s. CA, TX, VA

p. 326

CEDAR WAXWING — 526

Casual west to s.cen. AK

Somewhat nomadic; winter abundance varies from year to year depending on food supply

Very rare breeder south of mapped range

p. 326

PHAINOPEPLA — 527

Casual or accidental north and east to s. BC, KS, WI, RI

Complex seasonal movements where "resident"

p. 326

OLIVE WARBLER — 528

Casual in w. TX

p. 328

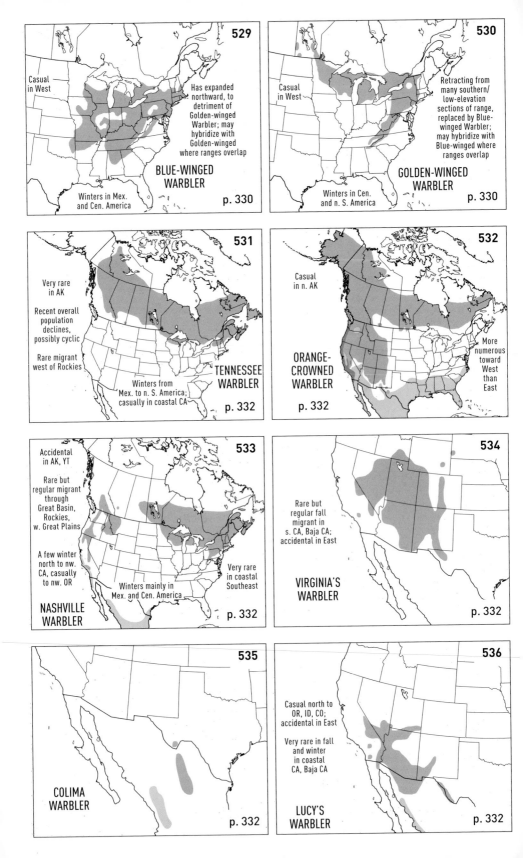

529

Casual in West

Has expanded northward, to detriment of Golden-winged Warbler; may hybridize with Golden-winged where ranges overlap

BLUE-WINGED WARBLER

Winters in Mex. and Cen. America

p. 330

530

Casual in West

Retracting from many southern/ low-elevation sections of range, replaced by Blue-winged Warbler; may hybridize with Blue-winged where ranges overlap

GOLDEN-WINGED WARBLER

Winters in Cen. and n. S. America

p. 330

531

Very rare in AK

Recent overall population declines, possibly cyclic

Rare migrant west of Rockies

Winters from Mex. to n. S. America; casually in coastal CA

TENNESSEE WARBLER

p. 332

532

Casual in n. AK

More numerous toward West than East

ORANGE-CROWNED WARBLER

p. 332

533

Accidental in AK, YT

Rare but regular migrant through Great Basin, Rockies, w. Great Plains

A few winter north to nw. CA, casually to nw. OR

Winters mainly in Mex. and Cen. America

Very rare in coastal Southeast

NASHVILLE WARBLER

p. 332

534

Rare but regular fall migrant in s. CA, Baja CA; accidental in East

VIRGINIA'S WARBLER

p. 332

535

COLIMA WARBLER

536

Casual north to OR, ID, CO; accidental in East

Very rare in fall and winter in coastal CA, Baja CA

LUCY'S WARBLER

p. 332

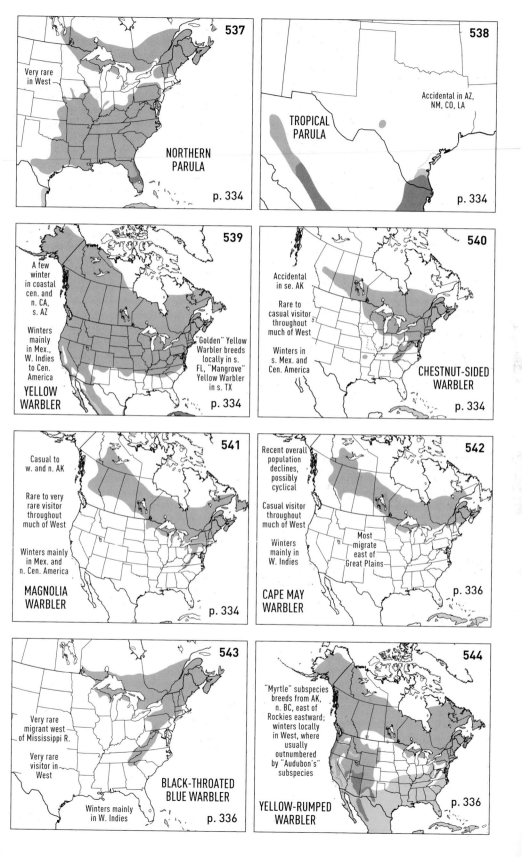

537

Very rare in West

NORTHERN PARULA

p. 334

538

TROPICAL PARULA

Accidental in AZ, NM, CO, LA

p. 334

539

A few winter in coastal cen. and n. CA, s. AZ

Winters mainly in Mex., W. Indies to Cen. America

"Golden" Yellow Warbler breeds locally in s. FL, "Mangrove" Yellow Warbler in s. TX

YELLOW WARBLER

p. 334

540

Accidental in se. AK

Rare to casual visitor throughout much of West

Winters in s. Mex. and Cen. America

CHESTNUT-SIDED WARBLER

p. 334

541

Casual to w. and n. AK

Rare to very rare visitor throughout much of West

Winters mainly in Mex. and n. Cen. America

MAGNOLIA WARBLER

p. 334

542

Recent overall population declines, possibly cyclical

Casual visitor throughout much of West

Winters mainly in W. Indies

Most migrate east of Great Plains

CAPE MAY WARBLER

p. 336

543

Very rare migrant west of Mississippi R.

Very rare visitor in West

BLACK-THROATED BLUE WARBLER

Winters mainly in W. Indies

p. 336

544

"Myrtle" subspecies breeds from AK, n. BC, east of Rockies eastward; winters locally in West, where usually outnumbered by "Audubon's" subspecies

YELLOW-RUMPED WARBLER

p. 336

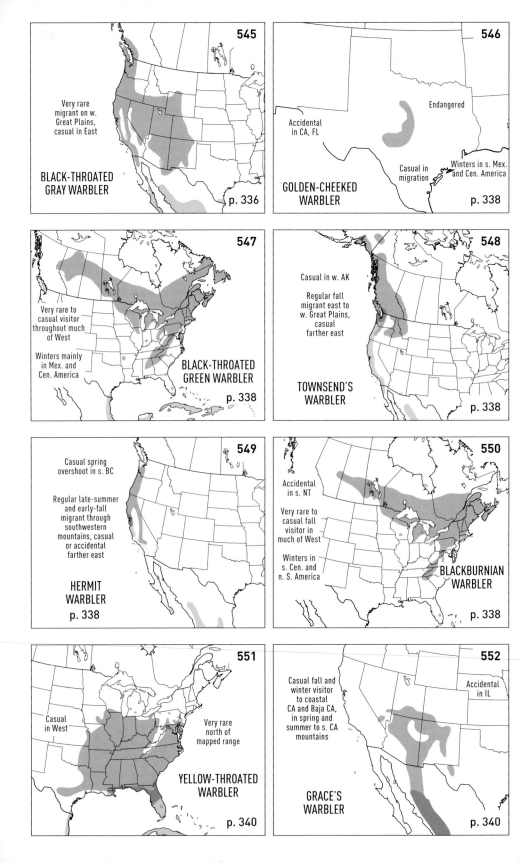

545

Very rare migrant on w. Great Plains, casual in East

BLACK-THROATED GRAY WARBLER

p. 336

546

Endangered

Accidental in CA, FL

Casual in migration

Winters in s. Mex. and Cen. America

GOLDEN-CHEEKED WARBLER

p. 338

547

Very rare to casual visitor throughout much of West

Winters mainly in Mex. and Cen. America

BLACK-THROATED GREEN WARBLER

p. 338

548

Casual in w. AK

Regular fall migrant east to w. Great Plains, casual farther east

TOWNSEND'S WARBLER

p. 338

549

Casual spring overshoot in s. BC

Regular late-summer and early-fall migrant through southwestern mountains, casual or accidental farther east

HERMIT WARBLER

p. 338

550

Accidental in s. NT

Very rare to casual fall visitor in much of West

Winters in s. Cen. and n. S. America

BLACKBURNIAN WARBLER

p. 338

551

Casual in West

Very rare north of mapped range

YELLOW-THROATED WARBLER

p. 340

552

Casual fall and winter visitor to coastal CA and Baja CA, in spring and summer to s. CA mountains

Accidental in IL

GRACE'S WARBLER

p. 340

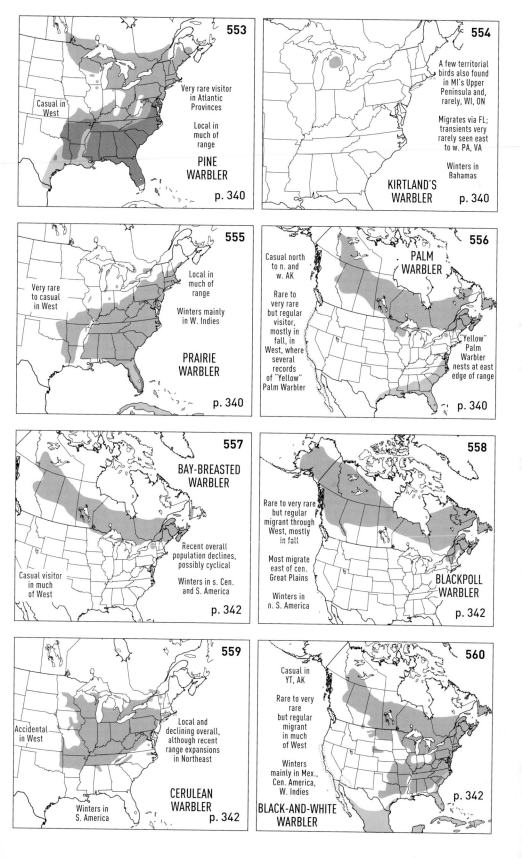

553

Casual in West

Very rare visitor in Atlantic Provinces

Local in much of range

PINE WARBLER

p. 340

554

A few territorial birds also found in MI's Upper Peninsula and, rarely, WI, ON

Migrates via FL; transients very rarely seen east to w. PA, VA

Winters in Bahamas

KIRTLAND'S WARBLER

p. 340

555

Very rare to casual in West

Local in much of range

Winters mainly in W. Indies

PRAIRIE WARBLER

p. 340

556

PALM WARBLER

Casual north to n. and w. AK

Rare to very rare but regular visitor, mostly in fall, in West, where several records of "Yellow" Palm Warbler

"Yellow" Palm Warbler nests at east edge of range

p. 340

557

BAY-BREASTED WARBLER

Recent overall population declines, possibly cyclical

Winters in s. Cen. and S. America

Casual visitor in much of West

p. 342

558

Rare to very rare but regular migrant through West, mostly in fall

Most migrate east of cen. Great Plains

Winters in n. S. America

BLACKPOLL WARBLER

p. 342

559

Accidental in West

Local and declining overall, although recent range expansions in Northeast

CERULEAN WARBLER

Winters in S. America

p. 342

560

Casual in YT, AK

Rare to very rare but regular migrant in much of West

Winters mainly in Mex., Cen. America, W. Indies

BLACK-AND-WHITE WARBLER

p. 342

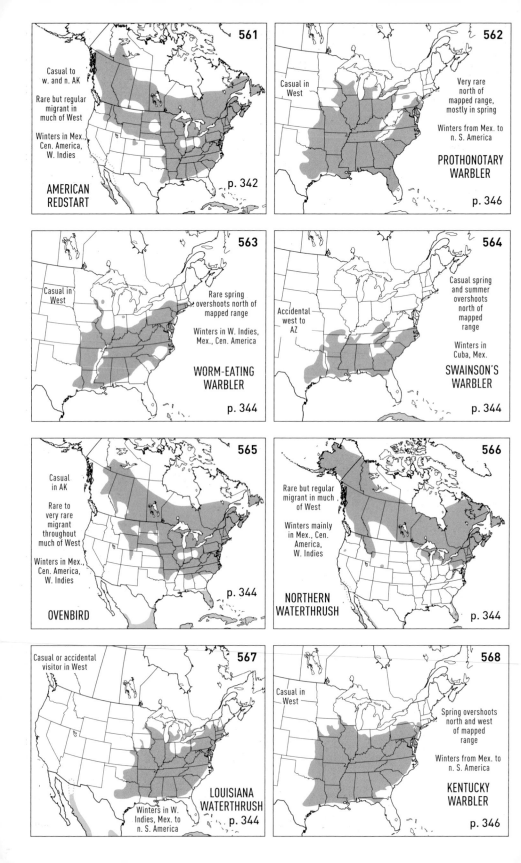

561

Casual to
w. and n. AK

Rare but regular
migrant in
much of West

Winters in Mex.,
Cen. America,
W. Indies

AMERICAN
REDSTART

p. 342

562

Casual in
West

Very rare
north of
mapped range,
mostly in spring

Winters from Mex. to
n. S. America

PROTHONOTARY
WARBLER

p. 346

563

Casual in
West

Rare spring
overshoots north of
mapped range

Winters in W. Indies,
Mex., Cen. America

WORM-EATING
WARBLER

p. 344

564

Accidental
west to
AZ

Casual spring
and summer
overshoots
north of
mapped
range

Winters in
Cuba, Mex.

SWAINSON'S
WARBLER

p. 344

565

Casual
in AK

Rare to
very rare
migrant
throughout
much of West

Winters in Mex.,
Cen. America,
W. Indies

OVENBIRD

p. 344

566

Rare but regular
migrant in much
of West

Winters mainly
in Mex., Cen.
America,
W. Indies

NORTHERN
WATERTHRUSH

p. 344

567

Casual or accidental
visitor in West

LOUISIANA
WATERTHRUSH

Winters in W.
Indies, Mex. to
n. S. America

p. 344

568

Casual in
West

Spring overshoots
north and west
of mapped
range

Winters from Mex. to
n. S. America

KENTUCKY
WARBLER

p. 346

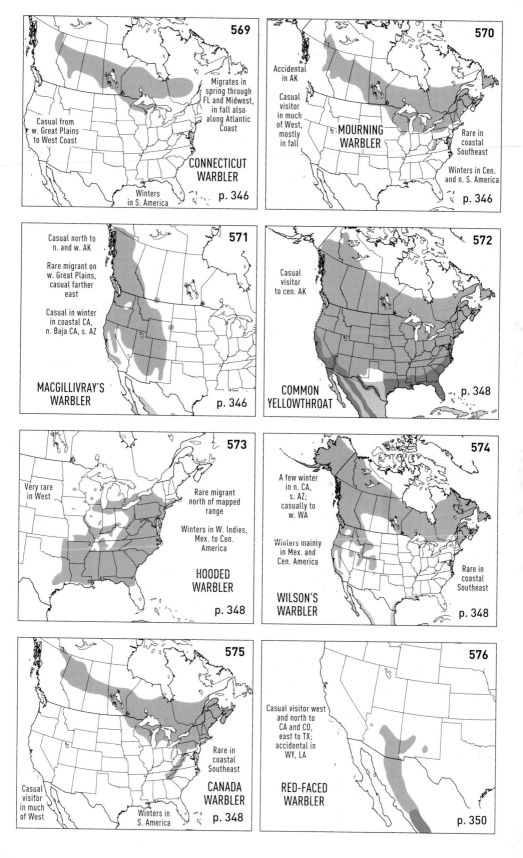

569

Migrates in spring through FL and Midwest, in fall also along Atlantic Coast

Casual from w. Great Plains to West Coast

CONNECTICUT WARBLER

Winters in S. America

p. 346

570

Accidental in AK

Casual visitor in much of West, mostly in fall

MOURNING WARBLER

Rare in coastal Southeast

Winters in Cen. and n. S. America

p. 346

571

Casual north to n. and w. AK

Rare migrant on w. Great Plains, casual farther east

Casual in winter in coastal CA, n. Baja CA, s. AZ

MACGILLIVRAY'S WARBLER

p. 346

572

Casual visitor to cen. AK

COMMON YELLOWTHROAT

p. 348

573

Very rare in West

Rare migrant north of mapped range

Winters in W. Indies, Mex. to Cen. America

HOODED WARBLER

p. 348

574

A few winter in n. CA, s. AZ; casually to w. WA

Winters mainly in Mex. and Cen. America

Rare in coastal Southeast

WILSON'S WARBLER

p. 348

575

Casual visitor in much of West

CANADA WARBLER

Rare in coastal Southeast

Winters in S. America

p. 348

576

Casual visitor west and north to CA and CO, east to TX; accidental in WY, LA

RED-FACED WARBLER

p. 350

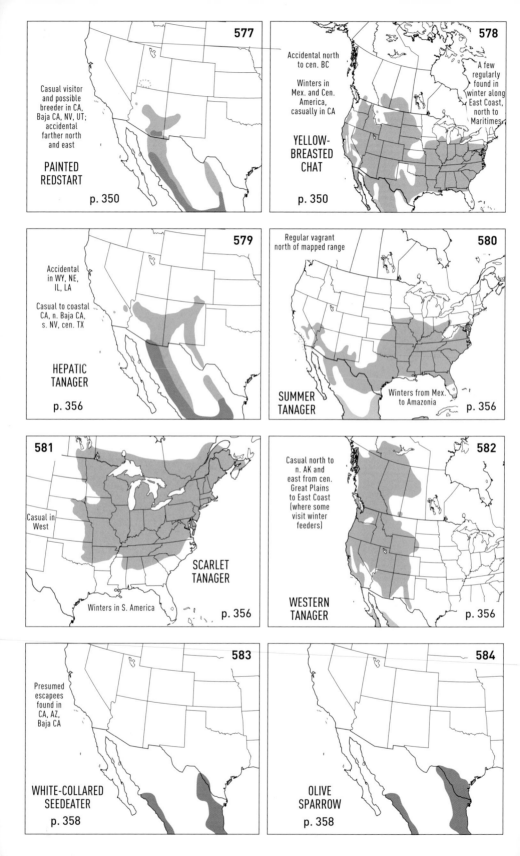

577

Casual visitor and possible breeder in CA, Baja CA, NV, UT; accidental farther north and east

PAINTED REDSTART

p. 350

578

Accidental north to cen. BC

Winters in Mex. and Cen. America, casually in CA

A few regularly found in winter along East Coast, north to Maritimes

YELLOW-BREASTED CHAT

p. 350

579

Accidental in WY, NE, IL, LA

Casual to coastal CA, n. Baja CA, s. NV, cen. TX

HEPATIC TANAGER

p. 356

580

Regular vagrant north of mapped range

Winters from Mex. to Amazonia

SUMMER TANAGER

p. 356

581

Casual in West

SCARLET TANAGER

Winters in S. America

p. 356

582

Casual north to n. AK and east from cen. Great Plains to East Coast (where some visit winter feeders)

WESTERN TANAGER

p. 356

583

Presumed escapees found in CA, AZ, Baja CA

WHITE-COLLARED SEEDEATER

p. 358

584

OLIVE SPARROW

p. 358

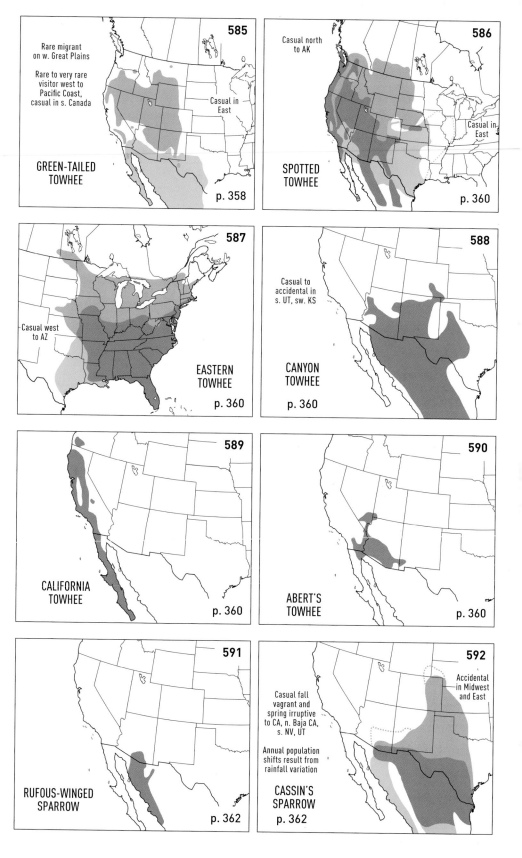

585

Rare migrant on w. Great Plains

Rare to very rare visitor west to Pacific Coast, casual in s. Canada

Casual in East

GREEN-TAILED TOWHEE

p. 358

586

Casual north to AK

Casual in East

SPOTTED TOWHEE

p. 360

587

Casual west to AZ

EASTERN TOWHEE

p. 360

588

Casual to accidental in s. UT, sw. KS

CANYON TOWHEE

p. 360

589

CALIFORNIA TOWHEE

p. 360

590

ABERT'S TOWHEE

p. 360

591

RUFOUS-WINGED SPARROW

p. 362

592

Casual fall vagrant and spring irruptive to CA, n. Baja CA, s. NV, UT

Annual population shifts result from rainfall variation

Accidental in Midwest and East

CASSIN'S SPARROW

p. 362

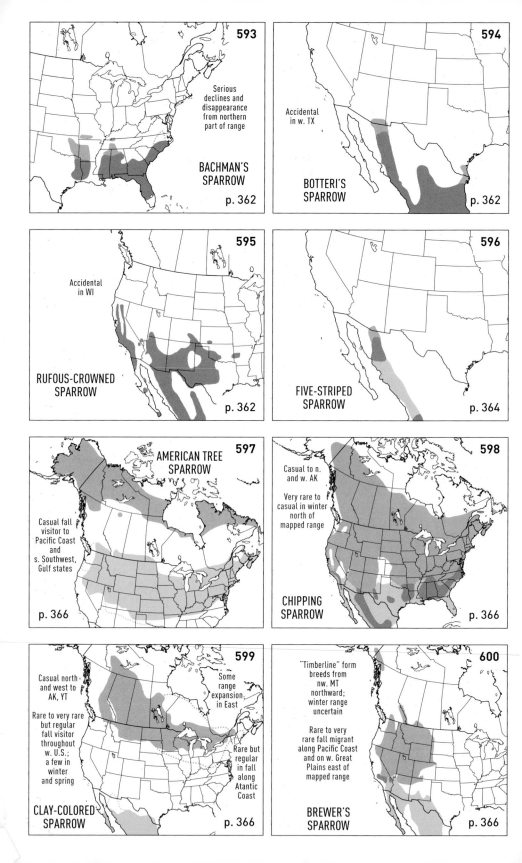

593

Serious declines and disappearance from northern part of range

BACHMAN'S SPARROW
p. 362

594

Accidental in w. TX

BOTTERI'S SPARROW
p. 362

595

Accidental in WI

RUFOUS-CROWNED SPARROW
p. 362

596

FIVE-STRIPED SPARROW
p. 364

597

AMERICAN TREE SPARROW

Casual fall visitor to Pacific Coast and s. Southwest, Gulf states

p. 366

598

Casual to n. and w. AK

Very rare to casual in winter north of mapped range

CHIPPING SPARROW
p. 366

599

Casual north and west to AK, YT

Rare to very rare but regular fall visitor throughout w. U.S.; a few in winter and spring

Some range expansion in East

Rare but regular in fall along Atlantic Coast

CLAY-COLORED SPARROW
p. 366

600

"Timberline" form breeds from nw. MT northward; winter range uncertain

Rare to very rare fall migrant along Pacific Coast and on w. Great Plains east of mapped range

BREWER'S SPARROW
p. 366

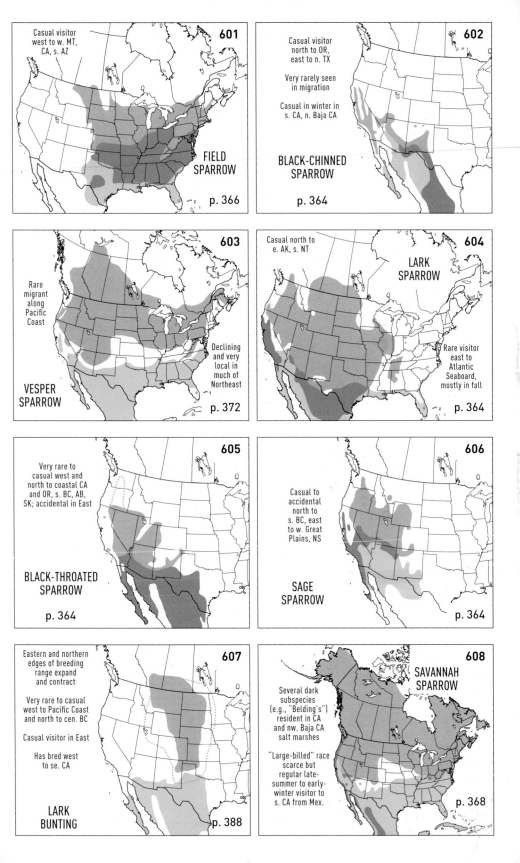

601

Casual visitor west to w. MT, CA, s. AZ

FIELD SPARROW

p. 366

602

Casual visitor north to OR, east to n. TX

Very rarely seen in migration

Casual in winter in s. CA, n. Baja CA

BLACK-CHINNED SPARROW

p. 364

603

Rare migrant along Pacific Coast

Declining and very local in much of Northeast

VESPER SPARROW

p. 372

604

Casual north to e. AK, s. NT

LARK SPARROW

Rare visitor east to Atlantic Seaboard, mostly in fall

p. 364

605

Very rare to casual west and north to coastal CA and OR, s. BC, AB, SK; accidental in East

BLACK-THROATED SPARROW

p. 364

606

Casual to accidental north to s. BC, east to w. Great Plains, NS

SAGE SPARROW

p. 364

607

Eastern and northern edges of breeding range expand and contract

Very rare to casual west to Pacific Coast and north to cen. BC

Casual visitor in East

Has bred west to se. CA

LARK BUNTING

p. 388

608

SAVANNAH SPARROW

Several dark subspecies (e.g., "Belding's") resident in CA and nw. Baja CA salt marshes

"Large-billed" race scarce but regular late-summer to early-winter visitor to s. CA from Mex.

p. 368

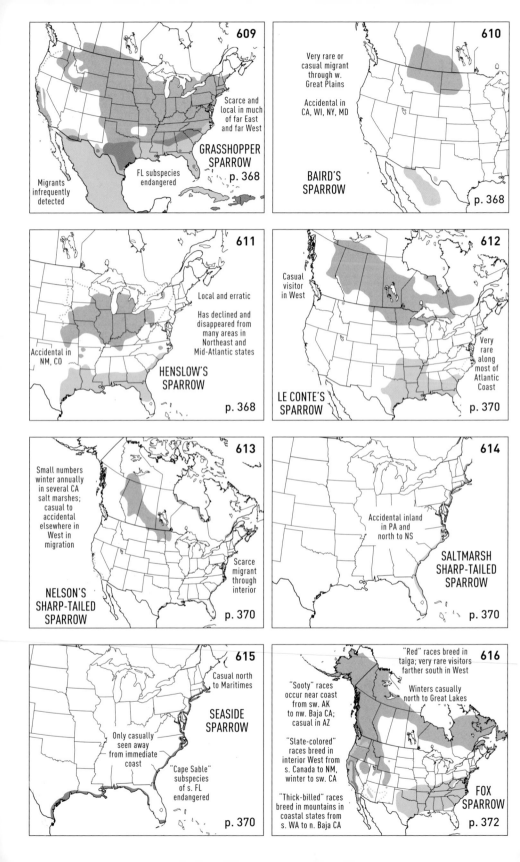

609

Scarce and local in much of far East and far West

Migrants infrequently detected

FL subspecies endangered

GRASSHOPPER SPARROW p. 368

610

Very rare or casual migrant through w. Great Plains

Accidental in CA, WI, NY, MD

BAIRD'S SPARROW p. 368

611

Local and erratic

Has declined and disappeared from many areas in Northeast and Mid-Atlantic states

Accidental in NM, CO

HENSLOW'S SPARROW p. 368

612

Casual visitor in West

Very rare along most of Atlantic Coast

LE CONTE'S SPARROW p. 370

613

Small numbers winter annually in several CA salt marshes; casual to accidental elsewhere in West in migration

Scarce migrant through interior

NELSON'S SHARP-TAILED SPARROW p. 370

614

Accidental inland in PA and north to NS

SALTMARSH SHARP-TAILED SPARROW p. 370

615

Casual north to Maritimes

Only casually seen away from immediate coast

"Cape Sable" subspecies of s. FL endangered

SEASIDE SPARROW p. 370

616

"Red" races breed in taiga; very rare visitors farther south in West

Winters casually north to Great Lakes

"Sooty" races occur near coast from sw. AK to nw. Baja CA; casual in AZ

"Slate-colored" races breed in interior West from s. Canada to NM, winter to sw. CA

"Thick-billed" races breed in mountains in coastal states from s. WA to n. Baja CA

FOX SPARROW p. 372

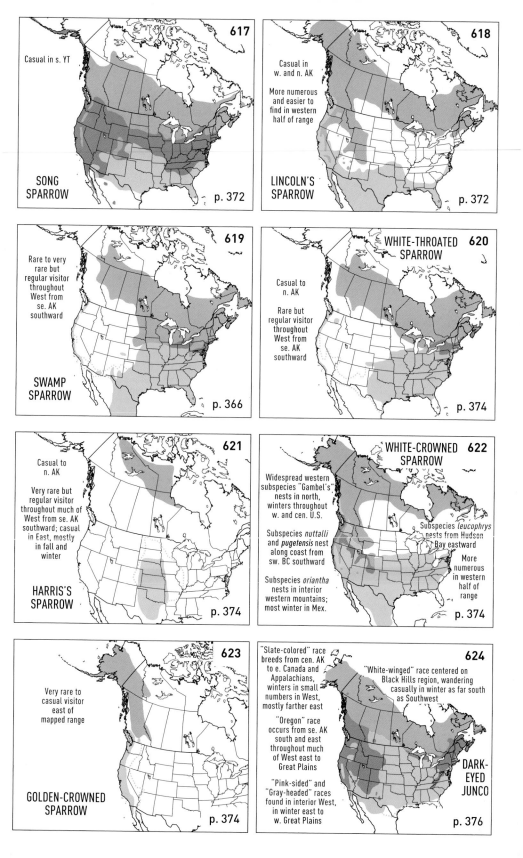

617

Casual in s. YT

SONG
SPARROW

p. 372

618

Casual in
w. and n. AK

More numerous
and easier to
find in western
half of range

LINCOLN'S
SPARROW

p. 372

619

Rare to very
rare but
regular visitor
throughout
West from
se. AK
southward

SWAMP
SPARROW

p. 366

WHITE-THROATED **620**
SPARROW

Casual to
n. AK

Rare but
regular visitor
throughout
West from
se. AK
southward

p. 374

621

Casual to
n. AK

Very rare but
regular visitor
throughout much
of West from se.
AK southward; casual
in East, mostly
in fall and
winter

HARRIS'S
SPARROW

p. 374

WHITE-CROWNED **622**
SPARROW

Widespread western
subspecies "Gambel's"
nests in north,
winters throughout
w. and cen. U.S.

Subspecies *nuttalli*
and *pugetensis* nest
along coast from
sw. BC southward

Subspecies *oriantha*
nests in interior
western mountains;
most winter in Mex.

Subspecies *leucophrys*
nests from Hudson
Bay eastward

More
numerous
in western
half of
range

p. 374

623

Very rare to
casual visitor
east of
mapped range

GOLDEN-CROWNED
SPARROW

p. 374

624

"Slate-colored" race
breeds from cen. AK
to e. Canada and
Appalachians,
winters in small
numbers in West,
mostly farther east

"Oregon" race
occurs from se. AK
south and east
throughout much
of West east to
Great Plains

"Pink-sided" and
"Gray-headed" races
found in interior West,
in winter east to
w. Great Plains

"White-winged" race
centered on
Black Hills region, wandering
casually in winter as far south
as Southwest

DARK-
EYED
JUNCO

p. 376

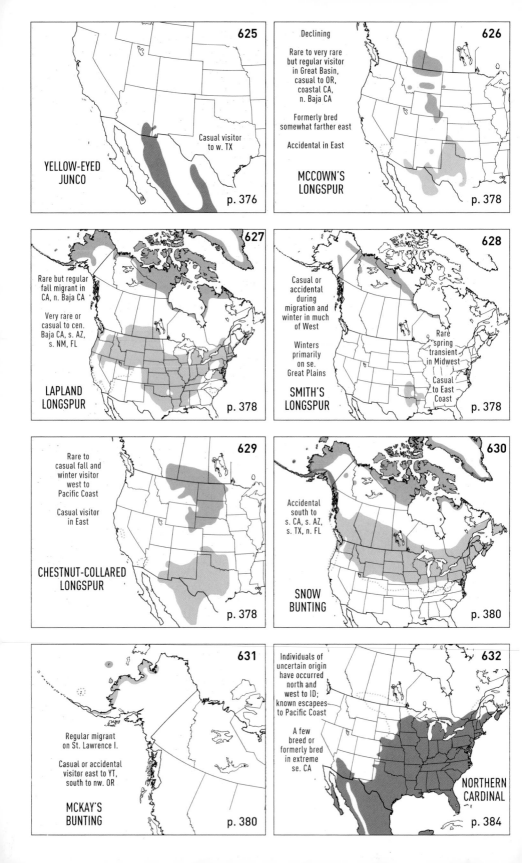

625

YELLOW-EYED
JUNCO

Casual visitor
to w. TX

p. 376

626

MCCOWN'S
LONGSPUR

Declining

Rare to very rare
but regular visitor
in Great Basin,
casual to OR,
coastal CA,
n. Baja CA

Formerly bred
somewhat farther east

Accidental in East

p. 378

627

LAPLAND
LONGSPUR

Rare but regular
fall migrant in
CA, n. Baja CA

Very rare or
casual to cen.
Baja CA, s. AZ,
s. NM, FL

p. 378

628

SMITH'S
LONGSPUR

Casual or
accidental
during
migration and
winter in much
of West

Winters
primarily
on se.
Great Plains

Rare
spring
transient
in Midwest

Casual
to East
Coast

p. 378

629

CHESTNUT-COLLARED
LONGSPUR

Rare to
casual fall and
winter visitor
west to
Pacific Coast

Casual visitor
in East

630

SNOW
BUNTING

Accidental
south to
s. CA, s. AZ,
s. TX, n. FL

p. 380

631

MCKAY'S
BUNTING

Regular migrant
on St. Lawrence I.

Casual or accidental
visitor east to YT,
south to nw. OR

p. 380

632

NORTHERN
CARDINAL

Individuals of
uncertain origin
have occurred
north and
west to ID;
known escapees
to Pacific Coast

A few
breed or
formerly bred
in extreme
se. CA

p. 384

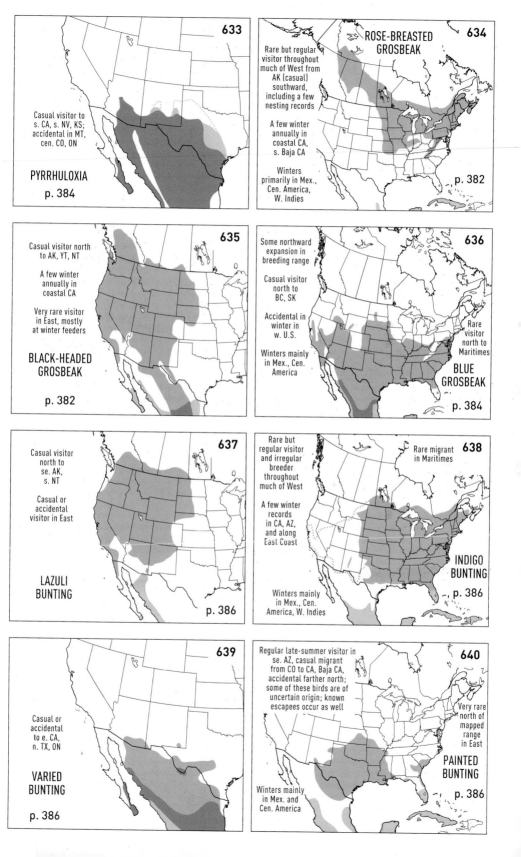

633

Casual visitor to
s. CA, s. NV, KS;
accidental in MT,
cen. CO, ON

PYRRHULOXIA
p. 384

**ROSE-BREASTED
GROSBEAK**

634

Rare but regular
visitor throughout
much of West from
AK (casual)
southward,
including a few
nesting records

A few winter
annually in
coastal CA,
s. Baja CA

Winters
primarily in Mex.,
Cen. America,
W. Indies

p. 382

635

Casual visitor north
to AK, YT, NT

A few winter
annually in
coastal CA

Very rare visitor
in East, mostly
at winter feeders

**BLACK-HEADED
GROSBEAK**

p. 382

636

Some northward
expansion in
breeding range

Casual visitor
north to
BC, SK

Accidental in
winter in
w. U.S.

Winters mainly
in Mex., Cen.
America

Rare
visitor
north to
Maritimes

**BLUE
GROSBEAK**

p. 384

637

Casual visitor
north to
se. AK,
s. NT

Casual or
accidental
visitor in East

**LAZULI
BUNTING**

p. 386

638

Rare but
regular visitor
and irregular
breeder
throughout
much of West

A few winter
records
in CA, AZ,
and along
East Coast

Rare migrant
in Maritimes

Winters mainly
in Mex., Cen.
America, W. Indies

**INDIGO
BUNTING**

p. 386

639

Casual or
accidental
to e. CA,
n. TX, ON

**VARIED
BUNTING**

p. 386

640

Regular late-summer visitor in
se. AZ, casual migrant
from CO to CA, Baja CA,
accidental farther north;
some of these birds are of
uncertain origin; known
escapees occur as well

Very rare
north of
mapped
range
in East

Winters mainly
in Mex. and
Cen. America

**PAINTED
BUNTING**

p. 386

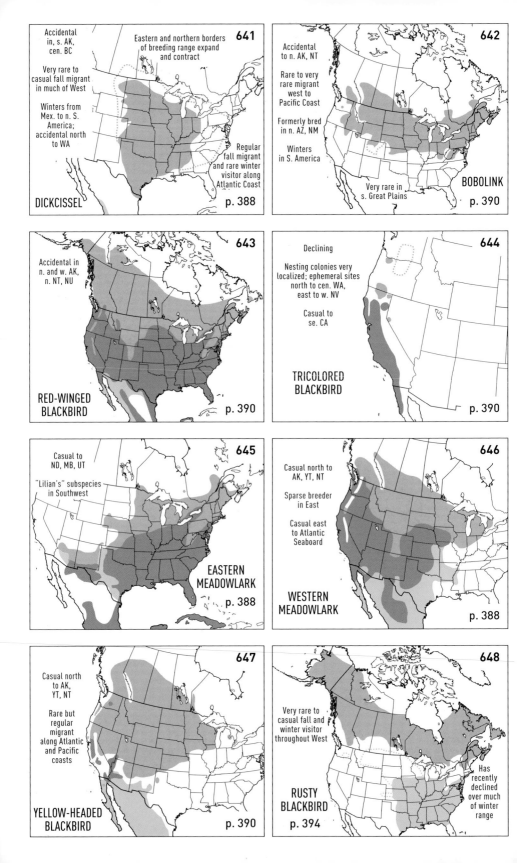

641

Accidental in, s. AK, cen. BC

Eastern and northern borders of breeding range expand and contract

Very rare to casual fall migrant in much of West

Winters from Mex. to n. S. America; accidental north to WA

Regular fall migrant and rare winter visitor along Atlantic Coast

DICKCISSEL
p. 388

642

Accidental to n. AK, NT

Rare to very rare migrant west to Pacific Coast

Formerly bred in n. AZ, NM

Winters in S. America

Very rare in s. Great Plains

BOBOLINK
p. 390

643

Accidental in n. and w. AK, n. NT, NU

RED-WINGED BLACKBIRD
p. 390

644

Declining

Nesting colonies very localized; ephemeral sites north to cen. WA, east to w. NV

Casual to se. CA

TRICOLORED BLACKBIRD
p. 390

645

Casual to ND, MB, UT

"Lilian's" subspecies in Southwest

EASTERN MEADOWLARK
p. 388

646

Casual north to AK, YT, NT

Sparse breeder in East

Casual east to Atlantic Seaboard

WESTERN MEADOWLARK
p. 388

647

Casual north to AK, YT, NT

Rare but regular migrant along Atlantic and Pacific coasts

YELLOW-HEADED BLACKBIRD
p. 390

648

Very rare to casual fall and winter visitor throughout West

Has recently declined over much of winter range

RUSTY BLACKBIRD
p. 394

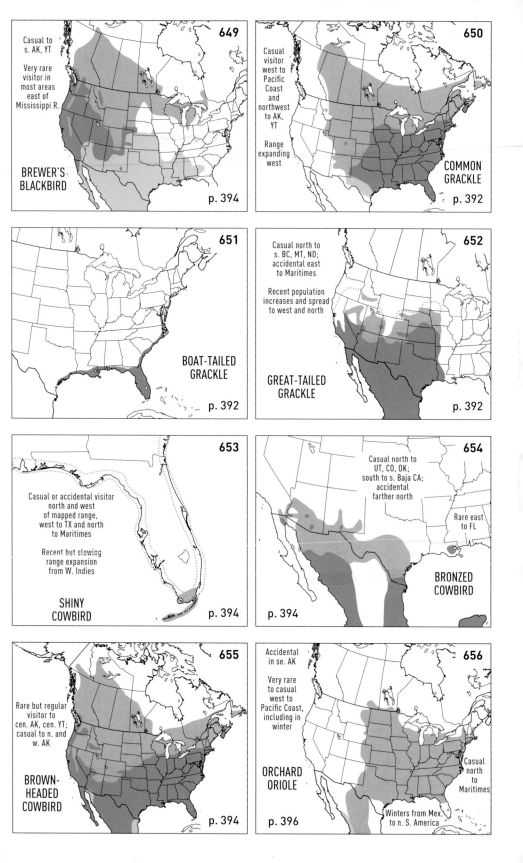

649

Casual to s. AK, YT

Very rare visitor in most areas east of Mississippi R.

BREWER'S BLACKBIRD

p. 394

650

Casual visitor west to Pacific Coast and northwest to AK, YT

Range expanding west

COMMON GRACKLE

p. 392

651

BOAT-TAILED GRACKLE

p. 392

652

Casual north to s. BC, MT, ND; accidental east to Maritimes

Recent population increases and spread to west and north

GREAT-TAILED GRACKLE

p. 392

653

Casual or accidental visitor north and west of mapped range, west to TX and north to Maritimes

Recent but slowing range expansion from W. Indies

SHINY COWBIRD

p. 394

654

Casual north to UT, CO, OK; south to s. Baja CA; accidental farther north

Rare east to FL

BRONZED COWBIRD

p. 394

655

Rare but regular visitor to cen. AK, cen. YT; casual to n. and w. AK

BROWN-HEADED COWBIRD

p. 394

656

Accidental in se. AK

Very rare to casual west to Pacific Coast, including in winter

Casual north to Maritimes

ORCHARD ORIOLE

Winters from Mex. to n. S. America

p. 396

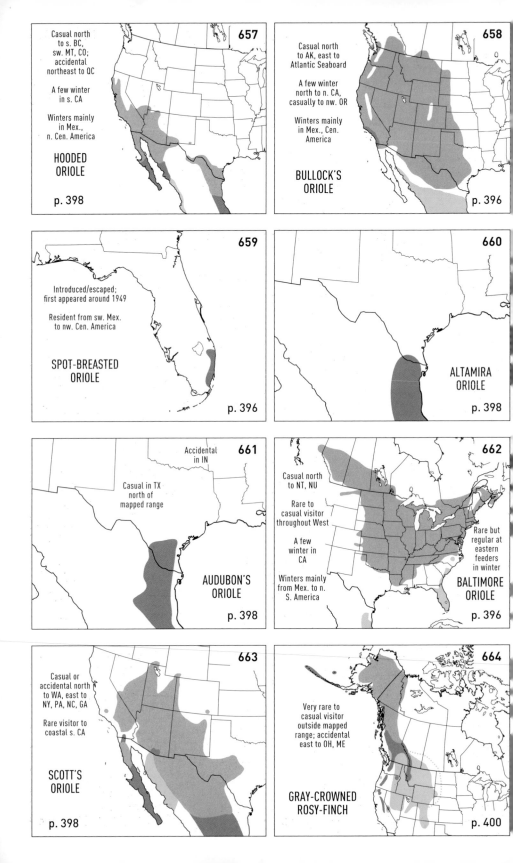

657

Casual north to s. BC, sw. MT, CO; accidental northeast to QC

A few winter in s. CA

Winters mainly in Mex., n. Cen. America

HOODED ORIOLE

p. 398

658

Casual north to AK, east to Atlantic Seaboard

A few winter north to n. CA, casually to nw. OR

Winters mainly in Mex., Cen. America

BULLOCK'S ORIOLE

p. 396

659

Introduced/escaped; first appeared around 1949

Resident from sw. Mex. to nw. Cen. America

SPOT-BREASTED ORIOLE

p. 396

660

ALTAMIRA ORIOLE

p. 398

661

Accidental in IN

Casual in TX north of mapped range

AUDUBON'S ORIOLE

p. 398

662

Casual north to NT, NU

Rare to casual visitor throughout West

A few winter in CA

Winters mainly from Mex. to n. S. America

Rare but regular at eastern feeders in winter

BALTIMORE ORIOLE

p. 396

663

Casual or accidental north to WA, east to NY, PA, NC, GA

Rare visitor to coastal s. CA

SCOTT'S ORIOLE

p. 398

664

Very rare to casual visitor outside mapped range; accidental east to OH, ME

GRAY-CROWNED ROSY-FINCH

p. 400

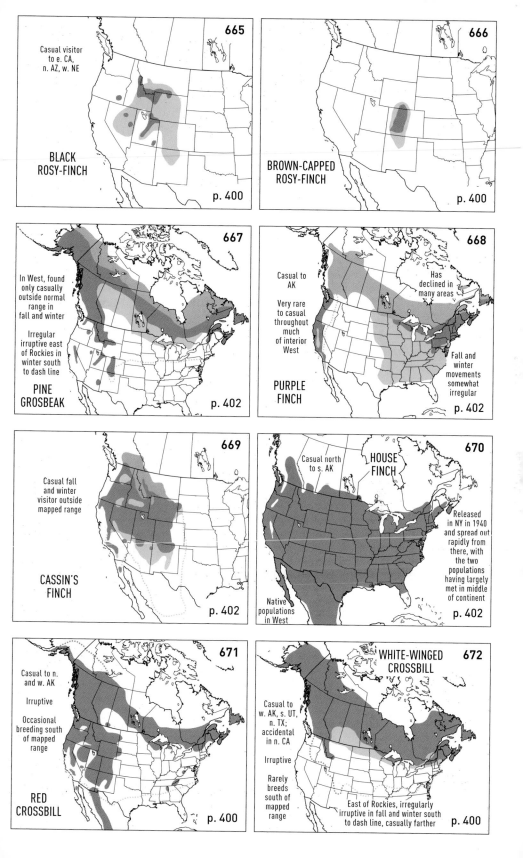

665

Casual visitor to e. CA, n. AZ, w. NE

BLACK ROSY-FINCH

p. 400

666

BROWN-CAPPED ROSY-FINCH

p. 400

667

In West, found only casually outside normal range in fall and winter

Irregular irruptive east of Rockies in winter south to dash line

PINE GROSBEAK

p. 402

668

Casual to AK

Very rare to casual throughout much of interior West

Has declined in many areas

Fall and winter movements somewhat irregular

PURPLE FINCH

p. 402

669

Casual fall and winter visitor outside mapped range

CASSIN'S FINCH

p. 402

670

HOUSE FINCH

Casual north to s. AK

Released in NY in 1940 and spread out rapidly from there, with the two populations having largely met in middle of continent

Native populations in West

p. 402

671

Casual to n. and w. AK

Irruptive

Occasional breeding south of mapped range

RED CROSSBILL

p. 400

672

WHITE-WINGED CROSSBILL

Casual to w. AK, s. UT, n. TX; accidental in n. CA

Irruptive

Rarely breeds south of mapped range

East of Rockies, irregularly irruptive in fall and winter south to dash line, casually farther

p. 400

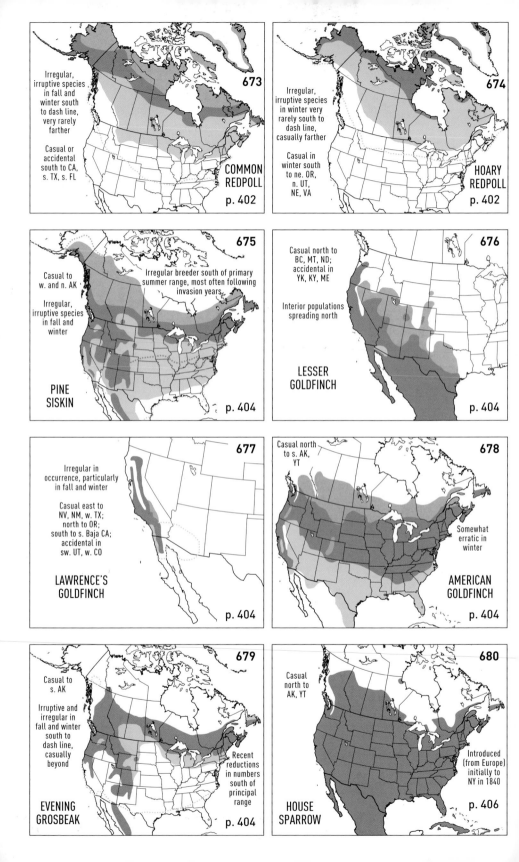

673

Irregular, irruptive species in fall and winter south to dash line, very rarely farther

Casual or accidental south to CA, s. TX, s. FL

COMMON REDPOLL

p. 402

674

Irregular, irruptive species in winter very rarely south to dash line, casually farther

Casual in winter south to ne. OR, n. UT, NE, VA

HOARY REDPOLL

p. 402

675

Casual to w. and n. AK

Irregular, irruptive species in fall and winter

Irregular breeder south of primary summer range, most often following invasion years

PINE SISKIN

p. 404

676

Casual north to BC, MT, ND; accidental in YK, KY, ME

Interior populations spreading north

LESSER GOLDFINCH

p. 404

677

Irregular in occurrence, particularly in fall and winter

Casual east to NV, NM, w. TX; north to OR; south to s. Baja CA; accidental in sw. UT, w. CO

LAWRENCE'S GOLDFINCH

p. 404

678

Casual north to s. AK, YT

Somewhat erratic in winter

AMERICAN GOLDFINCH

p. 404

679

Casual to s. AK

Irruptive and irregular in fall and winter south to dash line, casually beyond

Recent reductions in numbers south of principal range

EVENING GROSBEAK

p. 404

680

Casual north to AK, YT

Introduced (from Europe) initially to NY in 1840

HOUSE SPARROW

p. 406

LIFE LIST

Keep a Life List. Check off the birds you have seen.

The list on the following pages includes all of the birds shown on the plates, except for some of the accidentals that have not been verified.

For a checklist of all the birds of North America, see the *ABA Checklist: Birds of the Continental United States and Canada,* compiled by the Checklist Committee of the American Birding Association, PO Box 6599, Colorado Springs, CO 80934. It lists every species that has occurred north of the Mexican border.

In the following list, birds are grouped first under orders (identified by the Latin ending *-formes*), followed by families (*-dae* ending), and then species. Sequencing of orders and families follows the American Ornithologists' Union's Check-list of North American Birds (1998 through the 48th supplement, from 2007), as do the scientific names for genus and species. Scientific names are not given below but can be found in the species accounts throughout the book. The vernacular names given here are the ones decided upon by the ABA Checklist Committee. They are essentially the same as those adopted by the AOU.

Species marked with an asterisk are exotic and unestablished. Though not countable on official ABA lists, they are included here because birders may encounter them and wish to record their sightings.

RDER ANSERIFORMES

ucks, Geese, and Swans (Anatidae)

_____Black-bellied Whistling-Duck
_____Fulvous Whistling-Duck
_____Bean Goose
_____Pink-footed Goose
_____Greater White-fronted Goose
_____Lesser White-fronted Goose
_____Emperor Goose
_____Snow Goose
_____Ross's Goose
_____Brant
_____Barnacle Goose
_____Cackling Goose
_____Canada Goose

_____Mute Swan
_____Trumpeter Swan
_____Tundra Swan
_____Whooper Swan
_____Muscovy Duck
_____Wood Duck
_____Gadwall
_____Falcated Duck
_____Eurasian Wigeon
_____American Wigeon
_____American Black Duck
_____Mallard
_____Mottled Duck
_____Spot-billed Duck
_____Blue-winged Teal
_____Cinnamon Teal
_____Northern Shoveler
_____White-cheeked Pintail
_____Northern Pintail
_____Garganey
_____Baikal Teal
_____Green-winged Teal
_____Canvasback
_____Redhead
_____Common Pochard
_____Ring-necked Duck
_____Tufted Duck
_____Greater Scaup
_____Lesser Scaup
_____Steller's Eider
_____Spectacled Eider
_____King Eider
_____Common Eider
_____Harlequin Duck
_____Surf Scoter
_____White-winged Scoter
_____Black Scoter
_____Long-tailed Duck
_____Bufflehead
_____Common Goldeneye
_____Barrow's Goldeneye
_____Smew
_____Hooded Merganser
_____Common Merganser
_____Red-breasted Merganser
_____Masked Duck
_____Ruddy Duck

ORDER GALLIFORMES

Curassows and Guans (Cracidae)
_____Plain Chachalaca
Partridges, Grouse, Turkeys, and Old World Quail (Phasianidae)
_____Chukar
_____Himalayan Snowcock
_____Gray Partridge
_____Ring-necked Pheasant
_____Ruffed Grouse
_____Greater Sage-Grouse
_____Gunnison Sage-Grouse
_____Spruce Grouse
_____Willow Ptarmigan
_____Rock Ptarmigan
_____White-tailed Ptarmigan
_____Dusky Grouse
_____Sooty Grouse
_____Sharp-tailed Grouse
_____Greater Prairie-Chicken
_____Lesser Prairie-Chicken
_____Wild Turkey
New World Quail (Odontophoridae)
_____Mountain Quail
_____Scaled Quail
_____California Quail
_____Gambel's Quail
_____Northern Bobwhite
_____Montezuma Quail

ORDER GAVIIFORMES

Loons (Gaviidae)
_____Red-throated Loon
_____Arctic Loon
_____Pacific Loon
_____Common Loon
_____Yellow-billed Loon

ORDER PODICIPEDIFORMES

Grebes (Podicipedidae)
_____Least Grebe
_____Pied-billed Grebe
_____Horned Grebe
_____Red-necked Grebe
_____Eared Grebe
_____Western Grebe
_____Clark's Grebe

ORDER PROCELLARIIFORMES

Albatrosses (Diomedeidae)
_____ Yellow-nosed Albatross
_____ Shy Albatross
_____ Black-browed Albatross
_____ Wandering Albatross
_____ Laysan Albatross
_____ Black-footed Albatross
_____ Short-tailed Albatross

Shearwaters and Petrels (Procellariidae)
_____ Northern Fulmar
_____ Great-winged Petrel
_____ Herald Petrel
_____ Murphy's Petrel
_____ Mottled Petrel
_____ Bermuda Petrel
_____ Black-capped Petrel
_____ Galápagos/Hawaiian ("Dark-rumped") Petrel
_____ Fea's/Zino's Petrel
_____ Cook's Petrel
_____ Stejneger's Petrel
_____ Bulwer's Petrel
_____ Streaked Shearwater
_____ Cory's Shearwater
_____ Cape Verde Shearwater
_____ Pink-footed Shearwater
_____ Flesh-footed Shearwater
_____ Greater Shearwater
_____ Wedge-tailed Shearwater
_____ Buller's Shearwater
_____ Sooty Shearwater
_____ Short-tailed Shearwater
_____ Manx Shearwater
_____ Black-vented Shearwater
_____ Audubon's Shearwater
_____ Little Shearwater

Storm-Petrels (Hydrobatidae)
_____ Wilson's Storm-Petrel
_____ White-faced Storm-Petrel
_____ European Storm-Petrel
_____ Black-bellied Storm-Petrel
_____ Fork-tailed Storm-Petrel
_____ Leach's Storm-Petrel
_____ Ashy Storm-Petrel
_____ Band-rumped Storm-Petrel
_____ Wedge-rumped Storm-Petrel
_____ Black Storm-Petrel
_____ Least Storm-Petrel

ORDER PELECANIFORMES

Tropicbirds (Phaethontidae)
_____ White-tailed Tropicbird
_____ Red-billed Tropicbird
_____ Red-tailed Tropicbird

Boobies and Gannets (Sulidae)
_____ Masked Booby
_____ Blue-footed Booby
_____ Brown Booby
_____ Red-footed Booby
_____ Northern Gannet

Pelicans (Pelecanidae)
_____ American White Pelican
_____ Brown Pelican

Cormorants (Phalacrocoracidae)
_____ Brandt's Cormorant
_____ Neotropic Cormorant
_____ Double-crested Cormorant
_____ Great Cormorant
_____ Red-faced Cormorant
_____ Pelagic Cormorant

Darters (Anhingidae)
_____ Anhinga

Frigatebirds (Fregatidae)
_____ Magnificent Frigatebird
_____ Great Frigatebird
_____ Lesser Frigatebird

ORDER CICONIIFORMES

Bitterns, Herons, and Allies (Ardeidae)
_____ American Bittern
_____ Yellow Bittern
_____ Least Bittern
_____ Great Blue Heron
_____ Great Egret
_____ Chinese Egret
_____ Little Egret
_____ Western Reef-Heron
_____ Snowy Egret
_____ Little Blue Heron
_____ Tricolored Heron
_____ Reddish Egret
_____ Cattle Egret
_____ Chinese Pond-Heron

_____Green Heron
_____Black-crowned Night-Heron
_____Yellow-crowned Night-Heron

Ibises and Spoonbills (Threskiornithidae)
_____White Ibis
_____Scarlet Ibis
_____Glossy Ibis
_____White-faced Ibis
_____Roseate Spoonbill

Storks (Ciconiidae)
_____Jabiru
_____Wood Stork

New World Vultures (Cathartidae)
_____Black Vulture
_____Turkey Vulture
_____California Condor

ORDER PHOENICOPTERIFORMES

Flamingos (Phoenicopteridae)
_____Greater Flamingo

ORDER FALCONIFORMES

Hawks, Kites, Eagles, and Allies (Accipitridae)
_____Osprey
_____Hook-billed Kite
_____Swallow-tailed Kite
_____White-tailed Kite
_____Snail Kite
_____Mississippi Kite
_____Bald Eagle
_____White-tailed Eagle
_____Steller's Sea-Eagle
_____Northern Harrier
_____Sharp-shinned Hawk
_____Cooper's Hawk
_____Northern Goshawk
_____Crane Hawk
_____Common Black-Hawk
_____Harris's Hawk
_____Roadside Hawk
_____Red-shouldered Hawk
_____Broad-winged Hawk
_____Gray Hawk
_____Short-tailed Hawk
_____Swainson's Hawk

_____White-tailed Hawk
_____Zone-tailed Hawk
_____Red-tailed Hawk
_____Ferruginous Hawk
_____Rough-legged Hawk
_____Golden Eagle

Caracaras and Falcons (Falconidae)
_____Collared Forest-Falcon
_____Crested Caracara
_____Eurasian Kestrel
_____American Kestrel
_____Merlin
_____Eurasian Hobby
_____Aplomado Falcon
_____Gyrfalcon
_____Peregrine Falcon
_____Prairie Falcon

ORDER GRUIFORMES

Rails, Gallinules, and Coots (Rallidae)
_____Yellow Rail
_____Black Rail
_____Corn Crake
_____Clapper Rail
_____King Rail
_____Virginia Rail
_____Sora
_____Paint-billed Crake
_____Spotted Rail
_____Purple Gallinule
_____Common Moorhen
_____Eurasian Coot
_____American Coot

Limpkins (Aramidae)
_____Limpkin

Cranes (Gruidae)
_____Sandhill Crane
_____Common Crane
_____Whooping Crane

ORDER CHARADRIIFORMES

Thick-knees (Burhinidae)
_____Double-striped Thick-knee

Lapwings and Plovers (Charadriidae)
_____Northern Lapwing
_____Black-bellied Plover

_____European Golden-Plover
_____American Golden-Plover
_____Pacific Golden-Plover
_____Lesser Sand-Plover
_____Greater Sand-Plover
_____Collared Plover
_____Snowy Plover
_____Wilson's Plover
_____Common Ringed Plover
_____Semipalmated Plover
_____Piping Plover
_____Little Ringed Plover
_____Killdeer
_____Mountain Plover
_____Eurasian Dotterel

Oystercatchers (Haematopodidae)
_____Eurasian Oystercatcher
_____American Oystercatcher
_____Black Oystercatcher

Stilts and Avocets (Recurvirostridae)
_____Black-winged Stilt
_____Black-necked Stilt
_____American Avocet

Jacanas (Jacanidae)
_____Northern Jacana

Sandpipers, Phalaropes, and Allies (Scolopacidae)
_____Terek Sandpiper
_____Common Sandpiper
_____Spotted Sandpiper
_____Green Sandpiper
_____Solitary Sandpiper
_____Gray-tailed Tattler
_____Wandering Tattler
_____Spotted Redshank
_____Greater Yellowlegs
_____Common Greenshank
_____Willet
_____Lesser Yellowlegs
_____Marsh Sandpiper
_____Wood Sandpiper
_____Common Redshank
_____Upland Sandpiper
_____Little Curlew
_____Eskimo Curlew
_____Whimbrel
_____Bristle-thighed Curlew

_____Far Eastern Curlew
_____Slender-billed Curlew
_____Eurasian Curlew
_____Long-billed Curlew
_____Black-tailed Godwit
_____Hudsonian Godwit
_____Bar-tailed Godwit
_____Marbled Godwit
_____Ruddy Turnstone
_____Black Turnstone
_____Surfbird
_____Great Knot
_____Red Knot
_____Sanderling
_____Semipalmated Sandpiper
_____Western Sandpiper
_____Red-necked Stint
_____Little Stint
_____Temminck's Stint
_____Long-toed Stint
_____Least Sandpiper
_____White-rumped Sandpiper
_____Baird's Sandpiper
_____Pectoral Sandpiper
_____Sharp-tailed Sandpiper
_____Purple Sandpiper
_____Rock Sandpiper
_____Dunlin
_____Curlew Sandpiper
_____Stilt Sandpiper
_____Spoon-billed Sandpiper
_____Broad-billed Sandpiper
_____Buff-breasted Sandpiper
_____Ruff
_____Short-billed Dowitcher
_____Long-billed Dowitcher
_____Jack Snipe
_____Wilson's Snipe
_____Common Snipe
_____Pin-tailed Snipe
_____Eurasian Woodcock
_____American Woodcock
_____Wilson's Phalarope
_____Red-necked Phalarope
_____Red Phalarope

Pratincoles (Glareolidae)
_____Oriental Pratincole

Gulls, Terns, and Skimmers (Laridae)

_____ Laughing Gull
_____ Franklin's Gull
_____ Little Gull
_____ Black-headed Gull
_____ Bonaparte's Gull
_____ Heermann's Gull
_____ Gray-hooded Gull
_____ Belcher's Gull
_____ Black-tailed Gull
_____ Mew Gull
_____ Ring-billed Gull
_____ California Gull
_____ Herring Gull
_____ Yellow-legged Gull
_____ Thayer's Gull
_____ Iceland Gull
_____ Lesser Black-backed Gull
_____ Slaty-backed Gull
_____ Yellow-footed Gull
_____ Western Gull
_____ Glaucous-winged Gull
_____ Glaucous Gull
_____ Great Black-backed Gull
_____ Kelp Gull
_____ Sabine's Gull
_____ Black-legged Kittiwake
_____ Red-legged Kittiwake
_____ Ross's Gull
_____ Ivory Gull
_____ Brown Noddy
_____ Black Noddy
_____ Sooty Tern
_____ Bridled Tern
_____ Aleutian Tern
_____ Least Tern
_____ Large-billed Tern
_____ Gull-billed Tern
_____ Caspian Tern
_____ Black Tern
_____ White-winged Tern
_____ Whiskered Tern
_____ Roseate Tern
_____ Common Tern
_____ Arctic Tern
_____ Forster's Tern
_____ Royal Tern
_____ Sandwich Tern
_____ Elegant Tern
_____ Black Skimmer

Skuas (Stercorariidae)

_____ Great Skua
_____ South Polar Skua
_____ Pomarine Jaeger
_____ Parasitic Jaeger
_____ Long-tailed Jaeger

Auks, Murres, and Puffins (Alcidae)

_____ Dovekie
_____ Common Murre
_____ Thick-billed Murre
_____ Razorbill
_____ Black Guillemot
_____ Pigeon Guillemot
_____ Long-billed Murrelet
_____ Marbled Murrelet
_____ Kittlitz's Murrelet
_____ Xantus's Murrelet
_____ Craveri's Murrelet
_____ Ancient Murrelet
_____ Cassin's Auklet
_____ Parakeet Auklet
_____ Least Auklet
_____ Whiskered Auklet
_____ Crested Auklet
_____ Rhinoceros Auklet
_____ Atlantic Puffin
_____ Horned Puffin
_____ Tufted Puffin

ORDER COLUMBIFORMES

Pigeons and Doves (Columbidae)

_____ Rock Pigeon
_____ Scaly-naped Pigeon
_____ White-crowned Pigeon
_____ Red-billed Pigeon
_____ Band-tailed Pigeon
_____ Oriental Turtle-Dove
_____ Eurasian Collared-Dove
_____ African Collared-Dove*
_____ Spotted Dove
_____ White-winged Dove
_____ Zenaida Dove

_____Mourning Dove
_____Inca Dove
_____Common Ground-Dove
_____Ruddy Ground-Dove
_____White-tipped Dove
_____Key West Quail-Dove
_____Ruddy Quail-Dove

ORDER PSITTACIFORMES

Lories, Parakeets, Macaws, and Parrots (Psittacidae)

_____Budgerigar
_____Rose-ringed Parakeet*
_____Monk Parakeet
_____Green Parakeet
_____Mitred Parakeet*
_____Black-hooded Parakeet*
_____Thick-billed Parrot
_____White-winged Parakeet
_____White-fronted Parrot*
_____Yellow-chevroned Parakeet*
_____Red-crowned Parrot
_____Lilac-crowned Parrot*
_____Yellow-headed Parrot*
_____Red-lored Parrot*

ORDER CUCULIFORMES

Cuckoos, Roadrunners, and Anis (Cuculidae)

_____Common Cuckoo
_____Oriental Cuckoo
_____Yellow-billed Cuckoo
_____Mangrove Cuckoo
_____Black-billed Cuckoo
_____Greater Roadrunner
_____Smooth-billed Ani
_____Groove-billed Ani

ORDER STRIGIFORMES

Barn Owls (Tytonidae)

_____Barn Owl

Typical Owls (Strigidae)

_____Flammulated Owl
_____Oriental Scops-Owl
_____Western Screech-Owl
_____Eastern Screech-Owl
_____Whiskered Screech-Owl
_____Great Horned Owl
_____Snowy Owl
_____Northern Hawk Owl
_____Northern Pygmy-Owl
_____Ferruginous Pygmy-Owl
_____Elf Owl
_____Burrowing Owl
_____Mottled Owl
_____Spotted Owl
_____Barred Owl
_____Great Gray Owl
_____Long-eared Owl
_____Stygian Owl
_____Short-eared Owl
_____Boreal Owl
_____Northern Saw-whet Owl

ORDER CAPRIMULGIFORMES

Goatsuckers (Caprimulgidae)

_____Lesser Nighthawk
_____Common Nighthawk
_____Antillean Nighthawk
_____Common Pauraque
_____Common Poorwill
_____Chuck-will's-widow
_____Buff-collared Nightjar
_____Whip-poor-will
_____Gray Nightjar

ORDER APODIFORMES

Swifts (Apodidae)

_____Black Swift
_____White-collared Swift
_____Chimney Swift
_____Vaux's Swift
_____White-throated Needletail
_____Common Swift
_____Fork-tailed Swift
_____White-throated Swift
_____Antillean Palm-Swift

Hummingbirds (Trochilidae)

_____Green Violet-ear
_____Green-breasted Mango
_____Broad-billed Hummingbird
_____White-eared Hummingbird

_____ Xantus's Hummingbird
_____ Berylline Hummingbird
_____ Buff-bellied Hummingbird
_____ Cinnamon Hummingbird
_____ Violet-crowned Hummingbird
_____ Blue-throated Hummingbird
_____ Magnificent Hummingbird
_____ Plain-capped Starthroat
_____ Bahama Woodstar
_____ Lucifer Hummingbird
_____ Ruby-throated Hummingbird
_____ Black-chinned Hummingbird
_____ Anna's Hummingbird
_____ Costa's Hummingbird
_____ Calliope Hummingbird
_____ Bumblebee Hummingbird
_____ Broad-tailed Hummingbird
_____ Rufous Hummingbird
_____ Allen's Hummingbird

ORDER TROGONIFORMES

Trogons (Trogonidae)
_____ Elegant Trogon
_____ Eared Quetzal

ORDER UPUPIFORMES

Hoopoes (Upupidae)
_____ Eurasian Hoopoe

ORDER CORACIIFORMES

Kingfishers (Alcedinidae)
_____ Ringed Kingfisher
_____ Belted Kingfisher
_____ Green Kingfisher

ORDER PICIFORMES

Woodpeckers and Allies (Picidae)
_____ Eurasian Wryneck
_____ Lewis's Woodpecker
_____ Red-headed Woodpecker
_____ Acorn Woodpecker
_____ Gila Woodpecker
_____ Golden-fronted Woodpecker
_____ Red-bellied Woodpecker
_____ Williamson's Sapsucker
_____ Yellow-bellied Sapsucker

_____ Red-naped Sapsucker
_____ Red-breasted Sapsucker
_____ Great Spotted Woodpecker
_____ Ladder-backed Woodpecker
_____ Nuttall's Woodpecker
_____ Downy Woodpecker
_____ Hairy Woodpecker
_____ Arizona Woodpecker
_____ Red-cockaded Woodpecker
_____ White-headed Woodpecker
_____ American Three-toed
          Woodpecker
_____ Black-backed Woodpecker
_____ Northern Flicker
_____ Gilded Flicker
_____ Pileated Woodpecker
_____ Ivory-billed Woodpecker

ORDER PASSERIFORMES

Tyrant Flycatchers (Tyrannidae)
_____ Northern Beardless-Tyrannulet
_____ Greenish Elaenia
_____ Caribbean Elaenia
_____ Tufted Flycatcher
_____ Olive-sided Flycatcher
_____ Greater Pewee
_____ Western Wood-Pewee
_____ Eastern Wood-Pewee
_____ Cuban Pewee
_____ Yellow-bellied Flycatcher
_____ Acadian Flycatcher
_____ Alder Flycatcher
_____ Willow Flycatcher
_____ Least Flycatcher
_____ Hammond's Flycatcher
_____ Gray Flycatcher
_____ Dusky Flycatcher
_____ Pacific-slope Flycatcher
_____ Cordilleran Flycatcher
_____ Buff-breasted Flycatcher
_____ Black Phoebe
_____ Eastern Phoebe
_____ Say's Phoebe
_____ Vermilion Flycatcher
_____ Dusky-capped Flycatcher
_____ Ash-throated Flycatcher

_____Nutting's Flycatcher
_____Great Crested Flycatcher
_____Brown-crested Flycatcher
_____La Sagra's Flycatcher
_____Great Kiskadee
_____Social Flycatcher
_____Sulphur-bellied Flycatcher
_____Piratic Flycatcher
_____Variegated Flycatcher
_____Tropical Kingbird
_____Couch's Kingbird
_____Cassin's Kingbird
_____Thick-billed Kingbird
_____Western Kingbird
_____Eastern Kingbird
_____Gray Kingbird
_____Scissor-tailed Flycatcher
_____Fork-tailed Flycatcher
_____Rose-throated Becard
_____Masked Tityra

Shrikes (Laniidae)
_____Brown Shrike
_____Loggerhead Shrike
_____Northern Shrike

Vireos (Vireonidae)
_____White-eyed Vireo
_____Thick-billed Vireo
_____Bell's Vireo
_____Black-capped Vireo
_____Gray Vireo
_____Yellow-throated Vireo
_____Plumbeous Vireo
_____Cassin's Vireo
_____Blue-headed Vireo
_____Hutton's Vireo
_____Warbling Vireo
_____Philadelphia Vireo
_____Red-eyed Vireo
_____Yellow-green Vireo
_____Black-whiskered Vireo
_____Yucatan Vireo

Jays and Crows (Corvidae)
_____Gray Jay
_____Steller's Jay
_____Blue Jay
_____Green Jay

_____Brown Jay
_____Florida Scrub-Jay
_____Island Scrub-Jay
_____Western Scrub-Jay
_____Mexican Jay
_____Pinyon Jay
_____Clark's Nutcracker
_____Black-billed Magpie
_____Yellow-billed Magpie
_____Eurasian Jackdaw
_____American Crow
_____Northwestern Crow
_____Tamaulipas Crow
_____Fish Crow
_____Chihuahuan Raven
_____Common Raven

Larks (Alaudidae)
_____Sky Lark
_____Horned Lark

Swallows (Hirundinidae)
_____Purple Martin
_____Cuban Martin
_____Gray-breasted Martin
_____Southern Martin
_____Brown-chested Martin
_____Tree Swallow
_____Mangrove Swallow
_____Violet-green Swallow
_____Bahama Swallow
_____Northern Rough-winged
        Swallow
_____Bank Swallow
_____Cliff Swallow
_____Cave Swallow
_____Barn Swallow
_____Common House-Martin

Chickadees and Titmice (Paridae)
_____Carolina Chickadee
_____Black-capped Chickadee
_____Mountain Chickadee
_____Mexican Chickadee
_____Chestnut-backed Chickadee
_____Boreal Chickadee
_____Gray-headed Chickadee
_____Bridled Titmouse
_____Oak Titmouse

_____Juniper Titmouse
_____Tufted Titmouse
_____Black-crested Titmouse
Verdin (Remizidae)
_____Verdin
Bushtits (Aegithalidae)
_____Bushtit
Nuthatches (Sittidae)
_____Red-breasted Nuthatch
_____White-breasted Nuthatch
_____Pygmy Nuthatch
_____Brown-headed Nuthatch
Creepers (Certhiidae)
_____Brown Creeper
Wrens (Troglodytidae)
_____Cactus Wren
_____Rock Wren
_____Canyon Wren
_____Carolina Wren
_____Bewick's Wren
_____House Wren
_____Winter Wren
_____Sedge Wren
_____Marsh Wren
Dippers (Cinclidae)
_____American Dipper
Bulbuls (Pycnonotidae)
_____Red-whiskered Bulbul
Kinglets (Regulidae)
_____Golden-crowned Kinglet
_____Ruby-crowned Kinglet
Old World Warblers and Gnatcatchers (Sylviidae)
_____Middendorff's Grasshopper-Warbler
_____Lanceolated Warbler
_____Willow Warbler
_____Wood Warbler
_____Dusky Warbler
_____Yellow-browed Warbler
_____Arctic Warbler
_____Lesser Whitethroat
_____Blue-gray Gnatcatcher
_____California Gnatcatcher
_____Black-tailed Gnatcatcher
_____Black-capped Gnatcatcher

Old World Flycatchers (Muscicapidae)
_____Narcissus Flycatcher
_____Mugimaki Flycatcher
_____Dark-sided Flycatcher
_____Gray-streaked Flycatcher
_____Asian Brown Flycatcher
_____Spotted Flycatcher
Thrushes (Turdidae)
_____Siberian Rubythroat
_____Bluethroat
_____Siberian Blue Robin
_____Red-flanked Bluetail
_____Northern Wheatear
_____Stonechat
_____Eastern Bluebird
_____Western Bluebird
_____Mountain Bluebird
_____Townsend's Solitaire
_____Orange-billed Nightingale-Thrush
_____Black-headed Nightingale-Thrush
_____Veery
_____Gray-cheeked Thrush
_____Bicknell's Thrush
_____Swainson's Thrush
_____Hermit Thrush
_____Wood Thrush
_____Eurasian Blackbird
_____Eyebrowed Thrush
_____Dusky Thrush
_____Fieldfare
_____Redwing
_____Clay-colored Robin
_____White-throated Robin
_____Rufous-backed Robin
_____American Robin
_____Varied Thrush
_____Aztec Thrush
Babblers (Timaliidae)
_____Wrentit
Mockingbirds and Thrashers (Mimidae)
_____Gray Catbird
_____Northern Mockingbird
_____Bahama Mockingbird
_____Sage Thrasher

_____Brown Thrasher
_____Long-billed Thrasher
_____Bendire's Thrasher
_____Curve-billed Thrasher
_____California Thrasher
_____Crissal Thrasher
_____Le Conte's Thrasher
_____Blue Mockingbird

Starlings and Mynas (Sturnidae)
_____European Starling
_____Hill Myna*
_____Common Myna*

Accentors (Prunellidae)
_____Siberian Accentor

Wagtails and Pipits (Motacillidae)
_____Eastern Yellow Wagtail
_____Citrine Wagtail
_____Gray Wagtail
_____White Wagtail
_____Tree Pipit
_____Olive-backed Pipit
_____Pechora Pipit
_____Red-throated Pipit
_____American Pipit
_____Sprague's Pipit

Waxwings (Bombycillidae)
_____Bohemian Waxwing
_____Cedar Waxwing

Silky-Flycatchers (Ptilogonatidae)
_____Gray Silky-Flycatcher
_____Phainopepla

Olive Warbler (Peucedramidae)
_____Olive Warbler

Wood-Warblers (Parulidae)
_____Blue-winged Warbler
_____Golden-winged Warbler
_____Tennessee Warbler
_____Orange-crowned Warbler
_____Nashville Warbler
_____Virginia's Warbler
_____Colima Warbler
_____Lucy's Warbler
_____Crescent-chested Warbler
_____Northern Parula
_____Tropical Parula
_____Yellow Warbler

_____Chestnut-sided Warbler
_____Magnolia Warbler
_____Cape May Warbler
_____Black-throated Blue Warbler
_____Yellow-rumped Warbler
_____Black-throated Gray Warbler
_____Golden-cheeked Warbler
_____Black-throated Green Warbler
_____Townsend's Warbler
_____Hermit Warbler
_____Blackburnian Warbler
_____Yellow-throated Warbler
_____Grace's Warbler
_____Pine Warbler
_____Kirtland's Warbler
_____Prairie Warbler
_____Palm Warbler
_____Bay-breasted Warbler
_____Blackpoll Warbler
_____Cerulean Warbler
_____Black-and-white Warbler
_____American Redstart
_____Prothonotary Warbler
_____Worm-eating Warbler
_____Swainson's Warbler
_____Ovenbird
_____Northern Waterthrush
_____Louisiana Waterthrush
_____Kentucky Warbler
_____Connecticut Warbler
_____Mourning Warbler
_____MacGillivray's Warbler
_____Common Yellowthroat
_____Gray-crowned Yellowthroat
_____Hooded Warbler
_____Wilson's Warbler
_____Canada Warbler
_____Red-faced Warbler
_____Painted Redstart
_____Slate-throated Redstart
_____Fan-tailed Warbler
_____Golden-crowned Warbler
_____Rufous-capped Warbler
_____Yellow-breasted Chat

Bananaquits (Coerebidae)
_____Bananaquit

Tanagers (Thraupidae)
_____Hepatic Tanager
_____Summer Tanager
_____Scarlet Tanager
_____Western Tanager
_____Flame-colored Tanager
_____Western Spindalis
Emberizids (Emberizidae)
_____White-collared Seedeater
_____Yellow-faced Grassquit
_____Black-faced Grassquit
_____Olive Sparrow
_____Green-tailed Towhee
_____Spotted Towhee
_____Eastern Towhee
_____Canyon Towhee
_____California Towhee
_____Abert's Towhee
_____Rufous-winged Sparrow
_____Cassin's Sparrow
_____Bachman's Sparrow
_____Botteri's Sparrow
_____Rufous-crowned Sparrow
_____Five-striped Sparrow
_____American Tree Sparrow
_____Chipping Sparrow
_____Clay-colored Sparrow
_____Brewer's Sparrow
_____Field Sparrow
_____Worthen's Sparrow
_____Black-chinned Sparrow
_____Vesper Sparrow
_____Lark Sparrow
_____Black-throated Sparrow
_____Sage Sparrow
_____Lark Bunting
_____Savannah Sparrow
_____Grasshopper Sparrow
_____Baird's Sparrow
_____Henslow's Sparrow
_____Le Conte's Sparrow
_____Nelson's Sharp-tailed Sparrow
_____Saltmarsh Sharp-tailed Sparrow
_____Seaside Sparrow
_____Fox Sparrow
_____Song Sparrow

_____Lincoln's Sparrow
_____Swamp Sparrow
_____White-throated Sparrow
_____Harris's Sparrow
_____White-crowned Sparrow
_____Golden-crowned Sparrow
_____Dark-eyed Junco
_____Yellow-eyed Junco
_____McCown's Longspur
_____Lapland Longspur
_____Smith's Longspur
_____Chestnut-collared Longspur
_____Pine Bunting
_____Little Bunting
_____Rustic Bunting
_____Yellow-throated Bunting
_____Yellow-breasted Bunting
_____Gray Bunting
_____Pallas's Bunting
_____Reed Bunting
_____Snow Bunting
_____McKay's Bunting
Cardinals, Saltators, and Allies (Cardinalidae)
_____Crimson-collared Grosbeak
_____Northern Cardinal
_____Pyrrhuloxia
_____Yellow Grosbeak
_____Rose-breasted Grosbeak
_____Black-headed Grosbeak
_____Blue Bunting
_____Blue Grosbeak
_____Lazuli Bunting
_____Indigo Bunting
_____Varied Bunting
_____Painted Bunting
_____Dickcissel
Blackbirds (Icteridae)
_____Bobolink
_____Red-winged Blackbird
_____Tricolored Blackbird
_____Tawny-shouldered Blackbird
_____Eastern Meadowlark
_____Western Meadowlark
_____Yellow-headed Blackbird
_____Rusty Blackbird

_____Brewer's Blackbird
_____Common Grackle
_____Boat-tailed Grackle
_____Great-tailed Grackle
_____Shiny Cowbird
_____Bronzed Cowbird
_____Brown-headed Cowbird
_____Black-vented Oriole
_____Orchard Oriole
_____Hooded Oriole
_____Streak-backed Oriole
_____Bullock's Oriole
_____Spot-breasted Oriole
_____Altamira Oriole
_____Audubon's Oriole
_____Baltimore Oriole
_____Scott's Oriole

Fringilline and Cardueline Finches and Allies (Fringillidae)
_____Common Chaffinch
_____Brambling
_____Gray-crowned Rosy-Finch
_____Black Rosy-Finch
_____Brown-capped Rosy-Finch
_____Pine Grosbeak

_____Common Rosefinch
_____Purple Finch
_____Cassin's Finch
_____House Finch
_____Red Crossbill
_____White-winged Crossbill
_____Common Redpoll
_____Hoary Redpoll
_____Eurasian Siskin
_____Pine Siskin
_____Lesser Goldfinch
_____Lawrence's Goldfinch
_____American Goldfinch
_____European Goldfinch*
_____Oriental Greenfinch
_____Eurasian Bullfinch
_____Evening Grosbeak
_____Hawfinch

Old World Sparrows (Passeridae)
_____House Sparrow
_____Eurasian Tree Sparrow

Weavers (Ploceidae)
_____Orange Bishop*

Estrildid Finches (Estrildidae)
_____Nutmeg Mannikin*

INDEX

SHORE SILHOUETTES

1 Forster's Tern
2 Black Tern
3 Herring Gull
4 Cormorant
5 Loon
6 Great Blue Heron
7 Mallard
8 Pied-billed Grebe
9 Marbled Godwit
10 Greater Yellowlegs
11 Dowitcher
12 Clapper Rail
13 Whimbrel
14 Black-bellied Plover
15 Turnstone
16 Night-Heron
17 Phalarope
18 Least Sandpiper
19 Semipalmated Plover
20 Sanderling
21 Spotted Sandpiper
22 Killdeer
23 Coot
24 Green-backed Heron

FLIGHT SILHOUETTES

1	Barn Swallow	
2	Cliff Swallow	
3	Purple Martin	
4	Chimney Swift	
5	Starling	
6	Common Grackle	
7	Blackbird	
8	Bluebird	
9	Robin	
10	Goldfinch	
11	House Sparrow	
12	Belted Kingfisher	
13	Blue Jay	
14	Flicker	
15	Mourning Dove	
16	Meadowlark	
17	Bobwhite	
18	Ruffed Grouse	
19	Pheasant	
20	Nighthawk	
21	Crow	
22	Sharp-shinned Hawk	
23	Kestrel	
24	Killdeer	
25	Wilson's Snipe	
26	Woodcock